T0180422

The series Lecture Notes in Computer Science (LNCS), including its subseries Lecture Notes in Artificial Intelligence (LNAI) and Lecture Notes in Bioinformatics (LNBI), has established itself as a medium for the publication of new developments in computer science and information technology research, teaching, and education.

LNCS enjoys close cooperation with the computer science R & D community, the series counts many renowned academics among its volume editors and paper authors, and collaborates with prestigious societies. Its mission is to serve this international community by providing an invaluable service, mainly focused on the publication of conference and workshop proceedings and postproceedings. LNCS commenced publication in 1973.

Jean-Jacques Rousseau · Bill Kapralos
Editors

Pattern Recognition, Computer Vision, and Image Processing

ICPR 2022 International Workshops and Challenges

Montreal, QC, Canada, August 21–25, 2022
Proceedings, Part III

 Springer

Editors
Jean-Jacques Rousseau (iD)
York University
Toronto, ON, Canada

Bill Kapralos (iD)
Ontario Tech University
Oshawa, ON, Canada

ISSN 0302-9743   ISSN 1611-3349 (electronic)
Lecture Notes in Computer Science
ISBN 978-3-031-37730-3   ISBN 978-3-031-37731-0 (eBook)
https://doi.org/10.1007/978-3-031-37731-0

This Springer imprint is published by the registered company Springer Nature Switzerland AG
The registered company address is: Gewerbestrasse 11, 6330 Cham, Switzerland

Foreword

The organizers of the 26th International Conference on Pattern Recognition (ICPR 2022) are delighted to present the Proceedings of the event. The conference took place at Palais des Congrès de Montréal in Montreal, Canada, and we are thrilled to share the outcomes of this successful event.

We would like to express our heartfelt gratitude to the International Association for Pattern Recognition (IAPR) for sponsoring the conference, which allowed us to bring together a diverse group of researchers and experts in this field. Without their support, this conference would not have been possible.

We also want to extend our special thanks to the Workshop Chairs who provided excellent leadership in organizing the workshops. We appreciate the tireless efforts they put into making the workshops a success. We would also like to acknowledge the authors and presenters of the articles and workshops for their contributions. The high quality of their work and presentations enriched the conference.

Finally, we would like to thank the attendees for their participation, which made ICPR 2022 a truly collaborative and inspiring event. We hope that the Proceedings will serve as a valuable resource for those interested in pattern recognition and inspire future research in this field.

August 2022

Henrik I. Christensen
Michael Jenkin
Cheng-Lin Liu

Preface

The 26th International Conference on Pattern Recognition Workshops (ICPRW 2022) were held at the Palais des congrès de Montréal in Montreal, Quebec, Canada on Sunday August 21, 2022, one day earlier than the main ICPR conference. 27 workshop submissions were received and were carefully reviewed by the IAPR Conferences and Meetings committee and the workshop chairs. Considering their decisions and anticipated attendance, 24 workshops were selected and 21 workshops actually took place. Many of these workshops received a sponsorship or endorsement from the International Association for Pattern Recognition (IAPR).

ICPR 2022 marked the return of the conference to its in-person format (although workshops had the option of being held in person or remotely). This meant meeting colleagues face to face again, and making new connections to support scientific collaborations and (perhaps) even new friendships. The purpose of publishing the proceedings of a scientific conference such as ICPR 2022 include to:

- Establish a permanent record of the research presented;
- Report on the current research concerns and accomplishments of the conference participants;
- Make new research visible to scientific and other publics to promote collaboration, innovation, and discovery;
- Disseminate the latest research findings to a wider audience, in support of researchers, academics, industry, and other practitioners; and,
- Support the shared goal of staying up to date with developments in the fast moving field of artificial intelligence.

These volumes constitute the refereed proceedings of the twenty-one (21) workshops that were held in conjunction with ICPR 2022. The wide range of topics that it contains is a testament to the ever-widening concerns of AI researchers as they creatively find ways to apply artificial intelligence to domains further from its historical concerns. ICPR 2022 workshops covered domains related to pattern recognition, artificial intelligence, computer vision, and image and sound analysis. Workshop contributions reflected the most recent applications related to healthcare, biometrics, ethics, multimodality, cultural heritage, imagery, affective computing, and de-escalation. The papers included in these proceedings span four volumes and stem from the following workshops:

Volume I:

T-CAP 2022: Towards a Complete Analysis of People: From Face and Body to Clothes
HBU: 12th International Workshop on Human Behavior Understanding
SSL: Theories, Applications, and Cross Modality for Self-Supervised Learning Models
MPRSS 2022: Multimodal Pattern Recognition for Social Signal Processing in Human-Computer Interaction
FAIRBIO: Fairness in Biometric Systems

AIHA: Artificial Intelligence for Healthcare Applications
MDMR: Multimodal Data for Mental Disorder Recognition

Volume II:

MANPU 2022: 5th International Workshop on coMics ANalysis, Processing and Understanding
FOREST: Image Analysis for Forest Environmental Monitoring
MMFORWILD: MultiMedia FORensics in the WILD
IMTA: 8th International Workshop on Image Mining, Theory and Applications
PRHA: Pattern Recognition in Healthcare Analytics
IML: International Workshop on Industrial Machine Learning

Volume III:

PatReCH: 3rd International Workshop on Pattern Recognition for Cultural Heritage
XAIE: 2nd Workshop on Explainable and Ethical AI
PRRS: 12th Workshop on Pattern Recognition in Remote Sensing
CVAUI: Computer Vision for Analysis of Underwater Imagery
UMDBB: Understanding and Mitigating Demographic Bias in Biometric Systems

Volume IV:

AI4MFDD: Workshop on Artificial Intelligence for Multimedia Forensics and Disinformation Detection
AI4D: AI for De-escalation: Autonomous Systems for De-escalating Conflict in Military and Civilian Contexts
AMAR: 3rd International Workshop on Applied Multimodal Affect Recognition

Writing this preface, we were acutely aware of our special responsibilities towards those who will access the Proceedings for future reference. Unlike us and the contributors to these volumes, future readers will not have the benefit of having lived through the moment in which the research was conducted and presented. As background, leading to August 2022, there were two overarching meta-stories in the news: the COVID pandemic and social justice. COVID restrictions were lifted in piecemeal fashion leading to the conference dates, and began the long tail of the end of the pandemic. For conference attendees, wearing face masks was a live issue since masks indoors remained strongly recommended. International travel was still heavily impacted by COVID restrictions, with some participants being unable to travel either due to their COVID status or to the difficulty in meeting the range of COVID testing and inoculation requirements required. The public health theme continued with a new virus called 'Monkeypox' appearing on the scene.

On social justice, the May 25, 2020 murder of George Floyd by Minneapolis police officers continued to cast its shadow. During the summer of 2022, there continued to be protests and other actions to demand an end to anti-Black racism. In parallel, in Canada, Indigenous communities led protests and actions to demand an end to anti-Indigenous racism, and to acknowledge the historical circumstances that explain the discoveries of remains of children in unmarked burial sites at former residential schools. As conference attendees and participants, we lived through this cultural moment and were marked by it. However, future readers may need to supplement these volumes with research into the circumstances in which the research was conceptualized, conducted, and received. Philosophers of science make a relevant distinction here. Since Karl Popper, they speak of the context of discovery and the context of justification. Justification in science is relatively well understood, as it relates to the collection and analysis of data in pursuit of evidence for evaluating hypotheses in conformity with norms referenced to as the 'scientific method'. However, where do the initial questions or leaps of insights come from? The context of discovery is not as well understood. Still, it is widely believed that the social and personal conditions of researchers play an active role. We included a reference to the COVID-19 pandemic and social justice movements as widely shared preoccupations at the time of ICPR 2022 to aid a future reader who may wonder about the context of discovery of what is reported.

We acknowledge that future readers will no doubt enjoy benefits that we cannot enjoy. Specifically, they may be able to better assess which lines of research presented in the Proceedings proved the more beneficial. There are also concrete things: as we write, we do not know whether we are in a COVID pandemic hiatus or at its end; future readers will know the answer to this question.

The organization of such a large conference would not be possible without the help of many people. Our special gratitude goes to the Program Chairs (Gregory Dudek, Zhouchen Lin, Simone Marinai, Ingela Nyström) for their leadership in organizing the program. Thanks go to the Track Chairs and Area Chairs who dedicated their time to the review process and the preparation of the program. We also thank the reviewers who have evaluated the papers and provided authors with valuable feedback on their research work.

Finally, we acknowledge the work of conference committee members (Local Arrangements Chair and Committee Members, Finance Chairs, Workshop Chairs, Tutorial Chairs, Challenges Chairs, Publicity Chairs, Publications Chairs, Awards Chair, Sponsorship and Exhibition Chair) who strongly contributed to make this event successful. The MCI Group, led by Anjali Mohan, made great efforts in arranging the logistics, which is highly appreciated.

August 2022   Jean-Jacques Rousseau
                                                                              Bill Kapralos

Organization

General Chairs

Henrik I. Christensen   UC San Diego, USA
Michael Jenkin   York University, Canada.
Cheng-Lin Liu   Institute of Automation of Chinese Academy of
                              Sciences, China

Program Committee Co-chairs

Gregory Dudek   McGill University, Canada
Zhouchen Lin   Peking University, China
Simone Marinai   University of Florence, Italy
Ingela Nyström   Swedish National Infrastructure for Computing,
                              Sweden

Invited Speakers Chairs

Alberto Del Bimbo   University of Firenze, Italy
Michael Brown   York University, Canada
Steven Waslander   University of Toronto, Canada

Workshop Chairs

Xiang Bai   Huazhong University of Science and Technology,
                              China
Giovanni Farinella   University of Catania, Italy
Laurence Likforman   Télécom Paris, France
Jonathan Wu   University of Windsor, Canada

Tutorial Chairs

David Clausi   University of Waterloo, Canada
Markus Enzweiler   Esslingen University of Applied Sciences,
                                    Germany
Umapada Pal   Indian Statistical Institute, India

Local Arrangements Chair

Ioannis Rekleitis   University of South Carolina, USA

Finance Chairs

Rainer Herpers   Hochschule Bonn-Rhein-Sieg, Germany
Andrew Hogue   Ontario Tech University, Canada

Publication Chairs

Jean-Jacques Rousseau   York University, Canada
Bill Kapralos   Ontario Tech University, Canada

Awards Chair

Johana Hansen   McGill University, Canada

Sponsorship and Exhibition Chair

Hong Zhang   Southern University of Science and Technology
                                    (SUSTech), China

Challenges Chairs

Marco Bertini   University of Florence, Italy
Dimosthenis Karatzas   Universitat Autónoma de Barcelona, Spain

Track 1: Artificial Intelligence, Machine Learning for Pattern Analysis

Battista Biggio	Università degli Studi di Cagliari, Italy
Ambra Demontis	Università degli Studi di Cagliari, Italy
Gang Hua	Wormpex AI Research, University of Washington, USA
Dacheng Tao	University of Sydney, Australia

Track 2: Computer Vision and Robotic Perception

Olga Bellon	Universidade Federal do Parana, Brazil
Kosta Derpanis	York University, Canada
Ko Nishino	Kyoto University, Japan

Track 3: Image, Speech, Signal and Video Processing

Ana Fred	University of Lisbon, Portugal
Regina Lee	York University, Canada
Jingdong Wang	Baidu, China
Vera Yashina	Russian Academy of Sciences, Russian Federation

Track 4: Biometrics and Human-Computer Interaction

Kevin Bowyer	University of Notre Dame, USA
Kerstin Dautenhahn	University of Waterloo, Canada
Julian Fierrez	Universidad Autónoma de Madrid, Spain
Shiqi Yu	Southern University of Science and Technology, China

Track 5: Document Analysis and Recognition

Alexandra Branzan Albu	University of Victoria, Canada
Alicia Fornes	Universitat Autònoma de Barcelona, Spain
Koichi Kise	Osaka Prefecture University, Japan
Faisal Shafait	National University of Sciences and Technology, Pakistan

Track 6: Biomedical Imaging and Informatics

Hamid Abbasi   Auckland Bioengineering Institute, New Zealand
Ismail Bey Ayed   Ecole de Technologie Superieure (ETS), Canada
Lukas Käll   KTH Royal Institute of Technology, Sweden
Dinggang Shen   ShanghaiTech University, China

ICPR 2022 Workshops: Volume I

Towards a Complete Analysis of People: From Face and Body to Clothes (T-CAP)

Mohamed Daoudi	IMT Lille Douai, France
Roberto Vezzani	University of Modena and Reggio Emilia, Italy
Guido Borghi	University of Bologna, Italy
Marcella Cornia	University of Modena and Reggio Emilia, Italy
Claudio Ferrari	University of Parma, Italy
Federico Becattini	University of Florence, Italy
Andrea Pilzer	NVIDIA AI Technology Center, Italy

12th International Workshop on Human Behavior Understanding (HBU)

Albert Ali Salah	Utrecht University, The Netherlands
Cristina Palmero	University of Barcelona, Spain
Hugo Jair Escalante	National Institute of Astrophysics, Optics and Electronics, Mexico
Sergio Escalera	Universitat de Barcelona, Spain
Henning Müller	HES-SO Valais-Wallis, Switzerland

Theories, Applications, and Cross Modality for Self-Supervised Learning Models (SSL)

Yu Wang	NVIDIA, USA
Yingwei Pan	JD AI Research, China
Jingjing Zou	UC San Diego, USA
Angelica I. Aviles-Rivero	University of Cambridge, UK
Carola-Bibiane Schönlieb	University of Cambridge, UK
John Aston	University of Cambridge, UK
Ting Yao	JD AI Research, China

Multimodal Pattern Recognition of Social Signals in Human-Computer-Interaction (MPRSS 2022)

Mariofanna Milanova	University of Arkansas at Little Rock, USA
Xavier Alameda-Pineda	Inria, University of Grenoble-Alpes, France
Friedhelm Schwenker	Ulm University, Germany

Fairness in Biometric Systems (FAIRBIO)

Philipp Terhörst	Paderborn University, Germany
Kiran Raja	Norwegian University of Science and Technology, Norway
Christian Rathgeb	Hochschule Darmstadt, Germany
Abhijit Das	BITS Pilani Hyderabad, India
Ana Filipa Sequeira	INESC TEC, Portugal
Antitza Dantcheva	Inria Sophia Antipolis, France
Sambit Bakshi	National Institute of Technology Rourkela, India
Raghavendra Ramachandra	Norwegian University of Science and Technology, Norway
Naser Damer	Fraunhofer Institute for Computer Graphics Research IGD, Germany

2nd International Workshop on Artificial Intelligence for Healthcare Applications (AIHA 2022)

Nicole Dalia Cilia	Kore University of Enna, Italy
Francesco Fontanella	University of Cassino and Southern Lazio, Italy
Claudio Marrocco	University of Cassino and Southern Lazio, Italy

Workshop on Multimodal Data for Mental Disorder Recognition (MDMR)

Richang Hong	Hefei University of Technology, China
Marwa Mahmoud	University of Glasgow, UK
Bin Hu	Lanzhou University, China

ICPR 2022 Workshops: Volume II

5th International Workshop on coMics ANalysis, Processing and Understanding (MANPU 2022)

Jean-Christophe Burie	University of La Rochelle, France
Motoi Iwata	Osaka Metropolitan University, Japan
Miki Ueno	Osaka Institute of Technology, Japan

Image Analysis for Forest Environmental Monitoring (FOREST)

Alexandre Bernardino	Instituto Superior Técnico, Portugal
El Khalil Cherif	Instituto Superior Técnico, Portugal
Catarina Barata	Instituto Superior Técnico, Portugal
Alexandra Moutinho	Instituto Superior Técnico, Portugal
Maria João Sousa	Instituto Superior Técnico, Portugal
Hugo Silva	Instituto Superior de Engenharia do Porto, Portugal

MultiMedia FORensics in the WILD (MMFORWILD 2022)

Mauro Barni	University of Siena, Italy
Sebastiano Battiato	University of Catania, Italy
Giulia Boato	University of Trento, Italy
Hany Farid	University of California, Berkeley, USA
Nasir Memon	New York University, USA

Image Mining: Theory and Applications (IMTA-VIII)

Igor Gurevich	Federal Research Center Computer Science and Control of the Russian Academy of Sciences, Russian Federation
Davide Moroni	Institute of Information Science and Technologies, National Research Council of Italy, Italy

Maria Antonietta Pascali

Institute of Information Science and
Technologies, National Research Council of
Italy, Italy

Vera Yashina

Federal Research Center Computer Science and
Control of the Russian Academy of Sciences,
Russian Federation

International Workshop on Pattern Recognition in Healthcare Analytics (PRHA 2022)

Inci Baytas   Bogazici University, Turkey
Edward Choi   Korea Advanced Institute of Science and
                            Technology, South Korea
Arzucan Ozgur   Bogazici University, Turkey
Ayse Basar   Bogazici University, Turkey

International Workshop on Industrial Machine Learning (IML)

Francesco Setti   University of Verona, Italy
Paolo Rota   University of Trento, Italy
Vittorio Murino   University of Verona, Italy
Luigi Di Stefano   University of Bologna, Italy
Massimiliano Mancini   University of Tübingen, Germany

ICPR 2022 Workshops: Volume III

3rd International Workshop on Pattern Recognition for Cultural Heritage (PatReCH 2022)

Dario Allegra   University of Catania, Italy
Mario Molinara   University of Cassino and Southern Lazio, Italy
Alessandra Scotto di Freca   University of Cassino and Southern Lazio, Italy
Filippo Stanco   University of Catania, Italy

2nd Workshop on Explainable and Ethical AI (XAIE 2022)

Romain Giot   Univ. Bordeaux, France
Jenny Benois-Pineau   Univ. Bordeaux, France
Romain Bourqui   Univ. Bordeaux, France
Dragutin Petkovic   San Francisco State University, USA

12th Workshop on Pattern Recognition in Remote Sensing (PRRS)

Ribana Roscher   University of Bonn, Germany
Charlotte Pelletier   Université Bretagne Sud, France
Sylvain Lobry   Paris Descartes University, France

Computer Vision for Analysis of Underwater Imagery (CVAUI)

Maia Hoeberechts   Ocean Networks Canada, Canada
Alexandra Branzan Albu   University of Victoria, Canada

Understanding and Mitigating Demographic Bias in Biometric Systems (UMDBB)

Ajita Rattani   Wichita State University, USA
Michael King   Florida Institute of Technology, USA

ICPR 2022 Workshops: Volume IV

AI for De-escalation: Autonomous Systems for De-escalating Conflict in Military and Civilian Contexts (AI4D)

Victor Sanchez	University of Warwick, UK
Irene Amerini	Sapienza University of Rome, Italy
Chang-Tsun Li	Deakin University, Australia
Wei Qi Yan	Auckland University of Technology, New Zealand
Yongjian Hu	South China University of Technology, China
Nicolas Sidere	La Rochelle Université, France
Jean-Jacques Rousseau	York University, Canada

3rd Workshop on Applied Multimodal Affect Recognition (AMAR)

Shaun Canavan	University of South Florida, USA
Tempestt Neal	University of South Florida, USA
Saurabh Hinduja	University of Pittsburgh, USA
Marvin Andujar	University of South Florida, USA
Lijun Yin	Binghamton University, USA

Contents – Part III

2nd Workshop on Explainable and Ethical AI (XAIE 2022)

Computer Vision for Analysis of Underwater Imagery (CVAUI)

Understanding and Mitigating Demographic Bias in Biometric Systems (UMDBB)

3rd International Workshop on Pattern Recognition for Cultural Heritage (PatReCH 2022)

W15 - Pattern Recognition for Cultural Heritage (PatReCH 2022)

PatReCH is a forum for scholars who study Pattern Recognition applications for Cultural Heritage valorization and preservation. Pattern recognition is rapidly contaminating new areas of our life day by day. On the other hand, the management of Cultural Heritage is increasingly in need of new solutions to document, manage and visit (even virtually) the enormous number of artifacts and information that come from the past. Currently, Pattern Recognition technologies are already employed in the fields of Cultural Heritage preservation and exploitation. From these fields two main issues arise: The information contained in digital representations of physical objects like scanned documents, scanned artifacts, maps, digital music, etc. are not easy to exploit and advanced patter recognition analysis is required. At the same time, the production of digital material such as augmented reality, Cultural Heritage games, robotics applications, etc. need innovative techniques and methodologies. The above issues are leading PR researchers to develop new methodologies and applications, which are able to analyze the available data and learn mathematical models to generate new ones in a smart way (for augmented reality, serious games, etc.). The third edition of the International Workshop on Pattern Recognition for Cultural Heritage was virtually held in Montréal, Quebec, in conjunction with the 26th International Conference on Pattern Recognition (ICPR 2022). This year we received 16 submissions for reviews from authors belonging to 11 distinct countries. After an accurate and thorough peer-review, we selected 13 papers for presentation at the workshop. The review process focused on the quality of the papers, their scientific novelty, and the impact for Cultural Heritage valorization. The acceptance of the papers was the results of two different reviews. All the high-quality papers were accepted, and the acceptance rate was 81%.

August 2022

Dario Allegra
Mario Molinara
Alessandra Scotto di Freca
Filippo Stanco

Detecting 3D Texture on Cultural Heritage Artifacts

Iyyakutti Iyappan Ganapathi[1,2]([✉]), Sajid Javed[1], Taimur Hassan[1,2],
and Naoufel Werghi[1,2,3]

[1] Department of Electrical Engineering and Computer Science, Khalifa University,
Abu Dhabi 127788, UAE
{iyyakutti.ganapathi,sajid.javed,taimur.hassan,Naoufel.Werghi}@ku.ac.ae
[2] C2PS, Khalifa University, Abu Dhabi 127788, UAE
[3] KUCARS, Khalifa University, Abu Dhabi 127788, UAE

Abstract. Textures in 3D meshes represent intrinsic surface properties
and are essential for numerous applications, such as retrieval, segmentation, and classification. The computer vision approaches commonly used
in the cultural heritage domain are retrieval and classification. Mainly,
these two approaches consider an input 3D mesh as a whole, derive features of global shape, and use them to classify or retrieve. In contrast,
texture classification requires objects to be classified or retrieved based
on their textures, not their shapes. Most existing techniques convert 3D
meshes to other domains, while only a few are applied directly to 3D
mesh. The objective is to develop an algorithm that captures the surface variations induced by textures. This paper proposes an approach for
texture classification directly applied to the 3D mesh to classify the surface into texture and non-texture regions. We employ a hybrid method in
which classical features describe each facet locally, and these features are
then fed into a deep transformer for binary classification. The proposed
technique has been validated using SHREC'18 texture patterns, and the
results demonstrate the proposed approach's effectiveness.

Keywords: Texture · 3D · Classification · Feature descriptor · Deep
learning · Artifacts

1 Introduction

Advances in digital technology have been implemented in a wide range of
interdisciplinary fields. The cultural heritage domain digitally captures antique
objects such as sculptures, paintings, and drawings used for reconstruction,
restoration, segmentation, and detection [1,16]. Compared to texture and color
information from a 2D domain, data captured in the 3D domain provides geometric structure, which aids in performance improvement. Furthermore, the collected
data are in a proper 3D format, allowing various computer vision techniques to

Supported by a research fund from Khalifa University, Ref: CIRA-2019-047.

J.-J. Rousseau and B. Kapralos (Eds.): ICPR 2022 Workshops, LNCS 13645, pp. 3–14, 2023.
https://doi.org/10.1007/978-3-031-37731-0_1

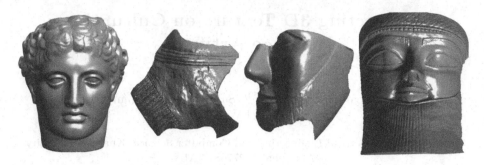

Fig. 1. Example patches from the SHREC'18 dataset with texture regions, such as the head region, eyebrows, and beards with substantial surface variations; and non-textured regions with smooth surface variations.

enhance and extract information. The texture classification is a unique problem that is based on the local components of any object, and their features rather than the overall shape [2,9]. In the literature, these issues have been addressed using classical and learning-based approaches, with most methods relying on classical techniques for feature extraction [3,10]. The techniques employed in the cultural heritage domain, particularly on 3D data, evaluate an input image globally and extract holistic features to classify or retrieve an image in either spatial or spectral-domain [2]. These features are derived primarily from the coordinates, normals, curvature, and shape index in the spatial domain. Normals provide information on orientation; curvature and shape index gives information on an object's surface variations. Hence, these geometric properties are commonly employed in the construction of features [6]. In contrast, in the spectral domain, descriptors depend primarily on the Laplace-Beltrami operator and its eigendecomposition [2]. Apart from these two approaches, a few adopting deep learning-based methods have lately been motivated by their success in computer vision [18].

This article introduces a hybrid technique for classifying texture and non-texture surfaces. The framework takes a 3D mesh as input and determines whether each facet belongs to texture or not. To the best of our knowledge, no work has been done in texture classification at the facet level. We propose a classical technique to extract facet-level information from a 3D mesh, which is then passed into a deep vision transformer for classification. At each facet, local depth (LD) and local facet orientations are utilized to create a grid structure resembling a 2D image by employing ordered ring facets (ORF) [22]. Unlike the other techniques [18] that convert a 3D mesh globally into 2D images, the proposed approach converts locally at the facet level to 2D images, utilizing the surface variations captured using local depth and spherical coordinates. These images are divided into a patch sequence to train a transformer, and the optimally learned parameters are then applied to classify a test facet. The obtained results demonstrate the efficiency of the proposed method.

2   Related Works

Numerous methods for defining texture patterns based on repeatability, randomness, and orientation have been developed in the 2D image domain [4,12]. For example, local descriptors are derived from convolution-based filtering operations, such as Gabor or Local Binary Pattern (LBP) [14]. Texture analysis is a mature field in the 2D domain, but it is still in its infancy in the 3D domain. Hence, several techniques described in the literature extend the 2D texture analysis to the 3D domain [2]. For instance, in [21], a 3D mesh convolution, an extended version of 2D, is introduced. Similarly, MeshHOG [25] and MeshLBP [22] are extensions of two of the most popular 2D techniques, HOG [4] and LBP.

Mesh local binary pattern (MeshLBP), and its applications are introduced in [22–24]. These techniques use ordered ring facets (ORF) at each facet, where the geometric difference between the facet and its neighboring facets is utilized in the MeshLBP computation. However, these techniques face difficulties with boundary facets that lack adjacent facets. Several other methods in SHREC'17, a track on relief patterns, utilize 2D images of 3D meshes and then apply image processing techniques, such as morphological operations, to determine the texture pattern. Those techniques performed better than many others, even though they are simple and easy to use. In [2], a covariance descriptor is presented utilizing 2D images derived from 3D mesh and used to compare texture patterns. Similarly, Giachetti *et al.* use a 2D raster image of 3D meshes and then apply an improved fisher vector (IFV) to the resulting 2D image to obtain the feature vectors [7]. Tatsuma and Aono extracted depth images from 3D meshes and converted them into LBP images, where a few statistical features are computed and concatenated to construct the final feature [2]. Sun *et al.* introduced a descriptor that utilizes the interior dihedral angle of mesh edges. The obtained angles are used to construct a histogram to identify similarities between texture patterns [2]. Texture-based applications are more prevalent in the 2D domain with wavelet transform. Masoumi *et al.* was inspired by this and developed a signature based on wavelets and geodesic distances [13].

The other category in texture analysis uses spectral descriptors, which are more robust to 3D object transformation. Limberger and Wilson presented a curvature-based Laplace Beltrami operator, which is decomposed to produce an enhanced wave kernel signature (IWKS) [11] and further encoded to find similarities between texture patterns. Signature Quadratic Form Distance (SQFD) introduces a distance metric for matching the local features of 3D objects to determine their similarity [19]. This method generated the features using the Laplace-Beltrami operator and evaluated the performance of the proposed distance metric using wave kernel descriptor variants. Spectral descriptors have drawbacks since they rely on the computation of the Laplace-Beltrami operator and its eigendecomposition; the complexity of these descriptors is directly proportional to the number of vertices in the input mesh. The input 3D samples can be downsampled to reduce complexity, however, this may result in loss of fine details and degrades performance in texture analysis.

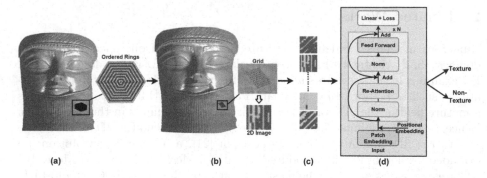

Fig. 2. Outline of the proposed approach. (a) Ordered ring facets, (b) 2D image for a facet generated employing a grid computed using the ordered rings, (c) 2D images generated for all facets, and (d) transformer fed with generated images to classify each facet as texture or non-texture.

Like MeshLBP, EdgeLBP uses concentric spheres with varying radii at each facet on a mesh surface. Twelve equidistant points are generated for each intersecting contour to compute a local binary pattern [20]. Similarly, mesh convolution is introduced in [8,21], where [8] performs convolution by tessellation modification, and [21] performs convolution through a grid and can be extended to texture classification. In SHREC'2021 [18], a track in retrieving cultural heritage objects, more techniques are based on deep learning than in previous years. Compared to the 3D domain, most of these techniques utilize the 2D domain to exploit the power of deep learning by transforming 3D mesh or point cloud into multi-view 2D images fed to off-the-shelf CNN models. Others reduce the image dimensions using an autoencoder for classification or retrieval. A few techniques apply directly on 3D meshes employing popular deep learning architectures such as PointNet [17].

3   Proposed Approach

Inspired by the performance of transformers in computer vision, we adopted a deep vision transformer to classify texture and non-textured regions on a surface. The proposed framework includes a feature descriptor to generate images at each facet is explained in Sect. 3. Further, Sect. 3.1 describes how these images are fed as input to a deep transformer for classification. The outline of the proposed framework is shown in Fig. 2.

Ordered Ring. For a 3D mesh, we first compute ordered ring facets for each facet by employing adjacent faces {1,2,3} and other faces, Fgap, as shown in Fig. 3(a). To normalize the starting position of a facet in a ring, we reorder it so that the first facet in each ring is closest to the centroid of the rings. A regular mesh with $R = r_1, r_2, ...r_n$ ordered rings, where r_1 represents the first ring

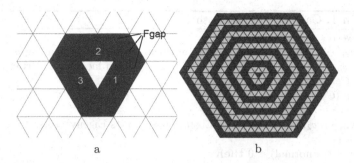

Fig. 3. Ordered ring facets. (a) Example of a ring constructed at a facet using the adjacent facets {1,2,3} and the Fgap facets and (b) example of ten rings constructed similarly using the adjacent and Fgap facets.

with 12 facets, r_2 represents the second ring with 24 facets, and r_n represents the nth ring with $n \cdot 12$ facets. The facets in each ring are described using the proposed features, which aid in describing the surface variations of the 3D mesh. Figure 3(a & b) depicts an illustration of one ring and ten rings generated on a mesh surface.

Local Features. Local depth, azimuth, and elevation are the local features computed at each facet. The local depth feature at a facet is computed using a covariance matrix which is constructed using vertices $C \in \mathcal{R}^{N \times 3}$ extracted from neighbouring facets. The covariance matrix is defined as $H = \hat{C}^T * \hat{C}$, where $\hat{C} = C - \bar{C}$ and $\bar{C}$ is the mean of vertices C. Further, eigenvalues and eigenvectors are obtained by decomposing H, where the eigenvector of the smallest eigenvalue is chosen as a normal. A plane is then constructed using the obtained normal and vertices C; it is used to find the local depth of any point by computing the distance between the point and the plane. Algorithm 1 provides pseudocode for implementation. Similarly, the azimuth and elevation features are computed using the normals converted from Cartesian to spherical coordinates as given in Algorithm 2.

Image Generation. At each facet, a 2D image of size $[2R \times 2R]$ is generated using the obtained local features where R is the number of rings. The ordered ring facets surrounding a central facet display a pattern of arithmetic progression that is utilized in a grid design. To construct a grid at a facet, $4R^2$ facets from the ordered rings are chosen. If the number of facets is less than $4R^2$, then the grid construction at that particular facet is skipped. Due to this constraint, grids are not constructed at border facets, and it is shown in Fig. 5(c). The grid has four quadrants, and each quadrant has its arithmetic pattern. We can extract the four quadrants that comprise the Mesh-Grid by determining the size of each quadrant. Each position in the obtained grid is filled with the obtained local features, local depth, azimuth, and elevation. Each forms a channel and is

---

Algorithm 1. Calculate LocalDepth

Require: vertex, face, RingList (R)

$R = r_1, r_2, \cdots r_n$ (R contains n number of rings, with each ring having $n \cdot 12$ facets)

$v_1, v_2, \cdots v_n \leftarrow f_1, f_2, \cdots f_n \leftarrow R$ (Obtain facets and vertices from R)

$C \leftarrow GetCenter(v_1, v_2 \cdots v_n)$

$\hat{C} \leftarrow mean(C)$

$H \leftarrow \hat{C}' * \hat{C}$

$[\lambda_1, \lambda_2, \lambda_3], [v_1, v_2, v_3] \leftarrow eig(H)$ (Eigenvalues and its Eigenvectors, $\lambda_1 < \lambda_2 < \lambda_3$)

normal $\leftarrow v_1$

if $sign([0 \; 0 \; 1] * \text{normal}) < 0$ **then**

     normal = -normal

end if

Construct a plane $Ax + By + Cz + D$ using $[v_1, v_2, \cdots v_n]$ and normal

LocalDepth $\leftarrow d = |Ax_0 + By_0 + Cz_0 + D|/\sqrt{(A^2 + B^2 + C^2)}$ (distance of a point x_0, y_0, z_0) to the plane

---

Algorithm 2. Calculate Azimuth and elevation

Require: vertex, face, RingList (R)

$R = r_1, r_2, \cdots r_n$ (R contains n number of rings, with each ring having $n \cdot 12$ facets)

$v_1, v_2, \cdots v_n \leftarrow f_1, f_2, \cdots f_n \leftarrow R$ (Obtain facets and vertices from R)

$normal(x, y, z) \leftarrow computeNormal(vertex, face)$ (Compute normal)

Azimuth $\leftarrow atan(y, x)$

Elevation $\leftarrow atan(z, \sqrt{(x^2 + y^2)})$

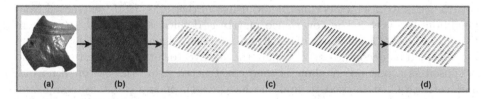

Fig. 4. Image generation (a) Grid at a facet highlighted in red box, (b) magnified grid where each position in the grid represents an index of a mesh facet, (c) using the index, each position in the grid is filled with local depth, azimuth, and elevation values (three images), and (d) final image obtained by concatenating images obtained in (c). (Color figure online)

finally concatenated to generate a three-channel 2D image. An example of a grid and the image generated at a facet is shown in Fig. 4.

3.1   Transformer Architecture

We use DeepVit [26] for classification, which is trained using 2D images generated at each facet. DeepVit is a modification of ViT [5] where the number of transformer blocks is higher than ViT, and the attention module is replaced with a Re-Attention module. The base transformer ViT has challenges in gaining

(a)   (b)   (c)   (d)

Fig. 5. An example of a training sample and its ground truth. (a) 3D mesh surface, (b) ground truth of texture in red and non-textured in yellow, (c & d) portion of the surface used in training and its corresponding ground truth. (Color figure online)

advantages from deeper architecture because the cosine similarity between the cross-layer attention head is high when the architecture becomes deeper. This shows that the architecture could not learn new features when the architecture is deeper. Therefore, DeepViT uses ReAttention and high embedded feature dimensions to allow deeper architecture.

$$\text{ReAttention(Q,K,V)} = Norm(\Theta^T(softmax(\frac{QK^T}{\sqrt{d}})))V \qquad (1)$$

where Q is the query, K and V are key-value pairs, and d is a scaling factor. $\Theta \in \mathcal{R}^{h \times h}$ is a learnable parameter that interacts between the attention heads h to seek complementary information to improve the performance. In general, multiplying Q and K produces an attention map containing similarities between all tokens within each layer. However, ReAttention's attention map is updated by the learnable parameter Θ before being multiplied by V. This learnable parameter increases the variability of the attention head and allows for a deeper architecture. The transformer block is shown in Fig. 2(d).

Training. The 2D image at each facet is constructed using $R = 15$ rings such that it can capture the texture pattern. Choosing a small ring number relatively does not cover the texture pattern, and on the other hand, selecting a higher number covers a large portion of the mesh and might cause losing the local properties. Through experimentation, we found the optimal ring value between 12 to 15. However, the ORF does not generate rings if any ring reaches the boundary. Due to this, we consider only the center portion of a 3D mesh surface for training. Using the grid structure, we generated an image of 30×30 and is resized to 224×224, and a patch size of 32 is used to train the transformer.

3.2 Training Loss

A binary cross-entropy loss function is chosen and minimized during training to learn a set of parameters. Consider the parameter vector θ corresponding to the task of locating the texture region is given as

$$\mathcal{L}(\theta) = \frac{1}{N} \sum_{i=1}^{N} -(y_i log(p_i) + (1 - y_i) log(1 - p_i)) \tag{2}$$

where p_i represents the probability of a textured region, $1 - p_i$ represents the probability of a non-textured region, and $y_i = 1$ represents the label for a textured region and $y_i = 0$ otherwise. By training, the optimal parameters are updated in each iteration, and the learned parameters are used to classify texture and non-texture regions in a test 3D mesh.

3.3 Implementation Details

The proposed network is implemented using PyTorch [15] on 2 RTX 2080 NVIDIA GPUs for 50 epochs. The training is conducted using an Adam optimizer with a learning rate of 0.00003 and a dropout of 0.1 to minimize the binary cross-entropy loss. Zero is assigned to non-textured regions, and one is assigned to textured regions in the annotated label used for training.

4 Experimental Evaluation

Using the SHREC'18 dataset, the performance of the proposed method is evaluated [3]. It comprises ten patches, three of which have multiple texture patterns, while the others have a single texture pattern. Aside from the non-textured region, there are 11 distinct texture patterns. MeshLab is used to label the faces as texture and non-texture. We discovered that the created training samples have more texture-related facets than non-textured facets. Therefore, we utilized augmented images from non-textured regions to balance the training samples to train the network. Since the task is a binary classification of texture and non-texture, patches comprising single and multiple textures are considered one class and non-textured as another. Figure 5(a & b) depicts an example of a surface and its ground truth, where red represents the texture region and yellow represents the non-textured region. The portion highlighted blue in Fig. 5 (c) is used to generate 2D images since ORF encounters difficulties near the boundary, and Fig. 5 (d) is the corresponding ground truth. Therefore, for each surface utilized in the experiment, only the center portion is used to generate the 2D images. It is possible to maximize portion coverage by selecting fewer rings; however, this reduces the description of texture and non-texture regions. We evaluate performance using precision, recall, and F1-score. Precision is the proportion of correctly predicted positive instances, recall is the fraction of correctly predicted positive cases to all positive cases, and F1-score combines precision and recall. We conducted experiments using DeepViT and ViT architecture and reported the quantitative and qualitative results. The objective is to classify whether each facet belongs to texture or not.

Table 1. Performance of the proposed approach on the SHREC'18 dataset. Five surfaces are used to validate using the metrics precision, recall, and F1-score. The best performance is highlighted in bold.

Surface	ViT [5]			DeepViT [26]		
	Precision	Recall	F1-Score	Precision	Recall	F1-Score
1	0.70	0.69	0.69	**0.72**	**0.70**	**0.71**
2	0.62	0.60	0.61	**0.70**	**0.66**	**0.68**
3	0.72	0.70	0.71	**0.78**	**0.76**	**0.77**
4	0.71	0.69	0.70	**0.76**	**0.72**	**0.75**
5	0.76	0.72	0.74	**0.81**	**0.76**	**0.79**

4.1 Quantitative Results

Three metrics, precision, recall, and F1-score, are computed on the SHREC'18 dataset to demonstrate the performance of the proposed technique. Table 1 shows the performance of the proposed approach. Five surfaces have been used to evaluate the proposed method's performance. As mentioned above, we consider all textures as one class and the non-textured as another. We chose ViT [5] and deep transformer [26] as the backbone to test the performance of the proposed approach and reported without comparison since no baseline classification techniques at the facet level exist in the literature to compare our technique. The classification results for most surfaces are above 75% using DeepViT and above 70% for ViT.

4.2 Qualitative Results

A few visual examples are provided to demonstrate the effectiveness of the proposed approach. Figure 6 shows ground truth and predicted results in the top, and bottom rows, respectively, where red represents the texture region and yellow represents the non-textured region. Due to boundary restrictions, only the central portion of a surface is used for training and testing. The proposed method produces better predictions; nonetheless, classification difficulties arise in locations where the transition from textured to non-textured areas occurs. This is because the ordered ring facets in the transition region cover texture and non-texture regions, and the images generated by these facets produce ambiguity during training. By selecting ordered rings of small size, the effect can be minimized; nevertheless, it does not adequately cover the texture region of a facet, and the resulting image may not accurately encode the texture and non-textured regions. Another reason is that non-textured regions are not smooth across all patches; therefore, a network should expose to a wide range of non-textured surfaces. Increasing the number of rings could improve the performance; nonetheless, determining the optimal number of rings is difficult; we use between 12 and 15. A large ring number generates a global feature representation rather than a

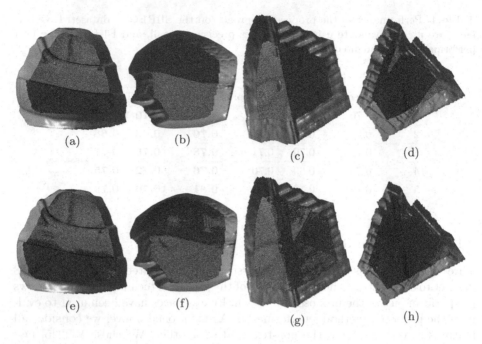

Fig. 6. Visual examples of classification facets. (a - d) 3D mesh surface with texture and non-textured ground truth; (e - h) predicted results of the proposed approach. The classification performance in (e,f, and h) is better than (g). In all cases, the facets near the transition encounter challenges in classification.

local representation. This issue can be addressed by using adaptive rings around a facet, given that a facet in the non-textured region requires fewer rings than one in the texture region.

5   Conclusion

A hybrid approach is proposed for classifying texture and non-texture regions in a 3D mesh. Each facet of a mesh is described using ordered rings generated from neighbor facets and is utilized to construct a grid where the grid positions are filled with the proposed features to generate a two-dimensional image. Further, the resulting image is fed to DeepViT, a deep transformer, to classify a facet. We have reported our results on the SHREC'18 dataset, even though no work on 3D texture classifications has yet been published. The results are encouraging, and DeepViT has demonstrated superior performance than ViT. Since there is a scarcity of 3D mesh data with labeled facets, we plan to annotate a few datasets with multiple classes and, in our future work, extend our current work to multi-class textures classification.

References

1. Andreetto, M., Brusco, N., Cortelazzo, G.M.: Automatic 3D modeling of textured cultural heritage objects. IEEE Trans. Image Process. **13**(3), 354–369 (2004)
2. Biasotti, S., et al.: Shrec'17 track: retrieval of surfaces with similar relief patterns. In: 10th Eurographics Workshop on 3D Object Retrieval (2017)
3. Biasotti, S., et al.: Shrec'18 track: recognition of geometric patterns over 3D models. In: Eurographics Workshop on 3D Object Retrieval, vol. 2, pp. 71–77 (2018)
4. Dalal, N., Triggs, B.: Histograms of oriented gradients for human detection. In: 2005 IEEE Computer Society Conference on Computer Vision and Pattern Recognition (CVPR'05), vol. 1, pp. 886–893 (2005)
5. Dosovitskiy, A., et al.: An image is worth 16x16 words: transformers for image recognition at scale. arXiv preprint arXiv:2010.11929 (2020)
6. Ganapathi, I.I., Javed, S., Fisher, R.B., Werghi, N.: Graph based texture pattern classification. In: 2022 8th International Conference on Virtual Reality (ICVR), pp. 363–369 (2022)
7. Giachetti, A.: Effective characterization of relief patterns. In: Computer Graphics Forum, vol. 37, pp. 83–92 (2018)
8. Hanocka, R., Hertz, A., Fish, N., Giryes, R., Fleishman, S., Cohen-Or, D.: Meshcnn: a network with an edge. ACM Trans. Graph. **38**(4), 1–12 (2019)
9. Hu, S., Li, Z., Wang, S., Ai, M., Hu, Q.: A texture selection approach for cultural artifact 3D reconstruction considering both geometry and radiation quality. Remote Sens. **12**(16), 2521 (2020)
10. Li, W., et al.: Shrec 2020 track: extended monocular image based 3D model retrieval (2020)
11. Limberger, F.A., Wilson, R.C.: Feature encoding of spectral signatures for 3D non-rigid shape retrieval. In: BMVC, pp. 56–61 (2015)
12. Lowe, D.G.: Distinctive image features from scale-invariant keypoints. Int. J. Comput. Vis. **60**(2), 91–110 (2004)
13. Masoumi, M., Li, C., Hamza, A.B.: A spectral graph wavelet approach for nonrigid 3D shape retrieval. Pattern Recogn. Lett. **83**, 339–348 (2016)
14. Ojala, T., Pietikainen, M., Harwood, D.: Performance evaluation of texture measures with classification based on kullback discrimination of distributions. In: Proceedings of 12th International Conference on Pattern Recognition, vol. 1, pp. 582–585 (1994)
15. Paszke, A., et al.: Pytorch: an imperative style, high-performance deep learning library. Adv. Neural Inf. Process. Syst. **32**, 8026–8037 (2019)
16. Pieraccini, M., Guidi, G., Atzeni, C.: 3D digitizing of cultural heritage. J. Cult. Heritage **2**(1), 63–70 (2001)
17. Qi, C.R., Su, H., Mo, K., Guibas, L.J.: Pointnet: deep learning on point sets for 3D classification and segmentation. In: Proceedings of the IEEE Conference on Computer Vision and Pattern Recognition, pp. 652–660 (2017)
18. Sipiran, I., et al.: Shrec 2021: retrieval of cultural heritage objects. Comput. Graph. **100**, 1–20 (2021)
19. Sipiran, I., Lokoc, J., Bustos, B., Skopal, T.: Scalable 3D shape retrieval using local features and the signature quadratic form distance. Vis. Comput. **33**(12), 1571–1585 (2017)
20. Thompson, E.M., Biasotti, S.: Description and retrieval of geometric patterns on surface meshes using an edge-based LBP approach. Pattern Recogn. **82**, 1–15 (2018)

21. Tortorici, C., Berretti, S., Obeid, A., Werghi, N.: Convolution operations for relief-pattern retrieval, segmentation and classification on mesh manifolds. Pattern Recogn. Lett. **142**, 32–38 (2021)
22. Werghi, N., Berretti, S., Del Bimbo, A.: The mesh-lbp: a framework for extracting local binary patterns from discrete manifolds. IEEE Trans. Image Process. **24**(1), 220–235 (2014)
23. Werghi, N., Tortorici, C., Berretti, S., Del Bimbo, A.: Local binary patterns on triangular meshes: Concept and applications. Comput. Vis. Image Understand. **139**, 161–177 (2015)
24. Werghi, N., Tortorici, C., Berretti, S., Del Bimbo, A.: Representing 3D texture on mesh manifolds for retrieval and recognition applications. In: Proceedings of the IEEE Conference on Computer Vision and Pattern Recognition, pp. 2521–2530 (2015)
25. Zaharescu, A., Boyer, E., Varanasi, K., Horaud, R.: Surface feature detection and description with applications to mesh matching. In: 2009 IEEE Conference on Computer Vision and Pattern Recognition, pp. 373–380 (2009)
26. Zhou, D., et al.: Deepvit: towards deeper vision transformer. arXiv preprint arXiv:2103.11886 (2021)

CIELab Color Measurement Through RGB-D Images

Furnari Giuseppe[1]($\boxtimes$) (ID), Allegra Dario[1] (ID), Gueli Anna[2,3] (ID),
and Stanco Filippo[1] (ID)

[1] Department of Mathematics and Computer Science (DMI), University of Catania,
Viale A. Doria 6, Catania, Italy
`giuseppe.furnari@phd.unict.it`
[2] Department of Physics and Astronomy "Ettore Majorana", University of Catania,
via S. Sofia 64, Catania, Italy
[3] INFN-CHNet Sez CT, via S. Sofia 64, Catania, Italy
`http://web.dmi.unict.it/`, `https://www.dfa.unict.it/`

Abstract. The color perception is a fundamental characteristic of humans. We use this capacity for an infinite number of activities. Even so, it has a strong subjective component, and many others factors can impact it. The color spaces were created to give an objective color measurement itself, one of the most used in the field of color measurement is the CIELab color space. The measurement of color combines multiple activities, from marketing, to dentistry, to cultural heritage; for instance color variations are used as degradation and conservation parameters. In this work, we propose a method to make automatic color measurements in a 3D context using a convolutional neural network to estimate the CIELab value of the acquired objects. In addition, a tool has been created to capture synthetic data for such research purposes. The proposed model has a very similar performance with the different illuminants that we explored.

Keywords: Color measurement · Color specification · CIELab

1 Introduction

The perception of color is certainly one of the fundamental skills of the human being. The color view, unlike the monochrome one, allows us to distinguish objects more easily. There has been a lot of discussion about the evolutionary reasons that led us to acquire this ability [2,3,9]. What we are sure of is that we could not imagine the human being without the perception of color. But color is not only seen as a tool that makes life easier, we usually associate emotions to color. Man has always used color as a means of communication through art. There is no work of art in which color has not been carefully chosen. In the modern era color is widely used in sales items to attract customers [8,13] as for smartphones, cars, but also in the food industry [4,10]. The color has an important role also in others contexts such as in the dentistry [7]. When we find

J.-J. Rousseau and B. Kapralos (Eds.): ICPR 2022 Workshops, LNCS 13645, pp. 15–20, 2023.
https://doi.org/10.1007/978-3-031-37731-0_2

ourselves in front of a work of art or, more generally, an object belonging to cultural heritage, one of the things that we cannot avoid is the color. From here, in the phase of acquisition and characterization of this object must definitely be inserted the color appropriately measured. This value can also be a valid indicator of the state of the conservation of the object [12]. The color measurement process is called color specification. Over the years, different color spaces have been created for this purpose, with different characteristics. One of the most common spaces for such activity is the CIELab color space. In this space it is possible to measure the difference between colors, this measure called ΔE_{ab}^*, it consists in the Euclidean distance between colors. The CIELab color space was born with the intention of being perceptively uniform. Differently from other measurements such as temperature, humidity, or quantity of certain substances, the colour does not simply depend on one factor, but on several factors including: the illuminant, the physical characteristics of the object, the place where it is placed. In addition, in the case of human color perception other factors can impact such as the background. As for the acquisition of digital images, other factors that impact the color rendering can be: the characteristics of the lens and the response of the sensors of the acquisition device [5]. What is clear from this premise is that color measurement clearly depends on multiple factors, which results in the impossibility of converting RGB to CIELab using a standard formula in every daily circumstance. For this purpose, different methods for measuring color have been proposed and developed over the years. One of the most used instruments for the measurement of color is the spectrophotometer which, resting directly on the object to be analyzed, constrains the impacting factors and simplifies the problem. These instruments are equipped with a light that reproduces a certain known illuminant, this light source illuminates the measuring surface in a "controlled" environment and then the instrument captures the electromagnetic response of the surface and determinates the corresponding coordinates in the CIELab color space. Although to date these instruments are the most precise and used in contexts where the measurement error must necessarily be low, they also have some cons, such as the need for physical contact with the object which is not always possible, the small measuring surface and the need for a flat surface on which to rest [10].

In the past years, also many innovative approaches have been presented to perform the RGB to CIELab transformation using computer vision and machine learning based methods. In [10] five models (direct, gamma, linear, quadratic and neural) are compared to solve the RGB to CIELab transformation. In previous studies [11] we performed experiments using Munsell Soil Charts as case study and performed conversion from HVC coordinates of the Munsell color space to the CIELab with the purpose to assist archaeologists. Color rendering depends heavily on the surface of the object and its geometric shape, this is the reason we took care of dealing with the transformation from RGB to CIELab using 3D data information such as RGB-D images and train a convolutional neural network (CNN) to perform the RGB-D to CIELab transformation [1], we observed better performance using the 3D information (adding the depth-map) compared to using RGB images only. To the best of our knowledge, there are no other similar methods that use 3D information such as depth map or 3D point clouds to perform color measurement in the CIELab color space. For this reason it is difficult to make a comparison with other state-of-the-art methods. In fact, our model uses the entire acquisition to determine the cielab value of the object Because of the difficulty and the long time required to acquire such types of data, in this work we build a python tool for Blender, a 3D modeling software, to acquire more data simulating different colors and brightness conditions. This tool allows us to train a previously studied model with a larger amount and variety of data. In the next section we will explain the dataset creation tool and the neural network used to perform the CIELab color transformation. In Sect. 3 we will discuss about experiments and results. And then, in Sect. 4 we will report our conclusions and future improvements.

2   Method

2.1   Dataset Creation Tool

Any machine learning method needs an adequate amount of data to be trained. In the color specification context, it is complicated and expensive to get such labeled data, even more in the case of three-dimensional data. Because, it is necessary to have a sufficient quantity of different colouring materials, measure the CIELab value using a spectrophotometer and capture 3D scans or RGB-D images in different brightness conditions. These reasons led us to choose to develop a tool to generate synthetic data in a controlled simulation environment. Blender was chosen as the software, in which a simple scene was recreated with an object in the center and a light source. The camera is designed to rotate around the object in order to acquire more views. To this scene was applied a python script used to vary the object in the center of the scene, its color and the illuminant. An example scene is shown in Fig. 1. This tool allow us also to change the simulated objects material.

2.2   Color Transformation Network

In order to perform the estimation of the CIELab values for each color/scene, we build a deep convolutional neural network using the ResNet V2 [6] as base model with a global average pooling layer followed by a fully connected layer (FC) with 1000 neurons using the ReLu activation function and dropout with 20% probability, we finally have a last FC layer with 3 neurons with linear activation function in order to estimate the CIELab coordinates.

3   Experiments and Result

We acquired six objects (cube, icosphere, cone, torus, Suzanne the Blender mascot and a sculpture) using the dataset creation tool varying four illuminants

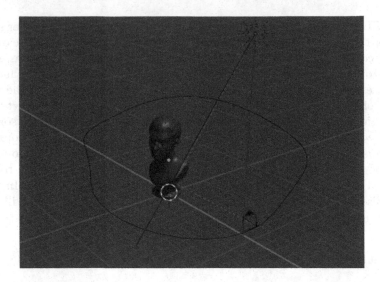

Fig. 1. Example of an acquired scene using Blender. The color is randomly generated by the python script and applied to the object. The approximately circular line indicates the path of the camera. Note how the color is different depending the surface.

(D50, D65, F11, F4) and 90 colors (nine hues and for each 10 variants changing the saturation and brightness). By performing all the combination of these parameters we obtained 2160 different 3D scenes, each scene was rendered as 30 RGB-D images by varying the position of the camera around it for each frame. For each illuminant we trained a color transformation network, with the assumption that the illuminant in the scene is known. In our experiments we used the 80% of the acquisitions as training set and the 20% as validation set, we also used a single hue variant for each hue as test set in order to test the performance on a color never seen from the model. The same subdivision has been repeated for all the illuminants experiments. The training phase lasted 50 epochs, using Adam as an optimizer with an initial learning rate of 1×10^{-3}. In Fig. 2 is shown the loss over epochs for each illuminant, this value refers to the mean squared error (MSE) over epochs. We used the ΔE_{ab}^* (color difference value for CIELab color space) as metric to monitor the performance of our models, this metrics are reported on Fig. 3. The minimum ΔE_{ab}^* value in the validation set is: 1.87, 1.84, 2.35, 2.16 respectively for D50, D65, F11 and F4, while in these points the test set ΔE_{ab}^* were: 6.86, 6.61, 6.47, 5.38 respectively for D50, D65, F11 and F4.

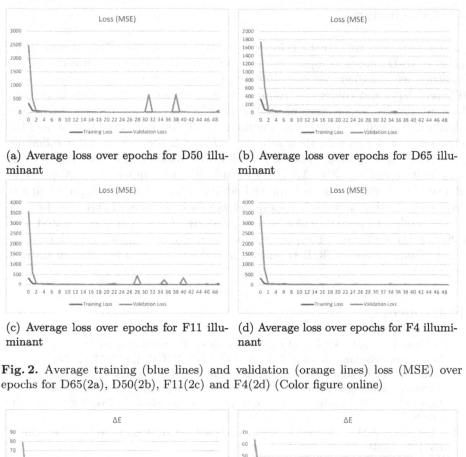

(a) Average loss over epochs for D50 illuminant

(b) Average loss over epochs for D65 illuminant

(c) Average loss over epochs for F11 illuminant

(d) Average loss over epochs for F4 illuminant

Fig. 2. Average training (blue lines) and validation (orange lines) loss (MSE) over epochs for D65(2a), D50(2b), F11(2c) and F4(2d) (Color figure online)

(a) Average ΔE_{ab}^* for D50

(b) Average ΔE_{ab}^* for D65

(c) Average ΔE_{ab}^* for F11

(d) Average ΔE_{ab}^* for F4

Fig. 3. Average training (blue lines), validation (orange lines) and test (gray lines) ΔE_{ab}^* over epochs for D65(3a), D50(3b), F11(3c) and F4(3d) (Color figure online)

4 Conclusion

In this work we explored the color specification task in the CIELab color space using RGB-D images as input and a deep convolutional neural network as color measurement method. We also build a tool in order to acquire objects with different light and colors condition, as results we saw that models have similar performance in the cases of studied illuminants, despite this the best value obtained was achieved with the illuminant D50. Results shows that model has high performance in validation set, $1 < \Delta E_{ab}^* < 2$ that means color difference perceptible only through close and careful observation, while does not perform very well on test set, $2 < \Delta E_{ab}^* < 10$ results on color difference perceptible at glance. The workflow can be improved adding a first phase of automatic illuminant classification, in addition more colors can be generated through the tool. Other models to perform color space transformation can be investigated with different types of training approach, such as multi-view input network or using point clouds instead of RGB-D images, in order to create a benchmark state on such task.

References

1. Allegra, D., et al.: A method to improve the color rendering accuracy in cultural heritage: preliminary results. J. Phys. Conf. Ser. **2204**(1), 012057 (2022)
2. Bompas, A., Kendall, G., Sumner, P.: Spotting fruit versus picking fruit as the selective advantage of human colour vision. i-Perception **4**(2), 84–94 (2013)
3. Bowmaker, J.K.: Evolution of colour vision in vertebrates. Eye **12**(3), 541–547 (1998)
4. Clydesdale, F.M.: Color as a factor in food choice. Crit. Rev. Food Sci. Nutr. **33**(1), 83–101 (1993)
5. Finlayson, G., Hordley, S., Schaefer, G., Tian, G.Y.: Illuminant and device invariant colour using histogram equalisation. Pattern Recogn. **38**(2), 179–190 (2005)
6. He, K., Zhang, X., Ren, S., Sun, J.: Identity mappings in deep residual networks. In: Leibe, B., Matas, J., Sebe, N., Welling, M. (eds.) ECCV 2016. LNCS, vol. 9908, pp. 630–645. Springer, Cham (2016). https://doi.org/10.1007/978-3-319-46493-0_38
7. Johnston, W.M.: Color measurement in dentistry. J. Dentist. **37**, e2–e6 (2009)
8. Labrecque, L.I., Milne, G.R.: Exciting red and competent blue: the importance of color in marketing. J. Acad. Market. Sci. **40**(5), 711–727 (2012)
9. Lamb, T.D., Collin, S.P., Pugh, E.N.: Evolution of the vertebrate eye: opsins, photoreceptors, retina and eye cup. Nat. Rev. Neurosci. **8**(12), 960–976 (2007)
10. Leon, K., Mery, D., Pedreschi, F., Leon, J.: Color measurement in l* a* b* units from rgb digital images. Food Res. Int. **39**(10), 1084–1091 (2006)
11. Milotta, F.L.M., et al.: Challenges in automatic munsell color profiling for cultural heritage. Pattern Recogn. Lett. **131**, 135–141 (2020)
12. Ramírez Barat, B., Cano, E., Molina, M.T., Barbero-Álvarez, M.A., Rodrigo, J.A., Menéndez, J.M.: Design and validation of tailored colour reference charts for monitoring cultural heritage degradation. Heritage Sci. **9**(1), 1–9 (2021). https://doi.org/10.1186/s40494-021-00511-6
13. Singh, S.: Impact of color on marketing. Manag. Decis. (2006)

Reconstruction of Cultural Heritage 3D Models from Sparse Point Clouds Using Implicit Neural Representations

Georgios Triantafyllou, George Dimas, Panagiotis G. Kalozoumis,
and Dimitris K. Iakovidis$^{(\boxtimes)}$

Department Computer Science and Biomedical Informatics, University of Thessaly,
Lamia, Greece
{gtriantafyllou,gdimas,pkalozoumis,diakovidis}@uth.gr

Abstract. Creating accessible museums and exhibitions is a key factor to today's society that strives for inclusivity. Visually-impaired people can benefit from manually examining pieces of an exhibition to better understand the features and shapes of these objects. Unfortunately, this is rarely possible, since such items are usually behind protective barriers due to their rarity, worn condition, and/or antiquity. Nevertheless, this can be achieved by 3D printed replicas of these collections. The fabrication of copies through 3D printing is much easier and less time-consuming compared to the manual replication of such items, which enables museums to acquire copies of other exhibitions more efficiently. In this paper, an accessibility-oriented methodology for reconstructing exhibits from sparse 3D models is presented. The proposed methodology introduces a novel periodic and parametric activation function, named WaveShaping (*WS*), which is utilized by a multi-layer perceptron (MLP) to reconstruct 3D models from coarsely retrieved 3D point clouds. The MLP is trained to learn a continuous function that describes the coarse representation of a 3D model. Then, the MLP is regarded as a continuous implicit representation of the model; hence, it can interpolate data points to refine and restore regions of the model. The experimental evaluation on 3D models taken from the ShapeNet dataset indicates that the novel *WS* activation function can improve the 3D reconstruction performance for given coarse point cloud model representations.

Keywords: 3D reconstruction · Machine Learning · Cultural Heritage

1 Introduction

The field of 3D printing has witnessed a booming interest during the last few decades. This interest has led to the development of state-of-the-art 3D printers

This work is supported by the project "Smart Tourist" (MIS 5047243) which is implemented under the Action "Reinforcement of the Research and Innovation Infrastructure", funded by the Operational Programme "Competitiveness, Entrepreneurship and Innovation" (NSRF 2014-2020) and co-financed by Greece and the European Union (European Regional Development Fund).

J.-J. Rousseau and B. Kapralos (Eds.): ICPR 2022 Workshops, LNCS 13645, pp. 21–35, 2023.
https://doi.org/10.1007/978-3-031-37731-0_3

that are cost-efficient, less time-consuming, and can use a wide variety of materials. Competition to attract more visitors has led museums to strive for a policy of interchangeable collections and exhibits [13]. Museums, cultural venues, and archaeological sites can benefit from the use of 3D printers to enrich their collections with exhibits from other sites without needing the original copy. This can be achieved by creating 3D printed replicas of theses objects. Another benefit of this approach is that it can broaden the accessibility and experience of visually-impaired people (VIP). More specifically, studies have shown that VIP can benefit from touchable exhibits, since this would encourage them to attend museums or exhibitions and assist them to better understand the nature of the exhibits [35]. Moreover, in [6], the notion of 3D printed replicas was perceived in a positive light for VIP. For the purposes of 3D printing, high-fidelity 3D models that may be inaccessible or require manual curation are preferred [4]. On the contrary, coarse 3D models are disadvantageous in terms of quality, but require less effort to produce. Thus, it would be important if a replica produced from a coarse 3D model could be qualitatively comparable to that produced by the high-fidelity version of the same model. As regards the 3D printing of archaic objects, the available research has primarily focused on acquiring detailed versions of exhibits through 3D laser scanning or digital photogrammetry [26]. Further processing of the obtained data, involves the use of 3D modelling-related software and manual curation [4,26,36]. The benefits of automation through the incorporation of machine learning have been highlighted in [14,15,24]; nevertheless, relative techniques, such as artificial neural networks (ANNs), have not been thoroughly utilized in the processing of sparse 3D models of archaic objects.

Deep learning has been extensively implemented in the 3D geometry reconstruction task. Initially the proposed approaches used voxels [12,37], meshes [3,17], or point clouds [32,38] to train ANNs. These methods require the use of discrete items and can be computationally demanding or lack understanding of complex shapes. Implicit representations have exhibited a capability to express shapes in the form of continuous functions with the use of ANNs [9,10,25,29] or convolutional neural networks (CNNs) [31]. These networks, which are known as implicit neural representations (INRs), are tasked to approximate implicit functions based on raw data, point clouds, or latent codes with or without supervision [25,29,34]. Signed distance functions (SDFs) have been recently utilized in INRs to infer different geometries [7,23,29,34]. However, many of these approaches require 3D supervision and they cannot use only raw point cloud data, since they depend on pre-processed input or pre-training defined output values. This problem can be tackled by using the Eikonal equation to approximate SDFs [16,34]. An advantage of this approach is that the raw data both on and off the surface are used for learning, without the need of localization or any auto-encoding/decoding scheme. Considering the capacity of multi-layer perceptrons (MLPs) to learn continuous implicit representations of 3D models, in this paper, we leverage this property on applications regarding the 3D printing of archaeological exhibits using sparse 3D models. More specifically, a deep MLP-based

INR is proposed, where the neural network is equipped with a novel activation function, called hereinafter WaveShaping (WS) activation function. The WS function, due to its smoothing effect on the shape representation of the sparse 3D model, improves the performance of recently-proposed periodic activation functions that have been used in INRs [34]. Moreover, the form of its first derivative benefits the training process, enabling the network to provide better reconstruction results during inference. To the best of our knowledge, this is the first time that INRs have been used for the 3D reconstruction of complex archaic objects.

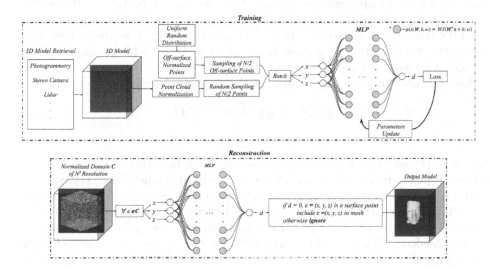

Fig. 1. Overview of the INR approach for the reconstruction of 3D models from sparse point clouds

2 Methods

The proposed methodology employs an MLP network tasked to learn an implicit continuous representation of a 3D model (Fig. 1). The MLP network utilizes a novel continuous activation function, abbreviated as WS, to learn an SDF which describes efficiently the 3D model that it aims to reconstruct [27]. In contrast to previous methodologies, the proposed approach can be efficiently trained given just a sparse point cloud of a 3D object, without the need of other information, *i.e.*, normals. The model, similarly to the SDF that is tasked to learn, receives as input a point $u = (x, y, z)^T$ of a 3D model and outputs a value approximating the respective SDF response. That value describes the distance of a point from the surface of the 3D model. After the training process, the model is capable to infer the 3D model at a higher resolution or restore any missing parts by predicting if a point in the defined 3D space belongs to the surface of the model, *i.e.*, its distance to the surface is 0.

2.1   Implicit Neural Representations and Mesh Reconstruction

Let $\boldsymbol{u} = (x, y, z)^T, x, y, z \in (-1, 1)$ be a point of a normalized point cloud $\boldsymbol{U}$ describing the 3D points that lie on the surface of a model. The surface of that model can be represented by the iso-surface of an SDF, $s(\cdot)$, where $s : \mathbb{R}^3 \to \mathbb{R}$ [27]. An SDF encodes the surface of a 3D model as the signed distance of a point $\boldsymbol{u}$ to the closest surface. The positive and negative values of an SDF indicate points that are outside and inside of the object surface at a distance $\pm d$, respectively, whereas a response $d = 0$ indicates that a point $\boldsymbol{u}$ lies on the surface of the 3D model. Since neural networks are universal function approximators, they can be trained to approximate an SDF that describes a particular 3D model. Subsequently, instead of representing the 3D model explicitly by the point cloud and the respective surface normals, the weights of the neural network are used to represent it implicitly through inference. Let $g(\cdot; \theta)$ be an MLP parametrized by θ, which is trained to approximate an SDF that describes a particular 3D model. Then, for different points in the 3D space, g predicts the following outputs:

$$g(\boldsymbol{u}; \theta) \approx s(\boldsymbol{u}) \approx 0, \forall \boldsymbol{u} \in \boldsymbol{U} \tag{1}$$

$$g(\boldsymbol{u}; \theta) \approx s(\boldsymbol{u}) \approx \pm d, \forall \boldsymbol{u} \notin \boldsymbol{U} \tag{2}$$

As Eqs. (1) and (2) suggest, $g(\cdot; \theta)$ needs to learn how the SDF responds for different points $\boldsymbol{u}$ that are on and off the surface of the model. Thus, the training dataset should be arranged to contain points $\boldsymbol{u}$ of the point cloud $\boldsymbol{U}$ that reside on the surface of the model, and random normalized samples of points $\boldsymbol{v} = (x, y, z)$ that occupy the rest of the spatial domain. These points $\boldsymbol{v}$ are samples from a random uniform distribution that comprises x, y, and z coordinates within the range of $[-1, 1]$. Each training batch is composed of $\frac{N}{2}$ samples of points $\boldsymbol{u}$ and $\boldsymbol{v}$, respectively, where N is the total batch size. For the training of the MLP, a variation of the loss function that was proposed in [34], which does not take the surface normals into consideration, has been adopted. The fitting of the network to the SDF is related to the solution of an Eikonal boundary value problem. The loss L that is used is defined as follows:

$$L = \sum_{\boldsymbol{U} \cup \boldsymbol{V}} \|\|\nabla_{\boldsymbol{u}} g(\boldsymbol{u}; \theta) - 1\|\| + \sum_{\boldsymbol{U}} \|g(\boldsymbol{u}; \theta)\| + \sum_{\boldsymbol{V}} \psi(g(\boldsymbol{v}; \theta)) \tag{3}$$

where $\boldsymbol{U}$ and $\boldsymbol{V}$ denote the sets of the points $\boldsymbol{u}$ and $\boldsymbol{v}$, respectively, that are included in the training. The first two terms of Eq. 3 are used to satisfy the condition of the Eikonal boundary value problem so that $g(\boldsymbol{u}; \theta)$ approximates an SDF. Specifically, the first term satisfies the need for the gradient norm $|\nabla_{\boldsymbol{u}} g(\boldsymbol{u}; \theta)|$ to be equal to 1 almost everywhere. The second term is added due to the condition that $s(\boldsymbol{u}) = 0, \forall \boldsymbol{u} \in \boldsymbol{U}$. Lastly, the third term is added to penalize the network when it predicts SDF values close to 0 for off-surface points. This is achieved by using $\psi(g(\boldsymbol{v}; \theta)) = e^{-\alpha * g(\boldsymbol{u}; \theta)}$, where $\alpha \gg 1$. Once $g(\cdot; \theta)$ is trained with points characterizing both the surface and the rest of the domain of a particular 3D model, $g(\cdot; \theta)$ can be used to reconstruct the model at different resolutions. Let $\boldsymbol{C}$ be a cubical normalized point cloud with a density n^3

and with points $c = (x, y, z)^T, x, y, z \in [-1, 1]$. By predicting the SDF values $\forall$ $c \in C$ using the trained network, we can reconstruct the model that was used for training by examining the responses of the network. The zero responses indicate that a point c is a surface point and thus it is included in the reconstructed mesh, whereas non-zero responses are off-surface points and they are ignored. In this way, sparse models can be reconstructed in different resolutions and missing parts can be restored. This process is possible since C is composed of points that originate from the same distribution as the training samples u and v. It should be noted that the proposed methodology can only interpolate data points that fall within the range of the training dataset distribution and it has no extrapolation capabilities.

Once a WS-equipped MLP has been trained to approximate an SDF of a 3D model, we can predict a point cloud whose points lie on the surface of that model. The trained model generates the point cloud according to the methodology described above. However, a raw point cloud containing only the vertex coordinates is not sufficient by itself to produce a 3D mesh, as it does not contain any information about the faces. For this purpose the Lewiner implementation of the marching cubes algorithm is employed to produce a 3D mesh given a predicted point cloud [22]. This way, the faces and vertices of the 3D model are estimated, enabling the reconstruction of its mesh.

2.2 WaveShaping Activation Function

Recently, the use of periodic activation functions, and particularly the sinusoidal (*sine*), for enhancing the performance of INRs has been proposed in the literature [34]. The utilization of *sine* as an activation function by the neurons of an MLP appears to substantially improve its representation capacity among different applications. In this paper, a periodic, parametric activation function, called WaveShaping function, is introduced to further improve the implicit representation performance of 3D models.

The proposed WS function is implemented by applying the hyperbolic tangent (*tanh*) as a "wave-shaper" to the *sine* activation function. The *tanh* has been chosen due to its wide application as a wave-shaper in various signal processing applications [18,20,28]. The proposed WS activation function and its derivative can be expressed as follows:

$$WS(x; \omega) = \frac{e^{sin(\omega x)} - e^{-sin(\omega x)}}{e^{sin(\omega x)} + e^{-sin(\omega x)}} \tag{4}$$

$$\frac{\partial WS(X; \omega)}{\partial x} = \frac{4\omega e^{2sin(\omega x)} cos(\omega x)}{(e^{2sin(\omega x)} + 1)^2} \tag{5}$$

where $\omega \in \mathbb{R}$ is a learnable parameter of WS in contrast to [34], where it is applied manually as a constant throughout the training and inference processes. Equation (2.2) describes the first derivative of the WS function.

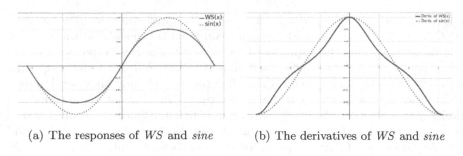

(a) The responses of WS and $sine$ (b) The derivatives of WS and $sine$

Fig. 2. Graphical representation of the proposed WS and $sine$

As it can be seen in Fig. 2a, given that $\omega = 1$, the proposed WS function can be characterized as an approximate scaled version of $sine$. Hence, it maintains the properties of $sine$, i.e., it has the same phase as $sine$, it is periodic and it has both upper and lower bounds. Nevertheless, as it can be observed in Fig. 2b, the derivation of the WS function produces a more complex expression. This leads to different computation of gradients during the training process compared to $sine$. This claim is further substantiated by the experimental evaluation in Sect. 3, which demonstrates that an MLP equipped with the WS learns efficiently an SDF even with a small sample of data points and without the incorporation of normals in the training process. Considering the above, a neuron $\phi(\cdot; W, b)$ of the MLP used in this work can be formally written as:

$$\phi(x; W, b, \omega) = WS(W^T x + b; \omega) \tag{6}$$

where $x, W \in \mathbb{R}^N$ represent the input and weight vectors, respectively, while $b \in \mathbb{R}$ is a bias term.

2.3   Experimental Setup

The proposed approach was evaluated both quantitatively and qualitatively with respect to its capacity to reconstruct 3D models from point cloud data. For this purpose, a subset of 12 categories obtained from the ShapeNet dataset was used to assess the reconstruction capabilities of the proposed method when applied on models of various shapes and resolutions [8]. From the 12 categories of the ShapeNet dataset, 2 models were randomly selected from each category. Dense and sparse point clouds of the meshes of the selected 3D models were automatically generated using the Monte Carlo (initial sampling) and Poisson disk (subsampling) algorithms implemented in the Meshlab software [11]. More specifically, for each model, a dense point cloud with 50,000 points was constructed through Monte Carlo sampling. These dense point clouds were sub-sampled by Poisson disk sampling to generate sparse point clouds with 1%, 5%, 10%, and 20% of the original point density; in total, 96 different objects were generated. The sub-sampling process was performed to simulate low-quality 3D representations of objects with various resolutions.

A different *WS*-based MLP-INR was trained on each point cloud and subsequently used to generate a mesh as described in Sub-sect. 2.1. In addition, two different activation functions, namely *sine* and Rectified Linear Unit (*ReLU*), were employed to comparatively analyze the performance of the proposed approach. These activation functions have been previously incorporated in MLPs for the reconstruction of 3D objects [29,34].

To demonstrate the capacity of *WS*-based MLP-INRs to reconstruct 3D features, two sparse models of archaic artifacts were used, namely a clay figurine of the Mycenaean period (1400 - 1050 B.C.) and part of a chryselephantine statuette (6th century B.C.). The two models were reconstructed from multiple photographs captured at different angles of artifacts displayed in the Archaeological Museum of Delphi in Greece [1] using the photogrammetry method (Meshroom v.2021.1.0) [2]. Figure 3 illustrates the actual artifacts and the reconstructed 3D models. To emulate the behaviour of low-quality 3D representations, the obtained meshes were sub-sampled and sparse point clouds were used to train MLP-INRs for each sub-sampling threshold.

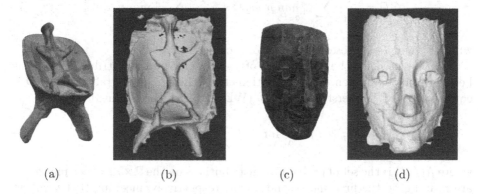

(a)   (b)   (c)   (d)

Fig. 3. Ancient artifacts exhibited in the museum of Delphi, Greece. (a) and (c) are photographs of the actual artifacts with removed background; (b) and (d) are the corresponding 3D models reconstructed using the photogrammetry method.

In all experiments, the architecture of the neural network comprised 4 hidden layers, with 256 neurons each, utilizing the proposed WS activation function and a linear output layer. Moreover, in all trials, the ω parameter of the WS was initialized before training with a value of 30 and the α parameter of the loss function with a value of $1e + 2$. To ensure the stability of the training, the point clouds were normalized with respect to the centroid of their x, y, and z coordinates in the $[-1, 1]$ region. For every point cloud, an MLP-INR was trained for 400 epochs with a learning rate equal to $1e - 4$ and batch size of 1024. The MLP-INRs trained with point clouds composed of less than 1024 points were trained using a batch size equal to the total number of points in the point cloud.

In addition, the reconstruction was performed at a resolution of 256^3 and the resulted point clouds were denormalized in order for the original and produced 3D models to coincide in terms of scale and origin. The experiments were performed using a computer system equipped with an AMD Ryzen 5 3400G 3.70GHz processor, 16.00 GB RAM and the NVIDIA 2060 Super GPU. The deep learning framework PyTorch v1.5 [30] was used for training the proposed neural network.

2.4 Evaluation Metrics

To quantitatively evaluate the proposed method, the Chamfer Distance (CD) [5] and Earth's Mover Distance (EMD) [33] metrics were employed. Both evaluation metrics have been widely used to evaluate the performance of 3D reconstruction methods. Given two different point clouds, CD is used to evaluate the distances between their closest points. Then, all the distances for both point clouds are squared and summed up. CD is formally formulated as:

$$CD = \frac{1}{|P_1|} \sum_{p \in P_1} \| \min_{q \in P_2} p - q \|_2^2 + \frac{1}{|P_2|} \sum_{q \in P_2} \| \min_{p \in P_1} p - q \|_2^2 \tag{7}$$

where P_1 and P_2 represent the two point clouds.

EMD is used for the comparison of two different data distributions. It has been proven that, when two distributions have the same integral, then EMD is equal to the 1st Wasserstein Distance (WD) [21], which is defined as [19]:

$$W_p(\mu, \zeta) = \inf_{\lambda \in \Lambda(\mu,\zeta)} \int_{\mathbb{R} \times \mathbb{R}} |x - y| \, d\lambda(x,y) \tag{8}$$

where $\Lambda(\mu, \zeta)$ is the set of probability distributions on the $\mathbb{R} \times \mathbb{R}$, whose marginals are μ and ζ on the first and second factor, respectively, meaning that $\forall$ subset $S \in \mathbb{R}$ $\lambda(S \times \mathbb{R}) = \mu(S)$ and $\lambda(\mathbb{R} \times S) = \zeta(S)$. In the context of this work, the probability distributions are replaced by the estimated and ground truth point clouds.

3   Results and Discussion

3.1   Quantitative and Qualitative Results

The quantitative results presented in Table 1 indicate that the *WS*-based MLPs achieve a better performance in reconstructing 3D objects given only a fraction of the original point cloud. However, as the density of the point cloud increases, the performance of the proposed approach becomes comparable to that of the *sine* function. A qualitative comparison among the utilization of *WS*, *sine*, and *ReLU* activation functions in the context of 3D model reconstruction is presented in

Table 1. Average CD ($\times 10^{-2}$) and EMD ($\times 10^{-2}$) for different thresholds of sub-sampled models from the 12 category subset of the ShapeNet dataset. Best results are indicated in boldface typesetting.

Sampled points (%)	Activation functions					
	WS		Sine		ReLU	
	CD	EMD	CD	EMD	CD	EMD
1	**3.53**	**1.61**	4.52	1.91	7.75	3.55
5	**2.30**	**1.40**	2.49	1.51	8.29	3.74
10	**1.69**	1.21	1.85	**1.20**	7.3	3.49
20	**1.49**	**1.06**	1.66	1.15	6.35	3.2

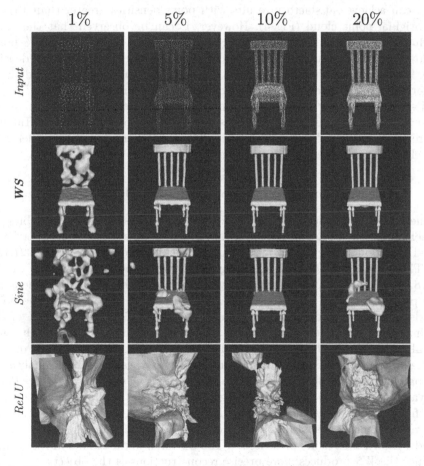

Fig. 4. 3D reconstruction results of a sample object (chair) from the ShapeNet dataset. The first row represents the training input for the INR and the rest show the result of the training using the *WS*, *sine*, and *ReLU*. The different columns correspond to different point cloud densities used as input.

Fig. 4. As it can be observed, the qualitative results reflect the results presented in Table 1, since the *WS* achieves a more precise reconstruction of the object given point clouds of different densities.

In general, the *WS*-based MLP-INRs appear to achieve a better performance in reconstructing 3D objects given only a fraction of the original point cloud, while, as the density of the point cloud increases, their performance becomes comparable to that of the *sine*-based ones. The resulted models depicted in Fig. 4 indicate that the proposed approach is able to better learn the shape of a 3D model for the 5%, 10%, and 20% point cloud densities. Moreover, under the 1% point cloud density, the *WS*-based MLP-INR is able to capture the shape of the model with more detail when compared to the *sine*-based MLP-INR. In addition, the *WS*-based MLP-INRs seem to provide more consistent results when applied to various point cloud densities, whereas the *sine*-based MLP-INRs can achieve satisfactory results with point densities greater than 10% of the original point cloud (Fig. 4). However, it can be observed that the mesh produced with the utilization of the *sine*-based MLP-INR on the 20% point cloud density is qualitatively worse than that in the 10% point cloud density case. This indicates that, in contrast to *WS*, *sine* is inconsistent regarding its performance on different point cloud densities. Furthermore, the *ReLU*-based MLP-INR is evidently struggling to produce a mesh comparable to those of the other two activation functions, which is also validated by the results in Table 1, where the numeric difference is significantly higher than that of the other two, as well as from the meshes illustrated in Fig. 4.

3.2 Application on Actual Exhibits from the Delphi Museum

As mentioned in Sub-sect. 2.3, two additional 3D models of museum exhibits [1], namely, a clay figurine and part of a chryselephantine statuette, were retrieved based on the photogrammetry method using the Meshroom software (v.2021.1.0) [2]. The retrieved 3D objects of clay figurine and statuette consisted of 81,698 and 81,630 points, respectively, and have been used in this study for demonstration purposes. In this case, due to the high number of initial points, the point clouds of the 3D objects were sub-sampled to 0.1%, 0.5%, 1%, and 10% of the original point cloud density. It should be noted that the difference in the sub-sampling percentages between the results in Fig. 4 and in Figs. 5 and 6 is related to the difference in the initial point cloud density of these objects. A qualitative comparison of the reconstructions of these objects using the *WS*, *sine*, and *ReLU* activation functions is presented in Figs. 5 and 6. As it is shown in the respective figures, the reconstructions that derive from models that employ the *WS* activation function are more precise even when resulted from low density point clouds. Lastly, the results presented in Table 2 validate the results in Figs. 5 and 6, since the *WS* produces more precise reconstructions of the objects.

Table 2. Average CD ($\times 10^{-2}$) and EMD ($\times 10^{-2}$) of the clay figurine and the statuette for different thresholds of sub-sampled models. Best results are indicated in boldface typesetting.

Sampled points (%)	Activation functions					
	WS		*Sine*		*ReLU*	
	CD	EMD	CD	EMD	CD	EMD
0.1	**11.11**	**5.49**	15.74	8.15	11.98	7.23
0.5	**3.38**	**2.65**	3.70	2.84	13.60	3.07
1	**3.34**	**2.69**	3.90	2.86	13.63	3.08
10	2.25	**2.10**	**2.20**	2.17	13.82	3.09

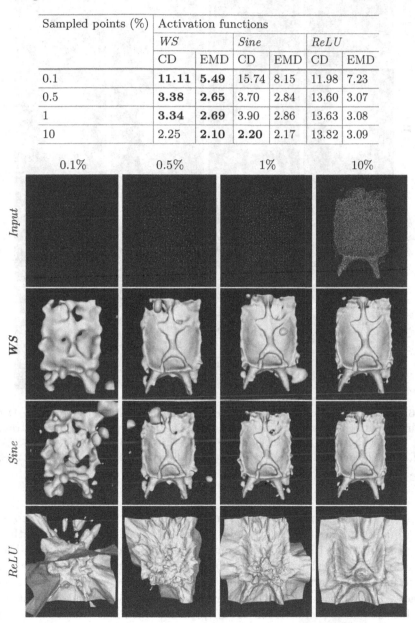

Fig. 5. 3D reconstruction results of the clay figurine from the Delphi museum for different sub-sampling thresholds. The first row represents the training input for the INR and the rest show the result of the training using the *WS*, *sine*, and *ReLU*. The different columns correspond to different point cloud densities used as input.

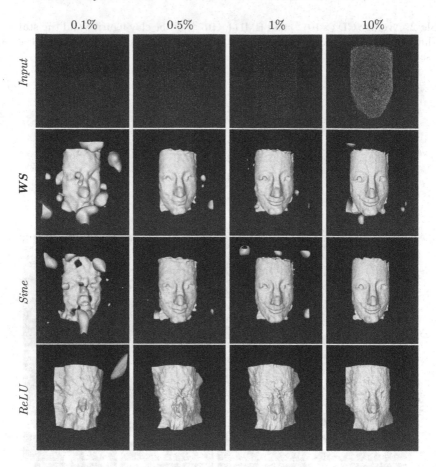

Fig. 6. 3D reconstruction results of the chryselephantine statuette from the Delphi museum for different subsampling thresholds. The first row represents the training input for the INR and the rest show the result of the training using the *WS*, *sine*, and *ReLU*. The different columns correspond to different point cloud densities used as input.

For the clay figurine, the results in Fig. 5 indicate that the *WS* produces higher quality meshes for all thresholds. More specifically, for the lowest threshold, the resulted mesh for the *WS* is quite comparable to the original mesh with only a few small unrelated artifacts. On the contrary, the result of *sine* is not able to fill missing parts of the model and contains more unrelated-to-the-mesh artifacts. The 3D model of the clay figurine has a smoother surface, thus showing that *WS* should be preferred for the 3D printing of similar objects or when the 3D printing of fine-detail objects is not of essence. For the statuette, the meshes reconstructed using *WS* and *sine* are on par, with only exception that, under the 0.1% threshold, the *WS* produces more artifacts; nevertheless, the mesh resembles more the original one than the one produced using the *sine* (Fig. 6). This might be caused by the nature of the object that has a more complex geometry compared to the clay figurine. Furthermore, the *sine* yields reconstructed meshes that are more crisp than the ones produced by the *WS*. This can both be considered advantageous in the case where the 3D printing of shapes with crisp characteristics is preferred, rather than smoother representations that may lack finer details. Lastly, it can be observed that the mesh reconstructed using the *ReLU* for the 10% threshold is of adequate quality compared to the other cases where the *ReLU* cannot adequately learn the 3D shape of the model.

4 Conclusions

In this paper, a novel activation function, abbreviated as *WS*, has been investigated, which enables MLPs to reconstruct 3D models from sparse point clouds. The 3D reconstruction of objects by *WS*-based MLP-INRs becomes easier, since it achieves better results than state-of-the-art activation functions that have been employed in the same context. This is achieved even for extremely sparse point clouds, without requiring the incorporation of normals in the training process. Nevertheless, the *sine* seems to provide results comparative to those of the *WS* when the number of available points is significantly larger. To evaluate the proposed method in absence of normals, the ShapeNet dataset was used. To demonstrate the performance of the method to generate high-quality 3D models from sparse point clouds, two archaic exhibits from the Delphi Museum in Greece were used. Ultimately, the capability of our method to generate meshes of 3D models is relative to the density of the retrieved point cloud, *i.e.*, the training on denser point clouds results in a more detailed reconstruction. Based on the results obtained from this study, it can be concluded that it is feasible to generate fine-quality 3D models for 3D printing of museum exhibits by using sparse point clouds.

References

1. 3D objects - Archaeological site of Delphi - Museum of Delphi. https://delphi.culture.gr/digital-tour/digital-objects-3d/
2. AliceVision: Meshroom: A 3D reconstruction software (2018). https://github.com/alicevision/meshroom
3. Bagautdinov, T., Wu, C., Saragih, J., Fua, P., Sheikh, Y.: Modeling facial geometry using compositional VAEs. In: Proceedings of the IEEE Conference on Computer Vision and Pattern Recognition, pp. 3877–3886 (2018)
4. Ballarin, M., Balletti, C., Vernier, P.: Replicas in cultural heritage: 3D printing and the museum experience. Int. Arch. Photogramm. Remote Sens. Spatial Inf. Sci. **42**(2), 55–62 (2018)
5. Barrow, H.G., Tenenbaum, J.M., Bolles, R.C., Wolf, H.C.: Parametric correspondence and chamfer matching: two new techniques for image matching. Technical report, Sri International Menlo Park CA Artificial Intelligence Center (1977)
6. Carrizosa, H.G., Sheehy, K., Rix, J., Seale, J., Hayhoe, S.: Designing technologies for museums: accessibility and participation issues. J. Enabling Technol. **14**(1), 31–39 (2020)

7. Chabra, R., et al.: Deep local shapes: learning local SDF priors for detailed 3D reconstruction. In: Vedaldi, A., Bischof, H., Brox, T., Frahm, J.-M. (eds.) ECCV 2020. LNCS, vol. 12374, pp. 608–625. Springer, Cham (2020). https://doi.org/10.1007/978-3-030-58526-6_36

8. Chang, A.X., et al.: ShapeNet: An Information-Rich 3D Model Repository. Technical report. arXiv:1512.03012, Stanford University – Princeton University – Toyota Technological Institute at Chicago (2015)

9. Chen, Z., Zhang, H.: Learning implicit fields for generative shape modeling. In: Proceedings of the IEEE/CVF Conference on Computer Vision and Pattern Recognition, pp. 5939–5948 (2019)

10. Chibane, J., Pons-Moll, G., et al.: Neural unsigned distance fields for implicit function learning. Adv. Neural. Inf. Process. Syst. **33**, 21638–21652 (2020)

11. Cignoni, P., Callieri, M., Corsini, M., Dellepiane, M., Ganovelli, F., Ranzuglia, G., et al.: Meshlab: an open-source mesh processing tool. In: Eurographics Italian Chapter Conference, Salerno, Italy, vol. 2008, pp. 129–136 (2008)

12. Dai, A., Ruizhongtai Qi, C., Nießner, M.: Shape completion using 3D-encoder-predictor CNNs and shape synthesis. In: Proceedings of the IEEE Conference on Computer Vision and Pattern Recognition, pp. 5868–5877 (2017)

13. Desvallées, A.: Key concepts of museology. Armand Colin (2010)

14. Fontanella, F., Colace, F., Molinara, M., Di Freca, A.S., Stanco, F.: Pattern recognition and artificial intelligence techniques for cultural heritage (2020)

15. Gomes, L., Bellon, O.R.P., Silva, L.: 3D reconstruction methods for digital preservation of cultural heritage: a survey. Pattern Recogn. Lett. **50**, 3–14 (2014)

16. Gropp, A., Yariv, L., Haim, N., Atzmon, M., Lipman, Y.: Implicit geometric regularization for learning shapes. arXiv preprint arXiv:2002.10099 (2020)

17. Groueix, T., Fisher, M., Kim, V.G., Russell, B.C., Aubry, M.: A papier-mâché approach to learning 3D surface generation. In: Proceedings of the IEEE Conference on Computer Vision and Pattern Recognition, pp. 216–224 (2018)

18. Huovilainen, A.: Non-linear digital implementation of the Moog ladder filter. In: Proceedings of the International Conference on Digital Audio Effects (DAFx 2004), pp. 61–64 (2004)

19. Kantorovich, L.V.: Mathematical methods of organizing and planning production. Manage. Sci. **6**(4), 366–422 (1960)

20. Lazzarini, V., Timoney, J.: New perspectives on distortion synthesis for virtual analog oscillators. Comput. Music. J. **34**(1), 28–40 (2010)

21. Levina, E., Bickel, P.: The earth mover's distance is the mallows distance: some insights from statistics. In: Proceedings Eighth IEEE International Conference on Computer Vision, ICCV 2001, vol. 2, pp. 251–256. IEEE (2001)

22. Lewiner, T., Lopes, H., Vieira, A.W., Tavares, G.: Efficient implementation of marching cubes' cases with topological guarantees. J. Graph. Tools **8**(2), 1–15 (2003)

23. Ma, B., Han, Z., Liu, Y.S., Zwicker, M.: Neural-pull: learning signed distance functions from point clouds by learning to pull space onto surfaces. arXiv preprint arXiv:2011.13495 (2020)

24. Mahmood, M.A., Visan, A.I., Ristoscu, C., Mihailescu, I.N.: Artificial neural network algorithms for 3D printing. Materials **14**(1), 163 (2020)

25. Mescheder, L., Oechsle, M., Niemeyer, M., Nowozin, S., Geiger, A.: Occupancy networks: learning 3D reconstruction in function space. In: Proceedings of the IEEE/CVF Conference on Computer Vision and Pattern Recognition, pp. 4460–4470 (2019)

26. Neumüller, M., Reichinger, A., Rist, F., Kern, C.: 3D printing for cultural heritage: preservation, accessibility, research and education. In: Ioannides, M., Quak, E. (eds.) 3D Research Challenges in Cultural Heritage. LNCS, vol. 8355, pp. 119–134. Springer, Heidelberg (2014). https://doi.org/10.1007/978-3-662-44630-0_9
27. Osher, S., Fedkiw, R., Piechor, K.: Level set methods and dynamic implicit surfaces. Appl. Mech. Rev. **57**(3), B15–B15 (2004)
28. Pakarinen, J., Yeh, D.T.: A review of digital techniques for modeling vacuum-tube guitar amplifiers. Comput. Music. J. **33**(2), 85–100 (2009)
29. Park, J.J., Florence, P., Straub, J., Newcombe, R., Lovegrove, S.: Deepsdf: learning continuous signed distance functions for shape representation. In: Proceedings of the IEEE/CVF Conference on Computer Vision and Pattern Recognition, pp. 165–174 (2019)
30. Paszke, A., et al.: Pytorch: an imperative style, high-performance deep learning library. In: Wallach, H., Larochelle, H., Beygelzimer, A., d' Alché-Buc, F., Fox, E., Garnett, R. (eds.) Advances in Neural Information Processing Systems, vol. 32, pp. 8024–8035. Curran Associates, Inc. (2019). https://papers.neurips.cc/paper/9015-pytorch-an-imperative-style-high-performance-deep-learning-library.pdf
31. Peng, S., Niemeyer, M., Mescheder, L., Pollefeys, M., Geiger, A.: Convolutional occupancy networks. In: Vedaldi, A., Bischof, H., Brox, T., Frahm, J.-M. (eds.) ECCV 2020. LNCS, vol. 12348, pp. 523–540. Springer, Cham (2020). https://doi.org/10.1007/978-3-030-58580-8_31
32. Qi, C.R., Su, H., Mo, K., Guibas, L.J.: Pointnet: deep learning on point sets for 3D classification and segmentation. In: Proceedings of the IEEE Conference on Computer Vision and Pattern Recognition, pp. 652–660 (2017)
33. Rubner, Y., Tomasi, C., Guibas, L.J.: A metric for distributions with applications to image databases. In: Sixth International Conference on Computer Vision (IEEE Cat. No. 98CH36271), pp. 59–66. IEEE (1998)
34. Sitzmann, V., Martel, J., Bergman, A., Lindell, D., Wetzstein, G.: Implicit neural representations with periodic activation functions. Adv. Neural. Inf. Process. Syst. **33**, 7462–7473 (2020)
35. Vaz, R., Freitas, D., Coelho, A.: Blind and visually impaired visitors' experiences in museums: Increasing accessibility through assistive technologies. Int. J. Inclusive Mus. **13**(2), 57 (2020)
36. Wilson, P.F., Stott, J., Warnett, J.M., Attridge, A., Smith, M.P., Williams, M.A.: Evaluation of touchable 3D-printed replicas in museums. Curator Mus. J. **60**(4), 445–465 (2017)
37. Wu, Z., et al.: 3D shapenets: a deep representation for volumetric shapes. In: Proceedings of the IEEE Conference on Computer Vision and Pattern Recognition, pp. 1912–1920 (2015)
38. Yuan, W., Khot, T., Held, D., Mertz, C., Hebert, M.: PCN: point completion network. In: 2018 International Conference on 3D Vision (3DV), pp. 728–737. IEEE (2018)

A Simulator for Minero-Petrographic and Chemical Research Instruments

Diego Sinitò[1,2(✉)], Alessandro Verderame[2], Carmelo Lombardo[1],
Alessandro Treffiletti[3], Maura Fugazzotto[3], Dario Allegra[1],
Vito Santarcangelo[2], Filippo Stanco[1], and Germana Barone[3]

[1] Department of Mathematics and Computer Science, University of Catania,
Catania, Italy
{diego,allegra,fstanco}@dmi.unict.it
[2] iInformatica S.r.l., Trapani, Italy
{diego,verderame,vito}@iiinformatica.it
[3] Department of Biological, Geological and Environmental Science,
University of Catania, Catania, Italy
https://iinformatica.it

Abstract. In recent years, digital technologies and serious game have widely affected the cultural heritage sector, offering incredible opportunities to enhance the experiential value of heritage assets and improve cultural activities. Due to pandemic and the closure of museums the demand for new digital remote solutions for Cultural Heritage has seen a great increase. Thanks to a collaboration between University of Catania, the Museum of Mineralogy, Petrography and Volcanology and a local SME iInformatica S.r.l a serious game for dissemination of mineralogic and petrographic science was developed. The idea behind the project is to give to all the possibility to learn by doing. Through the simulator, users can assume the role of researchers in mineralogy and petrography and, thus, study the minerals constituting the rocks. Within the game a player can learn how to use a petrographic microscope and how to recognise a rock by analysing the single minerals that constitute it and, therefore, to identify the rock itself.

Keywords: Cultural Heritage · Museums · Mineralogy · Petrography · Serious Game

1 Introduction

Over the past three years due to pandemic caused by the spreading of SARS-Cov-2 virus, the society has had to reinterpret many aspects of daily life such as travels, work in the offices, entertainment and cultural events. The entire system has required a deep reorganisation and with the concept of digitisation became a key factor. At the beginning of pandemic, the school system transferred education from face-to-face into remote teaching, setting up an Emergency Remote learning (ERL) in few weeks [11] and consequently changing the way of teaching

© Springer Nature Switzerland AG 2023
J.-J. Rousseau and B. Kapralos (Eds.): ICPR 2022 Workshops, LNCS 13645, pp. 36–49, 2023.
https://doi.org/10.1007/978-3-031-37731-0_4

we were used to. Companies in the business world had to find quickly solutions in order to permit the employees to access all the work resources from home [3].

The same phenomenon that has overwhelmed school and work has also affected the world of Cultural Heritage and the industry of museums. From an analysis conducted on the trends of Google searches, we can notice how the period of first lockdown corresponds to an increase in Google searches correlated with museums and digital access as shown in Fig. 1. This burdened university's museums more because they strictly depend from the activity of universities that in Italy they were closed for almost one year. Furthermore, museums, particularly those belonging to universities and those regarding scientific contents, are not only places for education and entertainment, but also centres of researches. Their collections are used for training students in the field of scientific investigations and are object of new research topics or projects. Thus, during the pandemic arose the necessity to find a way to continue these activities even with museums being closes. And again, this has been obtained thanks to the digital method, all over the world.

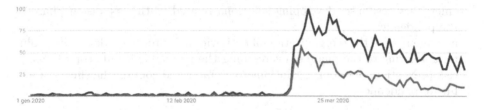

Fig. 1. The growth of the number of google searches for "museum virtual tour" (in blue) and "virtual museum" (in red) from 01/01/2020 to 01/05/2020 exacted from Google Trends. (Color figure online)

Fortunately, the transition to digital method in Cultural Heritage started many years before the pandemic caused by Covid-19. In the last decades, most of the musealisation processes took the advantage of digital techniques such as 3D modelling, Augmented Reality (AR), Virtual Reality (VR), digital platforms [2,7]. In [1], Morgantina Silver Treasure is acquired and analysed; then, 3D models and analysis results were made available through an ad-hoc web platform. In [19], the authors conducted a study about Kouros of Lentinoi and proposed a web application to make it accessible to the users. Other applications were developed to get benefits from augmented reality: in [20,21] the user is able to interact with ancient artefacts, digitally restored, through a mobile device.

The previous experience of collaboration among geologists, conservators and computer scientists led to the implementation of a web application called I-PETER: Interactive Platform to Experience Tours and Education on the Rocks [17], a turning point for the Museum of Mineralogy, Petrography and Volcanology of the University of Catania, with the goal of promoting a new interactive system which could facilitate the diffusion of its cultural contents towards a broader range of visitors, of different ages, countries and cultural background using their smartphone or any device equipped with a web browser. The visitor can decide to virtually observe rocks or minerals exposed at the museum and then explore their external application on monuments, or he/she can choose to make a tour in the interactive map, focusing on a particular monument and from there make the virtual reverse path from the macro to the micro scale until the study of the mineralogical or petrographic sample under microscope. Since I-PETER has had a good success among museum visitors, we decided to continue developing digital content for the museum.

The project DREAMIN (Digital REmote Access to Museums and research INfrastructures) was born as response to the need of the Italian Ministry of University and Research, that in May 2020 opened a call for project proposal aimed at addressing the new needs and issues raised by the spread of the SARS-Cov-2 virus and Covid-19 infection. The project proposals had to have as their objective the definition of product, methodological or process solutions, relating to the health, social, institutional, training, legal, economic, inclusion, or production context, with respect to at least one of the following areas:

- emergency response, developing solutions related to the expansion phase of the pandemic;
- management of the reorganisation of activities and processes, developing solutions relating to the phase of overcoming the pandemic in safe conditions;
- risk prevention, developing solutions to counter and contain the effects of any future pandemics.

The main goal of the project is to guarantee the remote access and the possibility to interact with the vast cultural and museum heritage of the University of Catania and its research centres. This was possible thanks to the cooperation between the Departments of Biological, Geological and Environmental Sciences (DSBGA), Physic and Astronomy (DFA), Civil Engineering and Architecture (DICAR) and Mathematics and Computer Sciences (DMI) of University of Catania, together with some Museums belonging to the University Museums Network (Sistema Museale d'Ateneo - SiMuA), that means Museum of Knowledge and Sicilian Mirabilia, Museum of Mineralogy, Petrography and Volcanology, Museum of Representation and City of Science; and the Innovative small and medium-sized enterprise (SME) iInformatica S.r.l.. Each of them made available their specific expertise required by the multidisciplinarity of the project. The project outcomes were focused on three different areas: digitisation and cataloguing of museums artefacts and collections, simulation and virtualisation of research instruments, virtual tour and digital reconstruction of museums and city monuments. The outcomes of the DREAMIN project are available on the digital hub website[1].

This paper presents a serious game aimed to spread the knowledge of mineralogic and petrographic science and research instruments and techniques that are used by researchers in this field. The game, in italian language, is free

---

[1] Digital HUB website: https://dreamin.unict.it.

available on-line[2]. Users of our simulator are able to analyse different thin sections of rocks using a microscope equipped with a polarising filter in order to discover those minerals which compose the rock. Than, users can conduct different type of non-invasive analysis to identify the mineral.

This paper is structured as follows: in Sect. 2 we report other studies of how serious game are used in Cultural Heritage and more in general for teaching purpose; in Sect. 3 we discuss the scientific analytical techniques we want to simulate (minero-petrographic and chemical); in Sect. 4 we introduce and detail the developed simulator game; future works and conclusion are included in Sect. 5.

2 Related Works

Computer games are a powerful mechanism to engage the large public into an active state of learning where spectators are motivated to create their own knowledge rather than to receive information passively. Games with educational purposes - namely Serious Games - are now becoming more and more popular. Serious games provide amusing and compelling experiences and keep the player focused for long lasting sessions. For this reason are widely used in many learning context: mathematics and science [15, 23], computational thinking and computer programming [10], history, etc.

In [6] a simulation tool was created by science teachers to help teach and learn physics. Easy Java Simulations (EJS) allows science students, teachers, and researchers to create simulations of scientific experiment only with a basic knowledge of programming. Using EJS even those who cannot afford the big investment of time, needed to create a complete graphical simulation, can obtain a good result in the style of similar software programs which can be easily found nowadays on internet.

Serious game can be used also to involve people in experience in hostile environments such as seabeds. The game Dive in the Past Serious Game [5] which allows users to simulate a virtual dive into the Mediterranean Sea to explore accurate and life-sized 3D reconstructions of underwater archaeological sites. The purpose of the game is twofold: to engage diver and non-diver tourists into a virtual interactive exploration of underwater sites through digital storytelling and challenges; to increase awareness and knowledge on Mediterranean UCH.

In [18], JDoc is presented. This is an interactive, computer-based 1st-3rd person junior doctor simulator where senior doctors can train and teach junior doctors interpersonal skills, communication skills, medical information, decision making skills etc. The purpose of the JDoc is to familiarise junior doctors with the day-to-day stress of a hectic hospital by simulating patients and creating scenarios using basic parameters provided by senior doctors. JDoc establishes what the player will learn through prior research with many experienced doctors who have first-hand experience and knowledge of the relevant areas for junior doctor education.

In [22], a systems for simplify teaching of computer algorithms foundations is proposed. The proposed solution face up the difficult encountered by students

---

[2] Simulator website: https://dreamin.unict.it/microscopio/.

during the learning of complex algorithms for trees, in particular algorithms applied to AVL trees. In traditional teaching approach algorithm's abstract concepts are presented and the learners find difficult to make the relation between the real world and the abstract concepts that are presented. Researchers presented video game with "Super Mario" style whose main purpose is learning AVL trees. It allows the user to learn while having fun algorithmic concepts specific to these trees. They tried to highlight and materialise the abstract concepts to explain them to the learner by an active way who favours his learning and also different from that which is presented in a theoretical course.

In all the examples analysed it was possible to appreciate how the use of serious games has contributed to improve and make teaching more interactive in sectors and with a completely different audience.

3   Minero-Petrographic and Chemical Research Instruments and Data Collection

In order to make the simulation as real as possible we decided to reconstruct all the chain of actions that a researcher need to do when he/she performs an analysis by using a specific instrumentation. Four kinds of analytical instrumentation, usually employed for investigating minerals and rocks, were considered. The petrographic microscope is the petrographic instrument for excellence, the most antique and the most used. It is an instrument that allows to observe objects at enlarged scale. It is possible to perform a series of operations which could reveal the optical characteristics of minerals, allowing their identifications. In case of rocks, the observation of thin sections of the sample will allow to identify the single minerals that constitute it, therefore to identify the rock itself [13]. A thin section is a 20–30 μ thickness section, obtained by cutting a rock sample in order to make it observable by transmitted light (Fig. 2).

In particular research topics, the observation by petrographic microscope could also help to identify clues related to the provenance of that particular sample or, in case of ceramics and further artificial materials, to understand the technological methods used to create it [4,8]. A sequence of mandatory actions carried out to use a microscope for petrographic investigations is reported as example. The sequence has been simplified and schematised, as scientific investigations are always dependent on the characteristics of materials that is investigated. In fact a unique path, always valid, does not actually exist. The simplified sequence for investigations by petrographic microscope is hereafter reported:

1. Choose the thin section of a sample to investigate;
2. Put the thin section on the microscope's rotating plate;
3. Turn on the light source;
4. Choose a microscope optic, in order to decide the level of magnification of the investigation;
5. Adjust the focus by using the specific knobs on the sides of the microscope.

Fig. 2. Microscope and observation of a basalt thin section at low magnification trough the eyepieces of the microscope.

Once these actions are completed, a researcher will be able to look through the eyepieces of the microscope and observe the structure of the sample. The microscope offers also the possibility to add a polarising filter, placed between the light source and the sample base. It can be activated or deactivated by means of a special lever. It allows to convert the light from non-polarises to polarises in order to collect univocal data for the recognition of the mineral. In order to observe the variables linked to the optic characteristics of the minerals observed in the sample, it could be useful/necessary to rotate the plate where the thin section is placed. In the example used for the microscope simulator, the thin section is a thin section of a Basalt rock, and looking inside through the microscope it is possible to recognise different kind of minerals, among which those centred in the image, which according to the observed features is hypothesised to be an olivine, as shown in Fig. 3.

Further techniques that allow the characterisation of minerals and rocks are X-ray Fluorescence (XRF), Fourier-Transform Infrared-Spectroscopy (FTIR) and Raman Spetroscopy (Raman).

XRF is a chemical technique that could be performed on a powdered material prepared in a pill, or in a non-invasive way just putting in contact the instrument with the surface of the rock/mineral that we want to study. This instrument allows the acquisition of the chemical composition of a sample, in terms of kind and percentage of chemical elements. X-Rays of a specific energy are collimated on the sample, determining different interactions. Among these, when the energy of the incident X-Rays is sufficient, a photoelectric phenomenon will occur. The incident light is completely absorbed by the material, which will in its turn emit further energy, in the field of X-Rays, called Fluorescence X-Rays. The ri-emitted X-Rays have a characteristic energy, depending on the chemical element involved in the photo-electric phenomenon. Thanks to the comparison

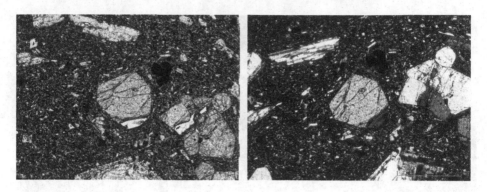

Fig. 3. Images acquired with microscope in non-polarised light (left) and polarised light (right) of the Basalt thin section with the olivine in the centre.

with appropriate databases, this characteristic energy will allow the system to identify the chemical element [16].

FTIR is a spectroscopic analytical technique which allows to find the molecular composition of a compound. Thanks to the interaction (absorption, transmission or reflection) of the substance with an incident infrared radiation, characteristics signals related to the kind of functional groups (e.g. -OH, -O-C-O; etc.) present in the sample are registered. The contemporary presence of different functional groups will allow the identification of the entire molecule. The results are interpreted thanks to an appropriate database [14].

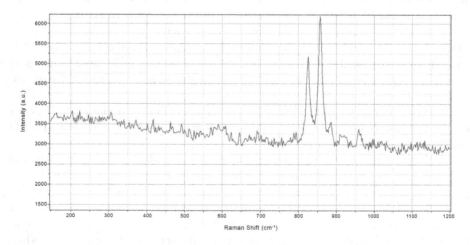

Fig. 4. Example of an olivine spectrum acquired by using Raman spectroscopy.

Raman is another spectroscopic technique, which exploits a different physical phenomenon with respect to FTIR, but at the same way it allows to see at the end of the analysis the signals related to the molecular composition of a substance and to definitely identify them by using a specific database [14]. For all these three analytical techniques the results are revealed as a spectrum, a linear image with peaks or bands that according to their position on the X-axis of the graph allows to understand their identity, and according to their value in the Y-axis allows to measure their relatively quantitative amount as shown in Fig. 4. As well as XRF, FTIR and Raman spectroscopy could be performed both on prepared samples or on the surface of them in a non-invasive way. The last method is preferable when we are investigating objects of museum interest, as in the case of this study. If for the microscope a specific sequence of action has been defined and simulated, for XRF, FTIR and Raman, the analyses are simulated by simply virtually touching the instrument for starting the acquisitions, and then by observing the formation of the related spectrum on the monitor of the computer.

3.1 Data Collection

Because we want to develop a simulator with the same results that can be obtained from the real instruments we need to collected the real data from real analysis: for each thin section observed using the microscope we collect different images changing the rotation of the plate, the magnification level and the type of light (polarised and not). It means that for each thin section we need to acquire 288 images. This number is given by this formulation: $n = 2(360/\alpha) \cdot l$; where α is the number of degrees of difference between two rotations, l is the number of level of magnification. In our configuration we use $\alpha = 10$ and $l = 4$ (2.5x, 10x, 20x, 40x). For the chemical investigations, a representative analytical spectrum resulted by the analyses conducted on an olivine sample is reported.

4 Proposed Solution

Starting from the good feedback obtained by visitors and users of I-PETER and in the context of the DREAMIN project, a new system for involving people in research topics has been developed. This could be imagined as a game, able to simulate a set of analytical instrumentation that are commonly used in mineralogical and petrographic researches. The analysis that we have considered are Optical Petrographic Microscopy, X-Ray Fluorescence Spectroscopy, Fourier-Transformed Infrared Spectroscopy and Raman Spectroscopy, already described. The idea at the base of the developing process was to create a product aimed at a school-age public that would allow children and young people to replicate the same studies that are carried out every day by researchers in the university laboratories. It would be a useful tool both for stimulate the curiosity of a common visitor toward the research field and for training in school that are not equipped with laboratories and instrumentation, as well as it would be a virtual solution for e-learning. It would be a tool with a simplified approach that could be used by every device (pc, smartphone, tablet, etc.).

Since the development of a video game is a very complicated process that requires different skills, it was essential to make some choices that kept development costs low but that could nevertheless allow to have a simple and effective tool. The development is based on the Unity game engine [9], a tool used at all scales of video games development, from the large studio to the hobbyist bedroom, such that over half of all new video games are reportedly being made with Unity [12]. Another feature, that was fundamental in our choice of Unity as game engine was the large compatibility of video games made with Unity. There is indeed the possibility to export the final product on the most spread platforms: Windows, iOS, Android, WebGL. Thanks to the possibility of using WebGL we were able to develop a web based build compatible with the most modern operating systems and browsers such as Chrome and Safari for desktop devices, but without additional effort we were able to produce APK that can be free downloaded and installed on mobile Android devices for better compatibility since WebGL is on experimental stage on mobile devices at the moment.

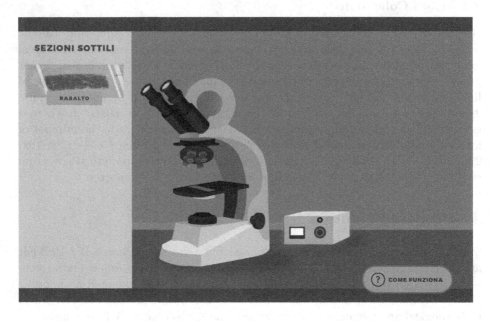

Fig. 5. A screenshot taken from the game where is possible to see on the left the side menu with the thin sections and on the right the main scene with the optical microscope and the light source control box. The game is in italian language, "Sezioni sottili" means Thin sections; "Basalto" means Basalt and "Come funziona?" means how does it work?

Unity offers the possibility to develop games both in 3D and 2D: since the use of 3D requires expert modellers that have to reconstruct the game environments and instruments used in the laboratory using computer graphics and this wasn't possible due the large time request and high costs this solution, it was chosen to use a two-dimensional graphic with a point and click approach widely used in many graphic adventures loved by a large audience of gamers.

The user interface (UI) has two sections: a side menu where the thin sections are drag and dropped on the rotating plate of the microscope by the player and a main panel that contains the main elements of the scenes: the microscope, the detail of the revolver of the microscope, all the analysis instruments and monitor where consult the result of analysis. To keep the design of the UI simple and even for the target of the users of our simulator it was decided to use a graphic style where all the objects in the scene are hand-drawn, faithfully reproducing the real objects that are present in the university laboratory, with a style similar to a comic.

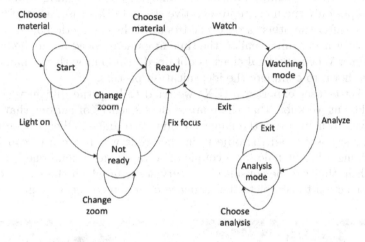

Fig. 6. Design of game interaction.

The game logic designed in collaboration with researcher of DSBGA is summarised in Fig. 6. At the begin of the game the player can drag a thin section from the menu on the left and put it to the rotating plate of the microscope (Fig. 5). Nevertheless, in order to proceed to the next scene it is mandatory that the player turns on the light source, as in the reality we cannot use the microscope since the light source is on. In scene two (Fig. 7a), the microscope with all the interactive parts is presented, the player can click on the eyepieces to observe the sample, click on the revolving nose-piece to add or remove the polarising filter or change the level of magnification (Fig. 7b), click on the knobs on the side of the microscope to adjust the focus. At the first time and after every change of magnification the player has to adjust the focus or a blur filter will applied to the image showed after the click on the eyepieces in order to simulate the lack of focus.

Scene three is where the real images obtained from the researchers can be observed (Fig. 7c). To simulate the observation of the thin section through the eyepieces a black frame is overlapped to the original image. Since we know that rotation is a key factor to find out more details, especially with the polarised light filter, two control points are implemented in order to give the user the possibility to rotate the plate and observe the same material with a different angle. When the user clicks on a control point a different image is loaded, each image is taken with an rotation of 10°. By clicking a mineral on the observed image it is possible to move to the laboratory to conduct further analysis and deeper the investigation.

The laboratory is presented in scene four (Fig. 7d). In this scene is possible to see all the instruments used to carry out XRF, FITR and Raman investigations and a personal computer where it is possible to observe the results. To start an analysis an user has to choose one instrument by clicking on it and turn on the computer. Since the result of all the analysis is a bi-dimensional chart containing the spectrum, that is acquired during the analysis process taking about 60 s, we decided to put only the most representative steps. In this case, a set of 6 images is shown one after the other, after every 10 s until the completion of the analysis. To make the waiting time smaller, the time in game is speed up at the double of the real time. When the final chart is obtained, a popup with the name of the mineral is shown to complete the identification process.

For a better user experience (UX) we tried to keep the difficulty as simple as possible, but we know that there are some sequences of actions that are not so intuitive. To help users, the game provides two different helps: the first one is given by suggesting all the objects in the scene which the user can interact simply adding a bright halo for a couple of seconds; the second one is a button with the help that can be consulted in every scene in which the player can find all the instruction to complete the sequence of action to get a result.

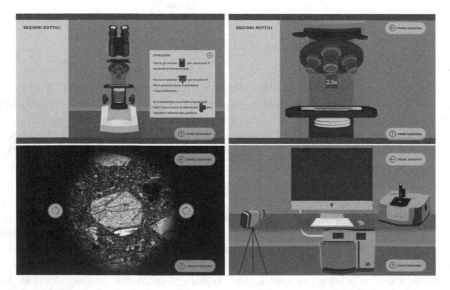

Fig. 7. a) scene two: microscope with all the interactive parts; b) scene two: a detail of the revolving nose-piece to change the magnification level; c) scene three: observation of a real sample of basalt; c) scene four: the laboratory with all the research instruments.

5   Conclusion and Future Work

Serious game carry the huge advantage of acquire information in an active playful environment that makes the learning process more interesting and less difficult compared with traditional methods such as listening or reading. Exploiting our simulator, users can easier assimilate knowledge in petrography and mineralogy and about laboratory instruments in a more interactive way following the principles of learn by doing. Users have the possibility to deep investigate how rocks are made and how to correctly recognise them, which tools are used everyday in research and what are the main functions of each of them. At this stage, all the software functionalities and the game logic passed the validation of researchers and developers. In the next phase, we can finally start to collect further real data in our lab in order to implement analysis of new rocks inside our simulator. The objective is to provide at least one mineral for each classification (e.g. one carbonate mineral, one silicate mineral and so on...). Than, we can easy import the new data in our simulator and provide and essential but useful database for investigation in mineralogy. Thanks to this effort students and young researchers will have the possibility to access real data that can't be easy find even in the enormous vastness of internet. Moreover, simulator provides chemical and spectroscopic analysis results that can be performed only inside professional laboratories with expensive instruments, difficult to find in primary or middle schools.

Acknowledgements. This project was funded by FISR 2020 "Fondo integrativo speciale per la ricerca" grant, CUP: E65F20001710001.

References

1. Alberghina, M.F., et al.: Integrated three-dimensional models for noninvasive monitoring and valorization of the Morgantina silver treasure (Sicily). J. Electron. Imaging **26**(1), 011015 (2016). https://doi.org/10.1117/1.jei.26.1.011015
2. Allegra, D., et al.: Virtual unrolling using X-ray computed tomography. In: European Signal Processing Conference (EUSIPCO), pp. 2864–2868 (2015). https://doi.org/10.1109/EUSIPCO.2015.7362908
3. Barabaschi, B., Barbieri, L., Cantoni, F., Platoni, S., Virtuani, R.: Remote working in Italian SMEs during COVID-19. Learning challenges of a new work organization. J. Workplace Learn. **34**(6), 497–512 (2022). https://doi.org/10.1108/JWL-10-2021-0132
4. Barone, G., Fugazzotto, M., Mazzoleni, P., Raneri, S., Russo, A.: Color and painting techniques in Etruscan architectural slabs. Dyes Pigm. **171**, 107766 (2019). https://doi.org/10.1016/j.dyepig.2019.107766. https://www.sciencedirect.com/science/article/pii/S0143720819307193
5. Cozza, M., et al.: Dive in the past: a serious game to promote the underwater cultural heritage of the mediterranean sea. Heritage **4**(4), 4001–4016 (2021). https://doi.org/10.3390/heritage4040220. https://www.mdpi.com/2571-9408/4/4/220

6. Esquembre, F.: Easy java simulations: a software tool to create scientific simulations in java. Comput. Phys. Commun. **156**(2), 199–204 (2004). https://doi.org/10.1016/s0010-4655(03)00440-5
7. Fontanella, F., Colace, F., Molinara, M., Scotto Di Freca, A., Stanco, F.: Pattern recognition and artificial intelligence techniques for cultural heritage. Pattern Recognit. Lett. **138**, 23–29 (2020). https://doi.org/10.1016/j.patrec.2020.06.018. https://www.sciencedirect.com/science/article/pii/S0167865520302361
8. Fugazzotto, M., et al.: Ceramic technology and paintings of archaic architectural slabs, louteria and antefixes from the palatine hill in Rome (Italy). Archaeometry **64**(1), 118–133 (2021). https://doi.org/10.1111/arcm.12684
9. Haas, J.: A history of the unity game engine. Diss. Worcester Polytechnic Institute (2014)
10. Kazimoglu, C., Kiernan, M., Bacon, L., Mackinnon, L.: A serious game for developing computational thinking and learning introductory computer programming. Procedia Soc. Behav. Sci. **47**, 1991–1999 (2012). https://doi.org/10.1016/j.sbspro.2012.06.938
11. Khlaif, Z.N., Salha, S., Kouraichi, B.: Emergency remote learning during COVID-19 crisis: students' engagement. Educ. Inf. Technol. **26**(6), 7033–7055 (2021). https://doi.org/10.1007/s10639-021-10566-4
12. Nicoll, B., Keogh, B.: The unity game engine and the circuits of cultural software. In: Nicoll, B., Keogh, B. (eds.) The Unity Game Engine and the Circuits of Cultural Software, pp. 1–21. Springer, Cham (2019). https://doi.org/10.1007/978-3-030-25012-6_1
13. Peccerillo, A., Perugini, D.: Introduzione alla Petrografia Ottica. Morlacchi Editore, Perugia (2003)
14. Rubinson, K.A., Rubinson, J.F.: Chimica analitica strumentale. Zanichelli Editore, Bologna (2002)
15. Schäfer, A., Holz, J., Leonhardt, T., Schroeder, U., Brauner, P., Ziefle, M.: From boring to scoring - a collaborative serious game for learning and practicing mathematical logic for computer science education. Comput. Sci. Educ. **23**(2), 87–111 (2013). https://doi.org/10.1080/08993408.2013.778040
16. Seccaroni, C., Moioli, P.: Fluorescenza X. Prontuario per l'analisi XRF portatile applicata a superfici policrome. Nardini Editore, Firenze (2001)
17. Sinitò, D., et al.: I-peter (interactive platform to experience tours and education on the rocks): a virtual system for the understanding and dissemination of mineralogical-petrographic science. Pattern Recogn. Lett. **131**, 85–90 (2020). https://doi.org/10.1016/j.patrec.2019.12.002
18. Sliney, A., Murphy, D.: JDoc: a serious game for medical learning. In: First International Conference on Advances in Computer-Human Interaction. IEEE (2008). https://doi.org/10.1109/achi.2008.50
19. Stanco, F., Tanasi, D., Allegra, D., Milotta, F.L.M., Lamagna, G., Monterosso, G.: Virtual anastylosis of Greek sculpture as museum policy for public outreach and cognitive accessibility. J. Electron. Imaging **26**(1), 011025 (2017). https://doi.org/10.1117/1.JEI.26.1.011025
20. Stanco, F., Tanasi, D., Gallo, G., Buffa, M., Basile, B.: Augmented perception of the past - the case of hellenistic syracuse. J. Multimed. **7**(2), 211–216 (2012). https://doi.org/10.4304/jmm.7.2.211-216
21. Stanco, F., Tanasi, D., Buffa, M., Basile, B.: Augmented perception of the past: the case of the telamon from the Greek theater of Syracuse. In: Grana, C., Cucchiara, R. (eds.) MM4CH 2011. CCIS, vol. 247, pp. 126–135. Springer, Heidelberg (2012). https://doi.org/10.1007/978-3-642-27978-2_11

22. Wassila, D., Tahar, B.: Using serious game to simplify algorithm learning. In: International Conference on Education and e-Learning Innovations. IEEE (2012). https://doi.org/10.1109/iceeli.2012.6360569
23. Wouters, P., van Oostendorp, H., ter Vrugte, J., Vandercruysse, S., de Jong, T., Elen, J.: The effect of surprising events in a serious game on learning mathematics. Br. J. Educ. Technol. **48**(3), 860–877 (2016). https://doi.org/10.1111/bjet.12458

Virtualization of the Chiurazzi Sculpture Collection at the John and Mable Ringling Museum of Art (Sarasota, Florida)

Madeleine Kraft[1], Kaitlyn Kingsland[1], Stephan Hassam[1],
Paolino Trapani[2], and Davide Tanasi[1(✉)]

[1] Institute for Digital Exploration, University of South Florida,
Tampa, FL 33620, USA
dtanasi@usf.edu

[2] Dipartimento di Studi Umanistici, Università degli Studi di Catania, Sicily, Italy

Abstract. The concept of using replicas as teaching tools and works of art in and of themselves is not new. Replicas of sculpture and other cultural heritage artifacts have been created for important or iconic originals for centuries, with these displayed in some of the most prominent museums around the world. The Chiurazzi Foundry is one workshop of note in the creation of replicas in the 19th century. A large number of these Chiurazzi replicas of statuary from Pompeii and Herculaneum, as well as other Roman and Greek sites, are displayed and housed at the John and Mable Ringling Museum of Art. The Ringlings, of circus fame, purchased 50 authentic replicas from the Chiurazzi Foundry in the early 20th century. These bronze copies are still on display at the museum. With the rise of digitization and the impact of the COVID-19 pandemic, the use for these physical replicas in education and accessibility looks increasingly to the educational space. Digital replicas hold the same value as the physical replicas and, in this way, the need to digitize these Chiurazzi sculptures for access and education is demonstrated. In the Fall of 2020, the Institute for Digital Exploration (IDEx) at the University of South Florida (USF) used digital photogrammetry for the purposes of generating a digital collection of the most representative Chiurazzi statues at the Ringling Museum. This paper discusses the best practices and the technical issues in digitizing large-scale bronze statuary and explores the methods for dissemination of a collection for public consumption.

Keywords: digital archaeology · digital photogrammetry · cultural heritage · sculpture · virtual collections

1 Introduction

The practice of creating replicas of masterpieces of the Classical statuary to offer a more direct experience with ancient art, for training art history scholars

J.-J. Rousseau and B. Kapralos (Eds.): ICPR 2022 Workshops, LNCS 13645, pp. 50–63, 2023.
https://doi.org/10.1007/978-3-031-37731-0_5

and educate the public, has a long tradition that goes back to the 18th century. With the publication in 1764 of Johann Joachim Winckelmann's seminal work, *History of the Art of Antiquity* [34], the ideology that the study of antiquity must be conducted through art became dominant in the European scholarly world. Such ideology put an emphasis on sculpture and on the significance of casts as a primary tool of investigation, where direct access to the originals was not possible because they were held in a distant location or no longer exist. Winckelmann himself praised the value of Roman casts of the Greek statues and of the Renaissance-era copies of the Roman ones that he saw in Rome and Florence during his *grand tour* in Italy in 1755 [29]. In the following decades, major European museums started a systematic process of producing copies of Classical statues to expand their cast collections or gathering scattered casts into homogeneous groups, contributing immensely to the popularization of Classical art and enhancing its' physical accessibility. As a result, dedicated exhibits of casts, such as the Cast Gallery at the Ashmolean Museum in Oxford [1] and the Collection of Classical Antiquities at the Bern Museum [2], as well as entire museums, such as the Museum of Casts of Classical Studies in Munich [4] and the Museum of Classical Art of the Università Sapienza in Rome [5], gradually came to be. Such phenomenon initially failed to expand to the United States, remaining a trait of European artistic culture of the 19th century.

The Fonderia Chiurazzi was established in Naples (Italy) in 1870, as an artisan foundry specializing in lost-wax casting. Their impressive casting techniques earned them a reputation in Italy for creating reproductions of very well-known works from the collections of the Louvre, the Vatican Museums and, of course, the Museo Archeologico Nazionale di Napoli. In the early 20th century, wealthy American tycoons and antiquities lovers, such as John Ringling (1866–1936) and Jean Paul Getty Sr. (1892–1976) started collecting Chiurazzi casts, initially with the idea of decorating their luxury mansions in Florida and California, but later contributing to the creation of the Chiurazzi collections of the John and Mable Ringling Museum in Sarasota (Florida) and The Getty Museum in Malibu (California). Starting in the 1920's, those trailblazing collections contributed to rediscovery of the Classical culture by the American public, making accessible masterpieces of ancient art from across the Atlantic Ocean.

The Chiurazzi collection at John and Mable Ringling Museum of Art in Sarasota (established in 1927) is one the largest collections in the world of casts of Classical statues produced by the Neapolitan foundry with over 70 examples. It has served for almost a century as a beacon of Classical art in the United States and has been used by entire generations of American classicists and art historians as a visual encyclopedia.

On 16 March 2020, the John and Mable Ringling Museum in Sarasota announced its closure to the public to help prevent the spread of coronavirus amidst the COVID-19 pandemic. It remained shut down until 27 May, when it reopened with new restrictions to mitigate health risks. Travel bans and warning as well as the general sense of uncertainty caused a significant decrease in the visitors to the museum. As a result, the Chiurazzi statues remained inaccessible or only partially accessible for over one and a half years and, with it, the importance in education and exploration of ancient sculpture casts.

In the Fall of 2020, the University of South Florida's Institute for Digital Exploration (USF IDEx) undertook, a digital photogrammetry virtualization project of 24 of the most representative bronze statues with the goal to create a curated digital collection of 3D models as a medium to enhance digital global accessibility. In pursuing that goal, best practices were applied for data capture and processing of outdoor bronze statues. A secondary objective of the project was to implement a system of monitoring of the degradation of the metallic surfaces of the statues, consistently exposed to Florida's atmospheric agents, to inform future conservation decisions.

2 The Fonderia Chiurazzi and the Collection at the Ringling Museum

2.1 Historical Background

Gennaro Chiurazzi Sr. founded the Fonderia Chiurazzi in 1870. The Fonderia Chiurazzi was one of many artisan foundries established in Naples, Italy during the 19th century [19]. Chiurazzi Sr. was trained as a Neapolitan engraver. He began his work in sculpture apprenticing with Pietro Masulli, after which he established his own art schools and galleries. He chose to focus on the art of casting from molds, using lost-wax casting. This type of casting has been practiced for thousands of years; however, it had a significant revival all over Europe in the 19th century [18,20,33].

As the Chiurazzi mold and cast collection grew and the foundry gained popularity, he was able to expand the foundry and open a storefront [25]. As a result of the craftsmanship shown by the foundry, Chiurazzi was given permission to create molds of sculptures from the National Archaeological Museum in Naples, Italy. This museum has historically housed a great number of artifacts excavated from Pompeii and Herculaneum, all with incredible archaeological and art historical significance. Thus, the Foundry became known for their replicas of sculptures excavated at these sites, gaining the workshop notoriety. Chiurazzi was eventually given similar permissions by international museums, adding other acclaimed sculptures to their collection [13].

The Chiurazzi Foundry thrived during the early 20th century due to an increased interest in cultural heritage tourism and authentic replicas, especially in Italy and the sites of Pompeii and Herculaneum. Sometimes called "Pompeii-mania," Chiurazzi became popular in both the public and private sectors where these authentic replicas were utilized in decorative elements and public art [23]. Jean Paul Getty commissioned a large number of sculptures from Chiurazzi in the 1970s to place in the Getty Villa in Malibu [31], something not unusual for wealthy collectors.

At the height of the foundry, it employed almost 2,000 artisans. A number of galleries and storefronts also operated under the Chiurazzi name [25]. After being evicted from their location in 1918, the Foundry was forced to move, taking a toll on productivity and their reputation. The Foundry noted a significant decline in the demand for replicas from museums and collectors during World War II. The Foundry was largely dormant after this time, mostly acting as caretakers for the collection and occasionally taking commissions during a minor revival in the 20th century. Despite this minor revival, the foundry remained financially unstable and eventually went bankrupt.

In 2000, the foundry and its contents of over 1,650 molds were sold to Clemente Setaro at public auction, maintaining the involvement of Elio Chiurazzi, the grandson of Gennaro Chiurazzi, until his death in 2003. It was eventually purchased by Chiurazzi Srl in 2010 and, in 2012, it was purchased by Experience Art and Design Inc in Nevada [13]. The Foundry, under the name Chiurazzi Internazionale Srl, is currently located in Casoria, Italy where it continues to produce casts of original sculptures and serve as an archive of sorts for Italian sculpture. A number of museums with significant Chiurazzi collections continue to showcase the craftsmanship of these replicas as masterpieces themselves. These museums include the Louvre in Paris, the Vatican Museums in Vatican City, the Philadelphia Museum of Art, the Field Museum in Chicago, the Getty Museum in Malibu, and the John and Mable Ringling Museum of Art in Sarasota, Florida [25].

2.2 The John and Mable Ringling Museum of Art and the Chiurazzi Collection

John Ringling established the John and Mable Ringling Museum of Art in 1931, shortly after his wife's death, as a means to commemorate her and showcase their unique art collection. The museum was housed on a 20-acre plot of land in Sarasota, Florida, which John and his wife Mable had purchased in 1911 [32]. During the 1920s, Ringling became one of the richest men alive, earning his wealth and fame from the traveling circus business, enabling him to build impressive works of architecture and to purchase collections of art to decorate their Gilded Age mansion in Sarasota, much of which they acquired during their travels [28]. The mansion, named the Ca'd'Zan, was built on the very same property that would become the museum. The collections were spread between the mansion and the original gallery.

In 1925, John Ringling purchased a collection of 50 bronze Chiurazzi statues, costing millions of Italian liras at the time. Federico Chiurazzi recounts his first meeting with Ringling, noting that he doubted if the payment provided was legitimate, based solely on Ringling's disheveled appearance at the time of purchase. Upon requesting the director of the bank in Naples affirm with Ringling's bank, they received in response: "John Ringling, a man good for any amount" [25]. Ringling's purchase included sculptures of ancient and Renaissance origins. While the collection was initially located on Ringling's estate, the sculptures were moved to the initial museum gallery at its dedication in 1927.

Four of those 50 sculptures, cast in bronze and finished with Herculaneum patina, were molded from marble originals, including the 5.25-meter-high replica of Michelangelo's David. When Ringling purchased them, it was proclaimed the largest collection of Chiurazzi casts ever put together. The collection was only surpassed in size by Getty's purchase in the 1970s [25]. Currently, the Ringling houses 71 sculptures attributed to the Fonderia Chiurazzi [7], the majority of which are located in courtyard of the Art Museum (Fig. 1) and constituting the Museum of Art Courtyard Sculpture Collection [8]. Others from the collection can be seen at St. Armand's Circle in Sarasota, Florida and at the Florida State University campus in Tallahassee.

Fig. 1. John and Mable Ringling Museum of Art Courtyard

3 Virtual Chiurazzi Project: Creation, Curation and Dissemination of a 3D Digital Cultural Heritage Collection

The University of South Florida's Institute for Digital Exploration began the digitization of the Chiurazzi Sculpture Collection at the John and Mable Ringling Museum of Art in the Fall 2020, working at a time when the museum was open but under strict restrictions to mitigate the spread of the coronavirus.

3.1 3D Capturing, 3D Processing and Post-processing: Methodologies and Challenges

In capturing the data for these objects, USF IDEx utilized hand-held digital photogrammetry. This method was chosen in accordance with the standards laid out in the London Charter [16], Seville Principles [15], and Bordeaux White Paper [14] which describes proposed best practices for digitization and visualization in cultural heritage and the humanities. Each of the three documents emphasize the importance of choosing the appropriate methodology for the desired outcome. Given the material, scale, lighting and position of the individual sculptures in the courtyard, it was determined that digital photogrammetry would be most effective for the project. Given the intended uses for the virtual collection, digital photogrammetry would allow for an accurate and high-resolution texture for the 3D models that would enable scholarly research and educational purposes for the collection [24].

For this project, four DSLRs were employed: Nikon D3400, Nikon D5600, Canon EOS REBEL T3i, and a Nikon D800. Three lenses were utilized with these cameras: AF-P Nikon 18–55 mm 1:3.5-5.6G, Canon EF 24 mm f/2,8 and Nikkor 20 mm/2.8 (Fig. 2). For each sculpture, anywhere between 89 photos to 549 photos per sculpture depending on the complexity and the physical accessibility of the object. There were a few challenges encountered during the capturing of the data. The first challenge was environmental factors such as the presence of water collected on the sculptures as well as the consistently changing lighting. To mitigate these issues, IDEx team members were sure to carefully dry sculptures if there was water from rain or condensation that would have affected the quality of the data. Another issue encountered were objects larger than life-size. Ladders were provided by the Ringling Museum to lessen this issue and enable the capture of the top of the sculpture (Fig. 2).

Fig. 2. IDEx members capturing the *Dying Gaul* (left), *Praying Boy* (center), and *Laccoon* (right) with digital photogrammetry

Another challenge was the placement of sculptures up against walls or in corners. Many of the sculptures are placed around the loggia in the courtyard of the Ringling Museum of Art, making it impossible to complete full rotations around the object. For some sculptures, like the *Capitoline Wolf* or *Seated Hermes*, there was the possibility of carefully reaching the camera around the object without physically walking around the object. However, one particular statute, the *Laocoon*, is placed in a corner. Given the scale of the object and its placement, IDEx members were not able to capture any data on the backside of the object. This issue, as explained below, was addressed in data collection to post-processing methods.

With respect to processing the datasets, initial attempts were done employing Agisoft Metashape v.1.8.0 (build 13257). The results, however, would have required significant extra time doing manual reconstruction work. The processing algorithms in each photogrammetry software differ, making it sometimes useful to attempt to datasets in other programs prior to spending resources in manual reconstruction [22]. The major benefits of Metashape are in the form of control and cost. Tests have determined that the level of control in not only the ability to create and generate chunks for small-scale digitization-that being done with a turntable and light box-but also in texture selection and masking. Metashape similarly provides benefits to drone photogrammetry where digital elevation maps can be created within the software itself, without the need to employ external geographic information systems (GIS) programs. This is contrasted to RealityCapture which thrives in situations where chunks and different artifact positions are not required and where GIS applications are not the focus [21].

In this project, RealityCapture's algorithm was able to more accurately reconstruct the point cloud and texture without much manual intervention. In comparison with the manual intervention of the processed photogrammetric 3D models of the Chiurazzi statues required by Metashape, the outcomes processed in RealityCapture required almost none (Fig. 3 and 4) and for this reason the latter was employed in most of the cases. Upon reconstruction in RealityCapture, only a small amount of cleaning to remove stray points and decimation to under 3.5 million triangles-so that the final model is small enough to disseminate on online platforms-was required. The decimation did not change the shape or quality of the mesh.

Fig. 3. Sparse cloud (left), cleaned dense cloud (middle), and mesh (right) of *Dying Gaul*

Due to the varying conditions of an outdoor setting and special cases, such as objects against a wall or placed in a corner, required post-processing. The issues that photogrammetric software can have related to creating point clouds for reflective or transparent surfaces [17] are also present as these statues are reflective bronze. These problems are compounded under certain atmospheric conditions, such as high relative humidity (in our case 77%) or direct sunlight.

Fig. 4. Final textured model of *Dying Gaul*

Morning dew on the surface of the metal can evaporate unevenly, creating a "dirty" effect that compromises the color rendering of the photogrammetric software [27].

Some of the protocols adopted to mitigate some of those issues is the postprocessing of the statue of the *Boxer*. The original dataset for this model consisted of 225 images, which were processed using four principal steps: 1) photographic postproduction, 2) photogrammetric processing, 3) postprocessing of the mesh, 4) postprocessing of the texture. The dataset of images is first subjected to postproduction in order to soften the differences in lighting between the parts of the statue in direct sunlight and those in shadow [26], using Adobe Lightroom Classic 2019. In this specific instance, the dataset processed using the Agisoft Metashape Professional v.1.8.0 (build 13257), bore better results. The front and rear of the statue were processed separately and united before moving on to the creation of the mesh and texturing of the model. Holes in the model or noisy data were concentrated in shadowed or difficult to capture areas for operator to capture, including as the shoulders, fist, crest of the head, and the fists, which translated into the texture of the model (Fig. 5).

The fourth step required the creation of new texture based on the original, mirroring the bronze patina of high-quality texture in the original model, in order not to let the blemished texture affect the photorealism of the model. Ambient Adobe Substance Painter was used by combining various material settings in the software with various filters to obtain an acceptable bronze patina effect (Fig. 6). In this case, we reproduced the bronze texture of the original while staying true to the light conditions under which the dataset was captured. By virtue of the flexibility of the software, the texture file generated has a wide range of customization that will allow for the rendering to be reused or altered in the future. Minor edits, such as smoothing, and texture edits, such as removing imposing colors from the walls of the Ringling Museum, and construction of background walls and planes mimicking the ground were also done using Blender 2.92.

Fig. 5. 3D model of the Chiurazzi *Boxer* featuring critical areas found during the build texture phase

Fig. 6. Stages of the process of re-texturizing the model the 3D model of the Chiurazzi *Boxer*

3.2   Digital Data Curation

Data curation is an important part of any digital project. All standards that have been formulated for cultural heritage digital projects stress the importance of transparency in the form of metadata and paradata, as well as longevity of the data. There are no absolute standards for classes of data, as the data curation plan must be tailored to the goals of the project. IDEx has adopted the Dublin Core Metadata Element Set (DCMES) with minor adjustments to its standards for recording metadata, paradata, and otherwise curating the data in the spirit of the Charters and Bordeaux White Paper to ensure continued accessibility to the data [14–16].

The Virtual Karam Collection [30] was used as a model for the Virtual Chiurazzi Collection, though the latter required more nuanced inputs and research due to their provenance from a foundry that is not very well documented in academic scholarship. A standard form of historical metadata had to be compiled using museum documentation, including object summaries, catalogues, and location and display information regarding the collection, which were revised and standardized to fit the metadata schema (Fig. 7) Original historical research was an important part of compiling the relevant data to recreate the provenance of each of the Chiruazzi foundry's reproductions. Contracts and sales records provided a great deal of information about museum partnerships established by the Fonderia Chirazzi, their unique molding technique, and history of ownership of the company. In addition, the objects' status as reproductions required research on the original objects that they reproduced, creating a layered history for each object.

Paradata about the objects was recorded in order to inform the end user of the technical choices made in the creation of the digital models. The technology

Metadata Report

SOUTH FLORIDA
College of Arts & Sciences
Institute for Digital Exploration

IDEX Code: JMR20.007	**Record creation:** 1/21/2021	**Collection Date:** 10/7/2020
Object Title: Dying Gaul	**Country:** Italy	**Alternative Title:** SN5088
Time Period: 20th Century	**Location:** Sarasota, Florida	**Cultural Heritage Type:** Italian
Subject: Bronze Statue		
Height (in cm): 94	**Width (in cm):** 91.4	**Length (in cm):** 194.3
Materials: Bronze		

Description: This bronze statue is a 20th century copy of the Roman marble statue given to the City of Sarasota in 1936 by John Ringling. It is a copy of a Hellenistic statue that is no longer extant. The figure is depicted laying on his shield with a sword puncture wound in his chest. A sword, belt and trumpet are next to him. The original Hellenistic bronze dates to around the 3rd century BCE and the Roman marble was created in the 1st-2nd century CE. The Roman copy was found in the 1600s at the Villa Ludovisi in Rome and is currently held in the Capitoline Museum in Rome, Italy.

Institution: University of South Florida

CHO ID: John and Mable Ringling Museum of Art

Institution ID: https://history.usf.edu/idex

Resource link: https://sketchfab.com/3d-models/peplophorus-sn5090-930c70aed67e41f998b967239eb4c925

Keywords: Bronze, sculpture, replica, Chiurazzi, Roman, Hellenistic, Gaul, figure

Images:

Paradata:
Digital Photogrammetry; Madeleine Kraft: Processor; Kaitlyn Kingsland, Madeleine Kraft: Imaging equipment: Nikon D 3400, Rendering Software: Reality Capture; Editing Software: Blender 2.9

Fig. 7. Metadata and paradata report for the *Dying Gaul*

software, and post-processing procedures (as elaborated above) are all important aspects of the reproducibility of the project and transparency for the public about the visualization of the digital object.

3.3 Dissemination of the Digital Collection

In continuing to follow the model for the Virtual Karam Collection, Virtual Chiurazzi exists as a living collection. All of the models, a total of 24, have been uploaded into a collection on the popular repository Sketchfab and made globally accessible [3]. The description of each model has a brief summary of the metadata and paradata for the object. Subsequently a dedicated web platform has been designed as section of the USF IDEx website [11]. The landing page of the web platform features a brief overview of the project, including a description of each major step in the creation and completion of the project: 3D data capturing, 3D data processing, metadata curation, and curation of the digital collection (Fig. 8). From it, the collection of 24 3D models can be browsed and reports of the standardized metadata and paradata can be downloaded.

Fig. 8. Screenshots of *Virtual Chiurazzi* 3D collection with the collection front page (right) and browsing the collection (left)

The ultimate goal for this data would be, in the near future, for it to be integrated through the USF Libraries archives system, Digital Commons, to ensure longevity and maintenance of the data, as has been previously done with the Virtual Karam Project, by which the Virtual Chiurazzi was inspired [12]. This is especially important given the emphasis on accessibility for this virtualization project. By establishing and enacting a plan to manage and maintain the data, it is available in perpetuity for research or reuse, enabling its sustainability.

4 Conclusion

In virtualizing the Chiurazzi sculpture collection at the John and Mable Ringling Museum of Art, USF IDEx complied with the standards for visualization in cultural heritage in an attempt to address important issues in the field, including accessibility to cultural heritage and scientific transparency.

The Fonderia Chiurazzi, despite a tumultuous past, remains an extremely important establishment for historical and archaeological documentation and accessibility. Laws enacted by the Italian government in 1972 prohibit the creation of molds from original artworks housed in museums. Thus, the Chiurazzi Foundry is one of few establishments with molds of these sculptures. With over 1,650 molds of original works the collection has the ability to showcase works of art to a much wider international audience by providing replicas to institutions around the world, such as the Ringling Museum [13].

Accessibility of these models also contributes to the Ringling's commitment to inclusion, diversity, equity, and access [9]. John Ringling, upon the opening of the museum to the public in 1931, stated that he hoped the museum would "promote education and art appreciation, especially among our young people" [10]. The Ringling museums take an active role in ensuring their collections are truly accessible. The accessibility aid tool on the Ringling website, catering to hearing and visually impaired individuals during museum programs, providing ASL interpreters, and more indicate the dedication the Ringling Museum has to maintaining John Ringling's hopes for the institution [6]. The development of digital replicas enables institutions to increase their own standards of accessibility to break physical and intellectual barriers in heritage tourism and contribute to the democratization of knowledge.

The Fonderia Chiurazzi and the Ringling Museum both have unique histories that make them intrinsically valuable both as cultural institutions and for the contents that the Fonderia originally produced. Gennaro Chiurazzi established a foundry that would later serve as a means of spreading awareness and increasing the accessibility of original artworks. The Ringling Museum, housing many of these bronze copies, allows those with reduced access due to socioeconomic reasons or disabilities to view sculptures with incredible historical, archaeological, and artistic significance.

Through 3D digitization via digital photogrammetry, this project carried out by USF IDEx, in coordination with the Ringling Museum, aims to continue to increase accessibility to these works while adhering to standards that aid in addressing the issue of authenticity, context, and transparency of digital objects. In doing so, this project carries on a legacy of reproductive media while also carrying out the Ringling's mission to provide accessible collections for appreciation and education, just as John Ringling had hoped. The Virtual Chiurazzi collection enables a singular platform that houses the models as well as their associated metadata to address these open issues and showcase the potential of reproductive digital media as a means to solve these issues and guarantee global digital accessibility.

Acknowledgements. The authors are very thankful to the curatorial and conservation staff of the John and Mable Ringling Museum for their help in support in the development of the project and, in particular, to Dr. Sarah Cartwright (Ulla R. Searing

Curator of Collections), Emily Brown (Conservator of Sculpture & Decorative Arts) and Kyle Mancuso (former Curatorial Research Fellow).

References

1. Cast museum at the ashmolean museum at oxford. https://www.ashmolean.org/cast-gallery-department
2. Collection of classical antiquities at the bern museum. https://www.museen-bern.ch/de/institutionen/museen/antikensammlung-bern
3. Idex sketchfab: Virtual chiurazzi collection at the ringing. https://sketchfab.com/usfidex/collections/fonderia-chiurazzi-collection-at-the-ringling
4. Museum of casts of classical studies in Munich. https://www.abgussmuseum.de
5. Museum of classical art of the università sapienza in rome. https://web.uniroma1.it/polomuseale/museo-arte-classica
6. The ringling: Accessibility. https://www.ringling.org/accessibility. Accessed 20 Jan 2022
7. Ringling e-museum. https://emuseum.ringling.org/emuseum/collections
8. Ringling e-museum courtyard sculpture collection. https://emuseum.ringling.org/emuseum/collections/96302/museum-of-art-courtyard-sculpture
9. The ringling: Equity statement. https://www.ringling.org/equitystatement. Accessed 20 Jan 2022
10. The ringling: History of the ringling. https://www.ringling.org/history-ringling. Accessed 20 Jan 2022
11. Virtual chiurazzi collection. https://history.usf.edu/idex/chiurazz.html
12. Virtual karam collection at the USF libraries. https://digitalcommons.usf.edu/karam
13. Experience art and design, Inc: Form 8-k/a. Report (Filed 2 May 2013). https://www.sec.gov/Archives/edgar/data/1514888/000155724013000261/exad-8ka1.htm
14. Alliez, P., et al.: Digital 3D objects in art and humanities: challenges of creation, interoperability and preservation. White paper (2017). https://hal.inria.fr/hal-01526713
15. Bendicho, V.M.L.-M.: International guidelines for virtual archaeology: the Seville principles. In: Corsi, C., Slapšak, B., Vermeulen, F. (eds.) Good Practice in Archaeological Diagnostics. NSA, pp. 269–283. Springer, Cham (2013). https://doi.org/10.1007/978-3-319-01784-6_16
16. Bentkowska-Kafel, A., Denard, H., Baker, D.: The London Charter for the Computer-Based Visualisation of Cultural Heritage (Version 2.1, February 2009), book section 7, pp. 73–78. Routledge, London (2012). https://doi.org/10.4324/9781315599366
17. Bici, M., Gherardini, F., Campana, F., Leali, F.: A preliminary approach on point cloud reconstruction of bronze statues through oriented photogrammetry: the "principe ellenistico" case. IOP Conf. Ser. Mater. Sci. Eng. **949**(1), 012117 (2020). https://doi.org/10.1088/1757-899x/949/1/012117
18. Bochicchio, L.: Transported art: 19th-century Italian sculptures across continents and cultures. Mater. Cult. Rev. **74–75**, 70–85 (2012). https://id.erudit.org/iderudit/mcr74_75art05
19. Fucito, L.: Fonderia artistica Chiurazzi: la forma dell'arte. Altrastampa, Napoli (2001)
20. Hunt, L.B.: The long history of lost wax casting. Gold Bull. **13**(2), 63–79 (1980). https://doi.org/10.1007/BF03215456

21. Kingsland, K.: A comparative analysis of two commercial digital photogrammetry software for cultural heritage applications. In: Cristani, M., Prati, A., Lanz, O., Messelodi, S., Sebe, N. (eds.) ICIAP 2019. LNCS, vol. 11808, pp. 70–80. Springer, Cham (2019). https://doi.org/10.1007/978-3-030-30754-7_8

22. Kingsland, K.: Comparative analysis of digital photogrammetry software for cultural heritage. Digit. Appl. Archaeol. Cult. Herit. **18**, e00157 (2020). https://doi.org/10.1016/j.daach.2020.e00157

23. Kovacs, C.L.: Pompeii and its material reproductions: the rise of a tourist site in the nineteenth century. J. Tour. Hist. **5**(1), 25–49 (2013). https://doi.org/10.1080/1755182X.2012.758781

24. Magnani, M., Douglass, M., Schroder, W., Reeves, J., Braun, D.R.: The digital revolution to come: photogrammetry in archaeological practice. Am. Antiq. **85**(4), 737–760 (2020). https://doi.org/10.1017/aaq.2020.59

25. Mattusch, C.C., Lie, H.: The Villa dei Papiri at Herculaneum: life and afterlife of a sculpture collection. J. Paul Getty Museum, Los Angeles (2005)

26. Menna, F., Rizzi, A., Nocerino, E., Remondino, F., Gruen, A.: High resolution 3D modeling of the behaim globe. Int. Arch. Photogramm. Remote Sens. Spatial Inf. Sci. **XXXIX-B5**, 115–120 (2012). https://doi.org/10.5194/isprsarchives-XXXIX-B5-115-2012

27. Nicolae, C., Noccrino, E., Menna, F., Remondino, F.: Photogrammetry applied to problematic artefacts. Int. Arch. Photogramm. Remote Sens. Spatial Inf. Sci. **XL-5**, 451–456 (2014). https://doi.org/10.5194/isprsarchives-XL-5-451-2014

28. Ormond, M., et al.: John Ringling: dreamer, builder, collector. Legacy of the circus king, John and Mable Ringling Museum of Art, Sarasota, Florida (1996)

29. Paolucci, F.: Winckelmann nella Galleria delle Statue, pp. 87–106. Edizioni ETS, Pisa (2018)

30. Tanasi, D., Hassam, S.N., Kingsland, K.: Virtual karam collection: 3D digital imaging and 3D printing for public outreach in archaeology. In: Visual Heritage 2018, Conference on Cultural Heritage and New Technologies (CHNT) 23, 2018. https://www.chnt.at/wp-content/uploads/eBook_CHNT23_Tanasi_Learningthroughobjects.pdf

31. True, M., Silvetti, J.: The Getty Villa. Getty Publishing, Los Angeles (2007)

32. Wetenhall, J.: A museum once forgotten: rebirth of the John and Mable Ringling Museum of Art. Florida State University, Tallahassee (2007)

33. Wiegartz, V.: The Subtlety of the Surface: Thoughts on the Revival of the Lost Wax Technique in Late Nineteenth-Century Germany, book section 4, pp. 93–114. Brill, Leiden (2020). https://doi.org/10.1163/9789004439931_006

34. Winckelmann, J.J., Potts, A.: History of the Art of Antiquity. Texts & Documents, Getty Research Institute, Los Angeles (2006)

Multimodal Strategies for Image and Audio Music Transcription: A Comparative Study

María Alfaro-Contreras[✉], Jose J. Valero-Mas, José M. Iñesta, and Jorge Calvo-Zaragoza

U.I for Computer Research, University of Alicante, Alicante, Spain
{malfaro,jjvalero,inesta,jcalvo}@dlsi.ua.es

Abstract. The mere availability of most musical heritage as image documents or audio recordings does not enable tasks such as indexing or editing unless they are transcribed into a structured digital format. Given the cost and time required for manual transcription, Optical Music Recognition (OMR) and Automatic Music Transcription (AMT) deal with the aforementioned situation by computational means. Their historically different approaches have recently shifted towards a common sequence labeling formulation framework, which enables research on a combined paradigm. In this respect, multimodal image and audio music transcription attempts to appropriately integrate the information depicted by image and audio modalities. This work explores whether combining the individual features of each modality—early multimodal fusion—or merging the hypotheses obtained by end-to-end OMR and AMT systems—late multimodal fusion—brings any additional benefits regarding the standard unimodal frameworks. The results obtained for a series of evaluation scenarios—in which the music sources were available in either one or both modalities—showed that while the feature-level approach worsens the single-modality transcription systems, the decision-level combination provides a meaningful improvement if, and only if, the corresponding unimodal approaches do not greatly differ in performance. This opens up a new promising, yet challenging, research path towards multimodality in music transcription.

Keywords: Optical Music Recognition · Automatic Music Transcription · Multimodality · Deep Learning · Connectionist Temporal Classification · Sequence Labeling

1 Introduction

Music is part of human tradition and represents a valuable element of cultural heritage that has been transmitted by two means: through sound and using written documents. Nonetheless, most of the existing music sources (either audio recordings or music documents) have never been transcribed into a structured

J.-J. Rousseau and B. Kapralos (Eds.): ICPR 2022 Workshops, LNCS 13645, pp. 64–77, 2023.
https://doi.org/10.1007/978-3-031-37731-0_6

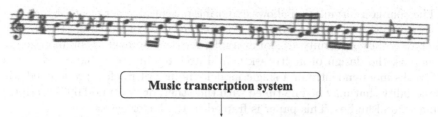

Music transcription system

clef-G2 keySignature-GM timeSignature-3/4 note-B4_eighth. gracenote-B4_sixteenth ...

(a) Optical Music Recognition: music transcription using score images as inputs and a music-representation language as output.

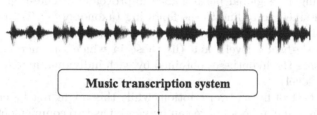

Music transcription system

clef-G2 keySignature-GM timeSignature-3/4 note-B4_eighth. gracenote-B4_sixteenth ...

(b) Automatic Music Transcription: music transcription using audio recordings as inputs and the same language as output.

Fig. 1. End-to-end music transcription framework. OMR techniques deal with images and AMT techniques deal with audio signals; however, both tasks have to provide a result in a symbolic format that represents a piece of music.

digital format that enables their indexing, retrieval, and processing with computational means. Similar to the case of human language processing with speech recognition and optical character recognition technologies, the music scenario invites automation as well.

Optical Music Recognition (OMR) and Automatic Music Transcription (AMT) are the research fields that investigate how to computationally transcribe music score images and audio recordings, respectively, into machine-readable formats encoding symbolic data [2,3]. Despite having a similar purpose, these two fields have historically evolved in a disjoint manner owing to differences in the nature of the data, which has resulted in specific task-oriented recognition frameworks that are most typically based on multi-stage procedures [6].

However, some recent proposals in the related literature frame transcription problems in a sequence labeling formulation that approaches the task in a holistic or end-to-end manner [4,11]: the input data—either scores or acoustic pieces—are directly decoded into a sequence of music-notation symbols. This makes it possible to address OMR and AMT tasks with similar recognition models that differ only in terms of the input data used to train the system. A graphic illustration of these recognition approaches is provided in Fig. 1.

The common formulation allows exploring potential synergies that may exist between image and audio domains. Possible avenues of research [1] yet to be explored by the community are, for example, the development of common linguistic models, the design of multi-task neural architectures capable of addressing both tasks independently in a single model, the use of models pre-trained with one modality that may be fine-tuned with the other, or multimodal transcription of images and audios. This paper is framed in the latter case.

Multimodal recognition frameworks, which are defined as those that take different representations or modalities of the same piece of data as input, have led to improvements in many fields [12,15,16]. The multiple modalities in these schemes are expected to bring complementary information to the system, ultimately resulting in a global performance improvement. These approaches are commonly classified according to the following taxonomy [5]: (i) those in which the individual features of the modalities are in some respects directly merged (*feature* or *early-fusion* level), and (ii) those in which the merging process is carried out using the hypotheses obtained by each individual modality (*decision* or *late-fusion* level).

In the context of music transcription, while this might not be entirely true, both a recording and a score image can be viewed as two complementary modalities of the same piece of music. On the one hand, the image contains all the information that was intended to store, but it is in a graphical domain that must be decoded in order to interpret it as music. On the other hand, the audio contains information about the musical performance, but certain aspects are difficult to retrieve due to human interpretation or certain unavoidable ambiguities (such as the clef or the time signature). If the original composition were in the form of both an image and a recording, the two could be combined in a synergistic manner to exploit the transcription advantages of each modality. The development of systems capable of efficiently combining the information conveyed by the image and the audio of the same piece of music for their joint transcription is, therefore, a promising task that has, with a few exceptions [6], barely been addressed in literature.

This work explores multimodality in neural end-to-end music transcription involving image scores and audio recordings given that the objective in both domains is to retrieve the same symbolic representation. More precisely, we propose and study different multimodal transcription approaches within the aforementioned early and late fusion frameworks to determine whether they can provide an advantage with respect to existing unimodal recognition cases. Additionally, we thoroughly analyze the individual advantages that each type of combination may report to this transcription task.

The remainder of the paper is organized as follows: Sect. 2 introduces the proposed approach for unimodal recognition and thoroughly develops the multimodal image and audio transcription framework considered. Section 3 describes the experimental setup and Sect. 4 presents and analyses the results. Finally, Sect. 5 concludes the work and discusses possible ideas for future research.

2   Methodology

This section formally presents the neural end-to-end recognition for the stand-alone and multimodal OMR and AMT processes addressed in this work. Considering the aforementioned *sequence labeling* formulation, our goal is to retrieve the most likely series of symbols from the input data—either a score image or an audio recording or both, as appropriate. Some notations will now be introduced in order to properly describe these design principles.

Let $\mathcal{T} = \{(x_m, \mathbf{z}_m) : x_m \in \mathcal{X}, \mathbf{z}_m \in \mathcal{Z}\}_{m=1}^{|\mathcal{T}|}$ represent a set of data in which sample x_m drawn from space $\mathcal{X}$ corresponds to symbol sequence $\mathbf{z}_m = (z_{m1}, z_{m2}, \ldots, z_{mN})$ from space $\mathcal{Z}$, considering the underlying function $g : \mathcal{X} \rightarrow \mathcal{Z}$. Note that the latter space is defined as $\mathcal{Z} = \Sigma^*$, where Σ represents the score-level symbol vocabulary.

2.1   Unimodal Neural End-to-End Music Transcription

We have considered a Convolutional Recurrent Neural Network (CRNN) scheme with the Connectionist Temporal Classification (CTC) training algorithm [7] in order to approximate the function g due to its competitive performance in the related literature. In the aforementioned approach, the convolutional stage—namely, CNN—extracts the most appropriate features for the case in hand, while the recurrent part—known as RNN—models the temporal (or spatial) dependencies of these symbols. The CTC method allows training the CRNN using unsegmented sequential data. In a practical sense, this mechanism requires only the different input signals and their associated sequences of symbols from Σ as its expected output, without any specific input-output alignment. It is important to mention that CTC demands an additional *"blank"* token within the set of symbols, i.e., $\Sigma' = \Sigma \cup \{blank\}$, to enable the detection of consecutive repeated elements.

Since CTC assumes that the architecture contains a fully-connected network of $|\Sigma'|$ neurons with a *softmax* activation, the actual output is a *posteriorgram* $p \in \mathbb{R}^{|\Sigma'| \times K}$, where K represents the number of frames given by the recurrent layer. The final predicted sequence $\hat{\mathbf{z}}$ is most commonly obtained out of this posteriogram using a *greedy* approach that retrieves the most probable symbol per step and a posterior squash function that merges consecutive repeated symbols and removes the *blank* label.

2.2   Multimodal Neural End-to-End Music Transcription

Multimodal frameworks attempt to leverage the information depicted by each input modality in a synergistic manner [14]. This combination can be implemented at two levels: at the feature level (or *early-fusion*) or at the decision level (or *late-fusion*). The first approach merges the data "as is"—the multiple input modalities are pre-processed in order to extract their corresponding features, which are then fused and fed into a single processing algorithm. The second approach, however, combines the predictions of various ad-hoc algorithms, one for each modality.

Let superscripts i and a identify the image and audio domains, respectively. There are consequently two different representation spaces, $\mathcal{X}^i$ and $\mathcal{X}^a$, which are related to the image scores and audio signals, respectively, with a single output vocabulary Σ.

Early Multimodal Fusion. The proposed feature-level multimodal policy aims to learn the possible common representation space by combining the corresponding single-modality features. Such a combination involves the use of a multiple-input, single-output model that depicts three differentiated parts: a first one devised for extracting the modality-specific features of the input data, i.e., two complete CNN blocks specialized on a certain type of modality (either image or audio); a second one in charge of joining the previous spaces of information; and a third one which comprises a RNN stage meant to process the combined features for the eventual recognition. A graphic illustration of this process is provided in Fig. 2.

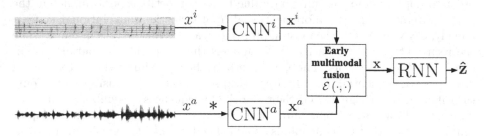

Fig. 2. Graphical example of the proposed early multimodal fusion framework: the feature vectors, $\mathbf{x}^i$ and $\mathbf{x}^a$, computed by the CNN^i image and the CNN^a audio feature extractors, respectively, are integrated into a joint $\mathbf{x}$ embedding through function $\mathcal{E}$. A common RNN block is used to model the temporal dependencies of these features, eventually predicting the final $\hat{\mathbf{z}}$ symbol sequence. The (*) symbol in the audio branch denotes that the signal undergoes a time-frequency transformation to obtain a spectrogram-based representation, which constitutes the input to the CNN^a module.

Given an input pair (x^i, x^a) representing a score image and an audio signal of the same piece of music, we obtain their corresponding feature vectors in the respective embedding spaces, by considering a pair of functions $f^i : \mathcal{X}^i \rightarrow \mathcal{X}^i_e$ and $f^a : \mathcal{X}^a \rightarrow \mathcal{X}^a_e$ given by the CNN^i image and the CNN^a audio feature extractors, respectively. The retrieved single-modality feature vectors, $\mathbf{x}^i$ and $\mathbf{x}^a$, are combined by means of function $\mathcal{E} : \mathcal{X}^i_e \times \mathcal{X}^a_e \rightarrow \mathcal{X}_e$, hence producing a joint vector $\mathbf{x}$. In preliminary experiments carried out for the current work, we observed that simply averaging the corresponding components of the resulting unimodal vectors yielded the most promising results. We, therefore, use $\mathcal{E}(\mathbf{x}^i, \mathbf{x}^a) = (x^i_j + x^a_j)/2$, for every feature j, as the combination function in the early multimodal fusion approach. Finally, this vector of merged features $\mathbf{x}$ is passed through the recurrent block to model the spatial dependencies and eventually output the final predicted $\hat{\mathbf{z}}$ transcription.

The considered early multimodal fusion framework entails a constraint as regards the dimension of the feature vectors: it must be identical for $\mathbf{x}^i$ and $\mathbf{x}^a$ in order to properly combine them. In this work, we meet this condition by ensuring that both CNN^i image and CNN^a audio feature extractors have the same architecture. We assume that it is possible to set a good configuration for both modalities.

Late Multimodal Fusion. The proposed decision-level multimodal policy combines the hypotheses given by each single-modality recognition system. Such a fusion involves the use of two single-input, single-output models devised to solve the OMR and the AMT tasks, respectively. A graphic illustration of this process is provided in Fig. 3.

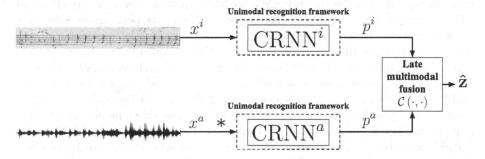

Fig. 3. Graphical example of the proposed late multimodal fusion framework: the posteriorgrams, p^i and p^a, computed by the $CRNN^i$ image and the $CRNN^a$ audio transcription models, respectively, are combined according to a certain combination function $\mathcal{C}(\cdot, \cdot)$. This combination results in the predicted $\hat{\mathbf{z}}$ symbol sequence. The (*) symbol in the audio branch denotes that the signal undergoes a time-frequency transformation to obtain a spectrogram-based representation, which constitutes the input to the $CRNN^a$ module.

Formally, let $CRNN^i$ and $CRNN^a$ denote the two CRNN transcription models introduced in Sect. 2.1 that deal with the source domain of the image and audio data, respectively. Given an input pair $\left(x^i, x^a\right)$ representing a score image and an audio signal of the same piece of music, respectively, we obtain their respective p^i and p^a posteriorgrams by employing the aforementioned $CRNN^i$ and $CRNN^a$ unimodal recognition methods. Function $\mathcal{C}(\cdot, \cdot)$, which combines two posteriorgrams and decodes the resulting structure, is then applied to p^i and p^a, and the predicted sequence is obtained as $\hat{\mathbf{z}} = \mathcal{C}\left(p^i, p^a\right)$.

In this work, we consider a $\mathcal{C}(\cdot, \cdot)$ combination approach based on the Minimum Bayes Risk (MBR) criterion [17]. The objective of MBR decoding is to find the sequence that minimizes the expected risk for a given loss function. In our case, the loss function is the string edit distance [9], and MBR, therefore, retrieves the set median string of the distribution provided by the hypothesis space of the model. In late-fusion combination scenarios, MBR performs this search by considering the weighted distributions of the hypothesis spaces.

3   Experimental Setup

This section presents the definition of the different layers of the neural models, the evaluation protocol used, and the corpus considered.

3.1   Neural Network Configuration

While the presented sequence labeling paradigm allows considering a common formulation for both OMR and AMT tasks, in practice there is no universal CRNN architecture capable of achieving state-of-the-art performances in both cases. Generally, these configurations are conditioned to the particular corpus considered, the amount of accessible data, or the computational resources available, among others. In this work, we consider different architectures for the convolutional block—based on those used in recent works addressing the individual OMR and AMT tasks as a sequence labeling problem [4,10]—while sharing a common composition for the recurrent stage. Given that the proposed early multimodal fusion approach requires that the CNN^i image and the CNN^a audio feature extractors have the same architecture, we also study which standard configuration—either the OMR one or that of AMT—is more appropriate under a multimodal framework. Table 1 depict the actual composition of each layer.

All the models in this work were trained using the backpropagation method provided by CTC for 150 epochs using the ADAM optimizer [8] with a fixed learning rate of 0.001.

3.2   Performance Metrics

The performance of the recognition schemes presented is assessed by considering the Symbol Error Rate (SER), as occurred in previous works addressing end-to-end transcription tasks [4,13]. This figure of merit is computed as the average number of elementary editing operations (insertions, deletions, or substitutions) required in order to match the sequence predicted by the model with that in the ground truth, normalized by the length of the latter. In mathematical terms, this is expressed as:

$$\text{SER}\ (\%) = \frac{\sum_{m=1}^{|\mathcal{S}|} \text{ED}\,(\hat{\mathbf{z}}_m,\ \mathbf{z}_m)}{\sum_{m=1}^{|\mathcal{S}|} |\mathbf{z}_m|} \tag{1}$$

Table 1. Layer-wise description of the CNN and RNN blocks used in the different CRNN schemes considered. Notation: Conv($f, w \times h$) represents a convolution layer of f filters of size $w \times h$ pixels, BatchNorm performs the normalization of the batch, LeakyReLU(α) represents a Leaky Rectified Linear Unit activation with a negative slope of value α, MaxPool($w \times h$) represents the max-pooling operator of dimensions $w \times h$ pixels with $w \times h$ striding factor, BLSTM(n, d) denotes a bidirectional Long Short-Term Memory unit with n neurons and d dropout value parameters, Dense(n) is a fully-connected layer of n neurons, and Softmax($\cdot$) represents the softmax activation. Σ' denotes the alphabet considered, including the CTC-blank symbol.

	Layer 1	Layer 2	Layer 3	Layer 4
CNN$_{\text{OMR}}$	Conv(64, 5 × 5) BatchNorm LeakyReLU(0.20) MaxPool(2 × 2)	Conv(64, 5 × 5) BatchNorm LeakyReLU(0.20) MaxPool(1 × 2)	Conv(128, 3 × 3) BatchNorm LeakyReLU(0.20) MaxPool(1 × 2)	Conv(128, 3 × 3) BatchNorm LeakyReLU(0.20) MaxPool(1 × 2)
CNN$_{\text{AMT}}$	Conv(8, 2 × 10) BatchNorm LeakyReLU(0.20) MaxPool(2 × 2)	Conv(8, 5 × 8) BatchNorm LeakyReLU(0.20) MaxPool(1 × 2)		
RNN	BLSTM(256) Dropout(0.50)	BLSTM(256) Dropout(0.50)	Dense($|\Sigma'|$) Softmax($\cdot$)	

where $\mathcal{S} \subset \mathcal{X} \times \mathcal{Z}$ is a set of test data—from either the image or the audio domains—, ED : $\mathcal{Z} \times \mathcal{Z} \to \mathbb{N}_0$ represents the string edit distance, and $\hat{\mathbf{z}}_m$ and $\mathbf{z}_m$ denote the estimated and target sequences, respectively.

3.3 Corpus

We have considered the Camera-based Printed Images of Music Staves (Camera-PrIMuS) database [4]. This corpus contains 87,678 real music staves of monophonic incipits[1] extracted from the *Répertoire International des Sources Musicales* (RISM), a repository documenting extant historical music sources from all over the world.[2] Different representations are provided for each incipit: an image with the rendered score (both plain and with artificial distortions), several encoding formats for the symbol information, and a MIDI file for driving a synthesizer to play the score.

Each transcription architecture considers a particular type of data: on the one hand, the OMR model takes the artificially distorted staff image of the incipit as input, and on the other, each MIDI file in the AMT case is synthesized using the FluidSynth software[3] and a piano timbre, considering a sampling rate of 22,050 Hz. A time-frequency representation based on the Constant-Q Transform was obtained, with a hop length of 512 samples, 120 bins, and 24 bins per octave,

---

[1] Short sequences of notes, typically the first measures of the piece, used to index and identify a melody or musical work.
[2] https://rism.info/.
[3] https://www.fluidsynth.org/.

which is eventually embedded as an image that serves as the input. The height of the input considered is scaled to 64 pixels for image data, or to 256 pixels for audio data, maintaining the aspect ratio (which implies that each sample might differ in width) and converted to grayscale, with no further preprocessing.

Since this corpus was originally devised for OMR tasks, a data cleaning process was carried out to adapt it to the multimodal transcription framework presented, resulting in 22,285 incipits.[4] We eventually derive three non-overlapping partitions—train, validation, and test—which correspond to 60%, 20%, and 20% of the latter amount of data, respectively. Note that, since the same corpus is considered for both image and audio data, both recognition tasks depict the same label space of $|\Sigma^i| = |\Sigma^a| = 1{,}166$ tokens.

4   Results

Multimodality seeks to leverage the possible synergies that may exist in situations where the same information is represented in different modalities. However, in practice, we generally find ourselves in scenarios where there is an uneven distribution of the observations of the multiple representations. Given that we aim to provide insights into the possible benefits that multimodality can bring to music transcription, we evaluate the proposed multimodal approaches taking into account the mentioned limitation. We specifically consider two evaluation cases: a first one, denoted as *Scenario A*, that assesses the performance of the recognition models when the existence of both modalities is assumed for all samples; and a second one, namely *Scenario B*, that studies the modality imbalance problem. In all cases, the figures provided represent those obtained with the test partition when the validation data achieved its best performance. In order to facilitate their analysis, the following notation is introduced for the two multimodal frameworks considered: *Early*$_{OMR}$ and *Early*$_{AMT}$ correspond to the feature-level fusion method, when using the standard OMR architecture and the common AMT configuration, respectively, for both CNN^i and CNN^a (Sect. 2.2), and *Late* is used for the decision-level approach based on MBR-decoding (Sect. 2.2).[5]

4.1   Scenario A: Balance

The first scenario posed studied the impact of multimodality on the overall recognition performance under the assumption of the existence of image and audio domain representations for all the samples of the corpus considered. For that, we analyzed how the training set size influenced the transcription results. Specifically, we explored how the proposed multimodal approaches leverage the possible synergies and commonalities between the image and audio modalities

---

[4] This is the case of samples containing long multi-rests, which barely extend the length of the score image but take many frames in the audio signal.

[5] The code developed in the work is publicly available for reproducible research at: https://github.com/mariaalfaroc/early-vs-late-multimodal-music-transcription.git.

under scenarios depicting data scarcity. The results obtained in terms of the SER metric are presented in Table 2.

Table 2. Transcription results obtained in terms of Symbol Error Rates (%) for different sizes of the train partition. The 80% of the set was used to train the corresponding model, while the remaining 20% served as a validation set. Best results are highlighted in bold type.

	Size of train corpus				
	100	500	1000	2000	Whole
Unimodal					
OMR	88.6	25.3	12.3	**6.8**	**1.5**
AMT	**59.4**	40.7	34.8	30.1	22.9
Multimodal					
Early$_{OMR}$	62.7	25.4	13.9	8.1	2.4
Early$_{AMT}$	92.6	55.6	36.2	18.8	11.4
Late	60.9	**24.9**	**12.2**	**6.8**	**1.5**

A first point that may be checked is that the increment of the training set size resulted in a steep decline in the error rate for both OMR and AMT approaches considered. Such a result denotes the need for having annotated data in order to obtain an adequate transcription rate by these neural methods. In this regard, it may be observed that, when considering 500 or more training samples, OMR depicted a substantially better recognition performance than AMT—somehow expected since the image modality of the dataset is deemed to be simpler than the audio domain samples.

Under these performance results showed by the unimodal schemes, the outcome of the multimodal framework depended on the chosen combination approach. We observed that the late fusion of the hypotheses yielded by both OMR and AMT models obtained lower error rates than processing the joint single-modality features. We shall now analyze each multimodal method in detail.

Focusing on the feature-level multimodal approach, it may be checked that, at best, it only improved the recognition rate of the worst-performing single-modality transcription system. We also observe in Table 2 that the architecture chosen for the feature extractor highly affected the performance of the model, since the best results were obtained when the CNN followed the architecture devised for image data. While *Early*$_{OMR}$ managed, at best, to reduce the error of the worst-performing single-modality transcription system independently of the training set size, *Early*$_{AMT}$ needed at least 2000 samples to do so whilst still yielding worse transcription results than its counterpart.

The late multimodal fusion policy analyzed in this work behaved in a synergistic manner as long as the size used for the training set exceeded 100 samples. If so, the performance of the two unimodal frameworks was improved. If not, the recognition rate of the best-performing single-modality transcription system reached a glass ceiling. Please note that in the first case, however, the improvement was extremely narrow and it does not compensate for the effort of using two systems to transcribe a piece of music. The last point to remark is that, when models that differ greatly in performance were combined, the decision-level policy tended to give more weight to the best-performing system, leading to rates similar to those of using that system alone (e.g., when train corpus considers 2000 or larger amounts of samples in which the results of the late fusion equal those of the stand-alone OMR method).

4.2   Scenario B: Imbalance

As stated, it might not be always possible to have both modalities for all the pieces of training data. A modality imbalance problem limits the application of multimodal frameworks to late fusion approaches since both modalities are processed by the same single music transcription system under a feature-level multimodal scenario. To simulate this scenario, we specifically combined the audio music transcription trained with the whole available training partition of Sect. 4.1 with the image recognition system, when the latter was trained with the set of increasing sizes considered in Sect. 4.1. With the aforementioned experimentation, this work aims to provide insights into how the differences among the performances of the stand-alone transcription models affect the outcome of the combined paradigm. Table 3 reports transcription results in terms of the SER metric.

Table 3. Transcription results obtained in terms of the Symbol Error Rate (%) for different sizes of the image training partition. The 80% of the given set is actually used to train the corresponding model, while the remaining 20% serves as a validation set. Note that, for all the aforementioned scenarios, a fixed AMT model was used—the whole training partition was considered. Best results are highlighted in bold type.

	Size of image train corpus			
	100	500	1000	2000
Unimodal				
OMR	88.6	25.3	12.3	6.8
AMT (fixed)	**22.9**	22.9	22.9	22.9
Multimodal				
Late	33.9	**18.0**	**11.2**	**6.3**

Inspecting the reported results, a first point to remark is that, as previously observed in Scenario A, the OMR task cannot be solved with only 100 training samples. Such acute performance differences among the unimodal recognition frameworks remarkably impact that of the fusion approach: it did not find any commonalities between the image and audio domains and it ultimately worsens the results of the latter.

Regarding the case when both music transcription systems showed a similar performance level—as observed when OMR used 500 training samples—, the decision-level policy successfully solved the image and audio music transcription process. More precisely, this multimodal approach achieved around a 21% of relative error improvement with respect to the best-performing single-modality system.

Finally, in all other cases, the image music transcription model outperformed its audio counterpart since the more samples considered for the image modality, the bigger the differences were between OMR and AMT. The main consequence is, therefore, that of Scenario A: the recognition rates yielded by the late multimodal framework were noticeably similar to those of the image model, which did not make up for the effort inherent in the late combined paradigm.

5 Conclusions

The transcription into a structured digital format of existing musical heritage, available only as either written or printed documents, or audio recordings, is a necessary activity for their better preservation, access, and dissemination. Two lines of research address this challenge: Optical Music Recognition (OMR), when the input data are images of digitized scores, and Automatic Music Transcription (AMT), when considering the input data as audio signals from digitized recordings. While these fields have historically evolved separately, their recent definition within a sequence labeling formulation results in a common representation for their expected outputs. OMR and AMT tasks can be, therefore, addressed within a multimodal recognition framework.

In this work, we empirically studied the impact of different multimodal frameworks to solve the image and audio music transcription task. More specifically, we explored two scenarios: (i) a first one in which an early fusion approach averages the single-modality features to process the joint embedding vector; and (ii) a second one in which a late-fusion method merges the hypotheses depicted by the individual OMR and AMT systems following the Minimum Bayes Risk criterion. The results obtained with monophonic music data show that the feature-level multimodal system fails to outperform the single-modality recognition frameworks whereas the decision-level combination provides a meaningful improvement if, and only if, the corresponding unimodal approaches do not greatly differ in performance.

As future work, we plan to follow different research avenues. For instance, it would be interesting to additionally explore different combination functions for both early and late multimodal fusion frameworks. Experimentation may also be extended to more challenging data, such as handwritten scores, different instrumentation, or polyphonic music.

Acknowledgments. This paper is part of the I+D+i PID2020-118447RA-I00 (MultiScore) project, funded by MCIN/AEI/10.13039/501100011033. The first author is supported by grant FPU19/04957 from the Spanish Ministerio de Universidades. The second author is supported by grant APOSTD/2020/256 from "Programa I+D+i de la Generalitat Valenciana".

References

1. Alfaro-Contreras, M., Valero-Mas, J.J., Iñesta, J.M., Calvo-Zaragoza, J.: Insights into transfer learning between image and audio music transcription. In: Proceedings of the 19th Sound and Music Computing Conference (Accepted). Axea sas/SMC Network (2022)
2. Benetos, E., Dixon, S., Duan, Z., Ewert, S.: Automatic music transcription: an overview. IEEE Signal Process. Mag. **36**(1), 20–30 (2018)
3. Calvo-Zaragoza, J., Hajič, J., Jr., Pacha, A.: Understanding optical music recognition. ACM Comput. Surv. (CSUR) **53**(4), 1–35 (2020)
4. Calvo-Zaragoza, J., Rizo, D.: Camera-PrIMuS: neural end-to-end optical music recognition on realistic monophonic scores. In: Proceedings of the 19th International Society for Music Information Retrieval Conference, Paris, France, pp. 248–255 (2018)
5. Dumas, B., Signer, B., Lalanne, D.: Fusion in multimodal interactive systems: an HMM-based algorithm for user-induced adaptation. In: Proceedings of the 4th ACM SIGCHI Symposium on Engineering Interactive Computing Systems, pp. 15–24 (2012)
6. de la Fuente, C., Valero-Mas, J.J., Castellanos, F.J., Calvo-Zaragoza, J.: Multimodal image and audio music transcription. Int. J. Multimedia Inf. Retrieval 1–8 (2021)
7. Graves, A., Fernández, S., Gomez, F., Schmidhuber, J.: Connectionist temporal classification: labelling unsegmented sequence data with recurrent neural networks. In: Proceedings of the 23rd International Conference on Machine Learning, ICML 2006, pp. 369–376. ACM, New York (2006)
8. Kingma, D.P., Ba, J.: Adam: a method for stochastic optimization. In: Bengio, Y., LeCun, Y. (eds.) 3rd International Conference on Learning Representations, ICLR 2015, San Diego, CA, USA, 7–9 May 2015, Conference Track Proceedings (2015)
9. Levenshtein, V.I.: Binary codes capable of correcting deletions, insertions, and reversals. Soviet physics doklady **10**(8), 707–710 (1966)
10. Liu, L., Benetos, E.: From audio to music notation. In: Miranda, E.R. (ed.) Handbook of Artificial Intelligence for Music, pp. 693–714. Springer, Cham (2021). https://doi.org/10.1007/978-3-030-72116-9_24
11. Liu, L., Morfi, V., Benetos, E.: Joint multi-pitch detection and score transcription for polyphonic piano music. In: ICASSP 2021–2021 IEEE International Conference on Acoustics, Speech and Signal Processing (ICASSP), pp. 281–285. IEEE (2021)
12. Pitsikalis, V., Katsamanis, A., Theodorakis, S., Maragos, P.: Multimodal gesture recognition via multiple hypotheses rescoring. In: Escalera, S., Guyon, I., Athitsos, V. (eds.) Gesture Recognition. TSSCML, pp. 467–496. Springer, Cham (2017). https://doi.org/10.1007/978-3-319-57021-1_16
13. Román, M.A., Pertusa, A., Calvo-Zaragoza, J.: A holistic approach to polyphonic music transcription with neural networks. In: Proceedings of the 20th International Society for Music Information Retrieval Conference, Delft, The Netherlands, pp. 731–737 (2019)

14. Simonetta, F., Ntalampiras, S., Avanzini, F.: Multimodal music information processing and retrieval: survey and future challenges. In: 2019 International Workshop on Multilayer Music Representation and Processing (MMRP), pp. 10–18. IEEE (2019)

15. Singh, A., Sangwan, A., Hansen, J.H.: Improved parcel sorting by combining automatic speech and character recognition. In: 2012 IEEE International Conference on Emerging Signal Processing Applications, pp. 52–55. IEEE (2012)

16. Toselli, A.H., Vidal, E., Casacuberta, F.: Multimodal Interactive Pattern Recognition and Applications. Springer, London (2011). https://doi.org/10.1007/978-0-85729-479-1

17. Xu, H., Povey, D., Mangu, L., Zhu, J.: Minimum Bayes risk decoding and system combination based on a recursion for edit distance. Comput. Speech Lang. **25**(4), 802–828 (2011)

Learning Similarity for Discovering Inspirations of Western Arts in Japanese Culture

Phongtharin Vinayavekhin[1], Vorapong Suppakitpaisarn[2,3]($\boxtimes$),
Philippe Codognet[2,3], Torahiko Terada[4], and Atsushi Miura[4]

[1] Bangkok, Thailand
[2] Graduate School of Information Science and Technology,
The University of Tokyo, Tokyo, Japan
{vorapong,codognet}@is.s.u-tokyo.ac.jp
[3] Japanese-French Laboratory for Informatics (JFLI), CNRS, Tokyo, Japan
[4] Graduate School of Arts and Sciences, The University of Tokyo, Tokyo, Japan

Abstract. Several paintings by Japanese artists in the beginning of 20th century were largely inspired by works of western artists. Finding correspondences between the Japanese and the western artworks can reveal how the western arts were introduced in Japan. Until now, to discover such correspondences, art historians usually annotated them manually. This is a tedious process which generally requires a lot of effort and time. In computer vision literature, there are several techniques that can find similarities in images. To find such similarities some techniques are based on objects appearing in the images, while some techniques compare fine-grain details. However, inspirations in art illustrations are sometimes from global outlines of the images. Another difficulty is that annotations of correspondences are rare in historical data. This makes a lot of techniques which are based on supervised learning not applicable. In this paper, we propose a novel technique to find correspondences between two related artworks, which compares the global outlines information. It is based on Siamese neural networks (SNNs) and self-supervised learning method. In addition, we create a dataset of illustrations from two different types of artworks: one from Japanese artists, Seiki Kuroda, and one from western artists, Raphaël Collin. Correspondence annotations are also given. We evaluate the algorithm using recall@k as metrics, and also qualitatively show that the proposed method provides profiles of image correspondences different from the state of the art.

Keywords: Application of deep learning to digital humanities ·
Computer vision for fine arts · Art history and computer vision · Image similarities

1 Introduction

During the Edo period (15th century - 19th century), Japan had very limited contacts with foreigners and the culture thus developed in a unique way [14].

P. Vinayavekhin—Independent Researcher.

J.-J. Rousseau and B. Kapralos (Eds.): ICPR 2022 Workshops, LNCS 13645, pp. 78–92, 2023.
https://doi.org/10.1007/978-3-031-37731-0_7

By the time Japan reopened to foreigners during the Meiji restoration (the middle of 19th century), its unique culture was admired by many westerners and indeed inspired some trends in European arts and paintings. There was even a word "Japanism" or "Japonisme" to describe the excitement of westerners to Japanese culture at that period [11].

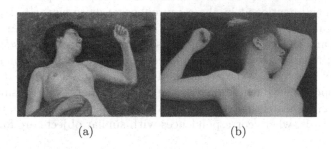

           (a)   (b)

Fig. 1. (a) "The Fields" by Seiki Kuroda (b) "The Sleep" by Raphaël Collin. It is known that the painting (b) inspires the painting (a).

On the other hand, it was also the first time in centuries that Japanese artists had a chance to see European paintings. Many of them, such as Seiki Kuroda, Keiichiro Kume, and Saburosuke Okada, went to study at salons in European countries. Some of them brought the western style of paintings back to Japan and several of their works were largely inspired by works by European artists. For example, the work named "The Fields" by Kuroda Seiki, shown in Fig. 1a, is known to be inspired by the work named "The Sleep" by Raphaël Collin, shown in Fig. 1b [18].

Art historians have found several western paintings that may have inspired Japanese arts in that period, a comprehensive discussion can be found in [16,23]. Each of those inspiration paintings gives us a deeper understanding of Japanese art history during that period. To find these style influences, one of the crucial information for the historians are the correspondences between the paintings. This is very difficult as an artist usually draws many paintings in their entire career. We aim to create a software tool to help the art historians find such correspondences automatically. This work is the first step toward that goal.

Artists took inspirations from paintings in various forms. In art historians' point of view, two paintings can be in correspondence either by possessing the same objects or they could have different objects with similar picture layout [16]. This is quite challenging for existing techniques which consider either a local [13] or global [9] similarity. As far as we know, none of them considers both at the same time. Furthermore, it is rare for historical data to have correspondence annotations [13]. This makes it challenging to use conventional learning approaches which require datasets with labels.

Our contributions are three-folds:

1. We propose a method to find image correspondences in two art collections. Because we do not have sufficient labels in our dataset, we choose to use

a self-supervised machine learning algorithm, called SimSiam [4]. We algorithmically train or fine-tune neural networks in order to produce a vector representation of each image. Similar images have similar vector representations from the neural network, so we can find similarities between two images based on the similarities of the vector representations.

2. We create two datasets. The first dataset is the Japanese paintings and western paintings mentioned in the comprehensive discussion [16,23]. The second is obtained from the collection of paintings by a Japanese artist *Kuroda Seiki* [23] and the collection of paintings by a French artist *Raphaël Collin* [8].

3. The experiments show that the proposed method can obtain similar precision as those of the state of the art method in some datasets. More importantly, the correspondence images found by the proposed methods have similar global outlines. This means that our results could complement the results found by other methods, where correspondences with similar objects are found.

2   Related Works

Given an input image, several methods are proposed to find an image in a collection that is the most similar to the input image. Many of them such as Shen et al. [21] and Kaoua et al. [13] are specially proposed for western paintings. However, many of them match deep local features which are obtained from small boxes/grids of the paintings. In those methods, two images are considered to be similar if there are several small boxes with similar patterns in two of the images. This works perfectly when two images are considered similar only if they contain the same object - which is the case for both [21] and [13].

(a)   (b)

Fig. 2. (a) "Portrait of a Woman" by Seiki Kuroda (b) "The Beggar" by Jules Bastien-Lepage. Although the two paintings do not contain the same object, it is known that the painting (b) inspires the painting (a).

However, a western artwork that inspires a Japanese one does not need to have same objects. Consider "Portrait of a Woman" by Seiki Kuroda in Fig. 2a and "The Beggar" by Jules Bastien-Lepage in Fig. 2b. Although art historians describe that "Portrait of a Woman" is inspired by "The Beggar", the two paintings do not contain any same object. It is their global layouts which make the two paintings similar in the historians' point of view. We cannot use the previous algorithms to detect the similarity.

Several algorithms are proposed to calculate the image similarities based on the global layout such as [2,17]. Many of them are specially for western painting [12,19,20]. When image similarities are defined by objects appearing on paintings, we can use image captions in the collections to help the similarity annotations. On the other hand, when the similarities are defined by the global layout, it becomes harder to use those image captions. The only possible way is manual labeling by art historians. Because of that, most image similarity algorithms using the global layouts are proposed for dataset without annotations. They use unsupervised learning. Their task is to cluster the paintings into several groups, which is the task that the unsupervised learning is good at.

On the other hand, our aim is to find matchings in two different sets of paintings. Although not very large in number, we have some similarity annotations from art historians, which are useful for this task. We then decide to use self-supervised learning for our task. As far as we know, our work is the first self-supervised learning algorithm for capturing the global layout of paintings.

3   Dataset and Task Setup

3.1   Dataset

We created two new datasets, that we present in this section.

The first dataset, called I1-I2, is created from articles by art historians in [16,23]. The articles discuss how Japanese artists were influenced by western paintings during the Meiji era. They give several pairs of paintings that indicate the influences with detailed discussions. In total, there are 44 pairs of paintings discussed there. We obtain images of those pairs manually from several public painting collections such as [1]. From those pairs, I1 is a set of 44 images from Japanese artists and I2 is a set of 44 images from western artists. As [23] discusses only works by Seiki Kuroda and western works that influenced him, more than half of paintings in I2 are Seiki Kuroda's paintings.

The relationship is not one-to-one. Some paintings give influence to many, and some paintings are influenced by multiple paintings. To simplify our dataset, we exclude paintings that would cause the many-to-many relationships. We remove all but one Japanese paintings that are influenced by the same western painting, and all but one western paintings that influence the same Japanese art. There remain 25 pairs of paintings after the removals.

While the first dataset is selective, organized, and annotated, the second dataset, called I3-I4, is not. The set of images I3 are obtained from the collection *Seiki Kuroda, Master of Modern Japanese Painting: The 150th Anniversary of*

His Birth [23]. We manually crop all 386 figures from the 320-page collection to create the set of images. Similarly, the set of images I4 is a set of 473 figures in the collection *Raphaël Collin Catalogue*, which has 306 pages [8]. The manual crops are done using the software called VGG Image Annotator (VIA) [7]. The same paintings may appear multiple times in this dataset and some paintings of Seiki Kuroda and Raphaël Collin do not appear there. We believe that, when art historians use our software to find a western painting that influences a Japanese painting, their datasets should look like I3-I4. We, then, use I3-I4 not for training our model or developing our algorithm, but to confirm that our algorithm can apply to the dataset that art historians may have.

3.2 Evaluation

Assume that our input is x_i from the set of images $X = \{x_1, \ldots, x_n\}$. Suppose that we want to find the most similar image to x_i in the the other set of images $Y = \{y_1, \ldots, y_m\}$. For $k \geq 1$, all algorithms considered in this paper give k images in Y which they predict to be the most similar to x_i. Let us denote the set of images given by the algorithm as $K(x_i) \subseteq Y$. We note that $|K(x_i)| = k$. We call the set of images X referenced dataset, and the set of images Y targeted dataset.

There is one image in Y which is matched with x_i in our annotation. Let us denote it by $y(x_i) \in Y$. It is important to note that $y(x_i)$ need not be the best match of x_i in Y. When $X, Y \in \{I1, I2\}$, art historians know that there is a relationship between x_i and $y(x_i)$, but we do not know if $y(x_i)$ would be an image with the strongest relationship.

We evaluate algorithms based on the number of $y(x_i)$ that the algorithm can find in their output $K(x_i)$, i.e. our evaluation is $|\{i : y(x_i) \in K(x_i)\}|/n$. If $k = 1$ and $|K(x_i)| = 1$, we can consider our evaluation as recall, which is the evaluation used in [13]. Also, suppose that $S(x_i)$ is the set of all images in Y that have relationships with x_i. We can consider our evaluation as recall@k which is $|S(x_i) \cap K(x_i)|/(n|S(x_i)|)$ when $S(x_i) = \{y(x_i)\}$. Because it is likely that $\{y(x_i)\} \subsetneq S(x_i)$, our evaluation is slightly different from recall@k. However, for the sake of simplicity, we call our evaluation as recall@k in the remaining part of this paper.

4   Self-supervised Image Similarity Learning

Siamese neural network [5] is a common approach to learn similarities of images. Each image is mapped into a feature vector using a convolutional neural network. We expect that the vectors obtained from the mapping satisfy the following conditions:

1. a distance between vectors for two similar images, called a positive pair, should be small, and
2. a distance between vectors for two different images, called a negative pair, should be large.

To have a network with the properties specified in the previous paragraph, one may use a technique called similarity learning [3]. In this technique, they use image augmentations [6] to create positive and negative pairs. Although they do not need an effort to annotate the data in this technique, training the network using this technique requires long time and consumes large amount of memory. That is because they need a large number of negative pairs in the training process. SimSiam [4], which is the technique used in this work, solves the issue by using stop gradient. Indeed, we do not need those negative pairs during the training process. The basic ideas of the SimSiam technique are explained in Fig. 3 and in the next paragraph.

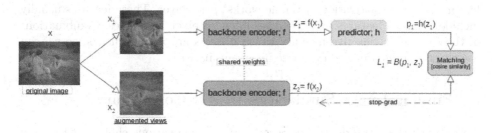

Fig. 3. Outline of Self-supervised Similarity Learning using SimSiam.

Recall from Sect. 3 that we consider two art collections, the referenced dataset X and the targeted dataset Y. In SimSiam, each illustration $x \in X$ is applied with two random augmentations to create two views, called $x^{(1)}$ and $x^{(2)}$. We consider the two views as a positive pair. They are then passed through the backbone encoder f and prediction network h to create vectors $z^{(1)}$, $z^{(2)}$, $p^{(1)}$ and $p^{(2)}$ as shown in Fig. 3. Let $B(u, v)$ represents the cosine similarity between vectors u and v, let $L_1 := -\frac{1}{2}B(p^{(1)}, z^{(2)})$, and let $L_2 := -\frac{1}{2}B(p^{(2)}, z^{(1)})$. Symmetric loss, defined as an average of two negative cosine similarities, can be written as:

$$L = \frac{1}{2}(L_1 + L_2) \tag{1}$$

Stop-gradient operation treats $z^{(1)}$ and $z^{(2)}$ in Eq. (1) as constants. Considering the portion of the loss L_1, during back-propagation, the backbone encoder of $x^{(2)}$ does not obtain a gradient value from $x^{(2)}$, but only from $p^{(1)}$. Similarly, the backbone encoder of $x^{(1)}$ does not obtain a gradient value from $x^{(1)}$, but only from $p^{(2)}$. In this training, the backbone encoder can either be trained from random weights or pre-trained weights. More details can be found in the original publication [4]. Note that we use L only for the training process. For the evaluation process, that is to find similarities between two images, we use other similarity functions defined in Sect. 5.

SimSiam uses global features to detect similarity between two images. The backbone encoder f is a combination of two sub-networks:

(i) f_1, a feature extractor, followed by
(ii) f_2, a projection MLP head [3].

The sub-network f_1 usually uses an architecture similar to other conventional networks such as ResNet [10] or VGG [22]. The networks have all layers of those conventional networks before the linear classifier layer. It is known [15] that those layers can capture a high-level information such as objects and their arrangements in the image. On the other hand, previous works in the fine art area, such as [13], often uses local features. In those works, they extract the features from the activation of the networks' prior layer. These features usually include low-level features such as edges, lines, or pixels in images. Combinations of those features can give us clues which objects are in the images, so we can use those combinations to calculate image similarities.

5   Finding Image Similarities in Art Collections

Considering the setup defined in Sect. 3.2, we define various choices of function to calculate a similarity between each image $x_i \in X$ and each image $y_j \in Y$. From the discussion in Sect. 4, we obtain two feature vectors p_{xi} and z_{xi} for each image x_i. Also, we have p_{yj} and z_{yj} for each image y_j. Recall that $B(u,v)$ is a cosine similarity between vector u and vector v. We can find similarities of x_i and y_j, denoted by $S(x_i, y_j)$, by the following three ways:

– *NLoss*: This is a negation of the loss in Eq. (1):

$$S_{NLoss}(x_i, y_j) := \frac{1}{2}B(p_{xi}, z_{yj}) + \frac{1}{2}B(p_{yj}, z_{xi}) \qquad (2)$$

– *CSimP*: a cosine similarity between the vectors p_{xi} and p_{yj}:

$$S_{CSinP}(x_i, y_j) := B(p_{xi}, p_{yj}) \qquad (3)$$

– *CSimZ*: a cosine similarity between the vectors z_{xi} and z_{yj}:

$$S_{CSinZ}(x_i, y_j) = B(z_{xi}, z_{yj}) \qquad (4)$$

We resized images into various scales before putting them into our neural networks. Let the scales of the resizing be $\{s_1, \ldots, s_L\}$. We calculate a similarity matrix of the datasets $X = \{x_1, \ldots, x_n\}$ and $Y = \{y_1, \ldots, y_m\}$, denoted by $M_{(X,Y)} = (m_{pq})$ for $1 \le p \le n$ and $1 \le q \le m$ in the following ways:

– Calculating similarity matrix $M_{X \succ Y}^{\ell} = (w_{pq}^{\ell}); \ell \in [1, L]$ by resizing illustrations $x_p \in X$ with the scale $s_{\lceil \frac{L}{2} \rceil}$ and find the similarity with the illustrations $y_q \in Y$ which are resized with the scale s_{ℓ}.

- Calculating similarity matrix $M_{X \succ Y} = (w_{pq})$ by taking

$$w_{pq} = \max_{\ell \in [1,L]} w_{pq}^{\ell} \qquad (5)$$

- We then do the same for $M_{Y \succ X} = (v_{qp})$. Then, we add $M_{X \succ Y}$ with $M_{Y \succ X}$ to obtain the similarity matrix $M_{(X,Y)}$, i.e.

$$m_{pq} = w_{pq} + v_{qp} \qquad (6)$$

We find a maximum matching between illustrations in dataset X and Y from the similarity matrix $M_{(X,Y)}$. To improve the matching results, we apply normalization and information propagation techniques as described in Kaoua et al. [13].

5.1 Fine-Tuning Weights for Alternative Similarity Functions

Alternatively, SimSiam training can be used to fine-tune weights of the neural network before using it to extract local features of images. Originally, Image Collation [13] uses the pre-trained weights from ImageNet as the feature extractor. Here, SimSiam is used to adjust those weights to be familiar with illustrations in the art collection. The network is, in turn, used to extract local features which is then used with the similarity function, transformation dependent similarity (Trans.), proposed in Image Collation [13].

6 Experiments

6.1 Experimental Protocols

We conduct experiments on the following datasets:

- Physiologus manuscripts (P1, P2, P3) described in [13]. We use the dataset P1 for our hyperparameter search.
- Japanese and western art collections (I1, I2, I3, I4) as described in Sect. 3.

The network architecture is the same as that of SimSiam [4]. As previously discussed, the backbone encoder f is a combination of two sub-networks, f_1 and f_2. The sub-network f_1 uses a ResNet (either 18 or 50) architecture until the average pool layer, while f_2 is a threefold repetition of linear, batchnorm and ReLu layers (except the last layer). The prediction network h is a combination of linear, batchnorm, ReLu, and another linear layer.

The hyperparameters of our ResNet-18 and ResNet-50 networks are parameters which minimize loss on P1 data. The hyperparameters are listed in Table 1. In addition to those parameters, we found that SGD with batch size of 32 is the best optimizer for the P1 dataset. We choose to train our neural network for 200 epochs. If we do not state otherwise, the network is fine-tuned from weights pre-trained from the ImageNet dataset. During inferences, we apply 5 scalings to each of illustrations. The values of those scales are $0.8, 0.95, 1.1, 1.25, 1.40$.

Table 1. Hyperparameters for ResNet-18 and ResNet-50 backbone.

Backbone	Image Size	Augmentation	lr	Weight Decay
ResNet-18	227	daugment0	0.0810	1.75e-4
ResNet-50	224	daugment1	0.0923	3.00e-5

All results shown in this section are means and standard deviations of recalls obtained from ten random seeds.

For each experiment, the results of image collation techniques [13] are used as a comparison. The following notations are used throughout the experimental result section.

- Model: *ResNet18* and *ResNet50* are the models whose weights are pre-trained from the ImageNet dataset. *SimSiam-rn18* and *SimSiam-rn50* are the model of which weights are fine-tuned from ResNet18 and ResNet50 respectively, using the SimSiam method.
- **NLoss, CSimP** and **CSimZ** are the inference results using the similarity functions explained in Sect. 5 (in red).
- **CSimZ (Norm.)** and **CSimZ (Prop.)** use normalization and information propagation techniques [13] to improve the similarity matrix. There are several normalization techniques proposed in the paper. However, as the authors state that the simple maximization is the best for their dataset, we choose to use the normalization technique in our experiments. (in red).
- **Image Collation** refers to results acquired from using similarity functions on the local features [13] (in green). Alternatively, the results obtained from the technique mentioned in Sect. 5.1 are also reported (in blue).

6.2   Results and Discussion

Table 2. Results on P2-P3 dataset; net_{P2}; means (and standard deviations) of recall@k=1 obtained from ten random seeds

Model	NLoss	CSimP	CSimZ	CSimZ		Image Collation [13]		
				Norm.	Prop.	Trans.	Norm.	Prop.
ResNet18						99.8 (0.6)	100 (0)	100 (0)
ResNet50						100 (0)	100 (0)	100 (0)
SimSiam-rn18	80.5 (5.1)	81.5 (4.9)	86.9 (4.0)	91.5 (4.1)	88.0 (1.7)	99.8 (0.4)	100 (0)	100 (0)
SimSiam-rn50	77.2 (4.7)	81.0 (4.6)	83.7 (4.9)	88.7 (4.1)	86.2 (1.4)	100 (0)	100 (0)	100 (0)

Results on Dataset P2-P3. Table 2 shows recall@$k = 1$ for correspondences between (P2, P3). In this experiment, it is very clear that similarity functions using local features perform best. The *SimSiam* fine-tuning also provides a competitive result, but we cannot see any improvement on the recall; hence the effect of SimSiam fine-tuning on local features can be ignored. The proposed similarity functions based on SimSiam fine-tuning underperform in all cases. **CSimZ** performs best among the proposed function and the **Norm.** technique can help improve the recall.

Table 3. Results on I1-I2 dataset; net_{I1}.

Model	NLoss	CSimP	CSimZ	CSimZ		Image Collation [13]		
				Norm.	Prop.	Trans.	Norm.	Prop.
ResNet18						24.4 (2.5)	27.2 (2.5)	32.6 (4.7)
ResNet50						26.2 (2.7)	31.2 (3.8)	36.4 (5.8)
SimSiam-rn18	21.8 (5.9)	22.0 (6.1)	23.0 (5.2)	26.2 (8.7)	29.6 (9.3)	20.8 (3.0)	31.6 (4.6)	37.2 (8.2)
SimSiam-rn50	19.8 (4.3)	18.8 (4.8)	18.6 (4.2)	20.2 (4.3)	23.8 (5.8)	27.0 (5.0)	32.4 (5.8)	38.6 (5.6)

(a) means (and standard deviations) of recall@k=1 from ten random seeds

Model	NLoss	CSimP	CSimZ	CSimZ		Image Collation [13]		
				Norm.	Prop.	Trans.	Norm.	Prop.
ResNet18						62.6 (3.0)	73.6 (1.8)	76.0 (4.2)
ResNet50						61.6 (1.8)	71.8 (3.5)	75.2 (3.9)
SimSiam-rn18	58.4 (9.3)	58.0 (8.4)	58.4 (9.6)	60.2 (8.8)	65.2 (9.7)	69.6 (4.9)	74.4 (1.8)	79.6 (4.9)
SimSiam-rn50	52.2 (5.7)	51.0 (6.0)	52.2 (6.6)	52.4 (4.4)	57.0 (8.0)	66.6 (4.1)	69.0 (4.2)	73.4 (6.2)

(b) means (and standard deviations) of recall@k=5 from ten random seeds

Results on Dataset I1-I2. Finding correspondences between (I1, I2) are challenging. Both results on recall@$k = 1$ and $k = 5$ are shown in Tables 3a and 3b. Again, the similarity functions based on local features perform better than the proposed function. The best performance in Table 3a which can be achieved by the fine-tuned model is 38%. Similar results can be observed in Table 3b. There, the model without fine-tuning achieve the best results at 78%. The results in Table 3 also suggest that the recalls do not have a correlation to the size of the network. One observation why ResNet50 performs poorly could be the amount of training data which is very small (25 pairs).

Figure 4 shows the recall@k for all $k \in [1, 25]$. Similar to the results in Table 3a and Table 3b, image collation with information propagation, with or without SimSiam fine-tuning, shows the best recalls for all k. The graph suggests that the value of $k \in [5, 10]$ could be the best for a recommendation system to support art historians. We have fairly large recalls when $k \in [5, 10]$, and five to ten recommendations are not too many that the historians can choose the best annotations from them manually in seconds.

Results on Dataset I3-I4. The results for (I3, I4) are shown in Fig. 5. It can be seen that images recommended by our technique as the first choices look similar to the reference images. The second to the fifth choices might not be very similar to the reference images. We can even consider them as another cluster of images. Those bad suggestions include the second and the third suggestions for the reference image #250, and also the second and fifth suggestions for the

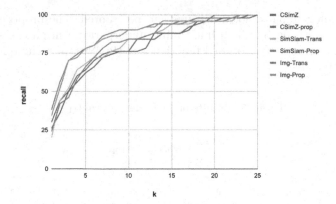

Fig. 4. Recall@k for various algorithms on I1-I2 dataset.

reference image #290. One intuitive explanation for this could be the lack of negative pairs during SimSiam training. Since SimSiam treats each sample in the reference collection as one class and train it independently, vector representations of two different classes could be very similar by the technique.

Figure 6 shows qualitative comparisons between the proposed similarity functions which use global features and the similarity functions based on the local features [13]. Although the proposed method might provide incorrect suggestions, in most cases, the illustrations that are matched have similar global impressions. In addition, it can be seen that the suggestions provided from the two methods can be totally different and could be complementary to each others.

Because we have only six annotations for I3-I4, we omit showing recalls for the dataset in this paper. Indeed, the small number of annotations leads to small recall values. For all algorithms, the means of recall@k are no more than 15%, even when we set k to 100.

Using Alternative Collection as Training Data. When we consider a pair of collections (I1, I2), we can train our neural networks by only I1, by only I2, and by both I1 and I2. Table 4 compares the recall@$k = 5$ of those choices. For our technique, we obtain better results when our neural networks are trained with a single collection. When using both collections as a training set, the total number of classes increases. It could be more likely that different classes are mapped to similar vectors in SimSiam.

On the other hands, for similarity functions on the local features [13], training with both collections provides the best result. This could result from the larger number of training data. It seems that those networks can perceive all of those training data during the training process.

reference image   5 nearest neighbors from target collection (sorted)

Fig. 5. Samples of 5 nearest neighbors of the reference illustrations from I3 to I4.

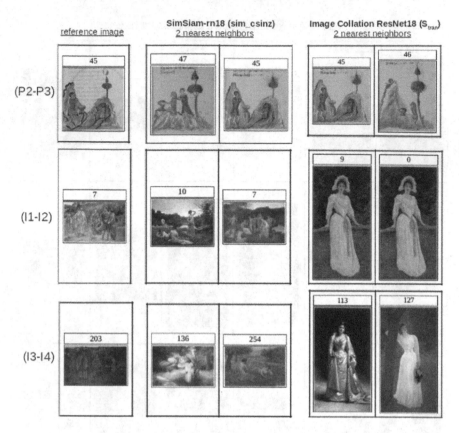

Fig. 6. Comparisons of the results from our proposed method (SimSiam) and the results obtained from the previous work (Image Collation).

Table 4. Comparison: using I1 vs I2 vs I1+I2 as training data; means (and standard deviations) of recall@k=5 from ten random seeds

Model	NLoss	CSimP	CSimZ	CSimZ		Image Collation [13]		
				Norm.	Prop.	Trans.	Norm.	Prop.
Training data : I1 (net_{I1})								
SimSiam-rn18	58.4 (9.3)	58.0 (8.4)	58.4 (9.6)	60.2 (8.8)	65.2 (9.7)	69.6 (4.9)	74.4 (1.8)	79.6 (4.9)
SimSiam-rn50	52.2 (5.7)	51.0 (6.0)	52.2 (6.6)	52.4 (4.4)	57.0 (8.0)	66.6 (4.1)	69.0 (4.2)	73.4 (6.2)
Training data : I2 (net_{I2})								
SimSiam-rn18	66.6 (5.9)	65.6 (7.5)	67.0 (5.0)	68.6 (5.2)	73.0 (4.6)	70.2 (4.8)	72.0 (5.5)	76.6 (4.6)
SimSiam-rn50	61.4 (6.5)	61.0 (6.9)	62.8 (5.4)	63.4 (5.9)	66.4 (6.2)	67.6 (3.2)	69.8 (2.9)	73.6 (6.0)
Training data : I1+I2 (net_{I1+I2})								
SimSiam-rn18	63.0 (5.4)	63.4 (6.1)	62.8 (6.9)	63.6 (6.2)	67.4 (6.0)	69.4 (4.5)	72.8 (4.1)	75.6 (7.0)
SimSiam-rn50	51.8 (7.1)	51.4 (7.4)	52.8 (8.0)	53.4 (8.2)	56.2 (8.0)	68.8 (3.8)	72.0 (4.8)	75.6 (6.0)

Discussion. We can conclude the following points from the experimental results:

1. Most results, as displayed in Tables 2 and 3, show quantitatively that image collation [13], a similarity function based on local features, provides better recalls than the proposed method which is based on the global features. Only Table 4 shows competitive results between both methods.
2. On the other hand, there might be some advantages of the fine-tuning using the SimSiam methods. Compared to the pre-trained ResNet networks when using similarity functions based on local features, the method gives the top performance for (I1, I2) dataset in Tables 3 and 4.
3. Although our results do not give better recalls in most cases, as seen in Fig. 5 and Fig. 6, we can give totally different recommendation results from those of [13]. We give the recommendations based on global outlines on images, while the previous works give the recommendations based on local features.

7 Conclusion

This paper considered a task of finding image correspondences in collections of paintings. It is a first step to automatically discover the influences of the western arts to the Japanese culture. In this work, we created new datasets based on collections of works by Japanese and western artists. We then proposed to use the self-supervised technique SimSiam for the task. Quantitatively, the proposed method under-performed baseline approaches, which find similarities using local features, in most experiments. However, qualitatively, by global features, the method found correspondences which have different profiles than those techniques. Currently, we aim to combine methods which use global features and methods which use local features. We hope that the combination would give a method which is strong to detect both global outlines and local objects.

The main goal of this project is a user-friendly software that helps art historians in finding the correspondences. Inputs of the software will be, similar to the dataset I3-I4, scan photos of art collections, while outputs will be suggested correspondences as shown in Fig. 5.

Acknowledgement. This work is supported by the project "IXT Encouragement - Support for project that delivers IT technology to other research areas", Graduate School of Information Science and Technology, the University of Tokyo.

References

1. Cultural Japan. https://cultural.jp/. Accessed 24 Jan 2022
2. Brown, A., Xie, W., Kalogeiton, V., Zisserman, A.: Smooth-AP: smoothing the path towards large-scale image retrieval. In: Vedaldi, A., Bischof, H., Brox, T., Frahm, J.-M. (eds.) ECCV 2020. LNCS, vol. 12354, pp. 677–694. Springer, Cham (2020). https://doi.org/10.1007/978-3-030-58545-7_39

3. Chen, T., Kornblith, S., Norouzi, M., Hinton, G.: A simple framework for contrastive learning of visual representations. In: ICML 2020, pp. 1597–1607 (2020)
4. Chen, X., He, K.: Exploring simple siamese representation learning. arXiv preprint arXiv:2011.10566 (2020)
5. Chopra, S., Hadsell, R., LeCun, Y.: Learning a similarity metric discriminatively, with application to face verification. In: CVPR 2005, vol. 1, pp. 539–546 (2005)
6. Dosovitskiy, A., Springenberg, J.T., Riedmiller, M., Brox, T.: Discriminative unsupervised feature learning with convolutional neural networks. In: NIPS 2014, pp. 766–774 (2014)
7. Dutta, A., Zisserman, A.: The VIA annotation software for images, audio and video. In: MM 2019 (2019)
8. Fukuoka Art Museum: Raphaël Collin Catalogue (1999). (in Japanese)
9. Gordo, A., Almazán, J., Revaud, J., Larlus, D.: End-to-end learning of deep visual representations for image retrieval. Int. J. Comput. Vision **124**, 237–254 (2017)
10. He, K., Zhang, X., Ren, S., Sun, J.: Deep residual learning for image recognition. In: 2016 IEEE Conference on Computer Vision and Pattern Recognition (CVPR), pp. 770–778 (2016). https://doi.org/10.1109/CVPR.2016.90
11. Irvine, G., Belgin, T.: Japonisme and the Rise of the Modern Art Movement: The Arts of the Meiji Period: the Khalili Collection (2013)
12. Jangtjik, K.A., Ho, T.T., Yeh, M.C., Hua, K.L.: A CNN-LSTM framework for authorship classification of paintings. In: ICIP 2017, pp. 2866–2870 (2017)
13. Kaoua, R., Shen, X., Durr, A., Lazaris, S., Picard, D., Aubry, M.: Image collation: matching illustrations in manuscripts. In: ICDAR 2021, pp. 351–366 (2021)
14. Kazui, T., Videen, S.D.: Foreign relations during the Edo period: Sakoku reexamined. J. Jpn. Stud. **8**(2), 283–306 (1982)
15. Mahendran, A., Vedaldi, A.: Understanding deep image representations by inverting them. In: CVPR, pp. 5188–5196. IEEE Computer Society (2015)
16. Miura, A.: Arts in Migration: Japonisme, Collin, and Contemporary Japanese Western Art (2020). (in Japanese)
17. Ng, T., Balntas, V., Tian, Y., Mikolajczyk, K.: SOLAR: second-order loss and attention for image retrieval. In: Vedaldi, A., Bischof, H., Brox, T., Frahm, J.-M. (eds.) ECCV 2020. LNCS, vol. 12370, pp. 253–270. Springer, Cham (2020). https://doi.org/10.1007/978-3-030-58595-2_16
18. POLA Museum of Art: Connections - Inspirations beyond Sea, 150 years of Japan and France (2020). (in Japanese)
19. Sandoval, C., Pirogova, E., Lech, M.: Two-stage deep learning approach to the classification of fine-art paintings. IEEE Access **7**, 41770–41781 (2019)
20. Shamir, L., Macura, T., Orlov, N., Eckley, D.M., Goldberg, I.G.: Impressionism, expressionism, surrealism: automated recognition of painters and schools of art. ACM Trans. Appl. Percept. (TAP) **7**(2), 1–17 (2010)
21. Shen, X., Efros, A.A., Aubry, M.: Discovering visual patterns in art collections with spatially-consistent feature learning. In: CVPR 2019, pp. 9278–9287 (2019)
22. Simonyan, K., Zisserman, A.: Very deep convolutional networks for large-scale image recognition. In: Bengio, Y., LeCun, Y. (eds.) 3rd International Conference on Learning Representations, ICLR, San Diego, CA, USA, 7–9 May 2015 (2015)
23. Tokyo National Museum: Seiki Kuroda, Master of Modern Japanese Painting: The 150th Anniversary of His Birth (2016). (in Japanese)

Few-Shot Music Symbol Classification via Self-Supervised Learning and Nearest Neighbor

Antonio Rios-Vila$^{(\boxtimes)}$, María Alfaro-Contreras, Jose J. Valero-Mas, and Jorge Calvo-Zaragoza

U.I for Computer Research, University of Alicante, Alicante, Spain
{arios,malfaro,jjvalero,jcalvo}@dlsi.ua.es

Abstract. The automatic labeling of music symbols in a score, namely music symbol classification, represents one of the main stages in Optical Music Recognition systems. Most commonly, this task is addressed by resorting to deep neural models trained in a supervised manner, which report competitive performance rates at the expense of large amounts of labeled data to be trained. Such a particularity generally limits their applicability when addressing historical manuscripts with early music notation, for which annotated data is considerably scarce. In this regard, this work proposes a self-supervised scheme for few-shot music symbol classification that comprises two stages: (i) a first one which retrieves a neural-based feature extractor in a self-supervised manner with the so-called Variance-Invariance-Covariance Regularization loss; and (ii) a second phase in which the k-Nearest Neighbor rule performs the classification task considering a limited set of reference data. The experiments carried out on a reference music corpus in mensural notation show that the proposal is capable of outperforming the contemplated baseline strategies even with a remarkably reduced number of labeled examples for the classification task.

Keywords: Music Symbol Classification · Optical Music Recognition · Self-Supervised Learning · Few-shot Learning

1 Introduction

Music represents a key element of cultural heritage and one of the main means of human expression. Due to this, there exists a large number of music collections scattered in libraries, cathedrals, museums, and historical archives that have been carefully preserved over the centuries. However, the different conservation processes before the breakthrough of current digital resources mainly relied on physical documents, which not only severely suffer from degradation due to environmental factors but also exhibit an accessibility limitation as they are only

---

A. Rios-Vila and M. Alfaro-Contreras—Equal contribution.

J.-J. Rousseau and B. Kapralos (Eds.): ICPR 2022 Workshops, LNCS 13645, pp. 93–107, 2023.
https://doi.org/10.1007/978-3-031-37731-0_8

physically available in the actual place they are stored. In this regard, the advantages and possibilities offered by access to digitized versions of these collections over their physical use *in situ* are undeniable, from their better preservation to their remote availability through broadband networks.

The different institutions that preserve music collections are investing considerable efforts to transfer their original sources to digital files [12]. However, image digitization—scanning the physical document to store it—is only the first stage towards the digital transition that these libraries and historical archives carry out and the services they can offer by applying digital humanities [21]: while these digitized files can be transmitted, copied, and viewed without suffering any deterioration in each operation, they do not allow any algorithm to work with the musical information they contain. For this, the actual content must be first extracted and encoded in structured formats such as, for instance, MusicXML or Music Encoding Initiative (MEI) [14]. Note that the problem is that such an encoding, if performed manually, is very time-consuming and prone to errors.

The alternative to the commented manual encoding process of the music content is to resort to state-of-the-art technology based on artificial intelligence, which performs an automated reading of documents, similar to the Optical Character Recognition (OCR) for written text. In the context of music documents, this technology is known as Optical Music Recognition (OMR) [5] and, despite being a long-standing research field that has been developed for decades, existing approaches historically yielded poor results [26]. According to Byrd and Simonsen [4], the main reason for that is that the problem faced in OMR systems is much more complex than that of OCR: on the one hand, music notation is a multidimensional visual language that is not only read from left to right as in text; on the other hand, there exist a great number of notations, especially in the context of historical OMR (e.g., neumatic or mensural), that may resemble modern notation but follow different principles [2].

Recently, the use of modern artificial intelligence and, particularly, machine learning techniques brought a paradigm shift that has partially unblocked this situation [6,24], especially when dealing with collections in early notations. In these cases, it has been empirically assessed that the manual digitization considering an initial OMR-based transcription considerably reduces the annotation effort compared to its disregarding [1].

However, even assuming a particular notation, the input of an OMR system can be quite varied as regards the printing mechanisms, writing style, ink types, document layouts, etc. Although the use of machine learning offers a remarkable advantage over other existing ad-hoc approaches, these models require to be specifically trained on the graphical domain that which the system is intended to be applied to. This means that, in order to transcribe a given collection, it is necessary to manually annotate a representative portion of data to serve as a training corpus. Given the inherent inefficiency that this workflow exhibits, an open objective in OMR is that of exploring alternative methodologies which tackle such a limitation.

The so-called Self-Supervised Learning (SSL) paradigm stands as one of the most recent, yet competitive strategies, within the machine learning field for palliating the high requirements of data in deep neural models [30]. These methods generally aim to learn general representative features from large-scale unlabeled data that may be later exploited by other downstream tasks.

Considering all the above, this work frames in a scenario that is quite common in practice: all the images of the collection to be transcribed are available from the beginning, but none are labeled. In this context, we propose a music symbol classification workflow that comprises two stages: (i) a first one that pre-trains a deep neural model via SSL for its use as a feature extractor; and (ii) a second one that, considering the feature extractor of the former stage, classifies a given query resorting to the k-Nearest Neighbor (kNN) rule [11] using a remarkably reduced reference set of labeled data—namely, few-shot classification—annotated by the user. Note that this reference set is expected to be considerably reduced so that the invested effort in annotating data remains as low as possible. In our experiments, which consider the use of old manuscripts with early music notation, our proposal attains high success rates with only a few labeled samples from the collection to be transcribed, thus remarkably outperforming the baseline and state-of-the-art systems considered for comparative purposes.

The remainder of the paper is structured as follows: we provide the background of our contribution in Sect. 2; the proposed methodology is presented in Sect. 3; our experiments are described in Sect. 4; the analysis of the results is provided Sect. 5; and finally, conclusions and future work are given in Sect. 6.

2 Background

This section defines the task of music symbol classification within OMR as well as a description of the self-supervised learning field considered in the work.

2.1 Optical Music Recognition for Early Notation

While most commercial OMR systems, such as PhotoScore[1], ScanScore[2], and PlayScore[3], focus on modern staff notation, there exists a need for developing strategies that deal with early music manuscripts: as aforementioned, a large number of music documents that are scattered around the world only exist as physical documents, hence requiring of a digitization process now only for its preservation but also for its ubiquitous access.

The Aruspix software [25] represents one of the first early-notation OMR systems publicly distributed for its general use. Despite its popularity, the fact that this method was devised for a specific music notation results in high error rates when addressing alternative scenarios [6]. More recently, the *Music Recognition,*

---

[1] https://www.neuratron.com/photoscore.htm.
[2] https://scan-score.com/.
[3] https://www.playscore.co/.

Encoding, and Transcription (MuRET) tool [27] was released and is becoming widely adopted within academia due to its high-performance capabilities reported in the literature [10,29]. However, since this tool relies on the use of deep neural models, its applicability is limited to the availability of labeled sets of data suitable for the task at hand. It must be noted that the proposal presented in this work is directed oriented toward the improvement of capabilities in this MuRET system, more precisely with the aim of facilitating its adaptation to new contexts without requiring huge data annotation campaigns.

Music Symbol Classification. Symbol classification, the task of automatically labeling the symbols in a given music score, stands as one of the main stages in many OMR pipelines [13,19,28]. Given its relevance, much research effort has been invested in this task, being deep neural networks the main approach considered by state-of-the-art methods [5]. Given the large amount of labeled data requirements such neural models depict, they are generally limited by the availability of annotated corpora. In this sense, the OMR community has stated the need for devising strategies that can equally perform with considerably less annotated data, which stands as a remarkable challenge in the field [20].

2.2 Self-Supervised Learning

Self-Supervised Learning (SSL) represents one of the existing paradigms within the broad machine learning field that aim to palliate the large amounts of labeled data required by deep neural models [17]. Note that, while traditional supervised learning relies on human-annotated corpora, SSL is meant to learn an appropriate representation space for one or more downstream tasks (e.g., classification process) considering no labeled data [23].

Depending on the considered principle for training the model, SSL methods are associated with one of the two following categories:

- *Contrastive SSL*: Representation learning technique based on the concept of *anchor*, *positive*, and *negative* (APN) sample differentiation [16]. In this methodology, given a base image—anchor sample—, a positive sample is commonly understood as its augmented version (a classifier should predict the same label for both elements), whereas any other sample from the corpus is considered as a negative sample. From a high-level perspective, this learning approach aims to gather a representation space that gathers same-class samples—positive and anchor images—and pushes away representations from different images—negative samples. Most generally, this is usually achieved by applying a contrastive loss function based on a certain dissimilarity metric (generally, cosine similarity) between embedded representations.
- *Non-contrastive SSL*: Generalization of the *Contrastive SSL* principle not restricted to sample-disposal scheme or similarity loss function. Most successful approaches consider the use of *teacher-student* schemes [7] or distribution properties [8].

In this paper, we focus our work on non-contrastive SSL. More precisely, we consider the use of the so-called *Variance-Invariance-Covariance Regularization* (VICReg) method by Bardes et al. [3] as it constitutes one of the most recent, yet competitive, approaches for Non-contrastive SSL in the literature.

3   Methodology

The devised few-shot music symbol classification proposal comprises two sequential stages: (i) an initial *Self-Supervised neural feature extraction* phase that trains a neural-based feature extractor—specifically, a Convolutional Neural Network (CNN)—via self-supervised learning with an unlabeled set of images; and (ii) the *Classification* stage that, given both an image query and a set of labeled data, maps the data to a common representation space using the CNN model and performs the classification resorting to the k-Nearest Neighbor (kNN) rule. Figure 1 graphically shows this proposal.

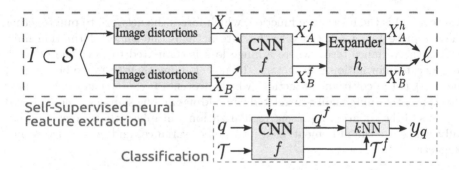

Fig. 1. Graphical representation of the methodology proposed.

Considering this scheme, the remainder of the section thoroughly describes the two stages of the proposed method. For the sake of clarity in these explanations, let $\mathcal{X}$ denote a space of images and let $\mathcal{Y}$ be a finite set of discrete categories. Additionally, let $\mathcal{S} \subset \mathcal{X}$ and $\mathcal{T} \subset \mathcal{X} \times \mathcal{Y}$ respectively denote the sets of unlabeled and labeled images used in the different stages of the process.

3.1   Stage I: Self-supervised Neural Feature Extraction

The first stage of the process aims to obtain a CNN-based feature extractor in a self-supervised manner. For that, we resort to the so-called Variance-Invariance-Covariance Regularization (VICReg) method [3] due to its reported competitive performance in the related literature. In a broad sense, this strategy allows training a neural model in a self-supervised fashion whose embeddings meet certain conditions based on the concepts of variance, invariance, and covariance. The gist of this method is now introduced.

As observed in Fig. 1, VICReg initially draws an N-size batch of unlabeled images $I \subseteq S$ that undergoes two independent image distortion processes, hence retrieving collections X_A and X_B. Note that, since these processes perform some controlled distortions in each of the images in the batch, the number of images for each collection remains the same, i.e., $|X_A| = |X_B| = N$.

After that, sets X_A and X_B are mapped to an m-dimensional space by considering a function $f : \mathcal{X} \rightarrow \mathbb{R}^m$ given by a CNN scheme, thus obtaining collections X_A^f and X_B^f, respectively. Note that this neural model represents the actual feature extractor to be retrieved as a result of this first stage of the proposal.

Following this, an additional neural model—namely, *expander*—applies a transformation $h : \mathbb{R}^m \rightarrow \mathbb{R}^{m'}$ to sets X_A^f and X_B^f, hence producing X_A^h and X_B^h. It must be pointed out that, while not strictly necessary, this step is considered to improve the convergence of the scheme.

Finally, the expanded sets X_A^h and X_B^h are used for computing the following loss function:

$$\ell\left(X_A^h, X_B^h\right) = \lambda s\left(X_A^h, X_B^h\right) + \mu\left[v(X_A^h) + v(X_B^h)\right] + \phi\left[c(X_A^h) + c(X_B^h)\right] \quad (1)$$

where $s(\cdot, \cdot)$ is the invariance function, which forces the network to pull together these representations in space as they are actually the same information unit, $v(\cdot)$ is the variance term, where a hinge loss is computed to force the network to generate information-rich vectors—by not enabling their terms to be equal—, and $c(\cdot)$ is the covariance function, which prevents the *informational collapse* effect, i.e., obtaining highly-correlated embeddings among samples. The λ, μ, and ϕ terms of the equation represent regularization multipliers that are experimentally tuned for the aforementioned invariance, variance, and covariance terms, respectively.

3.2   Stage II: Classification

The second phase of the proposal performs the actual music symbol classification considering the CNN-based feature extractor previously obtained. For that, we resort to the kNN classifier [11], which hypothesizes about the class of a given query attending to the labels of its closest k neighbors, based on a certain dissimilarity measure.

Formally, the initial query q as well as the labeled set of data $\mathcal{T}$ are mapped to the target m-dimensional representation space as q^f and $\mathcal{T}^f$ using the CNN model obtained in the first stage of the proposal. After that, the kNN rule estimates the class y_q of query q as:

$$y_q = \text{mode}\left(\zeta\left(\underset{\forall t \in \mathcal{T}^f}{\text{argmin}}_k\{d\left(q^f, t\right)\}\right)\right) \quad (2)$$

where $d : \mathbb{R}^m \times \mathbb{R}^m \rightarrow \mathbb{R}_0^+$ represents a dissimilarity measure, $\zeta(\cdot)$ stands for the function that outputs the label of the element in the argument, and mode$(\cdot)$ denotes the mode operator.

4   Experimental Setup

This section presents the music symbol corpus, the details of the proposed self-supervised neural feature extraction together with a set of existing strategies for comparatively assessing the goodness of our proposal, and the particularities of the classification stage.

4.1   Corpus

We consider the *Capitan* corpus [6] for evaluating our proposal, which represents a manuscript from the 17th century of a *missa* (sacred music) in mensural notation.[4] Each page of the manuscript is provided with the annotations, at the bounding box level, of the individual symbols in the different music staves within. Hence, it serves as an excellent benchmark for comparison with the state of the art of music symbol classification. Figure 2 shows different examples of these symbols.

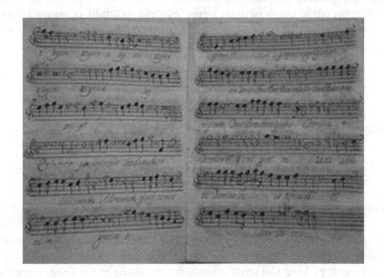

Fig. 2. Music page from *Capitan* handwritten dataset.

The corpus contains a total number of 17,112 running symbols of 53 different classes. As in previous works addressing this task with the same dataset [22], we resize each symbol image to 40×40 pixels without any other further preprocessing. Finally, we use a data split of 50% of the samples as a training set, 25% for validation, and 25% for testing. It must be noted that, except for the supervised method, the test set is the only one that contains the labels of the symbols.

---

[4] The music notation system that was used for most of the XVI and XVII centuries in Europe.

4.2 Self-supervised Classification Approach

We now introduce the implementation details of the proposal presented in the work. For the sake of clarity, we separately detail the feature extraction and classification stages.

Feature Extraction Stage. The self-supervised learning stage of the proposal requires the definition of two neural models: (i) the CNN scheme, which replicates the feature extraction stage of the supervised state-of-the-art architecture by Nuñez-Alcover et al. [22] for symbol classification; and (ii) the Expander block, which considers that by Bardes et al. [3]. Table 1 provides the precise definitions of these neural models.

Table 1. Layer-wise description of the CNN feature extractor and the Expander block considered. Notation: $Conv(f, w \times h)$ represents a convolution layer of f filters of size $w \times h$ pixels, $ReLU(\cdot)$ stands for a Rectified Linear Unit activation layer, $MaxPool(w \times h)$ denotes the max-pooling operator of dimensions $w \times h$ pixels, $BatchNorm(\cdot)$ performs the normalization of the batch of data, $Dense(n)$ denotes a fully-connected network of n neurons, and $Dropout(p)$ performs the dropout operation with p probability.

Model	Layer 1	Layer 2	Layer 3	Layer 4	Layer 5
CNN(f)	Conv(32, 3 × 3) ReLU(·)	Conv(32, 3 × 3) ReLU(·) MaxPool(2 × 2) Dropout(0.25)	Conv(64, 3 × 3) ReLU(·)	Conv(64, 3 × 3) ReLU(·) MaxPool(2 × 2) Dropout(0.25)	Dense(m)
Expander(h)	Dense(m') BatchNorm(·) ReLU(·)	Dense(m') BatchNorm(·) ReLU(·)	Dense(m')		

For comparative purposes, as will be later commented on, we consider a value of $m = 1,600$ for the target feature space (function f) given that it represents the same dimensionality than considering the raw input image as features for the classifier. Regarding the Expander target dimensionality (function h), we fix $m' = 1,024$ as it yielded the most promising results in preliminary experiments.

Regarding the image distortion processes, we have resorted to a subset of those suggested in the work by Bardes et al. [3] as they are proved to provide an adequate convergence of the neural model. Figure 3 shows an example of the different distortion processes considered in the work.

Finally, in order to gather more insights into the behavior of the method, different λ, μ, and ϕ weights are tested for the loss function in Eq. 1.

Classification Stage. To simulate a few-shot classification scenario in the reference $\mathcal{T}$ labeled set of images, we sub-sample the train partition by randomly selecting L samples—experimentation parameter—per class. For our

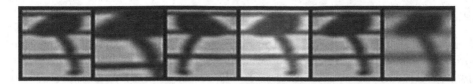

Fig. 3. Example of distortions applied to a given symbol image. From left to right: (i) original symbol image; (ii) random crop of the previous image resized to the original size; (iii) horizontally flipped version of the symbol image; (iv) color-jittered version of the symbol image, that is, the brightness, contrast, saturation, and hue of the original image have been randomly changed; (v) original symbol image converted to grayscale; and, (vi) blurred version of the original symbol image.

experiments we assess the influence of this particular parameter by considering $L \in \{1, 5, 10, 15, 20, 25, 30\}$ samples per class.

Regarding the kNN classifier, we set a value of $k = 1$ to ensure the condition $k \leq L$, i.e., the number of examples of the same class is always higher than—or, at least, equal to—the number of requested neighbors. Note that higher values may result in $k > L$, which would remarkably hinder the performance of the scheme.

4.3   Comparative Approaches

We now introduce two different feature extraction strategies considered that serve as baselines for comparatively assessing the goodness of the proposal:

- The first one, denoted as *Flatten*, in which the input image is flattened among its height and width. Note that this approach serves as a reference on how the *Classification* stage considered performs without a feature extraction process, i.e., raw unprocessed images.
- The second case is a ResNet-34 residual network [15] pre-trained with the ImageNet dataset [9], which is currently one of the state-of-the-art models for image classification. This baseline, which is denoted as *ResNet34* throughout the rest of the paper, establishes a reference on how performing transfer learning—a common approach for few-shot learning—works for our specific problem.

In addition to these methods, we contemplate the proposal by Nuñez-Alcover et al. [22], which is referred to as *Nuñez-Alcover* in the remainder of the work, as it currently represents the state of the art in isolated music symbol classification. Note that, for a fair comparison with the rest of the considered strategies, this method is trained with the same few-shot $\mathcal{T}$ set. In this regard, this strategy is expected to provide insights into the effectiveness of traditional supervised learning in a few-shot scenario of the commented classification task.

5   Results

The results in terms of classification rate for the few-shot classification proposal—denoted as VICReg—as well as the different baseline strategies are presented in Fig. 4. Note that different results are provided for the self-supervised proposal in terms of the studied λ, μ, and ϕ weights for the loss function.

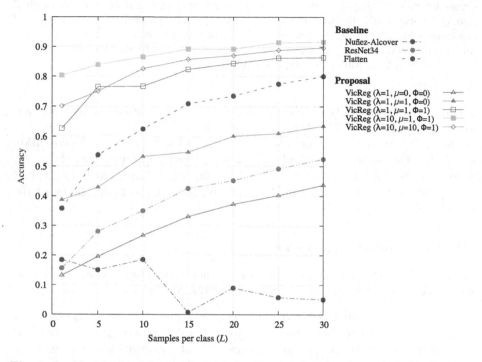

Fig. 4. Results obtained for the presented self-supervised music symbol classification strategy and the different reference methods considered when varying the L number of reference samples per class.

Focusing on the considered supervised baseline approaches, it can be first observed that the *Nuñez-Alcover* state-of-the-art method does not adequately perform in this few-shot scenario, most likely due to being set $\mathcal{T}$ insufficient for the neural model to converge. The *RestNet34*, while still depicting low classification rates, shows a better overall performance than that achieved by the *Nuñez-Alcover* method due to the pre-training phase of the model. The *Flatten* case, in spite of not performing any feature extraction process on the initial image, achieves the best performance among the supervised baseline alternatives considered, obtaining almost an 80% of accuracy when considering $L = 30$ samples per class.

Regarding the self-supervised scheme, the first point to be highlighted is that, when properly configured, our proposal is capable of outperforming the considered supervised baseline strategies. More precisely, the best performing model—the one with parameters $\lambda = 10$, $\mu = 1$, and $\phi = 1$—achieves a higher accuracy performance than that of the *Flatten* case with just $L = 1$ samples per class. Note that, when the number of samples is increased to $L = 30$, the performance of this self-supervised method boosts to a 90% of accuracy, which constitutes the best overall classification rate score among the alternatives considered. These results support the initial hypothesis that pre-training the neural feature extraction model with unlabeled data is capable of generating an adequate representation space which may be later exploited by a supervised classifier to yield good classification results with very few samples per class.

It should be also highlighted that the particular regularization multipliers in the self-supervised scheme—weights λ, μ, and ϕ—play a key role in the success of the task. More precisely, attending to the results obtained, it may be observed that the performance of the proposal clearly degrades when at least one of the coefficients is canceled (i.e., given a value of 0). In contrast to this, when all parameters are given the same weight, the method depicts a remarkable improvement since such cases outperform all supervised baselines. Among these configurations, the best performing case is when the invariance term is weighted above the rest of the components (i.e., $\lambda = 10$, $\mu = 1$, and $\phi = 1$).

In order to extract some additional insights about the proposal, we have considered the visualization of the embedded spaces of the $\mathcal{T}$ partition generated by the different configurations considered. For that, we have resorted to the t-distributed Stochastic Neighbor Embedding (t-SNE) [18] analysis, whose results are depicted in Fig. 5. For the sake of comparison, this analysis is also shown for the two best-performing supervised strategies in the previous analysis, i.e., the *Flatten* and *ResNet34* cases. Note that we consider the case of $L = 30$ samples per class for this particular case.

As can be observed, the considered supervised schemes (Figs. 5a and 5b) generate rather sparse representation spaces as the graphs do not show an adequate grouping of the samples according to their labels. This is somehow an expected outcome since the *Flatten* case directly relies on the image pixels as features while the representation space obtained when pre-training the *ResNet34* scheme with the ImageNet set does not match that of the posed music symbol classification task.

In relation to the self-supervised case, it can be checked that, when adequately adjusted, the method obtains a suitable representation for the classification task at hand since the resulting groups of samples do, in general terms, belong to a single category. Moreover, these individual groups are generally well separated in the space with minor overlapping among the different class sets, which also does benefit the latter classification stage. Note that, as expected due to the previously commented results, for the case in which at least one of the weights in the training loss is canceled—Fig. 5c in which $\phi = 0$—the generated space shows a great overlapping among the different classes, which remarkably hinders the performance of the posterior recognition model.

104   A. Rios-Vila et al.

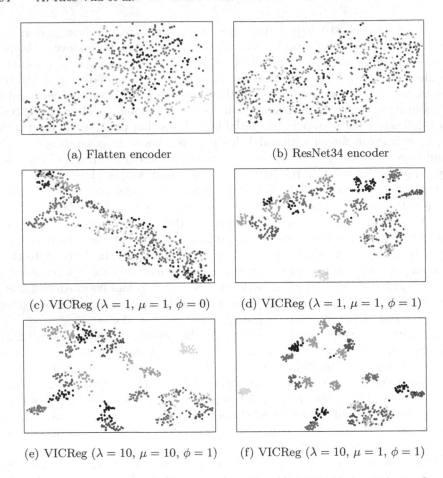

(a) Flatten encoder

(b) ResNet34 encoder

(c) VICReg ($\lambda = 1$, $\mu = 1$, $\phi = 0$)

(d) VICReg ($\lambda = 1$, $\mu = 1$, $\phi = 1$)

(e) VICReg ($\lambda = 10$, $\mu = 10$, $\phi = 1$)

(f) VICReg ($\lambda = 10$, $\mu = 1$, $\phi = 1$)

Fig. 5. Representations of the elements in set T using t-SNE when considering $L = 30$ samples per class for different configurations of the proposal as well as the *Flatten* and *ResNet34* supervised baseline cases. Colors in the samples denote their respective ground-truth labels.

Considering all the above, it can be concluded that the self-supervised approach with parameters $\lambda = 10$, $\mu = 1$ and $\phi = 1$ stands as the most competitive approach among the ones studied in the work for few-shot music symbol classification: on the one hand, according to the results in Fig. 4, this particular strategy quantitatively outperforms the rest of the considered cases; on the other hand, in a more qualitative analysis, the representation space Fig. 5f shows to adequately group the same-class samples according to their features while achieving an appropriate inter-class separation of the different groups obtained.

6   Conclusions

Music symbol classification, the task of automatically labeling the symbols in a given music score, represents one of the most relevant stages in the general pipeline of Optical Music Recognition systems. Currently, state-of-the-art systems capable of adequately addressing this task mainly rely on deep neural models trained in a supervised manner, which generally require large amounts of labeled data to be trained.

In this paper, we propose an alternative self-supervised scheme suited for few-shot music symbol classification tasks with the aim of reducing the need for annotated data. The proposed methodology comprises two sequential stages: (i) a first one in which a neural-based feature extractor is trained in a self-supervised manner considering the so-called Variance-Invariance-Covariance Regularization loss to generate an adequate representation space; and (ii) a second phase in which the k-Nearest Neighbor is considered for performing the classification task with a considerably limited set of reference data. The experiments carried out on a reference music corpus in mensural notation show that, when adequately adjusted, the proposal outperforms the contemplated baseline strategies in terms of classification accuracy. More precisely, this strategy achieves nearly an 80% of accuracy considering one single example per class in the reference set, being this figure improved up to 90% when the number of reference examples per class increased to thirty.

In light of the benefits of SSL, we believe it can be deemed as a suitable solution to the data scarcity problem, which notably affects more complex tasks such as layout analysis, holistic transcription, or end-to-end full page recognition. As future work, we plan to extend the mentioned SSL framework for these tasks.

Acknowledgments. This paper is part of the project I+D+i PID2020-118447RA-I00, funded by MCIN/AEI/10.13039/501100011033. Some of the computing resources used in this project are provided by Valencian Government and FEDER through IDIFEDER/2020/003. The first and third authors are supported by "Programa I+D+i de la Generalitat Valenciana" through grant ACIF/2021/356 and APOSTD/2020/256, respectively. The second author is supported by the Spanish Ministerio de Universidades through grant FPU19/04957.

References

1. Alfaro-Contreras, M., Rizo, D., Iñesta, J.M., Calvo-Zaragoza, J.: OMR-assisted transcription: a case study with early prints. In: Proceedings of the 22nd International Society for Music Information Retrieval Conference, pp. 35–41 (2021)
2. Apel, W.: The notation of polyphonic music: 900–1600. Cambridge Mass (1949)
3. Bardes, A., Ponce, J., LeCun, Y.: Vicreg: variance-invariance-covariance regularization for self-supervised learning. CoRR abs/2105.04906 (2021)
4. Byrd, D., Simonsen, J.G.: Towards a standard testbed for optical music recognition: definitions, metrics, and page images. J. New Music Res. **44**(3), 169–195 (2015)
5. Calvo-Zaragoza, J., Hajic Jr., J., Pacha, A.: Understanding optical music recognition. ACM Comput. Surv. **53**(4), 77:1–77:35 (2020)

6. Calvo-Zaragoza, J., Toselli, A.H., Vidal, E.: Hybrid hidden Markov models and artificial neural networks for handwritten music recognition in mensural notation. Pattern Anal. Appl. **22**(4), 1573–1584 (2019). https://doi.org/10.1007/s10044-019-00807-1
7. Caron, M., et al.: Emerging properties in self-supervised vision transformers (2021)
8. Chen, X., He, K.: Exploring simple siamese representation learning. In: Proceedings of the IEEE/CVF Conference on Computer Vision and Pattern Recognition, pp. 15750–15758 (2021)
9. Deng, J., Dong, W., Socher, R., Li, L.J., Li, K., Fei-Fei, L.: Imagenet: a large-scale hierarchical image database. In: 2009 IEEE Conference on Computer Vision and Pattern Recognition, pp. 248–255. IEEE (2009)
10. Desmond, K., Pugin, L., Regimbal, J., Rizo, D., Sapp, C., Thomae, M.: Encoding polyphony from medieval manuscripts notated in mensural notation. In: Music Encoding Conference Proceedings 2021 (2021)
11. Duda, R.O., Hart, P.E., Stork, D.G.: Pattern Classification, 2nd edn. Wiley, Hoboken (2001)
12. Duval, E., van Berchum, M., Jentzsch, A., Chico, G.A.P., Drakos, A.: Musicology of early music with Europeana tools and services. In: Müller, M., Wiering, F. (eds.) Proceedings of the 16th International Society for Music Information Retrieval Conference, pp. 632–638 (2015)
13. Fujinaga, I., Vigliensoni, G.: The art of teaching computers: the SIMSSA optical music recognition workflow system. In: 2019 27th European Signal Processing Conference (EUSIPCO), pp. 1–5 (2019)
14. Hankinson, A., Roland, P., Fujinaga, I.: The music encoding initiative as a document-encoding framework. In: Klapuri, A., Leider, C. (eds.) Proceedings of the 12th International Society for Music Information Retrieval Conference, pp. 293–298. University of Miami (2011)
15. He, K., Zhang, X., Ren, S., Sun, J.: Deep residual learning for image recognition. In: Proceedings of the IEEE Conference on Computer Vision and Pattern Recognition, pp. 770–778 (2016)
16. Jaiswal, A., Babu, A.R., Zadeh, M.Z., Banerjee, D., Makedon, F.: A survey on contrastive self-supervised learning. Technologies **9**(1), 2 (2021)
17. Jing, L., Tian, Y.: Self-supervised visual feature learning with deep neural networks: a survey. IEEE Trans. Pattern Anal. Mach. Intell. **43**(11), 4037–4058 (2020)
18. Van der Maaten, L., Hinton, G.: Visualizing data using t-SNE. J. Mach. Learn. Res. **9**(11) (2008)
19. Mas-Candela, E., Alfaro-Contreras, M., Calvo-Zaragoza, J.: Sequential next-symbol prediction for optical music recognition. In: Lladós, J., Lopresti, D., Uchida, S. (eds.) ICDAR 2021. LNCS, vol. 12823, pp. 708–722. Springer, Cham (2021). https://doi.org/10.1007/978-3-030-86334-0_46
20. Mateiu, T.N., Gallego, A.-J., Calvo-Zaragoza, J.: Domain adaptation for handwritten symbol recognition: a case of study in old music manuscripts. In: Morales, A., Fierrez, J., Sánchez, J.S., Ribeiro, B. (eds.) IbPRIA 2019. LNCS, vol. 11868, pp. 135–146. Springer, Cham (2019). https://doi.org/10.1007/978-3-030-31321-0_12
21. Müller, C.: Between Digital Transformation in Libraries and the Digital Humanities: New Perspectives on Librarianship, pp. 379–384. De Gruyter (2020)
22. Nuñez-Alcover, A., de León, P.J.P., Calvo-Zaragoza, J.: Glyph and position classification of music symbols in early music manuscripts. In: Morales, A., Fierrez, J., Sánchez, J.S., Ribeiro, B. (eds.) IbPRIA 2019. LNCS, vol. 11868, pp. 159–168. Springer, Cham (2019). https://doi.org/10.1007/978-3-030-31321-0_14

23. Ohri, K., Kumar, M.: Review on self-supervised image recognition using deep neural networks. Knowl.-Based Syst. **224**, 107090 (2021)
24. Pacha, A., Choi, K.Y., Coüasnon, B., Ricquebourg, Y., Zanibbi, R., Eidenberger, H.: Handwritten music object detection: open issues and baseline results. In: 13th International Workshop on Document Analysis Systems, pp. 163–168 (2018)
25. Pugin, L.: Editing Renaissance Music: The Aruspix Project, pp. 147–156. De Gruyter (2009)
26. Rebelo, A., Fujinaga, I., Paszkiewicz, F., Marcal, A.R., Guedes, C., Cardoso, J.D.S.: Optical music recognition: state-of-the-art and open issues. Int. J. Multimedia Inf. Retrieval **1**(3), 173–190 (2012)
27. Rizo, D., Calvo-Zaragoza, J., Iñesta, J.M.: MuRET: a music recognition, encoding, and transcription tool. In: Page, K.R. (ed.) Proceedings of the 5th International Conference on Digital Libraries for Musicology, pp. 52–56. ACM (2018)
28. Stoessel, J., Collins, D., Bolland, S.: Using optical music recognition to encode 17th-century music prints: the canonic works of paolo agostini (c.1583-1629) as a test case. In: Proceedings of the 7th International Conference on Digital Libraries for Musicology, pp. 1–9. ACM (2020)
29. Thomae, M.: The Guatemalan Choirbooks: Facilitating Preservation, Performance, and Study of the Colonial Repertoire. Rowman & Littlefield (2021)
30. Zbontar, J., Jing, L., Misra, I., LeCun, Y., Deny, S.: Barlow twins: self-supervised learning via redundancy reduction. In: International Conference on Machine Learning, pp. 12310–12320. PMLR (2021)

A Multi-modal Registration and Visualization Software Tool for Artworks Using CraquelureNet

Aline Sindel[(✉)], Andreas Maier, and Vincent Christlein

Pattern Recognition Lab, FAU Erlangen-Nürnberg, Erlangen, Germany
`aline.sindel@fau.de`

Abstract. For art investigations of paintings, multiple imaging technologies, such as visual light photography, infrared reflectography, ultraviolet fluorescence photography, and x-radiography are often used. For a pixel-wise comparison, the multi-modal images have to be registered. We present a registration and visualization software tool, that embeds a convolutional neural network to extract cross-modal features of the crack structures in historical paintings for automatic registration. The graphical user interface processes the user's input to configure the registration parameters and to interactively adapt the image views with the registered pair and image overlays, such as by individual or synchronized zoom or movements of the views. In the evaluation, we qualitatively and quantitatively show the effectiveness of our software tool in terms of registration performance and short inference time on multi-modal paintings and its transferability by applying our method to historical prints.

Keywords: Multi-modal registration · Visualization · Convolutional neural networks

1 Introduction

In art investigations often multiple imaging systems, such as visual light photography (VIS), infrared reflectography (IRR), ultraviolet fluorescence photography (UV), and x-radiography (XR), are utilized. For instance, IR is used to reveal underdrawings, UV to visualize overpaintings and restorations, and XR to highlight white lead. Since the multi-modal images are acquired using different imaging systems, we have to take into account different image resolutions and varying viewpoints of the devices. Thus, for a direct comparison on pixel level, image registration is crucial to align the multi-modal images.

Image registration methods for art imaging can mainly be split into intensity-, control point- and feature-based approaches. The intensity-based method of Cappellini et al. [4] uses mutual information to iteratively register multispectral images. The control point- and feature-based methods compute a geometric transform based on detected correspondences in both images. Murashov [12] detects local grayscale maxima as control points in VIS-XR image pairs and

© Springer Nature Switzerland AG 2023
J.-J. Rousseau and B. Kapralos (Eds.): ICPR 2022 Workshops, LNCS 13645, pp. 108–121, 2023.
https://doi.org/10.1007/978-3-031-37731-0_9

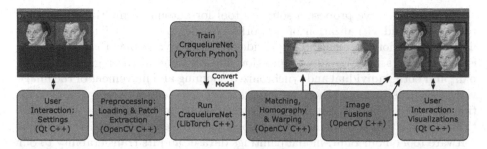

Fig. 1. Our multi-modal registration and visualization tool CraquelureNetApp. Users can select the images and registration options in the GUI. The registration itself is performed fully automatically using the CraquelureNet, a CNN for multi-modal keypoint detection and description, which was ported from PyTorch to C++. Due to the high-resolution images of paintings, the CraquelureNet is applied patch-wise. The registration results are depicted inside the GUI and the users can interact with the visualizations, *e.g.* joint zooming of the views. Image sources: Workshop Lucas Cranach the Elder, Katharina of Bora (Detail), visual light and UV-fluorescence photographs, captured by Ulrike Hügle, Stiftung Deutsches Historisches Museum, Berlin, Cranach Digital Archive, KKL-No IV.M21b, all rights reserved

applies coherent point drift [13]. Conover *et al.* [6] uses Wavelet transform, phase correlation, and disparity filtering for control point detection in sub-images of VIS, IR, and XR. The feature-based method of Zacharopoulos *et al.* [19] uses SIFT [11] to align multispectral images of artworks. CraquelureNet [17] uses a convolutional neural network (CNN) to detect keypoints and descriptors based on branching points in the crack structure (craquelure) of the paint, as it is visible by all imaging systems, in contrast to the depicted image content that can be very different in the multi-modal images.

More and more museums or art projects provide the ability to inspect their artworks in interactive website viewers. Specifically for multi-modal images website viewer have been designed that allow a synchronized scrolling and zooming of the image views [1,10] or a curtain viewer [1] that allows to interactively inspect multiple images in a single view. For these projects, the specific multi-modal images of artworks were pre-registered offline.

For the daily work, it would be practical for art technologists and art historians to have a tool, with which they can easily perform the registration themselves and also can interactively inspect the registered images. In the field of medical 2D-2D or 3D-3D registration, there are open source tools such as MITK [18] that provides a graphical user interface (GUI) application for iterative rigid and affine registration and also a developer software framework. Since these software tools are very complex, domain knowledge is required to adapt the algorithms for multi-modal registration of paintings. The ImageOverlayApp [16] is a small and easy to handle GUI application that allows the direct comparison of two registered artworks using image superimposition and blending techniques. However, here as well as in the online viewers, image registration is not provided.

In this paper, we propose a software tool for automatic multi-modal image registration and visualization of artworks. We designed a GUI to receive the user's registration settings and to provide an interactive display to show the registration results, such as superimposition and blending of the registered image pair, and both, individual and synchronized zooming and movement of the image views. As registration method, we integrate the keypoint detection and description network CraquelureNet into our application by porting it to C++. A quantitative evaluation and qualitative examples show the effective application of our software tool on our multi-modal paintings dataset and its transferability to our historical prints dataset.

2   Methods

In this section, the software tool for multi-modal registration and visualization is described.

2.1   Overview of the Registration and Visualization Tool

In Fig. 1, the main building blocks of the CraquelureNetApp are shown, consisting of the GUI, the preprocessing such as data loading and patch extraction, the actual registration method, which is split into the keypoint detection and description network CraquelureNet that was ported from PyTorch to LibTorch and into descriptor matching, homography estimation, and image warping, and the computation of visualizations of the registration results and its interactions with the user.

2.2   Registration Method

CraquelureNet [17] is composed of a ResNet backbone and a keypoint detection and a keypoint description head. The network is trained on small $32 \times 32 \times 3$ sized image patches using a multi-task loss for both heads. The keypoint detection head is optimized using binary cross-entropy loss to classify the small patches into "craquelure" and "background", i.e. whether the center of the patch (a) contains a branching or sharp bend of a crack structure ("craquelure") or (b) contains it only in the periphery or not at all ("background"). The keypoint description head is trained using bidirectional quadruplet loss [17] to learn cross-modal descriptors. Using online hard negative mining, for a positive keypoint pair the hardest non-matching descriptors are selected in both directions within the batch. Then, the positive distances (matching keypoint pairs) are minimized while the negative distances (hardest non-matching keypoint pairs) are maximized.

For inference, larger image input sizes can be fed to the fully convolutional network. Due to the architectural design, the prediction of the keypoint detection head and description head are of lower resolution than the input image and hence are upscaled by a factor of 4 using bicubic interpolation for the

Menu

Registration
toolbar items

Visualization
toolbar items

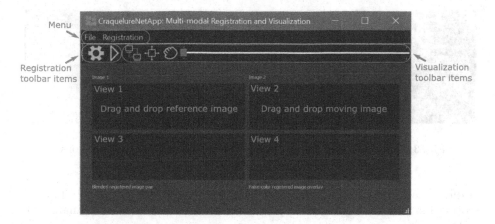

Fig. 2. The graphical user interface (GUI) of our CraquelureNetApp. The different elements of the GUI are marked in orange: the menu, the toolbar items for registration and visualization and the views.

keypoint heatmap and bilinear interpolation for the descriptors based on the extracted keypoint positions. Keypoints are extracted using non-maximum suppression and by selecting all keypoints with a confidence score higher than τ_{kp} based on the keypoint heatmap. Since the images can be very large, CraquelureNet is applied patch-based and the keypoints of all patches are merged and reduced to the N_{max} keypoints with the highest confidence score. Then, mutual nearest neighbor descriptor matching is applied and Random Sample Consensus (RANSAC) [9] is used for homography estimation [17].

CraquelureNet [17] is completely implemented in Python using PyTorch and OpenCV. To transfer the trained PyTorch model to C++, we made use of the TorchScript conversion functionality and restructured the source code accordingly using a combination of TorchScript modules and Tracing. We have directly reimplemented the other parts of the registration pipeline in C++ using the same OpenCV functions as in Python.

For homography estimation, we provide the option to choose between different robust estimators of the OpenCV library: RANSAC [9] which is already used in [15,17] is the default option. RANSAC is an iterative method to estimate a model, here homography, for data points that contain outliers. In each iteration, a model is estimated on a random subset of the data and is scored using all data points, $i.e.$ the number of inliers for that model is computed. In the end, the best model is selected based on the largest inlier count and can optionally be refined. Universal RANSAC (USAC) [14] includes different RANSAC variants into a single framework, $e.g.$ different sampling strategies, or extend the verification step by also checking for degeneracy. We use the USAC default method of OpenCV 4.5.5 that applies iterative local optimization to the so far best models [5]. Further, we enable two RANSAC variants which are also included in the OpenCV USAC framework: Graph-Cut RANSAC (GC-RANSAC) [2] uses the

Fig. 3. The menu and dialogs to configure registration and save options.

graph-cut algorithm for the local optimization and MAGSAC++ [3] applies a scoring function that does not require a threshold and a novel marginalization method.

2.3 Graphical User Interface

The GUI is implemented in C++ as a Qt5 desktop application. In Fig. 2 the main GUI elements are marked in orange. The user can interact with the GUI using the menu or the toolbar that provides items specified for the registration and visualization task or can also directly interact with the views. The size of the views depends on the size of the application window.

User Interaction Prior to Registration: To perform registration, two images have to be selected. They can either be chosen via the menu (Fig. 3a) using a file opener or per drag and drop of the image file to the image view. The selected images are visualized in the two image views in the top row. Per click on the configure button in the menu (Fig. 3b) or on the registration toolbar ("gear" icon), a user dialog (Fig. 3c) is opened to choose the registration options, such as patch size, number of maximum keypoints N_{max}, image input size, method for homography estimation (RANSAC, USAC, GC-RANSAC, or MAGSAC++), whether to run on the GPU (using CUDA) or on the CPU and whether to visualize keypoint matches. Custom settings of patch size, input image size, and maximum number of keypoints are also possible when the predefined selections are not sufficient. The settings are saved in a configuration file to remember the user's choice. It is always possible to restore the default settings. The registration is started by clicking the run button in the menu (Fig. 3b) or in the toolbar ("triangle" icon).

Visualizations and User Interaction: We include two different superimposition techniques to visually compare the registration results, a false-color image overlay (red-cyan) of the registered pair and a blended image overlay, similarly to [16]. After registration, the views in the GUI are updated with the transformed moving image (view 2) and the image fusions in the bottom row (view 3 and 4). The red-cyan overlay (view 4), stacks the reference image (view 1) into the red

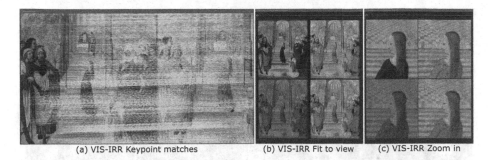

(a) VIS-IRR Keypoint matches   (b) VIS-IRR Fit to view   (c) VIS-IRR Zoom in

Fig. 4. VIS-IRR registration of paintings using CraquelureNetApp. In (a) the keypoint matches between the reference image (VIS) and moving image (IRR) are visualized as yellow lines. In (b) the registered image pair and the blended overlay and the false color overlay are depicted as complete images and in (c) they are synchronously zoomed in. Image sources: Meister des Marienlebens, Tempelgang Mariä, visual light photograph and infrared reflectogram, Germanisches Nationalmuseum, Nuremberg, on loan from Wittelsbacher Ausgleichsfonds/Bayerische Staatsgemäldesammlungen, Gm 19, all rights reserved (Color figure online)

and the transformed moving image (view 2) into the green and blue channel. The blended image (view 3) is initially shown with alpha value 0.5. By moving the slider in the visualization toolbar, the user can interactively blend between both registered images. For the optional visualization of the keypoint matches, a separate window is opened that shows both original images with superimposed keypoints as small blue circles and matches as yellow lines using OpenCV.

Additionally to the image overlays, we have implemented a synchronization feature of the views that enriches the comparison. It can be activated by the "connect views" icon in the visualization toolbar. All interactions with one view are propagated to the other views. Using the mouse wheel the view is zoomed in or out with the focus at the current mouse position. Using the arrow keys the image view can be shifted in all directions. By activating the "hand mouse drag" item in the toolbar, the view can be shifted around arbitrarily. By pressing the "maximize" icon in the toolbar, the complete image is fitted into the view area preserving aspect ratio. This can also be useful after asynchronous movement of single views to reset them to a common basis.

To save the registration results to disk, the user can click the "save" button in the menu (Fig. 3a) to choose the files to save in a dialog (Fig. 3d) or the "save all" button to save them all.

3   Applications and Evaluation

In this section, we apply the CraquelureNetApp to multi-modal images of paintings and to images of different prints of the same motif. We use the test parameters as defined in [17]: GPU, patch size of 1024, $N_{\max} = 8000$, $\tau_{\mathrm{kp}} = 0$, resize to same width, and RANSAC with a reprojection error threshold $\tau_{\mathrm{reproj}} = 5$.

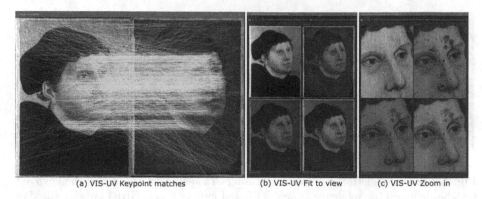

Fig. 5. VIS-UV registration of paintings using CraquelureNetApp. In (a) the keypoint matches of VIS and UV are densely concentrated at the craquelure in the facial region. (b) and (c) show the registered pair and image fusions of the complete images and synchronized details. Image sources: Workshop Lucas Cranach the Elder or Circle, Martin Luther, visual light photograph, captured by Gunnar Heydenreich and UV-fluorescence photograph, captured by Wibke Ottweiler, Lutherhaus Wittenberg, Cranach Digital Archive, KKL-No I.6M3, all rights reserved

For the quantitative evaluation, we measure the registration performance based on the success rate of successfully registered images. The success rate is computed by calculating the percentage of image pairs for which the error distance of manual labeled control points of the registered pair using the predicted homography is less or equal to an error threshold ϵ. As metric for the error distance, we use the mean Euclidean error (ME) and maximum Euclidean error (MAE) [15].

As comparison methods, we use the conventional keypoint and feature descriptor SIFT [11] and the pretrained models of the two deep learning methods, SuperPoint [7] and D2-Net [8], which we apply patch-based to both the paintings and prints. SuperPoint is a CNN with a keypoint detection head and a keypoint description head and is trained in a self-supervised manner by using homographic warpings. D2-Net simultaneously learns keypoint detection and description with one feature extraction CNN, where keypoints and descriptors are extracted from the same set of feature maps. For all methods, we use the same test settings as for our method (patch size, N_{max}, RANSAC).

3.1 Multi-modal Registration of Historical Paintings

The pretrained CraquelureNet [17], which we embedded into our registration tool, was trained using small patches extracted from multi-modal images of 16th century portraits by the workshop of Lucas Cranach the Elder and large German panel paintings from the 15th to 16th century. We use the images of the test split from these multi-modal datasets (13 pairs per domain: VIS-IRR, VIS-UV, VIS-XR) and the corresponding manually labeled control point pairs (40 point pairs per image pair) [17] to test the CraquelureNetApp.

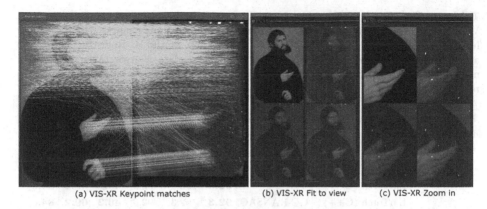

(a) VIS-XR Keypoint matches   (b) VIS-XR Fit to view   (c) VIS-XR Zoom in

Fig. 6. VIS-XR registration of paintings using CraquelureNetApp. In (a) the keypoint matches of VIS and XR are mostly concentrated at the craquelure in the lighter image area such as the face, hands, and green background. (b) and (c) show the qualitative registration results as overall view and as synchronized zoomed details. Image sources: Lucas Cranach the Elder, Martin Luther as "Junker Jörg", visual light photograph, Klassik Stiftung Weimar, Museum, X-radiograph, HfBK Dresden (Mohrmann, Riße), Cranach Digital Archive, KKL-No II.M2, all rights reserved

The qualitative results of three examples (VIS-IRR, VIS-UV and VIS-XR) are shown in Figs. 4, 5 and 6. For each example, the keypoint matches, the complete images (Fit to view option in the GUI), and a zoomed detail view in the synchronization mode are depicted showing good visual registration performance for all three multi-modal pairs.

Secondly, we compare in Table 1 the success rates of ME and MAE of the registration for the C++ and PyTorch implementation of CraquelureNet using RANSAC for homography estimation or alternatively using USAC, GC-RANSAC, or MAGSAC++. The C++ implementation using RANSAC achieves comparable results as the PyTorch implementation (both $\tau_{reproj} = 5$): For VIS-IRR and VIS-UV, all images are registered successfully using ME with an error threshold $\epsilon = 5$ (PyTorch) and $\epsilon = 7$ (C++). For VIS-XR, 12 (C++) or 11 (PyTorch) out of 13 images were successfully registered using ME ($\epsilon = 7$). The small deviations between the two models are due to slightly different implementations e.g. of non-maximum suppression that were necessary for the conversion to C++. Using the more recent USAC, GC-RANSAC, or MAGSAC++ is slightly less robust for VIS-IRR and VIS-UV, since not more than 12 out of 13 image pairs can be registered using ME ($\epsilon = 7$) as one image pair fails completely. VIS-XR registration is the most difficult part of the three domain pairs due to the visually highly different appearance of the VIS and XR images. Here, we can observe similar performance of ME, with a slightly higher percentage of USAC, GC-RANSAC, and especially MAGSAC++ for $\epsilon = 3$, but for $\epsilon = 7$ those are on par with the PyTorch model and are slightly inferior to the C++ model using RANSAC. Regarding the success rates of MAE, we observe a bit higher values

Table 1. Quantitative evaluation for multi-modal registration of paintings for the VIS-IRR, VIS-UV, and VIS-XR test datasets (each 13 image pairs) using CraquelureNet with different robust homography estimation methods. Registration results are evaluated with the success rates (SR) of mean Euclidean error (ME) and maximum Euclidean error (MAE) of the control points for different error thresholds ϵ. Best results are highlighted in bold.

Multi-modal Dataset	CraquelureNet Model	Homography Method	SR of ME [%] ↑			SR of MAE [%] ↑		
			$\epsilon = 3$	$\epsilon = 5$	$\epsilon = 7$	$\epsilon = 6$	$\epsilon = 8$	$\epsilon = 10$
VIS-IRR	PyTorch (Python)	RANSAC	84.6	**100.0**	**100.0**	38.5	**69.2**	**84.6**
	LibTorch (C++)	RANSAC	**92.3**	92.3	**100.0**	38.5	**69.2**	**84.6**
	LibTorch (C++)	USAC	**92.3**	92.3	92.3	**46.2**	**69.2**	**84.6**
	LibTorch (C++)	GC-RANSAC	**92.3**	92.3	92.3	**46.2**	**69.2**	**84.6**
	LibTorch (C++)	MAGSAC++	**92.3**	92.3	92.3	**46.2**	**69.2**	**84.6**
VIS-UV	PyTorch (Python)	RANSAC	**92.3**	**100.0**	**100.0**	46.2	53.8	61.5
	LibTorch (C++)	RANSAC	84.6	92.3	**100.0**	**53.8**	53.8	53.8
	LibTorch (C++)	USAC	**92.3**	92.3	92.3	**53.8**	**69.2**	**69.2**
	LibTorch (C++)	GC-RANSAC	**92.3**	92.3	92.3	**53.8**	**69.2**	**69.2**
	LibTorch (C++)	MAGSAC++	84.6	92.3	92.3	46.2	61.5	**69.2**
VIS-XR	PyTorch (Python)	RANSAC	69.2	**84.6**	84.6	23.1	38.5	61.5
	LibTorch (C++)	RANSAC	53.8	**84.6**	**92.3**	**30.8**	46.2	61.5
	LibTorch (C++)	USAC	76.9	**84.6**	84.6	23.1	38.5	**76.9**
	LibTorch (C++)	GC-RANSAC	76.9	**84.6**	84.6	23.1	38.5	**76.9**
	LibTorch (C++)	MAGSAC++	**84.6**	**84.6**	84.6	15.4	**53.8**	**76.9**

for USAC, GC-RANSAC, and MAGSAC++ than for both RANSAC models for VIS-UV and VIS-XR ($\epsilon = \{8, 10\}$), while for VIS-IRR they are the same.

In Fig. 7, the multi-modal registration performance of our C++ CraquelureNet (RANSAC) is measured in comparison to SIFT [11], SuperPoint [7], and D2-Net [8]. CraquelureNet achieves the highest success rates of ME and MAE for all multi-modal pairs. D2-Net is relatively close to CraquelureNet for VIS-IRR with the same SR of ME but with a lower SR of MAE. For VIS-IRR and VIS-UV, all learning-based methods are clearly better than SIFT. For the challenging VIS-XR domain, the advantage of our cross-modal keypoint detector and descriptor is most distinct, since for $\epsilon = 7$, CraquelureNet still achieves high success rates of 92.3 % for ME and 61.5 % for MAE, whereas for $\epsilon = 7$, D2-Net only successfully registers 61.5 % for ME and 15.3 % for MAE, SuperPoint only 23 % for ME and none for MAE, and lastly, SIFT does not register any VIS-XR image pair successfully. D2-Net was developed to find correspondences in difficult image conditions, such as day-to-night or depiction changes [8], hence it also is able to detect to some extend matching keypoint pairs in VIS-XR images. SuperPoint's focus is more on images with challenging viewpoints [7,8], thus the pretrained model results in a lower VIS-XR registration performance. In our prior work [17], we fine-tuned SuperPoint using image patches extracted

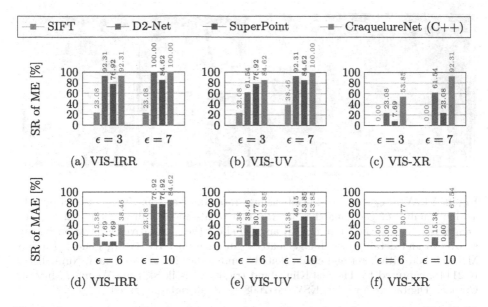

Fig. 7. Quantitative evaluation for our multi-modal paintings dataset using SR of ME with $\epsilon = 3, 7$ and SR of MAE with $\epsilon = 6, 10$.

from our manually aligned multi-modal paintings dataset, which did not result in an overall improvement. On the other hand, CraquelureNet is robust for the registration of all multi-modal pairs and does not require an intensive training procedure, as it is trained in efficient time only using very small image patches.

The execution time of CraquelureNet (C++ and PyTorch) for the VIS-IRR registration (including loading of network and images, patch extraction of size $1024 \times 1024 \times 3$ pixels, network inference, homography estimation using RANSAC and image warping) was about 11 s per image pair on the GPU and about 2 min per image pair on the CPU. We used an Intel Xeon W-2125 CPU 4.00 GHz with 64 GB RAM and one NVIDIA Titan XP GPU for the measurements. The comparable execution times of the C++ and PyTorch implementation of CraquelureNet (the restructured one for a fair comparison) is not surprising, as PyTorch and OpenCV are wrappers around C++ functions. The relatively fast inference time for the registration of high-resolution images makes CraquelureNet suitable to be integrated into the registration GUI and to be used by art technologists and art historians for their daily work.

3.2 Registration of Historical Prints

To evaluate the registration performance for prints, we have created a test dataset of in total 52 images of historical prints with manually labeled control point pairs. The dataset is composed of 13 different motifs of 16th century prints with each four exemplars that may show wear or production-related differences in the print. For each motif a reference image was selected and the other

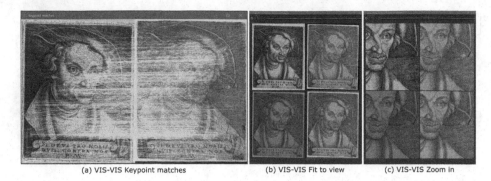

Fig. 8. VIS-VIS registration of prints using CraquelureNetApp. CraquelureNet detects a high number of good matches for the two prints in (a), although it did not see images of prints during training. (b) and (c) show the qualitative registration results as overall and detail views. Image sources: Monogramist IB (Georg Pencz), Philipp Melanchthon with beret and cloak, (left) Germanisches Nationalmuseum, Nuremberg, K 21148, captured by Thomas Klinke and (right) Klassik Stiftung Weimar, Museen, Cranach Digital Archive, DE_KSW_Gr-2008-1858, all rights reserved

three copies will be registered to the reference, resulting in 39 registration pairs. For each image pair, 10 control point pairs were manually annotated.

We test the CraquelureNet, that was solely trained on paintings, for the 16th century prints. One qualitative example is shown in Fig. 8. CraquelureNet also finds a high number of good matches in this engraving pair, due to the multitude of tiny lines and branchings in the print as CraquelureNet is mainly focusing on these branching points.

For the quantitative evaluation, we compute the success rates of ME and MAE for the registration of the print dataset using our CraquelureNet C++ model in comparison to using SIFT [11], SuperPoint [7], and D2-Net [8]. For the registration, the images are scaled to a fixed height of 2000 pixel, as then the structures in the prints have a suitable size for the feature detectors. In the GUI of CraquelureNetApp this option is "resize to custom height". The results of the comparison are depicted in Fig. 9. The CNN-based methods obtain clearly superior results to SIFT for both metrics. Overall, CraquelureNet and SuperPoint show the best results, as both achieve a success rate of ME of 100 % at error threshold $\epsilon = 4$, where they are closely followed by D2-Net at $\epsilon = 5$ and all three methods achieve a success rate of MAE close to 100 % at $\epsilon = 10$. For smaller error thresholds, CraquelureNet is slightly superior for MAE and SuperPoint for ME. As none of the methods was fine-tuned for the print dataset, this experiment shows the successful possibility of applying the models to this new dataset.

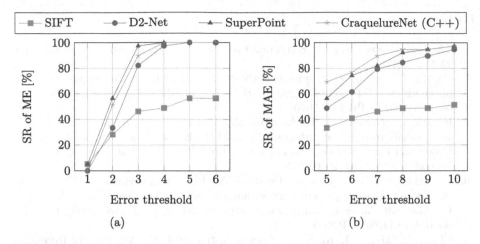

Fig. 9. Quantitative comparison of success rates for registration of prints (39 image pairs). For all methods RANSAC with $\tau_{\mathtt{reproj}} = 5$ was used. None of the methods was fine-tuned for the print dataset. In (a) the success rate of mean Euclidean error (ME) for the error thresholds $\epsilon = \{1, 2, ..., 6\}$ and in (b) the success rate of maximum Euclidean error (MAE) for the error thresholds $\epsilon = \{5, 6, ..., 10\}$ is plotted.

4 Conclusion

We presented an interactive registration and visualization tool for multi-modal paintings and also applied it to historical prints. The registration is performed fully automatically using CraquelureNet. The user can choose the registration settings and can interact with the visualizations of the registration results. In the future, we could extend the application by including trained models of CraquelureNet on other datasets, such as the RetinaCraquelureNet [15] for multi-modal retinal registration. A further possible extension would be to add a batch processing functionality to the GUI to register a folder of image pairs.

Acknowledgements. Thanks to Daniel Hess, Oliver Mack, Daniel Görres, Wibke Ottweiler, Germanisches Nationalmuseum (GNM), and Gunnar Heydenreich, Cranach Digital Archive (CDA), and Thomas Klinke, TH Köln, and Amalie Hänsch, FAU Erlangen-Nürnberg for providing image data, and to Leibniz Society for funding the research project "Critical Catalogue of Luther portraits (1519 - 1530)" with grant agreement No. SAW-2018-GNM-3-KKLB, to the European Union's Horizon 2020 research and innovation programme within the Odeuropa project under grant agreement No. 101004469 for funding this publication, and to NVIDIA for their GPU hardware donation.

References

1. The Bosch Research and Conservation Project. https://boschproject.org. Accessed 25 May 2022
2. Baráth, D., Matas, J.: Graph-cut RANSAC. In: 2018 IEEE Conference on Computer Vision and Pattern Recognition (CVPR), pp. 6733–6741 (2018). https://doi.org/10.1109/CVPR.2018.00704
3. Baráth, D., Noskova, J., Ivashechkin, M., Matas, J.: MAGSAC++, a fast, reliable and accurate robust estimator. In: 2020 IEEE/CVF Conference on Computer Vision and Pattern Recognition (CVPR), pp. 1301–1309 (2020). https://doi.org/10.1109/CVPR42600.2020.00138
4. Cappellini, V., Del Mastio, A., De Rosa, A., Piva, A., Pelagotti, A., El Yamani, H.: An automatic registration algorithm for cultural heritage images. In: IEEE International Conference on Image Processing 2005 2, pp. II-566 (2005). https://doi.org/10.1109/ICIP.2005.1530118
5. Chum, O., Matas, J., Kittler, J.: Locally optimized RANSAC. Pattern Recognit. 236–243 (2003). https://doi.org/10.1007/978-3-540-45243-0_31
6. Conover, D.M., Delaney, J.K., Loew, M.H.: Automatic registration and mosaicking of technical images of old master paintings. Appl. Phys. A **119**(4), 1567–1575 (2015). https://doi.org/10.1007/s00339-015-9140-1
7. DeTone, D., Malisiewicz, T., Rabinovich, A.: SuperPoint: self-supervised interest point detection and description. In: 2018 IEEE Conference on Computer Vision and Pattern Recognition (CVPR) Workshops, pp. 224–236 (2018). https://doi.org/10.1109/CVPRW.2018.00060
8. Dusmanu, M., et al.: D2-Net: a trainable CNN for joint description and detection of local features. In: 2019 IEEE/CVF Conference on Computer Vision and Pattern Recognition (CVPR), pp. 8084–8093 (2019). https://doi.org/10.1109/CVPR.2019.00828
9. Fischler, M.A., Bolles, R.C.: Random sample consensus: a paradigm for model fitting with applications to image analysis and automated cartography. Commun. ACM **24**(6), 381–395 (1981). https://doi.org/10.1145/358669.358692
10. Fransen, B., Temmermans, F., Currie, C.: Imaging techniques and methodologies for acquisition, processing and distribution of multimodal image data from the oeuvre of Jan van Eyck. In: Optics, Photonics and Digital Technologies for Imaging Applications VI, vol. 11353, pp. 68–81 (2020). https://doi.org/10.1117/12.2556260
11. Lowe, D.G.: Distinctive image features from scale-invariant keypoints. Int. J. Comput. Vision **60**(2), 91–110 (2004). https://doi.org/10.1023/B:VISI.0000029664.99615.94
12. Murashov, D.: A procedure for automated registration of fine art images in visible and X-ray spectral bands. In: Proceedings of the International Conference on Computer Vision Theory and Applications (VISAPP-2011), pp. 162–167 (2011)
13. Myronenko, A., Song, X.: Point set registration: coherent point drift. IEEE Trans. Pattern Anal. Mach. Intell. **32**(12), 2262–2275 (2010). https://doi.org/10.1109/TPAMI.2010.46
14. Raguram, R., Chum, O., Pollefeys, M., Matas, J., Frahm, J.M.: USAC: a universal framework for random sample consensus. IEEE Trans. Pattern Anal. Mach. Intell. **35**(8), 2022–2038 (2013). https://doi.org/10.1109/TPAMI.2012.257
15. Sindel, A., et al.: A keypoint detection and description network based on the vessel structure for multi-modal retinal image registration. Bildverarbeitung für die Medizin **2022**, 57–62 (2022). https://doi.org/10.1007/978-3-658-36932-3_12

16. Sindel, A., Maier, A., Christlein, V.: A visualization tool for image fusion of artworks. In: 25th International Conference on Cultural Heritage and New Technologies (2020)
17. Sindel, A., Maier, A., Christlein, V.: CraquelureNet: matching the crack structure in historical paintings for multi-modal image registration. In: IEEE International Conference on Image Processing 2021, pp. 994–998 (2021). https://doi.org/10.1109/ICIP42928.2021.9506071
18. Stein, D., Fritzsche, K., Nolden, M., Meinzer, H., Wolf, I.: The extensible opensource rigid and affine image registration module of the medical imaging interaction toolkit (MITK). Comput. Methods Programs Biomed. **100**(1), 79–86 (2010). https://doi.org/10.1016/j.cmpb.2010.02.008
19. Zacharopoulos, A., et al.: A method for the registration of spectral images of paintings and its evaluation. J. Cult. Herit. **29**, 10–18 (2018). https://doi.org/10.1016/j.culher.2017.07.004

Virtualization and 3D Visualization of Historical Costume Replicas: Accessibility, Inclusivity, Virtuality

Angela Costello[1] , Kaitlyn Kingsland[1] , Bernice Jones[2],
and Davide Tanasi[1]([✉])

[1] Institute for Digital Exploration, University of South Florida, Tampa, FL, USA
dtanasi@usf.edu
[2] Archaeological Institute of American, Tampa Bay Society, FL, USA

Abstract. Digitization in cultural heritage has been established as an important method for research, preservation, documentation, and dissemination of knowledge. Largely this research has been done on archaeological sites and artifacts made of durable materials using a variety of 3d digitization methods, from digital photogrammetry to laser scanning to and structured light 3D scanning. One class of artefacts less interested by 3D visualization applications of that of ancient textiles. The perishable nature of these materials and consequently their limited availability in museum collections has not encouraged many studies, with the exception of some significant case studies of digital restoration and 3D capturing. This paper aims at critically revising the available 3D digitization and 3D visualization approaches for the study of ancient textiles and present an example of how such technology can be successfully used to achieve global digital dissemination of knowledge among the general public and that public affected by disabilities that can hinder the learning process. In the Spring of 2022, a team from the Institute for Digital Exploration (IDEx) at the University of South Florida (USF) scanned eight items from a collection of Minoan and Mycenaean garment replicas created by Dr. Bernice Jones, a unique collection, subject of several national and international exhibitions, that has become the primarily visual interpretative tool for the study of Minoan and Mycenaean fashion. Using structured light 3D scanning to generate accurate and realistic replicas, Augmented Reality (AR) and Virtual Reality solutions have been applied to create a digital companion for future exhibitions.

Keywords: structured light 3D scanning · Augmented Reality · Virtual Reality · accessibility · inclusivity

1 Introduction

The digitization of cultural heritage artifacts continues to expand and grow rapidly. Techniques of digital photogrammetry, laser scanning, and structured light 3D scanning are accepted methods of digitization of both archaeological

© Springer Nature Switzerland AG 2023
J.-J. Rousseau and B. Kapralos (Eds.): ICPR 2022 Workshops, LNCS 13645, pp. 122–130, 2023.
https://doi.org/10.1007/978-3-031-37731-0_10

sites and artifacts [17]. 3D modelling is also largely used to post-process the 3D data generated by those techniques and deliver results more suited for public outreach purposes [3].

Ancient textiles, however, profoundly differ from other classes of artifacts, due to their fragility and serious conservation issues, and for their study the usual digital methods are often applied from novels perspectives. 3D modelling protocols are used for the digital restoration of ancient textiles using dataset obtained via advanced image analyses [5], often in tandem with machine learning methods for automatic reconstruction of complex patterns [4]. Digital photogrammetry, according to a research study [18], is the most used 3D digitization techniques for the virtualization of historical costumes and ancient textiles for its main characteristic of generating highly-realistic digital replicas even of very intricately shaped examples [13]. Laserscanning technology is largely used in this case more to assess the capability of the devices on a challenging material than to generate new historical research [15], although the application of laser-based 3D profilometers to map the topography of woven fabrics, for example, bore significant results [14]. More promising are the application of structured light 3D scanning to case studies of historical or archaeological textiles. An attempt at establishing best practices in this case is the recent work conducted on the Emir of Bukhara's costume at the Samarkand State Historical-Architectural and Art Museum-Reserve in Samarkand, Uzbekistan [16], the first to illustrate a full methodology of practice and observations. Born as a test project to validate if structured-light scanning could be successful in creating 3D models of historic clothing, it focused on developing a comprehensive methodology to do so. While overcoming problems regarding display were improved on site, the authors of the research were still able to successfully complete the scanning within a limited time frame prior to the exhibition opening to the public. The main take-away of this seminal work is that, while earlier computer-aided design (CAD) projects were focused on manually modeling and had to determine appearance and apply it during post-processing, the use of structured-light scanning allows for the inclusion of this data, creating an accurate representation of the textile's color, texture, and overall appearance of the Emir of Bukhara's complete outfit.

While the effectiveness of the main 3D digitization and 3D visualization is unquestionable with respect to documentation and study of ancient textiles, less emphasis is given to the scientific literature on the potential that 3D models of historical costumes for public outreach. Against this scenario, this paper presents an example of how such technology can be successfully employed to achieve global digital dissemination of knowledge among the general public and that public affected by disabilities that can hinder the learning process, using as a case study the collection of Minoan and Mycenaean costume replicas created by Dr. Bernice Jones, a unique collection, subject of several national and international exhibitions, that has become the primarily visual interpretative tool for the study of Minoan and Mycenaean fashion. In particular, Augmented Reality (AR) and Virtual Reality solutions will be discussed.

2   Case Study: Minoan and Mycenean Dress Replicas

The collection used as case study was created by Dr. Bernice Jones, a trail-blazing expert in Aegean art and dress history. As part of her research, she has constructed dozens of replica costumes of the Minoan and Mycenean civilizations, and has displayed them in several important world venues, from the National Archaeological Museum of Athens, the Herakleion Museum in Crete, and the Hellenic Museum in Melbourne (Australia) in 2018 with the most recent exhibition at the Institute of Antiquity at the University of Graz (Austria) in 2022. Jones' work, as exemplified in the opening of her seminal monograph on the Bronze Age Minoan and Mycenean civilizations, "attempts to define and understand the construction of the garments, to seek foreign or indigenous sources for the designs, to chart influences abroad, to resolve issues of dating, and where possible to determine the significance of dress and its identification with roles of women" [10]. The Minoan and Mycenean garments reconstructed by Jones are based on artwork dating from 2000 to 1250 BCE on the islands of Crete, Thera (present-day Santorini), and on the Greek mainland. While there are no extant textile finds dating to this period, an astonishing archaeological record including a variety of figures, vases, and frescoes provided Jones with the bedrock to begin her study, coupled with a close investigation of nearby civilizations such as Egypt and the Near East. Each ensemble consisted of at least two parts: a robe or *heanos*, and a skirt, either a double-axe-shaped kilt, or tiered skirt in the case of the interpretation of the Snake Goddess figure. Additional features could be an apron, bolero jacket, headband, or belt to add additional texture. Each garment was based off of an extant archaeological find or iconographic source.

3   3D Digitization, Processing and Online Dissemination

In the Spring of 2022, members of the Institute for Digital Exploration (IDEx) at the University of South Florida (www.usf.edu/idex) 3D scanned eight costumes of the larger collection of replicas. Each garment was scanned using the Artec Eva structured light scanner and processed in Artec Studio 13 Professional. The costumes were placed according to historical and archaeological knowledge on mannequins which were placed in relevant poses for each garment (Fig. 1). Scans were captured using default settings. Post-processing work was done with Geomagic Wrap 2021.

The Artec Eva was operated at a distance of two to four feet depending on the detail needing to be captured. At this range, the scanner was able to successfully image stitches, lose fibers, sheer fabrics, and fringe. Some fringe and netting details were difficult to process, but the texture wrapping algorithm still managed to provide enough information, and the ability to zoom in on the models to the point of seeing visible weaving structure of the textile is exciting. The visible texture of twill tape used as embellishment rendered perfectly to the point where even an amateur sewist with a basic understanding of materials would be able to recognize it as twill (Fig. 2). Variations in hand-dyed fabrics

Fig. 1. IDEx member using the Artec Eva to 3D scan the Snake Goddess ensemble (left) and the Crocus Gatherer ensemble (right)

were clear and visible, and even gentle creases from garment storage, and gathers of material into belts and under the arm of the mannequin were picked up with ease (Fig. 3).

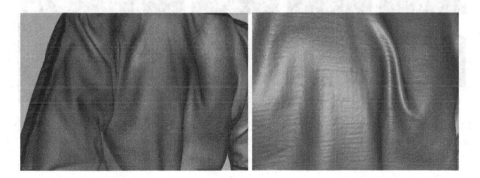

Fig. 2. Screenshots of the Crocus Gatherer ensemble showing the visible textile weaving structure of the in the mesh and texture

Once the processing of the 3D data was completed with Artec Studio 13, the eight 3d models of Minoan and Mycenaean garments were uploaded as a collection on IDEx account on the 3D cultural heritage oriented repository Sketchfab [8] (https://skfb.ly/ovXGq) for global digital dissemination, alongside archaeological metadata and technical paradata. The styled and accurately draped textiles can be found on the mannequins in the digital environment (Fig. 4).

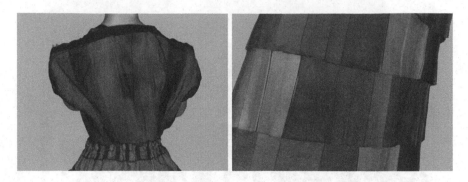

Fig. 3. Variation in the hand-dyed fabrics shown in the texture of the digitized Snake Goddess ensemble's blouse and skirt panels

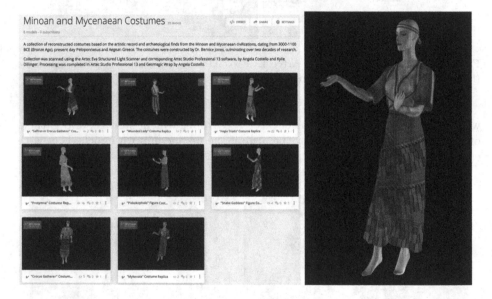

Fig. 4. Collection of the eight 3D scanned garments in the Sketchfab collection (left) and final 3D model of the Mykenaia ensemble (right)

4 Virtual Reality (VR) and Augmented Reality (AR) Applications

The availability of the 3D models of the garments allows for envisioning new communication strategies to reinforce the visual appeal of the exhibition and contributing to a more inclusive experience with less logistical implications. The design of VR and AR applications in a museum environment has in fact demonstrated the important role that those technologies can play with respect to public outreach.

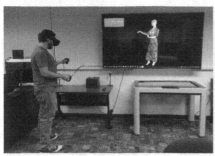 

Fig. 5. VR user experience with Oculus Rift (left) and AR visualization interface with Overly app on Android (right)

VR applications are on a growing trajectory in museum environments and for cultural tourism programs [11] thanks to the increased availability of low-cost headsets. Though AR user experiences are still hindered by the technological challenges of the BYOD practice (Bring Your Own Device) [12], their potential in terms of generating engagement across the spectrum of audience demographics is well known [1]. What makes VR and AR strongly appealing are also their effectiveness in enhancing the learning process in users with cognitive disabilities, a segment of the museum audience too often neglected by the mainstream communication strategies [2,9].

In order to provide a digital companion and more inclusive educational tool for the future exhibitions of the collection of Minoan and Mycenaean garments, it was chosen, for the online dissemination, to rely on Sketchfab for its popular VR-ready feature and the size limit for the 3D models that guarantees a smooth interaction with the 3D models even without internet broadband (Fig. 5). These models are accessible using VR via the Oculus Rift and, even using Google Cardboard, upon upload to Sketchfab. This basic tool on Sketchfab allows for the public to experience each costume to scale and to move around freely with the Oculus Rift headset. By providing this functionality, the VR experience provided with the online platform allow the user to more closely examine the garment and more organically interact with the object, producing higher levels of engagement.

With respect to AR, decimated versions in scale 1:1 of the eight digital replicas have been uploaded to the AR platform Overly (https://overlyapp.com) and linked to customized QR code for instant and ubiquitous visualization on mobile devices (Fig. 5). While this initiative requires the user to BYOD, the novelty and ability to place these QR codes within the museum settings allows for increased engagement with the garments that traditional displays do not allow [6]. Overly does require some dissemination in order to house these 3D models, however, seeing as the ability to view the models in AR is limited to whatever device the user has on hand at the time, it is likely that this will be done through a smartphone. Through using the texture files and normal maps, almost no information is lost and the AR experience is able to be run on most modern smartphones. Even though touch interaction in this AR platform is meditated through a digital screen, the public benefits from this ability to rotate, zoom, and examine the garment.

5   Conclusion

The ability to identify and capture minute details in the texture and mesh of the fabric proves incredibly valuable not only for researcher and conservators but also for the public. In terms of researchers and conservators, the ability to document the weaving structures, stitching, and overall condition of the fabrics provides a wealth of information. In examining weaving structures and stitching, researchers can provide a better hypothesis for how garments were constructed in historical periods, adding to or amending previous scholarship. For conservators, this information allows for a better ability to reconstruct and understand the garment construction and composition to enhance monitoring systems for decay or deterioration of the materials as well as to provide further understanding for reproduction if required. Similarly, the digital twins of fabrics provide an invaluable record for the fabric artifacts which are particularly vulnerable to decay. While the authors recognize that this collection is a series of reproductions based upon scholarship, the study demonstrates the value and ability for structured light scanning in documenting and digitally preserving textiles. These fragility of these materials makes them an ideal candidate for digitization. This record in the digital space produces information and a record of garments to assist in documentation and conservation as well as research and understanding of historic practices in the making of fabrics and clothes.

For the public, the digital models can be used for education, accessibility, and dissemination of knowledge. The history of fashion and dress is quite important in understanding culture and fabrics cannot, and indeed should not, be left out of the digitization movements in cultural heritage. These 3D objects can easily be zoomed in on, rotated, and examined at a much closer angle via public dissemination on websites such as Sketchfab, which also allows models to be embedded into different websites, such as virtual museum galleries. Additionally, the ability to fully rotate and explore the weaving structure of fabrics is engaging, as has been demonstrated with other archaeological materials in museums and educational spaces [7]. This increases accessibility to anybody with internet access, thus minimizing the need for expensive travel, or excessive handling of textile objects which can increase fragility. Additionally, objects that are too fragile for regular display can be digitized in a short period of time, minimizing further damage, as the light patterns from the scanner will only be in contact with the textile for an hour or less. It allows the public to better grasp how historic peoples lived while also allowing them to access the textile artifacts without risk of damaging the materials. Collections that may not have been able to be seen in person for years as a result of their deteriorating state can still be "displayed" virtually. Finally, the VR and AR developments of the virtual replicas of historical and archaeological garments can immensely contribute to share the knowledge about this peculiar class of artefacts to that disadvantaged public that often is left on the sidelines of the learning process, as this project has tried to point out.

References

1. Alelis, G., Bobrowicz, A., Ang, C.S.: Comparison of engagement and emotional responses of older and younger adults interacting with 3d cultural heritage artefacts on personal devices. Behav. Inf. Technol. **34**(11), 1064–1078 (2015). https://doi.org/10.1080/0144929X.2015.1056548
2. Bailey, B., Bryant, L., Hemsley, B.: Virtual reality and augmented reality for children, adolescents, and adults with communication disability and neurodevelopmental disorders: a systematic review. Rev. J. Autism Develop. Disord. **9**(2), 160–183 (2022) https://doi.org/10.1007/s40489-020-00230-x
3. Bentkowska-Kafel, A., MacDonald, L.: Digital Techniques for Documenting and Preserving Cultural Heritage, vol. 1. Arc Humanities Press, Leeds (2018)
4. Brown, L.P., Endruweit, A., Long, A., Jones, I.A.: Characterisation and modelling of complex textile geometries using texgen. IOP Conf. Ser. Mater. Sci. Eng. **406**, 012024 (2018). https://doi.org/10.1088/1757-899x/406/1/012024
5. Cybulska, M.: To See the Unseen: Computer Graphics in Visualisation and Reconstruction of Archaeological and Historical Textiles, pp. 213–228. IntechOpen, Rijeka (2012)
6. Di Giuseppantonio Di Franco, P., Camporesi, C., Galeazzi, F., Kallmann, M.: 3d printing and immersive visualization for improved perception of ancient artifacts. Presence **24**(3), 243–264 (2015). https://doi.org/10.1162/PRES_a_00229
7. Di Giuseppantonio Di Franco, P., Camporesi, C., Galeazzi, F., Kallmann, M.: 3d printing and immersive visualization for improved perception of ancient artifacts. Presence **24**(3), 243–264 (2015). https://doi.org/10.1162/PRES_a_00229
8. Flynn, T.: What Happens When You Share 3D Models Online (In 3D)?, vol. 3, pp. 73–86 (2019)
9. Jdaitawi, M.T., Kan'an, A.F.: A decade of research on the effectiveness of augmented reality on students with special disability in higher education. Contemp. Educ. Technol. **14**(1) (2022). https://doi.org/10.30935/cedtech/11369
10. Jones, B.R.: Ariadne's Threads The Construction and Significance of Clothes in the Aegean Bronze Age, vol. 38. Peeters Publishers (2019). https://doi.org/10.2307/j.ctv1q26qmh
11. Kang, Y., Yang, K.C.C.: Employing Digital Reality Technologies in Art Exhibitions and Museums: A Global Survey of Best Practices and Implications, Book Section 8, pp. 139–161. IGI Global, Hershey (2020). https://doi.org/10.4018/978-1-7998-1796-3.ch008
12. Marques, D., Costello, R.: Concerns and challenges developing mobile augmented reality experiences for museum exhibitions. Curator Museum J. **61**(4), 541–558 (2018). https://doi.org/10.1111/cura.12279
13. Marčiš, M., Barták, P., Valaška, D., Fraštia, M., Trhan, O.: Use of image based modelling for documentation of intricately shaped objects. Int. Arch. Photogramm. Remote Sens. Spatial Inf. Sci. **XLI-B5**, 327–334 (2016). https://doi.org/10.5194/isprs-archives-XLI-B5-327-2016, iSPRS-Archives

14. Matusiak, M.: Frącczak,: investigation of 3d woven fabric topography using laser-scanning. Fibres Text. Eastern Europe **26**(127), 81–88 (2018). https://doi.org/10.5604/01.3001.0010.7801
15. Montilla, M., Orjuela-Vargas, S., Philips, W.: State of the art of 3D scanning systems and inspection of textile surfaces, IS&T/SPIE Electronic Imaging, vol. 9018. SPIE (2014). https://doi.org/10.1117/12.2042552
16. Montusiewicz, J., Miłosz, M., Kęsik, J., Żyła, K.: Structured-light 3D scanning of exhibited historical clothing—a first-ever methodical trial and its results. Heritage Sci. **9**(1), 1–20 (2021). https://doi.org/10.1186/s40494-021-00544-x
17. Olson, B.R., Caraher, W.R.: Visions of Substance: 3D Imaging in Mediterranean Archaeology. The Digital Press @ The University of North Dakota, Grand Forks, North Dakota (2015)
18. Żyła, K., Kęsik, J., Santos, F., House, G.: Scanning of historical clothes using 3d scanners: comparison of goals, tools, and methods. Appl. Sci. **11**(12), 5588 (2021). https://doi.org/10.3390/app11125588

Datafication of an Ancient Greek City: Multi-sensorial Remote Sensing of Heloros (Sicily)

Davide Tanasi[1]([✉])(ID), Stephan Hassam[1](ID), Dario Calderone[2](ID),
Paolino Trapani[3], Nicola Lercari[2](ID), Gerardo Jiménez Delgado[4],
and Rosa Lanteri[5]

[1] University of South Florida, Institute for Digital Exploration (IDEx),
4202 E. Fowler Ave, Tampa, FL 33620, USA
dtanasi@usf.edu
[2] Ludwig Maximilian University of Munich, Institute for Digital Cultural Heritage
Studies, Geschwister-Scholl-Platz 1, Munich 80539, Germany
[3] Universitá di Catania, Dipartimento di Scienze Umanistiche, Piazza Dante
Alighieri, 24, Catania 95124, Italy
[4] Universidad Nacional Autónoma de México, Instituto de Investigaciones
Antropológicas,
Cto. Exterior, s/n Ciudad Universitaria, Ciudad de México 04510, Mexico
[5] Parco Archeologico e Paesaggistico di Siracusa, Eloro, Villa del Tellaro e Akrai,
Viale Teocrito 66, Siracusa 96100, Italy

Abstract. As 3D tools become increasingly used in archaeology and cultural heritage management, best practices are continuously developing to mediate their adoption. As part of an effort to revalorize the archaeological site of Heloros in southeastern Sicily, the authors have applied the concept of datafication to heuristically plan the approaches and objectives for its digitization. The process of datafication, i.e. the creation of new data through layered collection of natively digital and digitized legacy data, guided the collection of digital data aimed to consolidate archaeological and landscape data for the purposes of virtual reconstruction and planning of future interventions. The process of datafication, used here for the first time in a Mediterranean context led to the discovery of unpublished information about the previously excavated site of Heloros. Three-dimensional data were captured using terrestrial laser scanning, aerial and handheld photogrammetry, and integrated into a Geographic Information System to investigate and record the ancient Greek city of Heloros and individual elements of the site. Digitized legacy data were compared with the natively digital data of the site collected in 2021 and used to create a Digital Terrain Model. Bespoke GIS visualizations techniques were applied to identify as series of anomalies that were compared with legacy data. The preliminary results of this research led to the verification of hypotheses about the fortification system, previous excavation trenches, and the identification of possible further fortifications and unpublished use-phases of the site.

Keywords: Heloros · Greek Sicily · remote sensing · revalorization · datafication

© Springer Nature Switzerland AG 2023
J.-J. Rousseau and B. Kapralos (Eds.): ICPR 2022 Workshops, LNCS 13645, pp. 131–141, 2023.
https://doi.org/10.1007/978-3-031-37731-0_11

1   Introduction

The ancient Greek site of Heloros, named after the eponymous river (the modern Tellaro) and located south of Noto (Siracusa, Sicily) is mentioned only in passing in the historical sources. The excavations carried out in the early and mid-20th century unearthed a lively city in the Hellenistic period with fortification walls, a northern gate complex, a theater, the Sanctuary of Demeter, and some of the urban layout [24]. However, because the site has not been investigated with modern methods and lacks an authoritative publication, the potential to transform the park into a vessel for cultural heritage development is severely hindered and requires new investigations. Part of the Parco Archeologico e paesaggistico di Siracusa, Eloro, Villa del Tellaro e Akrai, the archaeological area of Heloros comprises about 10 hectares of gentle slopes overlooking the sea and beaches to the north and south. As part of the new investigations, it was decided to carry out a campaign of datafication that would serve both scientific and cultural purposes in the long run. The process of datafication, developed by Richards-Rissetto and Landau [19] and under continuous development [14], provides a reflexive practice for the planning, collection, and analysis of digital data with posterity in mind, allowing for multiple scales of analysis. In an effort to apply these principles in a Mediterranean context, various kinds of 2D and 3D digital data were collected in the summer of 2021 and inserted into a Geographic Information System (GIS) to better understand the urban layout of the ancient city, in the context of the HADES project (Heloros Advanced Digital Exploration and Surveying). Hundreds of low-altitude aerial photographs of Heloros' archaeological landscape were captured using an Unmanned Aerial System (UAS) and used to produce natively digital and derivative data through an Image-based Modeling pipeline. Hand-held digital photogrammetry (DP) and terrestrial laserscanning (TLS) were also employed to document specific features of the Sanctuary of Demeter and the North Gate city district. The integration of the native data and legacy data, its processing and translation into documentation about the site, and the application of visualization methods ultimately led to new discoveries.

1.1   Heloros

Greek colonization in the late 8th century BC was the beginning of centuries of strategic positioning of Greek city states on the eastern coast of Sicily. The most powerful of these, Syracuse, founded in 734 B.C., founded sub-colonies to extend its control and influence, including Akrai, Kasmenae, and Heloros. These sub-colonies, thought initially thought to have developed out of military encampments, became important city states in their own right, though they never left the shadow of their metropolis. The least well known of these is the city of Heloros, which is mentioned very little in ancient literary sources, and most often in conjunction with the river after which it was named [6]. Heloros is mentioned as a formal sub-colony of Syracuse [1], though the word "fortress" is used to describe it under Hiero II in the 3rd century BC. Positively identified by Paolo Orsi in 1899, excavations from that year and 1927, 1958–1959 and

1961 [17] revealed fortification walls, a theater and cult buildings located in the southern-western part of the hill and a vast cemeterial area dating to the 6th to 3rd centuries B.C. The site was subjected to new excavations between 1967 and 1980, for which several short reports were published [21–23] (Fig. 1). Research on the site has focused on the south-western sacred area, where at least two religious complexes attributed respectively to Demeter and Asclepios were investigated, and on the central sector of the hill, were a portion of the urban plan characterized by a possible small agora, intercepted by a major north-south axis (the *Helorine Odos* cited by the ancient sources) and a suburban sanctuary dedicated to Kore were also uncovered. More recently, new studies focused on the city's fortifications [12] and quarrying activity around the city [11]. The earliest finds from the site, Sikel Geometric and Proto-Corinthian cups, dating to the end of the 8th - beginning of the 7th century BC, and the irregular layout of the city led excavators to believe that the city was built around a holy road, though it could be evidence of an indigenous Greek settlement before it was transformed into a sub-colony [7]. Though the focus of all the investigations was on the ancient Greek periods of the city, a Byzantine *basilica* (Fig. 1) built over the sacred area and Paolo Orsi's mention of Roman *casupole* (huts) near the Northern Gate belie the long lasting settlement in the area and importance of the hill to the history of Sicily in this region [17].

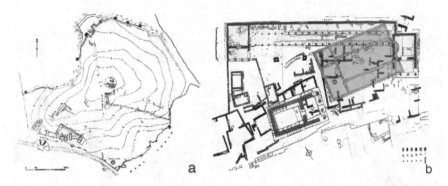

a   b

Fig. 1. Plan of the site (a); plan of the Sanctuary of Demeter with its main phases, red = Archaic, yellow = Hellenistic, blue = Byzantine (b) (after Voza 1999). (Color figure online)

2 Rationale

Due to a lack of resources, the archaeological area of Heloros has been inaccessible to the public for too long and repeatedly targeted by looters engaging in illegal excavation activities. There is an effort to revalorize the site through new investigations and dissemination of information among the general public. The previous excavations, while yielding a plan of the site and some chronological features, were never fully published and legacy data from the excavations are largely unavailable. It is therefore necessary to start anew with modern techniques. In 2021, University of South Florida's Institute for Digital Exploration

(IDEx; www.usf.edu/idex) signed an agreement with the Parco Archeologico di Siracusa, villa del Tellaro, Eloro e Akrai to conduct, in partnership with Ludwig-Maximilians-University of Munich to perform remote sensing surveys that would both update the current state of knowledge of the site and have the potential for creating an online presence for it. It was thus decided to carry out a campaign of datafication to generate new understandings and interpretations of the site.

2.1 Datafication

The topographical context of the hill of Heloros requires the use of modern digital methods. The archaeological site consists of a high number of ancient structures, the physiognomy of which, in certain cases, is made unclear by archaeological debris and thick vegetation. It was therefore necessary to isolate the various structural components in order to be able to analyze with precision the various parts of the walls with their relative phases that constitute the structure. Consequently, it was decided to use UAS and hand-held DP and TLS to create a digital 3D representation of some areas of the site (Fig. 2).

Fig. 2. Right: IDEx team employing a TLS to capture the Stoa in the south-western area of the Sanctuary of Demeter. Left: Geo-referencing points if the North Gate district.

3 Methods

3.1 Handheld Digital Photogrammetry

Well-established methods were followed in the planning process of the photogrammetric data capture of key points of the site [2]. Handheld photogrammetry was performed with a DSLR Canon Eos 2000D and a Sigma 10–20 mm f/4–5.6 EX DC HSM lens, set at a constant 10 mm with a focal aperture of f8. The wide-angle lens reduced the number of images generated making the subsequent phases of image processing and production of the 3d model less demanding in terms of time and computational power. Color correction and distortion correction were carried out with Adobe Lightroom Classic. Handheld DP was primarily used to 3D map a group of 51 architectural *disiecta membra* scattered in the sacred area, including column drums, cornices, foundation blocks with mason's marks and paneled ceiling elements, likely related with the *Stoa*, the major building of this part of the site, for future virtual anastylosis purposes (Fig. 3).

a   b

Fig. 3. Heloros Sanctuary of Demeter: foundation blocks with mason's marks (a); IDEx's Sketchfab collection for the 47 architectural disiecta membra (b)

A preliminary visualization of this aspect of the project can be found on an annotated 3D model of the sacred area with the links to the individual 51 3D models of the architectural elements in the IDEx's Sketchfab collection https://skfb.ly/oHyAW.

3.2   UAS Digital Photogrammetry

The capture of the site by aerial drone photogrammetry was based on established methods of aerial digital photogrammetry [8] using a DJI Phantom 4 PRO V2.0 drone. Photographs were taken in two data sets with multiple flights. The first dataset was captured from a height of 70 m covering the entire hill (about 12 ha). The second was captured from a height of 15m of altitude over the North Gate and Sanctuary of Demeter.

In the former area, this technique proved to be very effective for the mapping of a system of interconnected vats dug in the bedrock, located in the area comprised between the floor of the previously mentioned *Helorine Odos* and that of a novel secondary road, that will be discussed in the next section (Fig. 4) respectively to get more detailed images of those areas. To georeference the orthophoto and 3D model, selected control points were georeferenced using an Emlid Reach RS+ single-band RTK GNSS receiver [10]. The coordinates were used to insert the area into a GIS and create a DTM and the orthophotos were inserted into a GIS portal through which the detailed plans of the building, the road, and nearby structures were made.

Fig. 4. 3D model of the Northern Gate district made with drone photogrammetry. A system of interconnected vats dug in the bedrock, located in the area comprised between the Helorine Odos and that of a novel secondary road are highlighted.

3.3   Terrestrial Laser Scanning

Since drone photography is often unable to capture lower parts or overly shadowed parts of a structure, generating incomplete or overly sparse dense clouds, it was decided to employ terrestrial laser scanning for documentation and interpretative purposes [15]. In particular, such mapping techniques proved to be appropriate for the fortifications of the Northern Gate, where structures are taller than 2m and present complex masonry textures, and the Sanctuary of Demeter with its intricate overlay of architectural phases (Fig. 5). A Faro Focus M70 laser scanner was employed to capture 18 scans for the first area and 44 of the second one.

Fig. 5. 3D Point Cloud of the Sanctuary of Demeter obtained via terrestrial laserscanning.

4   Results and Discussion

With an eye towards pattern recognition this paper emphasizes the GIS-based visualization aspects of the research project and its related findings. As discussed below, the identification of novel features through one method were then able to be verified in other layers of data.

4.1   GIS-Based Visualization of Heloros' Landscape Features

Using low-altitude aerial photographs of Heloros' archaeological landscape that were captured by the UAS, we produced natively digital and derivative data through an Image-based Modeling pipeline. We created a Digital Terrain Model (DTM) (Fig. 6) of the site using the application Agisoft Metashape. In a GIS environment (QGIS 3.20.3), we transformed the DTM into GIS-based visualizations to improve the visual analysis of spatial features of interest related to archaeological resources. Using hill shading and various manipulations of the original DTM, we produced multiple visualizations that emphasize or smooth out features such as roads, paths, excavated features, defensive walls and gates, and other archaeological remains [13, 26]. Significantly, we applied a custom Local Relief Model (LRM) method to our DTMs [9] and obtained visualizations that isolate large landforms and buildings. We calculated the mean filter from the original DTM with an application radius of 50 pixels using the Whitebox Tools plug-in in QGIS. This low-pass filter was subtracted from our original DTM. The resulting LRM was combined with a slope model calculated in degrees. The latter was visualized in a palette of red or orange colors where the less pronounced slopes are displayed in light tones and the steepest in dark tones [14]. The fusion of both visualizations was produced in multiplication blending mode. Visually, the result is similar to the other visualization we produced using the Red Relief Image Map (RRIM), which is among the most common GIS-based visualization of archaeological airborne LiDAR data (Fig. 6). However, our custom Local Relief uses the LRM method to show positive and negative deviations to the surface trend instead of emphasizing concave and convex features of the relief as in the RRIM technique [5,25], allowing for the identification of new features marked in Fig. 4a as area 1 and 2.

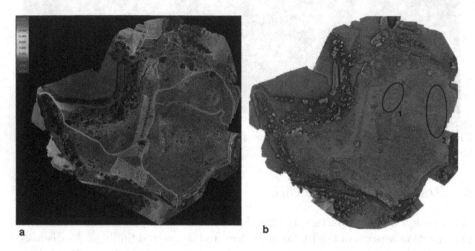

a   b

Fig. 6. GIS visualizations of Heloros: Digital Terrain Model (a); visualization obtained using custom Local relief blending a Slope Map with Local relief Model, areas 1 and 2 highlight the features identified (b).

4.2   Novel Archaeological Features and Old Issues

The 2021 remote sensing survey at Heloros, four decades after the last fieldwork campaign, focused primarily on 3D mapping the hill where the site is located and, at a smaller scale, the North Gate district and the area of the Sanctuary of Demeter characterized by the binomial temple of the goddess and Stoa.

The cataloguing and virtualization of the 47 scattered architectural elements in the sacred area via hand-held digital photogrammetry is the first step towards a reconstructive study of the Stoa aided by virtual anastylosis exercises [3]. The distribution pattern of those elements, some distance from the monument and on the periphery of the sacred area plateau, informs us about the occurrence of major natural and artificial events that took places in the post-classical era and contributed to the current poor conservation state of the Stoa. The above-mentioned Sketchfab platform will be critical for the interpretation of those patterns and will lay the foundation for tentative virtual reconstructions.

The identification and mapping via drone photogrammetry of the system of interconnected vats, previously unknown, is an important novelty that shares light on the post-Greek phases of life on the site. These installations should be interpreted as a grape-pressing facility which have comparisons everywhere in Sicilian countryside. Facilities of this type seem to have been excavated and used with minimal architectural and technical changes from the end of the Greek Classical period to the eleventh century CE [16], though they can be tentatively linked to the late antique and Byzantine periods, when formerly populated areas were reused for productive purposes, and when the climax of the presence of such facilities occurred [18]. A similar installation, likely dated to Roman era, was found in the territory of Noto (Siracusa) in Cava Cardinale-I Tre Fiumi and in the localities of Aguglia and Case Stallaini [20]. The reference offered by Orsi about Roman poor huts located in the area of the North Gate may offer good support for contextualizing this novel wine-pressing facility in the late Roman era. While that reference does not date the structures securely, and awaits further study, this minor discovery delivers on the effectiveness of the processes of datafication.

The application of the Red Relief Image Map and of a custom Local relief blending a Slope Map with Local relief Model visualizations methods on the DTM of the hill generated from the drone photogrammetry 3D model has allowed the identification of new features (Fig. 6b). In area 1, it is possible to identify a series of five irregular pits, located at a regular distance, that are not indicated in any of the prior excavation documentation produced and that are not directly linked with any known archaeological feature. It is very likely that those pits were dug by looters operating in that district of the ancient city, a hypothesis that, if supported by ground-truthing, would prove the effective application of the methodological approach presented in this paper for monitoring archaeological sites endangered by illegal excavations sponsored by criminal enterprises [4]. Of a different nature are the features observable in area 2, where large curvilinear cuts are visible, recalling excavations related to a defensive ditch or trench that could have been built during World War II. In this case, more importantly than the others, ground-truthing is required and has been already planned to be conducted in Summer 2022.

5 Conclusion

The process of datafication of an archaeological site, especially one as large and complex as Heloros, is an advance in archaeological methods for investigating large sites. Planning data capture through the lens of datafication led to the integration of multiple sources of remote sensing data that permitted the identification of anomalies and retrace older excavations, preparing the site for further investigation and ground truthing. Future campaigns seek to add additional layers of data to the datafication of the site, including LiDAR data collected with an UAS and Ground Penetrating Radar investigations to collect data on buried anomalies that will prepare the site for archaeological investigation. Significantly, this project has generated data that can be used for a myriad of applications in pattern recognition. Additionally, the potential to test reconstruction hypotheses virtually can now be done in a geolocated environment without materially affecting the site.

References

1. Diodorus Siculus. Library of History, 23.4.1
2. Sapirstein, P., Murray, S.: Establishing best practices for photogrammetric recording during archaeological fieldwork. J. Field Archaeol. **42**(4), 337–350 (2017)
3. Bennoui-Ladraa, B., Chennaoui, Y.: Use of photogrammetry for digital surveying, documentation and communication of the cultural heritage. Example regarding virtual reconstruction of the access doors for the nameless Temple of Tipasa (Algeria). Stud. Digit. Heritage **2**(2), 121–137 (2018). https://doi.org/10.14434/sdh.v2i2.24496
4. Ceschi, G.: Il ruolo della criminalita' organizzata nel traffico illecito di opere d'arte. Rivista di Studi e Ricerche sulla Criminalita' Organizzata **5**(3), 6–36 (2019)
5. Chiba, T., Kaneta, S.I., Suzuki, Y.: Red relief image map: new visualization method for three dimensional data. Int. Arch. Photogram. Remote Sens. Spat. Inf. Sci. **XXXVII**(B2), 1071–1076 (2008)
6. Copani, F.: Alle origini di eloro. l'espansione meridionale di siracusa arcaica. Acme: annali della Facoltà di lettere e filosofia dell'Università degli studi di Milano **58**(2), 245–264 (2005)
7. Copani, F.: 2. greci e indigeni ad eloro. In: Tréziny, H. (ed.) Grecs et indigènes de la Catalogne à la Mer Noire, pp. 689–693. Éditions Errance (2010)
8. Ferrari, V., Gaucci, P., Merico, A.: The use of drones in aerial archaeology. In: Ceraudo, G. (ed.) Studi Di Aerotopografia Archeologica, pp. 66–68. Claudio Grenzi Editoree (2015)
9. Hesse, R.: Using LiDAR-derived local relief models (LRM) as a new tool for archaeological prospection. In: Kluiving, S., Guttmann-Bond, E. (eds.) Landscape Archaeology between Art and Science, pp. 369–378. Amsterdam University Press, Amsterdam (2012)
10. Hill, A.C., Limp, F., Casana, J., Laugier, E.J., Williamson, M.: A new era in spatial data recording: low-cost GNSS. Adv. Archaeol. Pract. **7**(2), 169–177 (2019). https://doi.org/10.1017/aap.2018.50
11. Idà, L.: Eloro e la sua pietra. Cronache di Archeologia **38**, 217–230 (2019)
12. Karlsson, L.: Fortification Towers and Masonry Techniques in the Hegemony of Syracuse, 405–211 B.C., vol. 4 (1992)
13. Kokalj, Ž., Zakşek, K., Oštir, K.: Visualizations of lidar derived relief models. In: Opitz, R.S., Cowley, D. (eds.) Interpreting Archaeological Topography, pp. 100–114. Oxbow Books (2013)
14. Lercari, N., et al.: Building cultural heritage resilience through remote sensing: an integrated approach using multi-temporal site monitoring, datafication, and Web-GL visualization. Remote Sens. **13**(20), 4130 (2021). https://doi.org/10.3390/rs13204130
15. Chapman, H., Baldwin, E., Moulden, H., Lobb, M.: More than just a sum of the points: re-thinking the value of laser scanning data. In: Ch'ng, E., Gaffney, V., Chapman, H. (eds.) Visual Heritage in the Digital Age. SSCC, pp. 15–31. Springer, London (2013). https://doi.org/10.1007/978-1-4471-5535-5_2

Datafication of an Ancient Greek City   141

16. Magro, T., Scaravilli, M.: I palmenti rupestri nella valle dell'alcantara. In: Congiu, M., Miccichè, C., Modeo, S. (eds.) Cenabis bene. L'alimentazione nella Sicilia Antica, pp. 99–111. Edizioni Lussografica, Caltanissetta (2019)
17. Orsi, P., Curro, M.T., Militello, E., Piscione, V.: Eloro I–IV, Monumenti Antichi dei Lincei XLVII (1965)
18. Patti, D.: La facies rupestre nella sicilia centrale: aspetti metodologici e prospettive di ricerca. Mediaeval Sophia 13, 218–240 (2013)
19. Richards-Rissetto, H., Landau, K.: Digitally-mediated practices of geospatial archaeological data: transformation, integration, and interpretation. J. Comput. Appl. Archaeol. 2(1), 120–135 (2019)
20. Cugno, S.A.: Archeologia rupestre nel Territorio di Siracusa. BAR Publishing, Oxford (2020)
21. Voza, G.: L'attività della Soprintendenza alla antichità della Sicilia Orientale. Kokalos XIV–XV, 357–364 (1968–1969)
22. Voza, G.: L'attività della Soprintendenza alla antichità della Sicilia Orientale. Kokalos XVIII–XIX, 161–192 (1972–1973)
23. Voza, G.: L'attività della Soprintendenza alla antichità della Sicilia Orientale. Kokalos XXVI–XXVII, 674–693 (1980–1981)
24. Voza, G.: Nel segno dell'antico. Arnaldo Lombardi Editore, Palermo (1999)
25. Yokoyama, R., Shirasawa, M., Pike, R.J.: Visualizing topography by openness: a new application of image processing to digital elevation models. Photogramm. Eng. Remote. Sens. 68(3), 257–266 (2002)
26. Ştular, B., Kokalj, Ž., Oštir, K., Nuninger, L.: Visualization of lidar-derived relief models for detection of archaeological features. J. Archaeol. Sci. 39(11), 3354–3360 (2012). https://doi.org/10.1016/j.jas.2012.05.029

Geolocation of Cultural Heritage Using Multi-view Knowledge Graph Embedding

Hebatallah A. Mohamed[1]([✉]), Sebastiano Vascon[1,2]([✉]), Feliks Hibraj[2],
Stuart James[3], Diego Pilutti[1], Alessio Del Bue[3], and Marcello Pelillo[1,2]

[1] European Center for Living Technology (ECLT), Ca' Foscari University of Venice,
Venice, Italy
{hebatallah.mohamed,sebastiano.vascon}@unive.it
[2] Department of Environmental Sciences, Informatics and Statistics (DAIS), Ca'
Foscari University of Venice, Venice, Italy
[3] Pattern Analysis and Computer Vision (PAVIS), Istituto Italiano di Tecnologia,
Genova, Italy

Abstract. Knowledge Graphs (KGs) have proven to be a reliable way of
structuring data. They can provide a rich source of contextual information about cultural heritage collections. However, cultural heritage KGs
are far from being complete. They are often missing important attributes
such as geographical location, especially for sculptures and mobile or
indoor entities such as paintings. In this paper, we first present a framework for ingesting knowledge about tangible cultural heritage entities
from various data sources and their connected multi-hop knowledge into
a geolocalized KG. Secondly, we propose a multi-view learning model for
estimating the relative distance between a given pair of cultural heritage
entities, based on the geographical as well as the knowledge connections
of the entities.

Keywords: Cultural heritage · Geolocation · Knowledge graphs ·
Multi-view graph embedding

1 Introduction

The term cultural heritage includes tangible heritage, which can be further specified in *i)* movable (such as paintings, sculptures, coins); *ii)* immovable (such as
monuments, archaeological sites), and intangible heritage, such as traditions and
performing arts [7]. Preparing cultural heritage collections for exploration by a
wide range of users with different backgrounds requires to integrate heterogeneous data into modern information systems.

Knowledge graphs (KGs) have proven to be a reliable way of structuring
data in wide range of domains, including the cultural heritage domain [8,10].
KGs, such as Wikidata [17], are large directed network of real-world entities
and relationships between them, where facts are represented as triplets in the
form of (*head entity, relation, tail entity*). They enable to connect knowledge

J.-J. Rousseau and B. Kapralos (Eds.): ICPR 2022 Workshops, LNCS 13645, pp. 142–154, 2023.
https://doi.org/10.1007/978-3-031-37731-0_12

about cultural heritage collections, and enrich this knowledge with external data coming from heterogeneous sources.

A key challenge for KGs is the human annotation required, resulting in them remaining incomplete. Many general purpose KGs, such as Wikidata [17], are missing latitude and longitude coordinates for the entities representing tangible cultural heritage (especially the movable ones). In this paper, we present a method for estimating the relative distance between a given pair of cultural heritage entities in a KG. In particular, we propose a joint learning model to learn comprehensive and representative entity embeddings, based on entity geographical location and semantics. Moreover, we present a framework for ingesting city cultural heritage from multiple general purpose data sources into a geolocalized KG.

In brief, our main contributions are as follows:

- We present an ingestion tool and related system framework to create a geolocalized KG for cultural heritage exploration, by ingesting data from heterogeneous data sources based on city coordinates. The tool is based on Neo4j[1] graph-database and is published as open source on GitHub[2].
- We introduce new KG datasets for the geolocation prediction task, with a KG containing both spatial and non-spatial entities and relations.
- We propose a method that introduces a geospatial distance restriction to refine the embedding representations of geographic entities in a geolocalized KG, which fuses geospatial information and semantic information into a low-dimensional vector space. We then utilize this method for estimating the geographical distance between cultural heritage entities, where we outperform state-of-the-art methods.

2   Related Work

In this section, we discuss work related to cultural heritage KGs, and geolocation using KGs.

2.1   KGs for Cultural Heritage

There are some works that have proposed to use KGs to support cultural heritage exploration. For example, Pellegrino et al. have proposed [8], a general-purpose approach to perform Question-Answering on KGs for querying data concerning cultural heritage. They have assessed the system performance on domain-independent KGs such as Wikidata [17] and DBpedia [1]. The authors of [10] have proposed a semantic graph-based recommender system of cultural heritage places, by modeling a graph representing the semantic relatedness of cultural heritage places using tags extracted from the descriptive content of the places from Wikipedia[3].

---

[1] https://neo4j.com/.
[2] https://github.com/MEMEXProject/MEMEX-KG.
[3] https://www.wikipedia.org/.

In addition, there are some existing cultural heritage specific KGs, related to particular places or historical collections. For example, ArCO [2] is a KG that provides ontology to link people, events, and places about Italian artifacts and document collections. ArCO has been created from different data sources, including general purpose KGs such as Wikidata and DBpedia. Linked Stage Graph [14] which organizes and interconnects data about the Stuttgart State Theaters. ArDO [18] is an ontology to represent the dynamics of annotations of general archival resources. In our work, we propose a system framework for ingesting knowledge about any city cultural heritage using heterogeneous data coming from Wikidata [17], and any other geolocalized linked open data (LOD) such as Europeana [3], into a geolocalized KG.

2.2   Geolocation Using KGs

There have been only few works that have focused on the task of geographical KG construction. The Guo et al. have proposed GeoKG [4], a system framework for extracting geographical knowledge from geographic datasets and represent the knowledge by means of concepts and relations with the aid of GeoSPARQL[4]. However, this work has focused on specific semantic relationships such as *subclass_of* or *instance_of* to describe the subclass concepts of the geographical entities, such as *river* and *railway station*. In our work, we aim at constructing a geolocalized KG where tangible cultural heritage entities can be represented with richer semantic relations, such as *architectural_style*, *architect* and *exhibited_at*.

Moreover, there are works that focused on geographical KG completion and location prediction. For example, the authors of [11] have proposed a translational embedding model that has the ability to capture and embed the geospatial distance restriction with the semantic information of the geographical KG into a vector space. Then, the optimized model outputs the refined representations of geo-entities and geo-relations, which improves the completion performance on the sparse geographical KG. However, this work does not consider the existence of non geo-entity and non geo-relations in the KG. In our work, we aim at predicting the distance between two entities in a KG that contains both geographical and non-geographical entities and relations.

3   Data Curation for Geolocalized Knowledge Graph

In this section, we discuss details about our developed ingestion tool, and the related system framework for ingesting data about a given city and the cultural heritage it contains into a geolocalized KG.

---

[4] http://www.opengis.net/ont/geosparql.

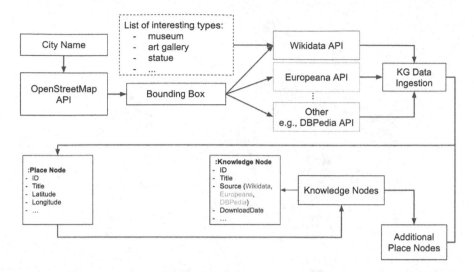

Fig. 1. Information extraction workflow.

3.1 Data Sources

In this work, Wikidata[5] and Europeana[6] have been selected for enriching our geolocalized KG, however other general purpose KGs and LOD can be incorporated. Wikidata is a public crowd-sourced knowledge base, with facts and figures about tens of millions of items (93,207,191). The data are offered freely, with no restriction on the reuse and modification (Creative Commons Zero). Wikidata provides its data openly in an easy to use standard Resource Description Framework (RDF). It provides much of its data in hundreds of languages. Already, large amounts of data about cultural assets are being shared with Wikidata by formal partnerships with Galleries, Libraries, Archives and Museums (GLAMS).

On the other hand, Europeana aims to facilitate the usage of digitized cultural heritage resources from and about Europe [5]. It seeks to enable users to access content in all European languages via the Europeana collections portal and allow applications to use cultural heritage metadata via its open APIs. Europeana holds metadata from over 3,700 providers [3], mostly GLAMS. However, it uses a strictly federated ontology limiting the diversity of the meta-data.

3.2 Information Extraction Workflow

We propose a localized approach that grows a KG based on association to known landmarks. We define two types of KG nodes: *Place* and *Knowledge*. The former represents tangible data while the latter represents intangible data. As shown in Fig. 1, first, we use OpenStreetMap (OSM)[7] to get the bounding box of the

---

[5] https://www.wikidata.org/.
[6] https://www.europeana.eu/.
[7] https://www.openstreetmap.org/.

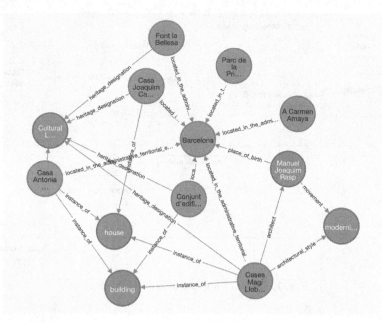

Fig. 2. A subset of our geolocalized KG (orange nodes are *Knowledge* and cyan ones are *Places*). (Color figure online)

target city. Then coordinates are used to query Wikidata to retrieve geo-entities within the selected scope, using Wikidata *coordinate_location (P625)* attribute. Moreover, a list of interesting entity types can be predefined by the user, to allow the ingestion tool to focus on specific cultural heritage related entities. We use the Wikidata *instance_of (P31) and subclass_of (P279)* attributes to select entities with specific types. These form the basis of our *Places* (node type is *Place*) where related additional properties are downloaded.

From each of the identified *Places*, we then query associated nodes based on all relations from Wikidata, this new set of nodes we refer to as *Knowledge*. This could be for example, the architect of a building. We repeat this step searching for new relationships a predefined number of times referred to as hops. We use the same approach to ingest data from Europeana. For a given city, we retrieve its coordinates using OSM, then a query is performed against Europeana API to identify content within the GPS region to add nodes in the KG. Figure 2 shows a small subset of our geolocalized KG.

3.3   NER for Data Integration

We utilize Named Entity Recognition (NER) technique in order to link KG entities from different sources of information. More precisely, we use spaCy[8], a

---

[8] https://www.spacy.io/.

Table 1. Named entity types used to integrate data from different sources.

Type	Meaning
GPE	Geopolitical entity, i.e., countries, cities, states
LOC	Non-GPE locations, mountain ranges, bodies of water
FAC	Buildings, airports, highways, bridges, etc
PER	People, including fictional ones

Python library with wide linguistic features. SpaCy annotates text with different types of named entities. We focus on the types listed in Table 1. For each entity ingested from Europeana, we apply NER to extract named entities from the title of Europeana entity. Then, we match those extracted named entities with the titles of Wikidata entities. If there is a match found, we create a relation (we name it *related_to*) between the matching Europeana and Wikidata entities. For example, when applying NER on a Europeana entity titled *"Carmen Amaya's last dance"*, the named entity *"Carmen Amaya"* of type PER will be extracted, and the Europeana entity will be linked to the entity titled *"A Carmen Amaya"* from Wikidata in the KG.

4 Geolocation Using Multi-view Graph Embedding

Given a geolocalized KG G, composed of a large number of triples in the form of *(head entity, relation, tail entity)*. All entities have associated type $\in \{Place,$ $Knowledge\}$, title $S = [w_1, w_2, ..., w_n]$ with n words. Additionally, most of the *Place* entities have a latitude and longitude information. From our KG we aim to predict the distance d_t between any two *Place* entities, u and v, where the latitude and longitude property is missing in at least one of those entities (i.e., the distance between is unknown). To achieve this, we propose a method to construct two types of *Place* entity correlations: 1) based on the geographical view using the *Place* nodes, and 2) based on entity semantics using the *Knowledge* nodes. An overview about our proposed approach is shown in Fig. 3, and more details are described in the following sections.

4.1 Geographical View

The geographical view aims at capturing the geographical relation between two geo-entities, *Places*, in the KG. To represent this view, we extract an induced subgraph around the two target entities. The subgraph represent how the two geo-entities are connected to each other, in terms of direct links or common nodes between the two target nodes. Since we are focusing on geographical view, we restrict the common nodes to *Place* node type. We then embed the extracted subgraph with a relational graph convolution network (R-GCN) [13] to represent the geographical relation between the target entities. In more details, we perform the following steps 1. Subgraph Extraction (Sect. 4.1), and 2. Node Representation (Sect. 4.1).

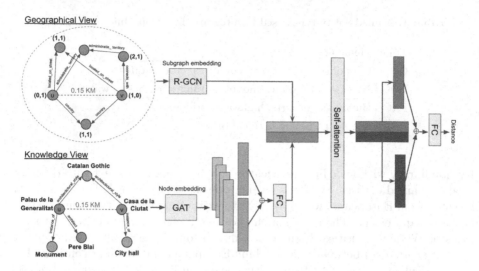

Fig. 3. The proposed approach for geographical location prediction.

Subgraph Extraction. We assume that the paths (i.e., geo-entities and geo-relations) on the KG connecting the two target nodes contain the information that could imply the distance between the two target entities. Hence, as a first step, we extract an enclosing subgraph around the target nodes. The enclosing subgraph between nodes u and v is the graph induced by all the nodes that occur on a path between u and v. The subgraph set is given by the intersection of neighbors of the two target nodes followed by a pruning procedure.

More precisely, let $N_k(u)$ and $N_k(v)$ be set of nodes in the k-hop (undirected) neighborhood of the two target nodes in the KG. We compute the enclosing subgraph by taking the intersection, $N_k(u) \cap N_k(v)$, of these k-hop neighborhood sets and then prune nodes that are isolated or at a distance greater than k from either of the target nodes. This results in all the nodes that occur on a path of length at most $k + 1$ between nodes u and v, where we refer to it as the induced subgraph $G(u, v)$.

Node Representation. We define an embedding for each entity (node) in the subgraph $G(u, v)$. Following [20], each node i in the subgraph is labeled with the tuple $(d(i, u), d(i, v))$, where $d(i, u)$ is the shortest distance between nodes i and u (likewise for $d(i, v)$). The two target nodes, u and v, are labeled $(0, 1)$, and $(1, 0)$ to be identifiable by the model. This scheme captures the position of each node in the subgraph with respect to the target nodes, as shown in Fig. 3. The node features are defined as $[\text{one-hot}(d(i, u)) \oplus \text{one-hot}(d(i, v))]$, representing the concatenation of the one-hot embedding of the labels.

Geographical View Embedding. We use multiple layers of the multi-relational R-GCN [13] to learn the embeddings of the extracted subgraph $G(u, v)$.

R-GCN adopts general message-passing scheme [19], where a node representation is iteratively updated by combining it with the aggregation of its neighbors' representation. The subgraph representation of $G(u,v)$ is obtained by average-pooling of all the node representations: In the k-th layer of our graph neural network (GNN), a_i^k represents the aggregated message from the neighbors of node i. The aggregation function is defined as:

$$a_i^k = \sum_{r=1}^{R} \sum_{s \in N_r(i)} \alpha_{r(s,i)}^k W_r^k h_s^{k-1}, \tag{1}$$

where R is the total number of unique relations, $N_r(i)$ represents the neighbors of node i under relation r, W_r^k is the transformation matrix of the k-th layer over relation r, and $\alpha_{r(s,i)}$ is the edge attention weight at the k-th layer corresponding to the edge between nodes s and i via relation r.

The latent representation of node i in the k-th layer is:

$$h_i^k = ReLU(W_0^k h_i^{k-1} + a_i^k), \tag{2}$$

where W_0 aims at retaining the information of the node itself using self-connection, and $ReLU$ is an activation function.

The subgraph representation of $G(u,v)$ is obtained by average-pooling of all the node representations:

$$h_{G(u,v)}^L = \frac{1}{|V|} \sum_{i \in V} h_i^L, \tag{3}$$

where V denotes the set of nodes in $G(u,v)$, and L represents the number of layers of message-passing.

4.2   Knowledge View

The knowledge view aims at representing the semantic relation between two target geo-entities, *Places*, in the KG, by means of their surrounding *Knowledge* nodes. We employ a graph attention network (GAT) [16] for representing each target entity semantics based on entity textual title. Then, we concatenate the representation of the two target entities and pass the concatenated representation into a linear layer. In more details, as with Geographical View, we perform: 1. Node Representation (Sect. 4.2), and 2. Node Embedding (Sect. 4.2).

Node Representation. For each node in G with title $S = [w_1, w_2, ..., w_n]$ (n is different for each node since each title might have different length), we initialize the embedding of each word w with a pre-trained word vector from GloVe [9]. Let p denote the dimension of each word vector. We obtain the sentence representation $\overrightarrow{S}$ by aggregating the embedding of each word, where $\overrightarrow{S} \in \mathbb{R}^p$. In aggregation, we use only simple averaging due to its validity [21].

Node Embedding. We employ a GAT to learn representations of nodes. GAT applies attention mechanism on graph-structured data. It updates the representation of a vertex by propagating information to its neighbors, where the weights of its neighbor nodes is learned by attention mechanism automatically. Formally, given the input vertex features $\left\{\vec{S_1}, \vec{S_2}, \ldots, \vec{S_n}\right\}$, a GAT layer updates the vertex representations by following steps:

$$e_{ij} = \exp\left(ReLU\left(a^T\left[W_k\vec{S_i} \oplus W_k\vec{S_j}\right]\right)\right) \tag{4}$$

$$\alpha_{ij} = softmax_j\left(e_{ij}\right) = \frac{\exp\left(e_{ij}\right)}{\sum_{k \in N_i} \exp\left(e_{ik}\right)} \tag{5}$$

$$h'_i = \sigma\left(\sum_{j \in N_i} \alpha_{ij} W_k h_j\right) \tag{6}$$

where W_k and a are learnable parameters, $\oplus$ is the concatenation operation.

Knowledge View Embedding. After calculating the embedding of each node in the graph, we concatenate the embeddings of the target entities, u and v. Then, we pass these concatenated representations through a linear layer, given by

$$h_{u,v} = [h'_u \oplus h'_v]W_s, \tag{7}$$

where $\oplus$ refers to the concatenation operation, and W_s is a learnable weight parameter.

4.3 Multi-view Embedding

In order to enable the cooperation among the different views during the learning process and effectively fuse multi-view representations, our model enables information sharing across all views via a scaled dot-product self-attention [15]. Given the representations from the different views as $\{\mathcal{E}_i\}_{i=1}^2$, we stack them into a matrix $X \in \mathbb{R}^{2 \times d}$ of dimension d. We associate query, key and value matrices Q, K and V as follows:

$$Q = XW_Q, \quad K = XW_K, \quad V = XW_V \tag{8}$$

where W_Q, W_K and W_V are weight matrices. We then propagate information among all views as follows:

$$Y = softmax\left(\frac{QK^T}{\sqrt{d_k}}\right)V \tag{9}$$

$\hat{\mathcal{E}}_i$ will then be the i-th row in matrix Y, which considered as the relevant global information for i-th view. To incorporate this information in the learning process, we concatenate the representations of the different views (geographical and

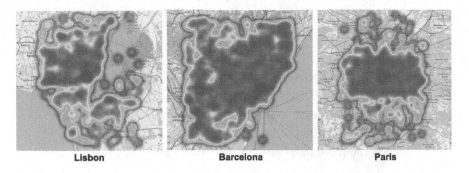

Lisbon   Barcelona   Paris

Fig. 4. Visualization of tangible cultural heritage on the map.

knowledge views) and pass it to a fully connected (FC) layer, to predict the distance $\hat{d}_t$ as follows:

$$\hat{d}_t = [\hat{\mathcal{E}}_1 \oplus \hat{\mathcal{E}}_2]W_m, \tag{10}$$

where $\oplus$ refers to the concatenation operation, and W_m is a learnable weight parameter.

4.4 Learning Objective

Given the ellipsoidal shape of the earth's surface, we apply the Haversine distance [12] to calculate the distance of two points represented by their latitude in range of $\{-90, 90\}$ and longitude in range of $\{-180, 180\}$. The Haversine distance is the great circle distance between two geographical coordinate pairs. We train our model to reduce the Mean Squared Error (MSE) loss based on the actual and predicted Haversine distance, d_t and $\hat{d}_t$.

5 Experiments

5.1 Datasets

In order to evaluate our model, we create three datasets using our ingestion tool described in Sect. 3. The datasets are about tangible (*Place*) and *Knowledge* of three main cities in Europe: Lisbon, Barcelona and Paris.

We set the number of hops to 3, since 3-hop contains sufficient information about each tangible cultural heritage entity. Statistics about the datasets, including the maximum distance between geo-entites representing cultural heritage related places are shown in Table 2. The maximum distance between the places in Barcelona dataset is less than in Lisbon and Paris. Lisbon dataset is the most challenging since it contains fewer number of nodes and relations. Moreover, Lisbon has the highest maximum distance between places. In Fig. 4, we visualise the location of the tangible cultural heritage of the different cites. We randomly split the links between *Places* into 80% and 20% sets with corresponding distances for training and testing, respectively. Hyper-parameters are optimised for the training set.

Table 2. Statistics of the city datasets.

	Lisbon	Barcelona	Paris
#*Place* Nodes	2,780	5,989	26,214
#*Knowledge* Nodes	5,860	9,140	35,885
#Links	21,253	37,384	196,898
#Relation types	377	708	578
#*Place-Place* links	5,077	6,907	48,954
Maximum distance	35.32 KMs	16.76 KMs	34.69 KMs

5.2 Baselines and Implementation Details

We compare our model against GAT [16] and R-GCN [13] as baselines when textual title of the *Place* and *Knowledge* nodes are used for message-passing to generate node embeddings. We also evaluate our model when using only the geographical view (Ours - geographical), utilizing enclosing subgraph embeddings with R-GCN. Moreover, we experiment our model without the attention layer (Ours - without att).

The latent embedding sizes used in all our models are set to 32. We set the number of layers in GAT and R-GCN to 3. To train our model, we use Adam optimizer [6] with a learning rate of 1e-4. We run our experiments on a machine with two Intel Xeon Gold 6230 CPUs running at 2.10 GHz with 128 GB of memory, and Nvidia Quadro RTX 5000 GPU with 16 GB of memory. Finally, we use Mean Absolute Error (MAE) and Root Mean Square Error (RMSE) to measure the prediction errors.

5.3 Results

In Table 3, we present the results of the different prediction methods in terms of MAE and RMSE. As shown, our proposed method outperform other baseline methods. Best results are achieved on Barcelona dataset, since the maximum distance between the places is less than the one in Lisbon and Paris.

The results show that GAT is outperforming R-GCN when applying the message-passing technique on the whole KG for extracting node embeddings. This indicates that GAT is able to focus on certain neighbors to represent a *Place* node due to its attention mechanism. However, when applying R-GCN on enclosing subgraphs (Ours - geographical), the performance is outperforming the R-GCN baseline since the model is focusing on fewer unique relation types representing the spatial relation. Finally, the results show that applying an attention layer helps to fuse the multiple views in our proposed model.

Table 3. The results showing MAE and RMSE of Haversine distance in km. Best results are in **Bold**.

	Lisbon		Barcelona		Paris	
	MAE	RMSE	MAE	RMSE	MAE	RMSE
GAT	1.95	2.64	1.43	1.87	0.70	1.23
R-GCN	2.30	3.12	1.48	1.90	1.21	1.63
Ours - geographical	2.23	3.10	0.48	0.75	0.83	1.42
Ours - without att	2.13	2.86	0.56	0.86	0.67	1.20
Ours	**1.90**	**2.50**	**0.42**	**0.71**	**0.59**	**1.05**

6 Conclusion

We present an ingestion tool and a framework to create a geolocalized KG for contextualising cultural heritage. In addition, we propose a method that introduces a geospatial distance restriction to refine the embedding representations of geographic entities in a geolocalized KG, which fuses geospatial information and semantic information into a low-dimensional vector space. We utilize this method for a geographical distance prediction task, where we outperform baseline methods.

Acknowledgments. This work was supported by MEMEX project funded by the European Union's Horizon 2020 research and innovation program under grant agreement No 870743.

References

1. Auer, S., Bizer, C., Kobilarov, G., Lehmann, J., Cyganiak, R., Ives, Z.: DBpedia: a nucleus for a web of open data. In: Aberer, K., et al. (eds.) ASWC/ISWC -2007. LNCS, vol. 4825, pp. 722–735. Springer, Heidelberg (2007). https://doi.org/10.1007/978-3-540-76298-0_52
2. Carriero, V.A., et al.: ArCo: the Italian cultural heritage knowledge graph. In: Ghidini, C., et al. (eds.) ISWC 2019. LNCS, vol. 11779, pp. 36–52. Springer, Cham (2019). https://doi.org/10.1007/978-3-030-30796-7_3
3. Freire, N., Voorburg, R., Cornelissen, R., de Valk, S., Meijers, E., Isaac, A.: Aggregation of linked data in the cultural heritage domain: a case study in the Europeana network. Information **10**(8), 252 (2019)
4. Guo, X., Qian, H., Wu, F., Liu, J.: A method for constructing geographical knowledge graph from multisource data. Sustainability **13**(19), 10602 (2021)
5. Haslhofer, B., Isaac, A.: data. europeana. eu: the Europeana linked open data pilot. In: International Conference on Dublin Core and Metadata Applications, pp. 94–104 (2011)
6. Kingma, D.P., Ba, J.: Adam: a method for stochastic optimization. CoRR abs/1412.6980 (2015)

7. Maietti, F., Di Giulio, R., Piaia, E., Medici, M., Ferrari, F.: Enhancing heritage fruition through 3D semantic modelling and digital tools: the inception project. In: IOP Conference Series: Materials Science and Engineering, vol. 364, p. 012089. IOP Publishing (2018)

8. Pellegrino, M.A., Scarano, V., Spagnuolo, C.: Move cultural heritage knowledge Graphsin everyone's pocket (2020)

9. Pennington, J., Socher, R., Manning, C.D.: Glove: global vectors for word representation. In: Proceedings of the 2014 Conference on Empirical Methods in Natural Language Processing (EMNLP), pp. 1532–1543 (2014)

10. Qassimi, S., Abdelwahed, E.H.: Towards a semantic graph-based recommender system. A case study of cultural heritage. J. Univers. Comput. Sci. **27**, 714–733 (2021)

11. Qiu, P., Gao, J., Yu, L., Lu, F.: Knowledge embedding with geospatial distance restriction for geographic knowledge graph completion. ISPRS Int. J. Geo Inf. **8**(6), 254 (2019)

12. Robusto, C.C.: The cosine-haversine formula. Am. Math. Mon. **64**(1), 38–40 (1957)

13. Schlichtkrull, M., Kipf, T.N., Bloem, P., van den Berg, R., Titov, I., Welling, M.: Modeling relational data with graph convolutional networks. In: Gangemi, A., et al. (eds.) ESWC 2018. LNCS, vol. 10843, pp. 593–607. Springer, Cham (2018). https://doi.org/10.1007/978-3-319-93417-4_38

14. Tietz, T., et al.: Linked stage graph. In: SEMANTICS Posters&Demos (2019)

15. Vaswani, A., et al.: Attention is all you need. In: Advances in Neural Information Processing Systems, vol. 30 (2017)

16. Veličković, P., Cucurull, G., Casanova, A., Romero, A., Lio, P., Bengio, Y.: Graph attention networks. arXiv preprint arXiv:1710.10903 (2017)

17. Vrandečić, D., Krötzsch, M.: Wikidata: a free collaborative knowledgebase. Commun. ACM **57**(10), 78–85 (2014)

18. Vsesviatska, O., et al.: Ardo: an ontology to describe the dynamics of multimedia archival records. In: Proceedings of the 36th Annual ACM Symposium on Applied Computing, pp. 1855–1863 (2021)

19. Xu, K., Hu, W., Leskovec, J., Jegelka, S.: How powerful are graph neural networks? arXiv abs/1810.00826 (2019)

20. Zhang, M., Chen, Y.: Link prediction based on graph neural networks. In: Bengio, S., Wallach, H., Larochelle, H., Grauman, K., Cesa-Bianchi, N., Garnett, R. (eds.) Advances in Neural Information Processing Systems, vol. 31. Curran Associates, Inc. (2018)

21. Zhu, X., Li, T., De Melo, G.: Exploring semantic properties of sentence embeddings. In: Proceedings of the 56th Annual Meeting of the Association for Computational Linguistics (Volume 2: Short Papers), pp. 632–637 (2018)

Masonry Structure Analysis, Completion and Style Transfer Using a Deep Neural Network

Yahya Ibrahim[1,2] (ID), Péter Szulovszky[1,2] (ID), and Csaba Benedek[1,2](✉) (ID)

[1] Institute for Computer Science and Control (SZTAKI), Budapest, Hungary
benedek.csaba@sztaki.hu
[2] Faculty of Information Technology and Bionics, Péter Pázmány Catholic
University, Budapest, Hungary

Abstract. In this paper, we present a novel deep learning-based fully automatic method for masonry wall analysis in digital images. The proposed approach is able to automatically detect and virtually complete occluded or damaged wall regions, it segments brick and mortar areas leading to an accurate model of the wall structure, and it can also perform wall-to-wall style transfer as well. Our method involves numerous sequential phases. Initially, a U-Net-based network is used to segment the wall images into brick, mortar, and occluded/damaged regions. Thereafter the hidden wall regions are predicted by a two-stage adversarial inpainting model: first, a schematic mortar-brick pattern is predicted, then the second network component adds color information to these areas, providing a realistic visual experience to the observer. Next, a watershed transform-based segmentation step produces accurate outlines of individual bricks in both the visible and the inpainted wall segments. Furthermore, we show that the second adversarial network can also be used for texture transfer: one can change the texture style of a given wall image, based on another wall image, and we can artificially color a schematic wall sketch map, based on the style of a sample wall image. Experiments revealed that the proposed method produces realistic results for various masonry wall types in terms of inpainting the occluded regions or style transfer.

Keywords: Masonry wall · Segmentation · Inpainting · Style transfer

1 Introduction

Ancient heritage sites have always been challenging to study, maintain, and model due to various destructed and altering regions produced by human interventions or natural forces over time, which should be carefully documented. Reassembling these destroyed sites necessitates a comprehensive understanding of the studied archaeological location's global basic structure.

This paper focuses on the investigation and examination of digital images taken from masonry walls, which are among the most fundamental and major components of ancient sites. Large historic walls frequently contain many ruined

© Springer Nature Switzerland AG 2023
J.-J. Rousseau and B. Kapralos (Eds.): ICPR 2022 Workshops, LNCS 13645, pp. 155–168, 2023.
https://doi.org/10.1007/978-3-031-37731-0_13

segments, while after the reconstruction process, the restored areas should follow the main construction patterns of the originally visible parts of the wall. When relying on archive wall images as a basis of reconstruction, it is also a common problem that some regions are hidden/occluded by covering items or other objects in the reference photos of the wall. Therefore the wall's original structural pattern is not visible in certain parts, thus it should be artificially synthesised during reconstruction or in visualization.

Archaeologists investigating masonry walls usually begin their analysis by separating and classifying the wall materials as either main components *(bricks)* or joints *(mortars)*. Next the observed wall structure should be understood and modelled, thereafter one can estimate the original layout of brick and mortar components in areas that have been damaged, discolored, or got covered by other items. Moreover, many historical documents of ancient walls are hand-drawn including only the structure information. When presenting a possible reconstruction view of these walls, archaeologists synthesize a texture style to these sketch drawings based on the style of other preserved ancient walls made from the same material.

In the recent years, we have observed a substantial increase of using machine learning and deep learning algorithms for cultural heritage applications, such as semantic segmentation for historical architectural elements [15] or classification of various segments of monuments [19].

In this paper, we propose a fully automatic end-to-end deep learning-based algorithm for masonry wall image analysis, virtual structure recovery and wall-to-wall style transfer. The proposed approach can be applied in different scenarios: First, given as input a wall image that is partially hidden by numerous irregular items, or contains some ruined/damaged regions, our algorithm detects these outlier areas, it predicts the brick-mortar pattern and wall color texture in these regions, and it extracts correct brick outlines, giving a meaningful structural representation for both the initially visible and the artificially inpainted sections of the wall (see Fig. 3).

The second scenario deals with style transfer and artificial coloring of schematic wall sketch maps. In particular, one can replace the coloring style (e.g. color and texture pattern of the bricks) of a wall image, with another wall's style, while maintaining the wall's original structural integrity. Given two images as inputs: a *content image* which is a color wall image or a binary image for the wall structure, and a *style image* which is a different wall image, the goal is to create a new image that incorporates both the structure of the *content image* and the texture style of the *style image* (see Fig. 4 and Fig. 5).

For both use-cases, our proposed algorithms are freely available for testing on our laboratory's public website[1].

Our contributions can be summarized as follows:

1. An end-to-end algorithm is proposed for inpainting and segmenting masonry wall images, as well as for style transfer from a given wall photo to another wall sample.

---

[1] http://imgproc.mplab.sztaki.hu/masonrydemo.

2. We provide a comprehensive qualitative evaluation to demonstrate the benefits of our approach in masonry wall inpainting and wall-to-wall style transfer.
3. We present a new web-based application, which can be used by the research community for widely testing and validating our proposed approach.

The initial steps of the presented approach have been described in our prior papers [4–6], which methods we extend here with further steps and real world application examples. More specifically, [4] focused purely on the brick segmentation step, and [6] described an initial occlusion detection and inpainting model that was verified mostly on synthetic data samples. The previously mentioned steps have been first used together and evaluated on real data in [5]. In the present paper, we introduce an extended model, additional experiments and novel use case options for wall image analysis with the proposed approach. In particular, we focus on new style transfer and sketch coloring applications that can widely help architects and archaeologists in many applications such as modeling or restoration.

The article is organized as follows: Sect. 2 reviews recent works related to state-of-the-art wall image delineation, image inpainting and style transfer algorithms; Sect. 3 demonstrates how we produce and augment our dataset; Sect. 4 explains our proposed model in detail; Sect. 5 shows the experimental results; Sect. 6 summarizes our results.

2 Related Work

In this section, we highlight three essential challenges linked to the discussed research topic, and provide a brief summary of recent image segmentation methods utilized for masonry wall delineation. Following that, we give an overview on the state-of-the-art in image inpainting techniques, focusing on their suitability for the task of completing the wall images. Finally, we discuss recent research on style transfer methods.

Several wall image delineation techniques are presented in the literature for various wall types. Many of them are working on 2D images of walls, relying on various image features and modeling approaches, such as a combination of object-oriented and pixel-based image processing technology [3], a color-based automated algorithm based on an improved marker-controlled watershed transform [16], a Hough transform-based delineation algorithm [14], a machine learning-based algorithm [9], and a deep neural-based network for stone-by-stone segmentation [7]. As for using 3D point clouds instead of images, [20] used a Continuous Wavelet Transform (CWT) applied on a 2.5D depth map to obtain the outlines of the bricks. Alternatively, [1] used different 3D local and global features for the wall segmentation. Nevertheless, none of the approaches mentioned have been tested on a wide range of wall image structures. On the contrary, in our research project we focused on involving a wide range of wall types and texture models.

Image inpainting is the process of filling in damaged, noisy, or missing areas of an image to create a completed image. Large datasets are often required to train and learn the hidden feature representation of the images, especially in the recent deep learning models [13,21,22]. GMCNN [21] is a generative multi-column convolutional neural network model which deals with global texture features and local details simultaneously, containing a multi-output model [22] which produces numerous image inpainting solutions with two GAN-based parallel paths. The recent EdgeConnect [13] method employs a two-stage adversarial network that fills in the gaps of an edge map created in the first stage. This algorithm is based either on the Canny detector or on the Holistically-Nested Edge Detection algorithm (HED) for initial edge information. However, neither of these two edge generators can provide semantic structural information about the masonry walls because their performance is sensitive to the internal edges inside the brick or mortar regions, resulting in a number of false edges that are unrelated to the wall structure pattern. In contrast, our solution uses in the first step a deep neural network to separate the wall components (brick, and mortar), allowing for a better observation of the entire wall structure in the following steps.

Style transfer approaches combine two images (a *content image* and a *style image*) so that the resulting output image keeps the content image's fundamental elements while appearing to be *painted* in the style of the reference *style image*. Li and Wand proposed a patch-based non-parametric Markov Random Field (MRF) approach [10], which has been proved to be effective in preserving coherent textures in complex images, however it worked less efficiently with non-textured styles. [2] combines independent network components to learn the corresponding content and style information, and uses a *StyleBank* layer which comprises mid-level convolutional filters to individually learn different styles, where style is coupled to a set of parameters. This algorithm provides the advantage of learning a new style as well as a flexible control over style fusion. However, it has a number of weaknesses, including the lack of details in the result images. Li et al. [11] attempt to use a sequence of feature transformations to transfer arbitrary styles without the need for style learning. However, when the used feature vector has a large dimension, the expensive matrix calculation in whitening and colouring modifications becomes a limitation. In contrast to the existing state-of-the-art algorithms, our solution uses a preliminary phase to extract the *content wall image*'s dominant structure, then we add the target wall image style to the model in a direct manner, as it will be detailed later in Sect. 4.2.

3   Dataset Generation

In our project, we created a unique dataset[2] with images of facades and masonry walls from both old and new buildings for training and evaluating the proposed algorithm. Among the collected images, there are examples for three forms of rubble masonry (Random, Square, and Dry), as well as two types of ashlar (Fine, Rough).

Our dataset consists of 532 different 512×512 wall images separated into a training set (310 images) and a test set (222 images). The training dataset

---

[2] The wall images and the manually annotated brick-mortar delineation masks used in the paper are available: http://mplab.sztaki.hu/geocomp/masonryWallAnalysis.

is made up of occlusion-free wall images with a manually segmented binary brick-mortar mask I_{wall_ftr} for each image. Synthetic objects are used to create occlusions for training phase during the data augmentation process which various perturbation steps, including (a) horizontal flip, (b) vertical flip, (c) both vertical and horizontal flips, (d) adding Gaussian noise (e) randomly increasing the average brightness, (f) randomly decreasing the average brightness, and (g) adding random shadows.

4 Proposed Approach

The proposed method's major use-cases are twofold: (i) a comprehensive *wall analysis* usage which includes extracting individual brick instances from masonry wall images automatically, detecting occluded/damaged wall segments and filling in their regions with a realistic brick-mortar pattern prediction, and (ii) *a style transfer* usage between different wall images. The following sections present the implementations of these two functionalities in details.

4.1 Wall Analysis

Our complete masonry wall analysis workflow is presented in Fig. 1. The input of the method should be a masonry wall image I_{in} that can be partially hidden by one or several foreground items, or may contain damaged regions. Our method generates a color image of the reconstructed wall I_{G2_out}, as well as it provides the contours of segmented individual bricks I_{out}. The proposed algorithm is divided into three stages.

Pre-processing Stage: The initial stage has two objectives: obtaining the delineation structure of the wall by separating the bricks from the mortar regions, and detecting the masks of potentially occluded or damaged wall parts that should be inpainted in the subsequent steps. A U-Net [18] network preforms this segmentation task, yielding a three-class segmented image $I_{wall\_ftr\_oclud}$ as its output, with class labels representing brick (white), mortar (black), and occluded (gray) parts. Then we construct two binary auxiliary images from the output I_{u_out}: a binary mask I_{mask} of the predicted occluded pixels, and a mask of the anticipated bricks I_{ftr_mskd} in the observed wall sections, where both the previously detected occluded and brick pixels have white labels, whilst the mortar pixels are black. The Adam optimizer is used to train the network over a joint loss that includes a cross-entropy loss and a feature-matching loss.

Inpainting Stage: There are two primary sub-steps in this stage: First, based on the mortar pattern detected in the I_{ftr_mskd} mask, the Hidden Feature Generator completes the mortar pixels in the area covered by the white parts of the predicted I_{mask} image. Second, the Image Completion step predicts the RGB color values of the pixels marked as occluded in the I_{mask} image, depending

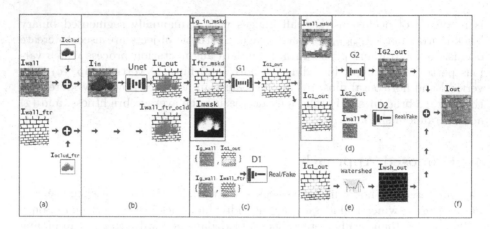

Fig. 1. Dataflow of our algorithm. (**a**) Data augmentation by adding synthetic occlusion (**b**) Pre-processing Stage (U-Net network). (**c**) Inpainting Stage - Hidden Feature Generator (GAN-based network $G1$).(**d**) Inpainting Stage - Image Completion (GAN-based network $G2$). (**e**) Segmentation Stage (Watershed Transform). (**f**) Brick segmentation map superimposed to the inpainted image output (I_{out}).

on the color information in the non-occluded regions of the I_{wall_mskd}, and the structural wall features extracted from the I_{G1_out} map in the occluded regions. The inpainting stage uses two separate generative adversarial networks (GANs), each of them has generator and discriminator components [8,13].

Hidden Feature Generator: Three images are used as inputs of the first generator (G_1): the output images of the two pre-processing stages (I_{mask}, I_{ftr_mskd}), and $I_{g\_in\_mskd}$, which is the masked grayscale version of the input image. The output I_{G1_out} represents the predicted wall structure, completing I_{ftr_mskd} with brick outlines under the occlusion mask regions.

The adversarial loss and the feature-matching loss are used to train the network. The adversarial loss is modeled as a two-player zero-sum game between the Generator G_1 and Discriminator D_1 networks, so that the generator attempts to minimize the loss and the discriminator attempts to maximize it.

Image Completion: The input of the second generator G_2 combines both the masked wall image (I_{wall_mskd}) and the output of the first generator (I_{G1_out}). The aim of the G_2 generator is creating an output image I_{G2_out} which is filled with predicted color information in the masked regions (see Fig. 1d). The inputs of the discriminator D_2 are I_{G2_out} and I_{wall}, while its goal is to predict whether the color pattern is true or not. The network is trained over a joint loss that consists of L_1 loss, adversarial loss, perceptual loss, and style loss.

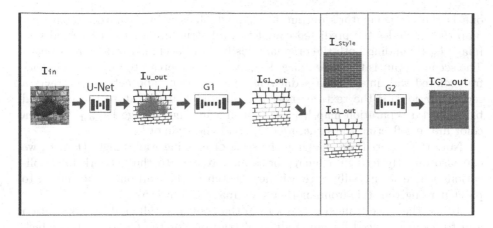

Fig. 2. Dataflow of the Style Transfer application

Segmentation Stage: This stage of the proposed algorithm extracts the accurate outlines of the brick instances, using the previously obtained Hidden Feature Generator delineation map I_{G1_out}. Although the separation maps are notably precise, they may be noisy at brick boundaries, and we can observe that some bricks are touching, making Connected Component Analysis CCA-based separation susceptible to errors. Therefore, we use a marker-based watershed [17] segmentation for robust brick separation to overcome these issues.

First, we calculate the obtained delineation map's (I_{G1_out}) inverse distance transform (IDT) image, then we apply the H–minima transform, which suppresses all minima under a given H-value since the IDT image may have numerous false local minima, we start flooding using the H–minima regions as a starting points (internal marker of the watershed algorithm), and take the inverse of I_{G1_out} (i.e., all mortar or non-wall pixels) as an external marker map, whose pixels are not compatible with any bricks. Finally, the obtained brick shapes can be displayed over the Image Completion output (see I_{out}).

4.2 Style Transfer

The goal of the style transfer component is to fill or modify the wall's texture style based on an image of another wall or wall segment. The workflow of this procedure is presented in Fig. 2. The style of the input image I_{in} is changed to match the style of another wall image sample called the *style image* I_{style}. Archaeologists can use this algorithm to modify some degraded segments of the studied wall that have become soiled or lost its original color over time due to environmental factors, relying in various style features extracted from the intact wall regions.

The proposed style transfer procedure uses the same G_1 and G_2 network components, that were previously introduced in the wall analysis section (Sect. 4.1). Here the *image completion* network G_2 has two inputs: the first one is the G_1 generator's output I_{G1_out}, which is a brick-mortar separation map that includes the predicted complete wall structure for the processed wall image I_{in} (including both the originally visible and occluded wall components). The second input is the style image I_{style}, which is represented by an occlusion-free colored wall image with a different texture style. The network extracts a representation for the texture style of I_{style} and transfers it to the predicted brick-mortar separation map I_{G1_out}, resulting in a new image I_{G2_out}, that is a color image reflecting the structure of I_{in} and the style of I_{style}.

Note that apart from changing the style of existing wall images (Fig. 4), we can also directly feed in a binary brick-mortar map to the network for applications where we initially have a binary sketch of the wall only, and intend to paint it using the style from another wall image (see Fig. 5).

To use the same trained network as in the previous wall analysis application and to avoid the need for any additional training for the G_2 generator, which is originally trained to paint exclusively the *occluded* (i.e. masked) regions of its input image (see Sect. 4.1 and Fig. 1), we add here virtual masks to the style images. The joint usage of two binary virtual masks - which are inverted variants of each other - ensures that the entire target image will be filled with the texture of the style image, so that the style image is fed twice to the network, each time with one of the masks.

5 Experiments

In this section, we analyze the performance of the proposed approach on the test data.

We begin with the discussion of the *wall analysis* application, where the results of applying our algorithm in real-world scenarios are presented. Figure 3 shows some qualitative results where the first row presents wall images with occluding objects (human-made items or plants), the second row shows the output of the pre-processing stage (U-net network) presented as a three-color images (gray: the occluding objects, black: the mortar, white: the bricks), the third row illustrates the G_1 output where the predicted mortar lines are in blue, the fourth row shows the results of the color inpainting algorithm, and the last row presents the results of the brick segmentation step where brick instances are separated by a green lines.

The results confirm that our technique is effective in recognizing the occluded wall regions in the images: we can see that the U-net network can accurately extract occluded image parts and nearly all occluding objects are properly detected. The results of the "Hidden Feature Generator" phase indicate our algorithm's efficiency in predicting the mortar lines in occluded regions. By examining the inpainted color images we can confirm that our algorithm manages to create realistic wall patterns in the occluded areas. Moreover, despite the wide variety of brick component sizes in the images, and image quality issues such as the poor contrast of the second sample, the output of the brick segmentation stage has a high quality.

Fig. 3. Results for wall analysis application step by step for three real-world samples, first row: input images, second row: Pre-Processing Stage output, third row: G_1 output, fourth row: G_2 output, last row: Segmentation Stage output.

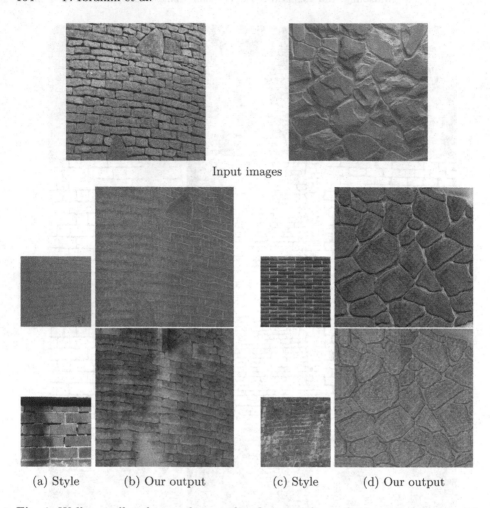

Input images

(a) Style   (b) Our output   (c) Style   (d) Our output

Fig. 4. Wall to wall style transfer samples, first row shows the input images, second and third rows represent the style image and our output side by side.

In Fig. 4, we show results for the *style transfer* application, where we present two different *content image* samples in the first row, and each of them is transformed in the process using two different *style images*. (The style images and the corresponding style transfer results are displayed side by side in the second and third rows.)

Next, We present the results of transforming a binary brick-mortar map to a wall image. Figure 5 displays two brick-mortar sketch maps, which can be drawn even by hand. Each of them is transformed to different colored wall images using two distinct *style images*, and the results are shown in the last two rows.

We can observe in both Fig. 4 and 5 how the algorithm manged to paint the style texture of the style image onto the brick-mortar pattern of the processed image or the handrawn sketch map, so that the mortar regions efficiently match

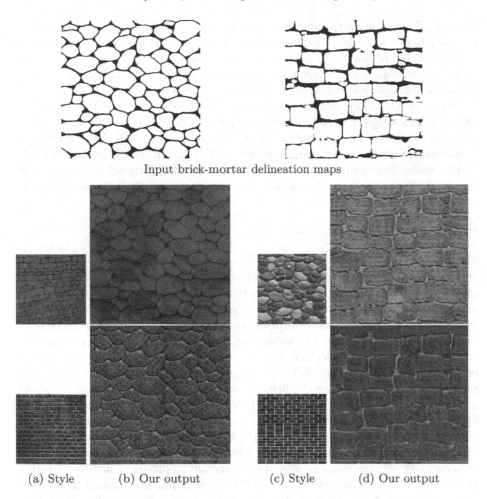

Input brick-mortar delineation maps

(a) Style   (b) Our output   (c) Style   (d) Our output

Fig. 5. brick-mortar map to a wall style transfer samples.

the color of the mortar, and the appearances of the brick regions match the brick texture of the style image. However there are a few error cases when some neighboring bricks are merged into a large brick object in the image as shown in the center part of Fig. 4(d).

Since in image inpainting tasks there are usually many alternative solutions, there is no clear numerical metric for evaluating image inpainting [12] and style transfer results. Therefore, similarly to our user survey regarding the image inpainting model in [5], we conducted a user survey to assess our proposed style transfer approach. Using 15 different style images and 15 content images (9 color wall images and 6 brick-mortar maps), we generated 15 stylized images by our network. We showed the outputs to 28 test subjects displaying the images side-by-side with the style images, and asked them to vote whether they find the result of our style transfer network visually appropriate or not. 18 out of 28 participants said that more than 66% of the seen images were transformed appropriately; 10 out of 15 images received more than 66% votes that it has been transferred appropriately. By summarizing all votes on all images, 70.47% (296/420) images were considered being transferred correctly.

Based on the above-mentioned study results, we can conclude that our algorithm provides high quality inpainting outputs for real-world wall images, when we need to expect that real occluding objects are present. We also get efficient segmentation results both in the originally visible and in the inpainted segments of the walls. Furthermore, the algorithm is capable of transferring the style between different wall structures and styles resulting a realistic image outputs.

6   Conclusion

This research presented a new approach for wall image processing, analysis and style transfer from one wall to another. Our network has two different ways of utilization: in the first one, the algorithm recognizes occluded or damaged wall portions and inpaints the corrupted segment with a realistic wall pattern. Moreover, for the inpainted wall image, the technique returns an instance level brick segmentation output. The second implementation able to transfer the texture and color style from an image to the another wall structure. Our approach is divided into three steps. A U-Net-based module is used in the initial pre-processing stage to separate the brick, mortar, and occluded areas of the input image. This preliminary segmentation is fed into the inpainting stage, which is comprises two GAN-based networks: the first one is responsible for the wall structure compilation, while the second is in charge of color image inpainting. The final stage employs the watershed algorithm, which ensures that the entire wall is accurately segmented. The algorithm's second application involves altering the second GAN's inputs to fit two different wall images. Numerous qualitative experiments have shown that the proposed approach is significantly robust against various artifacts in real-world applications regarding the specified challenges.

Acknowledgement. The authors acknowledge the support of the Hungarian National Research, Development and Innovation Office (NKFIH) via the projects OTKA K-143274 and TKP2021-NVA-01. The work was also supported by the European Union within the framework of the Artificial Intelligence National Laboratory (RRF-2.3.1-21-2022-00004).

References

1. Bosché, F., Valero, E., Forster, A., Wilson, L., Leslie, A.: Evaluation of historic masonry substrates: towards greater objectivity and efficiency (2016). https://doi.org/10.4324/9781315628011-8

2. Chen, D., Yuan, L., Liao, J., Yu, N., Hua, G.: Stylebank: an explicit representation for neural image style transfer. In: 2017 IEEE Conference on Computer Vision and Pattern Recognition (CVPR), pp. 2770–2779 (2017). https://doi.org/10.1109/CVPR.2017.296

3. Hemmleb, M., Weritz, A.F., Schiemenz, B.A., Grote, C.A., Maierhofer, C.: Multi-spectral data acquisition and processing techniques for damage detection on building surfaces. In: ISPRS Commission V Symposium, pp. 1–6 (2006)

4. Ibrahim, Y., Nagy, B., Benedek, C.: CNN-based watershed marker extraction for brick segmentation in masonry walls. In: International Conference on Image Analysis and Recognition, pp. 332–344 (2019)

5. Ibrahim, Y., Nagy, B., Benedek, C.: Deep learning-based masonry wall image analysis. Remote Sens. **12**(23) (2020). https://doi.org/10.3390/rs12233918. https://www.mdpi.com/2072-4292/12/23/3918

6. Ibrahim, Y., Nagy, B., Benedek, C.: A GAN-based blind inpainting method for masonry wall images. In: 2020 25th International Conference on Pattern Recognition (ICPR), pp. 3178–3185 (2021). https://doi.org/10.1109/ICPR48806.2021.9413009

7. Idjaton, K., Desquesnes, X., Treuillet, S., Brunetaud, X.: Stone-by-stone segmentation for monitoring large historical monuments using deep neural networks. In: Del Bimbo, A., et al. (eds.) ICPR 2021. LNCS, vol. 12667, pp. 235–248. Springer, Cham (2021). https://doi.org/10.1007/978-3-030-68787-8_17

8. Johnson, J., Alahi, A., Fei-Fei, L.: Perceptual losses for real-time style transfer and super-resolution. In: Leibe, B., Matas, J., Sebe, N., Welling, M. (eds.) ECCV 2016. LNCS, vol. 9906, pp. 694–711. Springer, Cham (2016). https://doi.org/10.1007/978-3-319-46475-6_43

9. Kajatin, R., Nalpantidis, L.: Image segmentation of bricks in masonry wall using a fusion of machine learning algorithms. In: Del Bimbo, A., et al. (eds.) ICPR 2021. LNCS, vol. 12667, pp. 446–461. Springer, Cham (2021). https://doi.org/10.1007/978-3-030-68787-8_33

10. Li, C., Wand, M.: Precomputed real-time texture synthesis with Markovian generative adversarial networks. In: Leibe, B., Matas, J., Sebe, N., Welling, M. (eds.) ECCV 2016. LNCS, vol. 9907, pp. 702–716. Springer, Cham (2016). https://doi.org/10.1007/978-3-319-46487-9_43

11. Li, Y., Fang, C., Yang, J., Wang, Z., Lu, X., Yang, M.H.: Universal style transfer via feature transforms. In: Guyon, I., et al. (eds.) Advances in Neural Information Processing Systems, vol. 30. Curran Associates, Inc. (2017). https://proceedings.neurips.cc/paper/2017/file/49182f81e6a13cf5eaa496d51fea6406-Paper.pdf

12. Liu, G., Reda, F.A., Shih, K.J., Wang, T.C., Tao, A., Catanzaro, B.: Image inpainting for irregular holes using partial convolutions. In: European Conference on Computer Vision (ECCV) (2018)

13. Nazeri, K., Ng, E., Joseph, T., Qureshi, F., Ebrahimi, M.: Edgeconnect: generative image inpainting with adversarial edge learning. In: International Conference on Computer Vision Workshop (ICCVW), pp. 3265–3274 (2019)

14. Oses, N., Dornaika, F., Moujahid, A.: Image-based delineation and classification of built heritage masonry. Remote Sens. **6**(3), 1863–1889 (2014). https://doi.org/10.3390/rs6031863

15. Pierdicca, R., et al.: Point cloud semantic segmentation using a deep learning framework for cultural heritage. Remote Sens. **12**(6), 1005 (2020). https://doi.org/10.3390/rs12061005

16. Riveiro, B., Conde, B., Gonzalez, H., Arias, P., Caamaño, J.: Automatic creation of structural models from point cloud data: the case of masonry structures. ISPRS Ann. Photogramm. Remote Sens. Spatial Inf. Sci. **II-3/W5**, 3–9 (2015). https://doi.org/10.5194/isprsannals-II-3-W5-3-2015

17. Roerdink, J.B., Meijster, A.: The watershed transform: definitions, algorithms and parallelization strategies. Fundam. Inf. **41**(1,2), 187–228 (2000). http://dl.acm.org/citation.cfm?id=2372488.2372495

18. Ronneberger, O., Fischer, P., Brox, T.: U-Net: convolutional networks for biomedical image segmentation. In: Navab, N., Hornegger, J., Wells, W.M., Frangi, A.F. (eds.) MICCAI 2015. LNCS, vol. 9351, pp. 234–241. Springer, Cham (2015). https://doi.org/10.1007/978-3-319-24574-4_28

19. Teruggi, S., Grilli, E., Russo, M., Fassi, F., Remondino, F.: A hierarchical machine learning approach for multi-level and multi-resolution 3D point cloud classification. Remote Sens. **12**(16), 2598 (2020). https://doi.org/10.3390/rs12162598

20. Valero, E., Bosché, F., Forster, A., Hyslop, E.: Historic digital survey: reality capture and automatic data processing for the interpretation and analysis of historic architectural rubble masonry. In: Aguilar, R., Torrealva, D., Moreira, S., Pando, M.A., Ramos, L.F. (eds.) Structural Analysis of Historical Constructions. RB, vol. 18, pp. 388–396. Springer, Cham (2019). https://doi.org/10.1007/978-3-319-99441-3_41

21. Wang, Y., Tao, X., Qi, X., Shen, X., Jia, J.: Image inpainting via generative multi-column convolutional neural networks. CoRR abs/1810.08771 (2018). http://arxiv.org/abs/1810.08771

22. Zheng, C., Cham, T., Cai, J.: Pluralistic image completion. In: IEEE Conference on Computer Vision and Pattern Recognition (CVPR), pp. 1438–1447 (2019)

2nd Workshop on Explainable and Ethical AI (XAIE 2022)

Preface

We are witnessing the emergence of an "AI economy and society" where AI technologies are increasingly impacting many aspects of business as well as everyday life. We read with great interest about recent advances in AI medical diagnostic systems, self-driving cars, ability of AI technology to automate many aspects of business decisions like loan approvals, hiring, policing etc. However, as evident by recent experiences, AI systems may produce errors, can exhibit overt or subtle bias, may be sensitive to noise in the data, and often lack technical and judicial transparency and explainability. These shortcomings have been documented in scientific but also and importantly in general press (accidents with self-driving cars, biases in AI-based policing, hiring and loan systems, biases in face recognition systems for people of color, seemingly correct medical diagnoses later found to be made due to wrong reasons etc.). These shortcomings are raising many ethical and policy concerns not only in technical and academic communities, but also among policymakers and general public, and will inevitably impede wider adoption of AI in society.

The problems related to Ethical AI are complex and broad and encompass not only technical issues but also legal, political and ethical ones. One of the key component of Ethical AI systems is explainability or transparency, but other issues like detecting bias, ability to control the outcomes, ability to objectively audit AI systems for ethics are also critical for successful applications and adoption of AI in society. Consequently, explainable and Ethical AI are very current and popular topics both in technical as well as in business, legal and philosophy communities.

The 2nd Workshop on Explainable and Ethical AI has been successfully held at ICPR 2022. 7 presentations (6 long and 1 short) has been done on various subjects related to explainability while one invited talk has been done on ethics on AI. Various explainability technics have been presented: features attribution (for classification and segmentation) with posthoc methods or attention, factual collection, counterfactuals generation, rule extraction. Two papers were related to evaluation. Ethics presentation was related to crowd workers and the impact of AI.

Each paper has undergone a single blind review with three expert reviewers in the domain of AI. Regarding the acceptance rate, 2 short papers have been submitted and 1 has been accepted, while 11 long papers has been submitted and 6 accepted. The following papers represent the state of the art in explainability for artificial intelligence.

August 2022

Romain Giot
Jenny Benois-Pineau
Romain Bourqui
Dragutin Petkovic

Organization

General Chairs

Jenny Benois-Pineau   University of Bordeaux, France
Romain Bourqui   University of Bordeaux, France
Romain Giot   University of Bordeaux, France
Dragutin Petkovic   University of San Fransisco State University, USA

Program Committee Chairs

Jenny Benois-Pineau   University of Bordeaux, France
Romain Bourqui   University of Bordeaux, France
Romain Giot   University of Bordeaux, France
Dragutin Petkovic   San Fransisco State University, USA

Program Committee

Alexandre Benoit   University Savoie Mont Blanc/LISTIC, France
André C. P. L. F. de Carvalho   University of Sao Paulo/ICMC, Brazil
Christophe Garcia   LIRIS, France
Christophe Hurter   Ecole Nationale de l'Aviation Civile, France
Théo Jaunet   LIRIS, France
Mark Keane   UCD Dublin/Insight SFI Centre for Data Analytics, Ireland
Stefanos Kollias   National Technical University of Athens/Image, Video and Multimedia Systems Lab, Greece
Sebastian Lapuschkin   Fraunhofer HHI, Germany
Harold Mouchère   Université de Nantes/LS2N, France
Noel E. O'Connor   DCU, Ireland
Nicolas Thome   CNAM/Cedric, France
Carlos Toxtli   Northeastern University, USA

Publication Chairs

Romain Bourqui	University of Bordeaux, France
Romain Giot	University of Bordeaux, France

Additional Reviewers

Alexandre Bruckert
Tristan Gomez
Adrien Halnaut
Gaëlle Jouis
Elias Ramzi

PARTICUL: Part Identification with Confidence Measure Using Unsupervised Learning

Romain Xu-Darme[1,2]([✉]), Georges Quénot[2], Zakaria Chihani[1], and Marie-Christine Rousset[2]

[1] Université Paris-Saclay, CEA, List, 91120 Palaiseau, France
`{romain.xu-darme,zakaria.chihani}@cea.fr`
[2] Université Grenoble Alpes, CNRS, Grenoble INP, LIG, 38000 Grenoble, France
`{georges.quenot,marie-christine.rousset}@imag.fr`

Abstract. In this paper, we present PARTICUL, a novel algorithm for unsupervised learning of part detectors from datasets used in fine-grained recognition. It exploits the macro-similarities of all images in the training set in order to mine for recurring patterns in the feature space of a pre-trained convolutional neural network. We propose new objective functions enforcing the locality and unicity of the detected parts. Additionally, we embed our detectors with a confidence measure based on correlation scores, allowing the system to estimate the visibility of each part. We apply our method on two public fine-grained datasets (Caltech-UCSD Bird 200 and Stanford Cars) and show that our detectors can consistently highlight parts of the object while providing a good measure of the confidence in their prediction. We also demonstrate that these detectors can be directly used to build part-based fine-grained classifiers that provide a good compromise between the transparency of prototype-based approaches and the performance of non-interpretable methods.

Keywords: Part detection · Unsupervised learning · Interpretability · Confidence measure · Fine-grained recognition

1 Introduction

With the development of deep learning in recent years, convolutional neural networks (CNNs) have quickly become the backbone of all state-of-the-art visual recognition systems. CNNs are highly efficient but also highly complex systems manipulating abstract (and often opaque) representations of the image - also called feature vectors - to achieve high accuracy, at the cost of transparency and interpretability of the decision-making process. In order to overcome these issues, a solution, explored in [1,3,6,7,10–12,17,19,22,27,34,41,44], consists in building an intermediate representation associating each input image with a set of semantic *attributes*. These attributes, usually representing an association between a part of an object (*e.g.*, head of a bird) and a property (*e.g.*, shape,

© Springer Nature Switzerland AG 2023
J.-J. Rousseau and B. Kapralos (Eds.): ICPR 2022 Workshops, LNCS 13645, pp. 173–187, 2023.
https://doi.org/10.1007/978-3-031-37731-0_14

color), can be either used by interpretable methods [3,22,27] to produce the decision, as *post-hoc* explanation [11,12] of a particular decision, or as supplementary information in order to discriminate similar categories in the case of fine-grained visual classification (FGVC) [7,10,19,41,44]. In practice, attributes are learned through fully supervised algorithms [1,6,7,10,19,34,41,44], using datasets with hand-crafted annotations. Such datasets are expensive to produce - using expert knowledge or online crowd-sourcing platforms - and prone to errors [13,23]. Therefore, a lot of effort [3,5,8,9,14,18,25,29,38,39,42,43] has been recently put into the development of more scalable techniques using less training information. In particular, the task of localizing different parts of an object, a prerequisite to attribute detection, can be performed in a weakly supervised (using the category of each image) or unsupervised manner. By focusing on general features of the objects rather than discriminative details, part detection represents an easier task than attribute detection. However, it must offer strong evidence of accuracy and reliability in order to constitute a solid basis for a trustworthy decision.

In this paper, we present PARTICUL[1] (Part Identification with Confidence measure using Unsupervised Learning), a plug-in module that uses an unsupervised algorithm in order to learn part detectors from FGVC datasets. It exploits the macro-similarities of all images in the training set in order to mine for recurring patterns in the feature space of a pre-trained CNN. We propose new objective functions enforcing the locality and unicity of the detected parts. Our detectors also provide a confidence measure based on correlation scores, allowing the system to estimate the visibility of each part. We apply our method on two public datasets, Caltech-UCSD Bird 200 (CUB-200) [35] and Stanford Cars [37], and show that our detectors can consistently highlight parts of the object while providing a good measure of the confidence in their prediction. Additionally, we provide classification results in order to showcase that classifiers based only on part detection can constitute a compromise between accuracy and transparency.

This paper is organized as follows: Sect. 2 presents the related work on part detection; Sect. 3 describes our PARTICUL model and Sect. 4 presents our results on two FGVC datasets. Finally, Sect. 5 concludes this paper and proposes several lines of research aiming at improving our approach.

2   Related Work

Part detection (and more generally attribute detection) is a problem which has been extensively studied in recent years, especially for FGVC which is a notoriously hard computer vision task. Learning how to detect object parts in this context can be done either in a fully supervised (using ground-truth part locations), weakly supervised (using image labels only) or unsupervised manner.

Weakly supervised approaches [3,5,8,14,16,18,21,25,30,36,38,42,43] produce part detectors as by-products of image classification *i.e.*, object parts are jointly learned with categories in an end-to-end manner to help distinguish very

---

[1] Patent pending.

similar categories. In particular, the OPAM approach presented in [25] obtains parts from candidate image patches that are generated by Selective Search [33], filtered through a dedicated pre-trained network, selected using an object-part spatial constraint model taking into account a coarse segmentation of the object at the image level, and finally semantically realigned by applying spectral clustering on their corresponding convolutional features.

Recently, unsupervised part detection methods have greatly benefited from the expressiveness and robustness of features extracted from images using deep CNNs. Modern approaches [15, 29, 39, 40, 42] mainly focus on applying clustering techniques in the feature space and/or identifying convolutional channels with consistent behaviors. More precisely, [15] produces part detectors through the sampling and clustering of keypoints within an estimation of the object segmentation produced by a method similar to GrabCut [26]. For a given image, [39] uses itemset mining to regroup convolutional channels based on their activation patterns, producing parts per image instead of globally (as in [25]) and thus requiring an additional semantic realignment - through clustering - for part-based classification. Rather than working on the full images, [40] and [29] use convolutional features of region proposals produced by Selective search [28]. [29] then learns the relation between regions and parts using clustering and soft assignment algorithms, while [40] builds part detectors from the top-k most activated filters across all regions of the training set. Due to the independent training of each detector, the latter approach produces tens of redundant part detectors which must be filtered out in a weakly unsupervised manner.

This issue is partially addressed in the MA-CNN approach [42], where part detectors are learned by performing a soft assignment of the convolutional channels of a pretrained CNN into groups that consistently have a peak response in the same neighborhood, then regressing the weight (importance) of each channel in each group through a fully convolutional layer applied on the feature map. Each part detector produces an activation map, normalized using a sigmoid function, corresponding to the probability of presence of the part at each location. By picking the location with the highest activation value for each detector, MA-CNN generates part-level images patches that are fed into a Part-CNN [2] architecture for classification. In practice, part detectors are initialized by channel grouping (using k-means clustering) and pre-trained in an unsupervised manner using dedicated loss functions enforcing the locality and unicity of each detector attention region. Finally, these detectors are fine-tuned during end-to-end learning of the image category. As such, this method falls into the category of unsupervised part learning with weakly supervised fine-tuning. More recently, the P-CNN approach [9] implements the part detection learning algorithm of MA-CNN, replacing the fully connected layer in charge of channel grouping by a convolution layer. Its classification pipeline uses Region-of-Interest (ROI) pooling layer around the location of maximum activation to directly extract part features and global features from the part detection backbone. In both cases, the channel grouping initialization requires first to process all images of the training set in order to cluster channels according to the location of their highest response. Moreover, for a given detector, only the area immediately surrounding the location of highest activation is taken into account (either to extract an image patch in [42] or a vector through ROI-pooling in [9]), thus reducing the ability to detect the same part at different scales.

Contributions. Our PARTICUL approach builds part detectors as weighted sums of convolutional channels extracted from a pre-trained CNN backbone. Our detectors are trained globally across the training set, instead of locally, contrary to [39] and [25] which require an additional semantic alignment phase. We develop objective functions that are specially crafted to ensure the compactness of the distribution of activation values for each part detector and the diversity of attention locations. Unlike [42] and [9], which propose similar functions, our approach does not require any fine-tuning of the backbone or an initial channel grouping phase. This induces a fast convergence during training and enables our module to be used with black-box backbones, in a plug-in fashion. Moreover, our detectors use a softmax normalization function, instead of sigmoid function, that simplifies the process of locating the part and enables us to detect parts at different scales. Finally, our detectors supply a measure of confidence in their decision based on the distribution of correlation scores across the training set. Importantly, this measure can also predict the *visibility* of a given part, a subject which is, to our knowledge, not tackled in any of the related work.

3   Proposed Model

In this section, we present PARTICUL, our proposal for unsupervised part learning from FGVC datasets. In practice, each part detector can be seen as a function highlighting dedicated attention regions on the input image, in accordance with the constraints detailed in this section.

Notations. For a tensor T inside a model $\mathcal{M}$, we denote $T(x)$ the value of T given an input x of $\mathcal{M}$. If T has H rows, W columns and C channels, we denote $T_{[h,w]}(x) \in \mathbb{R}^C$ the vector (or single feature) located at the hth row, wth column. We denote $*$ the convolution operation between tensors, σ the softmax normalization function. We define $\mathcal{I}$ as the set of all input images of a given dimension $H_{\mathcal{I}} \times W_{\mathcal{I}}$ and $\mathcal{I}_\mathcal{C} \subseteq \mathcal{I}$ as the subset of images in $\mathcal{I}$ containing an object of the macro-category $\mathcal{C}$. In our experiments, we denote $X_{train} = \{x_i \in \mathcal{I}_\mathcal{C} | i \in [1 .. n]\}$ the training set of size n. Although $\mathcal{I}_\mathcal{C}$ cannot usually be formally specified, we assume that X_{train} is representative of this set.

3.1   Part Detectors

As illustrated in Fig. 1, we first use a pre-trained CNN F to extract a $H \times W \times D$ feature map. Then, we build each of the p part detectors as a convolution with a $1 \times 1 \times D$ kernel $k^{(i)}$ (no bias is added), followed by a 2D spatial softmax layer, each part detector producing a $H \times W$ activation map

$$P(k^{(i)}, x) = \sigma\big(F(x) * k^{(i)}\big), \ \forall x \in \mathcal{I} \tag{1}$$

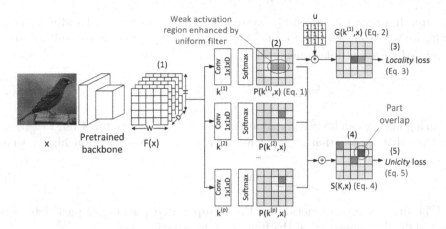

Fig. 1. Architecture of our PARTICUL model. (1) Convolutional features $F(x)$ are extracted from the image x. (2) Each part detector produces an activation map $P(k^{(i)}, x)$. (3) We apply a uniform kernel u to each part activation map before computing the Locality loss which ensures the compactness of activations. (4) All part activation maps are summed in $S(K, x)$. (5) Unicity loss is applied to ensure the diversity of part detectors. Here, part detectors 2 and p are very similar, leading to a high peak in bright red in $S(K, x)$. Best viewed in color.

We denote the set of all part detector kernels as $K = [k^{(1)}, k^{(2)}, \dots, k^{(p)}]$.

3.2 Objective Functions

Locality: For each part detector i, we force the network to learn a convolutional kernel $k^{(i)}$ which maximizes one region of the activation map for any training image x. In order to allow activations to be localized into a given neighborhood rather than in a single location in the $H \times W$ activation map, we first apply a 3×3 uniform filter u on $P(k^{(i)}, x)$. Let

$$G(k^{(i)}, x) = P(k^{(i)}, x) * \underbrace{\begin{pmatrix} 1 & 1 & 1 \\ 1 & 1 & 1 \\ 1 & 1 & 1 \end{pmatrix}}_{u} \qquad (2)$$

Learning all convolutional kernels K in order to enforce locality can be translated as the optimization of the objective function

$$\mathcal{L}_l(K) = -\frac{1}{p} \sum_{i=1}^{p} \frac{1}{n} \sum_{x \in X_{train}} \max_{h,w} \left(G(k^{(i)}, x)_{[h,w]} \right) \qquad (3)$$

Intuitively, solving the optimization problem in Eq. 3 using $G(k^{(i)}, x)$ rather than $P(k^{(i)}, x)$ relaxes the learning constraint and prevents the detectors from focusing on discriminative details between two adjacent feature vectors that would represent the same part.

Unicity. In order to prevent the system from learning only a handful of easy parts, we wish to ensure that each feature vector $F_{[h,w]}(x)$ is not simultaneously correlated with multiple convolutional kernels $k^{(i)}$. Let $S(K, x) \in \mathbb{R}^{H \times W}$ s.t.:

$$S_{[h,w]}(K, x) = \sum_{i=1}^{p} P(k^{(i)}, x)_{[h,w]} \tag{4}$$

Ensuring unicity can be translated as the following objective function, *i.e.*, making sure that no location (h, w) contains a cumulative activation higher than 1:

$$\mathcal{L}_u(K) = \frac{1}{n} \sum_{x \in X_{train}} \max \left(\max_{h,w} S_{[h,w]}(K, x) - 1, 0 \right) \tag{5}$$

The final objective function for the unsupervised learning of part detectors is a weighted composition of the functions described above:

$$\mathcal{L}(K) = \mathcal{L}_l(K) + \lambda \mathcal{L}_u(K) \tag{6}$$

where λ controls the relative importance of each objective function.

3.3   Confidence Measure and Visibility

Visibility is related to a measure of confidence in the decision provided by each of our detectors and based on the distribution of correlation scores across the training set. After fitting our detectors to Eq. 6, we employ the function

$$H_i : \mathcal{I} \to \mathbb{R}$$
$$x \to \max_{h,w} \left(F_{[h,w]}(x) * k^{(i)} \right) \tag{7}$$

returning the maximum correlation score of detector i for image x (before soft-max normalization). The distribution of values taken by H_i across $\mathcal{I}_C$ is modeled as a random variable following a normal distribution $\mathcal{N}(\mu_i, \sigma_i^2)$ estimated over X_{train}. We define the confidence measure of part detector i on image x as

$$C(x, i) = \Phi(H_i(x), \mu_i, \sigma_i^2) \tag{8}$$

where $\Phi(z, \mu, \sigma^2)$ is the cumulative distribution function of $\mathcal{N}(\mu_i, \sigma_i^2)$.

4   Experiments

In order to showcase the effectiveness of our approach, we apply our algorithm on two public FGVC datasets - the Caltech-UCSD Birds 200 (CUB-200) [35] dataset containing 11,788 images from 200 bird species (5994 training images, 5794 test images) and the Stanford Cars [37] dataset containing 16,185 images from 196 car models (8144 training images, 8041 test images). In addition to the object subcategory labels (bird species, car model), both datasets also provide additional information in the form of annotations (object bounding box, part locations in [35]). However, when learning and calibrating our part detectors, and unless specified otherwise, **we do not use any information other than the images themselves** and work in a fully unsupervised setting.

4.1 Unsupervised Learning of Part Detectors

In this section, we illustrate our unsupervised part detection algorithm using VGG19 [31] (with batch normalization) pretrained on the Imagenet dataset [4] as our extractor $F(.)$ (Eq. 1). For part visualization, we use SmoothGrad [32], filtering out small gradients using the method described in [24].

We train our detectors during 30 epochs, using RMSprop with a learning rate of 5×10^{-4} and a decay of 10^{-5}. These training parameters are chosen using cross-validation on the training set, with the goal of minimizing the objective function (Eq. 6). Since we do not need to fine-tune the extractor, only $p \times D$ convolutional weights are learned during training, which drastically reduces the computation time. Finally, for a given number of parts p, we supervise the importance λ of the unicity constraint (Eq. 6) by measuring the overall attention across the feature map after training. More precisely, we compute the value

$$\mathcal{E}(X_{train}, K) = \frac{1}{|X_{train}|} \sum_{x \in X_{train}} \frac{1}{p} \sum_{h,w} \max_{i \in [1..p]} P(k^{(i)}, x)_{[h,w]} \qquad (9)$$

corresponding to the average contribution of each detector. $\mathcal{E}(X_{train}, K) = 1$ corresponds to the ideal case where all detectors focus on different locations in the feature map $F(x)$, while $\mathcal{E}(X_{train}, K) = 1/p$ indicates a high redundancy of attention regions among detectors. As illustrated in Fig. 2, for both datasets the average contribution of each detector decreases with p, reflecting the growing difficulty of finding distinct detectors. The choice of p itself depends on the downstream task (*e.g.*, classification), where again increasing the number of parts might produce diminishing returns (see Sect. 4.3). Moreover, in both datasets the presence ($\lambda > 0$) of our unicity loss function (Eq. 5) is paramount to learning distinct detectors. Without the unicity constraint, in the case of CUB-200 all detectors systematically converge towards the same location inside of the feature map ($\mathcal{E}(X_{train}, K) \approx 1/p$) corresponding to the head of the bird; in the

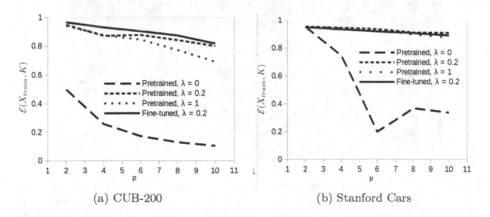

(a) CUB-200   (b) Stanford Cars

Fig. 2. $\mathcal{E}(X_{train}, K)$ v. number p of detectors for various values of λ, with pre-trained or fine-tuned extractor.

180   R. Xu-Darme et al.

case of Stanford Cars, where images contain more varied distinctive patterns, the number of unique detectors depends on the random initialization of their convolutional weights, but the average contribution per detector quickly drops with p. For both datasets, we choose $\lambda = 0.2$ which maximizes $\mathcal{E}(X_{train}, K)$ for all values of p. As a comparison, we also train our detectors after fine-tuning the extractor on each dataset (in this case, the learning process can be considered weakly supervised), leading to only marginally better results. This supports our claim that, in practice, our detectors do not require a fine-tuned extractor and can work as a plug-in module to a black-box extractor.

As illustrated in Fig. 3, our detectors consistently highlight recurring parts of the objects and are relatively insensitive to the scale of the part. Although we notice some apparent redundancy of the detected parts (*e.g.,* around the head of the bird), the relatively high corresponding value for $\mathcal{E}(X_{train}, K)$ (0.87 for $\lambda = 0.2$ and $p = 6$, see Fig. 2a) indicates that each detector actually focus

Fig. 3. Part visualization after training 6 detectors using the VGG19 extractor on Stanford cars (top) or CUB-200 (bottom). Using this visualizations, we can manually re-attach a semantic value to each detector, *e.g.,* the second part detector trained on CUB-200 is probably a "leg" detector. Best viewed in color.

on a different location of the feature map, leading to a richer representation of the object. Note that when training our detectors, we do not know beforehand towards which part each detector will converge. However, using part visualization, we can re-attach a semantic value to each detector after training.

4.2 Confidence Measure

After training our detectors, we perform a calibration of their confidence measure using the method presented in Sect. 3.3. In order to illustrate the soundness of our approach, we exploit the annotations provided by the CUB-200 dataset to extract a subset of images where the legs of the bird are non-visible (2080 images from both the training and test set, where the annotations indicate that the color of the legs is not visible). As shown on Fig. 4a, there is a clear difference in the distributions of maximum correlation scores between images with and without visible legs. This also confirms that images not containing the part tend to produce lower correlation scores, and by consequence our proposal for a confidence measure based on a cumulative distribution function (Eq. 8). In practice (Fig. 4b), a calibrated detector can detect the same part at different scales while ignoring images where the confidence measure is below a given threshold (2% in the example). It is interesting to note that for all images in the middle row, the annotations actually indicate that the legs are not visible, *i.e.*, our detectors can also be employed as a fast tool to verify manual annotations.

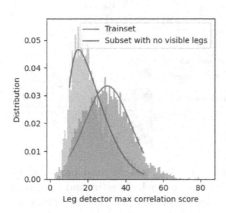

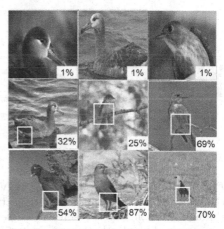

(a) Distribution of maximum correlation scores on the CUB-200 training set (in blue) and on a subset containing only images with non-visible legs (red).

(b) Confidence scores and part visualizations on images with non visible legs (top-row) and with visible legs (bottom rows).

Fig. 4. Confidence measure applied on a bird leg detector trained and calibrated on CUB-200 dataset. Best viewed in color.

4.3   Classification

In all related works closest to ours, the performance of part detectors is never evaluated independently but rather *w.r.t.* to the classification task, a method which is highly dependent on the architecture chosen for the decision-making process: *e.g.,* SVMs in [15] and [29], Part-CNN [2] in [42], Spatially Weighted Fisher Vector CNN (SWFV) in [40], multi-stream architecture in [39]. Nevertheless, in order to provide a basis of comparison with state-of-art techniques, we also provide classification results based on the extraction of part feature vectors. As illustrated in Fig. 5, we use a method similar to [41], where the feature map $F(X)$ is multiplied element-wise with the activation map produced by each detector to compute a set of part feature vectors that are used as inputs of p independent classifiers (each containing 2 intermediate layers - with 4096 neurons, ReLU activation and dropout - before the classification layer). As such, our detectors operate a form of semantic realignment and extraction of relevant feature vectors from the image. Note that, contrary to the fixed size ROI pooling used in [9], this method has the advantage of dynamically adjusting the number of feature vectors taken into account depending on the scale of the part. For the final decision, we sum up the logits of all part-based classifiers to produce prediction scores for each category. Therefore, the final decision can be directly traced back to the individual result of each part-based classifier. This approach does not provide the transparency [20] of prototype-based methods [3, 22], but constitutes a good compromise to non interpretable approaches using global features.

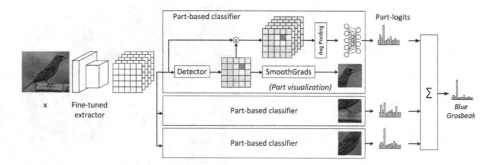

Fig. 5. Our classification model for FGVC datasets. The feature map produced by the extractor is masked out using the activation map of each detector and processed through a pooling layer, resulting in a set of part vector features. These vectors are processed independently through a set of fully connected layers to generate part-based logits that are summed up to produce the final prediction.

Table 1 summarizes the results obtained when using our part-based classifier, along with the results obtained on a fine-tuned VGG-19 (acting as a baseline) and other state-of-the-art methods. With 8 detectors, we outperform the prototype-based approach [22] - which uses a more efficient extractor (Resnet50) - on Stanford Cars and obtain similar results on CUB-200. When compared

Table 1. Classification accuracy on CUB-200 and Stanford Cars and comparison with related works, from less transparent to most transparent.

⟵ Transparency [20] ⟵

Method	Train anno.	Accuracy (%)	
		CUB-200	Stanford Cars
Global features only			
Baseline (VGG-19)		83.3	89.3
Part + global features			
UPM[39] (VGG19)		81.9	89.2
OPAM [25] (VGG-16)		85.8	92.2
MA-CNN [42] (VGG-19)		86.5	92.8
P-CNN [9] (VGG-19)		87.3	93.3
Part-based			
Ours (VGG-19)			
2 parts		70.1	76.0
4 parts		79.2	84.2
6 parts		81.5	87.5
8 parts		82.3	88.3
10 parts		82.3	88.6
OPAM [25] (parts-only, VGG-16)		80.7	84.3
No parts[15] (VGG19)	BBox	82.0	92.6
+ Test Bbox	BBox	82.8	92.8
PDFS[40] (VGG-19)		84.5	n/a
Prototypes			
ProtoPNet [3] (VGG-19)	BBox	78.0 ± 0.2	85.9 ± 0.2
ProtoTree [22] (Resnet-50)		82.2 ± 0.7	86.6 ± 0.2

with other methods using only part-level features, our PARTICUL model outperforms the OPAM [25] approach on both datasets. We also obtain comparable results to other methods requiring either the object bounding box [15] or to preselect detectors (in a weakly supervised manner) based on their classification accuracy [40]. When compared with less transparent methods using image-level (global) features in addition to part-level features - a method which usually has a significant impact on accuracy (*e.g.,* from 80.7% to 85.8% on CUB-200 using OPAM [25]) - again we achieve comparable results and even outperform the UPM [39] approach on CUB-200. Finally, it is also interesting to note that for both datasets, our classification results obtained by picking 10 feature vectors out of the $14 \times 14 = 196$ possible vectors of the extractor feature map correspond to a drop of less then 1% in accuracy when compared with the baseline, indicating that we are indeed selecting the most relevant vectors for the classification. Moreover, in 80% (resp. 77%) of these cases where only the baseline provides a correct prediction on the CUB-200 (resp. Stanford Cars) dataset, at least one of our individual part-based classifier does provide a correct prediction (see Fig. 6). Thus, our proposed model could be further improved by fine-tuning the relative importance of part logits (*e.g.,* using the confidence measure).

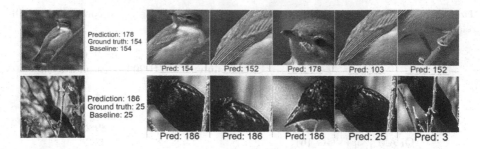

Fig. 6. Examples of images correctly classified by the baseline and incorrectly classified by our model (only 5 parts are shown for clarity). In both cases, at least one part-based classifier provides a correct prediction. Best viewed in color.

5   Conclusion and Future Work

In this paper, we presented our algorithm for unsupervised part learning using datasets for FGVC. We showed that our detectors can consistently highlight parts of an object while providing a confidence measure associated with the detection. To our knowledge, our method is the first to take the visibility of parts into account, paving the road for a solid attribute learning and ultimately for interpretable visual recognition. In the particular context of FGVC, our detectors can be integrated in a part-based classification architecture which constitutes a good compromise between the transparency of prototype-based approaches and the performance of non-interpretable methods. As a future work, we will study the integration of our detectors into a prototype-based architecture, learning prototypes from part feature vectors rather than from the entire image feature map. We will also study the impact of weighting part logits by the confidence score associated with the detected part on the overall accuracy of the system.

Acknowledgements. Experiments presented in this paper were carried out using the Grid'5000 testbed, supported by a scientific interest group hosted by Inria and including CNRS, RENATER and several Universities as well as other organizations. This work has been partially supported by MIAI@Grenoble Alpes, (ANR-19-P3IA-0003) and TAILOR, a project funded by EU Horizon 2020 research and innovation programme under GA No 952215. This work was financially supported by European commission through the SAFAIR subproject of the project SPARTA which has received funding from the European Union's Horizon 2020 research and innovation programme under GA No 830892, as well as through the CPS4EU project that has received funding from the ECSEL Joint Undertaking (JU) under GA No 826276.

References

1. Abdulnabi, A.H., Wang, G., Lu, J., Jia, K.: Multi-task CNN model for attribute prediction. IEEE Trans. Multimedia **17**(11), 1949–1959 (2015). https://doi.org/10.1109/TMM.2015.2477680. arXiv:1601.00400

2. Branson, S., Van Horn, G., Belongie, S., Perona, P.: Bird species categorization using pose normalized deep convolutional nets. In: Proceedings of the British Machine Vision Conference 2014, BMVC 2014, June 2014. arXiv:1406.2952
3. Chen, C., Li, O., Tao, C., Barnett, A.J., Su, J., Rudin, C.: This looks like that: deep learning for interpretable image recognition. In: Proceedings of the 33rd International Conference on Neural Information Processing Systems, pp. 8930–8941 (2019)
4. Deng, J., Dong, W., Socher, R., Li, L.J., Li, K., Fei-Fei, L.: ImageNet: a large-scale hierarchical image database. In: 2009 IEEE Conference on Computer Vision and Pattern Recognition, pp. 248–255. IEEE (2009)
5. Ding, Y., Zhou, Y., Zhu, Y., Ye, Q., Jiao, J.: Selective sparse sampling for fine-grained image recognition. In: 2019 IEEE/CVF International Conference on Computer Vision (ICCV), Seoul, South Korea, pp. 6598–6607. IEEE, October 2019. https://doi.org/10.1109/ICCV.2019.00670. https://ieeexplore.ieee.org/document/9008286/
6. Farhadi, A., Endres, I., Hoiem, D., Forsyth, D.: Describing objects by their attributes. In: 2009 IEEE Conference on Computer Vision and Pattern Recognition, pp. 1778–1785 (2009). https://doi.org/10.1109/CVPR.2009.5206772
7. Fukui, H., Hirakawa, T., Yamashita, T., Fujiyoshi, H.: Attention branch network: learning of attention mechanism for visual explanation. In: 2019 IEEE/CVF Conference on Computer Vision and Pattern Recognition (CVPR), pp. 10697–10706 (2019). https://doi.org/10.1109/CVPR.2019.01096
8. Ge, W., Lin, X., Yu, Y.: Weakly supervised complementary parts models for fine-grained image classification from the bottom up. In: 2019 IEEE/CVF Conference on Computer Vision and Pattern Recognition (CVPR), pp. 3029–3038 (2019)
9. Han, J., Yao, X., Cheng, G., Feng, X., Xu, D.: P-CNN: part-based convolutional neural networks for fine-grained visual categorization. IEEE Tran. Pattern Anal. Mach. Intell. **44**(2), 579–590 (2022). https://doi.org/10.1109/TPAMI.2019.2933510
10. Han, K., Guo, J., Zhang, C., Zhu, M.: Attribute-aware attention model for fine-grained representation learning. In: Proceedings of the 26th ACM International Conference on Multimedia (2018)
11. Hassan, M.U., Mulhem, P., Pellerin, D., Quénot, G.: Explaining visual classification using attributes. In: 2019 International Conference on Content-Based Multimedia Indexing (CBMI), pp. 1–6 (2019)
12. Hendricks, L.A., Akata, Z., Rohrbach, M., Donahue, J., Schiele, B., Darrell, T.: Generating visual explanations. In: Leibe, B., Matas, J., Sebe, N., Welling, M. (eds.) ECCV 2016. LNCS, vol. 9908, pp. 3–19. Springer, Cham (2016). https://doi.org/10.1007/978-3-319-46493-0_1
13. Jo, E.S., Gebru, T.: Lessons from archives: strategies for collecting sociocultural data in machine learning. In: Proceedings of the 2020 Conference on Fairness, Accountability, and Transparency, FAT* 2020, pp. 306–316. Association for Computing Machinery (2020). https://doi.org/10.1145/3351095.3372829
14. Korsch, D., Bodesheim, P., Denzler, J.: Classification-specific parts for improving fine-grained visual categorization. In: Fink, G.A., Frintrop, S., Jiang, X. (eds.) DAGM GCPR 2019. LNCS, vol. 11824, pp. 62–75. Springer, Cham (2019). https://doi.org/10.1007/978-3-030-33676-9_5
15. Krause, J., Jin, H., Yang, J., Fei-Fei, L.: Fine-grained recognition without part annotations. In: 2015 IEEE Conference on Computer Vision and Pattern Recognition (CVPR), pp. 5546–5555 (2015). https://doi.org/10.1109/CVPR.2015.7299194

16. Duan, K., Parikh, D., Crandall, D., Grauman, K.: Discovering localized attributes for fine-grained recognition. In: 2012 IEEE Conference on Computer Vision and Pattern Recognition, Providence, RI, pp. 3474–3481. IEEE, June 2012. https://doi. org/10.1109/CVPR.2012.6248089. http://ieeexplore.ieee.org/document/6248089/
17. Lampert, C.H., Nickisch, H., Harmeling, S.: Attribute-based classification for zero-shot visual object categorization. IEEE Trans. Pattern Anal. Mach. Intell. 36(3), 453–465 (2014). https://doi.org/10.1109/TPAMI.2013.140
18. Li, H., Zhang, X., Tian, Q., Xiong, H.: Attribute mix: semantic data augmentation for fine grained recognition. In: 2020 IEEE International Conference on Visual Communications and Image Processing (VCIP), pp. 243–246 (2020). https://doi. org/10.1109/VCIP49819.2020.9301763
19. Liang, K., Chang, H., Shan, S., Chen, X.: A unified multiplicative framework for attribute learning. In: 2015 IEEE International Conference on Computer Vision (ICCV), Santiago, Chile, pp. 2506–2514. IEEE, December 2015. https://doi.org/ 10.1109/ICCV.2015.288. http://ieeexplore.ieee.org/document/7410645/
20. Lipton, Z.C.: The mythos of model interpretability. Commun. ACM 61, 36–43 (2018)
21. Liu, X., Xia, T., Wang, J., Yang, Y., Zhou, F., Lin, Y.: Fine-grained recognition with automatic and efficient part attention. [Preprint] arXiv:1603.06765 [cs], March 2017
22. Nauta, M., van Bree, R., Seifert, C.: Neural prototype trees for interpretable fine-grained image recognition. In: 2021 IEEE/CVF Conference on Computer Vision and Pattern Recognition (CVPR), pp. 14928–14938 (2021)
23. Northcutt, C.G., Athalye, A., Mueller, J.: Pervasive label errors in test sets destabilize machine learning benchmarks. arXiv arXiv:2103.14749 (2021)
24. Otsu, N.: A threshold selection method from gray-level histograms. IEEE Trans. Syst. Man Cybern. 9(1), 62–66 (1979). https://doi.org/10.1109/TSMC.1979. 4310076
25. Peng, Y., He, X., Zhao, J.: Object-part attention model for fine-grained image classification. IEEE Trans. Image Process. 27(3), 1487–1500, March 2018. https:// doi.org/10.1109/TIP.2017.2774041. arXiv:1704.01740
26. Rother, C., Kolmogorov, V., Blake, A.: "GrabCut" - interactive foreground extraction using iterated graph cuts. In: ACM SIGGRAPH 2004 Papers (2004)
27. Rymarczyk, D., Struski, L., Tabor, J., Zieliński, B.: ProtoPShare: prototype sharing for interpretable image classification and similarity discovery. [preprint] arXiv:2011.14340 [cs], November 2020
28. van de Sande, K.E.A., Uijlings, J.R.R., Gevers, T., Smeulders, A.W.M.: Segmentation as selective search for object recognition. In: 2011 International Conference on Computer Vision, Barcelona, Spain, pp. 1879–1886. IEEE, November 2011. https://doi.org/10.1109/ICCV.2011.6126456. http://ieeexplore.ieee.org/ document/6126456/
29. Sicre, R., Avrithis, Y., Kijak, E., Jurie, F.: Unsupervised part learning for visual recognition. In: 2017 IEEE Conference on Computer Vision and Pattern Recognition (CVPR), Honolulu, HI, pp. 3116–3124. IEEE, July 2017. https://doi.org/10. 1109/CVPR.2017.332. http://ieeexplore.ieee.org/document/8099815/
30. Simon, M., Rodner, E.: Neural activation constellations: unsupervised part model discovery with convolutional networks. 2015 IEEE International Conference on Computer Vision (ICCV), pp. 1143–1151 (2015)
31. Simonyan, K., Zisserman, A.: Very deep convolutional networks for large-scale image recognition. CoRR abs/1409.1556 (2015)

32. Smilkov, D., Thorat, N., Kim, B., Viégas, F.B., Wattenberg, M.: SmoothGrad: removing noise by adding noise. arXiv:1706.03825 (2017)
33. Uijlings, J.R.R., van de Sande, K.E.A., Gevers, T., Smeulders, A.W.M.: Selective search for object recognition. Int. J. Comput. Vis. **104**, 154–171 (2013)
34. Wang, J., Zhu, X., Gong, S., Li, W.: Attribute recognition by joint recurrent learning of context and correlation. In: 2017 IEEE International Conference on Computer Vision (ICCV), pp. 531–540 (2017)
35. Welinder, P., et al.: Caltech-UCSD Birds 200. Technical report. CNS-TR-2010-001, California Institute of Technology (2010)
36. Xiao, T., Xu, Y., Yang, K., Zhang, J., Peng, Y., Zhang, Z.: The Application of two-level attention models in deep convolutional neural network for fine-grained image classification. In: 2015 IEEE Conference on Computer Vision and Pattern Recognition (CVPR), pp. 842–850 (2015)
37. Yang, L., Luo, P., Loy, C.C., Tang, X.: A large-scale car dataset for fine-grained categorization and verification. In: 2015 IEEE Conference on Computer Vision and Pattern Recognition (CVPR), pp. 3973–3981 (2015)
38. Yang, Z., Luo, T., Wang, D., Hu, Z., Gao, J., Wang, L.: Learning to navigate for fine-grained classification. In: Ferrari, V., Hebert, M., Sminchisescu, C., Weiss, Y. (eds.) Computer Vision – ECCV 2018. LNCS, vol. 11218, pp. 438–454. Springer, Cham (2018). https://doi.org/10.1007/978-3-030-01264-9_26
39. Zhang, J., Zhang, R., Huang, Y., Zou, Q.: Unsupervised part mining for fine-grained image classification [preprint]. arXiv:1902.09941 (2019)
40. Zhang, X., Xiong, H., Zhou, W., Lin, W., Tian, Q.: Picking deep filter responses for fine-grained image recognition. In: 2016 IEEE Conference on Computer Vision and Pattern Recognition (CVPR), pp. 1134–1142 (2016)
41. Zhao, X., et al.: Recognizing part attributes with insufficient data. In: 2019 IEEE/CVF International Conference on Computer Vision (ICCV), Seoul, South Korea, pp. 350–360. IEEE, October 2019. https://doi.org/10.1109/ICCV.2019.00044. https://ieeexplore.ieee.org/document/9009781/
42. Zheng, H., Fu, J., Mei, T., Luo, J.: Learning multi-attention convolutional neural network for fine-grained image recognition. In: 2017 IEEE International Conference on Computer Vision (ICCV), Venice, pp. 5219–5227. IEEE, October 2017. https://doi.org/10.1109/ICCV.2017.557. http://ieeexplore.ieee.org/document/8237819/
43. Zhou, X., Yin, J., Tsang, I.W.H., Wang, C.: Human-understandable decision making for visual recognition. In: PAKDD (2021)
44. Zhu, J., Liao, S., Lei, Z., Li, S.: Multi-label convolutional neural network based pedestrian attribute classification. Image Vis. Comput. **58**, 224–229 (2017)

Explaining Classifications to Non-experts: An XAI User Study of Post-Hoc Explanations for a Classifier When People Lack Expertise

Courtney Ford[1,3](✉) and Mark T. Keane[1,2]

[1] School of Computer Science, University College Dublin, Dublin, Ireland
courtney.ford@ucdconnect.ie, mark.keane@ucd.ie
[2] Insight Centre for Data Analytics, UCD, Dublin, Ireland
[3] ML Labs, SFI CRT, Dublin, Ireland

Abstract. Very few eXplainable AI (XAI) studies consider how users' understanding of explanations might change depending on whether they know more/less about the to-be-explained domain (i.e., whether they differ in their expertise). Yet, expertise is a critical facet of most high-stakes, human decision-making (e.g., understanding how a trainee doctor differs from an experienced consultant). Accordingly, this paper reports a novel, user study (N = 96) on how people's expertise in a domain affects their understanding of post-hoc explanations-by-example for a deep-learning, black-box classifier. The results show that people's understanding of explanations for correct and incorrect classifications changes dramatically, on several dimensions (e.g., response times, perceptions of correctness and helpfulness), when the image-based domain considered is familiar (i.e., MNIST) as opposed to unfamiliar (i.e., Kannada-MNIST). The wider implications of these new findings for XAI strategies are discussed.

Keywords: Explainable AI · Expertise · Deep Learning

1 Introduction

As Artificial Intelligence (AI) extends its automated decision-making capabilities to tasks that impact our everyday lives, there is an urgency to solve the problem of explaining the operation of these systems to human end-users using Explainable AI (XAI). Furthermore, opaque deep learning models are increasingly used for high-stakes decision-making tasks (e.g., cancer detection [9] and crime occurrence [15]); decisions that need to be explainable to audiences with varying levels of expertise. However, very little hard evidence exists on whether people with different levels of domain knowledge understand automated explanations differently. In this paper, we consider how *domain expertise* changes people's understanding of automated, post-hoc example-based explanations of a deep learner's classifications of images of written numbers with which users have differential familiarity (i.e., MNIST and Kannada-MNIST).

© Springer Nature Switzerland AG 2023
J.-J. Rousseau and B. Kapralos (Eds.): ICPR 2022 Workshops, LNCS 13645, pp. 246–260, 2023.
https://doi.org/10.1007/978-3-031-37731-0_15

1.1 Post-Hoc Explanation of Unfamiliar Images

Consider a medical scenario where a black-box classifier analyzes MRI images for cancer detection. The system might explain a detection of a cancerous mass by showing end-users similar historical images with the same diagnosis (i.e., so-called post-hoc, example-based explanations [20]). Alternatively, it might highlight a critical region in the MRI to show the key features leading to the diagnosis (i.e., feature-importance explanations [23, 26]). Although many XAI methods generate such explanations, there is a dearth of user studies on how people understand these explanations and whether they really work as intended (e.g., see [16]). Even fewer user studies have considered whether different users who have different expertise in a domain, understand automated explanations differently.

However, intuitively, expertise is likely to be important to people's understanding of explanations. For instance, a medical consultant with many years' experience will engage very differently with an MRI image from a student doctor. The consultant may "read" the image quicker, find critical features more readily, and reach different diagnostic conclusions based on their deeper expertise. So, automated explanations may need to consider expertise differences in what the model presents to users to support decision making. Unfortunately, most XAI methods assume a one-size-fits-all approach to explanation, that all users should receive the same explanation irrespective of their background. In this paper, we present a study that reveals wholly-new evidence on how users' perceptions of explanations can change based on their expertise with an image-based domain analyzed by an AI classifier.

The present study examines post-hoc, example-based explanations for classifications made by a convolutional neural network (CNN) involving images of written numbers (from the MNIST and Kannada-MNIST datasets). Kenny et al. [19, 20] have previously shown that correct and incorrect MNIST classifications by this CNN can be explained by finding nearest-neighboring examples to a query-image from the training data, using their twin-systems XAI method (see Fig. 1). These example-based explanations give users insight into why the model classified an image in a certain way (see Fig. 2). In a series of user studies, Kenny et al. [18] showed that people who were given these explanations judged misclassifications differently to those who did not receive explanations. Specifically, they found that explanations led people to judge misclassifications as being more correct, even though they still recognized them as incorrect (n.b., similar effects did not occur in correct classifications). They also showed that people experienced algorithmic aversion; users trust in the model decreased when they were shown more and more misclassifications. However, these results involved written Arabic numerals commmonly used by English-speaking participants (i.e., the MNIST dataset), a well-learned domain from an early age, regularly practiced when reading handwritten information. So, everyone was an deep-expert with these written-numbers image-data. This paper examines how a Western, English-speaking population responds to example-based explanations from an unfamiliar, Indian number system (i.e., the Kannada-MNIST dataset). By performing matched tests with explanations of the CNN's classifications for these two different written-numeral systems, we aim to assess cognitive differences that arise from differences in expertise.

We report a large user study examining the effect of domain expertise on example-based explanations for classifications made by a CNN. The key manipulation used to test for expertise effects involved presenting participants with familiar (i.e., Arabic numerals from the MNIST dataset) or unfamiliar (i.e., Indian numerals from the Kannada-MNIST dataset) written numbers. In the following subsection, we quickly describe the main differences between these two image datasets (see Subsect. 1.2), before outlining the structure of the paper (see Subsect. 1.3).

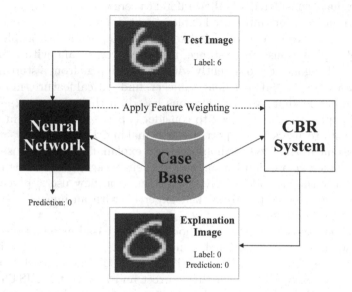

Fig. 1. Twin-Systems XAI (Adapted from [19,20]): Feature weights from a CNN classifier are mapped to a twinned Case Based Reasoner (i.e., a k-NN), so the classification of the test image is explained post-hoc by close examples from the dataset/case-base.

1.2   A Tale of Two Written-Number Systems

The MNIST dataset consists of 70,000 images of handwritten, single-digit Arabic numerals. MNIST is a ubiquitous machine learning dataset; its simplicity and "too perfect" data features (i.e., the images uniformly centered with the digits of equal sizes) routinely results in accuracies >99% for many models [1]. MNIST has also been heavily explored in the XAI literature, often user-tested in a "classifier debugging" task of the sort used here (e.g., see [10,18,28]).

Several newer datasets address MNIST's limitations. One such dataset, the Kannada-MNIST [25], is comprised of ten classes of data (representing Arabic numerals 0–9) in the Kannada script. The Kannada language is spoken in Karnataka, India, and its single-digit numeral system is comparable to MNIST in its

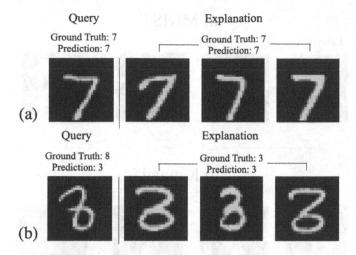

Fig. 2. Examples of post-hoc, example-based explanations for (a) a correct and (b) incorrect classification. The query image gives the CNN's prediction, along with three nearest neighbours in the dataset that influenced the classification made [19,20].

relative simplicity (i.e., most characters are single-stroke). Over 200 published AI papers have used the Kannada-MNIST dataset since 2019; however, to our knowledge, no XAI studies using the dataset have been completed.

Figure 3 shows samples of the MNIST and Kannada-MNIST datasets. These different written-numeral datasets give us an intuitive sense of how expertise might impact people's understanding of them. Readers familiar with the symbol "two" in Fig. 3a understand that the first two symbols, beside the printed number (i.e., in the blue box), can be a "two" even though the second contains a loop feature absent in the others. We also know that even though an "eight" has a similar loop, it is a different number-class to "two", because it has a closed upper-loop that the "two" lacks. So, expertise with these written numbers allows us to judge "acceptable variations" in the class instances and judge the class boundaries between classes when progressive changes make it a different number.

Now, consider the unfamiliar Kannada dataset, assuming you are an English-speaking Westerner with no knowledge of Indian languages. Figure 3b shows the Kannada symbol "mūru" (the symbol for the number 3). Without domain expertise, it is hard to judge whether the three symbols to the right of the printed number (i.e., in the blue box) are valid variants of "mūru" or whether they are from different number-classes. In fact, the third symbol (in the orange box) is from a different number-class, though it is very similar. As in MRI interpretation by doctors, non-expert users may not easily determine which classifications are correct or incorrect. Non-experts may not notice subtle differences between images and, indeed, may find explanations harder to understand. It is these aspects of the user experience that we explore in the present study.

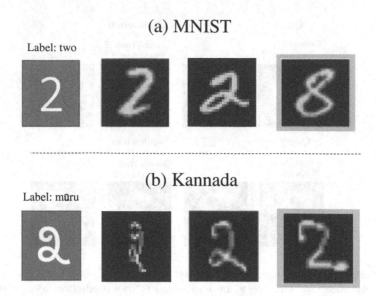

Fig. 3. Examples of variation within a class for the (a) MNIST and (b) Kannada datasets. Images outlined in orange are numbers from different, but similar, classes. (Color figure online)

1.3   Outline of Paper

The following section outlines related work on expertise and how it might impact AI systems (see Sect. 2). In the remainder of the paper, we report a user study that examines the effect of domain expertise and example-based explanations on people's judgments of a CNN's correct and incorrect classifications using the MNIST and Kannada datasets (see Sects. 3, 4, and 5). The study tests the local effects of domain expertise using a comparison of the MNIST versus Kannada-MNIST (henceforth, Kannada) dataset. This research is wholly novel in the current XAI literature (see Sect. 2) and reveals how expertise impacts several different psychological measures. In Sect. 6, we consider the broader implications of these findings for the interpretability of black-box models.

2   Related Work

Experts are individuals who have superior knowledge of a domain, and their expertise is generally assumed to be acquired through learned experience [36]. Evidence from cognitive science suggests that experts profit from perceptual processes that aid in the storage, retrieval, and analysis of domain-familiar stimuli. One such process called "chunking" enables experts to store units of information in a single, compact group rather than as separate individual entities [5,6,12]. Though experts can exploit chunking for goal-oriented tasks (e.g., expert chess players use goal-oriented chunking to recall and anticipate moves more clearly and quickly than less experienced players [7]), chunking is primarily a subconscious, perceptual process learned from experience [11]. For example, readers and writers of languages with complex character systems (e.g., Chinese) perceptually chunk "semantic-phonetic" compound characters as a cohesive unit rather than separate parts; a skill that develops gradually alongside improving language expertise in vocabulary and grammar [2]. Other aspects of perceptual expertise, such as visual search, also appear to develop over time. Krupinski et al. [22], in a longitudinal study, found that resident pathologists became increasingly more efficient at viewing domain-familiar images and focusing on key image details over the term of their residencies.

There is a considerable literature on the impact of domain expertise on people's perceptual processing of images. Consistent findings suggest that experts outperform non-experts in reaction time [34], visual span [4,34], and change detection [35]. In a series of user studies, Thompson and Tangen [30] manipulated the amount of perceptual information (i.e., image quality and time) available to fingerprint experts and novices. The experts outperformed novices in measures of accuracy and time despite image noise and temporal spacing; their results suggested that experts benefit from "non-analytic" processing of domain-familiar data that supersedes information quality. However, this advantage disappears for non-domain-related images [17]. Searston and Tangen [29] found that domain experts have an accuracy and speed advantage over novices when identifying matches and outliers in familiar stimuli (i.e., fingerprint images), but show the same behaviour as novices when identifying non-domain images (i.e., inverted faces). So, the improved perceptual abilities and task performance of experts only holds when the domain is familiar to them; experts and non-experts perform the same when the domain is unfamiliar to both groups. To that end, it is possible that non-experts could benefit from feature signaling (e.g., highlighted data features [21]), or by presenting tasks as similarity judgments [27].

The wealth of cognitive research on expertise suggests that it influences analytic and decision-making tasks. But, what if analyses and decisions are made by an AI system? Recently, a small number of papers have directly investigated the role of domain expertise on trust in an AI system. Nourani, King, and Ragan [24] report a user study on the role of expertise and AI-system first-impressions on users' trust. They found that domain experts are sensitive to system error based on their first impressions of an AI system; experts who saw correct classifications at the start of the system interaction reported higher trust in the overall system than experts who first viewed system errors. Novices, on the other hand, were not sensitive to material-type order, but over-estimated the system's accuracy despite viewing multiple misclassifications. Bayer, Gimpel, and Markgraf [3] found that explanations of a decision-support system contributed to higher trust in the overall system for domain experts but failed to improve trust in non-experts. It appears that experts augment the system's explanation with their domain knowledge, whereas the same explanation has little significance to someone with no or limited domain understanding. Dikman and Burns [8] reported a user study in which participants (all of whom were non-experts) were provided with an occasionally faulty AI Assistant for an investing task; the experimental condition additionally received domain information that stated why a given factor influences the decision. They found that participants made fewer risky investments when provided with domain information, sometimes in opposition to the AI assistant. In fact, these participants reported less trust in the AI system [8]. Therefore, it appears that augmenting expertise throughout a user-system interaction improves user performance at the expense of trust if the system is repeatedly inaccurate or provides faulty recommendations.

The literature described above indicates fundamental perceptual differences between experts and non-experts that impact the effectiveness of XAI explanation strategies. Experts process familiar information faster and more accurately than novices, though this advantage disappears in unfamiliar domains. Therefore, some explanation strategies may slow experts down (i.e., if the data is familiar), while others assume a higher level of knowledge or experience than the user possesses. Experts also seem to be sensitive to domain-familiar system errors, an issue possibly resolved by an alternate, error-specific explanation strategy. Non-experts, on the other hand, may require an alternative explanation strategy to experts. Though novices generally perform worse than experts in the experts' domain, consistent findings show that novices are just as accurate as experts in unfamiliar domains. From an XAI perspective, these findings suggest that explanations for novices could close the accuracy gap through supplemental information or guided assistance. Recently, Herchenbach et al. [13] have argued that the explanation strategy for experts using these domains should use class-specific prototypes, near misses (i.e., counterfactuals) and near hits (i.e., semi-factuals) and show how these can be computed. However, their proposals are not grounded in any user analysis and some caution is warrented in juggling so many different explanation options [32,33]. The current study explores the impact of domain expertise on the efficacy of post-hoc, example-based explanations by varying the familiarity of the domains presented to a single group.

3 User Study: Expertise in Image Classification

Kenny et al. [18] user tested post-hoc example-based explanations of a CNN's classifications of image data (i.e., MNIST data). They extracted correct and incorrect classifications from a CNN, explaining them with nearest neighbours using their twin-systems method. In a "classifier debugging" task, participants judged the correctness of classifications with and without explanations and it was shown that example-based explanations changed people's perception of misclassifications (but not correct classifications); people given explanations viewed these errors as "less incorrect" than those not getting explanations. So, explanations partly mitigated people's perception of errors made by the AI system. However, these tests were performed on a familiar dataset (the Arabic numerals of MNIST). At present, no evidence in the literature exists on how people respond to an unfamiliar, image dataset (such as the Kannada-MNIST one).

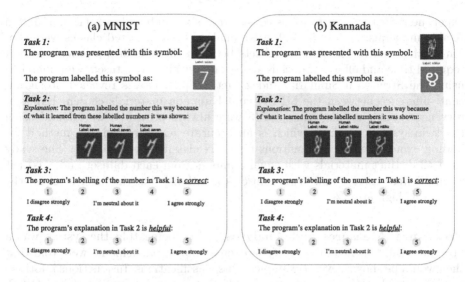

Fig. 4. Sample materials used in the study showing (a) MNIST and (b) Kannada-MNIST misclassifications along with explanations showing three nearest neighbours.

3.1   Method

The present study compares people's performance on the MNIST dataset to a matched set of images from the Kannada dataset, using the measures used before (Correctness, Trust, Satisfaction) and several new measures (Helpfulness and Response Time). In the study, people were presented with matched number-images from the MNIST and Kannada datasets and post-hoc, example-based explanations. Participants then judged the correctness of the model's classifications and provided other subjective judgments (e.g., helpfulness of explanations and trust and satisfaction in the overall system after each dataset). Figure 4 shows sample materials as they were presented to participants in the study.

Participants (N = 96) were recruited on the Prolific crowdsourcing site. Eligibility criteria were that the participants had to be over 18 years old, native English speakers, and residents in the USA, UK, or Ireland. Participants were randomly assigned to the conditions of the study. These chosen N was based on a power analysis for a moderate effect size. Ethical clearance was provided by the University's Ethics Panel (LS-E-21-214-Ford-Keane).

Materials used were the actual classifications (correct and incorrect) produced by a CNN trained separately on MNIST and Kannada-MNIST datasets. The model has a high accuracy for both domains ($\sim$96%); therefore, multiple runs were used to produce materials. The misclassifications were system mislabels to a class different from the ground-truth label. The image-instances used in the experiment for the classifications consisted of six number classes (1, 3, 4, 5, 6 in Arabic numerals; 2, 4, 5, 7, 8, 9 in Kannada). These selected classes were chosen on the need to match material sets between the domains, a procedure that required time and effort. Materials across and within the datasets were matched using the Structural Similarity Index Metric[1] [31]; t-tests revealed no significant difference between the MNIST and Kannada materials chosen. Explanatory nearest-neighboring examples (3 were always provided) were found using the twin-systems method, which is an accurate feature-weighting method for finding example-based explanations for CNN classifiers (see [19,20]. The study used 42 distinct materials with equal numbers from each dataset and class (21 each; 12 were correct and 9 were misclassifications). So, the error-level for the study was high at 43%.

Procedure, Measures and Analyses. After being told the system was a program that "learned" to classify written symbols, participants were told that they would be shown several examples of its classifications. Instructions informed participants that they would see two different groups of symbols (the MNIST and Kannada symbols) in two different sections of the study (i.e., two distinct blocks of items counterbalanced across groups for order). Before beginning each section, participants were provided with the centroid images and written labels of each number-class of the dataset being tested. They were also told that these symbols could be written in different ways. For each presented item, they were told that their task was to rate the correctness of the presented classification on a 5-point Likert-scale from "I disagree strongly" (1) to "I agree strongly" (5), as well as the helpfulness of the system's explanation on another 5-point Likert scale (see Fig. 4 for sample materials). After rating all of the presented classifications, participants filled out Hoffman et al.'s [14] DARPA trust (8 questions) and satisfaction (8 questions) surveys. The 4 measures analyzed were:

- *Correctness.* Mean 5-point Likert-scale ratings of perceived correctness of correct system classifications and misclassifications.
- *Helpfulness.* Mean 5-point Likert-scale ratings of perceived explanation helpfulness of correct system classifications and misclassifications.
- *Response Time.* Time (in seconds) spent on each page of the experiment (i.e., each material item), including viewing the presented image and explanatory images, and performing Correctness and Helpfulness judgements.
- *Trust and Satisfaction.* Ratings from the DARPA Trust and Satisfaction surveys analyzed question-by-question. This variable was repeated after each dataset (MNIST and Kannada datasets).

Design was a 2 (Order: MNIST-first, or Kannada-first, a between-subjects variable) × 2 (Dataset: MNIST or Kannada, a within-subjects variable) × 2 (Classification Type: correct/incorrect classification, a within-subjects variable).

---

[1] SSIM distances were calculated from each test instance to its centroid, and its three explanatory cases to their respective centroid.

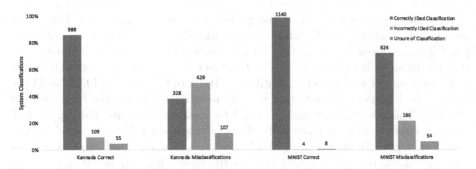

Fig. 5. Percent of user identifications by type-of-classification. Scores from the Correctness ratings were re-coded categorically as "identified-as-correct" (if rated ≥ 4 on the correctness scale) or "identified-as-error" (if rated ≤ 2 on the correctness scale).

3.2 Results and Discussion

The results of this experiment show that people are profoundly affected by their lack of expertise with an unfamiliar domain relative to a familiar one. When interacting with an unfamiliar domain (the Kannada dataset), participants experienced greater difficulty accurately identifying correct and incorrect classifications. Their judgments of system correctness and explanation helpfulness also changed, and response times were longer. Non-experts can perceptually compare a written-number image to its ideal-printed image of the number class, irrespective of the domain. However, they have limited background knowledge about how these written numbers can vary within the labeled number-class before transitioning to another number-class (hence, their judgmental uncertainty)[2].

Correctness. The three-way mixed measures ANOVA revealed a significant two-way interaction between Dataset and Classification Type, $F(1,94) = 310.58$, $p < 0.001$, partial $\eta^2 = 0.77$. Simple main effects of Dataset revealed that participants judged correctly-predicted MNIST predictions as significantly more correct ($M = 4.8$, $SD = 0.3$) than the correctly-predicted Kannada items ($M = 4.26$, $SD = 0.6$, $p < 0.001$). Conversely, participants rated Kannada misclassifications as significantly more correct ($M = 3.15$, $SD = 0.82$) than MNIST misclassifications ($M = 2.15$, $SD = 0.68$, $p < 0.001$). So, when people are less familiar with a domain, they are less sure about judging the correctness of items; for the Kannada data, judgments of correct and incorrect classifications move towards the center of the 5-point scale reflecting this uncertainty.

Participants were also less sure about correct and incorrect items in the unfamiliar domain relative to the familiar one (see Fig. 5). This effect is revealed when we re-code their correctness ratings categorically as "identified-as-correct" (if rated ≥ 4 on the correctness scale) or "identified-as-error" (if rated ≤ 2

---

[2] Note, the Order variable is not reported as it had no effect on the analyses reported; that is, the presentation of one dataset before the other did not affect performance.

on the correctness scale). Then, using this re-coding we can show how many item-classifications in each dataset were correctly or incorrectly identified by participants. Figure 5a graphs this data and shows how people's performance on the two datasets differs. For the MNIST dataset items that were correctly classified by the model are correctly identified (~100% of the time, 1140 out of 1144), but for the Kannada dataset they are only identified (90% of the time, 988 out of 1097). This effect is even more marked for misclassifications. For the MNIST dataset, items that were incorrectly classified by the model (i.e., misclassifications) are correctly identified (77% of the time), but for the Kannada dataset they are only correctly identified (43% of the time). So, people encounter some difficulty spotting correctly-classified items and have major difficulties identifying incorrectly-classified items in the unfamiliar Kannada images. An *a posteriori* chi-square test of this data found a significant association between Dataset and participants' correct identification of the CNN's classifications as either correct or incorrect, $\chi^2(1) = 37.71$, $p < 0.0001$; an association of $\phi = 0.11$ ($p < 0.0001$).

Helpfulness. People's rating of how helpful they found the system explanations also varied for the familiar versus unfamiliar datasets. A three-way mixed measures ANOVA analysis of Helpfulness revealed a significant two-way interaction of Dataset with Classification Type, $F(1, 94) = 51.9$, $p < 0.01$, partial $\eta^2 = 0.36$. Simple main effects revealed a counter-intuitive result: that nearest-neighbor example explanations were perceived as more helpful when judging correct classifications for MNIST items ($M = 4.77$, $SD = 0.39$), compared to correct classifications for Kannada items ($M = 4.37$, $SD = 0.63$, $p < 0.001$). Furthermore, for the MNIST items alone, these explanations were perceived as more helpful when provided for correct classifications ($M = 4.77$, $SD = 0.39$) compared to misclassifications ($M = 3.49$, $SD = 0.87$, $p < .001$). The same pattern is found within Kannada items with simple main effects showing that explanations were perceived as more helpful when provided for correct classifications ($M = 4.37$, $SD = 0.63$) than for misclassifications ($M = 3.71$, $SD = 0.77$). These results suggest that examples might not be appropriate for explaining classifications in unfamiliar domains, as users' perceptions of helpfulness seem to follow ease-with-the-task. People may simply think explanations are more helpful just because they can readily identify them as correct.

Response Time. The differences caused by expertise were also seen in the mean response times to items in the different conditions[3]. A three-way mixed measures ANOVA revealed a significant two-way interaction of Dataset with Classification Type, $F(1, 94) = 10.1$, $p < 0.01$, partial $\eta^2 = 0.097$. Simple main effects revealed significantly longer response times for correct Kannada materials ($M = 13.26$, $SD = 7.79$) than for correct MNIST materials ($M = 11.54$, $SD = 4.84$, $p < .01$; see Fig. 6). For the MNIST dataset, response times were significantly shorter for

---

[3] Outlier responses (3 SDs from the mean for a given item) were removed before mean times were analyzed.

correct classifications ($M = 11.54$, $SD = 4.82$) than misclassifications ($M = 15.38$, $SD = 6.19$, $p < 0.001$). Similarly, for Kannada dataset, response times were significantly shorter for correct classifications ($M = 13.26$, $SD = 5.79$) than misclassifications ($M = 15.43$, $SD = 6.94$, $p < 0.001$). When these results are combined with the accuracy differences in users identification of correct and incorrect classifications, it appears that longer response times improve users' accuracy in "identifying-as-correct" correct classifications of unfamiliar data. Conversely, users spent approximately the same time analyzing MNIST and Kannada misclassifications, despite struggling to "identify-as-error" the system misclassifications of unfamiliar data. These results suggest that there may be a speed versus accuracy trade-off occurring for misclassifications.

Trust and Satisfaction. Repeated-measures ANOVA analyses of Trust and Satisfaction (respectively) provided no significant effects across the conditions, but the questions differed significantly within each questionnaire. There is insufficient space to discuss the significance of these measures here.

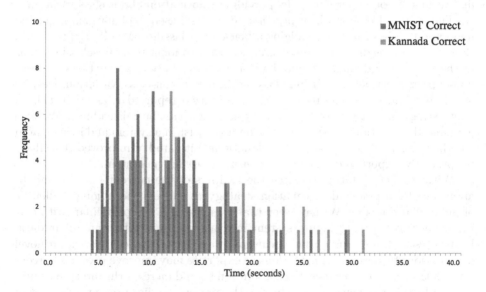

Fig. 6. Distribution of response time (in seconds) for correctly classified MNIST and Kannada materials.

4   General Discussion

The present study reveal several novel findings on the impact of domain expertise on people's perception of a classifier's decisions when post-hoc, example-based explanations are provided. We found that (i) domain familiarity significantly impacts users judgments of a classifier, (ii) example-based explanations assist users with judging correct system classifications of an unfamiliar domain, but (iii) people have significant difficulties dealing with misclassifications in an unfamiliar domain (uneased by the provision of explanations).

This study determines the impact of domain familiarity on user judgments of an AI system's classifications. As expected, users displayed an accuracy and speed advantage in their judgments of correct classifications for the familiar domain over the unfamiliar one. Users were slower (albeit still accurate) at positively identifying correct, unfamiliar classifications but notably struggled with judging and identifying unfamiliar misclassifications. In fact, they tend to perceive Kannada misclassifications as being correct (and making this decision quickly). These results echo those of Searson and Tangen [29], who found that experts are adept at identifying matches and outliers in domain-familiar data and consistently have an accuracy and speed advantage over non-experts. This ability may stem from chunking variations for a familiar class; in other words, experts may be perceptually aware of the bounds of a familiar class. This suggests that modifications to an explanation strategy should address the perceptual limitations of non-experts (e.g., by providing information about class variation).

The study also shows how post-hoc, example-based explanations impacted non-experts' performance in judging a black-box classifier. Manifestly, we found that explanations did not improve user accuracy in identifying misclassifications in the unfamiliar domain. It may be that example-based explanations improve non-experts' accuracy for within-class, but not between-class, variation. Despite this limitation, users who received an explanation reported it as being helpful (suggesting that in this context the explanation can be misleading). We also explored the effect of domain expertise on user trust in a system and investigated whether post-hoc, example-based explanations mitigated or improved this effect. Surprisingly, expertise did not change users' trust in the system.

With respect to future research the findings of the current study highlight an avenue for a modified explanation strategy to address the unique challenges of unfamiliar domains. We have seen that users struggle, in particular, with correctly identifying and judging system misclassifications with unfamiliar data. Future research focusing on improving people's performance, through an novel explanation strategy catering for domain expertise may improve people's perceptions of the system as a whole. Such a solution should increase the interpretability of deep learning systems. In conclusion, the present studies present a rich set of findings for a wider understanding of the dynamics of user interactions between explanation-strategies and domain expertise in XAI contexts.

Acknowledgement. This paper emanated from research funded by Science Foundation Ireland to the Insight Centre for Data Analytics (12/RC/2289P2) and SFI Centre for Research Training in Machine Learning (18/CRT/6183).

References

1. An, S., Lee, M., Park, S., Yang, H., So, J.: An ensemble of simple convolutional neural network models for MNIST digit recognition. preprint arXiv:2008.10400 (2020)
2. Anderson, R.C., Ku, Y.M., Li, W., Chen, X., Wu, X., Shu, H.: Learning to see the patterns in Chinese characters. Sci. Stud. Read. **17**(1), 41–56 (2013)
3. Bayer, S., Gimpel, H., Markgraf, M.: The role of domain expertise in trusting and following explainable AI decision support systems. J. Decis. Syst., 1–29 (2021)
4. Cañal-Bruland, R., Lotz, S., Hagemann, N., Schorer, J., Strauss, B.: Visual span and change detection in soccer: an expertise study. J. Cogn. Psychol. **23**(3), 302–310 (2011)
5. Chase, W.G., Simon, H.A.: The mind's eye in chess. In: Visual Information Processing pp. 215–281 (1973)
6. Chase, W.G., Simon, H.A.: Perception in chess. Cogn. Psychol. **4**(1), 55–81 (1973)
7. Connors, M.H., Burns, B.D., Campitelli, G.: Expertise in complex decision making: the role of search in chess 70 years after de Groot. Cogn. Sci. **35**(8), 1567–1579 (2011)
8. Dikmen, M., Burns, C.: The effects of domain knowledge on trust in explainable AI and task performance: a case of peer-to-peer lending. Int. J. Hum Comput Stud. **162**, 102792 (2022)
9. Fakoor, R., Ladhak, F., Nazi, A., Huber, M.: Using deep learning to enhance cancer diagnosis and classification. In: Proceedings of the International Conference on Machine Learning, vol. 28, pp. 3937–3949. ACM, New York (2013)
10. Glickenhaus, B., Karneeb, J., Aha, D.: DARPA XAI phase 1 evaluations report. DARPA Program (2019)
11. Gobet, F., et al.: Chunking mechanisms in human learning. Trends Cogn. Sci. **5**(6), 236–243 (2001)
12. de Groot, A.D.: Thought and Choice in Chess, 1st edn. Amsterdam University Press, Amsterdam (2008)
13. Herchenbach, M., Müller, D., Scheele, S., Schmid, U.: Explaining image classifications with near misses, near hits and prototypes. In: El Yacoubi, M., Granger, E., Yuen, P.C., Pal, U., Vincent, N. (eds.) Pattern Recognition and Artificial Intelligence, ICPRAI 2022. LNCS, vol. 13364, pp. 419–430. Springer, Cham (2022). https://doi.org/10.1007/978-3-031-09282-4_35
14. Hoffman, R.R., Johnson, M., Bradshaw, J.M., Underbrink, A.: Trust in automation. IEEE Intell. Syst. **28**(1), 84–88 (2013)
15. Kang, H.W., Kang, H.B.: Prediction of crime occurrence from multi-modal data using deep learning. PLoS ONE **12**(4), e0176244 (2017)
16. Keane, M.T., Kenny, E.M., Delaney, E., Smyth, B.: If only we had better counterfactual explanations: five key deficits to rectify in the evaluation of counterfactual XAI techniques. In: Proceedings of the 28th International Joint Conference on Artificial Intelligence, pp. 4466–4474 (2021)
17. Kelly, B., Rainford, L.A., McEntee, M.F., Kavanagh, E.C.: Influence of radiology expertise on the perception of nonmedical images. J. Med. Imaging **5**(3), 1–5 (2017)
18. Kenny, E.M., Ford, C., Quinn, M., Keane, M.T.: Explaining black-box classifiers using post-hoc explanations-by-example: the effect of explanations and error-rates in XAI user studies. Artif. Intell. **294**, 103459 (2021)

19. Kenny, E.M., Keane, M.T.: Twin-systems to explain artificial neural networks using case-based reasoning: comparative tests of feature-weighting methods in ANN-CBR twins for XAI. In: Proceedings of the 28th International Joint Conference on Artificial Intelligence, pp. 2708–2715 (2019)

20. Kenny, E.M., Keane, M.T.: Explaining deep learning using examples: optimal feature weighting methods for twin systems using post-hoc, explanation-by-example in XAI. Knowl. Based Syst. **233**, 107530 (2021)

21. Kneusel, R.T., Mozer, M.C.: Improving human-machine cooperative visual search with soft highlighting. ACM Trans. Appl. Percept. **15**(1), 1–21 (2017)

22. Krupinski, E.A., Graham, A.R., Weinstein, R.S.: Characterizing the development of visual search expertise in pathology residents viewing whole slide images. Hum. Pathol. **44**(3), 357–364 (2013)

23. Lundberg, S.M., Lee, S.I.: A unified approach to interpreting model predictions. In: Advances in Neural Information Processing Systems, vol. 30 (2017)

24. Nourani, M., King, J., Ragan, E.: The role of domain expertise in user trust and the impact of first impressions with intelligent systems. In: Proceedings of the AAAI Conference on Human Computation and Crowdsourcing, vol. 8, no. 1, pp. 112–121 (2020)

25. Prabhu, V.U.: Kannada-MNIST (2019)

26. Ribeiro, M.T., Singh, S., Guestrin, C.: "why should i trust you?" explaining the predictions of any classifier. In: Proceedings of the 22nd ACM SIGKDD International Conference on Knowledge Discovery and Data Mining, pp. 1135–1144 (2016)

27. Roads, B.D., Mozer, M.C.: Improving human-machine cooperative classification via cognitive theories of similarity. Cogn. Sci. **41**(5), 1394–1411 (2017)

28. Ross, A., Doshi-Velez, F.: Improving the adversarial robustness and interpretability of deep neural networks by regularizing their input gradients. Proc. AAAI Conf. Artif. Intell. **32**(1), April 2018

29. Searston, R.A., Tangen, J.M.: Expertise with unfamiliar objects is flexible to changes in task but not changes in class. PLOS ONE **12**(6), 1–14 (2017)

30. Thompson, M.B., Tangen, J.M.: The nature of expertise in fingerprint matching: experts can do a lot with a little. PLOS ONE **9**(12), 1–23 (2014)

31. Wang, Z., Bovik, A., Sheikh, H., Simoncelli, E.: Image quality assessment: from error visibility to structural similarity. IEEE Trans. Image Process. **13**(4), 600–612 (2004)

32. Warren, G., Keane, M.T., Byrne, R.M.J.: Features of explainability: how users understand counterfactual and causal explanations for categorical and continuous features in XAI. In: IJCAI-22 Workshop on Cognitive Aspects of Knowledge Representation, CAKR 2022 (2022)

33. Warren, G., Smyth, B., Keane, M.T.: "Better" counterfactuals, ones people can understand: psychologically-plausible case-based counterfactuals using categorical features for explainable AI (XAI). In: Proceedings of the 30th International Conference on Case-Based Reasoning (2022)

34. Waters, A.J., Underwood, G., Findlay, J.M.: Studying expertise in music reading. Percept. Psychophys. **59**(4), 477–488 (1997)

35. Werner, S., Thies, B.: Is "change blindness" attenuated by domain-specific expertise? An expert-novices comparison of change detection in football images. Vis. Cogn. **7**(1–3), 163–173 (2000)

36. Winegard, B., Winegard, B., Geary, D.C.: The evolution of expertise. In: The Cambridge Handbook of Expertise and Expert Performance, pp. 40–48 (2018)

Motif-Guided Time Series Counterfactual Explanations

Peiyu Li[1](✉), Soukaïna Filali Boubrahimi[1], and Shah Muhammad Hamdi[2]

[1] Utah State University, Logan, UT 84322, USA
peiyu.li@usu.edu
[2] New Mexico State University, Las Cruces, NM 88003, USA

Abstract. With the rising need of interpretable machine learning methods, there is a necessity for a rise in human effort to provide diverse explanations of the influencing factors of the model decisions. To improve the trust and transparency of AI-based systems, the EXplainable Artificial Intelligence (XAI) field has emerged. The XAI paradigm is bifurcated into two main categories: feature attribution and counterfactual explanation methods. While feature attribution methods are based on explaining the reason behind a model decision, counterfactual explanation methods discover the smallest input changes that will result in a different decision. In this paper, we aim at building trust and transparency in time series models by using motifs to generate counterfactual explanations. We propose Motif-Guided Counterfactual Explanation (MG-CF), a novel model that generates intuitive post-hoc counterfactual explanations that make full use of important motifs to provide interpretive information in decision-making processes. To the best of our knowledge, this is the first effort that leverages motifs to guide the counterfactual explanation generation. We validated our model using five real-world time-series datasets from the UCR repository. Our experimental results show the superiority of MG-CF in balancing all the desirable counterfactual explanations properties in comparison with other competing state-of-the-art baselines.

Keywords: Counterfactual explanations · Explainable Artificial Intelligence (XAI) · time series motifs

1 Introduction

Recently, time-series data mining has played an important role in various real-life applications, such as healthcare [10], astronomy [3], and aerospace [11]. The availability of big data provides researchers the unprecedented opportunity to deploy high accurate models in real-life applications. The success of deep learning time series models has been validated by their high accuracy. However, the black-box nature makes the decision-making process of high accuracy models less explained [1]. This represents a big barrier for decision makers in trusting the system. For example, in life-changing decisions such as critical disease management, it is important to know the reasons behind the critical decision of choosing

© Springer Nature Switzerland AG 2023
J.-J. Rousseau and B. Kapralos (Eds.): ICPR 2022 Workshops, LNCS 13645, pp. 203–215, 2023.
https://doi.org/10.1007/978-3-031-37731-0_16

a treatment line over another one [9]. An inappropriate treatment decision can cost human lives in addition to a substantial monetary loss [26]. Therefore, it is vital to understand the opaque models' decision process by either prioritizing interpretability during the model development phase, or developing post-hoc explanation solutions.

To build trust between humans and decision-making systems, EXplainable Artificial Intelligence (XAI) methods are increasingly accepted as effective tools to explain machine learning models' decision-making processes. XAI methods aim at increasing the interpretability of the models whilst maintaining the high-performance levels. There are two XAI dominant paradigms: intrinsic interpretable and post-hoc explanations for opaque models [29]. Examples of intrinsic interpretable models include linear regression, decision trees, rule sets, etc. On the other hand, examples of post-hoc explanation methods include LIME [19], native guide, and SHAP [23,24]. In this paper, we focus only on post-hoc XAI methods. A lot of efforts have been made to provide post-hoc XAI for image and vector-represented data while significantly less attention has been paid to time series data [18]. The complex and time-evolving nature of time series makes the explanation models one of the most challenging tasks [5].

On the light of desirable counterfactual method properties, we propose a Motif-Guided Counterfactual Explanation (MG-CF), a novel model that generates interpretable, intuitive post-hoc counterfactual explanations of time series classification predictions that balance between validity, proximity, interpretability, contiguity and efficiency. The contributions are the following:

1. We incorporate motif mining algorithms for guiding the counterfactual search. In particular, we make full use of the interpretability power of motifs to provide interpretable information in the decision-making process. Our method does not require the use of class activation maps to search for the counterfactual explanation, which makes it model-agnostic.
2. We conduct experiments on six real-life datasets from various domains (image, spectro, ECG, and motion) and show the superiority of our methods over state-of-the-art models.

To the best of our knowledge, this is the first effort to leverage the a-priori mined motifs to produce counterfactual explanations for time series classification. The rest of this paper is organized as follows: in Sect. 2, background and related works are described. Section 3 introduces the preliminary concepts. Section 4 describes our proposed method in detail. We present the experimental results and evaluations in comparison to other baselines in Sect. 5. Finally, we conclude our work in Sect. 6.

2 Background and Related Work

In the post-hoc interpretability paradigm, one of the most prominent approaches is to identify important features given a prediction through local approximation, such as LIME [19], LORE [7], TS-MULE [21], and SHAP [14]. In particular,

LIME is a feature-based approach that operates by fitting an interpretable linear model to the classifier's predictions of random data samples, weighted based on their distance to the test sample. LORE is an extension work based on LIME, which is a local black box model-agnostic explanation approach based on logic rules. TS-MULE is also an extension to LIME with novel time series segmentation techniques and replacement methods to enforce a better non-informed values exchange. SHAP is a unified framework that operates by calculating feature importance values using model parameters. In addition, visualizing the decision of a model is also a common technique for explaining model predictions [16]. In the computer vision domain, visualization techniques have been widely applied to different applications successfully, such as highlighting the most important parts of images to class activation maps (CAM) in convolutional neural networks [15]. Schlegel et al. [20] tested the informativeness and robustness of different feature-importance techniques in time series classification. LIME was found to produce poor results because of the large dimensionality by converting time to features; in contrast, saliency-based approaches and SHAP were found to be more robust across different architectures.

An alternative method to feature-based methods has been proposed by Wachter et al. [25], which aims at minimizing a loss function and using adaptive Nelder-Mead optimization to encourage the counterfactual to change the decision outcome and keep the minimum Manhattan distance from the original input instance. Similarly, another method that is used to deal with the plausibility and feasibility issues of the generated counterfactual explanation has been proposed, which is called GeCo. The model achieves the desirable counterfactual properties by introducing a new plausibility-feasibility language (PLAF) [22]. Both GeCo and wCF focus on structured tabular datasets. Since these two methods explore a complete search space, they are not adequate to be used in a high dimensional feature space such as in the case of time-series data.

Recently, an instance-based counterfactual explanation for time series classification has been proposed [5]. The instance-based counterfactual explanation uses the explanation weight vector (from the Class Activation Mapping) and the in-sample counterfactual (NUN) to generate counterfactual explanations for time series classifiers. The proposed technique adapts existing training instances by copying segments from other instances that belong to the desired class. More recently, MAPIC, an interpretable model for TSC based on Matrix Profile, shapelets, and decision tree has been proposed by [6]. Finally, a counterfactual solution for multivariate time series data called CoMTE has been proposed by Etes et al. [2], which focuses on observing the effect of turning off one variable at a time.

3 Preliminary Concepts

Notation. *We define a time series* $T = \{t_1, t_2, ..., t_m\}$ *as an ordered set of real values, where m is the length, then we can define a time series dataset* $\boldsymbol{T} = \{T_0, T_1, ..., T_n\}$ *as a collection of such time series where each time series has* *mapped to a mutually exclusive set of classes $C = \{c_1, c_2, ..., c_l\}$ and used to train a time series classifier $f : \boldsymbol{T} \rightarrow C$, where $\boldsymbol{T} \in \mathbb{R}^k$ is the k-dimensional feature space. For each T_i in time series dataset $\boldsymbol{T}$ associated with a class $f(T_i) = c_i$, a counterfactual explanation model $\mathcal{M}$ generates a perturbed sample T_i' with the minimal perturbation that leads to $f(T_i') = c_i'$ such that $c_i \neq c_i'$.*

According to [5,13], a desire counterfactual instance x_{cf} should obey the following initial properties :

- **Validity**: The prediction of the to-be-explained model f on the counterfactual instance x_{cf} needs to be different from the prediction of the to-be-explained model f on the original instance x (i.e., if $f(x) = c_i$ and $f(x_{cf}) = c_j$, then $c_i \neq c_j$).
- **Proximity**: The to-be-explained query needs to be close to the generated counterfactual instance, which means the distance between x and x_{cf} should be minimal.
- **Sparsity**: The perturbation δ changing the original instance x_0 into $x_{cf} = x_0 + \delta$ should be sparse (i.e., $\delta \approx \epsilon$).
- **Model-agnosticism**: The counterfactual explanation model should produce a solution independent of the classification model f, high-quality counterfactuals without prior knowledge of the gradient values derived from optimization-based classification models should be generated.
- **Contiguity**: The counterfactual instance $x_{cf} = x + \delta$ needs to be perturbed in a single contiguous segment which makes the solution semantically meaningful.
- **Efficiency**: The counterfactual instance x_{cf} needs to be found fast enough to ensure it can be used in a real-life setting.

4   Motif-Guided Counterfactual Explanation (MG-CF)

In this section, we describe our proposed Motif-Guided Counterfactual Explanation method. The general architecture is illustrated in Fig. 1, there are two main steps: motifs mining and counterfactual explanation generation.

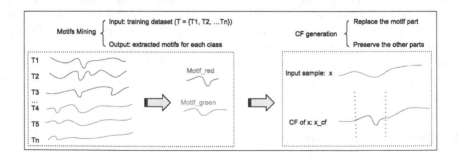

Fig. 1. Motif-Guided Counterfactual Explanation

4.1   Motif Mining

Motifs, also known as shapelets, are time series sub-sequences that are max-imally representative of a class [27]. Motifs provide interpretable information beneficial for domain experts to better understand their data. To mine the most prominent motifs, we apply the Shapelet Transform (ST) algorithm proposed by [12]. To generate the most prominent motifs, a set of candidate motifs need to be generated, a distance measure between a motif and each time series instance should be defined, and a measure of the discriminatory power of the mined motifs [12] need to be defined. The details of the algorithm is shown in Algorithm 1. The algorithm starts by sampling specific-length intervals from the time series instance to generate candidate motifs (line 7). The motifs' discriminatory power is then estimated by first computing their distance to all the instances from each class (line 9), and then computing the distance correlation to the target class (line 10). Finally, the motifs are sorted and only the best motif from each class is retained (lines 14, 16). Figure 2a and 2b show the two extracted motifs of different classes from ECG 200 dataset.

Candidates Generation. Given a time series T with length m, a subsequence S of length l of time series T is a contiguous sequence of l points in T, where $l \leq m$. For a given m-lengthed time series, there are $(m-l)+1$ distinct subsequences of length l. The set of all subsequences of length l for a dataset is described as:

$$W_l = \{W_{1,l}, ..., W_{n,l}\}, \tag{1}$$

where $W_{i,l}$ is defined as the set of all subsequences of length l for time series T_i. To speed up the process of finding motifs, instead of considering all the lengths that range in (3, m), similar to [12], we only consider 0.3, 0.5 and 0.7 percent length of the whole time series for each dataset. In this case, the set of all candidate motifs for data set T is:

$$W = \{W_{0.3m}, W_{0.5m}, W_{0.7m}\}, \tag{2}$$

We denote the candidates generation as *generateCandidates* in Algorithm 1.

Measuring Distances. The distance between two subsequences S and R of length l is defined as

$$dist(S, R) = \sum_{i=1}^{l} (s_i - r_i)^2 \tag{3}$$

To calculate all distances between a candidate motif S and all series in T, we denote $d_{i,s}$ as the distance between a subsequence S of l and time series T_i, then

$$d_{i,S} = \min_{R \in W_{i,l}} dist(S, R) \tag{4}$$

$$D_S = < d_{1,S}, d_{2,S}, ..., d_{n,S} > \tag{5}$$

We denote the process of measuring distance as *findDistances* in Algorithm 1.

Measuring the Discriminatory Power of a Motif. Information gain has been used to evaluate the quality of a motif in the previous shapelet papers [17,27,28]. Firstly, the distance list D_S, defined in Eq. 5, is sorted, then the information gain is evaluated on the class values for each possible split value. Ye et al. propose to use an early abandon technique on calculating D_S through maintaining an upper bound on the quality of the candidate whilst generating D_S [28]. If the upper bound falls below the best found so far, the calculation of D_S can be abandoned. After each $d_{i,S}$ is found, the current best information gain split is calculated and the upper bound is found, assuming the most optimistic division of the remaining distances. We denote the process of measuring the discriminatory power of a motif as *assessCandidate* in Algorithm 1.

Algorithm 1. Motifs mining

Input: Training set samples **T** with labeled binary classes C = [0, 1]
Output: Extracted motifs for each class
1: Motifs = ∅
2: N = length(**T**[0])   ▷ Number of time series samples
3: m = length(**T**[0][0])   ▷ Length of time series
4: **for** $\mathbf{T}_i \leftarrow \mathbf{T}_1$ to $\mathbf{T}_N$ **do**
5:      Motifs ← ∅
6:      **for** l in [0.3m, 0.5m, 0.7m] **do**
7:          $W_{i,l}$ ← generateCandidates($\mathbf{T}_i$, l)
8:          **for** all subsequences S in $W_{i,l}$ **do**
9:              D_S ← findDistances(S, $W_{i,l}$)
10:             quality ← assessCandidate(S, D_S)
11:             Motifs.add(i,start_idx, end_idx, S, quality)   ▷ The index of time series, the start idx and end idx of motifs will be stored
12:         **end for**
13:     **end for**
14:     sortByQuality(Motifs)
15: **end for**
16: **return** $[[i\_0, start\_idx\_0, start\_idx\_0], [i\_1, start\_idx\_1, start\_idx\_1]]$ ▷ return the index information for motifs of different classes

---

4.2   CF Generation

After motifs are extracted from the training dataset, the next step is to generate CF explanations. In this section, we introduce the counterfactual explanation generation process as outlined at Algorithm 2. The CF generation starts by using the pre-trained model f to predict the classification result of the test dataset *samples* (line 1). We set the target classes of the test dataset as the opposite label of the prediction results (line 2). To generate an explanation of a query time series X, we consider the motif's existing segment from the target class as the most prominent segment (lines 4–7). Therefore, we replace the motif existing part with the target class motif and preserve the remaining parts (line 9). In this case, the counterfactual explanation for the input query time series is generated (line 10). It is important to note that MG-CF does not require the use of class activation maps which makes it a model-agnostic model. Figure 2 shows examples of generated counterfactual explanations for the ECG 200 dataset of the Myocardial Infarction and Normal Heartbeat class.

Algorithm 2. CF generation

Input: Test set samples *samples*, pretrainined time series classifier f, extracted motifs for each class from Motif mining algorithm

Output: CF, Counterfactual explanation for each sample in test set

1: preds = f.predict(*samples*)   ▷ Applying the test data on f to get the prediction results
2: targets= the opposite label of the preds   ▷ Get the target labels based on the prediction results
3: **for** *sample* ← *samples* **do**
4:     **if** target(sample) == 0 **then**
5:         i, start_idx, end_idx = [i_0, start_idx_0, end_idx_0]   ▷ extracted index information of the motif from class 0
6:     **else**
7:         i, start_idx, end_idx = [i_1, start_idx_1, end_idx_1]   ▷ extracted index information of the motif from class 1
8:     **end if**
9:     sample[start_idx, end_idx] = T[i][start_idx, end_idx]
10:     cf_sample = sample
11:     CF.append(cf_sample)
12: **end for**
13: **return CF**

---

5   Experimental Evaluation

In this section, we outline our experimental design and discuss our findings. We conduct our experiments on the publicly-available univariate time series data sets from the University of California at Riverside (UCR) Time Series Classification Archive [4]. We test our model on five real-life datasets from various domains (image, spectro, ECG, and motion). The number of labels of each dataset is binary and the time series classes are evenly sampled across the training and testing partitions. The length of the time series in the data sets varies between 96 and 512. Table 1 shows all the dataset details (number of classes, time series length, training size, testing size, and the type of time series).

5.1   Baseline Methods

We evaluate our proposed SG-CF model with two other baselines, namely, Alibi [8] and Native guide counterfactual explainers [5].

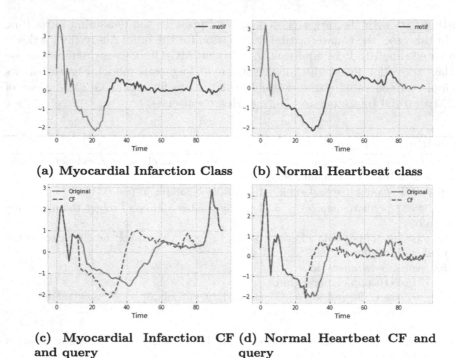

(a) Myocardial Infarction Class   (b) Normal Heartbeat class

(c) Myocardial Infarction CF and query   (d) Normal Heartbeat CF and query

Fig. 2. Example MG-CF explanations for the ECG200 dataset

– **Alibi Counterfactual (Alibi):** The Alibi generates counterfactuals by optimizing a new objective function that includes class prototypes generated from encoders [8]. The method leverages the resulting autoencoder reconstruction error after decoding the counterfactual instance x_{cf} as a measure of fitness to the training data distribution. The additional loss term L_{AU} penalizes out-of-distribution counterfactual instances.

– **Native guide counterfactual (NG-CF):** NG-CF is the latest time series counterfactual method that perturbs the query time series by inserting segments from the opposing class [5]. Although the method is model agnostic, the method reaches its full potential when class activation weights are available. NG-CF uses Dynamic Barycenter (DBA) averaging of the query time series x and the nearest unlike neighbor from another class to generate the counterfactual example.

The source code of our model, competing baselines, and the experimental dataset are available on the MG-CF project website[1].

---

[1] https://sites.google.com/view/naive-shapelets-guided-cf.

Table 1. UCR datasets metadata (each dataset is binary labeled)

ID	Dataset Name	TS length	DS train size	DS test size	Type
0	ECG200	96	100	100	ECG
1	Coffee	286	28	28	SPECTRO
2	GunPoint	150	50	150	MOTION
3	BeetleFly	470	20	20	IMAGE
4	BirdChicken	512	20	20	IMAGE

5.2   Experimental Results

The goal of our experiments is to assess the performance of the baseline methods with respect to all the desired properties of an ideal counterfactual method. To evaluate our proposed method, we compare our method with the other two baselines in terms of several metrics: L1 distance (proximity), sparsity level, number of independent segments is perturbing (contiguity), the label flip rate (validity), and the run time (efficiency).

L1 distance, which is defined in Eq. 6, measures the distance between the counterfactuals and the original samples, a smaller L1 distance is desired.

$$proximity = \|x_{cf} - x\| \qquad (6)$$

Sparsity level, which indicates the level of time series perturbations. A high sparsity level that is approaching 100% is desirable, which means the time series perturbations made in x to achieve x_{cf} is minimal. We computed the sparsity level using a new metric that we formulate in Eqs. 7 and 8.

$$sparsity = 1 - \frac{\sum_{i=0}^{len(x)} g(x_{cf_i}, x_i)}{len(x)} \qquad (7)$$

$$g(x, y) = \begin{cases} 1, & \text{if } x \neq y \\ 0, & \text{otherwise} \end{cases} \qquad (8)$$

The number of independent non-contiguous segments is also investigated to show the contiguity, which is shown in Fig 3. The lower the number of independent non-contiguous segments the better. Finally, we define the validity metric by comparing the label flip rate for the prediction of the counterfactual explanation result, we computed the flip rate following the formula of Eq. 9.

$$flip\_rate = \frac{num\_flipped}{num\_testsample}, \qquad (9)$$

where we denote the num_flipped as the number of generated counterfactual explanation samples that flip the label, and the num_testsample is the total number of samples in the test dataset that we used to generate counterfactual explanation samples. The closer the label flip rate is to 1, the better.

Figure 3 and 4 show the evaluation results on the CF desired properties assessed using the aforementioned metrics. Since our proposed method relies on an instance-based counterfactual explanation, which generates a CF for each time series in the dataset, we calculate the mean value and the standard deviation for all CF samples for each dataset to show the overall performances. We note that Alibi achieves the lowest L1 distance (proximity) in the four datasets, which is highly desirable. However, Alibi minimizes proximity in the cost of sparsity level, contiguity (number of independent segments), and efficiency (running time). Alibi achieves the lowest sparsity level and run time, which entails that the method generates CF explanations with less proximity, contiguity, and efficiency.

We also note that NG-CF results in highly valid counterfactual explanations that are guaranteed to have the desired class. Since the method does not rely on any optimization function to generate new shapes, it simply copies fragments from existing training time series instances that the prediction model f has already learned. Therefore, it is expected that the prediction model f recognizes the copied segments with high confidence. Although highly valid, NG-CF sacrifices the other metrics (sparsity, contiguity) for maximizing validity. Figures 3 and 4 show that our proposed MG-CF results in a higher sparsity level,

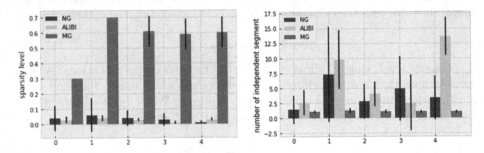

Fig. 3. The sparsity level (the higher the better) and number of independent segments (the lower the better) of the CF explanations

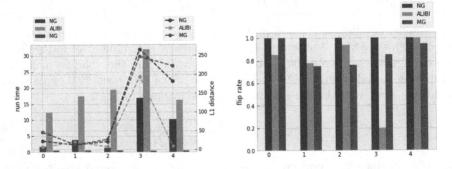

Fig. 4. The average running time (the lower the better), average L1 distance (the lower the better), and the label flip rate (the higher the better) of the CF explanations

a lower number of independent perturbed segments (contiguity), and a lower running time (efficiency) compared to NG-CF and Alibi. Finally, although Alibi and NG-CF can lead to high proximity and validity counterfactuals, they are not valid and sparse respectively. Thus, MG-CF shows a good balance across all the metrics without maximizing one property and compromising the other.

6 Conclusion

In this paper, we propose a novel model that derives intuitive, interpretable post-hoc counterfactual explanations of time series classification models that finds balance between validity, proximity, sparsity, contiguity, and efficiency desirable properties. The main limitation of current time series explainers is that they produce perturbations that maximize a metric on the cost of others. This shortcoming limits the interpretability of their resulting counterfactual explanations. We address these challenges by proposing MG-CF, a motif-based model that produces high-quality counterfactual explanations that are contiguous and sparse. The MG-CF method guides the perturbations on the query time series resulting in significantly sparse and more contiguous explanations than other state-of-the-art methods. This is the first effort to leverage the a-priori mined motifs to produce high-quality counterfactual explanations. There are spaces for extensions of our work with time series datasets with high dimensionality and multiple-classes case. As a future direction of this work, we would like to extend our work to multiple-class case time series dataset and also focus on generating the counterfactual explanations for high dimensional time series data.

References

1. Adadi, A., Berrada, M.: Peeking inside the black-box: a survey on explainable artificial intelligence (XAI). IEEE Access **6**, 52138–52160 (2018)
2. Ates, E., Aksar, B., Leung, V.J., Coskun, A.K.: Counterfactual explanations for multivariate time series. In: 2021 International Conference on Applied Artificial Intelligence (ICAPAI), pp. 1–8. IEEE (2021)
3. Boubrahimi, S.F., Aydin, B., Schuh, M.A., Kempton, D., Angryk, R.A., Ma, R.: Spatiotemporal interpolation methods for solar event trajectories. APJs **236**(1), 23 (2018)
4. Dau, H.A., et al.: The UCR time series archive. IEEE/CAA J. Automat. Sin. **6**(6), 1293–1305 (2019)
5. Delaney, E., Greene, D., Keane, M.T.: Instance-based counterfactual explanations for time series classification. In: Sánchez-Ruiz, A.A., Floyd, M.W. (eds.) ICCBR 2021. LNCS (LNAI), vol. 12877, pp. 32–47. Springer, Cham (2021). https://doi.org/10.1007/978-3-030-86957-1_3
6. Guidotti, R., D'Onofrio, M.: Matrix profile-based interpretable time series classifier. Front. Artif. Intell. **4** (2021)
7. Guidotti, R., Monreale, A., Ruggieri, S., Pedreschi, D., Turini, F., Giannotti, F.: Local rule-based explanations of black box decision systems. arXiv preprint arXiv:1805.10820 (2018)

8. Klaise, J., Looveren, A.V., Vacanti, G., Coca, A.: Alibi explain: algorithms for explaining machine learning models. J. Mach. Learn. Res. 22(181), 1–7 (2021), http://jmlr.org/papers/v22/21-0017.html
9. Kundu, S.: AI in medicine must be explainable. Nat. Med. **27**(8), 1328–1328 (2021)
10. Lin, J., Keogh, E., Fu, A., Van Herle, H.: Approximations to magic: finding unusual medical time series. In: 18th IEEE Symposium on Computer-Based Medical Systems (CBMS'05), pp. 329–334. IEEE (2005)
11. Lin, J., Keogh, E., Lonardi, S., Lankford, J.P., Nystrom, D.M.: Visually mining and monitoring massive time series. In: Proceedings of the 10th ACM SIGKDD International Conference on Knowledge Discovery and Data Mining, pp. 460–469 (2004)
12. Lines, J., Davis, L.M., Hills, J., Bagnall, A.: A shapelet transform for time series classification. In: Proceedings of the 18th ACM SIGKDD International Conference on Knowledge Discovery and Data Mining, pp. 289–297 (2012)
13. Van Looveren, A., Klaise, J.: Interpretable counterfactual explanations guided by prototypes. In: Oliver, N., Pérez-Cruz, F., Kramer, S., Read, J., Lozano, J.A. (eds.) ECML PKDD 2021. LNCS (LNAI), vol. 12976, pp. 650–665. Springer, Cham (2021). https://doi.org/10.1007/978-3-030-86520-7_40
14. Lundberg, S.M., Lee, S.I.: A unified approach to interpreting model predictions. Adv. Neural Inf. Process. Syst. **30** (2017)
15. Mahendran, A., Vedaldi, A.: Understanding deep image representations by inverting them. In: Proceedings of the IEEE Conference on Computer Vision and Pattern Recognition, pp. 5188–5196 (2015)
16. Mothilal, R.K., Sharma, A., Tan, C.: Explaining machine learning classifiers through diverse counterfactual explanations. In: Proceedings of the 2020 Conference on Fairness, Accountability, and Transparency, pp. 607–617 (2020)
17. Mueen, A., Keogh, E., Young, N.: Logical-shapelets: an expressive primitive for time series classification. In: Proceedings of the 17th ACM SIGKDD International Conference on Knowledge Discovery and Data Mining, pp. 1154–1162 (2011)
18. Nguyen, T.T., Le Nguyen, T., Ifrim, G.: A model-agnostic approach to quantifying the informativeness of explanation methods for time series classification. In: Lemaire, V., Malinowski, S., Bagnall, A. Guyet, T., Tavenard, R., Ifrim, G. (eds.) AALTD 2020. LNCS (LNAI), vol. 12588, pp. 77–94. Springer, Cham (2020). https://doi.org/10.1007/978-3-030-65742-0_6
19. Ribeiro, M.T., Singh, S., Guestrin, C.: "Why should i trust you?" explaining the predictions of any classifier. In: Proceedings of the 22nd ACM SIGKDD International Conference on Knowledge Discovery and Data Mining, pp. 1135–1144 (2016)
20. Schlegel, U., Arnout, H., El-Assady, M., Oelke, D., Keim, D.A.: Towards a rigorous evaluation of XAI methods on time series. In: 2019 IEEE/CVF International Conference on Computer Vision Workshop (ICCVW), pp. 4197–4201. IEEE (2019)
21. Schlegel, U., Vo, D.L., Keim, D.A., Seebacher, D.: Ts-mule: local interpretable model-agnostic explanations for time series forecast models. In: Joint European Conference on Machine Learning and Knowledge Discovery in Databases, pp. 5–14. Springer, Cham (2021). https://doi.org/10.1007/978-3-030-93736-2_1
22. Schleich, M., Geng, Z., Zhang, Y., Suciu, D.: Geco: quality counterfactual explanations in real time. arXiv preprint arXiv:2101.01292 (2021)
23. Slack, D., Hilgard, S., Jia, E., Singh, S., Lakkaraju, H.: How can we fool lime and shap? adversarial attacks on post hoc explanation methods (2019)
24. Verma, S., Dickerson, J., Hines, K.: Counterfactual explanations for machine learning: a review. arXiv preprint arXiv:2010.10596 (2020)

25. Wachter, S., Mittelstadt, B., Russell, C.: Counterfactual explanations without opening the black box: automated decisions and the GDPR. Harv. JL Tech. **31**, 841 (2017)
26. Xu, Y., et al.: Deep learning predicts lung cancer treatment response from serial medical imaging. Clin. Cancer Res. **25**(11), 3266–3275 (2019)
27. Ye, L., Keogh, E.: Time series shapelets: a new primitive for data mining. In: Proceedings of the 15th ACM SIGKDD International Conference on Knowledge Discovery and Data Mining, pp. 947–956 (2009)
28. Ye, L., Keogh, E.: Time series shapelets: a novel technique that allows accurate, interpretable and fast classification. Data Mining Knowl. Discov. **22**(1), 149–182 (2011)
29. Zhou, Z., Hooker, G., Wang, F.: S-lime: stabilized-lime for model explanation. In: Proceedings of the 27th ACM SIGKDD Conference on Knowledge Discovery and Data Mining, pp. 2429–2438 (2021)

Comparison of Attention Models and Post-hoc Explanation Methods for Embryo Stage Identification: A Case Study

Tristan Gomez[1]([✉])(iD), Thomas Fréour[2], and Harold Mouchère[1]

[1] Nantes Université, Centrale Nantes, CNRS, LS2N, 44000 Nantes, France
{tristan.gomez,harold.mouchere}@univ-nantes.fr
[2] Nantes University Hospital, Inserm, CRTI, Inserm UMR 1064,
44000 Nantes, France
thomas.freour@chu-nantes.fr

Abstract. An important limitation to the development of AI-based solutions for In Vitro Fertilization (IVF) is the black-box nature of most state-of-the-art models, due to the complexity of deep learning architectures, which raises potential bias and fairness issues. The need for interpretable AI has risen not only in the IVF field but also in the deep learning community in general. This has started a trend in literature where authors focus on designing objective metrics to evaluate generic explanation methods. In this paper, we study the behavior of recently proposed objective faithfulness metrics applied to the problem of embryo stage identification. We benchmark attention models and post-hoc methods using metrics and further show empirically that (1) the metrics produce low overall agreement on the model ranking and (2) depending on the metric approach, either post-hoc methods or attention models are favored. We conclude with general remarks about the difficulty of defining faithfulness and the necessity of understanding its relationship with the type of approach that is favored.

1 Introduction

Infertility is a global health issue worldwide [18]. One of the most common treatments for infertile couples is In Vitro Fertilization (IVF). This procedure notably consists of embryo culture for 2–6 days under controlled environmental conditions, leading to intrauterine transfer or freezing of embryos identified as having a good implantation potential by embryologists. To allow continuous monitoring of embryo development, Time-lapse imaging incubators (TLI) were first released in the IVF market around 2010. This time-lapse technology provides a dynamic overview of embryonic in vitro development by taking photographs of each embryo at regular intervals throughout its development. TLI

Supported by Nantes Excellence Trajectory (NExT).

J.-J. Rousseau and B. Kapralos (Eds.): ICPR 2022 Workshops, LNCS 13645, pp. 216–230, 2023.
https://doi.org/10.1007/978-3-031-37731-0_17

appears to be the most promising solution to improve embryo quality assessment methods, and subsequently, the clinical efficiency of IVF [27]. In particular, the unprecedented high volume of high-quality images produced by TLI systems has already been leveraged using deep learning (DL) methods. Previous work has notably focused on designing models that automatically identify the embryo development stages, a crucial task to identify embryos with low live-birth potential [21,28]. However, an important limitation to the development of AI-based solutions for IVF is the black-box nature of most state-of-the-art models, due to the complexity of deep learning architectures, which raises potential bias and fairness issues [1]. The need for interpretable AI has risen not only in the IVF field but also in the deep learning community in general. This has started a trend in literature where authors confront users with models' decisions along with various explanations to determine which fits better the users' needs on a particular application [3,31,32]. However, the financial cost and the difficulty of establishing a correct protocol make this approach difficult. Because of these issues, another trend focuses on designing objective metrics and protocols to evaluate generic explanation methods [5,13,19,26]. In this paper, we follow this trend and study the behavior of objective faithfulness metrics recently proposed applied to the problem of embryo stage identification. We apply faithfulness metrics to attention models and further show empirically that (1) the metrics produce low overall agreement on the model ranking and (2) depending on the metric approach, either post-hoc methods or attention models are favored.

First, we describe the attention models, post-hoc methods, and faithfulness metrics we use in this work. Secondly, we compute an extensive benchmark and study the behavior of the metrics on 9 saliency approaches, including 5 post-hoc methods and 4 attention models. We conclude with general remarks about the difficulty of defining faithfulness and the necessity of understanding its relationship with the type of approach that is favored.

2 Method

2.1 Saliency Map Generation Approaches

We now describe the models and methods used to generate saliency maps. First, we list several attention models as they integrate the computation of a saliency map (called an attention map) that is used to guide the decision process. Secondly, we list generic post-hoc explanation methods that can generate saliency maps for a wide range of models and architectures without requiring model training.

Attention Models. In this category, we include models featuring a spatial attention layer in their inference phase. Note that we do not include visual transformers [10] as they are difficult to interpret due to their non-local heads, as opposed to the local CNN kernels. Hu et al. [16] proposed a variant of the model originally proposed by Lin et al. [22] with a convolutional module that processes the feature maps and outputs the attention map. In the rest of this paper, this model is designated as the Bilinear-CNN (B-CNN). Fukui et al. [11] proposed another variant of Lin et al.'s architecture called Attention Branch Network (ABN) where the attention module is also trained to correctly predict the object class along with the regular classification head. This was applied to the problem of embryo quality prediction [29], a problem related to the one studied here.

Another line of work proposes to use prototypes to increase interpretability. Notably, Interpretability By Parts (IBP) [17] is a model that improves upon Chen et al.'s work [6] by encouraging the model to generate prototypes presence probabilities close to 0 or 1, to generate more accurate attention maps and improve interpretability.

The last attention model included in this study is called Bilinear Representative Non-Parametric Attention (BR-NPA) [14] and proposes to generate attention maps to guide the model spatially without any dedicated parameter, contrary to the models mentioned above which feature either a convolution attention module or parametric prototypes.

Post-hoc Explanation Methods. This category proposes generic methods that can be applied to any CNN with feature maps and does not require training the model, contrarily to the attention modules mentioned above. Class Activation Map (CAM) [34] was proposed to visualize the areas that contributed the most to the prediction of one specific class. Grad-CAM [30] improves upon CAM and proposes to compute the gradients of the feature maps relatively to the class score to identify the maps that contributed the most to the decision. A weighted average of the maps is then computed to obtain the saliency map. The first method included here is Grad-CAM++ [5], which further replaces feature-wise gradients with pixel-wise positive partial derivatives to compute the saliency map. We also use Score-CAM [33] and Ablation-CAM [9] later proposed to remove gradients by evaluating each feature map's importance by masking the input image according to the activated areas of the map or by ablation analysis.

We also apply RISE [26], a method that uses random masks to find the areas that impact the class score the most. The last method is a baseline that we call Activation Map (AM) which consists to visualize the average activation map by computing the mean of the last layer's feature maps.

2.2   Faithfulness Metrics

The input image is a 3D tensor $I \in \mathbb{R}^{H \times W \times 3}$ and the saliency map is a 2D matrix $S \in \mathbb{R}^{H' \times W'}$ with a lower resolution, $H' < H$ and $W' < W$. We study the following faithfulness metrics.

Increase In Confidence (ICC) [5]

The IIC metrics measures how often the confidence of the model in the predicted class increases when highlighting the salient areas. First, the input image is masked with the explanation map as follows:

$$I_m = \text{norm}(\text{upsamp}(S)) \bullet I, \tag{1}$$

where $\text{norm}(S)$ is the min-max normalization function, defined as $\text{norm}(S) = \frac{S - min(S)}{max(S) - min(S)}$, $\text{upsamp}(S)$ is a function that upsample S to the resolution of I, and • is the element-wise product. The IIC metric is defined as:

$$IIC = \mathbf{1}_{[c_I < c_{I_m}]},\tag{2}$$

where c_I is the score of the predicted class with I as input and c_{I_m} is the score of the same class with I_m as input. The intuition is that a good saliency map S highlights areas such that when the non-salient areas are removed, the class score increases. Note that this metric is a binary value and is only useful when computing its mean value over a large number of images, as in Sect. 4. Therefore, maximizing the mean of this metric corresponds to an improvement.

Average Drop (AD) [5]. Similar to IIC, this metric measures the average score drop when highlighting the salient areas. Using the same masking of the input image, the AD metric computes the relative score difference between the two images I and I_m:

$$AD = \frac{max(0, c_I - c_{I_m})}{c_I}\tag{3}$$

Given that when highlighting the salient areas the class score is not supposed to decrease, minimizing this metric corresponds to an improvement. Note that the metric name implies computing an average value over several images, as is done in Sect. 4. However, we did not include the averaging operator in the AD definition to keep notation simple and uniform throughout this section.

Average Drop in Deletion (ADD) [19]. Jung et al. proposed a variant of the preceding metric which consists to mask the salient areas instead of the non-salient areas. To do this, the image is masked with the inverse of the saliency map, which highlights the non-salient areas:

$$I_{1-m} = (1 - norm(upsamp(S))) \bullet I\tag{4}$$

The ADD metric is then defined as follows:

$$ADD = \frac{max(0, c_I - c_{I_{1-m}})}{c_I},\tag{5}$$

where $c_{I_{1-m}}$ is the score with I_{1-m}. Contrarily to AD, this metric removes the salient areas and the class score is expected to decrease, which means that maximizing this metric results in an improvement. Also, as for AD, we dropped the averaging operator to keep notation simple.

Deletion Area Under Curve (DAUC) [26]. This metric evaluates the reliability of the saliency maps by progressively masking the image starting with the most important areas according to the saliency map and finishing with the least important. First, S is parsed from the highest element to the lowest element. At each element $S_{i'j'}$, we mask the corresponding area of I by multiplying it by a mask $M^{i'j'} \in \mathbb{R}^{H \times W}$, where

$$M_{ij}^{i'j'} = \begin{cases} 0, & \text{if } i'r < i < i'(r+1) \text{ and } j'r < j < j'(r+1) \\ 1, & \text{otherwise,} \end{cases}\tag{6}$$

and $r = H/H' = W/W'$. After each masking operation, the model m runs an inference with the updated version of I, and the score of the initially predicted class is updated, producing a new score c_k:

$$c_k = m(I \cdot \prod_{\tilde{k}=(1,1)}^{\tilde{k}=k} M^{\tilde{k}}), \tag{7}$$

where $k = (i', j')$. Secondly, once the whole image has been masked, the scores c_k are normalized by dividing them by the maximum $\max_{k} c_k$ and then plotted as a function of the proportion p_k of the image that is masked. The DAUC is finally obtained by computing the area under the curve (AUC) of this graph. The intuition behind this is that if a saliency map highlights the areas that are relevant to the decision, masking them will quickly result in a large decrease in the initially predicted class score, which in turn will minimize the AUC. Therefore, minimizing this metric corresponds to an improvement.

Insertion Area Under Curve (IAUC) [26]. Instead of progressively masking the image, the IAUC metric starts from a blurred image and then progressively unblurs it by starting from the most important areas according to the saliency map. Similarly, if the areas highlighted by the map are relevant for predicting the correct category, the score of the corresponding class (obtained using the partially unblurred image) is supposed to increase rapidly. Maximizing this metric corresponds to an improvement.

Deletion Correlation (DC) [13]. The DC metric also consists of gradually masking the input image by following the order suggested by the saliency map, but instead of computing the area under the class score/pixel rank curve, it computes the linear correlation of the class score variations and the saliency scores. Once the scores c_k have been computed, we compute the variation of the scores $v_k = c_k - c_{k+1}$. The DC metric is obtained by the linear correlation coefficient between the v_k and the s_k where s_k is the saliency score of the area masked at step k. As it represents the correlation between the saliency of a pixel and its impact on the class score, maximizing this metric is an improvement.

Insertion Correlation (IC) [13]. Similarly, the IC metric is inspired by IAUC and starts from a blurred image, and gradually reveals the image according to the saliency map. Once the image is totally revealed, the score variations are computed $v_k = c_{k+1} - c_k$ and the linear correlation of the v_k with the s_k is computed. This correlation metric should also be maximized to correspond to an improvement.

2.3   The Embryo Development Stage Dataset

The images used in this work are microscopic images of growing embryos between their first and fifth day of development in vitro [12]. During these five days, the embryo grows through 16 successive development stages that we note sPB2, sPNa, sPNf, s2, s3, s4, s5, s6, s7, s8, s9+, sM, sSB, sB, sEB, and sHB. These stages are delimited by 16 events called tPB2, tPNa, tPNf, t2, t3, t4, t5, t6, t7, t8, t9+, tM, tSB, tB, tEB, tHB and defined by Ciray et al. [7]. The timings of each event are valuable information to determine if the quality of the embryo is high enough to be transferred to the uterus [27].

The raw dataset consists of 704 videos that we split equally into one training/validation set and one test set. From each set and each video, we extract one-third of the frames regularly spaced the video. The images are in grayscale with a 500 × 500 resolution. The total size of each set is 29843 images for the training/validation set and 28282 images for the test set.

We choose to model this problem as an image classification task. The models studied in this paper are trained to process an embryo image and infer which development stage the embryo is at. Note that the video recording starts at the tPB2 event which means that the first frames show the sPB2 stage. The class distribution and some samples are shown respectively in Fig. 1 and Fig. 2.

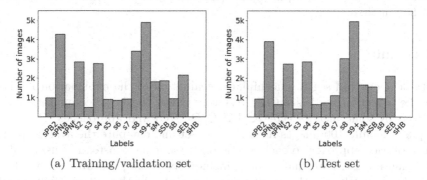

(a) Training/validation set   (b) Test set

Fig. 1. The class distribution of the dataset used. There are only 5 and 15 sHB samples respectively in the training/validation set and the test set as this stage usually occurs after the video recording has been stopped.

3   Implementation Details

The backbone used for all networks is ResNet-50 [15] pretrained on ImageNet. Images are augmented during training using a random 448×448 crop and random horizontal flipping. During the test, we extract a center crop of size 448×448. We use 10% of the training set images for validation. The models are trained with regular cross-entropy during 10 epochs and the best model on the validation set is restored for the test phase. The following hyperparameters were searched on the validation set using the Optuna python framework ([2]) with the default sampler (a Tree-structured Parzen Estimator algorithm): the learning rate, momentum, optimizer, batch size, dropout on the classification layer, and weight decay.

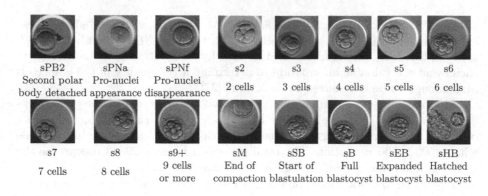

sPB2	sPNa	sPNf	s2	s3	s4	s5	s6
Second polar body detached	Pro-nuclei appearance	Pro-nuclei disappearance	2 cells	3 cells	4 cells	5 cells	6 cells

s7	s8	s9+	sM	sSB	sB	sEB	sHB
7 cells	8 cells	9 cells or more	End of compaction	Start of blastulation	Full blastocyst	Expanded blastocyst	Hatched blastocyst

Fig. 2. Illustrations of the 16 development stages used.

We use Pytorch 1.10.2 [8] and two P100 GPUs. Following the original work of Petsiuk et al. [26], we sampled 4000 masks at a 7×7 resolution for the RISE post-hoc method.

4   Results

In Table 1 one can see the faithfulness evaluation of the explanation methods and the attention models on the test set. Given the large computation time required by some metrics (DAUC/IAUC/DC/IC) and approaches (RISE), we sample randomly 100 images from the test set and compute the average performance of each approach to each metric on these images instead of using all the test images. First, note that we also include the average accuracy per video of the trained models over the whole test set to highlight that all models have similar accuracies. This means that the differences in faithfulness observed can not be explained by different levels of accuracy but only by the approach (attention model/post-hoc method) or the metrics. Secondly, the faithfulness metrics do not agree on which model is the best. For example, depending on the metric, the most faithful explanation method is BR-NPA, RISE, Ablation-CAM, ABN, or Score-CAM and the least faithful is ABN, InterByParts, RISE, BR-NPA, or AM.

Quantifying the Metrics Disagreement. We propose to use the Kendall-tau correlation coefficient [20] to obtain a better idea of the disagreement between the metrics. This correlation coefficient indicates if two variables have a monotonic relationship with each other. When close from 1/-1, the variables have an increasing/decreasing relationship, and when close to 0, they are independent. We represent each metric using the 9 mean performances they have attributed to each approach. Let x and y be two such lists of performance for two metrics. We define a concordant pair, which is a pair of approaches A and B that are ranked the same in x and y, i.e. metrics x and y agree that A is better or worse than B. We also define a discordant pair, where x and y disagree on the ranking of A and B. Furthermore, we say that a pair is a tie according to x if they have

Table 1. Performance of the studied models and methods.

Model	Viz. Method	DAUC	IAUC	DC	IC	IIC	AD	ADD	Accuracy
CNN	AM	0.134	0.308	−0.174	0.075	0.19	0.397	0.325	71.0
	Grad-CAM++	0.1162	0.333	−0.101	0.032	0.52	0.14	0.383	
	RISE	0.113	**0.457**	−0.221	−0.077	0.5	0.137	0.436	
	Score-CAM	0.1079	0.315	−0.123	0.081	0.52	**0.108**	0.362	
	Ablation-CAM	0.0954	0.329	**0.272**	−0.071	**0.57**	0.111	0.328	
ABN	-	0.1464	0.249	−0.186	**0.136**	0.12	0.591	0.475	71.0
InterByParts	-	0.0876	0.115	0.196	−0.255	0.08	0.901	0.879	**71.3**
B-CNN	-	0.0772	0.221	−0.208	0.124	0.13	0.491	0.482	70.2
BR-NPA	-	**0.0709**	0.261	0.185	−0.146	0.04	0.91	**0.887**	70.7

the same ranking in x. Finally, the Kendall-tau correlation coefficient between two metrics x and y is computed as follows:

$$\tau(x,y) = \frac{(P-Q)}{\sqrt{P+Q+U} * \sqrt{P+Q+T}}, \tag{8}$$

where P is the number of concordant pairs, Q the number of discordant pairs, T the number of ties only in x, and U the number of ties only in y. If a tie occurs for the same pair in both x and y, it is not added to either T or U. The coefficient values obtained between each pair of metrics are shown in Fig. 3. Overall, there is a low correlation value between metrics. This means that metrics globally disagree on the model ranking, with many metrics producing independent ranking (DC and IC have a close from 0 correlation with AD, ADD, IIC, and IAUC) and some metrics even ranking models in reversed order (AD and ADD, ADD and IIC, IC, and DC). However, some metrics offer similar rankings like AD with IIC or IAUC.

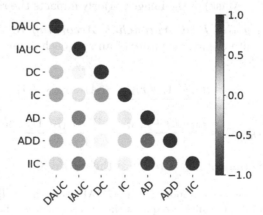

Fig. 3. Kendall-tau correlation coefficient between the metrics.

Visualizing the Metrics Disagreement. To obtain a clear representation of metrics' similarities with each other, we propose to use a dimension reduction algorithm like t-SNE [23]. Each pair of image/metric is represented by a vector of size 9 (the 9 explanations) and projected in 2d using t-SNE. Note that we exclude the IIC metric as it is a binary metric and will not provide a meaningful ranking on a single image. We obtain 6 point clouds in a 9-dimensional space, where each cloud is composed of 100 points and represents one metric, for a total of 600 points. We use t-SNE to reduce the dimension of the 600 points at the same time and visualize the result on a single 2D plot. Note that an appropriate distance function has to be chosen, given that each point represents a ranking. Instead of the default Euclidean distance, we use the following distance function based on Kendall's tau correlation:

$$D(x,y) = -\log\left(\frac{1}{2}(\tau(x,y)+1)\right), \tag{9}$$

where $\tau(\cdot,\cdot)$ is the Kendall's tau correlation. With this metric, we ensure a distance that goes from 0 to $+\infty$ when the correlation $\tau(x,y)$ goes from 1 to -1. Furthermore, when $\tau = -1$ we replace its value by -0.999 to prevent any numerical errors.[1]

The plot in Fig. 4 shows that the metrics are arranged in two groups: {DAUC, DC, ADD}, {IAUC, IC, AD}. This structure is not surprising given that DAUC, DC and ADD all consist to mask the important areas of the image, measure the score drop, and favor the model with the lowest class score once the mask(s) are applied. Similarly, IAUC, IC, and AD all highlight/reveal the important areas and favors models for which the class score is the highest possible once the important areas have been revealed. This is why we call 'Mask' and 'Highlight' the two groups of metrics obtained: {DAUC, DC, ADD} and {IAUC, IC, AD, IIC}. Note that we also include IIC in the Highlight group as it also consists to highlight the salient areas of the image and expects a score increase as a consequence. This demonstrates that the method used to measure the impact of an area (Highlight or Mask) of the image majorly impacts the ranking produced.

We Now Identify the Best Aproaches According to Each Group of Metrics. We compute the average rank of an approach A on the Highlight and Mask groups as follows:

$$r_{Mask}(A) = \frac{r_{DC}(A) + r_{DAUC}(A) + r_{ADD}(A)}{3}$$
$$r_{Highlight}(A) = \frac{r_{IC}(A) + r_{IAUC}(A) + r_{AD}(A) + r_{IIC}(A)}{4}, \tag{10}$$

where $r_X(A)$ is the rank of A according to the metric X.

---

[1] Note that we did not use the more recent UMAP algorithm [24] because the only UMAP implementation available requires the custom distance function to be compiled with Numba, which is currently not possible with the Kendall's tau implementation of the Scikit-Learn python package [25].

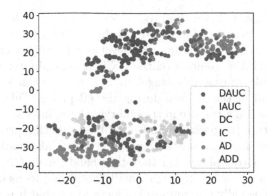

Fig. 4. t-SNE projection of the ranking given by metrics on the 100 images. The distance between points is computed using a metric based on Kendall's tau correlation.

Table 2 shows the average ranks computed. One can see a link between metric type and approach type where the Mask group seems to favor the Attention models whereas the Highlight group favors the generic post-hoc methods. We also identify the most faithful approaches according to each metric group: BR-NPA and Score-CAM.

Table 2. Average ranking of the methods according to the two metrics groups: Mask and Highlight. Attention models and post-hoc methods are respectively highlighted in orange and cyan.

Mask			Highlight		
Average rank	Approach	Type	Average rank	Approach	Type
1.67	BR-NPA	Attention	2.75	Score-CAM	Post-Hoc
2.33	InterByParts	Attention	3.0	Ablation-CAM	Post-Hoc
4.33	B-CNN	Attention	3.25	Grad-CAM++	Post-Hoc
4.33	Ablation-CAM	Post-Hoc	3.75	RISE	Post-Hoc
5.67	Grad-CAM++	Post-Hoc	4.75	AM	Post-Hoc
5.67	Score-CAM	Post-Hoc	5.5	ABN	Attention
6.67	ABN	Attention	5.5	B-CNN	Attention
6.67	RISE	Post-Hoc	8.0	BR-NPA	Attention
7.67	AM	Post-Hoc	8.5	InterByParts	Attention

Visualizing the Saliency Maps. Next, we propose to examine the maps they generate to determine which model seems the most reliable between BR-NPA and the CNN, using the Score-CAM algorithm to explain the CNN's decision. By reliable, we mean a model which uses biologically relevant features in the image.

Figure 5 shows examples of saliency maps generated by BR-NPA and Score-CAM during 3 stages: sPNa (Fig. 5a), s4 (Fig. 5b) and sB (Fig. 5c). In Fig. 5a,

BR-NPA focuses distinctly on the Pro-Nuclei (PN) (the nuclei of a sperm or an egg cell during the process of fertilization) during the sPNa stage whereas the focus of the CNN seems to be at an upper level as it highlights the whole embryo. The focus of BR-NPA's attention on the PN is biologically relevant because the PN are only visible during this stage. In Fig. 5c one can see that BR-NPA focuses on the wall of the embryo during the sB phase. This stage marks the beginning of a new cell structure in the embryo where, instead of being arranged as a pack, cells start to specialize and notably some cells form the wall of the embryo. Therefore, focusing on the embryo's wall is also biologically relevant as it is a marker of this phase. On the other hand, Score-CAM produces low-resolution maps that can not highlight small details and focus on the embryo as a whole, a less biologically relevant level of focus given that it is visible during all stages. Globally, BR-NPA's saliency maps are sharp and precise and highlight biologically relevant elements of the image. However, this does not imply that BR-NPA focuses on more biologically relevant features than the CNN. Indeed, the blurriness of Score-CAM's saliency maps is probably due at least to the low resolution of the CNN's feature maps (14×14) compared to the resolution of BR-NPA's which is higher (56×56). This shows the interest in using high-resolution attention maps like BR-NPA maps to disambiguate the model's focus.

5 Discussion

Bastings et al. [4] argue that post-hoc methods should be privileged over attention models when it comes to faithfulness, as post-hoc methods take the whole computation path into account whereas attention maps only reflect input importance at one point in the computation. However, we showed here that depending on the way the map is evaluated (Highlight or Mask), attention models can provide superior faithfulness.

Also, the intuitions behind the metrics discussed here should be examined. For example, the IIC metric suggests that the class score should increase once the salient parts of the image have been highlighted. However, it is unclear if such a phenomenon would happen in practice. Indeed, filling the masked areas with black pixels generates out-of-distribution samples that can induce an unexpected behavior of the model [13]. Moreover, ICC suggests that the confidence is increased by the presence of salient areas and decreased by the presence of non-salient areas, but the non-salient areas could also play a neutral role and not affect the confidence much.

More generally, the major difficulty in designing these metrics resides in measuring the impact of an area of the input image reliably. Measuring the impact of an area by masking it is difficult because the score variation depends on if the other areas of the image are masked or not. To reach a consensus on how this measure should be done, the community has first yet to understand how exactly the score variation depends on the masking of other areas. Moreover, the metrics studied here were all developed to quantify faithfulness but in practice adopt two distinct behaviors and seems to favor different methods: attention models for

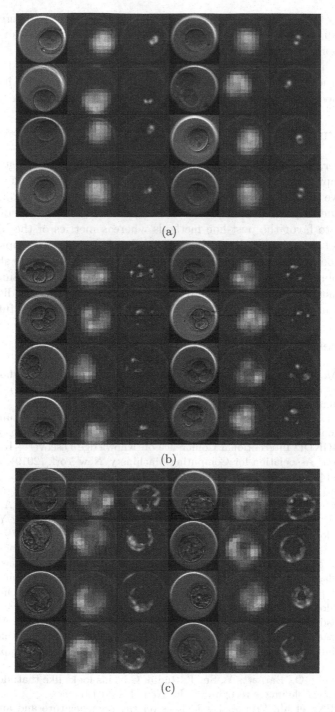

Fig. 5. The saliency maps generated by the Score-CAM method and BR-NPA model (respectively middle and right columns) on stages sPNa (a), s4 (b), and sB (c).

the Mask group and post-hoc methods for the Highlight group. Therefore, there should also be future works on the definition of faithfulness and its relationship with the approach type (attention models or post-hoc methods).

Finally, the practical relevance of the faithfulness metrics should be evaluated in a user study. To what extent the reliability of the maps can improve, for example, the acceptability of the decision by a user remains an open question.

6   Conclusion

In this paper, we compared the faithfulness of the saliency maps generated by 9 different approaches, including 4 attention models and 5 post-hoc explanation methods. We showed low overall agreement between the metrics proposed in the literature and in particular demonstrated the tendency of metrics of the Highlight group to favor the post-hoc methods whereas metrics of the Mask group favor instead attention models. We then visualized the saliency maps generated by the two best approaches, namely Score-CAM and BR-NPA, and showed that the low resolution of Score-CAM limits the insights that can be obtained whereas BR-NPA's maps highlight biologically relevant features. Finally, we discussed the difficulty of measuring the impact of each image part reliably and future work.

References

1. Afnan, M., et al.: Interpretable, not black-box, artificial intelligence should be used for embryo selection. Human Reprod. Open **2021**(4), hoab040 (2021). https://doi.org/10.1093/hropen/hoab040
2. Akiba, T., Sano, S., Yanase, T., Ohta, T., Koyama, M.: Optuna: a next-generation hyperparameter optimization framework. In: Proceedings of the 25th ACM SIGKDD International Conference on Knowledge Discovery (KDD'19), pp. 2623–2631. Association for Computing Machinery, New York (2019). https://doi.org/10.1145/3292500.3330701
3. Alqaraawi, A., Schuessler, M., Weiß, P., Costanza, E., Berthouze, N.: Evaluating Saliency Map Explanations for Convolutional Neural Networks: A User Study (IUI '20), pp. 275–285. Association for Computing Machinery, New York (2020). https://doi.org/10.1145/3377325.3377519
4. Bastings, J., Filippova, K.: The elephant in the interpretability room: why use attention as explanation when we have saliency methods? In: Proceedings of the Third BlackboxNLP Workshop on Analyzing and Interpreting Neural Networks for NLP, pp. 149–155. Association for Computational Linguistics, Online (2020). https://doi.org/10.18653/v1/2020.blackboxnlp-1.14
5. Chattopadhay, A., Sarkar, A., Howlader, P., Balasubramanian, V.N.: Grad-cam++: generalized gradient-based visual explanations for deep convolutional networks. In: 2018 IEEE Winter Conference on Applications of Computer Vision (WACV) (2018). https://doi.org/10.1109/wacv.2018.00097
6. Chen, C., Li, O., Barnett, A., Su, J., Rudin, C.: This looks like that: deep learning for interpretable image recognition. In: NeurIPS (2019)
7. Ciray, H.N., et al.: Proposed guidelines on the nomenclature and annotation of dynamic human embryo monitoring by a time-lapse user group. Human Reprod. **29**(12), 2650–2660 (2014). https://doi.org/10.1093/humrep/deu278

8. Collobert, R., Kavukcuoglu, K., Farabet, C.: Torch7: a matlab-like environment for machine learning. In: BigLearn, NIPS Workshop (2011)
9. Desai, S., Ramaswamy, H.G.: Ablation-cam: Visual explanations for deep convolutional network via gradient-free localization. In: 2020 IEEE Winter Conference on Applications of Computer Vision (WACV), pp. 972–980 (2020). https://doi.org/10.1109/WACV45572.2020.9093360
10. Dosovitskiy, A., et al.: An image is worth 16x16 words: Transformers for image recognition at scale. In: International Conference on Learning Representations (2021). https://openreview.net/forum?id=YicbFdNTTy
11. Fukui, H., Hirakawa, T., Yamashita, T., Fujiyoshi, H.: Attention branch network: learning of attention mechanism for visual explanation. In: 2019 IEEE/CVF Conference on Computer Vision and Pattern Recognition (CVPR), pp. 10697–10706 (2019). https://doi.org/10.1109/CVPR.2019.01096
12. Gomez, T., et al.: A time-lapse embryo dataset for morphokinetic parameter prediction. Data Brief **42** (2022). https://doi.org/10.1016/j.dib.2022.108258
13. Gomez, T., Fréour, T., Mouchère, H.: Metrics for saliency map evaluation of deep learning explanation methods. In: International Conference on Pattern Recognition and Artificial Intelligence (2022). https://doi.org/10.48550/ARXIV.2201.13291
14. Gomez, T., Ling, S., Fréour, T., Mouchère, H.: Br-npa: a non-parametric high-resolution attention model to improve the interpretability of attention (2021). https://doi.org/10.48550/ARXIV.2106.02566
15. He, K., Zhang, X., Ren, S., Sun, J.: Deep residual learning for image recognition. In: 2016 IEEE Conference on Computer Vision and Pattern Recognition (CVPR), pp. 770–778 (2016)
16. Hu, T., Qi, H.: See better before looking closer: Weakly supervised data augmentation network for fine-grained visual classification. arXiv preprint arXiv:1901.09891 (2019)
17. Huang, Z., Li, Y.: Interpretable and accurate fine-grained recognition via region grouping. In: The IEEE/CVF Conference on Computer Vision and Pattern Recognition (CVPR) (2020)
18. Inhorn, M.C., Patrizio, P.: Infertility around the globe: new thinking on gender, reproductive technologies and global movements in the 21st century. Human Reprod. Update **21**(4), 411–426 (2015). https://doi.org/10.1093/humupd/dmv016
19. Jung, H., Oh, Y.: Towards better explanations of class activation mapping. In: Proceedings of the IEEE/CVF International Conference on Computer Vision (ICCV), pp. 1336–1344 (2021)
20. Kendall, M.G.: The treatment of ties in ranking problems. Biometrika **33**(3), 239–251 (1945). http://www.jstor.org/stable/2332303
21. Khan, A., Gould, S., Salzmann, M.: Deep convolutional neural networks for human embryonic cell counting. In: Hua, G., Jégou, H. (eds.) ECCV 2016. LNCS, vol. 9913, pp. 339–348. Springer, Cham (2016). https://doi.org/10.1007/978-3-319-46604-0_25
22. Lin, T.Y., RoyChowdhury, A., Maji, S.: Bilinear CNN models for fine-grained visual recognition. In: Proceedings of the 2015 IEEE International Conference on Computer Vision (ICCV) (ICCV '15), pp. 1449–1457. IEEE Computer Society, Washington, DC (2015). https://doi.org/10.1109/ICCV.2015.170
23. van der Maaten, L., Hinton, G.: Visualizing data using t-sne. J. Mach. Learn. Res. **9**(86), 2579–2605 (2008). http://jmlr.org/papers/v9/vandermaaten08a.html
24. McInnes, L., Healy, J., Saul, N., GroSSberger, L.: Umap: Uniform manifold approximation and projection. J. Open Source Softw. **3**(29), 861 (2018). https://doi.org/10.21105/joss.00861

25. Pedregosa, F., et al.: Scikit-learn: machine learning in Python. J. Mach. Learn. Res. **12**, 2825–2830 (2011)
26. Petsiuk, V., Das, A., Saenko, K.: Rise: randomized input sampling for explanation of black-box models. In: BMVC (2018)
27. Pribenszky, C., Nilselid, A.M., Montag, M.: Time-lapse culture with morphokinetic embryo selection improves pregnancy and live birth chances and reduces early pregnancy loss: a meta-analysis. Reprod. BioMed. Online **35**, 511–520 (2017)
28. Rad, R.M., Saeedi, P., Au, J., Havelock, J.: Blastomere cell counting and centroid localization in microscopic images of human embryo. In: 2018 IEEE 20th International Workshop on Multimedia Signal Processing (MMSP), pp. 1–6 (2018). https://doi.org/10.1109/MMSP.2018.8547107
29. Sawada, Y., et al.: Artificial intelligence with attention branch network and deep learning can predict live births by using time-lapse imaging of embryos after in vitro fertilisation. Reprod. BioMed. Online (2021). https://doi.org/10.1016/j.rbmo.2021.05.002
30. Selvaraju, R.R., Cogswell, M., Das, A., Vedantam, R., Parikh, D., Batra, D.: Grad-CAM: visual explanations from deep networks via gradient-based localization. Int. J. Comput. Vis. **128**(2), 336–359 (2019). https://doi.org/10.1007/s11263-019-01228-7
31. Tsai, C.H., Brusilovsky, P.: Evaluating Visual Explanations for Similarity-Based Recommendations: User Perception and Performance, pp. 22–30. Association for Computing Machinery, New York (2019)
32. van der Waa, J., Nieuwburg, E., Cremers, A., Neerincx, M.: Evaluating XAI: a comparison of rule-based and example-based explanations. Artif. Intell. **291**, 103404 (2021). https://doi.org/10.1016/j.artint.2020.103404
33. Wang, H., et al.: Score-cam: score-weighted visual explanations for convolutional neural networks. In: 2020 IEEE/CVF Conference on Computer Vision and Pattern Recognition Workshops (CVPRW), pp. 111–119. IEEE Computer Society, Los Alamitos (2020). https://doi.org/10.1109/CVPRW50498.2020.00020
34. Zhou, B., Khosla, A., Lapedriza, A., Oliva, A., Torralba, A.: Learning deep features for discriminative localization. In: The IEEE Conference on Computer Vision and Pattern Recognition (CVPR) (2016). https://doi.org/10.1109/CVPR.2016.319

Graph-Based Analysis of Hierarchical Embedding Generated by Deep Neural Network

Korlan Rysbayeva⬤, Romain Giot$^{(\boxtimes)}$⬤, and Nicholas Journet⬤

Univ. Bordeaux, Bordeaux INP, CNRS, LaBRI, UMR5800, 33400 Talence, France
{korlan.rysbayeva,romain.giot,nicholas.journet}@u-bordeaux.fr

Abstract. In a previous work, we have developed a framework for the multimodal and hierarchical classification of images from soil remediation reports. We extended this work using Deep Metric Learning (DML) as an additional training step to improve embeddings quality and obtained 84.24% of weighted F1 score for the level 5th hierarchical level. However, the standard classifier performance metrics are insufficient to explain the decision process reasoning. So far of our knowledge, there are no methods to analyze hierarchical classification algorithms. In this work, we propose a method of graph analysis to describe the embeddings that represent the extended classifier, which we believe properly interprets the obtained results than classification metrics. We illustrate the method of analyzing hierarchical classification algorithms on private dataset, but the method remains generic enough to be used in other contexts.

Keywords: Graph analysis · Hierarchical embeddings · eXplainable Artificial Intelligence

1 Introduction

Machine Learning (ML) is used in various applications [5] with an emphasis on Deep Learning (DL) [6] since a decade ago. Their models are error-prone due to various factors such as willingness to generalize, lack of expressiveness of the model, inappropriate training dataset. For these reasons, their architects, or users, dispose of various evaluation metrics [20] to assess the quality of the models. However, such metrics are only able to express its quality (*i.e.*, if it tends to do few or lots of errors); they are unable to explain errors and successes.

This is where eXplainable Artificial Intelligence (XAI) is relevant [1]. These techniques go beyond the standard evaluation by trying to explain these errors and successes. Several methods have been proposed by the ML [5] and the Visual Analytics (VA) [13] communities in parallel. We can classify them with methods doing a *single sample analysis* (mainly from the ML community) or a *database analysis* (mainly from the VA community). *Single sample analysis* regroups methods that compute: *features attribution* of the input sample

This work is supported by Abai-Verne scholarship and Innovasol Consortium.

J.-J. Rousseau and B. Kapralos (Eds.): ICPR 2022 Workshops, LNCS 13645, pp. 231–245, 2023.
https://doi.org/10.1007/978-3-031-37731-0_18

for white boxes [2,19,25] or black boxes [23], *factual* and *counterfactual examples* [14–16]. *Database analysis* regroup methods that compute *learned features* by a DL model [21] or methods that try to extract some behavior of the model [11,18]. Despite the studies in other areas, the majority of XAI works target image or text classification.

We have developed a multi-modal and hierarchical classifier [24], which is able to classify images in documents from soil depollution reports. Each image is (a) described by its raw pixels, optional text caption in the document and the OCR extracted text, and (b) classified along 5 hierarchy levels defined by soil remediation experts. We extend this work using Deep Metric Learning (DML) [12] as additional training step to improve the quality of embeddings and the overall recognition performance. The classifier performance is acceptable in regard to our application, but we lack the understanding of its behavior. In this paper, we are interested in analyzing this model within its usage context to understand if it behaves properly, or if its predictions are not consistent with the dataset. To do so, we will follow a *database analysis* to build and analyze a graph of embeddings, as well as a *single sample analysis* to collect counterfactuals from it.

So far of our knowledge, this is the first paper to describe the embedding relations of a multilevel classifier. Several papers in the literature stick to the use of umap or tsne projections of their embedding [22], whereas we use a graph-based approach.

2   Context

The classifier [24] we have developed aims to get the embeddings from data specified by multiple modalities and hierarchical structure. As mentioned earlier, it was recently extended with DML to improve the quality of its embeddings. Thereby, our model is completed in training in two successive steps, (i) with a multi-modal hierarchical classification system, where the last vector of embedding layers is extracted and presented to (ii) a deep metric learning system. Figure 1 presents the framework of the training process, where the *classification network* contains one branch for each modality (image, caption and embedded text) working in parallel. All three branches compose of feature extraction F, embedding E and classification C layers. The feature extraction F is specific for each modality. In embedding E layer, the information from one hierarchy level is transferred to another in top-down manner by concatenating the activations of last embedding layers of one hierarchy level with feature representation of next level. Moreover, the embeddings of different modalities (image, caption, embedded text) are concatenated creating multi-modal embeddings for each hierarchy level and present to *DML network* for further training. For each hierarchy level, the final prediction of classification network is calculated by fusion of softmax tensors coming from three modalities by weighted averaging technique.

The described framework was tested on a real world private dataset. We processed 35 reports and automatically extracted 700 valid images with corresponding caption. Additionally, we manually extracted 500 images without a caption.

All images have been processed with Tesseract OCR engine [26] to obtain their embedded text. Images dimension range from 100×100 to 2000×2000 pixels and are resized to 256×256 pixels. The average caption length is 44 words, embedded text length is 100–300 words. Any sample in the dataset is assigned with one class of each level along its hierarchical path. The hierarchical classification with five levels is depicted in Fig. 2. Level 1 labels correspond to *Cross section*, *Maps*, *Graphs and tables* and *Photos*. Node size is proportional to the number of samples per hierarchy level. The number of samples goes from 505 for class 0 of level 1 to 6 for class 8 of level 4.

Due to the low amount of data, prediction experiments have been executed using a stratified k-fold mechanism [7]. It means the dataset has been split to six subsets sharing the same ratio of samples per class than in the complete dataset. Five subset are used to train a model that serve for the inference with the 6th one. The classification results are computed globally by fusing 6 folds results. We report 84.24% of weighted F1 score for the 5th hierarchical level. F1 score with weighted averaging is the output average accounted for the contribution of each class as weighted by the number of examples of that given class. However, the results we received were hard to interpret and understand. Consequently, we have analysed the model by describing the embeddings relation of different hierarchical levels by building a K-graph, and generating the similar and counterfactual examples. For that we have used part of the embeddings that was extracted at point ② shown in the Fig. 1, precisely the embeddings coming from each separate levels.

3 Proposed Analysis

This section presents the data structure and main visual encoding we have chosen to use to represent the result of our model and the questions we want to answer.

3.1 Data Structure

The database S contains around $1, 2K$ samples described by three modalities, labeled on five levels. We are interested in the multi-modal embedding generated at each level: each sample $s_i \in S$ is described by five embeddings $\{emb_i^l, 1 <= l <= 5\}$ of size 512 for each level l and annotated by its groundtruth gt_i^l and prediction $pred_i^l$ that are level dependent.

For each level l, we build a proximity graph (also called k-graph) $G_l = (S, E_l)$ that encodes the nodes proximity related to the multi-modal embeddings of level l. Each node i represents a sample $s_i \in S$. There is an edge $(s_s, s_t) \in E_l$ between s_s and s_t if emb_t^l is among the k closest samples of emb_s^l in terms of Euclidean distance. Such mathematical object represents well the proximity between the objects.

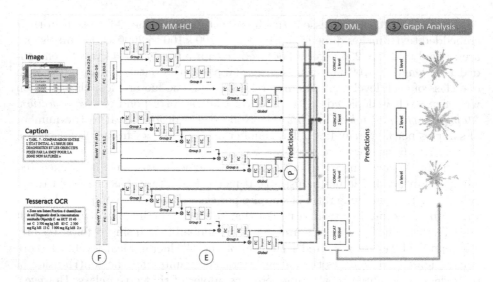

Fig. 1. Architecture of the analysed model. Training process is accomplishes in steps ① that corresponds to multi-modal hierarchical classification (MM-HCl) system following DML approach (step ②). For each hierarchical level the multi-modal hierarchical embeddings is extracted at step ② which is analyzed using K-graphs in step ③.

3.2 Visual Encoding

We want to depict graphs on screen to manually extract patterns and information. For this reason, we use the FM^3 [10] algorithm to compute the layout of each node on screen, followed by Fast Overlap Removal [9] to ensure there is no node-node overlap. The edges are colored in gray with alpha-transparency to reduce the visual clutter and the nodes can be colored according to the expected information (the groundtruth, the prediction, the fact it is an error, or any other metric). Our experiments have shown that such way of visualizing samples is of higher quality than the standard 2d projection with PCA, UMAP or T-SNE [17] depicted in a scatter plot.

The image representation of samples is not depicted on screen because it would take too much space. However, the graphs are visualized using the interactive tool Tulip [3] that allows to interactively obtain it (*i.e.* by hovering a node).

3.3 Questions of Interest

Several questions arise and are treated in independent evaluations.

Does the Embedding is Consistent over the Training Folds? Since prediction experiments have been executed using a stratified k-fold (6 folds) mechanism, we would like to verify if the embedding space is consistent among the folds. If so, we can assume the embedding space is stable and the full dataset

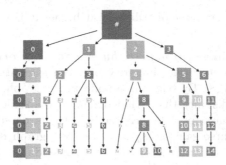

Fig. 2. Hierarchical classification of the data. 5 levels of classification are expected. Each level refines the concepts of the previous ones for a subset of the classes. Node size illustrates the balanced issue of the dataset.

can be analyzed as a whole for the rest of the paper. Otherwise, it implies that the embedding is not stable other than on the trainings because it is sensitive to the training samples and each fold should be analyzed separately.

To verify this stability, the proximity graph is built using all samples, regardless of the fold they belong to. We then compare two representations of the drawn graph by coloring the nodes with their fold number and their groundtruth, and manually analyze visual patterns.

Does the Embedding Align with Knowledge from the Data? The visualization of the k-graphs for each fold on 5 levels allows to quickly grasp the proximity of samples. We expect samples of the same class to be densely connected and depicted close together.

How the Embeddings of One Level Perform on the Other Levels? As we are addressing a hierarchical classification problem, we could expect the embeddings to follow a hierarchical pattern. To analyze them, we train some Random Forest classifiers to predict the classes of a target hierarchical level from the embeddings of a source level. To target the imbalanced data, for RF we have weighted classes such that rarely observed groups/classifications are more likely to be selected in bootstrap samples. We evaluate the classification using the weighted F1 score. We expect to obtain the best performance when the embedding and label levels are the same.

Does the Embedding of Successive Levels Makes Sense? We should observe patterns of interest. Another experiment consists of analysis of neighborhoods in the K-graph of the nodes over the layers. We expect to have similar neighbours of the same node at two successive layers. This can be verified by computing the Intersection Over the Union of the neighbors. It is a number from 0 to 1 that specifies the amount of overlap between the neighbors of one node at the current level and the next level. The more the network learns to represent the data the more it is consistent, and it relies on knowledge acquired on previous levels, thereby we expect large distribution at higher IOU values than on deeper hierarchy levels.

Does the Embeddings Influenced by Modalities over Different Levels? To be able to detect the similarity between samples, we propose to use Breadth First Search [8]. By selecting a node in the graph, the user can obtain the closest node by distance that is labelled with the same class for exemplars and with different class for counterfactuals. This is possible because we can assume that while three samples s_a, s_b, s_c follow graph distances constraints $distance_{G_l}(s_a, s_b) < distance_{G_l}(s_a, s_c)$, the embedding's Euclidean distances follow the constraints $norm\left(emb^l_{s_a} - emb^l_{s_b}\right) < norm\left(emb^l_{s_a} - emb^l_{s_b}\right)$. Thus, from the requested node, the exemplars and counterfactuals can be found by browsing the graph using a Breadth First Search. Similar examples (resp. counterfactuals) are collected by keeping only nodes belonging to the same (resp. to a different) prediction than the input; the search stop after collecting the appropriate number of samples. Eventually, the 1-top neighbors can be visited by ascending distance to input order. Since level 1 labels are visually distinguished, we expect to have similar and counterfactual examples, which are visually close. We also expect the embeddings contain more information from caption and embedded text for deeper hierarchy levels.

4   Results

The section presents the analysis results based on the evaluations presented in Sect. 3.3.

Does the Embedding is Consistent over the Training Folds? Figure 3 presents the k-graph colored per fold and groundtruth for the first and last levels of the hierarchy. The color range in Figs. 3a and 3b corresponds to the number of folds. For each fold from Figs. 3a and 3b we can see the corresponding nodes in Figs. 3c and 3d accordingly, where colors are defined by the groundtruth. For example, the nodes colored in yellow from Fig. 3a contains 204 classified images (nodes), which corresponds to the same nodes at the same location in Fig. 3c. Since we have four classes in level 1, we can see from Fig. 3c that these 204 images are correctly projected among an equal number of classes. The same pattern applies for other folds (colors) of Fig. 3a.

The representation of other levels follows the same trends. The patterns from the fold-colored graphs prove that the embedding is fold-sensitive: indeed, we clearly identify clusters of folds; it means that samples of the same fold are closer to each other than the samples from different folds. The comparison between patterns from gt-colored graphs and fold-colored graphs shows that the embedding is also able to recognize samples of the same class as soon as they come from the same fold. This is not an issue for an operational system, since only a single model (and thus family of embeddings) would be used, but the remaining analysis must then done on a fold basis rather than using the full dataset as a whole.

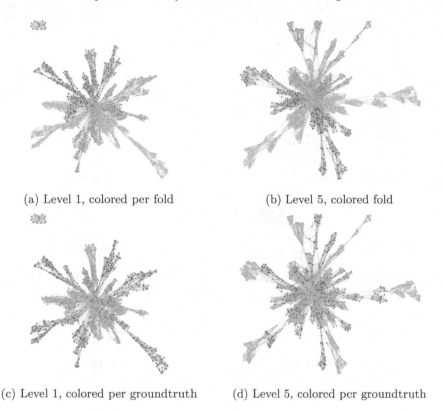

(a) Level 1, colored per fold

(b) Level 5, colored fold

(c) Level 1, colored per groundtruth

(d) Level 5, colored per groundtruth

Fig. 3. Comparison of fold (a, c) and groundtruth (b, d) assignment on the full dataset for the first and last level of the hierarchical classification on the K-graph representation.

Does the Embedding Align with Knowledge from the Data? Figure 4 illustrates the k-graph of the first fold with nodes colored by their groundtruth. For *Level* 1, according to the placement of samples, we can clearly see that embeddings of nodes are generated such that they have high intra-class similarity. However, the *Maps* (orange) and *Graph and tables* (pink) class embeddings are very close to each other and has common close neighbors (Fig. 4a). In Fig. 4b, we identify that selected samples of mentioned classes are clearly distance away from each other by embeddings on *Level 2*. Moreover, Fig. 4c shows the example of a sample that has been wrongly classified on *Level 3*, but the embeddings of this sample progressively gets better in deeper hierarchy levels and still being wrongly predicted recognize by embedding towards correct class. However, it is true the other way around.

How the Embeddings of One Level Perform on the Other Levels? The random forest has been individually tested on each fold of the dataset with respect to results on the embedding consistency. Figure 5 presents the global (*i.e.* computed on the whole result rather than on per fold aggregated result) weighted

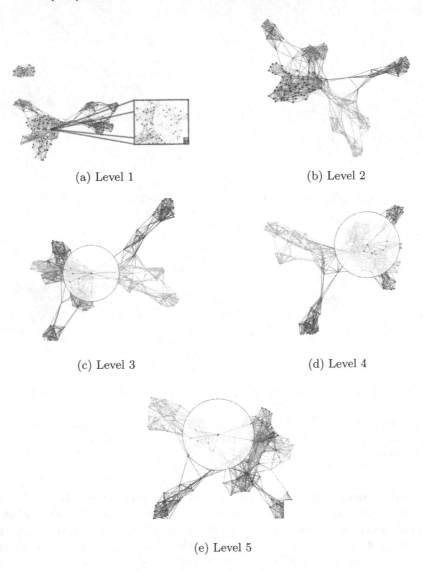

(a) Level 1 (b) Level 2

(c) Level 3 (d) Level 4

(e) Level 5

Fig. 4. K-graph of the embeddings from five levels of fold 1. The other folds have similar cluster behavior. The samples are colored according to their predicted labels on each level. In (a) and (b), the selected samples (nodes with blue borders) are true (groundtruth) labels from class *Graphs and tables*. (c–e) show the chosen example of a sample embeddings on one level that close to embeddings of other class samples in *Level 3*, but progressively gets better in deeper hierarchy levels. (Color figure online)

f1 score and the balanced accuracy for all the combinations of embedding/label combinations. By looking at the weighted f1 score, we can make the following observations. Some semantics (even if it is still an open problem to properly

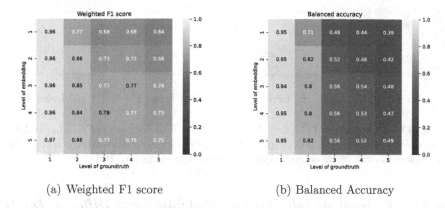

(a) Weighted F1 score   (b) Balanced Accuracy

Fig. 5. Weighted F1-score of a Random Forest trained to recognize the label of level x when using the embedding of level y.

identify them) have been properly extracted by the network. To predict the labels of a given level, it is better to use the embeddings of this specific level or the embedding of a deeper level (read the matrix per column). Indeed, some levels (1 and 3) have slightly better performance with the deepest embeddings; the network has not specialized enough properly generate these embeddings. By looking at the balanced accuracy, we can make the following observations. The problem gets more severe on deepest levels (look at the diagonal) until quickly reaching a point where several classes are not properly classified (level 3). There is a strong effect of the unbalanced dataset.

Does the Embedding of Successive Levels Makes Sense? According to Fig. 5 the embeddings of a level systematically perform worst (or equal) on the next level than their true level (read the lines for left to right starting by the groundtruth of the same level): the network has learned the appropriate level of details to make the classification for this specific level. The embeddings of a level systematically perform better on the previous levels than their true level (read the lines for right to left starting by the groundtruth of the same level): the information provided by the next levels are consistent with the previous ones.

Figure 6 illustrates this aspect at a sample level by depicting the IOU of neighbors for the whole dataset. The graphs are shown for the first four levels, since IOU values are calculated among two successive levels. The distribution of IOU values calculated from 0 and 1 for all samples. By looking at the graphs, we see that the distribution of IOU increases to the right. For example, in Fig. 6a, we see that around 350 samples have around $IOU = 0.4$, which means Level 1 and Level 2 samples have less common neighbors compared to Fig. 6c where the largest distribution at $IOU = 0.8$. Since we have more classes at the Level 5 and the largest distribution at higher IOU among the same number of samples, we can they that the embeddings of Level 5 is consistent according to Fig. 6d.

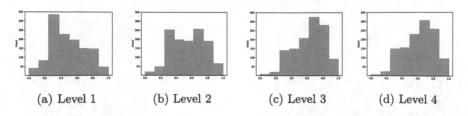

(a) Level 1   (b) Level 2   (c) Level 3   (d) Level 4

Fig. 6. IOU distribution of the first 4 levels. Taking into account the number of labels in the deepest hierarchical level, figure (d) shows that level 5 embeddings is consistent and acquire knowledge from embeddings of level 4 according to IOU value.

Does the Embeddings Influenced by Modalities over Different Levels?
Tables 1, and 2 provide the results of breadth-first-search to extract examples of Similar and Counterfactual for different levels for the same sample on each table. We have selected samples from *Maps*, and *Graphs and tables* classes as targeted samples, since they are mostly mis-classified. Each row corresponds to examples for the same node but different hierarchy levels (1 and 5 for maps, 1, 3, 5 for graphs and tables).

Table 1 targets the examples from *Maps* class. For Level 1 examples, since we have only four classes on this level, the examples should be easily distinguished visually. However, we see clear difference in counterfactual examples, meaning that this photo has close embeddings with targeted map. Moreover, if we consider the caption and OCR information, the targeted example shows the geo-location of the field, whereas Similar example for Level 1 illustrates the concentration levels of pollutant on the specific area, and for level 5 the illustration of the geo-location. Thereby, we can conclude that the embeddings of level 5 is more defined that the embeddings of Level 1.

Table 2 targets the sample taken from *Graphs and tables* class that show the evolution of total injected volume in wells. Taking into account caption and embedded text of the provided samples, the Similar example for Level 1 shows the evolution of groundwater level (height of water) which is again easily distinguished visually, that it belongs to *Graph and tables* class. On the other hand, the Counterfactual example shows the map of geo-location of treated zone. For level 3, the Similar example illustrates the evolution of pollution, which is close to the evolution of injected water by the meaning observed from caption and embedded text, whereas the map of water level was selected as Counterfactual example. For level 5, the evolution of water level but given in table for Similar example check the meaning of thie sentence, whereas Counterfactual illustrates the contamination level, which is very close to the targeted sample label, but it is illustrated as a map.

The overall conclusion from the table is that for *graphs and tables* the tendency is the same, in lower hierarchy levels the embeddings contain more visual information, but in the deeper hboxhierarchy level the embeddings have more information taken from captions and embedded text. The Counterfactual examples could be easily distinguished visually for lower levels, but the deeper the

Table 1. Exemplars of similar and counterfactual search for one node in level 1 and level 5 of *maps* class. Each sample is depicted by a thumbnail of its visual representation, an extract of its caption, and an extract of the text embedded in the image. *Some parts of the data are hidden under black box for confidentiality issues.

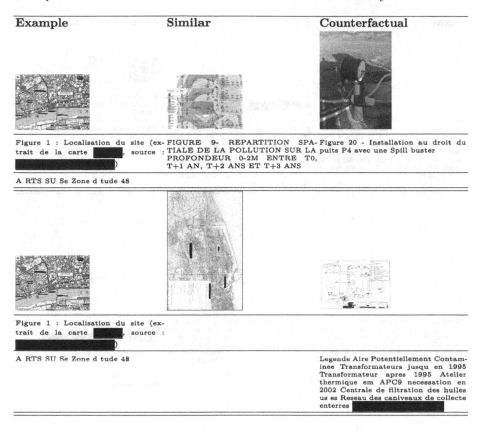

Example	Similar	Counterfactual

Figure 1 : Localisation du site (ex-
trait de la carte ███████, source

A RTS SU Se Zone d tude 48

FIGURE 9- REPARTITION SPA-
TIALE DE LA POLLUTION SUR LA
PROFONDEUR 0-2M ENTRE T0,
T+1 AN, T+2 ANS ET T+3 ANS

Figure 20 - Installation au droit du
puits P4 avec une Spill buster

Figure 1 : Localisation du site (ex-
trait de la carte ███████, source :
███████████████)

A RTS SU Se Zone d tude 48

Legende Aire Potentiellement Contam-
inee Transformateurs jusqu en 1995
Transformateur apres 1995 Atelier
thermique em APC9 necessation en
2002 Centrale de filtration des huiles
us es Reseau des caniveaux de collecte
enterres ████████████████

hierarchy level is the more similarity is observed regarding captions and embedded text.

5 Discussion

Studying the results with the k-graphs which are built using embeddings obtained by our classifier makes it possible to draw the following conclusions. It would be interesting to have a model with an improved stability other the training folds. However it is not straightforward to define a strategy to achieve it by keeping the same training data distribution. One solution could rely on the definition of dedicated losses.

The network slightly failed to provided level-specific embedding for level 1 and level 2 as using deepest embeddings allow to obtain better results. To overcome this issue, we should add a component to the loss that take into account

Table 2. Exemplars of similar and counterfactual search for one node in level 1, 3, 5 of *graphs and table* class. Each sample is depicted by a thumbnail of its visual representation, an extract of its caption and an extract of the text embedded in the image. *Some parts of the data are hidden under black box for confidentiality issues.

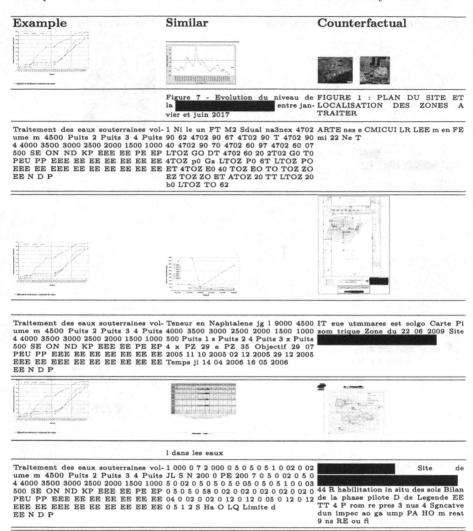

Example	Similar	Counterfactual
	Figure 7 - Evolution du niveau de la ▮▮▮▮ entre jan-vier et juin 2017	FIGURE 1 : PLAN DU SITE ET LOCALISATION DES ZONES A TRAITER
Traitement des eaux souterraines volume m 4500 Puits 2 Puits 3 4 Puits 4 4000 3500 3000 2500 2000 1500 1000 500 SE ON ND KP EEE EE PE EP PEU PP EEE EE EE EE EE EE EEE EE EEE EE EE EE EE EE EE EE N D P	1 Ni le un FT M2 Sdual na3nex 4702 90 62 4702 90 67 4T02 90 T 4702 90 40 4702 90 70 4702 60 97 4702 60 07 LTOZ GO DT 4702 60 20 2T02 G0 T0 4TOZ p0 Gz LTOZ P0 6T LTOZ PO ET 4TOZ E0 40 TOZ EO TO TOZ ZO EZ TOZ ZO ET ATOZ 20 TT LTOZ 20 b0 LTOZ TO 62	ARTE nes e CMICUI LR LEE m en FE mi 22 Ne T
Traitement des eaux souterraines volume m 4500 Puits 2 Puits 3 4 Puits 4 4000 3500 3000 2500 2000 1500 1000 500 SE ON ND KP EEE EE PE EP PEU PP EEE EE EE EE EE EE EEE EE EEE EE EE EE EE EE EE EE N D P	Teneur en Naphtalene jg l 9000 4500 4000 3500 3000 2500 2000 1500 1000 500 Puits 1 s Puits 2 4 Puits 3 x Puits 4 x PZ 29 e PZ 35 Objectif 29 07 2005 11 10 2005 02 12 2005 29 12 2005 Temps ji 14 04 2006 16 05 2006	IT eue utmmares est solgo Carte Pi zom trique Zone du 22 06 2009 Site ▮▮▮▮
	l dans les eaux	
Traitement des eaux souterraines volume m 4500 Puits 2 Puits 3 4 Puits 4 4000 3500 3000 2500 2000 1500 1000 500 SE ON ND KP EEE EE PE EP PEU PP EEE EE EE EE EE EE EEE EE EEE EE EE EE EE EE EE EE N D P	1 000 0 7 2 000 0 5 0 5 0 5 1 0 02 0 02 JL S N 200 0 PE 200 7 0 5 0 02 0 5 0 5 0 02 0 5 0 5 0 05 0 05 0 5 0 5 1 0 0 03 0 5 0 5 0 58 0 02 0 02 0 02 0 02 0 02 0 04 0 02 0 02 0 12 0 12 0 05 0 12 0 12 0 5 1 2 S Ha O LQ Limite d	▮▮▮▮ Site de 44 R habilitation in situ des sols Bilan de la phase pilote D de Legende EE TT 4 P rom re pres 3 nus 4 Sgncatve dun impec ao ga ump PA HO m reat 9 ns RE ou fi

this specialization. The unbalanced dataset effect should be overcame in the future by using dedicating methods [4].

A mixture of Sankey diagram and parallel coordinates would help to better understand the hierarchal treatment of the input samples by the network. The axes would be the depth of the hierarchy, the flows would be the samples clustered by prediction at each level.

The distribution of IOU showed the consistency of embeddings in deepest level taking into account the number of classes in the last hierarchy level, however, by the examplars and counterfactuals sometimes we observed that level 4 embeddings more truthworthy than the last hierarchy level for the prediction as well as defining semantic similarities. Thereby, adding one more modality from the text around the images could improve the network performance on the deepest hierarchical level. The other solution could be to re-define the level 4 and level 5 labels.

6   Conclusion

The training of multi-modal and hierarchical classifier [24] for images from soil remediation reports were extended by DML to improve the embeddings quality. The obtained results using classification network was acceptable, but we faced the problem of interpreting them by the classification metrics. Thereby, in this work we are interested in analyzing this model within its usage context to understand if it behaves properly or if its predictions are not consistent with our knowledge of the database. To do so, we describe the embedding relations of a multilevel classifier by database analysis to build and analyze a graph of embeddings as well as single sample analysis to collect counterfactuals from it.

First, we observed that the embeddings are fold-sensitive and not consistent among six stratified folds. The generated embeddings followed a hierarchical pattern, thereby it is better to use the embeddings of this specific level or the embedding of a deeper level. Moreover, we showed that the more the network learns to represent the data the more it is consistent, and it relies on the knowledge acquired on previous levels. Finally, we expect to see the impact of visual information on initial levels and more on semantic information by the influence of caption and embedded text. By generating exemplars and counterfactuals, we saw the pattern for Similar examples in which at lower hierarchy levels the embeddings contain more visual information, but the deeper in the hierarchy level the embeddings have more information taken from captions and embedded text.

For the future work, it is worth to study the consistency between the levels using the global embeddings, which we have not used in this work. These embeddings consider all classes in hierarchical tree at once and processes the hierarchy dependency in loss function. This global embeddings correspond to the last (violet) line of each modality in Fig. 1.

References

1. Adadi, A., Berrada, M.: Peeking inside the black-box: a survey on explainable artificial intelligence (XAI). IEEE Access **6**, 52138–52160 (2018)
2. Ahmed Asif Fuad, K., Martin, P.E., Giot, R., Bourqui, R., Benois-Pineau, J., Zemmari, A.: Features understanding in 3D CNNs for actions recognition in video. In: 2020 Tenth International Conference on Image Processing Theory, Tools and Applications (IPTA), pp. 1–6 (2020)

3. Auber, D., et al.: Tulip 5. In: Alhajj, R., Rokne, J. (eds.) Encyclopedia of Social Network Analysis and Mining, pp. 3185–3212. Springer, New York (2018). https://doi.org/10.1007/978-1-4939-7131-2_315

4. Batista, G.E., Prati, R.C., Monard, M.C.: A study of the behavior of several methods for balancing machine learning training data. ACM SIGKDD Explorations Newsl. **6**(1), 20–29 (2004)

5. Dargan, S., Kumar, M., Ayyagari, M.R., Kumar, G.: A survey of deep learning and its applications: a new paradigm to machine learning. Arch. Comput. Methods Eng. **27**(4), 1071–1092 (2020)

6. Deng, L., Yu, D.: Deep learning: methods and applications. Found. Trends Signal Process. **7**(3–4), 197–387 (2014)

7. Diamantidis, N., Karlis, D., Giakoumakis, E.A.: Unsupervised stratification of cross-validation for accuracy estimation. Artif. Intell. **116**(1–2), 1–16 (2000)

8. Dietterich, T.G., Michalski, R.S.: A comparative review of selected methods for learning from examples. In: Michalski, R.S., Carbonell, J.G., Mitchell, T.M. (eds.) Machine Learning, pp. 41–81. Morgan Kaufmann, San Francisco (1983)

9. Dwyer, T., Marriott, K., Stuckey, P.J.: Fast node overlap removal. In: Healy, P., Nikolov, N.S. (eds.) GD 2005. LNCS, vol. 3843, pp. 153–164. Springer, Heidelberg (2006). https://doi.org/10.1007/11618058_15

10. Hachul, S., Jünger, M.: Drawing large graphs with a potential-field-based multilevel algorithm. In: Pach, J. (ed.) GD 2004. LNCS, vol. 3383, pp. 285–295. Springer, Heidelberg (2005). https://doi.org/10.1007/978-3-540-31843-9_29

11. Halnaut, A., Giot, R., Bourqui, R., Auber, D.: Deep dive into deep neural networks with flows. In: Proceedings of the 15th International Joint Conference on Computer Vision, Imaging and Computer Graphics Theory and Applications (VISIGRAPP 2020): IVAPP, vol. 3, pp. 231–239 (2020)

12. Hoffer, E., Ailon, N.: Deep metric learning using triplet network. In: Feragen, A., Pelillo, M., Loog, M. (eds.) SIMBAD 2015. LNCS, vol. 9370, pp. 84–92. Springer, Cham (2015). https://doi.org/10.1007/978-3-319-24261-3_7

13. Hohman, F., Kahng, M., Pienta, R., Chau, D.H.: Visual analytics in deep learning: an interrogative survey for the next frontiers. IEEE Trans. Vis. Comput. Graph. (TVCG) **25**(8), 2674–2693 (2018)

14. Karimi, A.H., Barthe, G., Schölkopf, B., Valera, I.: A survey of algorithmic recourse: definitions, formulations, solutions, and prospects. arXiv preprint arXiv:2010.04050 (2020)

15. Keane, M.T., Kenny, E.M., Delaney, E., Smyth, B.: If only we had better counterfactual explanations: five key deficits to rectify in the evaluation of counterfactual XAI techniques. arXiv preprint arXiv:2103.01035 (2021)

16. Kenny, E.M., Keane, M.T.: Explaining deep learning using examples: optimal feature weighting methods for twin systems using post-hoc, explanation-by-example in XAI. Knowl.-Based Syst. **233**, 107530 (2021)

17. Kobak, D., Berens, P.: The art of using t-SNE for single-cell transcriptomics. Nat. Commun. **10**(1), 1–14 (2019)

18. Liu, M., Liu, S., Su, H., Cao, K., Zhu, J.: Analyzing the noise robustness of deep neural networks. In: 2018 IEEE Conference on Visual Analytics Science and Technology (VAST), pp. 60–71. IEEE (2018)

19. Montavon, G., Binder, A., Lapuschkin, S., Samek, W., Müller, K.-R.: Layer-wise relevance propagation: an overview. In: Samek, W., Montavon, G., Vedaldi, A., Hansen, L.K., Müller, K.-R. (eds.) Explainable AI: Interpreting, Explaining and Visualizing Deep Learning. LNCS (LNAI), vol. 11700, pp. 193–209. Springer, Cham (2019). https://doi.org/10.1007/978-3-030-28954-6_10

20. Novaković, J.D., Veljović, A., Ilić, S.S., Papić, Ž, Milica, T.: Evaluation of classification models in machine learning. Theory Appl. Math. Comput. Sci. **7**(1), 39–46 (2017)
21. Olah, C., Mordvintsev, A., Schubert, L.: Feature visualization. Distill **2**(11), e7 (2017)
22. Rauber, P.E., Fadel, S.G., Falcao, A.X., Telea, A.C.: Visualizing the hidden activity of artificial neural networks. IEEE Trans. Visual Comput. Graphics **23**(1), 101–110 (2016)
23. Ribeiro, M.T., Singh, S., Guestrin, C.: "why should i trust you?" explaining the predictions of any classifier. In: Proceedings of the 22nd ACM SIGKDD International Conference on Knowledge Discovery and Data Mining, pp. 1135–1144 (2016)
24. Rysbayeva, K., Giot, R., Journet, N.: Hierarchical and multimodal classification of images from soil remediation reports. In: Lladós, J., Lopresti, D., Uchida, S. (eds.) ICDAR 2021. LNCS, vol. 12821, pp. 160–175. Springer, Cham (2021). https://doi.org/10.1007/978-3-030-86549-8_11
25. Selvaraju, R.R., Cogswell, M., Das, A., Vedantam, R., Parikh, D., Batra, D.: Gradcam: visual explanations from deep networks via gradient-based localization. In: Proceedings of the IEEE International Conference on Computer Vision, pp. 618–626 (2017)
26. Smith, R.: An overview of the tesseract OCR engine. In: ICDAR '07: Proceedings of the Ninth International Conference on Document Analysis and Recognition, pp. 629–633. IEEE Computer Society, Washington, DC (2007)

Explainability of Image Semantic Segmentation Through SHAP Values

Pierre Dardouillet[1]([✉])[iD], Alexandre Benoit[1][iD], Emna Amri[1,2][iD],
Philippe Bolon[1], Dominique Dubucq[2][iD], and Anthony Credoz[2][iD]

[1] LISTIC, Polytech Annecy-Chambery, University of Savoie Mont-Blanc,
B.P. 80439, 74944 Annecy le Vieux Cedex, France
{pierre.dardouillet,alexandre.benoit,emna.amri,
philippe.bolon}@univ-smb.com
[2] TotalEnergies S.E, Avenue Larribau, 64018 Pau Cedex, France
{emna.amri,dominique.dubucq,anthony.credoz}@totalenergies.com

Abstract. The introduction of Deep Neural Networks in high-level
applications is significantly increasing. However, the understanding of
such model decisions by humans is not straightforward and may limit
their use for critical applications. In order to address this issue, recent
research work has introduced explanation methods, typically for classification and captioning. Nevertheless, for some tasks, explainability methods need to be developed. This includes image segmentation that is an
essential component for many high-level applications. In this paper, we
propose a general workflow allowing for the adaptation of a state of
the art explainability methods, especially SHAP, to image segmentation
tasks. The approach allows for explanation of single pixels as well image
areas. We show the relevance of the approach on a critical application
such as oil slick pollution detection on the sea surface. We also show
the applicability of the method on a more standard multimedia domain
semantic segmentation task. The conducted experiments highlight the
relevant features on which the models derive their local results and help
identify general model behaviours.

Keywords: Model Explainability · Image Segmentation · Shapley
Values · SAR Images

1 Introduction

Artificial intelligence (AI) models are increasingly used for many applications,
as they have demonstrated their potential to solve complex tasks previously performed by humans. However, their high performance comes at a cost: AI models
are often very complex and their decision processes cannot be clearly understood
by humans, which impacts on their reliability and acceptability. To date, this

This work was supported by TotalEnergies company and also relied on HPC resources
from GENCI-IDRIS (Grant 2021-AD011011418R1).

J.-J. Rousseau and B. Kapralos (Eds.): ICPR 2022 Workshops, LNCS 13645, pp. 188–202, 2023.
https://doi.org/10.1007/978-3-031-37731-0_19

major drawback is one of the obstacles in AI subfields such as Deep Learning [7]. Thus, for tasks where confidence in the results obtained is as important as the results, the use of AI models is compromised. Then, the **eXplainable Artificial Intelligence** (XAI) field has been subject of growing interest and already gathers a multitude of methods designed to open those black boxes [11].

This paper focuses on image segmentation tasks for which explainability methods are for now limited. Image semantic segmentation is widely used as a preliminary process for various image types and applications, such as radar images for remote sensing [2], multimedia images for automatic driving [10], medical images for health diagnosis [21], and so on. This semantic segmentation task is complex and is nowadays addressed by deep neural networks. As a base application component, associated explanation methods become mandatory. However, few works have been dedicated to the understanding of such segmentation model decisions [11]. The main issue is related to the complexity of the explanation method since one expects any pixel or region-level decision to be explained with respect to the entire input image and maybe some metadata. In addition, it is thus required to provide relevant explanation in a timely manner.

To address this challenge, we propose an adaptation of an explainability method, called SHapley Additive exPlanations (SHAP). This method represents one of the most widely used post-hoc explainability methods [11] but its adaptation to semantic segmentation is not straightforward. Our approach can consider any type of image as input. It can identify features that inhibit or excite a model decision, i.e. negative or positive contributions to the decision. The resulting explanations are consistent with human intuition to the extent that they are built on Shapley values [17]. We base our approach on an agnostic implementation of SHAP, called Kernel SHAP [12], which we refer to hereafter as SHAP.

In this paper, two application domains are considered for experiments. We first focus on offshore oil slick detection illustrated in Fig. 1 for which we explain the predictions provided by a state-of-the-art semantic segmentation model proposed in [3]. This represents a typical critical application for environmental pollution monitoring for which detection results can induce strong and costly actions. In this context, oil slicks are generally detected from Synthetic Aperture Radar (SAR) images from which they appear as dark spots on the sea surface as shown in the left image of Fig. 1. Current detection methods rely on SAR analysis and is performed by photo-interpreters or automatically by deep neural network models [3]. In this context, automatic detection must be explained to decision makers. Our proposal is then to provide comprehensible explanations as coloured maps highlighting the input image areas that contributed to the model decision for a selected pixel or region. As illustrated in Fig. 1, the good detection related to the red region (no oil, left image) is explained on the right image. One observes that the local area close and within the region of interest contribute negatively to classification as oil slicks (red colours) while the dark neighbouring slick areas provide a positive influence (green colours). Then, the sum of these contributions yields the oil detection probability, here close to zero that explains classification as a sea area.

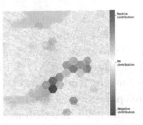

Fig. 1. An input Synthetic Aperture Radar image (left) is processed by a model for oil slick detection (centre). In order to explain prediction for a given region (red polygon on the left), the proposed SHAP based method provides a coloured map showing each image area's contribution (right). (Color figure online)

Finally, in order to show the applicability of the method to other domains, a second experimental case study is proposed. We consider semantic segmentation in urban scene from RGB images relying on the CityScapes dataset [6] and a state-of-the-art model, HardNet-MSeg [8]. More specifically, we show the interest of the method to explain the competition between probable classes in different situations.

The article is organized as follows: first, a state of the art in post-hoc methods for model applicability in machine learning is presented. Then, a general framework for the adaptation of occlusion based explanation methods to semantic segmentation is presented. We then integrate the kernel SHAP method as well as RISE [14] as a comparison baseline. Finally, results are presented and discussed, demonstrating the relevance of our approach and its sensitivity to hyper-parameter choices.

2   Related Works

2.1   Model Explainability Methods

As shown in recent surveys such as [4], the field of AI explainability includes methods having different approaches, such as post-hoc methods that aims to explain complex models, intrinsic methods that aims to create understandable models, methods used to enhance model fairness, or methods used to test model sensitivity. Also, most of these methods are applicable to tasks that provide a prediction that is global with respect to the input data i.e. image classification, captioning and so on. Explanation on local predictions as for pixel level or region classification is scarce. This work focuses exclusively on post-hoc interpretation methods applicable to images. Related methods do not modify or influence the model process nor apply some specific processing on the optimized model. In this context, three main categories of post-hoc explanation methods can be identified:

Back propagation based methods that are typically suitable for neural networks models. Several methods based on backpropagation are reported in the literature, such as Guided Backpropagation [19], LRP [13], or DeepLIFT [18]. These methods aim to produce explanations by back propagating a network output score (e.g. a class probability) through the network to the first layer. In this way, the input image pixels that contributed the most to the network decision are highlighted and thus produce a heat map also referred to as saliency maps in some papers. These methods compute a rather fast and precise explanation (at the pixel level). However, they have some limitations in terms of flexibility, as they are mainly used for classification neural networks. Moreover, the obtained saliency map often results from a tradeoff between human understandability and fidelity to the network decision process.

Activation based methods combine the feature maps of a considered neural network layer to produce explanations presented as a coarse heat map. One of the best-known methods in this category is Grad-CAM [16]. The intuition behind activation-based explainability methods is to combine only feature maps that have patterns considered important by the network for an output. Selecting only these feature maps highlights the relevant areas of the input image with respect to the network. The obtained heat maps are relatively easy to interpret since they are coarse. However, they are also inaccurate and not suitable for fine-grained explanations. An adaptation of this approach to semantic segmentation has been recently introduced in [20].

Occlusion based methods are the only type of model-agnostic methods and rely on perturbation approaches. The intuition is that if a sample feature, for instance an image area, contains relevant information, then occluding such area will harm the model output. Thus, occlusion based methods, such as LIME [15], RISE [14] and SHAP [12] compute input feature importance estimates relying on model response when masking them. For this purpose, occluded versions of the input image are computed and passed through the model to compute an output value. This approach then leads to a significant computation overhead compared to the other methods. Nevertheless, it has the advantage of creating more global and understandable results, independent of model type and architecture.

In this work, we focus on occlusion based methods, as they provide more information while not being dependent on the model internal processes.

2.2   Comparison of Occlusion Based Explanation Methods

LIME and SHAP are based on the same algorithm described in [15], create a linear decision model g_x, that aims to approximate the black-box model f for a given input x. Applied to image analysis problems, such approach relies on the input image division into super-pixels (image regions), which are further occluded to examine their impacts ϕ_i on the model output. The general formulation has been introduced in [12] as:

$$g_x(x') = \phi_0 + \sum_{i=1}^{M} \phi_i x_i' \tag{1}$$

where x' corresponds to the mapping of the input x through the function h_x, such that $x' = h_x(x)$. Formally, $x' \in \{0,1\}^M$ is a vector representing the presence or absence of input super-pixels and M is the number of super-pixels.

Differences between LIME and SHAP reside in the importance value attributed to each super-pixel: while LIME use heuristic coefficients to compute its contribution values, SHAP relies on Shapley values [17], a game-theory approach that leads contribution values to be better aligned with human intuition, and results in more relevant explanations.

RISE [14] is another occlusion based explanation method. It does not rely on a rigid super-pixel structure but applies occlusions relying on random mask generation. This has the advantage of reducing the potential bias caused by a rigid organization of image features. However, it also leads to coarser explanation maps comparable to those produced by Grad-CAM. Given a set of s masks M and the model output value *scalar* o_i, when the input image is masked with M_i, the final *Heatmap* is computed as the sum of the image masks weighted by the corresponding model output maps, multiplied by a coefficient C for normalization purposes.

$$Heatmap = \frac{C}{S} * \sum_{i \in s} o_i \times M_i \tag{2}$$

A limitation of RISE is the fact that this method does not provide information on the type of feature contribution (i.e. excitation or inhibition effect) on the prediction.

3   Occlusion Methods Adaptation to Semantic Segmentation

From state of the art, the SHAP method appears the most relevant. However, its adaptation to image segmentation is not straightforward. We first propose a general framework for the adaptation of any occlusion based method, from which we detail some steps, specific to our SHAP adaptation.

3.1   Proposed Approach

The proposed general workflow is illustrated in Fig. 2. It relies on four steps.

The first step generates masked samples of the original image. Masks are occluding super-pixels whose shape and number are controlled by dedicated hyper-parameters. Resulting masked images are processed in the second step by a black-box image semantic segmentation model (e.g. a deep neural network) that provides one prediction for each masked image. For the applications presented in this paper, we always consider probability maps as the model output but model output logits or binary classification results could also be considered. The third step consists in the selection of the regions and classes of interest (RoIs) for which model output explanation must be computed. Lastly, occlusion

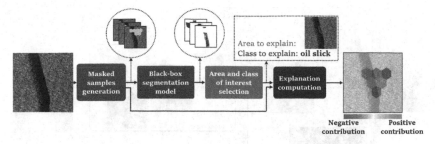

Fig. 2. Workflow of occlusion based explanation methods adapted to image segmentation.

based explanation methods are applied on the RoIs making use of the mask configurations and the selected model outputs. Finally, an explanation is generated, presented as a heat-map pointing areas of the input image that contributed the most to the model decision.

As illustrated in Fig. 2, the model decision for the red polygonal RoI, is explained. The red colour range is assigned to areas decreasing the target class probability value for the given RoI (negative contribution, or *inhibition*), while the green colour range is assigned to areas increasing this value (positive contribution, or *excitation*). Colour saturation is related to the amplitude of the contribution value.

The region selection step is specific to the image segmentation case. In contrast to the image classification case, explaining the whole model decision would not make sense. Therefore, the proposed method explains prediction related to a region of interest selected by the user, which is more naturally relevant.

Any occlusion method can be involved in this framework. RISE, as an example, only inputs the area and class of interest selection for its adaptation to segmentation: the masking step and explanation computation are already defined in the function to follow Eq. 2. As a comparison, SHAP method requires more information about the image sample mask configurations as described in the following.

3.2   SHAP Case Study

Implementation

The application of the kernel SHAP method to the framework is described in Fig. 3. The adaptation consists in associating the explanation computation with the mask sample generation steps in order to comply with Shapley values equation [12]. SHAP indeed relies on a set of predefined and static features, here super-pixels. Also, for each masked image sample, feature state (i.e. masked or unmodified) must be known.

The input image is then clustered into a set of uniformly organized and non-overlapping hexagons, having an identical area. This choice is more detailed in the next section and facilitates the readability of the result relying on super-pixels of equal importance and more homogeneous neighbourhood relations.

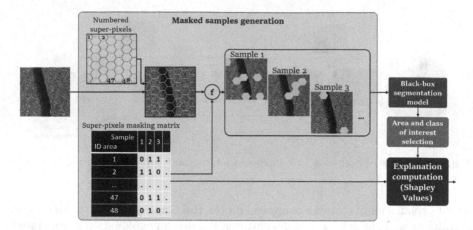

Fig. 3. The *Masked samples generation* step from Fig. 2 detailed for our SHAP adaptation. Each super-pixel is delimited following a hexagonal grid. Then, masked samples are generated via function *f*, using a masking matrix to occlude a given super-pixel, on a given sample.

In our experiments, considering images of size 512×512, the input image is typically clustered in $M = 224$ super-pixels of about 1170 pixels.

On the Relevance of Super-Pixel Shapes
The most critical parameter for the SHAP method applied to image analysis models is the delimitation of the input super-pixels. Several experiments were conducted as presented in Fig. 4. We first considered a method based on a configurable k-means-based clustering algorithm, SLIC [1]. Tests were performed applying SLIC on the input data with different parameters as illustrated in Fig. 4A and 4B. Clustering has also been applied from ground truth images for more homogeneous clustering while making use of class boundaries as shown in Fig. 4C. From preliminary results and visual analysis, we conclude that all those automatic clustering based methods cannot provide consistent and stable clustering and could not provide homogeneous super-pixel delimitation of dark patches and sea areas. In addition, SHAP values also depend on super-pixels surface, meaning that more homogeneity in super-pixel shapes would facilitate human interpretation. We thus suggest clustering pixels regions, not relying on the image content but rather making use of regular grids that yield super-pixels homogeneous in shape and size. Experiments on regular grid shapes were performed, comparing a standard square grid and a hexagonal one. These results showed that hexagonal grid are more suited for visual explanations, mainly due to its connectivity pattern [5]. Finally, we rely on a hexagonal grid (Fig. 4D).

3.3 Explaining Predictions on Images Regions

From a practical point of view, user consider RoIs as image regions while limiting to a single pixel is a scarce case study. As an example, on the oil slick detection

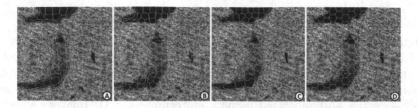

Fig. 4. Tested super-pixels for SHAP method, delimited in green. One compares automatic clustering approaches (A–C) and a predefined hexagonal grid (D). (Color figure online)

problem, photo-interpreters for now manually delimit large regions surrounding the slicks they detect. Conversely, when it comes to assessing automatic detection, such experts, expect models to follow similar behaviours. Finally, explanations that would assist experts in their assessment should also be compliant with such behaviours and thus provide a regular approach for all case studies.

The explanation of regions can be performed in a variety of ways and we focus on an approach that makes sense with respect to the application context while not increasing the computational cost compared to a single pixel explanation. When explaining a pixel classification, SHAP estimates the sensitivity of its target class prediction probability with respect to the super-pixel coalition changes. Similarly, when willing to explain the prediction on a group of connected pixels, i.e. a region, we propose to estimate the sensitivity of the average target class predicted probability over that region. The semantics remain the same but for a wider region of interest. From an implementation point of view, it consists in a limited change at the third step of the workflow depicted in Fig. 2, 'Area and class of interest selection': the SHAP implementation remains the same but receives either a single pixel of interest probability or the average probability of the pixels within the region of interest.

4   Experiments

The proposed method has been evaluated on real application case studies. The first one relates to oil slick detection at the sea surface. It involves the application of a semantic segmentation model applied to SAR images used on operations. This is a critical environmental and safety case study where oil detection can generate very strong and costly responses. Thus model predictions explanations make real sense. The second case study relates to semantic segmentation of multiple object categories in urban scenes on the standard Cityscapes dataset [6], relying on RGB images. In this section, we push emphasis on the first case study and show the applicability of the same method on the more classical second case study. We then first detail the experimental setup for oil slick detection with the data and the models considered. Second, we present and discuss the results obtained from different perspectives.

4.1   Oil Slicks Detection Experimental Setup

We build on the model and data collections presented in [3] that are dedicated to offshore oil slick semantic segmentation at the sea surface from SAR data. The model involved is based on the FC-Densenet architecture [9] and is trained in a supervised manner on a large collection of images extracted from real monitoring scenarios and annotated by photo-interpreters. SAR Imagery allows for day-and-night detection of oil slicks that appear as patches darker than their neighbourhood thanks to radar response on their surface. In this paper, no more details on the model and related optimization are provided in order to keep the focus on the explanation methods. Paper [3] provides more details on the model that we consider here as black box. The aim is indeed to bring transparency to such models from an application point of view. Then, one considers the predictions of this preliminary trained model on new images not involved in the training process as for real monitoring scenarios. In this specific case study, the background colour applied to masked pixels cannot be black: It would induce a bias in explanations, as masked super-pixels would be detected as an oil slick. Then, background value is set to the input image average grey level.

4.2   Oil Slicks Detection Explanation Results and Discussions

First, we compare our adapted SHAP and RISE approaches for the explanation of predictions of the same model on the same samples. Then, focusing on the SHAP approach, we study the impact of the super-pixel size on the explanation. We finally show the consistency of the pixel and region-level explanations.

SHAP vs. RISE
RISE adaptation to semantic segmentation is made following the workflow presented in Fig. 2. Default RISE hyper-parameters are kept, such that $C = 2$, typical masks (occlusion cells) are of size 64×64, i.e. 4096 pixels at most, and the number of samples remains $S = 2000$. Considering the same model and the same output selection, a comparison of the explanations provided by the SHAP and RISE based methods is presented in Fig. 5.

First, one can observe that high RISE explanation values tend to correspond to the super-pixels with a positive contribution obtained with SHAP. Surprisingly, RISE additionally reports diffuse areas with low contribution values that can be very distant from the RoIs. However, negatively contributing features reported by SHAP are not highlighted by RISE. Also, relevant regions reported by RISE have more spatial extent and are poorly contrasted such that this reduces the explanation precision. This can be explained by internal mask subsampling process, and by RISE occlusion masks, four times the size of those in SHAP.

As a first conclusion, while RISE and SHAP report highly positive contributions to the decision in a consistent way, SHAP provides more detailed and more relevant explanations both in terms of resolution and contribution type.

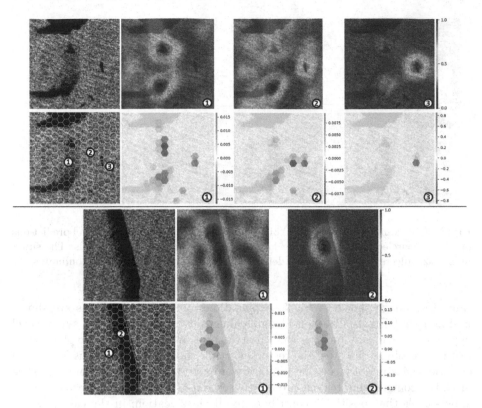

Fig. 5. For 2 image examples (top, bottom), explanation maps on the model decision for some pixels of interest (red enumerated circles) with either RISE (top-right images) or SHAP (bottom-right) adapted methods. SHAP provides more local contributions, less noise while making the difference between exciting and inhibiting features. (Color figure online)

Super-Pixel Size Impact on Explanation

Focusing on the SHAP based method, we examine the impact of the super-pixel size on the explanation relevance. Figure 6 shows explanation maps on the same model prediction but with different super-pixel sizes.

One observes that large super-pixels may cover patterns of different target categories and thus yields a loss of information regarding the contribution type (excitation or inhibition). On the other hand, too small super-pixels may also cause a loss of information, when they provide a partial view of large objects in the visual scene. The relevance of the explanation then actually depends on the image content and the super-pixel spatial distribution but rigid super-pixel grids already provide a good compromise.

From Pixel Level to Region Explanation

As described in Sect. 3.1, the proposed approach allows for the explanation of single pixels and regions in a unified way. Considering the same model and the

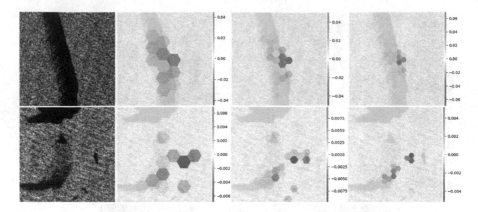

Fig. 6. Two examples (top, bottom) of adapted SHAP explanation of model predictions on the red circled pixel considering large, medium and small super-pixels. The super pixels size affects the explanations details and consistency. (Color figure online)

same test image shown in Fig. 5, explanations of predicted regions are shown in Fig. 7 and Fig. 1. The considered regions actually surround a single pixel explained previously and one can observe the consistency of the explanations: in the case of the sea area, the region affecting the model decision is large, and considers slick regions as either inhibition or excitation; in the case of an oil slick area, the contributing regions are mostly restricted to the neighbouring oil slick super-pixels that positively contribute to oil classification; in the case of an in between area, the model combines both behaviours.

Conclusions on Model Behaviours

Using SHAP explanations presented in this section, one can understand the model behaviour when confronted to different cases:

For RoIs classified as sea, close sea super-pixels have inhibitory effects to classify as oil while neighbouring super-pixels containing oil have an excitatory effect. Overall, these effects are extremely low and balance each other, making the final classification as sea.

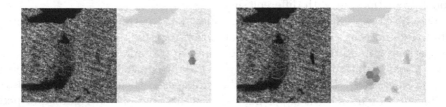

Fig. 7. Explanation provided for two regions: oil (left) and oil and sea mixture (right). Figure 1 shows a clean sea area in the same experimental conditions. These results illustrate that the region-level explanations are consistent with pixel-level explanations.

Fig. 8. Urban scene semantic segmentation example: input (left), coloured ground truth (centre), predicted segmentation (right). Model does not predict on crop boundaries, 3 circled pixels in the predicted area are subject to explanation.

For RoIs classified as slick, both model decisions are based on a limited number of super-pixels containing oil, close to the explained RoIs. They almost always have an excitatory effect, with high intensity.

For ROIs in between slick and sea, models tend to consider contextual information over the whole image, and specifically contrasted patterns. However, if no salient features are present in the image, the model relies on a very local area.

4.3   Urban Scene Segmentation Results and Discussions

One considers an implementation of the state-of-the-art HardNet-Mseg model [8] trained to perform semantic segmentation of the 34 visual concepts of the Cityscapes dataset [6] (people, cars, road signs and so on) from RGB images. Figure 8 shows a typical visual scene from the validation set with associated ground truth and a model prediction. Compared to the previous case study, this multi-class segmentation problem must consider more numerous and diverse overlapping class instances. Then, relying on the same configuration (image size of 512×512 pixels, same hexagonal grid), we show the applicability of the method for a very different context.

SHAP super-pixel size is kept medium for these experiments, and the background masking value is set to zero (black) as usually done for such multimedia data. Three pixels of interest are considered for explanation, one on a car that is well predicted, one on a person also predicted well. The last one is more ambiguous. It is annotated as sidewalks but lies at the frontier between sidewalk, concrete, ground and vegetation and is predicted as *static* (a class regrouping indistinguishable objects that correspond to none of the other classes). For each pixel, two explanation maps are provided, for two different classes of interest.

Figure 9 first presents explanation maps for the selected pixel classified as 'person' (probability=94%). It shows a significant positive contribution focused on the front and upper part of the body, which is an expected phenomenon. However, the hexagon containing the explained pixel has a negative contribution. It covers a homogeneous white area around the person shoulder with some contours on its left boundaries. This is explained by the second explanation map, related to the 'dynamic' class that gathers movable objects. This class has a similar

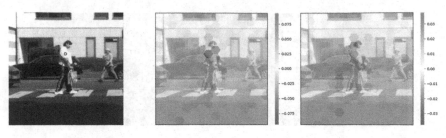

Fig. 9. SHAP explanation for the pixel circled in red in the input image. Middle image corresponds to the class 'person', and right image to the class 'dynamic'. (Color figure online)

Fig. 10. SHAP explanation for the pixel circled in red in the input image. Middle image corresponds to the class 'car', and right image to the class 'sidewalk'. (Color figure online)

Fig. 11. SHAP explanation for the pixel circled in red in the input image. Middle image corresponds to the class 'static', and right image to the class 'dynamic'. (Color figure online)

spatial distribution than the 'person' class, but with opposed signs. From these two explanations, we can conclude that the shoulder super-pixel alone help the model detect the pixel as a dynamic object, but neighbouring information (head, arm and low chest) contribute more significantly to classification as a person.

Figure 10 shows explanation on the pixel detected as a car (probability = 69%). The first explanation map, representing the car class, shows that the vehicle windowed part increases the car class probability, while the car bodywork decreases it. However, in this region, 'sidewalk's explanation map class report opposite values. This shows that the car bodywork, without a larger view of the vehicle, can be interpreted as a sidewalk by the model, which may appear natural in light of its homogeneous dark colour.

Figure 11 focuses on a misclassified pixel as 'static' (probability = 34%), at the frontier on the sidewalk and vegetation with visible concrete and ground. This is a typical area subject to difficult annotation. One can observe the explanation of the two dominant classes for this pixel, 'static' and 'dynamic'. Static class is excited by the pixel surroundings, while the dynamic class seems to be inhibited by the road below the pixel. On the other side, the explanation maps for sidewalks and vegetation do not report significant values. Then, the two most probable classes are finally relevant for such complex region and highlight the difficulty of the annotation.

These results show the relevance of the approach on a very different case study but relying on the same explanation method hyper-parameters. Further refined analysis could be proposed to provide more details on the local patterns impact on the decision by adjusting super-pixel size and the number of samples on explanation maps. However, this depends on the expected explanation level. Typically, smaller super-pixels may lead to more intuitive explanations, as it would better fit to various small objects and features of input images. Moreover, increasing the number of masked samples along the explanation process has proven to reduce noise in the explanation maps particularly present in Fig. 10.

5   Conclusion

This work presents a general workflow that allows for the adaptation of SHAP and RISE explainability methods to the semantic segmentation task. SHAP based method provides more relevant explanations and allows for refined understanding of model behaviours. Experiments were conducted to assess the parameters choice of the presented method and detail its advantages and pitfalls. The developed method was tested on deep neural networks trained for remote sensing oil slick segmentation, as well as urban scene segmentation on the public Cityscapes dataset. Explanations permitted to identify general model rules for specific input data configurations. Future works will focus on the extraction of relevance metrics such as deletion/insertion [14], as well as model behaviour comparison using SHAP explanation. Finally, SHAP super-pixel delimitation strategies need to be studied more deeply for different applications, as it may lead to better explanations.

References

1. Achanta, R., Shaji, A., Smith, K., Lucchi, A., Fua, P., Süsstrunk, S.: Slic superpixels compared to state-of-the-art superpixel methods. IEEE Trans. Pattern Anal. Mach. Intell. **34**(11), 2274–2282 (2012). https://doi.org/10.1109/TPAMI.2012.120
2. Amri, E., Benoit, A., Bolon, P., Migebielle, V., Conche, B., Oppenheim, G.: Offshore oil slicks detection from SAR images through the mask-RCNN deep learning model. In: 2020 International Joint Conference on Neural Networks (IJCNN), pp. 1–8 (2020). https://doi.org/10.1109/IJCNN48605.2020.9206652

3. Amri, E., et al.: Automatic offshore oil slick detection based on deep learning using SAR data and contextual information. In: Remote Sensing of the Ocean, Sea Ice, Coastal Waters, and Large Water Regions 2021, vol. 11857, pp. 35–42. SPIE (2021)
4. Arrieta, A.B., et al.: Explainable artificial intelligence (XAI): concepts, taxonomies, opportunities and challenges toward responsible AI. Inf. Fusion **58**, 82–115 (2020)
5. Birch, C.P., Oom, S.P., Beecham, J.A.: Rectangular and hexagonal grids used for observation, experiment and simulation in ecology. Ecol. Model. **206**(3–4), 347–359 (2007)
6. Cordts, M., et al.: The cityscapes dataset for semantic urban scene understanding. In: Proceedings of the IEEE Conference on Computer Vision and Pattern Recognition (CVPR) (2016)
7. Doshi-Velez, F., Kim, B.: Towards a rigorous science of interpretable machine learning. arXiv preprint arXiv:1702.08608 (2017)
8. Huang, C.H., Wu, H.Y., Lin, Y.L.: HarDNet-MSEG: a simple encoder-decoder polyp segmentation neural network that achieves over 0.9 mean dice and 86 FPS. arXiv preprint arXiv:2101.07172 (2021)
9. Jégou, S., Drozdzal, M., Vazquez, D., Romero, A., Bengio, Y.: The one hundred layers tiramisu: fully convolutional densenets for semantic segmentation. In: Proceedings of the IEEE Conference on Computer Vision and Pattern Recognition Workshops, pp. 11–19 (2017)
10. Li, J., et al.: Lane-deeplab: lane semantic segmentation in automatic driving scenarios for high-definition maps. Neurocomputing **465**, 15–25 (2021)
11. Linardatos, P., Papastefanopoulos, V., Kotsiantis, S.: Explainable AI: a review of machine learning interpretability methods. Entropy **23**(1), 18 (2021)
12. Lundberg, S.M., Lee, S.I.: A unified approach to interpreting model predictions. In: Proceedings of the 31st International Conference on Neural Information Processing Systems, pp. 4768–4777 (2017)
13. Montavon, G., Samek, W., Müller, K.R.: Methods for interpreting and understanding deep neural networks. Digit. Signal Process. **73**, 1–15 (2018)
14. Petsiuk, V., Das, A., Saenko, K.: Rise: randomized input sampling for explanation of black-box models. arXiv preprint arXiv:1806.07421 (2018)
15. Ribeiro, M.T., Singh, S., Guestrin, C.: "why should i trust you?" explaining the predictions of any classifier. In: Proceedings of the 22nd ACM SIGKDD International Conference on Knowledge Discovery and Data Mining, pp. 1135–1144 (2016)
16. Selvaraju, R.R., Cogswell, M., Das, A., Vedantam, R., Parikh, D., Batra, D.: Grad-cam: visual explanations from deep networks via gradient-based localization. In: Proceedings of the IEEE ICCV, pp. 618–626 (2017)
17. Shapley, L.S.: A Value for N-person Games. Princeton University Press, Princeton (2016)
18. Shrikumar, A., Greenside, P., Kundaje, A.: Learning important features through propagating activation differences. In: International Conference on Machine Learning, pp. 3145–3153. PMLR (2017)
19. Springenberg, J.T., Dosovitskiy, A., Brox, T., Riedmiller, M.: Striving for simplicity: the all convolutional net. arXiv preprint arXiv:1412.6806 (2014)
20. Vinogradova, K., Dibrov, A., Myers, G.: Towards interpretable semantic segmentation via gradient-weighted class activation mapping (student abstract). In: Proceedings of the AAAI Conference on AI, vol. 34, pp. 13943–13944 (2020)
21. Yang, X., et al.: Towards automatic semantic segmentation in volumetric ultrasound. In: Descoteaux, M., Maier-Hein, L., Franz, A., Jannin, P., Collins, D.L., Duchesne, S. (eds.) MICCAI 2017. LNCS, vol. 10433, pp. 711–719. Springer, Cham (2017). https://doi.org/10.1007/978-3-319-66182-7_81

Comparing Feature Importance and Rule Extraction for Interpretability on Text Data

Gianluigi Lopardo[✉] and Damien Garreau

Université Côte d'Azur, Inria, CNRS, LJAD, Nice, France
glopardo@unice.fr

Abstract. Complex machine learning algorithms are used more and more often in critical tasks involving text data, leading to the development of interpretability methods. Among local methods, two families have emerged: those computing importance scores for each feature and those extracting simple logical rules. In this paper we show that using different methods can lead to unexpectedly different explanations, even when applied to simple models for which we would expect qualitative coincidence. To quantify this effect, we propose a new approach to compare explanations produced by different methods.

Keywords: Interpretability · Explainable Artificial Intelligence · Natural Language Processing

1 Introduction

In recent years, increased complexity seems to have been the key to obtain state-of-the-art performance in natural language processing. Language models such as BERT [4] or GPT-3 [3] typically rely on billions of parameters and complex architecture choices to make accurate predictions. The availability of huge datasets and the computational capacity available today make this growth in complexity of algorithms possible. On the other hand, the opacity of these models hinders their usage in sensitive domains, such as healthcare or legal.

Indeed, there is a lack of adequate explanations to support individual predictions, preventing the social acceptance of these decisions. In order to provide interpretability, numerous methods have been proposed in the last five years [5,8]. In this paper, we focus on local, *post hoc* explanations, that is, methods explaining one decision in particular for a model which is already trained. There is a great diversity among these methods which we summarize briefly here. Perhaps the easiest to understand compute the gradient (or a variation thereof) of the model with respect to the input [1]. Other methods, such as LIME [15] and kernel SHAP [11] give attribution scores to each feature by fitting a linear model on the presence or absence of a feature. Rule-based methods such as Anchors [16] determine a small set of rules satisfied by the instance and provide

J.-J. Rousseau and B. Kapralos (Eds.): ICPR 2022 Workshops, LNCS 13645, pp. 261–268, 2023.
https://doi.org/10.1007/978-3-031-37731-0_20

it as explanation. Their principle is to learn decision sets that jointly maximizes their interpretability and predictive accuracy [6]. Explanations in form of rules are typically preferred by users [7]. Let us also mention that attention mechanisms [17], more and more frequently used in deep neural networks architectures, can be leveraged to get interpretability.

One main problem in interpretability is the lack of adequate metrics to measure the quality of explanations. While some studies propose a framework for comparing feature importance methods [2,14] and others for comparing rule-based methods [13], the comparison between methods of different classes is more challenging. Moreover, the problem is particularly understudied on textual data.

In this paper, we focus on perturbative and rule-based approaches, specifically LIME and Anchors. Our goal is to pin-point differences in their results which can be easily overlooked. Our motivation for doing so is the following: for a user working with a specific model and instance, the results of LIME and Anchors are qualitatively similar—both will highlight a subset of the words used in the document. It is tempting to think that these two subsets should roughly match. Focusing on the sentiment prediction task, we show empirically that this is not the case, even for very simple classifiers such as logistic models.

The paper is organized as follows: we first recall briefly the methods that we are scrutinizing in Sect. 2. We then present our main findings in Sect. 3, before concluding in Sect. 4. The code used for the comparison is available at https://github.com/gianluigilopardo/anchors_vs_lime_text, where our experiments are reproducible.

Notation. In all the paper, we will consider a model f applied to text documents z of length b (z contains b words). We let d denote the number of unique words of z, which is potentially smaller than b. For a given corpus $\mathcal{C}$, we define $\mathcal{D} = \{w_1, \ldots, w_D\}$ as the global dictionary with cardinality $D = |\mathcal{D}|$, containing the distinct words of each document in $\mathcal{C}$. For any given document z, we can define a *local dictionary* $\mathcal{D}(z)$, containing a subset d of $\mathcal{D}$. We set m_j the multiplicity of word j in z (in particular, $m_j = 0$ if word w_j does not appear in document z). Finally, for any integer k, we set $[k] = \{1, \ldots, k\}$.

2   Methods

In this section, we briefly recall the operation procedure of LIME (Sect. 2.1) and Anchors (Sect. 2.2), introducing our notation in the process. Our main assumption going into that description is that the classifier f takes as input the TF-IDF [10] vectorization of the words. We denote by ϕ this mapping.

2.1   LIME for Text Data

LIME [15] provides explanation in the form of feature attribution for the presence or absence of a unique word in the document to explain ξ. Since our choice is set on a given vectorizer ϕ, the procedure is as follows:

1. create n $(= 10^3)$ perturbed samples from ξ by removing words at random;
2. get the predictions $y_i = f(\phi(x_i))$;
3. train a weighted linear model on the presence / absence of words.

Sampling. The sampling procedure is as follows: for each perturbed document x_i, draw s_i a number of deletions uniformly at random in $[d]$. Then draw uniformly at random a subset $S_i \subseteq \mathcal{D}(x)$ of size s_i and remove all corresponding words from the document. In particular, all occurrences of a given word selected by this procedure are removed.

Surrogate Model. Further, weights π_i are given to each perturbed sample x_i. Finally, a linear model is fitted on the y_i with inputs given by the indicator functions that word j belongs to x_i and weights π_i. The user is provided with a visualization of the weights of this linear model.

2.2   Anchors for Text Data

An *anchor* is defined by [16] as a logical condition that *sufficiently* approximates the model locally. In the case of textual data, anchors are simply a subset of the words in the example ξ. The precision of an anchor A for a prediction $f(\xi)$ is defined as $\mathrm{Prec}\,(A) = \mathbb{E}\left[\mathbb{1}_{f(x)=f(\xi)} \mid A\right]$, where the condition means that all words in A belong to x. Since $\mathrm{Prec}\,(A)$ is generally not available in practice, an empirical estimate of the precision is computed from new samples x_i of the text.

The core idea of Anchors is to pick an anchor with high precision, while preserving some notion of globality. More precisely, Anchors solves (approximately)

$$A \in \underset{\mathrm{Prec}(A)\geq 1-\varepsilon}{\arg\max}\ \mathrm{cov}(A), \tag{1}$$

where, by default $\varepsilon = 0.05$ and the coverage $\mathrm{cov}(A)$ is defined as the probability that A applies to samples. However, due to Anchors' sampling, maximizing the coverage is equivalent to minimizing the length of A (see [9] for more details).

Sampling. As for LIME, the idea is to look at the behaviour of the model f in a local neighborhood of ξ, while fixing the anchor. For a given document ξ and each candidate anchor $A \subseteq \xi$, the sampling is performed in the following steps:

1. a number n $(= 10)$ of identical copies $x_1, \ldots, x_n$ of ξ are generated;
2. for each word ξ_k not in A, any $x_{i,k}$ is selected with probability $1/2$;
3. selected words are then *removed* by replacing them with the token "UNK."

Finally, the model is queried on these samples and the empirical precision is computed. The user is provided with the shortest anchor satisfying the precision condition of Eq. (1) (note that it is not necessarily unique).

One main difference between LIME and Anchors lies in the sampling. LIME selects words to remove in the local dictionary $\mathcal{D}_\xi$: if a word is selected, all its occurrences in ξ will be removed. Anchors consider words in ξ as independent.

3 Main Results

We now present our main results, comparing LIME and Anchors for text data when applied to simple classifiers. We run experiments on three reviews datasets: Restaurants, Yelp, and IMDB, available on Kaggle. We work with (binary) sentiment analysis: label 1 denotes a positive review and 0 a negative one. Note that we always consider explaining positive predictions, *i.e.*, we look at examples ξ such that $f(\xi) = 1$. In Sect. 3.1, we present a qualitative comparison of LIME and Anchors, by looking at individual explanations. In Sect. 3.2 we propose the ℓ-index: a new metric to measure the quality of explanation on text. Unless otherwise specified, the figures will report the average LIME coefficient and occurrence count for Anchors, both out of 100 runs of the default algorithms.

3.1 Qualitative Evaluation

Simple Decision Trees. We first focus on simple decision trees relying on the presence or absence of given words. Such rules can be written in terms of indicator functions. We present four cases of increasing complexity.

Presence of a Given Word. Let us first look into the case of a simple decision tree returning 1 or 0 according to the presence or the absence of an individual word $w_j \in \mathcal{D}$, *i.e.*, $f(z) = \mathbb{1}_{w_j \in z} = \mathbb{1}_{\phi(z)_j > 0}$. Let us consider an example ξ such that $w_j \in \xi$, meaning $f(\xi) = 1$. In this case, **both methods behave as expected**: LIME attributes high weight to w_j and negligible weight to the others words, while Anchors extracts the anchor $A = \{w_j\}$, as showcased in Fig. 1.

Small Decision Tree. Let us consider now a small decision tree looking for the presence of the words w_1 and w_2 or word w_3, *i.e.*,

$$f(z) = \mathbb{1}_{(w_1 \in z \text{ and } w_2 \in z) \text{ or } w_3 \in x} .$$

We consider an example ξ such that $w_1, w_2, w_3 \in \xi$. LIME assigns the same positive weight to w_1 and w_2, a higher weight to w_3 and negligible weight to all

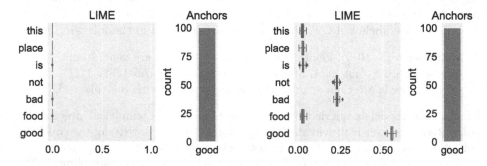

Fig. 1. Comparison on the classifiers $\mathbb{1}_{\text{good} \in z}$ (left panel) and $\mathbb{1}_{(\text{not} \in z \text{ and } \text{bad} \in z) \text{ or } \text{good} \in z}$ (right panel) applied to the same review. Anchors makes no difference between the two.

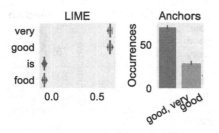 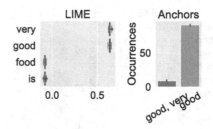

Fig. 2. Making a word disappear from the explanation by adding one occurrence. The classifier $\mathbb{1}_{(\text{very}\in z \text{ and } \text{good}\in z)}$ is applied when $m_{\text{very}} = 4$ (left) and $m_{\text{very}} = 5$ (right).

other words, as shown in [12]. Anchors only extracts the word w_3. In principle, we would expect the two methods to highlight the same words: they all seem important for the decision. Nevertheless, **Anchors is not considering w_1 and w_2 in its explanation, since the presence of word w_3 is *sufficient* to have a positive classification and $\{w_3\}$ is a shorter anchor than $\{w_1, w_2\}$.**

Presence of Several Words. Let us generalize the previous example by considering a model classifying documents according to the presence or absence of a set of words. Let $J = [k] \subseteq [d]$ be a set of distinct indices. We consider the model

$$f(z) = \prod_{j \in J} \mathbb{1}_{w_j \in z} = \prod_{j \in J} \mathbb{1}_{\phi(z)_j > 0}.$$

Then LIME will assign the same importance to any word in J, independently from their multiplicities (Proposition 3 in [12]). On the contrary, Anchors explanations are impacted by the multiplicities of words (Proposition 6 in [9]). In particular, **if the multiplicity of a word in J crosses a certain threshold, it disappears from the anchors** (see Fig. 2). This is quite surprising, and not a desired behavior (especially since we do not control this threshold).

Presence of Disjoint Subsets of Words. Let us consider now two disjoint sets of indices $J_1 = [k_1] \subseteq [d]$ and $J_2 = \{k_1 + 1, \ldots, k_2\} \subseteq [d]$ with the same cardinality $|J_1| = |J_2|$. We consider the model

$$f(z) = \prod_{j \in J_1} \mathbb{1}_{w_j \in z} \cdot \prod_{j \in J_2} \mathbb{1}_{w_j \in z} = \prod_{j \in J_1} \mathbb{1}_{\phi(z)_j > 0} \cdot \prod_{j \in J_2} \mathbb{1}_{\phi(z)_j > 0},$$

and an example ξ such that $w_j \in \xi$ for all $j \in J_1$ and for all $j \in J_2$. LIME gives the same weight to words in J_1 and words in J_2. Anchors' explanations depend, again, on the multiplicities involved, (see Fig. 3): as the occurrences of one word in J_1 (or in J_2) increase, the presence of other words in the same subset becomes *sufficient* to get a positive prediction.

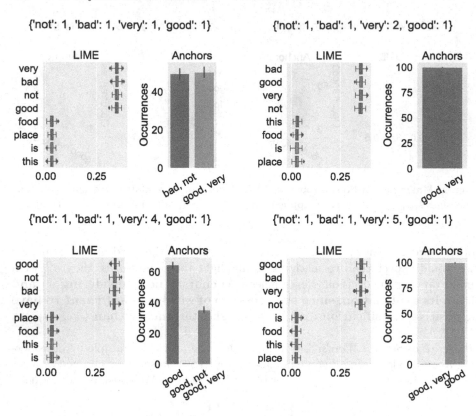

Fig. 3. Comparison on the classifier $\mathbb{1}_{(\text{not}\in z \text{ and } \text{bad}\in z) \text{ or } (\text{very}\in z \text{ and } \text{good}\in z)}$ when only m_{very} is changing. Anchors' explanations depend on multiplicities.

Logistic Models. We now focus on logistic models. Let $\sigma : \mathbb{R} \to [0,1]$ be the sigmoid function, that is, $t \mapsto 1/(1+e^{-t})$, $\lambda_0 \in \mathbb{R}$ an intercept, and $\lambda \in \mathbb{R}^d$ fixed coefficients. Then, for any document z, we consider $f(z) = \mathbb{1}_{\sigma(\lambda_0 + \lambda^\top \phi(z)) > \frac{1}{2}}$.

Sparse Case. We look at the case where only two coefficients $\lambda_1 > 0$ and $\lambda_2 < 0$ are nonzero, with $|\lambda_1| > |\lambda_2|$. LIME gives nonzero weights to w_1 and w_2, and null importance to the others, while Anchors only extract the word w_1 (see Fig. 4), as expected: w_1 is the only word that really matters for positive prediction.

Arbitrary Coefficients. Let us take $\lambda_1 \gg 0$, and $\lambda_j \sim \mathcal{N}(0,1)$, for $j \geq 2$. Then LIME gives a weight $\lambda_1 \gg 0$ and small weights to the others, while Anchors only extract $\{w_1\}$: the only word actually influencing the decision (see Fig. 4).

When applied to simple if-then rules based on the presence of given words, we showed that Anchors has an unexpected behaviour with respect to the multiplicities of these words in a document, while LIME is perfectly capable of extracting the support of the classifier. The experiments on logistic models in Fig. 4 show that, even when agreeing on the most important words, LIME is able to capture more information than Anchors.

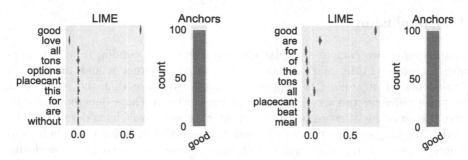

Fig. 4. Comparison on logistic model with $\lambda_{\text{love}} = -1$, $\lambda_{\text{good}} = +5$ and $\lambda_w = 0$ for the others (left), *vs* $\lambda_{\text{good}} = 10$ and $\lambda_w \sim \mathcal{N}(0, 1)$ for the others (right), applied to the same document. *good* is the most important word for the classification in both cases.

3.2 Quantitative Evaluation

When applying a logistic model f on top of a vectorizer ϕ, we know that the contribution of a word w_j is given by $\lambda_j \phi(z)_j$: we can unambiguously rank words in a document by importance. We propose to evaluate the ability of an explainer to detect the most important words for the classification of a document z by measuring the similarity between the N most important words for the interpretable classifier, namely $\Lambda_N(z)$, and the N most important words according to the explainer, namely $E_N(z)$. We define the ℓ-index for the explainer E as

$$\ell_E := \frac{1}{|\mathcal{C}|} \sum_{z \in \mathcal{C}} J\left(E_N(z), \Lambda_N(z)\right),$$

where $J(\cdot, \cdot)$ is Jaccard similarity and $\mathcal{C}$ is the test corpus.

Since we cannot fix N a priori for Anchors, we run the experiments as follows. For any document z, we call $A(z)$ the obtained anchor and we use $N = |A(z)|$, *i.e.*, we compute $J\left(A(z), \Lambda_{|A(z)|}(z)\right)$ for Anchors and $J\left(L_{|A(z)|}(z), \Lambda_{|A(z)|}(z)\right)$ for LIME. Table 1 shows the ℓ-index and the computing time for LIME and Anchors on three different datasets. LIME has high performance in extracting the most important words, while requiring less computational time than Anchors. **An anchor is a minimal set of words that is sufficient (with high probability) to have a positive prediction, but it does not necessarily coincide with the $|A|$ most important words for the prediction.**

Table 1. Comparison between LIME and Anchors in terms of ℓ-index and time.

	ℓ-index			time (s)		
	Restaurants	Yelp	IMDB	Restaurants	Yelp	IMDB
LIME	0.96 ± 0.17	0.95 ± 0.22	0.94 ± 0.23	0.21 ± 0.05	0.45 ± 0.22	0.73 ± 0.44
Anchors	0.67 ± 0.44	0.29 ± 0.43	0.22 ± 0.35	0.19 ± 0.27	3.83 ± 13.95	33.87 ± 165.08

4   Conclusion

In this paper, we compared explanations on text data coming from two popular methods (LIME and Anchors), illustrating differences and unexpected behaviours when applied to simple models. We observe that the results can be quite different: the set of words A extracted by Anchors does not coincide with the set of the $|A|$ words with largest interpretable coefficients determined by LIME. We proposed the ℓ-index to evaluate the ability of different explainers to identify the most important words. Our experiments show that LIME performs better than Anchors on this task, while requiring less computational resources.

Acknowledgments. Work supported by NIM-ML (ANR-21-CE23-0005-01).

References

1. Ancona, M., et al.: Towards better understanding of gradient-based attribution methods for deep neural networks. In: ICLR (2018)
2. Bhatt, U., Weller, A., Moura, J.: Evaluating and aggregating feature-based model explanations. In: IJCAI (2021)
3. Brown, T., et al.: Language models are few-shot learners. In: NeurIPS (2020)
4. Devlin, J., Chang, M., Lee, K., Toutanova, K.; Bert: pre-training of deep bidirectional transformers for language understanding. In: NAACL (2019)
5. Guidotti, R., Monreale, A., et al.: A survey of methods for explaining black box models. ACM Comput. Surv. (CSUR) **51**(5), 1–42 (2018)
6. Lakkaraju, H., Bach, S., Leskovec, J.: Interpretable decision sets: a joint framework for description and prediction. In: SIGKDD (2016)
7. Lim, B., Dey, A., Avrahami, D.: Why and why not explanations improve the intelligibility of context-aware intelligent systems. In: SIGCHI (2009)
8. Linardatos, P., Papastefanopoulos, V., Kotsiantis, S.: Explainable AI: a review of machine learning interpretability methods. Entropy **23**(1), 18 (2021)
9. Lopardo, G., Garreau, D., Precioso, F.: A sea of words: an in-depth analysis of anchors for text data. arXiv preprint arXiv:2205.13789 (2022)
10. Luhn, H.P.: A statistical approach to mechanized encoding and searching of literary information. IBM J. Res. Dev. **1**(4), 309–317 (1957)
11. Lundberg, S.M., Lee, S.: A unified approach to interpreting model predictions. In: NeurIPS (2017)
12. Mardaoui, D., Garreau, D.: An analysis of LIME for text data. In: AISTATS, PMLR (2021)
13. Margot, V., Luta, G.: A new method to compare the interpretability of rule-based algorithms. In: MDPI AI (2021)
14. Nguyen, A., Martínez, M.R.: On quantitative aspects of model interpretability. arXiv preprint arXiv:2007.07584 (2020)
15. Ribeiro, M.T., Singh, S., Guestrin, C.: Why should I trust you?: Explaining the predictions of any classifier. In: ACM SIGKDD (2016)
16. Ribeiro, M.T., Singh, S., Guestrin, C.: Anchors: High-precision model-agnostic explanations. In: AAAI (2018)
17. Vaswani, A., et al.; Attention is all you need. In: NeurIPS (2017)

12th Workshop on Pattern Recognition in Remote Sensing (PRRS)

Preface

The steady progress in developing new remote sensing sensors and technology has led to ever-increasing data, new opportunities, but also new challenges. Thus, the demand arises to apply current machine learning, and pattern recognition methods for analyzing and interpreting remotely sensed data, such as satellite and aerial imagery. This enables the processing of large datasets and promotes automation, but it can also lead to new insights derived from the data. One main goal of the PRRS workshops is to draw experts and researchers from the photogrammetry and remote sensing communities to the International Conference on Pattern Recognition (ICPR) and make them aware of the International Association for Pattern Recognition – fostering interdisciplinary cooperation.

The 2022 edition of PRRS was held in Montreal, Canada, in conjunction with 25th International Conference on Pattern Recognition. The workshop format includes two keynotes and nine oral presentations about the accepted papers. 11 manuscripts were submitted to the workshop and reviewed using a single-blind review process by a program committee of international experts. Nine papers were accepted, and all were presented as orals (virtual or on-site) during the workshop. This year, two keynotes were given that addressed current challenges in remote sensing. One keynote was given by Prof. Elif Sertel (Istanbul Technical University) about 'Earth Observation Data for Geospatial Artificial Intelligence' and the other keynote was given by Claudia Paris (University of Twente) with the title 'The Scarcity of Labels for Satellite Images: Opportunity and Challenges of Multi-source Geo-tagged Data'.

The papers were presented in three sessions: 'Learning with Multiple Models and Inputs', 'Analyzing and Interpreting SAR Imagery', and 'Semantic Segmentation and Detection'. The papers cover a wide range of remote sensing application areas, including solar wind prediction, sea ice motion estimation, sea ice classification, road segmentation, tree detection, and utility network segmentation. The type of data considered by the papers varies from different sensors (optical and radar) to distinct remote sensing platforms (satellites, airborne). Overall, the contributions of the nine accepted papers are in terms of new machine learning frameworks and novel neural network architectures. This includes, for example, novel and recent approaches for uncertainty quantification, few-shot learning, or self-training.

We take this opportunity to thank the program committee members for their efforts in the paper review. We also thank all the authors and the keynote speakers for their contributions, ESA Phi-Lab, IAPR, and the ISPRS for their sponsorship. We are grateful to the local organizers of ICPR 2022 for their assistance.

August 2022

Ribana Roscher
Charlotte Pelletier
Sylvain Lobry

Organization

Program Committee Chairs

Ribana Roscher	University of Bonn, Germany
Charlotte Pelletier	Université Bretagne Sud, France
Sylvain Lobry	Paris Descartes University, France

Program Committee

Alper Yilmaz	Ohio State University, USA
Benjamin Lucas	University of Colorado Boulder, USA
Bertrand Le Saux	European Space Agency (ESA), Italy
Camille Kurtz	University of Paris, France
Cem Ünsalan	Marmara Üniversitesi, Turkey
Clément Rambour	CNAM, France
David Clausi	University of Waterloo, Canada
Diego Marcos	Wageningen University, Netherlands
Dino Ienco	INRAE, France
Jenny Q. Du	Mississippi State University, USA
Eckart Michaelsen	Fraunhofer-IOSB, Germany
Emanuele Dalsasso	Telecom Paris, France
Fabio Dell'Acqua	University of Pavia, Italy
Flora Weissgerber	ONERA, France
Florence Tupin	Telecom Paris, France
Franz Rottensteiner	Leibniz Universitat Hannover, Germany
Gunho Sohn	York University, Canada
Helmut Mayer	Bundeswehr University Munich, Germany
Jan Dirk Wegner	University of Zurich, Switzerland
Jocelyn Chanussot	Grenoble Institute of Technology, France
John Kerekes	Rochester Institute of Technology, USA
Lloyd Hughes	EPFL, Switzerland
Loic Landrieu	IGN, France
Lorenzo Bruzzone	University of Trento, Italy
Martin Weinmann	Karlsruhe Institute of Technology, Germany
Michael Schmitt	Bundeswehr University Munich, Germany
Michele Volpi	Swiss Data Science Center, ETH Zurich, Switzerland
Nathan Jacobs	Washington University in St. Louis, USA

Nicolas Audebert	CNAM, France
Paolo Gamba	University of Pavia, Italy
Sébastien Lefèvre	Université de Bretagne Sud/IRISA, France
Selim Aksoy	Bilkent University, Turkey
Xuezhi Yang	Hefei University of Technology, China

Physics-Informed Neural Networks
for Solar Wind Prediction

Rob Johnson, Soukaïna Filali Boubrahimi$^{(\boxtimes)}$, Omar Bahri,
and Shah Muhammad Hamdi

Department of Computer Science, Utah State University, Logan 84322, UT, USA
{rob.johnson,soukaina.boubrahimi,omar.bahri,s.hamdi}@usu.edu

Abstract. Solar wind modeling is categorized into empirical and physics-based models that both predict the properties of solar wind in different parts of the heliosphere. Empirical models are relatively inexpensive to run and have shown great success at predicting the solar wind at the L1 Lagrange point. Physics-based models provide more sophisticated scientific modeling based on magnetohydrodynamics (MHD) that are computationally expensive to run. In this paper, we propose to combine empirical and physics-based models by developing a physics-guided neural network for solar wind prediction. To the best of our knowledge, this is the first attempt to forecast solar wind by combining data-driven methods with physics constraints. Our results show the superiority of our physics-constrained model compared to other state-of-the-art deep learning predictive models.

Keywords: Physics-constrained modeling · OMNI data · Ohm's law · Multivariate time series

1 Introduction

With advancements in technology, space weather and the risks associated with it are becoming more prominent [6]. One of the latest executive orders related to space weather studies, issued by the former president of the United States, urges scientists to direct attention to develop a response plans to severe space weather conditions [10]. Different types of space weather events may have different impacts on Earth, as well as on space crew members and satellites that are not protected by the magnetosphere [4]. For example, Solar Energetic Particles (SEP) can penetrate instruments on satellites and pose a possible threat of magnetic saturation which can eventually lead to electrical failures [7]. Coronal Mass Ejections (CMEs) can induce currents in surface-based electronics which can deteriorate power grid operations down on the Earth [17]. Additionally, X-rays heat the Earth's outer atmosphere, causing it to expand, which can increase the effects of drag on lower orbiting satellites. As a chain effect, space weather will also impact people who rely on those technologies.

Solar wind is another space weather event of interest that is composed of a stream of charged matter originating from the sun. Accurately forecasting

© Springer Nature Switzerland AG 2023
J.-J. Rousseau and B. Kapralos (Eds.): ICPR 2022 Workshops, LNCS 13645, pp. 273–286, 2023.
https://doi.org/10.1007/978-3-031-37731-0_21

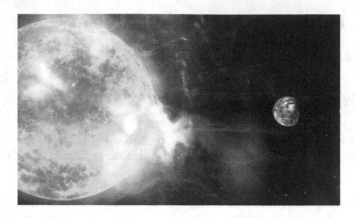

Fig. 1. Solar wind travelling to Earth at the speed of 300 km per second *(Image Courteousy from* [18])

solar wind can allow mission controllers to protect satellites and astronauts' health. Forecasts can also provide insight to enhance our understanding of the different physical processes that are responsible for solar wind acceleration and composition. The solar wind plasma can be considered an ideal plasma, or in other words, the electrostatic force controls the movements of the plasma more than the processes of ordinary gas kinetics [5]. While less effort has been invested in predicting solar wind characteristics using data-driven methods, most of the present studies rely on measurements of solar conditions to predict the solar wind. Our novelty in this work comes from the use of multivariate time series analysis to predict solar wind characteristics using physics constraints (Fig. 1).

2   Related Works

Since the discovery of solar wind over half a century ago, a number of studies have been conducted to predict solar wind [15]. One of the highly adopted physics-based solar wind forecasting mode is that of Wang-Sheely-Arge Enlil (WSA-Enlil) hybrid model - a three-dimensional magneto-hydrodynamic (MHD) model. WSA-Enlil starts by taking the input state of the sun at a given time and runs it through a few MHD equations. The model then propagates the result outward from the sun and forward in time to forecast solar wind speeds three to four days in advance [11].

A number of incremental works that build on the WSA-Enlil have been proposed. The increment is done either by slightly improving the accuracy of the model, or by making the MHD computations run faster. Yu et al. propose an improved WSA-Enlil by approximating the MHD computation through key assumptions. The improved WSA-Enlil was reduced from a three-dimensional problem into a one-dimensional problem without compromising significant accuracy [21]. Yu et al. focused their modeling only on predicting the slow solar wind.

The idea is that slow wind may have more sources than fast solar wind, which is relatively easily predicted by looking at the size of the coronal hole events that trigger it [24]. Finally, Liu et al. developed a new forecasting model that relies on dark areas of the sun to produce solar wind forecasts [16].

The advent of large neural networks has also allowed other researchers to improve over WSA-Enlil by using more data-driven methods, as opposed to purely physics-based systems used previously. Yang et al. achieved better results at 2.5 solar radii by using a three-layer fully connected network to establish the relationship between the polarized magnetic field and the electron density and solar wind velocity [26]. The same group also improved upon their work by enforcing self-consistent boundary conditions. Hemapriya et al. developed a convolutional neural network online model trained on solar images to gain a comprehensive knowledge of the solar activity prior to predicting solar wind velocities [23]. Leitner et al. found the distribution of solar wind to be quasi-invariant. Due to this nature, we propose to adopt a physics-guided neural network (PGNN) as a novel approach for solar wind prediction. Specifically, our paper contributions are summarized below:

1. We model the solar wind prediction problem as a multivariate time series prediction task and propose a novel loss function based on the adjusted Ohm's law for an ideal plasma.
2. We train multiple state-of-the-art deep learning forecasting models and show the superiority of our physics loss.
3. We explore multiple data normalizations and assess their effect on our model.
4. We made our source code open-source in a project website[1] that meets the principles of Findability, Accessibility, Interoperability, and Reusability (FAIR) [25].

The rest of the paper is organized as follows: Sect. 3 describes the data used in this study, Sect. 4 defines the Ohm's law constraint, followed by a description of the methods and experimental results in Sect. 5 and Sect. 6 respectively. Finally, Sect. 7 concludes the paper and shows potential directions for future works.

3 Data

Our data originates from the NASA OMNI multi-spacecraft data set of near-Earth solar wind parameters [22]. Table 3 summarizes the seven OMNI parameters that we used for prediction. Bx, By, and Bz are the three components of the magnetic field measured by a three-axis teslameter (Gauss meter). The velocity sensors measure the three-dimensional velocity distribution functions of electrons and ions (Vx, Vy, and Vz) [19]. Finally, the electric field parameter refers to the force exercised by the physical field that surrounds electrically charged particles.

The data set consists of a 5-minute time resolution multivariate time series data, which we preprocess by averaging into 1 h time resolution. We used 12 h

---

[1] https://sites.google.com/view/solarwindprediction/.

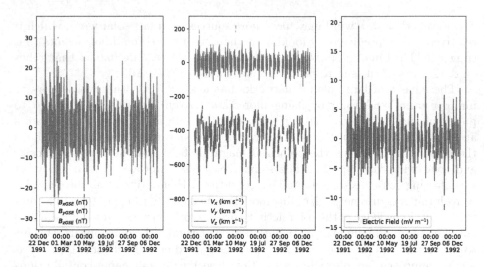

Fig. 2. OMNI time series data snapshot for the year 1992

(*prior*) as the number of hours prior to the solar wind event. The *prior* is the interval of time in the future when our model should be able to predict the parameters of the ambient solar wind. In other terms, we investigated the possibility of predicting the ambient solar wind characteristics from the electrical field, velocity, and magnetic field physical characteristics 12 h before its occurrence. We considered a *span* of 24 h, which corresponds to the number of hours we observe the solar wind characteristics. There is a direct correlation between the span duration and the length of the multivariate time series. Figure 2 illustrates the time series data of the seven solar wind physical parameter for the year 1992 (Table 1).

Table 1. OMNI features and metadata

Feature	Unit	Description
E	mV/m	Electric field
Vx	km/s	X component of the velocity
Vy	km/s	Y component of the velocity
Vz	km/s	Z component of the velocity
Bx	nT	X component of the magnetic field
By	nT	Y component of the magnetic field
Bz	nT	Z component of the magnetic field

3.1 Data Normalization

Neural networks are highly sensitive to variations in the input data [3]; therefore, data normalization is an important step prior to model training. In this paper, we considered three data normalization techniques in addition to the raw non-normalized data. Figure 3a shows the raw electric field (E) data as a function of $||v \times B||^2$. Figures 3b, 3c, and 3d show the same data when normalized using z-norm, 100 to 1000 norm, and the max-100 data normalization respectively.

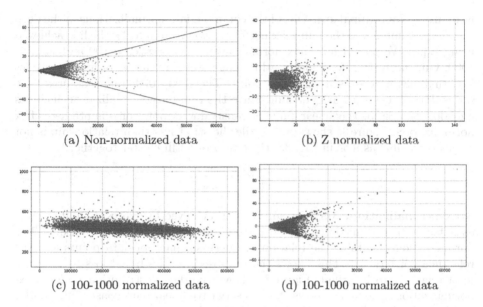

(a) Non-normalized data   (b) Z normalized data

(c) 100-1000 normalized data   (d) 100-1000 normalized data

Fig. 3. Scatterplots of E as a function of $||\hat{V} \times \hat{B}||^2$ under different data normalizations. The green lines show the relationship $|E| - \alpha ||\hat{V} \times \hat{B}||^2 = 0$ which follows the adapted Ohm's Law. (Color figure online)

No Normalization. To establish a coherent baseline, we considered raw non-normalized multivariate time series as the first data product for training our models [1,2,20]. The main limitation of using raw data stems from the different orders of magnitude of the input physical parameters. This introduces an inherent bias in the input data where the network weights the high magnitude parameters higher than the low magnitude ones. The raw non-normalized data follows physics Ohm's law ($|E| = ||\hat{V} \times \hat{B}||^2$) which constrains the range of possible values 6. To give a general sense of Ohm's law, the linear constraints are plotted in green as shown in Fig. 3.

Z Normalization. A common form of normalization that consists of fitting the data to a Gaussian distribution. The normalized values correspond to the number of standard deviations away from the mean. Standardization is achieved by subtracting the mean of all the data and dividing it by the standard deviation. In an ideal context, about 68% of the data reside in the range [−1,1]. The limitation of standardization is that it does not retain the inter-series relationships.

$$x' = \frac{x - \mu}{\sigma} \tag{1}$$

Min-max Normalization. One of the common data normalizations in the deep learning community is the min-max normalization from 0 to 1, which is achieved using Eq. 2. We used a min-max normalization with a $x_{min} = 100$ and $x_{max} = 1000$. Our motivation for choosing this range stems from our proposed physics loss that has a zero as a reference point. The [100–1000] range assures time series data values that are not null. Since the min-max normalization includes an additional step, the linear physics constraint is not well maintained after normalization. Figure 3c shows that while the strict less than relationship is not as clearly visible as it is in Fig. 3a, the data does still cluster together.

$$x' = \frac{x - x_{min}}{x_{max} - x_{min}} \tag{2}$$

Max-normalization. Max-normalization is achieved by expressing data points as a factor of the maximum value in the time series as shown in Eq. 3. The normalization maintains the relationship between pairs of data points and the reference point (zero). This allows the proposed physics-based loss to keep the data relationship invariant. Figure 3d shows the data distribution under max-normalization. The figure shows that conservative linear data constraints similar to Fig. 3a could easily be applied.

$$x' = \frac{x}{x_{max}} * 100 \tag{3}$$

4   Ohm's Law Constraint

In this work, we propose a guided neural network that relies on a fundamental underlying relationship in the data, known as Ohm's law for plasma as defined in Eq. 4 [5]

$$J = \sigma(E + V \times B), \tag{4}$$

where J is the current vector field, E is the electric vector field, V is the velocity vector field, and B is the magnetic vector field. Since the solar wind is made up of about equal parts electrons and protons, $J \approx 0$. Equation 5 shows the modified Ohm's law for solar wind.

$$- E \approx V \times B. \tag{5}$$

One of our data-level limitations is that while the velocity and magnetic field parameters are expressed as three vector quantities that they are, OMNI data only provides one scalar for the electric field. In order to combine all the parameters into Eq. 5 equality, we relaxed the equality into an inequality property. We used the knowledge that the magnitude norm of the product of three orthogonal component vectors is greater than or equal to the magnitude of the individual component vectors [8]. Since Eq. 5 is a vector equality, the norm of the product of the velocity field and the magnetic field must be greater than the magnitude of any single component vector of the electric field as defined in Eq. 6.

$$|E| - \alpha||\hat{V} \times \hat{B}||^2 \leq 0, \tag{6}$$

where α is a constant to allow for unit conversion.

5   Methodology

To develop a physics constrained neural network, we rely on a loss function that penalizes the network based on violations of physics laws, and a physics model input [13].

5.1   A Physics Based Loss Function

As discussed in Sect. 4, our data follows Ohm's law for an ideal plasma that we modified to Eq. 6. Since there is a negativity constraint, we use a rectified linear unit (ReLU) as shown in Eqs. 7 and 8.

$$\mathcal{L}_{PHY}(\hat{Y}) = ReLU(H(\hat{Y}, Y)) \tag{7}$$

$$H(E, V, B) = -(|E| - \alpha||\hat{V} \times \hat{B}||^2) \tag{8}$$

In addition to the physics loss, we used the Root Mean Square Error (RMSE) as the traditional loss used for continuous values as defined in Eq. 9. In order to find a balance between the two losses, we use a hyper-parameter λ. Our proposed combined physics constrained loss function is shown in Eq. 10.

$$\mathcal{L}_{RMSE}(\hat{Y}, Y) = \sqrt{\frac{1}{n}\sum_{i=1}^{n}(y_i - \hat{y}_i)^2} \tag{9}$$

$$\mathcal{L} = (1 - \lambda)\mathcal{L}_{RMSE}(\hat{Y}, Y) + \lambda * \mathcal{L}_{PHY} \tag{10}$$

5.2   Baselines

We consider five deep learning baselines in our study that we trained with our proposed $\mathcal{L}$ loss and without physics loss $\mathcal{L}_{phy}$. In this section, we outline the details of our baselines.

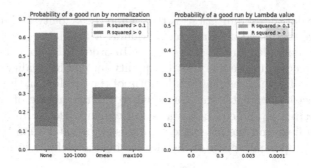

Fig. 4. Probabilities of achieving a given R squared threshold with a time based CNN. *(The maximum R squared achieved by this network was 0.178)*

Time-Based CNN. Convolutional Neural Networks (CNNs) work on data of sequential nature (e.g., images and maps) that have an underlying dependence between contiguous data points. Since our multivariate time series data is a sequence, we used a modified CNN for the prediction. The CNN modifications involve using two types of kernels: $1 \times n$ kernels that modify the univariate time series across the time dimension, and $m \times n$ kernels with dimension m being equal to the number of univariate time series contained in the multivariate time series. These changes allow our CNN to be aware of how the variables change with time, as well as how each variable relates to all other variables.

ResNet. Residual Neural Network model (ResNet) is a deeper model that learns how to modify the existing data to match their correct probability distribution. ResNet models utilize skip connections to jump over some layers to avoid the vanishing gradients problem. To augment the ResNet model for time series data, we used the same kernel shapes as used in the time based CNN.

RotateNet. RotateNet network takes the multivariate time series input and makes a neural model that learns how to distinguish between the different geometric transformations (rotations) performed on the normal multivariate time series matrix. RotateNet is the first method to discover multivariate time series anomalies by constructing a self-supervised classification model [12,14]. The auxiliary expertise learned by the model generates feature detectors that effectively forecast the next time steps.

LSTM. Long Short-Term Memory (LSTM) is a memory-based model that can handle the complexity of sequence dependence among the input variables by maintaining a state (memory) across very long sequences. One of the ways the model addresses the exploding and vanishing gradient problem is by having a forget mechanism that ignores data points based on a probabilistic model.

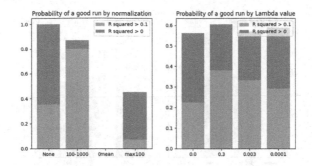

Fig. 5. Probabilities of achieving a given R squared threshold with a time constrained ResNet. *(The maximum R squared achieved by this network was 0.175)*

GRU. Gated Recurrent Unit (GRU) model has been developed to improve the LSTM model by adding extra gates to allow the network to extract important bits from sequences [9]. GRU is simpler and faster to train than the LSTM model as they do not require a memory unit. The GRU model generally performs better on short time sequences compared to the LSTM model.

6   Experimental Setup and Evaluation

To evaluate our proposed baselines with our proposed $\mathcal{L}$ loss and without physics loss $\mathcal{L}_{phy}$, we split the data into training, validation, and testing sets and used the R squared measure as defined in Eq. 11. Prior to training our models, we also performed a grid search over the architectures and hyper-parameters of the baseline models. The grid searches were run on data with a 60/30/10 split, where the first partition is used as a training data, the second as validation data, and the final withheld partition as a testing data. After seven hundred epochs of training, each network was evaluated on the testing data. We repeated the process three times, averaged the scores, and reported the aggregate score.

$$R^2 = 1 - \frac{\sum_i \left(y_i - \hat{y}_i\right)^2}{\sum_i \left(y_i - \bar{y}\right)^2} \tag{11}$$

6.1   Experimental Results

Figure 4 shows the R squared results of the time based CNN which is relatively a simple network with few parameters. We note that among the four normalization methods, the 100–1000 min-max normalization achieved the best results for a positive R squared and R squared >0.1. We also note that although the positive R squared probability is similar for the non-physics constrained CNN (i.e., $\lambda \neq 0$) and the physics constrained CNN for $\lambda = 0.3$, the constrained model provides better r squared probabilities of greater than 0.1. Figure 5 shows the results of the ResNet model. The ResNet model achieved significantly better performance

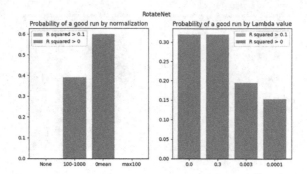

Fig. 6. Probabilities of achieving a given R squared threshold with a rotating ResNet implementation. *(The maximum R squared achieved by this network was 0.087)*

levels with the 100–1000 min-max normalization performing more than twice better than the second best normalization. The ResNet model achieves the best positive R squared probabilities with a constrained network with $\beta = 0.3$. Similar to CNN, the physics-constrained ResNet model is better than the unconstrained model on the R squared probabilities greater than 0.1.

Figure 6 shows the results of the RotateNet which requires significantly fewer hyper-parameters than the ResNet model (roughly one third of the number of parameters). ResNet performed the best using Z normalization (zero mean). Similar to the CNN and ResNets, RotateNet did not perform well with low values of λ. The network performed well either under a high λ or an unconstrained loss (i.e., $\lambda = 0$). Figure 8 shows the results of our experiments when trained using the LSTM baseline. The LSTM baseline performed the best when trained with Z normalized data and outperformed the other data normalizations by a large margin. While the LSTM did not need physics loss to produce a decent result, the physics loss provided to be useful in producing a better quality result that have a higher R squared probability of being greater than 0.1. Finally, Fig. 7 shows the results of the GRU. Similar to the LSTM recurrent neural network, the GRU network performed the best when trained on Z normalized data. The GRU model also benefited from the physics informed loss and achieved higher R squared values.

6.2   Discussion

All of the five deep learning baselines benefited from the use of the physics loss. The physics loss was especially important in fine-tuning the higher-performing baselines. This is likely because the RMSE is a quadratic function and dominates our proposed $\mathcal{L}$ when the predicted value is far from the actual value. Similarly, the physics loss dominates when the networks predict values closer to the true values. We note that the loss $\mathcal{L}$ is multiplied by the learning rate before being back-propagated through the network. Since non-normalized data have relatively high magnitudes, it results in larger $\mathcal{L}$ values. Hence, the model performs better

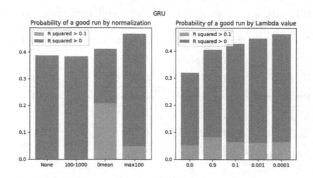

Fig. 7. Probabilities of achieving a given R squared threshold with GRU network. *(The maximum R squared achieved by this network was 0.158)*

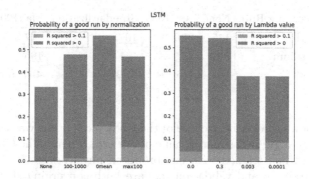

Fig. 8. Probabilities of achieving a given R squared threshold with an LSTM network. *(The maximum R squared achieved by this network was 0.173)*

with lower learning rates. On the other hand, Z normalized data will result in lower $\mathcal{L}_{RMSE}$, which requires the network to have a larger learning rate.

We also implemented a null model that predicts the future values by simply reporting the last snapshot of current values. The null model can be accurate only if the data is highly stationary. Table 2 contains the RMSE values of the null model and the five baselines. Most of the baselines perform better than the null model. Note that the RMSE values across columns are not comparable due to normalization effects.

Table 3 contains the results of all experiments on all the baselines, organized by normalization and relative learning rate. We can note that each normalization performs better under a preferred learning rate. A low learning rate is preferred when training a network on Z normalized or max-100 normalization method. The 100–1000 min-max normalization performs better when training the baselines under a high learning rate and non-normalized data are better fitted when the learning rate is medium. Comparing Table 2 and Table 3, we note that in general lower learning rate results in lower losses.

Table 2. RMSE values of baselines trained with different normalization methods

Network	None	100–1000	Standardization	Max-100
CNN	278	1800	0.560	68.9
ResNet	298	1710	0.567	62.0
RotateNet	443	1740	0.626	76.0
LSTM	286	2040	0.529	63.3
GRU	430	2260	0.634	77.1
Null Model	525	5730	1.23	227

Table 3. Number of runs with R squared above 0, by learning rate and normalization. *(The best values by columns are bolded and the runner-up is underlined)*

Learning Rate	None	100–1000	Standardization	Max100
high	<u>185</u>	**326**	<u>167</u>	17
medium	**329**	<u>267</u>	41	<u>196</u>
low	180	115	**372**	**467**

Figure 9 shows the learning curve of the CNN model that was captured from the run with the highest R squared value of our experiment. The CNN converges to lower losses when trained with our proposed physics loss $\mathcal{L}_{phy}$. The RMSE values of the training and validation sets are both converging showing a desirable transition from an underfitting model (at approximately 50 epochs) to an ideally trained model at the end of the seven hundred epoch. The plateauing of the validation loss indicates the end of convergence and the lack of overfitting problem.

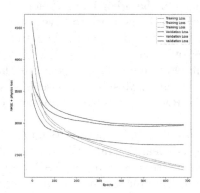

Fig. 9. 3-fold cross validation training loss (green) and validation loss (purple) of the time based CNN normalized using 100–1000 min-max and trained with a learning rate of 0.0001 and a physics weight $\beta = 0.003$. The first twenty epochs have been omitted from the graph to enhance readability. (Color figure online)

7   Conclusion

In this work, we propose an adjusted Ohm's law inequality that we used for building a new physics loss to guide deep learning models for the task of solar wind forecasting. To our best knowledge, this is the first effort to build a hybrid physics and deep learning model for solar wind prediction. Our findings support our hypothesis that physics loss helps fine-tune model prediction. In this work, we considered five baseline models that all showed improvement when informed with Ohm's law physics loss. As a future direction to this work, we would like to explore the inclusion of the WSA-ENLIL physics model forecasts as an input to our hybrid physics-guided model.

Acknowledgment. This project has been supported in part by funding from GEO and CISE directorates under NSF awards #2204363 and #2153379.

References

1. Angryk, R.A., et al.: Multivariate time series dataset for space weather data analytics. Sci. Data **7**(1), 1–13 (2020)
2. Bahri, O., Boubrahimi, S.F., Hamdi, S.M.: Shapelet-based counterfactual explanations for multivariate time series. arXiv preprint arXiv:2208.10462 (2022)
3. Bartlett, P.L., Foster, D.J., Telgarsky, M.J.: Spectrally-normalized margin bounds for neural networks. Adv. Neural Inf. Process. Syst. **30** (2017)
4. Board, S.S., Council, N.R., et al.: Severe Space Weather Events: Understanding Societal and Economic Impacts: a Workshop Report. National Academies Press, Washington (2009)
5. Boozer, A.H.: Ohm's law for mean magnetic fields. J. Plasma Phys. **35**(1), 133–139 (1986)
6. Boubrahimi, S.F., Aydin, B., Kempton, D., Angryk, R.: Spatio-temporal interpolation methods for solar events metadata. In: 2016 IEEE International Conference on Big Data (Big Data), pp. 3149–3157. IEEE (2016)
7. Boubrahimi, S.F., Aydin, B., Martens, P., Angryk, R.: On the prediction of 100 MEV solar energetic particle events using goes satellite data. In: 2017 IEEE International Conference on Big Data (Big Data), pp. 2533–2542. IEEE (2017)
8. Bresler, A., Joshi, G., Marcuvitz, N.: Orthogonality properties for modes in passive and active uniform wave guides. J. Appl. Phys. **29**(5), 794–799 (1958)
9. Cho, K., van Merrienboer, B., Bahdanau, D., Bengio, Y.: On the properties of neural machine translation: encoder-decoder approaches (2014). 10.48550/ARXIV.1409.1259, https://arxiv.org/abs/1409.1259
10. Eastwood, J., et al.: The economic impact of space weather: where do we stand? Risk Anal. **37**(2), 206–218 (2017)
11. Emmons, D., Acebal, A., Pulkkinen, A., Taktakishvili, A., MacNeice, P., Odstrcil, D.: Ensemble forecasting of coronal mass ejections using the WSA-ENLIL with coned model. Space Weather **11**(3), 95–106 (2013)
12. Golan, I., El-Yaniv, R.: Deep anomaly detection using geometric transformations. Adv. Neural Inf. Process. Syst. **31** (2018)
13. Karpatne, A., Watkins, W., Read, J.S., Kumar, V.: Physics-guided neural networks (PGNN): an application in lake temperature modeling. CoRR abs/1710.11431 (2017), https://arxiv.org/abs/1710.11431

14. Li, P., Boubrahimi, S.F., Hamdi, S.M.: Graph-based clustering for time series data. In: 2021 IEEE Big Data, pp. 4464–4467. IEEE (2021)
15. Li, P., Boubrahimi, S.F., Hamdi, S.M.: Shapelets-based data augmentation for time series classification. In: 2021 20th IEEE International Conference on Machine Learning and Applications (ICMLA), pp. 1373–1378. IEEE (2021)
16. Luo, B., Zhong, Q., Liu, S., Gong, J.: A new forecasting index for solar wind velocity based on EIT 284 Å observations. Solar Phys. **250**(1), 159–170 (2008)
17. Ma, R., Angryk, R.A., Riley, P., Boubrahimi, S.F.: Coronal mass ejection data clustering and visualization of decision trees. Astrophys. J. Suppl. Ser. **236**(1), 14 (2018)
18. Martin, S.: Solar winds travelling at 300km per second to hit earth today. www.express.co.uk/news/science/1449974/solar-winds-space-weather-forecast-sunspot-solar-storm-aurora-evg, Accessed 01 May 2022
19. Mukai, T., et al.: The low energy particle (LEP) experiment onboard the Geotail satellite. J. Geomag. Geoelectr. **46**(8), 669–692 (1994). https://doi.org/10.5636/jgg.46.669
20. Muzaheed, A.A.M., Hamdi, S.M., Boubrahimi, S.F.: Sequence model-based end-to-end solar flare classification from multivariate time series data. In: 2021 20th IEEE International Conference on Machine Learning and Applications (ICMLA), pp. 435–440. IEEE (2021)
21. Owens, M., et al.: A Computationally efficient, time-dependent model of the solar wind for use as a surrogate to three-dimensional numerical magnetohydrodynamic simulations. Solar Phys. **295**(3), 1–17 (2020). https://doi.org/10.1007/s11207-020-01605-3
22. Papitashvili, N., Bilitza, D., King, J.: Omni: a description of near-earth solar wind environment. In: 40th COSPAR Scientific Assembly, vol. 40, pp. C0–1 (2014)
23. Raju, H., Das, S.: CNN-based deep learning model for solar wind forecasting. Solar Phys. **296**(9), 1–25 (2021). https://doi.org/10.1007/s11207-021-01874-6
24. Shugai, Y.S.: Analysis of quasistationary solar wind stream forecasts for 2010–2019. Russian Meteorol. Hydrol. **46**(3), 172–178 (2021). https://doi.org/10.3103/S1068373921030055
25. Wilkinson, M.D., et al.: The fair guiding principles for scientific data management and stewardship. Sci. Data **3**(1), 1–9 (2016)
26. Yang, Y., Shen, F.: Modeling the global distribution of solar wind parameters on the source surface using multiple observations and the artificial neural network technique. Solar Phys. **294**(8), 1–22 (2019). https://doi.org/10.1007/s11207-019-1496-5

Less Labels, More Modalities: A Self-Training Framework to Reuse Pretrained Networks

Jean-Christophe Burnel[✉][ID], Luc Courtrai, and Sébastien Lefèvre[ID]

Université Bretagne Sud, UMR 6074 IRISA Campus de Tohannic,
56000 Vannes, France
jean-christophe.burnel@univ-ubs.fr

Abstract. Remote sensing largely benefits from recent advances in deep learning. Beyond traditional color imagery, remote sensing data often features some extra bands (e.g. multi or hyperspectral imagery) or multiple sources, leading to the so-called multimodal scenario. While multimodal data can lead to better performances, it also requires to design specific deep networks, to collect specifically-annotated datasets, and to perform full retraining of the models. However, a major drawback of deep learning is the large number of annotations that is required to ensure such a training phase. Besides, for some given task and modality combination, annotated data might not be available, thus requiring a tedious labeling phase. In this paper, we show how to benefit from additional modalities without requiring additional labels. We propose a self-training framework that allows us to add a modality to a pretrained model in order to improve its performance. The main features of our framework are the generation of pseudo-labels that act as annotations on the new modality, but also the generation of a pseudo-modality corresponding to the labeled monomodal dataset. Experiments on the ISPRS Potsdam dataset, where we complement color orthophotography with a digital surface model, shows the relevance of our approach, especially for land cover classes that can take advantage of the two modalities.

Keywords: Multimodal · Self-training · Remote sensing

1 Introduction

During the last decade, deep learning has become the standard framework for pattern recognition, for both the general case and specific contexts, such as remote sensing [23]. However, deep neural networks require a large number of examples for their training and, depending on the inputs and the task considered, open datasets are not always available. When applying a deep learning process to remote sensing data, an example is most often made of a color (or multispectral) image along with some ground truth. Such ground truth (a.k.a. reference data) can take the form of a label per image or per pixel, leading to the problems known as scene classification and semantic segmentation respectively. The latter is very popular in remote sensing, since it allows to provide land cover or land use maps. However, it also requires

J.-J. Rousseau and B. Kapralos (Eds.): ICPR 2022 Workshops, LNCS 13645, pp. 287–302, 2023.
https://doi.org/10.1007/978-3-031-37731-0_22

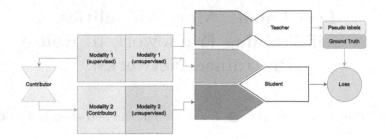

Fig. 1. Illustration of our self-training framework. Teacher is our pretrained model, and contributor is our modality mapping model. Both are used to train our student, i.e. a model able to use both modalities.

a long and tedious annotation phase since every single pixel should be labeled beforehand. To illustrate, let us consider an urban mapping scenario, that can be achieved using color orthophotography together with labels coming from OpenStreetMap. If the specific classes of interest are not available in OpenStreetMap, additional annotation should be conducted. Once these labels are made available, one can design, train, and evaluate a deep network. If the task is not trivial, some classes will likely be hardly distinguishable by relying on orthophotography alone. Enriching the input data with another modality would then be particularly relevant, e.g. adding infrared band to characterize vegetation, or digital surface models to distinguish between low and high vegetation.

While adding a modality would certainly lead to better performances, it also comes with some severe drawbacks. Indeed, the underlying deep network needs to be adapted to meet the new input. Beyond the design effort that is necessary, and that has received wide attention in the field these last years [3], it is also mandatory to conduct a full retraining of the model. Such a step often requires to annotate a new multimodal dataset, leading to additional labeling costs. We tackle here this issue and propose to reuse existing annotations done on the unimodal dataset, without requiring any new annotation to be done on the new multimodal dataset. To this end, we use a self-training framework where we add a new model called contributor, which goal is to find a mapping from the first modality to the second one. This framework makes use of pseudo-labels generated from the unlabeled multimodal dataset, but also of pseudo-modalities, allowing us to reuse the initial annotated monomodal dataset used to train the first model. While our framework can be applied to various tasks, we consider here the specific case of semantic segmentation given its importance in remote sensing (Fig. 1).

2   Related Work

2.1   Multimodal Deep Learning

Using multiple modalities to reach better performances have been widely explored [22], including in remote sensing [14]. But beyond such a performance gain, multimodality mainly helps a model to succeed even when one modality is not useful or reliable. For instance, fusion of Sentinel-1 (SAR) and Sentinel-2 (optical) data can deal with nighttime or cloudy situations while the sole use of Sentinel-2 would fail in such cases. Many research works have thus been conducted to design a deep architecture that makes full benefit of two modalities [3].

However, to the best of our knowledge, all existing models need to trained on a fully annotated multimodal dataset, thus limiting their applicability to some specific scenarios where such multimodal and related annotations are available.

2.2   Self-training

Using a network to train another network is known as the teacher-student paradigm. It has been widely explored in the deep learning community, mostly through knowledge distillation and self-training scenarios. The former aims to use a previously trained model as a teacher in order to train a smaller model (a.k.a. the student) that will be more compact or efficient than the original teacher [12]. In the context multimodal data, knowledge distillation has been used in cross-modal distillation [13], where the authors use a pretrained encoder (teacher) to train a second encoder dedicated to the additional modality (student). While the proposed method was applied to object detection, its design is generalist enough to be used in other tasks. But it ends with a final training phase that requires labels on multimodal data. Let us also mention [9], where knowledge distillation is used with multiple modalities to enable the drop of a modality at test time (i.e. opposite scenario to ours).

The other family of teacher-student methods is called self-training [6,21], a specific case of self-labelling [17] where we only have one teacher for one student in a single view setting. It differs from co-training [4] that requires multiple views to train different teachers by view. The main idea behind self-training is to first train a teacher model for a given task, and then use its predictions as labels (a.k.a. pseudo-labels) for an extra unlabeled dataset, thus allowing to train a student model on this unlabeled dataset. Despite being very promising, this core idea only leads to some performance increase when coupled with noise injection [2,20]. In the context of semantic segmentation, self-training has been used to adapt a model pretrained on synthetic data to some real data [24,25], thus solving an unsupervised domain adaptation problem. The authors rely on class-balanced label selection, which aims to ensure the distribution of pseudo-labels follows the distribution of original labels. To do so, they perform the label selection process for each class instead of selecting the best predictions on the global set. Besides, they use both hard [24] and soft [25] pseudo-labeling.

However, the potential of self-training for dealing with multimodal data remains to be explored yet. Our paper aims to fill this gap and show the relevance of self-training in order to add an additional modality without requiring new labels. In the sequel, we will denote as supervised modality the one coming with the original annotations, and as unsupervised modality the additional modality for which no labels are provided.

3   Method

We recall we aim to alleviate human labour when adding a modality $\mathcal{M}_2$ to a model already trained with some labels on a modality $\mathcal{M}_1$. As justified in the previous section, we will rely on self-training. In this section, we describe our method and provide insights regarding some of our technical choices.

3.1   Training of the Teacher

Since we assume a previously trained model, we first need to train such a model. We will refer to our first model $\mathcal{C}_\theta^s$ as the teacher in the rest of the paper. This teacher is trained in a supervised manner, using only one modality that we define as $\mathcal{M}_1$. This step is illustrated with Fig. 2a.

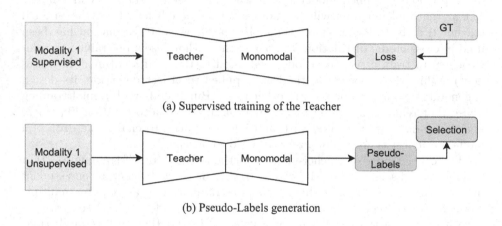

(a) Supervised training of the Teacher

(b) Pseudo-Labels generation

Fig. 2. Steps involving our teacher.

3.2   Pseudo-Labels

Pseudo-labels are labels that were not assigned by a human. To generate them, we start by retrieving prediction for every data that will be used in our unsupervised set (x_{uns}^1, x_{uns}^2) where $x_{uns}^1 \in \mathcal{M}_1$ and $x_{uns}^2 \in \mathcal{M}_2$. We apply the following equation to obtain $\boldsymbol{p}$ our set of all predictions:

$$\boldsymbol{p} = \mathcal{C}_\theta^s(x_{uns}^1) \tag{1}$$

Once done, we need to filter our predictions, in order to counter mistakes made by the teacher. To do so, we apply a class-balanced selection [24] as previously discussed. We start by computing our thresholds $\mathcal{T}$ for each class. Those thresholds are found by ordering all predictions using probability outputs and taking the value corresponding to the sought percentage of data to keep. We then define our filtering with

$$S(\boldsymbol{p}) = \{y : y \in \boldsymbol{p} \wedge \sum_{i=0}^{n} \max(0, y_i - \mathcal{T}_i) > 0\} \tag{2}$$

where n is the number of classes. Finally, and as illustrated in Fig. 2b, we can write our pseudo-labels as

$$PL = S(\mathcal{C}_{\theta}^s(\boldsymbol{x})) \tag{3}$$

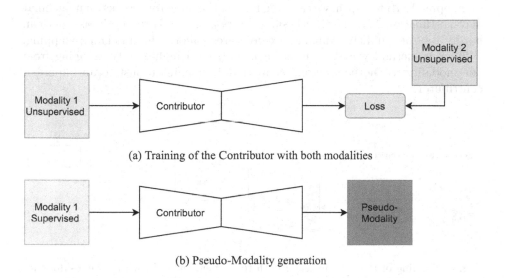

(a) Training of the Contributor with both modalities

(b) Pseudo-Modality generation

Fig. 3. Steps involving our contributor.

Soft vs Hard Pseudo-Labels In the previous step, we had two possibilities regarding pseudo-labeling. We could either go with soft labeling [25], where every label is a probability distribution based on the teacher's predictions. Or we could use hard labeling [24] where every label is one-hot encoded. Both choices have shown good results, and we chose to use hard labeling for efficiency reasons. To illustrate, let us consider a 100×100 image with 100 classes. On the one hand, soft labeling requires our labels to be coded as floating point values (e.g. float32), and furthermore needs to be saved in a 100×100×100 array. So the labels associated to our image will take up to 4MB. On the other hand, hard labeling can be simply coded as int8 and saved in a "small" 100×100 array, thus leading to a 10KB file. Hard labeling results in a 400× reduction of the memory footprint w.r.t. its soft-labeling counterpart.

3.3   Pseudo-Modality

As already stated, we include here another model $\mathcal{C}_\psi^c$ called contributor. The purpose of this model is to learn a mapping from $\mathcal{M}_1$ to $\mathcal{M}_2$:

$$\mathcal{C}_\psi^c : \mathcal{M}_1 \to \mathcal{M}_2 \tag{4}$$

and its role is illustrated in Fig. 3.

Learning to map a remote sensing modality into another has already been explored using GANs [16,19], since these models represent the most common solution for image-to-image translation. When dealing with the common scenario of mapping RGB to depth, we can even rely on the numerous works on monocular depth estimation [8,10,11]. But besides this popular RGB-to-depth task, one can hardly rely on publicly available architectures tailored for modality mapping. While our method would definitely benefit from a high-quality mapping from one modality to another, we will show that it remains robust to an imperfect contributor.

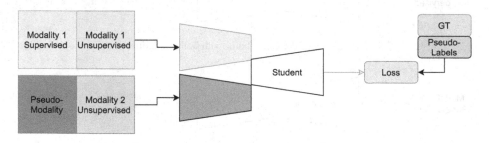

Fig. 4. Training of the student using both the supervised data with Pseudo-Modality (from the contributor) and the unsupervised data with Pseudo-Labels (from the teacher).

3.4   Student Training

Once our teacher and contributor networks have been trained, we can used them to train our student model. Let us recall that, at this step, we rely on both a supervised set (x_{sup}^1, y_{sup}) and an unsupervised set (x_{uns}^1, x_{uns}^2) where $x^1 \in \mathcal{M}_1$ and $x^2 \in \mathcal{M}_2$. To train the student, we then define a new dataset ds as follows:

$$ds = (x_{sup}^1, \mathcal{C}_\psi^c(x_{sup}^1), y_{sup}) \cdot (x_{uns}^1, x_{uns}^2, S(\mathcal{C}_\theta^s(x_{uns}^1))) \tag{5}$$

with $\cdot$ denotes the set concatenation operator.

We then use this dataset to train our student in a similar way that we would have done with a supervised dataset as shown with Fig. 4. However, since in our semantic segmentation scenario, the pseudo-labels come from a filtering step, some of the pixels in the image remain without label. This specific situation needs to be taken into account when defining the loss function in order to rely solely on pixel with either a label or a pseudo-label.

3.5 On the Use of Pre-training

Let us note that, since we use a previously trained model as the teacher, one can rely on its weights to initialize the student. Furthermore, as done in Cross-Modal Distillation [13], we can even initialize the weights for the new modality part of the model. To this end, we pretrain the second modality encoder to predict features similar to those returned by the first modality encoder. While this setup seems appealing, it may be counterproductive to "lock" different encoders to monomodal setups as it may reduce the benefits of multimodality. However, it remains hard to predict if the same effects occur for each scenario. Still, our training framework is compatible with such techniques.

4 Experiments

4.1 Settings

We evaluate our method on the ISPRS Potsdam dataset [1]. This dataset has the advantage of coming with several modalities, in particular orthophotos (RGB) as well as the associated digital surface model (DSM). We propose to modify this dataset in order to adapt it to our problem, where we need an RGB dataset with annotations as well as an RGB+DSM dataset without annotation. We show the splits used for our experiments in Fig. 5.

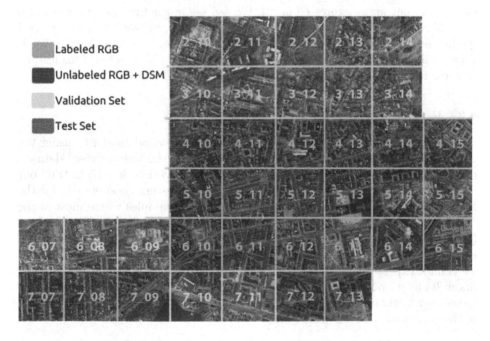

Fig. 5. Design of our dataset from ISPRS Potsdam [1].

As far as our Student and Teacher are concerned, we use networks based on Adapnet and SSMA [18], where we kept the ResNet downsampling layers and adjust the decoder accordingly, using upsampling layers instead of transposed convolutions. These networks have some properties that fit well our problems. Both unimodal and multimodal networks share the same decoder architecture. The decoder uses a eASPP module that has the same purpose as ASPP from DeepLab [5]. All encoders are based on ResNet. These backbones allow us to use publicly available ImageNet pretrain weights for their initialization. Furthermore, the principle of our method is to add a modality, and this architecture let us reuse the previously trained unimodal model.

We used ResNet-50 as backbone for both our Teacher and the RGB encoder of our Student, and ResNet-18 for the DSM encoder. We use a similar ResNet-50 network for our Contributor that we adapted for a regression task. Our multi-modal model also includes stochastic depth [15] to add noise during training. We also used several augmentations such as image scaling, color modification or geometrical changes.

4.2   Pseudo-labels

Because we choose to use a fully labeled dataset to test our method, we are able to precisely evaluate the different steps of our pipeline. Our first step is to generate pseudo-labels, and some examples are provided in Fig. 6. We then apply a filtering to keep only 5% of the labels, selecting the ones with the highest probability output as expressed in (2). We can see in the first four rows of Fig. 6 that this selection is able to erase errors in prediction, allowing us to keep good quality labels. However, as observed in the last two rows, when the Teacher is very confident on wrong areas, the whole area tends to be selected, thus leading to some images having a majority of wrongly assigned labels.

4.3   Pseudo-modality

The second step of our method is to estimate the second modality using the unlabeled dataset. We first train our contributor on the unsupervised dataset, using RGB as input and DSM as GT. We use scale-invariant loss [7] to train our contributor. Looking at Fig. 7, we can see the results seem good enough for the first three rows. However, the last three rows show examples where most of the DSM is null, we observe a lot of noise in the predictions. For DSM estimation (a.k.a. depth estimation in computer vision), we could have used a more sophisticated model in order to obtain better results. But in a more general scenario, we cannot expect dedicated models to be publicly available, so this contributor fits well our purpose. Because we have access to the true DSM, we are also able to test our method in the case of a perfect contributor and thus to see the impact of the contributor on the final results.

4.4 Results

Table 1. Experimental results on ISPRS Potsdam. We compare our teacher with multiple scenarios: direct application of our method as described in Sect. 3 (student), student weight initialization with both teacher and cross-modal weights (student pretrain), and possible result in case of a perfect contributor (considering ground truth DSM).

	Impervious surfaces	Building	Low vegetation	Tree	Car	Clutter/ background	mIOU
Teacher	79.56%	*82.05%*	**82.52%**	71.99%	71.31%	*34.63%*	56.96%
Student	*80.89%*	81.82	*80.12%*	**80.71%**	*86.02%*	29.68%	*57.25%*
Student PreTrain	76.43%	71.98%	67.11%	68.64%	83.59%	**48.50%**	52.50%
Student with perfect contributor	**82.03%**	**87.33%**	72.47%	*75.92%*	**89.85%**	*42.21%*	**59.56%**

The quantitative results are given in Table 1 using as evaluation metrics, the precision per pixel (accuracy) for each class, as well as the mean intersection over union (mIOU).

For the teacher results, we see that there are three classes that reached lower scores, namely tree, car and clutter. We expect our method to improve scores for these classes while not degrading the others. A full application of our method is thus given in the second line of the table. We note that, in this case, for the first three classes (impervious surfaces, buildings and low vegetation), the results are close to those of the teacher. However, for the next two (trees and cars), the performance significantly grows with the student. Finally, the last class (clutter) is much worse with the student. While those results seem to indicate that the student benefits from the addition of a modality, we could also expect a class like building to benefit more from our student.

Thus, further investigation through qualitative examples may help to see the benefit of our method as well as failure cases. This qualitative evaluation of segmentation maps produced by the different networks is illustrated in Fig. 8. Overall, the segmentation maps seem to be of higher quality with the student, and we can notice that even here the impervious surfaces and buildings classes seem to benefit from the addition of modality. Moreover, the student's predictions on the last two lines seem to indicate the presence of trees instead of low vegetation, as confirmed by the DSM. To understand the differences between qualitative and quantitative analyses, it is interesting to look at situations where the student is put in failure, as illustrated in Fig. 9. In the first example, where only the water class is present, the DSM is very noisy, and the student produces a segmentation map which is also very noisy. This example concerns the clutter class, a class where the student's performance is clearly worse than that of the teacher. In the test scenario, we notice that this situation occurs frequently, degrading the overall performance of the student. In the second row, one can see an image of a roof

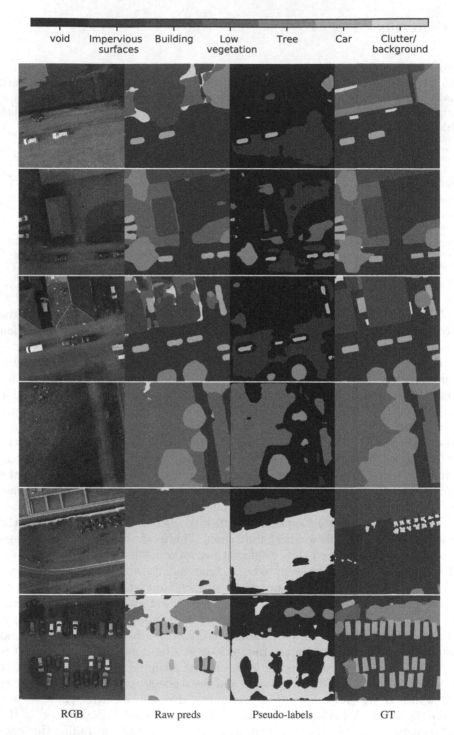

Fig. 6. Illustration of label selection: first four lines show when good labels remain after selection, while last two lines illustrate bad quality pseudo-labels.

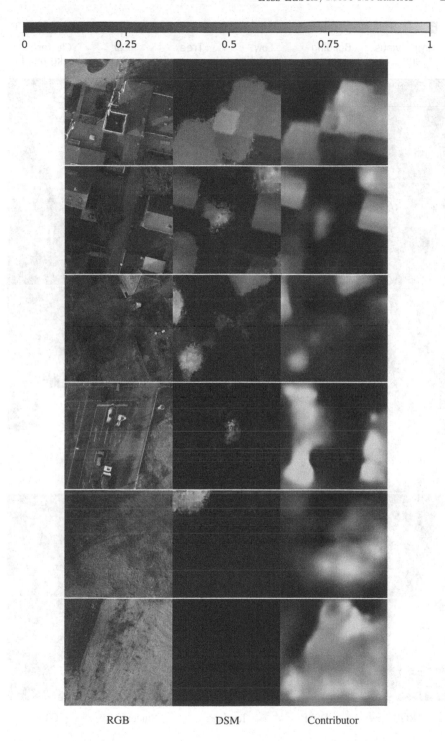

0   0.25   0.5   0.75   1

RGB   DSM   Contributor

Fig. 7. Contributor's prediction on the labeled set from our Potsdam split: first three lines show when contributor performances are acceptable, while last three rows illustrate when predictions are very far from the Ground Truth.

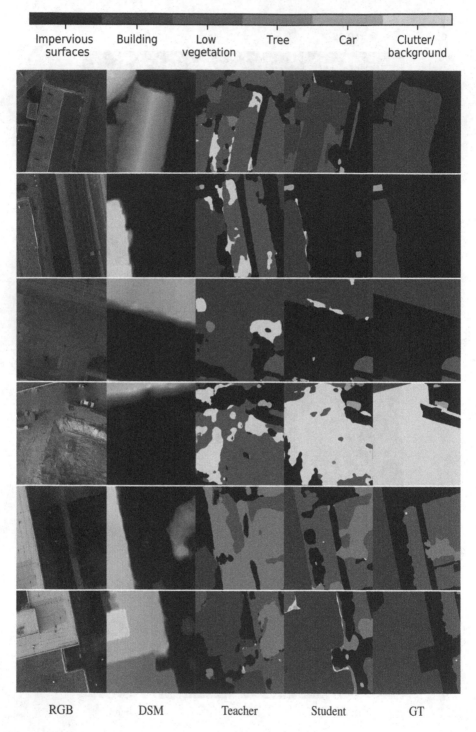

Fig. 8. Comparison between results from monomodal teacher and (largely outperforming) multimodal student network.

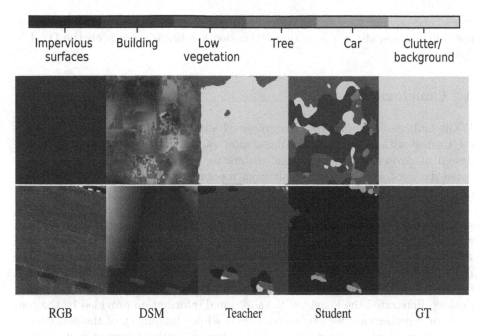

Fig. 9. Failure cases of the student w.r.t. teacher network.

with two elements standing out on the DSM. We also note that, for the roof, the DSM is not regular, whereas we could have expected one. The student confuses the two elements with cars and also predicts the roof as an impervious surface, going hand in hand with the presence of cars. Thus we notice that, unlike the teacher, the errors are more generalized here: the network is mistaken uniformly over an entire surface, which quantitatively harms the results, but gives more meaning to the visual analysis of the results.

We also tested the case where we initialized our model with pretrained weights from our teacher for the RGB part, as well as weights from distillation for the DSM part. While this model is the top performer for the clutter class, it is overall the worst model, even worse than the teacher. This seems to indicate that such initialisation may not be a good idea when encoders are expected to return different features.

Finally, our last test considers a perfect contributor. To do so, we use the ground truth for the DSM modality instead of the output from our contributor. We can see that in this case, the student had better performances for the building class as was expected, but performs very poorly on low vegetation and not that well on trees. Globally, the class that benefits a lot from DSM in all cases is the class car.

To conclude, adding a modality (even in an unsupervised way) allows us to obtain more consistent segmentation maps. For some classes such as trees or cars, which are rarer classes and whose instances are smaller (therefore more difficult classes), the student is more precise, thus confirming that the network takes good advantage of the DSM for the segmentation of these classes. However, the failure cases also show us that the network relies too much on the DSM in some cases.

5   Conclusion

While multimodal approaches have received a lot of attention due to their interest to deal with remote sensing data, most of the existing works focus on the design of novel architectures, that require to be trained on specifically annotated datasets, and do not benefit from monomodal deep networks pretrained on existing labeled datasets.

We advocate that adding a modality to a deep learning process can be achieved without the cost of an additional annotation phase. We support our claim through a novel self-training framework, that rely not only on teacher and student networks, but also includes a contributor network whose goal is to generate pseudo-modalities for the annotated data, thus making possible to reuse existing annotations in a multimodal scenario. Experiments conducted on the ISPRS Potsdam dataset illllustrated the benefit of the additional information provided by the contributor. Furthemore, we also showed that, while the quality of the contributor obviously matters, the model can still be enhanced without a good contributor.

In this study, we assumed that monomodal labeled and multimodal unlabeled datasets came from the same domain, i.e. correspond to the same geographical area. In future work, we aim to alleviate this assumption by including a domain adaptation strategy in our framework.

Acknowledgements. This work is funded by the region Bretagne and the GIS BreTel via the doctoral project ALTER, and by the FEAMP via the GAME OF TRAWLS project. This work benefited from access to the computing resources of IDRIS through the allocation of resources 2021-101245 allocated by GENCI.

References

1. ISPRS Potsdam. www.isprs.org/education/benchmarks/UrbanSemLab/2d-sem-label-potsdam.aspx. Accessed 18 Mar 2022
2. Arazo, E., Ortego, D., Albert, P., O'Connor, N.E., McGuinness, K.: Pseudo-labeling and confirmation bias in deep semi-supervised learning. In: International Joint Conference on Neural Networks (IJCNN) (2020). https://doi.org/10.1109/IJCNN48605.2020.9207304
3. Audebert, N., Le Saux, B., Lefèvre, S.: Beyond RGB: very high resolution urban remote sensing with multimodal deep networks. ISPRS J. Photogrammetry Remote Sens. **140**, 20–32 (2018)
4. Blum, A., Mitchell, T.: Combining labeled and unlabeled data with co-training. In: Proceedings of the Eleventh Annual Conference on Computational Learning Theory, pp. 92–100 (1998)

5. Chen, L.C., Papandreou, G., Kokkinos, I., Murphy, K., Yuille, A.L.: Deeplab: semantic image segmentation with deep convolutional nets, atrous convolution, and fully connected crfs. IEEE Trans. Pattern Anal. Mach. Intell. **40**(4), 834–848 (2017)
6. Dópido, I., Li, J., Marpu, P.R., Plaza, A., Bioucas Dias, J.M., Benediktsson, J.A.: Semisupervised self-learning for hyperspectral image classification. IEEE Trans. Geosci. Remote Sens. **51**(7), 4032–4044 (2013). https://doi.org/10.1109/TGRS.2012.2228275
7. Eigen, D., Fergus, R.: Predicting depth, surface normals and semantic labels with a common multi-scale convolutional architecture. In: Proceedings of the IEEE International Conference on Computer Vision (ICCV), pp. 2650–2658 (2015)
8. Fu, H., Gong, M., Wang, C., Batmanghelich, K., Tao, D.: Deep ordinal regression network for monocular depth estimation. In: Proceedings of the IEEE Conference on Computer Vision and Pattern Recognition (CVPR), June 2018
9. Garcia, N.C., Morerio, P., Murino, V.: Modality distillation with multiple stream networks for action recognition. In: Proceedings of the European Conference on Computer Vision (ECCV), pp. 103–118 (2018)
10. Godard, C., Mac Aodha, O., Brostow, G.J.: Unsupervised monocular depth estimation with left-right consistency. In: Proceedings of the IEEE International Conference on Computer Vision and Pattern Recognition (CVPR) (2017)
11. Godard, C., Mac Aodha, O., Firman, M., Brostow, G.J.: Digging into self-supervised monocular depth estimation. In: Proceedings of the IEEE International Conference on Computer Vision (ICCV) (2019)
12. Gou, J., Yu, B., Maybank, S.J., Tao, D.: Knowledge distillation: a survey. Int. J. Comput. Vis. **129**(6), 1789–1819 (2021)
13. Gupta, S., Hoffman, J., Malik, J.: Cross modal distillation for supervision transfer. In: Proceedings of the IEEE Conference on Computer Vision and Pattern Recognition (CVPR), pp. 2827–2836 (2016)
14. Hong, D., et al.: More diverse means better: multimodal deep learning meets remote-sensing imagery classification. IEEE Trans. Geosci. Remote Sens. **59**(5), 4340–4354 (2020)
15. Huang, G., Sun, Yu., Liu, Z., Sedra, D., Weinberger, K.Q.: Deep networks with stochastic depth. In: Leibe, B., Matas, J., Sebe, N., Welling, M. (eds.) ECCV 2016. LNCS, vol. 9908, pp. 646–661. Springer, Cham (2016). https://doi.org/10.1007/978-3-319-46493-0_39
16. Tasar, O., Happy, S., Tarabalka, Y., Alliez, P.: Semi2i: semantically consistent image-to-image translation for domain adaptation of remote sensing data. In: IEEE International Geoscience and Remote Sensing Symposium (IGARSS), pp. 1837–1840. IEEE (2020)
17. Triguero, I., García, S., Herrera, F.: Self-labeled techniques for semi-supervised learning: taxonomy, software and empirical study. Knowl. Inf. Syst. **42**(2), 245–284 (2015)
18. Valada, A., Mohan, R., Burgard, W.: Self-supervised model adaptation for multimodal semantic segmentation. Int. J. Comput. Vis. **128**(5), 1239–1285 (2019). https://doi.org/10.1007/s11263-019-01188-y
19. Voreiter, C., Burnel, J., Lassalle, P., Spigai, M., Hugues, R., Courty, N.: A cycle GAN approach for heterogeneous domain adaptation in land use classification. In: IEEE International Geoscience and Remote Sensing Symposium (IGARSS), pp. 1961–1964. IEEE (2020). https://doi.org/10.1109/IGARSS39084.2020.9324264

20. Xie, Q., Luong, M.T., Hovy, E., Le, Q.V.: Self-training with noisy student improves imagenet classification. In: Proceedings of the IEEE International Conference on Computer Vision and Pattern Recognition (CVPR) (2020)
21. Yarowsky, D.: Unsupervised word sense disambiguation rivaling supervised methods. In: 33rd Annual Meeting of the Association for Computational Linguistics, pp. 189–196 (1995)
22. Zhang, Y., Sidibé, D., Morel, O., Mériaudeau, F.: Deep multimodal fusion for semantic image segmentation: a survey. Image Vis. Comput. 104042 (2020)
23. Zhu, X.X., et al.: Deep learning in remote sensing: a comprehensive review and list of resources. IEEE Geosci. Remote Sens. Mag. 5(4), 8–36 (2017)
24. Zou, Y., Yu, Z., Kumar, B.V., Wang, J.: Unsupervised domain adaptation for semantic segmentation via class-balanced self-training. In: Proceedings of the European Conference on Computer Vision (ECCV) (2018)
25. Zou, Y., Yu, Z., Liu, X., Kumar, B.V., Wang, J.: Confidence regularized self-training. In: Proceedings of the IEEE/CVF International Conference on Computer Vision (ICCV), October 2019

Feature Transformation for Cross-domain Few-Shot Remote Sensing Scene Classification

Qiaoling Chen[1] , Zhihao Chen[1] , and Wei Luo[1,2]([⊠])

[1] South China Agricultural University, Guangzhou 510000, GD, China
[2] Pazhou Lab, Guangzhou 510330, GD, China
cswluo@gmail.com

Abstract. Effectively classifying remote sensing scenes is still a challenge due to the increasing spatial resolution of remote imaging and large variances between remote sensing images. Existing research has greatly improved the performance of remote sensing scene classification (RSSC) in recent years. However, these methods are not applicable to cross-domain few-shot problems where target domain is with very limited training samples available and has a different data distribution from source domain. To improve the model's applicability, we propose the feature-wise transformation module (FTM) in this paper. FTM transfers the feature distribution learned on source domain to that of target domain by a very simple affine operation with negligible additional parameters. Moreover, FTM can be effectively learned on target domain in the case of few training data available and is agnostic to specific network structures. Experiments on RSSC and land-cover mapping tasks verified its capability to handle cross-domain few-shot problems. By comparison with finetuning methods, FTM achieves better performance and possesses better transferability and fine-grained discriminability.

Keywords: Remote sensing scene classification · Few-shot learning · Cross-domain

1 Introduction

Remote sensing scene classification (RSSC) has attracted much attention in the field of optical remote sensing image processing and analysis in recent years, both due to the availability of high spatial-resolution images and its key role in wide applications, e.g., disaster detection [12], environmental monitoring [2], urban planning [37]. However, effectively classifying scenes from a newly obtained remote sensing image (RSI) is still nontrivial owing to the rich content brought by high-resolution, imaging conditions, seasonal changes and so on. Together with the difficulty of collecting sufficient labeled training samples, these factors make the robust-performance of RSSC a very challenging task.

To improve the performance of RSSC, deep learning methods [10,15,35] have been widely used in RSSC. The deep learning based RSSC methods made use of

© Springer Nature Switzerland AG 2023
J.-J. Rousseau and B. Kapralos (Eds.): ICPR 2022 Workshops, LNCS 13645, pp. 303–316, 2023.
https://doi.org/10.1007/978-3-031-37731-0_23

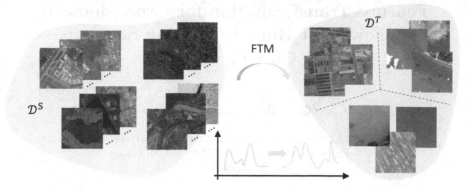

Fig. 1. Illustration of our motivation. Source domain $\mathcal{D}^S$ has sufficient training samples for each class as shown here airplane, forest, lake, and river. Target domain $\mathcal{D}^T$ may have different classes from $\mathcal{D}^S$ and provides only few training samples for each class (here 3 samples for paddy field, river, and lake, respectively). As shown here, $\mathcal{D}^S$ and $\mathcal{D}^T$ have a significant domain gap. The proposed FTM tries to transfer the feature distribution learned on $\mathcal{D}^S$ to matching that of $\mathcal{D}^T$ by an affine transformation with a negligible number of additional parameters, thus improving the applicability of models learned on $\mathcal{D}^S$ to cross-domain few-shot tasks.

the hierarchical network structure and feature abstraction ability of deep models to extract robust features for classification [3,17,26] and have achieved a great success, although they usually set aside the distribution differences between the training and testing data. While in a more realistic setting, the distribution difference was explicitly taken into consideration (under the framework of domain adaption) to build more applicable RSSC models like [23,28,46]. These methods usually require the same class distribution in the source and target domains. In addition, existing methods are almost all built on the prerequisite that sufficient training samples are available on target domain. This is, however, a very strict constraint on many real RSSC applications, especially in those target samples from a different distribution.

To address the difficulty of cross-domain RSSC tasks with few training samples, we propose a feature-wise transformation module (FTM) in deep CNNs with a two-stage training strategy. FTM borrows the idea from feature-wise linear modulation (FiLM) [29] but works in the unconditional setting and can be inserted in every convolutional layer. It attacks the cross-domain problem by transforming the distribution of features learned on source domain into matching that of target domain (see Fig 1). To achieve this, a pair of scale and shift vectors is applied to convolutional layers element-wisely. This pair of vectors, however, is not learned on source domain with the backbone network parameters, but instead trained on target domain without touching those already learned backbone parameters on source domain, which is different from [27,29,38] where the FiLM parameters are learned with the backbone network in an end-to-end manner. This two-stage training strategy can also alleviate the phenomenon of overfitting on target tasks with few labeled training samples due to the parsimonious parameters involved in the second training stage. Generally, the two-stage training strategy and the parsimonious usage of parameters in FTM make it well adapted to scenarios with limited labeled training samples and class distribution mismatching between domains. We compare FTM with finetuning methods in this study and show its better prediction performance, transferability, and fine-grained discriminability. We notice that there is no existing work to deal with this problem in RSSC and we approach this problem in this study with the following contributions:

– We propose FTM for cross-domain few-shot RSSC. FTM transforms the feature distribution of source data into that of matching the target data via an affine transformation.
– We propose a two-stage training strategy in which only FTM parameters are involved in the second training stage on target tasks, thus alleviating the overfitting problem.
– We validate the effectiveness of FTM on two cross-domain few-shot RSSC tasks and demonstrate its applicability to land cover mapping tasks.

2   Related Work

Remote sensing scene classification (RSSC) has gained great progress in recent years since the publication of several benchmark datasets such as AID [43] and NWPU [5], which promote the application of deep models in RSSC. In early studies, researches focus on directly transferring deep features [26] or exploring deep network structures to utilize multi-layer [11,17,24] or multi-scale features [21,22,42] for classification, thus fully exploiting granularity information in RSIs [41]. Another line of research highlights the importance of local structures and geometries and proposes to combine them with global features for more discriminative representation [18,19,45]. Recently, the attention mechanism is further incorporated in selectively attending informative areas [40] or assigning objects with different weights for feature fusion [3]. In addition, nonlocal attentions are also studied to integrate long-range spatial relationships for RSSC [9]. Although the mainstream deep learning methods are absorbed quickly by the RSSC field and much progress has been achieved, these methods, however, are not applicable to the setting in this paper where the training and testing data have different distributions.

Few-shot learning (FSL) has attracted much attention in recent years where the target tasks have very few training samples available. To tackle this problem, a large-scale labeled dataset is usually supposed to be available for prior knowledge learning and the learned prior knowledge can be adapted to guide the model learning on target tasks, thus alleviating the overfitting problem in few-shot scenarios. The methodologies can be roughly grouped into three categories. The metric-learning based methods [33,34,39] target at learning an embedding space where an off-the-shelf or learned metric can be performed well. In contrast, the meta-learning based methods [8,16,31] aim to make the learned model fast adapt to unseen novel tasks at the test stage. Recently, the finetuning based methods [4] report exciting results by exploiting multiple subspaces [20] or assembling multiple CNN features [6]. Meanwhile, FSL is also developed in settings like incremental learning [32,36], cross-domain learning [30,38], etc. However, very few works investigate FSL in RSSC while it is widely admitted as a practical problem in RSSC.

Domain adaption (DA) has gone through thorough studies and has been introduced to RSSC for a long time. The research on DA in RSSC mainly borrows ideas of existing DA approaches such as finetuning models on target domain [37], minimizing the maximum mean discrepancy between the source and target data distributions [28]. Specifically, [46] argues that the conditional distribution alignment is also important to cross-scene classification, thus they propose to combine the marginal and conditional distributions for more comprehensive alignment. To achieve fine-grained alignment, [47] tries to capture complex structures behind the data distributions for improved discriminability and reduce the local discrepancy of different domains to align the relevant category distributions. In addition, the class distribution misaligned problem is investigated in [23] by multisource compensation learning. Nevertheless, these methods assume sufficient training samples available on target domain. [44] studies the cross-domain task with limited target samples in RSSC, their training samples on the target domain is, however, orders of magnitude larger than ours.

3 Approaches

In this section, we propose FTM in deep CNNs that adapts the feature distribution learned on source domain to that of target domain. Assuming a well-labeled large-scale dataset and a newly acquired RS image with a small number of labeled samples annotated from it, we define two domains, the source domain $\mathcal{D}^S$ and the target domain $\mathcal{D}^T$, respectively. The data of the two domains may from different classes, $\mathcal{C}^S \neq \mathcal{C}^T$ and $\mathcal{C}^S \cap \mathcal{C}^T \neq \emptyset$. Our approach first learns a backbone network on $\mathcal{D}^S$, and then adapts the backbone feature maps by FTM on $\mathcal{D}^T$ without touching the backbone network parameters. In the following, we start by introducing FTM, followed by describing its training strategy, and then present the FTM network (Fig. 2).

3.1 Feature-Wise Transformation Module

Modern deep CNNs usually include BN [13] layers that reduce internal covariate shift and preserve feature distributions via a learned affine transformation for training efficiency. This operation inspires us to model different feature distributions by adjusting the feature map activations of a learned CNN, expecting it can perform well on a different domain with few training examples.

Supposing a backbone network has been trained on $\mathcal{D}^S$. Feature-wise transformation module (FTM) transforms the feature map by a pair of scale and shift vectors (γ, β). Concretely, assuming the feature map of an input $X \in \mathbb{R}^{3 \times H \times W}$

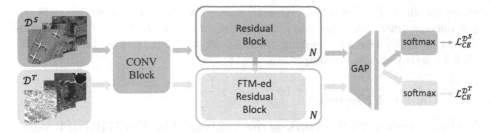

Fig. 2. Overview of the proposed FTM network. The detail of the FTM-ed residual block is depicted in Fig. 3(b). Our approach first trains a backbone network (shaded by gray blocks) on the source domain $\mathcal{D}^S$ and then uses it to initialize a corresponding FTM network (shaded by blue blocks). The aligned parts between the two networks are then fixed and only the remained parts of the FTM network are learned on the target domain $\mathcal{D}^T$ by $\mathcal{L}_{CE}^{\mathcal{D}^T}$. The light green blocks are shared. Best viewed in color. (Color figure online)

from the l-th layer is $\boldsymbol{f}^l \in \mathbb{R}^{C \times H' \times W'}$, FTM transforms the distribution of $\boldsymbol{f}^l$ by modulating its activations:

$$\tilde{\boldsymbol{f}}_c^l = \boldsymbol{\gamma}_c^l \odot \boldsymbol{f}_c^l + \boldsymbol{\beta}_c^l, \tag{1}$$

where the subscript c represents feature channel indices and $\odot$ means element-wise multiplication, $\boldsymbol{\gamma}^l, \boldsymbol{\beta}^l \in \mathbb{R}^C$ are learnable parameters. FTM approaches the change of distribution of $\boldsymbol{f}^l$ by independently changing the activations of each feature channel. Compared to FiLM [29], where $(\boldsymbol{\gamma}, \boldsymbol{\beta})$ are generated by a conditioning network, FTM works in a unconditional setting and simply initializes $\boldsymbol{\gamma}$ and $\boldsymbol{\beta}$ to $\mathbf{1}$ and $\mathbf{0}$, respectively. Moreover, FTM is learned on target domain instead of source domain. By noting that the BN transform recovers feature activations through an affine operation, FTM further adapts it to a larger range and recovers the BN transform at $\boldsymbol{\gamma} = \mathbf{1}$ and $\boldsymbol{\beta} = \mathbf{0}$.

3.2 Optimization

To alleviate the overfitting phenomenon of deep CNNs with FTM on target domain with few labeled training samples, we study a two-stage learning strategy for optimization. Recalling that our target is transforming the feature distribution learned on source domain into that of target domain, we prefer to keep the backbone parameters unchanged and only train FTM on target data. To this end, we first optimize the backbone network by regular training on $\mathcal{D}^S$, then we fix the backbone network parameters and optimize FTM parameters $\{\boldsymbol{\gamma}, \boldsymbol{\beta}\}$ on $\mathcal{D}^T$ through SGD.

Intuitively, we put FTM between the BN layers and nonlinear activations. It seems weird at first that applies two affine transformations – BN and FTM successively, but the separated mechanism can bring advantages to optimization and introduce different functions (see experiments). This operation, however, will cause the shift of mid-level feature activations if we keep the backbone network parameters untouched, thus complicating optimization. To this end, we free the statistics of BN layers by making them adapt to input changes and leave the shift in activations to be compensated by $\{\gamma, \beta\}$.

3.3 The FTM Network

We instantiate our FTM network on the backbone of ResNet-34 [10]. It is worth noting that FTM is agnostic to specific CNN structures and we choose ResNet-34 just for simplicity. ResNet-34 includes one convolutional stem and 4 stages with each several residual blocks. Each residual block has two convolutional layers to form a shortcut connection. We construct the corresponding FTM network by inserting FTM after the BN layer of the second convolutional layer of the last residual block in one or several stages. For simplicity, we insert FTM after the BN layer of the last stage in ResNet-34 to illustrate its strength in this work. The transformed feature maps are then rectified by ReLU [25] and globally averaged pooled to be fed into a softmax function for classification. Figure 3 shows the FTM-ed residual bock in conv5.

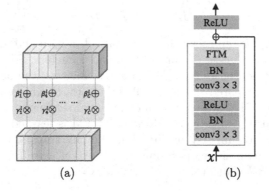

(a)   (b)

Fig. 3. (a) The shaded part is FTM, which operates on feature maps channel-wise. $\otimes$ and $\oplus$ represent element-wise multiplication and addition. (b) A FTM-ed residual block.

4   Experiments

In this section, we evaluate the transferability of the FTM network on two cross-domain few-shot applications: an RSSC task and a land-cover mapping task.

Table 1. Learning hyper-parameters of FTM and FT on $\mathcal{D}^T$.

	batch	epochs	lr	step	decay	opt
FT	64	50	0.001	15	0.1	Adam
FT-full	64	50	0.0001	15	0.1	Adam
FTM/FT-bn	64	50	0.003	15	0.1	Adam

4.1 Datasets

Two datasets – NWPU-RESISC45 [5] (hereinafter called NWPU) and AID [43] are separately employed as source domain $\mathcal{D}^S$ in our experiments. Both of them are collected from Google Earth RGB images but with different pixel resolution ranges. NWPU images are with pixel resolutions ranging from 30m to 0.5m. It has 700 sizes of 256×256 images for each class with a total of 45 scene classes such as residential areas, river, and commercial areas. AID has 220 to 420 images with each of size 600×600 and pixel resolutions ranging from 8m to 0.5m in each class with a total of 30 classes, e.g., farmland and port. The two datasets have 19 classes in common that share the same semantic label. In addition, NWPU captures more fine-grained labels than AID. For example, the farmland class in AID is further divided into circular farmland, rectangular farmland, and terrace in NWPU.

The target domain data are from the R, G, and B channels of GID [37] multispectral images, which are collected from Gaofen-2 satellite with a spatial resolution of 4m. GID provides two subsets – a large-scale classification set (Set-C) and a fine land-cover classification set (Set-F). Set-C includes 150 and 30 training and validation images of size 6800×7200 with each pixel annotated into 5 coarse categories. Set-F has a subset of $6,000$ image patches with train/val/testing $1500/3750/750$ respectively. The image patches are of size 224×224 and belong to 15 fine-grained categories, which are subcategories of the 5 coarse categories of Set-C. Set-F is used as $\mathcal{D}^T$ and Set-C is only used for land-cover mapping evaluation. We report the average performance over 5 trials on the RSSC tasks.

4.2 Implementation

We experiment with a FTM network based on the ResNet-34 backbone. The ResNet-34 pretrained on ImageNet [7] is first employed to learn on $\mathcal{D}^S$, where random crops of size 224×224 are used for training and 60 and 100 images from each class are kept for validation on AID and NWPU, respectively. We train ResNet-34 by Adam [14] on $\mathcal{D}^S$ for 30 epochs with batch size 128, lr 10^{-4}, and decay lr by 0.1 every 10 epochs. After this stage, we select the best-performed one to initialize the FTM network, keep the aligned parameters fixed, and learn the remained parameters on $\mathcal{D}^T$ for the few-shot RSSC tasks. The learning hyper-parameters are presented in Table 1.

For the land-cover mapping task, we classify every pixel into one of the 5 coarse classes by combining the output probabilities of subcategories that belong to the same coarse category.

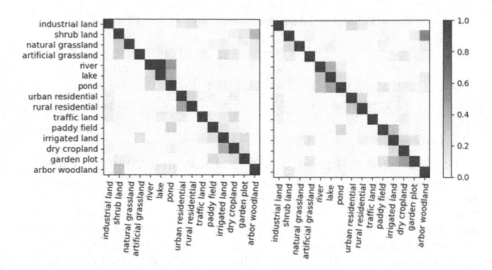

Fig. 4. Confusion matrices of FT-bn (left) and FTM (right) networks on the testing set of Set-F. Both networks are trained with 10 shots on Set-F.

Baseline: we compare FTM network with the finetuning (FT) method, which only finetunes the classification head of ResNet-34 trained on $\mathcal{D}^S$ on $\mathcal{D}^T$. In addition, FT-bn additionally finetunes the last BN layer on FT. See Table 1 for learning hyper-parameters.

4.3 Experimental Results

RSSC Results. Table 2 and 3 compare the performance of FT, FT-bn and FTM under various available shots on $\mathcal{D}^T$. The results are obtained from the testing set of Set-F, and show that FTM improves the performance over FT (and FT-bn) by $> 3.1\%$ and $> 4.0\%$ on average respectively, demonstrating the advantages of FTM. Interestingly, the performance of FT-bn is only comparable to FT, lagging behind FTM apparently. This illustrates the different functions of BN and FTM in a residual block and signifies that additional affine transformation after BN can achieve additional effects that are beyond the effects brought in by BN. In addition, Table 2 and 3 illustrate that the performance of FT, FT-bn and FTM can be steadily improved with more training shots and the improvement of FTM over FT and FT-bn is relatively stable independent of the number of available training shots. These observations validate that FTM possesses the ability to transform the feature distribution learned on $\mathcal{D}^S$ into that of target domain even with very limited training shots available on the target domain, thus alleviating the tendency to overfitting on target domain.

To understand which aspects of advantages brought by FTM, we make an analysis of the confusion matrices of FTM and FT-bn networks trained with 10 shots on Set-F and with $\mathcal{D}^S$ NWPU in Fig. 4. It can be seen that FTM has a more concentrated diagonal distribution than FT-bn, indicating its better

Table 2. Accuracy on Set-F under different shots with $\mathcal{D}^S$ NWPU ($\sqrt{\sigma} < 0.03$).

	3	5	10	15	20	30	50
FT	0.50	0.57	0.65	0.71	0.73	0.73	0.81
FT-bn	0.50	0.55	0.65	0.71	0.72	0.73	0.81
FTM	**0.53**	**0.59**	**0.69**	**0.73**	**0.77**	**0.77**	**0.84**

Table 3. Accuracy on Set-F under different shots with $\mathcal{D}^S$ AID ($\sqrt{\sigma} < 0.03$).

	3	5	10	15	20	30	50
FT	0.51	0.53	0.63	0.67	0.71	0.71	0.79
FT-bn	0.50	0.57	0.64	0.67	0.71	0.71	0.79
FTM	**0.55**	**0.59**	**0.67**	**0.73**	**0.75**	**0.75**	**0.83**

classification performance, especially in those subcategories belonging to the same coarse category. The same phenomenon is also observed on Set-F with $\mathcal{D}^S$ AID. Specifically, we find that FTM can well separate urban residential from rural residential and distinguish between river, lake, and pond effectively, which are respectively from the same coarse categories – built-up and water, while these are confused by the FT-bn. This signifies that FTM has the ability to transform the original feature space into a more delicate and discriminative space where the subtle differences between fine-grained categories can be better ascertained, even in the case of very limited training shots available.

Land Cover Mapping Results. To verify that FTM can improve models' applicability to across-domain tasks, we perform the land-cover mapping task on two randomly selected GID images from the Set-C validation set. The two GID images are taken from different locations and seasons showing a big domain gap to the images in $\mathcal{D}^S$. For simplicity, we do not annotate additional training samples from the two GID images as the target domain data but directly use the Set-F training samples as target domain data since they are obtained from the same satellite. In addition, we only compare FTM to FT in this task because of the better performance of FT than FT-bn in RSSC.

To achieve pixel-level mapping, we on the one hand segment the full GID image into 224×224 patches and classify them by using the FTM (or FT) networks, on the other hand, we segment the full GID image into 100 superpixels by using SLIC [1] and align them with the 224×224 patches. Finally, we assign labels to superpixels by assembling the labels of 224×224 patches within the corresponding superpixels and labeling them by winner-take-all.

Table 4 shows the average F1 scores of the FT and FTM networks evaluated on the 224×224 patches of the two GID images. By comparison, FTM shows a clear advantage over FT, achieving higher performance in all categories. Noting that there is no meadow class because the image has no pixels belonging to it. Further, it is worth special attention that the improvement on farmland is very significant raising from 55.3% to **86.3%**. These improvements further validate

Table 4. F1 scores (%) of FT and FTM networks on land-cover mapping tasks with 3 training samples each class.

	FT3	FTM3
Farmland	55.3	86.3
Built-up	80.6	90.0
Forest	35.2	53.0
Water	84.8	90.5
Average	64.0	80.0

the wide applicability of FTM to cross-domain few-shot tasks considering that we even do not annotate training samples from the target image.

Fig. 5. The land-cover mapping results. (a, e) are RGB images from GID validation set. (b, f) are ground-truth annotations. (c, g) and (d, h) are mapping results from FTM and FT, respectively. The numbers at the bottom of (c, d, g, h) are class average F1 scores evaluated on 224 × 224 image patches.

We further visualize the mapping results in Fig. 5. From it we find that large variances exist between GID images. This poses great challenges to models applicability where a large number of annotated training samples are usually needed to be recollected to retrain the model. However, FTM can alleviate the annotation requirements. The third and fourth columns of Fig. 5 show prediction results. By comparison, we conclude that FTM can effectively predict the main areas in the image and keep the smoothness between neighboring superpixels. In contrast, FT fails to achieve these effects and results in fragmented superpixels. For example, large areas of farmland are mismapped into built-up by FT while correctly mapped by FTM. This is because seasonal changes cause large differences between the source and target domains in the farmland class, thus when the labeling information of the target data is limited, it is incapable of FT to effectively represent contextual properties of this scene class. Although the visualization effects are far behind satisfaction, we, however, should note that our purpose is to validate the adaptability of FTM across domains while not the mapping accuracy, which can be achieved via much smaller image patches and more superpixels.

5   Conclusion

In this paper, we studied a feature-wise transformation module (FTM) that adapts feature distributions learned on source domain to that of target domain and verified that it has better transferability and fine-grained discriminability relative to fine-tuning methods, especially in cases of limited training shots available. Although it is simple, FTM shows great applicability to the RS field where large domain gaps exist and available training samples are extremely limited.

Problems remain. We notice that FTM still cannot well separate samples from visually similar classes, thus limiting its performance to a certain degree. This can be observed from the confusion matrices. The reason may be due in part to the affine transformation of FTM, which cannot nonlinearly scale features thus limiting its ability to explore more discriminative space. In addition, the performance of FTM still lacks robustness, although it performs better than FT and FT-bn on average. This is reflected in the land cover mapping tasks on Set-C, where the performance of FTM on different trials with different training samples varies. This phenomenon also indicates the weakness of FTM to reshape the feature space. We will explore these in our future work.

Acknowledgements. This work was supported in part by NSFGD (No.2020A15150 10813), STPGZ (No.202102020673), Young Scholar Project of Pazhou Lab (No.PZL2021KF0021), and NSFC (No.61702197).

References

1. Achanta, R., Shaji, A., Smith, K., Lucchi, A., Fua, P.V., Süsstrunk, S.: Slic superpixels compared to state-of-the-art superpixel methods. IEEE Trans. Pattern Anal. Mach. Intell. **34**, 2274–2282 (2012)
2. Alcántara, C., Kuemmerle, T., Prishchepov, A.V., Radeloff, V.C.: Mapping abandoned agriculture with multi-temporal modis satellite data. Remote Sens. Environ. **124**, 334–347 (2012)
3. Cao, R., Fang, L., Lu, T., He, N.: Self-attention-based deep feature fusion for remote sensing scene classification. IEEE Geosci. Remote Sens. Lett. **18**, 43–47 (2021)
4. Chen, W.Y., Liu, Y.C., Kira, Z., Wang, Y., Huang, J.B.: A closer look at few-shot classification. In: ICLR (2019)

5. Cheng, G., Han, J., Lu, X.: Remote sensing image scene classification: benchmark and state of the art. Proc. IEEE **105**, 1865–1883 (2017)
6. Chowdhury, A., Jiang, M., Jermaine, C.: Few-shot image classification: Just use a library of pre-trained feature extractors and a simple classifier. In: ICCV (2021)
7. Deng, J., et al.: Imagenet: a large-scale hierarchical image database. In: CVPR (2009)
8. Finn, C., Abbeel, P., Levine, S.: Model-agnostic meta-learning for fast adaptation of deep networks. In: ICML (2017)
9. Fu, L., Zhang, D., Ye, Q.: Recurrent thrifty attention network for remote sensing scene recognition. IEEE Trans. Geosci. Remote Sens. **59**, 8257–8268 (2021)
10. He, K., Zhang, X., Ren, S., Sun, J.: Deep residual learning for image recognition. In: CVPR (2016)
11. He, N., Fang, L., Li, S., Plaza, A.J., Plaza, J.: Remote sensing scene classification using multilayer stacked covariance pooling. IEEE Trans. Geosci. Remote Sens. **56**, 6899–6910 (2018)
12. Huang, X.Z., Han, X., Ma, S., Lin, T., Gong, J.: Monitoring ecosystem service change in the city of shenzhen by the use of high-resolution remotely sensed imagery and deep learning. Land Degrad. Dev. **30**(12), 1490–1501 (2019)
13. Ioffe, S., Szegedy, C.: Batch normalization: accelerating deep network training by reducing internal covariate shift. In: ICML (2015)
14. Kingma, D.P., Ba, J.: Adam: a method for stochastic optimization. CoRR abs/1412.6980 (2015)
15. Krizhevsky, A., Sutskever, I., Hinton, G.E.: Imagenet classification with deep convolutional neural networks. In: NIPS (2012)
16. Lee, K., Maji, S., Ravichandran, A., Soatto, S.: Meta-learning with differentiable convex optimization. In: 2019 IEEE/CVF Conference on Computer Vision and Pattern Recognition (CVPR), pp. 10649–10657 (2019)
17. Li, E., Xia, J., Du, P., Lin, C., Samat, A.: Integrating multilayer features of convolutional neural networks for remote sensing scene classification. IEEE Trans. Geosci. Remote Sens. **55**, 5653–5665 (2017)
18. Li, F., Feng, R., Han, W., Wang, L.: High-resolution remote sensing image scene classification via key filter bank based on convolutional neural network. IEEE Trans. Geosci. Remote Sens. **58**, 8077–8092 (2020)
19. Li, Z., Xu, K., Xie, J., Bi, Q., Qin, K.: Deep multiple instance convolutional neural networks for learning robust scene representations. IEEE Trans. Geosci. Remote Sens. **58**, 3685–3702 (2020)
20. Lichtenstein, M., Sattigeri, P., Feris, R.S., Giryes, R., Karlinsky, L.: Tafssl: task-adaptive feature sub-space learning for few-shot classification. In: ECCV (2020)
21. Liu, Q., Hang, R., Song, H., Li, Z.: Learning multiscale deep features for high-resolution satellite image scene classification. IEEE Trans. Geosci. Remote Sens. **56**, 117–126 (2018)
22. Liu, Y., Zhong, Y., Qin, Q.: Scene classification based on multiscale convolutional neural network. IEEE Trans. Geosci. Remote Sens. **56**, 7109–7121 (2018)
23. Lu, X., Gong, T., Zheng, X.: Multisource compensation network for remote sensing cross-domain scene classification. IEEE Trans. Geosci. Remote Sens. **58**, 2504–2515 (2020)
24. Lu, X., Sun, H., Zheng, X.: A feature aggregation convolutional neural network for remote sensing scene classification. IEEE Trans. Geosci. Remote Sens. **57**, 7894–7906 (2019)
25. Nair, V., Hinton, G.E.: Rectified linear units improve restricted boltzmann machines. In: ICML (2010)

26. Nogueira, K., Penatti, O.A.B., dos Santos, J.A.: Towards better exploiting convolutional neural networks for remote sensing scene classification. ArXiv abs/1602.01517 (2017)
27. Oreshkin, B.N., Rodriguez, P., Lacoste, A.: Tadam: task dependent adaptive metric for improved few-shot learning. In: NeurIPS (2018)
28. Othman, E., Bazi, Y., Melgani, F., Alhichri, H.S., Alajlan, N.A., Zuair, M.A.A.: Domain adaptation network for cross-scene classification. IEEE Trans. Geosci. Remote Sens. **55**, 4441–4456 (2017)
29. Perez, E., Strub, F., Vries, H.D., Dumoulin, V., Courville, A.: Film: visual reasoning with a general conditioning layer. In: AAAI (2018)
30. Phoo, C.P., Hariharan, B.: Self-training for few-shot transfer across extreme task differences. In: ICLR (2021)
31. Ravi, S., Larochelle, H.: Optimization as a model for few-shot learning. In: ICLR (2017)
32. Ren, M., Liao, R., Fetaya, E., Zemel, R.S.: Incremental few-shot learning with attention attractor networks. In: NeurIPS (2019)
33. Snell, J., Swersky, K., Zemel, R.S.: Prototypical networks for few-shot learning. In: NIPS (2017)
34. Sung, F., Yang, Y., Zhang, L., Xiang, T., Torr, P.H.S., Hospedales, T.M.: Learning to compare: relation network for few-shot learning. 2018 IEEE/CVF Conference on Computer Vision and Pattern Recognition, pp. 1199–1208 (2018)
35. Szegedy, C., et al.: Going deeper with convolutions. In: CVPR (2015)
36. Tao, X., Hong, X., Chang, X., Dong, S., Wei, X., Gong, Y.: Few-shot class-incremental learning. In: 2020 IEEE/CVF Conference on Computer Vision and Pattern Recognition (CVPR) (2020)
37. Tong, X.Y., et al.: Land-cover classification with high-resolution remote sensing images using transferable deep models. Remote Sens. Environ. **237**, 111322 (2018)
38. Tseng, H.Y., Lee, H.Y., Huang, J.B., Yang, M.H.: Cross-domain few-shot classification via learned feature-wise transformation. In: ICLR (2020)
39. Vinyals, O., Blundell, C., Lillicrap, T.P., Kavukcuoglu, K., Wierstra, D.: Matching networks for one shot learning. In: NeurIPS (2016)
40. Wang, Q., Liu, S., Chanussot, J., Li, X.: Scene classification with recurrent attention of VHR remote sensing images. IEEE Trans. Geosci. Remote Sens. **57**, 1155–1167 (2019)
41. Wang, S., Guan, Y., Shao, L.: Multi-granularity canonical appearance pooling for remote sensing scene classification. IEEE Trans. Image Process. **29**, 5396–5407 (2020)
42. Wang, X., Wang, S., Ning, C., Zhou, H.: Enhanced feature pyramid network with deep semantic embedding for remote sensing scene classification. IEEE Trans. Geosci. Remote Sens. **59**, 7918–7932 (2021)
43. Xia, G.S., Hu, J., Hu, F., Shi, B., Bai, X., Zhong, Y., pei Zhang, L., Lu, X.: Aid: a benchmark data set for performance evaluation of aerial scene classification. IEEE Trans. Geosci. Remote Sens. **55**, 3965–3981 (2017)
44. Yan, L., Zhu, R., Mo, N., Liu, Y.: Cross-domain distance metric learning framework with limited target samples for scene classification of aerial images. IEEE Trans. Geosci. Remote Sens. **57**, 3840–3857 (2019)
45. Yuan, Y., Fang, J., Lu, X., Feng, Y.: Remote sensing image scene classification using rearranged local features. IEEE Trans. Geosci. Remote Sens. **57**, 1779–1792 (2019)

46. Zhu, S., Du, B., pei Zhang, L., Li, X.: Attention-based multiscale residual adaptation network for cross-scene classification. IEEE Trans. Geosci. Remote Sens. **60**, 1–15 (2022)
47. Zhu, S., Luo, F., Du, B., pei Zhang, L.: Adversarial fine-grained adaptation network for cross-scene classification. In: 2021 IEEE International Geoscience and Remote Sensing Symposium IGARSS, pp. 2369–2372 (2021)

A Novel Methodology for High Resolution Sea Ice Motion Estimation

Kelsey Kaplan$^{(\boxtimes)}$ and Chandra Kambhamettu

Video/Image Modeling and Synthesis (VIMS) Lab, Department of Computer and
Information Sciences, University of Delaware, Newark 19716, DE, USA
{kelskap,chandrak}@udel.edu

Abstract. As changes in climate lead to rapid changes in Arctic sea ice
dynamics, there is a pressing need to provide methods for reliably monitoring sea ice motion. High-resolution sea ice motion estimation from
satellite imagery is a task still widely considered unresolved. While various algorithms exist, they are limited in their ability to provide dense
and accurate motion estimates with required spatial coverage. This paper
presents a novel, hybrid method using a combined feature tracking and
Optical Flow approach. It outperforms existing methods in sea ice literature in both density, providing a drift field with a resolution equal to
that of the image, and accuracy, with a displacement error of 74 m.

Keywords: Sea ice motion · High resolution · Tracking

1 Introduction

Over the last few decades, the Arctic's response to climate change has been
significant. Since satellite data first became available of the Arctic in 1979, sea
ice extent has steadily declined each decade [1], bringing with it a decrease in
sea ice concentration and an increase in sea ice drift velocity [14,21,25,29,33].
Understanding how these dynamics alter over time is a critical factor in uncovering the effects of climate change. Additionally, as ice retreat in the Arctic
brings increased opportunities for human activity, accurately characterizing current sea ice dynamics becomes vital for polar navigation, offshore operations,
and scientific research.

Sea ice dynamics are complex, as they are driven by a series of external factors in the ocean and atmosphere, and internal stresses inherent to the nature of
ice. The motion of sea ice is non-rigid and involves both continuous and discrete
particle motion. Its analysis can vary in spatial scale from meters to thousands of
kilometers, with each scale useful for some type of analysis. For example, when
looking at sea ice retreat over the entirety of the Arctic, extensive spatial coverage is required and the resolution of the dynamics will be much higher (~ 25 km).
Currently, there is a gap in the understanding of how sea ice dynamics relate to
small-scale processes occurring within the ice field [13]. High-resolution, dense,

© Springer Nature Switzerland AG 2023
J.-J. Rousseau and B. Kapralos (Eds.): ICPR 2022 Workshops, LNCS 13645, pp. 317–329, 2023.
https://doi.org/10.1007/978-3-031-37731-0_24

and accurate sea ice motion estimates are required to overcome this.

Estimating sea ice motion from satellite imagery began in the mid-1980s [12] and is still an active area of research today. In sea ice literature, methods used fall broadly into three categories referred to as pattern matching (PM), feature tracking (FT), and Optical Flow (OF).

PM techniques, such as normalized and maximum cross-correlation (NCC, MCC) [6,9,12,20,27], were the earliest employed. Thomas et al. [36] were the first to use Phase Correlation (PC), as it is illumination invariant and more computationally efficient. The algorithm consisted of a cascaded, multi-resolution motion estimation and interpolation scheme that uses a combination of PC and NCC. It was further developed by others [5,15,17].

Cross-correlation methods, however, struggle to reliably handle the rotational and deformational motion dynamics of sea ice. In most cases, an exhaustive search in which an image is iteratively rotated to compute cross-correlation at each angle must be performed [20]. Additionally, PM methods estimate block motion; a single motion vector is associated with a patch of pixels such that the spatial resolution of the estimated motion field is always coarser than the image resolution, and fine-scale motion details are lost.

On the other hand, FT methods can handle the non-linear motion of sea ice and independently estimate motion vectors for pixels in terms of position, magnitude, and orientation. FT methods are arguably the most widely used image matching techniques in Computer Vision (CV) and find correspondences between images by identifying geometric features, such as edges, corners, and blobs. In sea ice literature, both traditional features from CV algorithms, such as Scale-Invariant Feature Transform (SIFT) [23], Speeded-Up Robust Features (SURF), and Oriented FAST and Rotated BRIEF (ORB) [35], as well as hand-crafted features such as the geometric characteristics of extracted ice floes [19,20,22], have been used. However, FT is generally insufficient as ice features are often sparse, and resultant correspondences are unevenly distributed spatially. Therefore, to benefit from the advantages of both PM and FT methods, recent algorithms use FT as an initial step for coarse but reliable correspondences, after which they employ a PM approach to get a denser motion field [4,18,26,30,32,38].

The OF algorithm [16,24] and its adaptations [10,28] can efficiently find correspondences between images for every pixel, under the assumption that the brightness of a moving object remains constant [16]. This assumption of brightness constancy and small motion makes it sensitive to noisy images and unreliable when estimating large or discontinuous motion; therefore, it has not been as frequently used for sea ice analysis. Petrou and Tian [31] show that when paired with a preliminary FT step, these problems are less significant. They apply an edge detection algorithm to images to obtain sparse matches before applying OF to get dense motion estimates. Although they obtained sub-pixel motion, they applied this algorithm to higher resolution images of 250 m per pixel and obtained a relatively high displacement error of 5.7 km.

While all existing algorithms provide useful analysis in terms of fine-scale motion, they are either lacking in density, estimating drift fields at a resolution far greater than the image resolution, or in accuracy, with displacement errors greater than 100 m.

In this paper, we present a novel, hybrid method for sea ice motion estimation that is dense, providing a drift field with a resolution equal to that of the image, and highly accurate, with a displacement error within 2 pixels, of 74 m. Our method outperforms those presented in current sea ice literature in terms of quantitative error and spatial resolution of the drift field.

The paper is ordered as follows. We first provide the details of the data used and a description of our methodology, following which we present our experiments and results. We conclude with a brief discussion and summary of work we would like to undertake in the future.

2 Data

We use RADARSAT-2 satellite imagery and GPS buoy data acquired during the Sea Ice Dynamics Experiment (SIDEx) expedition, which took place in the Beaufort Sea in March 2021.

RADARSAT-2 is a C-band, Synthetic Aperture Radar (SAR) satellite launched by the Canadian Space Agency in 2007 [2]. SAR imagery is high resolution and unaffected by environmental conditions, penetrating cloud cover and capturing images at night. It is, however, affected by speckle noise and geolocation errors [8], which can significantly influence the appearance of ice features or the relative position of ice features to reference points, such as buoys, from one image to the next.

Fifty-nine images with HH polarization and a resolution of either 20 m or 50 m were acquired. The average time between consecutive images was 30.97 h. Higher resolution images were downsampled to a 50 m resolution, and all were cropped to a 40 km × 40 km area, centered around Buoy 23 at the SIDEx camp, as shown in Figs. 1 and 2. This puts the images and estimated motion into a Lagrangian Frame of Reference, removing the large-scale drift of the ice field such that only the differential motion relative to Buoy 23 needs to be estimated.
A total of 45 in-situ GPS buoys were deployed during the expedition, which we used for validation. To align buoy and satellite data, buoy locations at each image acquisition time were linearly interpolated.

3 Methodology

With the aim of both dense and accurate motion estimations in mind, we developed a hybrid algorithm that uses OF to provide dense estimates anchored by

Fig. 1. (a) A sample full-sized RADARSAT-2 image highlighting our area of interest, the SIDEx camp, centered around buoy 23 and (b) a 40 km × 40 km cropped RADARSAT-2 sample with all interpolated buoy points plotted.

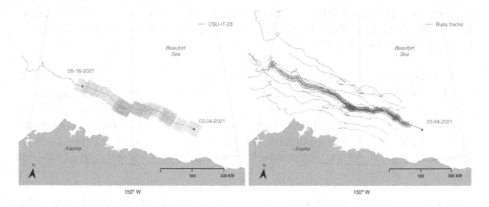

Fig. 2. (a) All acquired RADARSAT-2 images, cropped and plotted over the track of buoy 23 and (b) all buoy data collected during the SIDEx expedition.

FT correspondences for accuracy. As illustrated in Fig. 3, for each image pair, we obtain initial OF estimates for the entire image and a set of sparse but reliable FT correspondences. For each FT correspondence, we rerun OF on a small patch of each image, centered on the matching feature coordinates, and use this result to update the initial OF estimates.

As OF fails in the presence of large motion, our algorithm's primary consideration was obtaining a sufficient number of well-distributed FT correspondences to prevent the OF algorithm from tracking any significant large motion.

FT algorithms generally consist of a feature extraction stage, where features are detected and then described in some vector form, and a matching stage, in

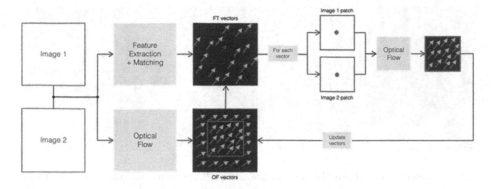

Fig. 3. The sea ice motion estimation algorithm pipeline, integrating FT, for accurate correspondences and OF, for dense matches.

Table 1. Results of Feature Extraction Evaluation for Each of the Approaches.

	Number of extracted features	Number of matches	Matched features [%]	Coverage [%]
Traditional	**10 057.14**	499.86	5.84	69.89
Learning-based	1681.86	759.57	45.13	80.56
Manual	961.00	**841.00**	**87.51**	**87.29**

which vectors are compared to find the best match. While traditional FT algorithms, such as SIFT, have been shown to reliably match descriptor vectors in a variety of domains, the large homogeneous regions present in sea ice images make the feature detection stage a challenging task, with traditional CV algorithms producing sparse and clustered features that are absent from large portions of the image. We consequently determined the first stage of the pipeline, feature extraction, to be the most crucial step of our algorithm.

We experiment with three methods to determine the best-suited approach to feature detection in the context of sea ice imagery. The first uses a traditional CV algorithm, SIFT, the second, a Deep Learning-based network, Greedily Learned Accurate Match Points (GLAMpoints) [37], which was developed to increase the spatial distribution of features detected on images with few features, and the third, bypasses an algorithmic approach to detection completely, manually defining features at specified locations.

Below we outline each of these approaches, after which we describe the remainder of the algorithm.

3.1 Feature Extraction

Traditional Feature Extraction. We used the SIFT algorithm, which performs feature detection by creating a scale-space of the image with Gaussian filtering to reduce image noise, finding the Difference of Gaussians to enhance image features, and employing NMS to detect local extrema points. For each detected feature, a 128-dimensional SIFT descriptor vector is created.

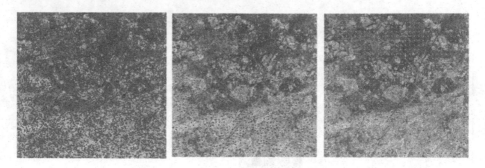

Fig. 4. Sample image from the test set showing all extracted features (red) and successfully matched features (green), using (a) traditional, (b) learning-based and (c) manual approaches. (Color figure online)

Learning-Based Feature Extraction. For a Learning-based approach, we implemented GLAMpoints [37]. It is trained for feature detection on the entire image matching pipeline but implements a traditional, SIFT-based approach for description and matching, enabling us to incorporate it into our pipeline easily. The network consists of a novel CNN-based framework, using a standard 4-level deep Unet architecture [34]. For each image I, a score map $S = f_\theta(I)$ is learnt. The score map has the same dimensions as the image, such that each score map coordinate has a one-to-one mapping with an image pixel. A high value on the score map is an indication of a good feature and is detected through an NMS filter. For each detection, a SIFT descriptor vector is created.

GLAMpoints learns in a semi-supervised manner, meaning it does not require ground truth data, and we could fine-tune the pre-trained network on sea ice images. Through experimentation, we found that the best results were obtained by training for an additional ten epochs with a batch size of 5. The 59 images were divided into a roughly 70:20:10 split for training, validation, and testing.

Manual Feature Extraction. With this approach, the SIFT descriptor is used in a PM-like manner. First, we manually designate features by creating SIFT descriptors on a regular grid in the first image. For each descriptor, we then create candidate matching descriptors for every pixel in a corresponding search window in the second image, from which we can select the best match.

We selected a 50×50 pixel search window, using the buoy tracks as a guide for the maximum sea ice motion and adding some padding. This method is not very computationally efficient, so we only obtain descriptors on a regular 25×25 pixel grid.

3.2 Feature Matching

The remainder of the pipeline for all three feature extraction methods is the same.

To match keypoints, we use a brute force matching scheme from OpenCV [7], BFMatcher, which compares descriptors in the first image to every candidate matching descriptor in the second image and, using the L1 norm as a distance measure, determines the best match by minimum vector distance.

To further improve matching, we utilize RootSIFT [3], which reduces large variations in the 128-vector SIFT descriptor by L1 normalizing each vector and taking the element-wise square root. This prevents larger values from dominating the descriptor and has been shown to boost matching performance [3].

Additionally, to ensure robust matches, we incorporate the ratio test recommended by Lowe [23]. A match is only accepted as valid if the distance from the descriptor in the first image to its best matching descriptor in the second image is smaller than 0.75 times the distance to the next best descriptor in the second image. This ensures the descriptor is sufficiently distinct and removes potentially ambiguous or incorrect matches.

As the manual extraction approach may select points that do not make good features, we added a step for outlier detection for this approach only. We compared the magnitude and orientation of matching pairs of points in vector form to that of its ten nearest neighbors to detect outliers. The vector was discarded if the difference was greater than some threshold for more than three neighbors. As discontinuities in the sea ice motion field mean neighboring vectors could have significantly differing values, these parameters had to be chosen carefully and were selected through experimentation and visual inspection of results.

3.3 OF Integration

In Optical Flow (OF), image pixel intensities I are considered functions of their spatial coordinates and time, $I(x, y, t)$. After time dt a pixel moves by (dx, dy), such that

$$I(x, y, t) = I(x + dx, y + dy, t + dt) \tag{1}$$

Using partial derivatives we get the OF equation

$$I_x u_x + I_y u_y + I_t = 0 \tag{2}$$

where $u_x = \frac{dx}{dt}$ and $u_y = \frac{dy}{dt}$. We used the Gunnar Farneback method [11] from OpenCV [7] to solve this equation for every pixel in the image.

For each FT match, we extracted a 25 × 25 pixel patch from the images to rerun OF and updated the estimates. This size patch was experimentally selected and appeared to provide the best balance between limiting OF to tracking only small motion and covering the majority of regions of the image based on the spatial coverage of FT points.

We also found that although initial OF estimates were altered using the patch update method, when overlapping patches occurred due to the proximity of FT points the OF estimates were so similar as to make the difference negligible. Therefore, we did not need to investigate methods of combining overlapping patch estimates.

4   Experiments and Results

Table 2. Mean Absolute Errors in EPE, Orientation and Magnitude, Averaged for All 208 Buoy Tracks Across 7 Test Images.

Method	EPE [pixels] (meters)	Orientation error [degrees]	Magnitude error [pixels] (meters)
Traditional	2.89 (144.5)	33.21	2.67 (133.5)
Learning-based	1.52 (76)	15.67	**0.92 (46)**
Manual	**1.47 (73.5)**	**12.61**	0.94 (47)

Table 3. Mean Absolute Errors in Displacement and Velocity Components for All 208 Buoy Tracks Across 7 Test Images.

	Displacement error (x) [m]	Displacement error (y) [m]	Velocity error (x) [cm/s]	Velocity error (y) [cm/s]
Traditional	80.07	94.27	0.11	0.13
Learning-based	40.83	42.77	**0.06**	**0.05**
Manual	**39.55**	**40.46**	0.06	0.05

Fig. 5. Sample buoy vectors (red) and motion estimation results (green) from (a) traditional, (b) learning-based and (c) manual approaches. (Color figure online)

We tested the three variations of our algorithm on the 7 test set image pairs, evaluating results quantitatively in terms of feature extraction and tracking accuracy.

4.1   Feature Extraction Evaluation

In the context of sea ice motion estimation we have two primary considerations for feature extraction, the spatial coverage of detected features and the quality of extracted features.

Spatial coverage is computed by assigning each matched feature a circle of 25 pixel radius, as used in GLAMpoints [37] and generating a mask over the image. We then calculate the percentage of masked image pixels.

By quality, we mean that we want to extract features that are likely to obtain a match. Detected features may be discarded during the matching stage if no match is found or due to the ratio test, indicating that the feature was not sufficiently distinct. Quality is therefore evaluated by calculating the percentage of detected features that are successfully matched.

Qualitatively, we can see improved coverage and spatial distribution of learning-based detections over traditional in Fig. 4, which shows clustered matched features that are almost completely absent from the darker homogeneous regions. The improvement is more clearly observed in Table 1, which shows that although the traditional approach has a far higher initial number of features extracted, only a small percentage are successfully matched. As expected, manual extractions provide the best coverage and distribution of features. The fact that they also have the highest percentage of successfully matched features is surprising, as points are not selected based on heuristics of what makes a good feature. We attribute this to the efficacy of SIFT descriptors and the search window, which limits the ability of the approach to select bad matches. This evaluation, however, is not a measure of matching accuracy but rather only whether a feature is matched. The former we evaluate in the following section.

4.2   Tracking Evaluation

We quantitatively evaluate sea ice motion estimation accuracy using buoy vectors. Given (x_1, y_1) are the coordinates of the buoy in image one, (x_2, y_2) are the coordinates of the buoy in image two, and $(\hat{x}_2, \hat{y}_2)$ the estimated corresponding point in image two, we evaluate endpoint error (EPE) as

$$EPE = \sqrt{(\hat{x}_2 - x_2)^2 + (\hat{y}_2 - y_2)^2} \qquad (3)$$

We also calculate errors in orientation and magnitude between the buoy and estimated vectors. If the vector magnitude was less than a pixel, the error in orientation was disregarded.

Displacement was defined in real terms by multiplying by the 50 m pixel resolution. We calculated displacement error for x and y components separately and found velocity error by dividing displacement by the difference in acquisition time between an image pair.

Tables 2 and 3 show that learning-based and manual approaches achieve competitive results, with the manual approach only slightly better in most categories.

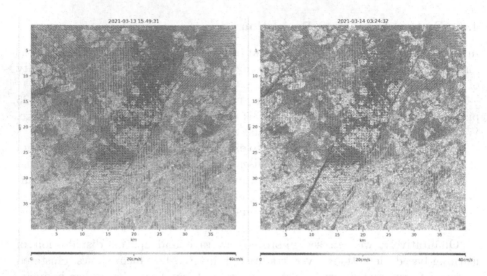

Fig. 6. Motion estimated results from the manual approach shown on a pair of images, with vectors color coded according to speed and buoys plotted in red. We can clearly see that motion is only incoherent across lead features and consistent across the rest of the image. (Color figure online)

Both achieve fewer than 2 pixels for EPE and less than a pixel in magnitude, which could be attributed to geolocation errors. Both of these methods outperform the traditional approach, and while an error difference of ~1.3 pixels is seemingly small, it becomes significant when converted to a real distance of 65 m.

Due to the limited number of buoys, we also performed a qualitative analysis. As seen in Fig. 5, the best results are clearly achieved with the manual approach. While challenging to see in static images, sudden inconsistencies in the motion field which are not clearly bordered by sea ice lead features are incorrect.

As the traditional approach produces a sparsity of correspondences, many regions of the estimated motion track incorrectly. While expanding the patch size of updates could, in theory, correct this, it also leads to the tracking of large motion and more incorrect estimates.

In the learning-based approach, we can see a smaller portion of incorrect regions, for example, towards the bottom right region, where no motion suddenly appears to be estimated.

The manual approach provides the most consistent and coherent motion field due to the better spatial distribution and coverage of initial FT points, despite these features not necessarily being good features to track.

In terms of efficiency, however, the learning-based approach outperforms the manual, extracting features in an average time of 1.34 s per image, while manual extraction takes 38.25 s per image. This could become a serious consideration if estimation needs to be included in a real-time tracking system.

5   Conclusions and Future Work

This paper presents the development and results of feature extraction and tracking methods for sea ice imagery. We have shown that feature extraction from SAR images with few features can benefit from a learning-based approach, improving spatial coverage with only a small amount of fine-tuning. Also, the efficacy of traditional SIFT descriptors allowed us to bypass algorithmic feature detection altogether, still finding reliable matches through manually defined features.

Our learning-based and manual approaches outperform existing high-resolution sea ice motion estimation algorithms in terms of spatial resolution of the motion field and quantitative error. We have vector estimates for every pixel resulting in a $50 \, m^2$ motion field, which is better than the current best we could find of $200 \, m^2$ from Petrou and Tian [31]. Our best EPE of 1.47 pixels, or 73.5 m, is superior to the previous best result of 150 m from Hollands [15].

Additionally, our method is effective even without preprocessing images to reduce speckle noise and, due to using OF, does not require incorporating algorithms for interpolating motion to increase drift estimate resolution.

Overall, the success of was surprising as much of the literature states it is not a viable method for sea ice motion estimation. This could be due to large motion in our study area being reduced through a Lagrangian Frame of Reference, or our area of study is in a Non-Marginal Ice Zone with comparatively less activity. The most likely reason, however, is that the high density of our FT points ensures OF does not have to estimate large motion.

In the future, we would like to further perform sub-pixel motion analysis by implementing a self-supervised Deep Learning network and using supersampling techniques. We would also like to develop a method to use estimated motion vectors to establish the boundaries of coherent motion of the ice field, which would enable the detection of active leads and better analysis of floe-floe interaction.

Acknowledgements. The authors would like to thank Dr. Jennifer Hutchings, Dr. Chris Polashenski, Dr. Andy Mahoney and the other members of the SIDEx team for their contributions to this work in the form of data collection and invaluable input and feedback. This work was supported by the Office of Naval Research (ONR), Arctic and Global Prediction Program as part of the Sea Ice Dynamics Experiment (SIDEx) under award number N00014-19-1-2606.

References

1. National snow and ice data center. https://nsidc.org/data/seaice_index/ (2020), https://nsidc.org/cryosphere/icelights/arctic-sea-ice-101, Accessed 03 Oct 2021

2. Agency, C.S.: What is radarsat-2. https://www.asc-csa.gc.ca/eng/satellites/radarsat2/what-is-radarsat2.asp, January 2021, https://www.asc-csa.gc.ca/eng/satellites/radarsat2/what-is-radarsat2.asp, Accessed 03 Dec 2021

3. Arandjelović, R., Zisserman, A.: Three things everyone should know to improve object retrieval. In: 2012 IEEE Conference on Computer Vision and Pattern Recognition, pp. 2911–2918. IEEE (2012)

4. Berg, A., Eriksson, L.E.: Investigation of a hybrid algorithm for sea ice drift measurements using synthetic aperture radar images. IEEE Trans. Geosci. Remote Sens. **52**(8), 5023–5033 (2013)

5. Berg, A., Eriksson, L.E., Borenäs, K., Lindh, H.: Observations and analysis of sea ice motion with the ice buoy driva during the 2010 spring field campaign in the bay of bothnia. Chalmers University of Technology, Technical Report (2011)

6. Bowen, M.M., Emery, W.J., Wilkin, J.L., Tildesley, P.C., Barton, I.J., Knewtson, R.: Extracting multiyear surface currents from sequential thermal imagery using the maximum cross-correlation technique. J. Atmos. Oceanic Technol. **19**(10), 1665–1676 (2002)

7. Bradski, G.: The OpenCV library. Dr. Dobb's J. Softw. Tools **25**(11), 120–123 (2000)

8. Dierking, W., Stern, H.L., Hutchings, J.K.: Estimating statistical errors in retrievals of ice velocity and deformation parameters from satellite images and buoy arrays. Cryosphere **14**(9), 2999–3016 (2020)

9. Emery, W., Radebaugh, M., Fowler, C., Cavalieri, D., Steffen, K.: A comparison of sea ice parameters computed from advanced very high resolution radiometer and landsat satellite imagery and from airborne passive microwave radiometry. J. Geophys. Res. Oceans **96**(C12), 22075–22085 (1991)

10. Farneback, G.: Very high accuracy velocity estimation using orientation tensors, parametric motion, and simultaneous segmentation of the motion field. In: Proceedings Eighth IEEE International Conference on Computer Vision. ICCV 2001, vol. 1, pp. 171–177. IEEE (2001)

11. Farnebäck, G.: Two-frame motion estimation based on polynomial expansion. In: Bigun, J., Gustavsson, T. (eds.) SCIA 2003. LNCS, vol. 2749, pp. 363–370. Springer, Heidelberg (2003). https://doi.org/10.1007/3-540-45103-X_50

12. Fily, M., Rothrock, D.: Sea ice tracking by nested correlations. IEEE Trans. Geosci. Remote Sens. **5**, 570–580 (1987)

13. Griebel, J.: Improvements and Analyzes of Sea Ice Drift and Deformation Retrievals from SAR Images. Ph.D. thesis, Universität Bremen (2020)

14. Hakkinen, S., Proshutinsky, A., Ashik, I.: Sea ice drift in the arctic since the 1950s. Geophys. Res. Lett. **35**(19) (2008)

15. Hollands, T., Dierking, W.: Performance of a multiscale correlation algorithm for the estimation of sea-ice drift from SAR images: initial results. Ann. Glaciol. **52**(57), 311–317 (2011)

16. Horn, B.K., Schunck, B.G.: Determining optical flow. Artif. Intell. **17**(1–3), 185–203 (1981)

17. Karvonen, J.: Operational SAR-based sea ice drift monitoring over the Baltic sea. Ocean Sci. **8**(4), 473–483 (2012)

18. Korosov, A.A., Rampal, P.: A combination of feature tracking and pattern matching with optimal parametrization for sea ice drift retrieval from SAR data. Remote Sens. **9**(3), 258 (2017)

19. Kwok, R., Schweiger, A., Rothrock, D., Pang, S., Kottmeier, C.: Sea ice motion from satellite passive microwave imagery assessed with ERS SAR and buoy motions. J. Geophys. Res. Oceans **103**(C4), 8191–8214 (1998)

20. Kwok, R., Curlander, J.C., McConnell, R., Pang, S.S.: An ice-motion tracking system at the Alaska SAR facility. IEEE J. Oceanic Eng. **15**(1), 44–54 (1990)
21. Kwok, R., Rothrock, D.: Decline in arctic sea ice thickness from submarine and ICESat records: 1958–2008. Geophys. Res. Lett. **36**(15) (2009)
22. Lopez-Acosta, R., Schodlok, M., Wilhelmus, M.: Ice floe tracker: an algorithm to automatically retrieve Lagrangian trajectories via feature matching from moderate-resolution visual imagery. Remote Sens. Environ. **234**, 111406 (2019)
23. Lowe, D.G.: Distinctive image features from scale-invariant keypoints. Int. J. Comput. Vision **60**(2), 91–110 (2004)
24. Lucas, B.D., Kanade, T., et al.: An iterative image registration technique with an application to stereo vision. Vancouver (1981)
25. Meier, W.N., et al.: Arctic sea ice in transformation: a review of recent observed changes and impacts on biology and human activity. Rev. Geophys. **52**(3), 185–217 (2014)
26. Muckenhuber, S., Sandven, S.: Open-source sea ice drift algorithm for sentinel-1 SAR imagery using a combination of feature tracking and pattern matching. The Cryosphere **11**(4), 1835–1850 (2017)
27. Ninnis, R., Emery, W., Collins, M.: Automated extraction of pack ice motion from advanced very high resolution radiometer imagery. J. Geophys. Res. Oceans **91**(C9), 10725–10734 (1986)
28. Nordberg, K., Farneback, G.: A framework for estimation of orientation and velocity. In: Proceedings 2003 International Conference on Image Processing (Cat. No. 03CH37429), vol. 3, pp. III-57. IEEE (2003)
29. Olason, E., Notz, D.: Drivers of variability in arctic sea-ice drift speed. J. Geophys. Res. Oceans **119**(9), 5755–5775 (2014)
30. Park, J.W., et al.: Feasibility study on estimation of sea ice drift from KOMPSAT-5 and COSMO-SkyMed SAR images. Remote Sens. **13**(20), 4038 (2021)
31. Petrou, Z.I., Tian, Y.: High-resolution sea ice motion estimation with optical flow using satellite spectroradiometer data. IEEE Trans. Geosci. Remote Sens. **55**(3), 1339–1350 (2016)
32. Qiu, Y.J., Li, X.M.: An adaptability for arctic sea ice drift retrieval from spaceborne SAR data. In: 2021 SAR in Big Data Era (BIGSARDATA), pp. 1–4. IEEE (2021)
33. Rampal, P., Weiss, J., Marsan, D.: Positive trend in the mean speed and deformation rate of arctic sea ice, 1979–2007. J. Geophys. Res. Oceans **114**(C5) (2009)
34. Ronneberger, O., Fischer, P., Brox, T.: U-net: convolutional networks for biomedical image segmentation. In: Navab, N., Hornegger, J., Wells, W.M., Frangi, A.F. (eds.) MICCAI 2015. LNCS, vol. 9351, pp. 234–241. Springer, Cham (2015). https://doi.org/10.1007/978-3-319-24574-4_28
35. Rublee, E., Rabaud, V., Konolige, K., Bradski, G.: Orb: an efficient alternative to sift or surf. In: 2011 International Conference on Computer Vision, pp. 2564–2571. IEEE (2011)
36. Thomas, M.V.: Analysis of Large Magnitude Discontinuous Non-Rigid Motion. Ph.D. thesis, USA (2008). aAI3337413
37. Truong, P., Apostolopoulos, S., Mosinska, A., Stucky, S., Ciller, C., Zanet, S.D.: Glampoints: greedily learned accurate match points. In: Proceedings of the IEEE/CVF International Conference on Computer Vision, pp. 10732–10741 (2019)
38. Zhang, M., An, J., Zhang, J., Yu, D., Wang, J., Lv, X.: Enhanced delaunay triangulation sea ice tracking algorithm with combining feature tracking and pattern matching. Remote Sens. **12**(3), 581 (2020)

Deep Learning-Based Sea Ice Lead Detection from WorldView and Sentinel SAR Imagery

Rohit Venkata Sai Dulam$^{(\boxtimes)}$, Kelsey Kaplan, and Chandra Kambhamettu

Video/Image Modeling and Synthesis (VIMS) Lab Department of Computer and Information Sciences, University of Delaware, Newark, DE 19716, USA
{rdulam,kelskap,chandrak}@udel.edu

Abstract. Sea ice leads are recurrent and elongated patches of open water, among the most distinguishing characteristics of sea ice cover. Leads act as a medium between the atmosphere above and seawater below, making it paramount to detect and understand them. We propose a deep learning-based approach for sea ice lead detection from visible-band WorldView and C-band Synthetic Aperture Radar Sentinel images using the U-Net deep neural network. We detect the boundaries of these leads due to their clear visual distinction from the neighboring sea ice. Furthermore, we show that our approach detects leads from multiple modalities using small amounts of training data. Finally, the proposed method is not susceptible to speckle noise in SAR imagery and produces accurate lead predictions.

Keywords: Sea Ice Leads · Deep Learning

1 Introduction

Sea ice is frozen seawater found mainly in the Arctic and Antarctic. It floats on the sea surface, insulating it from the sun's rays and stopping evaporation. Although polar regions contain most sea ice, it significantly influences global climatic conditions. Rising global temperatures have led to more significant sea ice melting, increasing seawater exposure to the sun. Unlike sea ice, seawater has a lower albedo resulting in less reflection of sunlight, in turn raising global temperatures further [1]. Hence, monitoring openings in sea ice cover is paramount in understanding the trend of rising global temperatures. Sea ice leads are elongated fractures in the sea ice cover that are hundreds of kilometers long, which expose seawater to the surface, making it one of the main phenomena of sea ice to monitor.

The World Meteorological Organization (WMO) defines a lead as a fissure in the ice more than 50 m wide, spanning several kilometers to hundreds of kilometers in length. Leads encourage a high heat and moisture exchange between the relatively warm water and the cold winter atmosphere. As a result, leads

© Springer Nature Switzerland AG 2023
J.-J. Rousseau and B. Kapralos (Eds.): ICPR 2022 Workshops, LNCS 13645, pp. 330–342, 2023.
https://doi.org/10.1007/978-3-031-37731-0_25

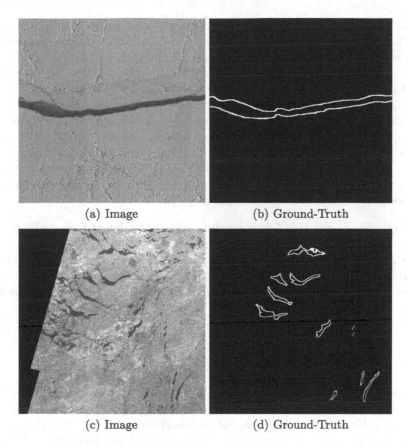

(a) Image   (b) Ground-Truth

(c) Image   (d) Ground-Truth

Fig. 1. (a) and (c) are the image patches used for training from WorldView and Sentinel, respectively. (b) and (d) indicate the ground truth annotations to be predicted by the deep learning model.

produce a significant amount of fresh ice, contributing to the seasonal sea-ice mass balance of the entire Arctic [1]. Leads have also been identified as a source of worldwide methane emissions, making them a potential greenhouse gas driver. Sea ice leads are also beneficial for navigation, as they have less ice cover making it easy for ice-breakers and submarines to go through the weaker ice formations. Finally, many animals like seals and whales rely on them for oxygen. Polar bears also rely on these leads for prey as animals come to the surface through these openings in sea ice for oxygen. Hence, a reliable and accurate system of automatic lead detection would aid in a better understanding of the Arctic and Antarctic environments.

Leads in the WorldView and Sentinel images are darker than sea ice, clearly demarcating the boundary between them. Hence, we detect the edges of these leads, which can be used to obtain the area covered by leads through additional post-processing. However, edge detectors like Canny [4] are susceptible to minute intensity changes due to a lack of context, thus producing noisy outputs. On the other hand, deep learning models learn context from data to distinguish between edges of leads and sudden intensity changes. Therefore, we propose an adaptive lead detection method using deep learning. We use the U-Net [17] deep learning model to output a binary map displaying the boundaries of leads, as shown in Fig. 1. Additionally, we use an edge detection-specific loss function to predict crisp and accurate boundaries. Finally, we train the U-Net model separately on two modalities: Worldview and Synthetic Aperture Radar (SAR) images. The results demonstrate that the proposed training pipeline can predict accurate lead boundaries in both modalities, providing a common framework to extend to other visual data-based lead detection. Our contributions can be summarized as follows -

1. We create a U-Net-based deep learning pipeline to detect boundaries of leads from WorldView and Sentinel SAR Imagery.
2. For accurate boundary maps, we use an edge detection-based loss function to train the deep learning model.
3. Our model predicts the precise boundaries of leads in both modalities from less training data.

2   Related Works

Multiple works have been proposed to detect sea ice leads. Schnell et al. [18] detect Arctic sea ice leads from lidar data using hydrometer plumes originating from them. Onana et al. [14] propose an algorithm called SILDAMS to detect clouds, extract leads and classify ice types from visual imagery. J. Rohrs et al. [16] proposed an algorithm to detect sea ice leads wider than 3 km using AMSR-E passive microwave imagery in the entire arctic ocean. Zakharova et al. [20] used SARAL/AltiKa (Satellite with ARgos and ALtiKa) altimeter to detect leads and monitor their spatio-temporal dynamics. Hoffman et al. [8] propose a lead detection method using satellite imagery's thermal infrared window channels. Reiser et al. [15] propose a lead detection algorithm from satellite thermal infrared images using Fuzzy logic. Similarly, machine learning approaches have also been proposed for lead detection. McIntire et al. [12] propose a three-stage feed-forward neural network-based model to classify Arctic sea ice, cloud water, and leads. They use .6-/spl mu/m data from the new Chinese Fengyun-1C satellite. Le et al. [10] have proposed a machine learning based system made of decision tree and random forest classifiers to detect leads from Cryosat-2 data using characteristics like stack standard deviation, stack skewness, stack kurtosis, pulse peakiness and backscatter sigma-0. Liang et al. [11] propose an entropy-weighted deep neural network for lead detection from Sentinel-1 SAR images. Different from above methods which work on a single type of data, we propose a generic deep learning pipeline that can detect leads from multiple modalities when trained separately.

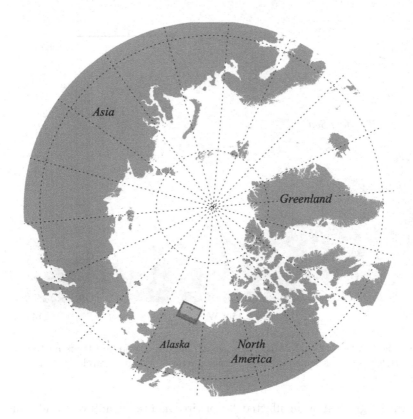

Fig. 2. Location of the SIDEx camp and acquired WorldView satellite imagery, north of Alaska in the Beaufort Sea.

3   Data

We obtained five sea ice images from the WorldView-1 and -2 satellites [2]. These commercial satellites are part of the WorldView constellation, acquiring high-resolution Earth observations. The satellites are visible-band, Very High Resolution (VHR) systems, providing panchromatic images with a resolution of less than a meter. We transformed the image data to the National Snow and Ice Data Center (NSIDC) Polar Stereographic projection for the Northern Hemisphere, EPSG 3413 [1]. All images were acquired during the Sea Ice Dynamics Experiment (SIDEx) project, which took place in the Beaufort Sea just north of Alaska, between March 13 and March 21, 2021, as seen in Figs. 2 and 3. The images roughly track the location of the SIDEx camp as it drifted westward, and each covers an area of approximately 15 km × 15 km. They show various lead features, varying in length and width from meters to kilometers in size.

Sentinel-1A is a C-band SAR satellite from the European Space Agency [3], providing images with a resolution of 40 m and wide swath width of roughly 290 km. While SAR imagery suffers from speckle noise due to the backscattering

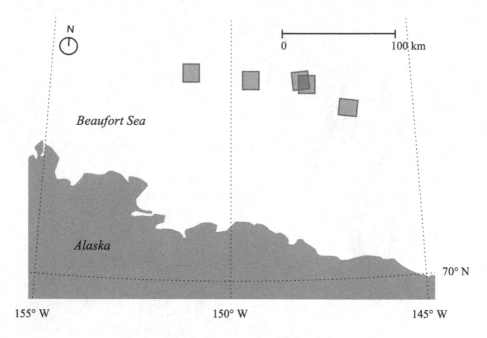

Fig. 3. The location of each WorldView image acquired, roughly tracking the location of the SIDEx camp as it drifted west between March 13 and March 21, 2021.

microwave signal, it is unaffected by environmental conditions and can capture images at night and penetrate cloud cover. Images were minimally preprocessed by reprojecting to the EPSG 3413 Polar Stereographic projection. Images acquired were from 29 and 30 September, and 1 and 8 October 2019, from various locations over the Arctic.

In this work, we annotate the five WorldView images shown in Fig. 2 to train and evaluate the deep learning model. For annotation, each WorldView image is divided into patches of size 512 × 512. Patches not containing a lead are discarded. After annotation, we obtain a total of 556 images. We further divide them into a train and test split. We use 540 images for training and the rest for testing. We further augment the training data by rotating each image in increments of 10°C, with the range of rotation being [−30, 30]. We use GIMP open-source image manipulation software for annotating our data. We treat the outermost layer of water touching the ice as the boundary of a lead and annotate it. We also annotate the boundaries of the freshly formed ice on top of open water as lead boundaries.

We also apply this method to Sentinel SAR-Imagery, where we annotate four images to train and test the U-Net deep learning model. We use the same annotation procedure used for WorldView imagery. While training, we use a patch size of 224 × 224. We do not apply additional preprocessing steps like speckle-noise reduction to our data.

4   Method

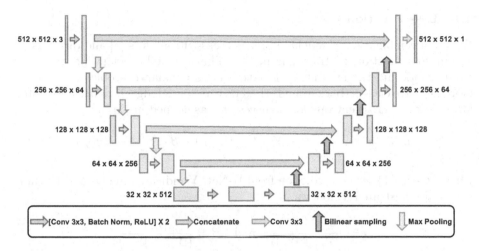

Fig. 4. U-Net deep learning architecture. The left half of the network depicts the encoding phase which sequentially encodes information and downsamples input to obtain global features. The decoding phase, the right half of the network, uses the encoded information to detect the boundary of leads. Conv 3×3 implies a convolution layer with 3×3 sized convolution weights. Patch size of 512×512 is used for illustration.

We use a U-Net [17] deep neural network to predict the boundaries of leads. Figure 4 illustrates the architecture of the model used. U-Net consists of two parts, an encoding phase and a decoding phase. The encoding phase, which follows the path of a typical convolutional neural network [7,19], takes the input and encodes features. The decoding phase uses these encoded features to predict the boundaries of these leads. The encoding phase consists of convolutional modules that contain two 3×3 convolutions and rectified linear unit (ReLU) [13] activation function applied sequentially. The network also uses a two-by-two max-pooling after each of the convolution blocks to reduce the spatial dimensions, just like other convolutional neural networks [7,19]. Slightly modifying the original architecture, we apply a batch normalization (BatchNorm) [9] layer right after the convolution layer and before the activation function. The decoding phase consists of similar convolution blocks used in the encoding phase. The only difference is the replacement of max-pooling layers with bilinear upsampling layers to increase the spatial resolution by two times in both the height and width dimensions. The convolutional block follows the upsampling operation. Additionally, features from the encoding phase are concatenated at each level as shown in Fig. 4. This concatenation operation guides the network by adding context information from the encoding phase. The network outputs a binary map containing the probability of each pixel. A higher probability of a pixel indicates that its part of a lead. We use a sigmoid layer at the end of our network to obtain these probabilities.

4.1 Loss Function

We use a combination of weighted binary cross-entropy loss [6] and dice loss [5] as our loss function to train our model. The probability maps produced by our network and the ground truth have a class imbalance problem. There are more negative classes (background) than positive ones (edges). Hence a weighted formulation of cross-entropy loss is necessary, as defined in Eq. 1.

$$L_{wbce} = -\alpha \cdot \sum_{i \in Y_-} (1 - Y) \cdot log(1 - \hat{y}_i) - \beta \cdot \sum_{i \in Y_+} Y \cdot log(\hat{y}_i) \tag{1}$$

where $\hat{y}_i \in \{0, 1\}$ is the prediction from U-Net. Y indicates the ground-truth. α and β are illustrated as follows -

$$\alpha = \frac{|Y_+|}{(|Y_+| + |Y_-|)} \quad \text{and} \quad \beta = \frac{|Y_-|}{(|Y_+| + |Y_-|)}$$

α and β indicate the proportion of positive and negative samples, respectively. Similarly, the dice loss is defined in Eq. 2 as follows,

$$L_{dice} = \frac{\sum_{i=1}^{N} p_i^2 + \sum_{i=1}^{N} g_i^2}{2 \cdot \sum_{i=1}^{N} p_i \cdot g_i} \tag{2}$$

where p_i and g_i indicate the prediction and ground-truth, respectively.

Dice-coefficient computes the similarity between the predicted binary map and ground truth. Using the reciprocal of this measure as a loss function has shown to benefit contour and edge, detection models. Adding this loss function to the weighted BCE loss primarily yields thinner and more precise boundaries compared to models trained only on the BCE loss. Equation 3 illustrates the final loss used to train the network.

$$L_{Final} = \lambda \cdot L_{wbce} + L_{dice} \tag{3}$$

In our experiments, we set λ to 0.001.

5   Experimental Setup and Evaluation

We train our model for 150 epochs and multiply the learning rate by 0.1 after every 30 epochs. We use an initial learning rate of 0.001. We use the weight initialization method in the original U-Net to initialize the weights of our network. We use two Titan X gpus of 12GB RAM each for training our network. To carry out our experiments, we use the PyTorch deep learning framework.

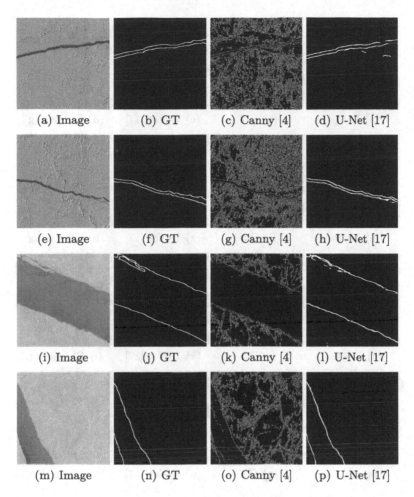

(a) Image	(b) GT	(c) Canny [4]	(d) U-Net [17]
(e) Image	(f) GT	(g) Canny [4]	(h) U-Net [17]
(i) Image	(j) GT	(k) Canny [4]	(l) U-Net [17]
(m) Image	(n) GT	(o) Canny [4]	(p) U-Net [17]

Fig. 5. Visual results of the U-Net deep learning model [17] compared to the Canny edge detector [4] on WorldView images. Our method demonstrates good results while being adaptive unlike Canny which needs a set of thresholds.

To evaluate our work, we use Mean Absolute Error (MAE). It computes the mean of absolute error between the predicted binary map and ground truth. Equation 4 shows the formula used to compute MAE.

$$MAE = \frac{\sum_{i=1}^{H} \sum_{j=1}^{W} |gt_{i,j} - pred_{i,j}|}{H * W} \tag{4}$$

Intersection-over-Union (IoU) is the second metric which determines the quality of our predictions by finding the overlap between the prediction and the ground-truth. We illustrate the formula for IoU in Eq. 5.

$$IoU = \frac{|A \cap B|}{|A \cup B|} \tag{5}$$

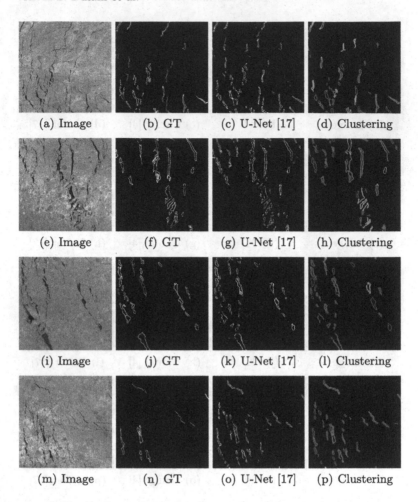

Fig. 6. Visual results of the U-Net deep learning model [17] on SAR images. We additionally cluster the predicted leads into three groups using height, width and orientation of these leads. K-means algorithm is used for clustering. Results from Canny edge detector are not included due to sub-optimal results.

A and B indicate the prediction and ground-truth, respectively.

We use F-measure as the third measure to illustrate the quality of our results. Precision is the ratio of true positives and the sum of true positives and false positives. Recall is the ratio of true positives to the sum of true positives and false negatives. Precision and recall values are obtained for all the images at every threshold from 0.01 to 0.99. F-measure is the weighted harmonic mean of Precision and Recall. Equation 6 illustrates the formula for calculating F-measure.

$$F - measure = \frac{(1 + \beta^2) \times Precision \times Recall}{\beta^2 \times Precision + Recall} \tag{6}$$

We report the maximum score over all the thresholds and β^2 is set to 0.3. Precision and Recall are illustrated in Eq. 7.

$$Precision = \frac{TP}{TP + FP} \quad \text{and} \quad Recall = \frac{TP}{TP + FN} \tag{7}$$

We report the max score over all the thresholds.

6 Results

Table 1. Empirical results of Canny edge detector and the U-Net deep learning model on worldview imagery. The values shown in the table are the average values computed for the 16 testing patches.

Method	MAE	IOU	max F-measure
Canny [4]	0.174	0.032	0.064
U-Net [17]	0.018	0.297	0.441

Table 2. IoU scores for images shown in Figure - 5

Method	Image	IOU
Canny [4]	Figure - 5 a	0.015
U-Net [17]	Figure - 5 a	0.466
Canny [4]	Figure - 5 e	0.013
U-Net [17]	Figure - 5 e	0.402
Canny [4]	Figure - 5 i	0.07
U-Net [17]	Figure - 5 i	0.414
Canny [4]	Figure - 5 m	0.016
U-Net [17]	Figure - 5 m	0.302

Table 3. Empirical results of the U-Net deep learning model on SAR imagery. The values shown in the table are the average values computed for the 27 testing patches.

Method	MAE	IOU	max F-measure
U-Net [17]	0.010	0.191	0.304

Table 4. IoU scores for images shown in Figure - 6

Method	Image	IOU
U-Net [17]	Figure - 6 a	0.274
U-Net [17]	Figure - 6 e	0.291
U-Net [17]	Figure - 6 i	0.270
U-Net [17]	Figure - 6 m	0.150

Figures 5 and 6 illustrate results of the proposed method. Unlike the output of the Canny edge detector in fig 5, the predictions of the deep learning model are agnostic to local intensity changes and thus look clearer. Fig 6 shows the results of the proposed model on SAR Imagery, which are again not affected by local illumination properties. Tables 1, 2, 3, and 4 illustrate the empirical results of our models. Table 1 shows the results of Canny and the proposed method on the 16 patches used for testing. As the proposed method can differentiate between the boundary of a lead and local intensity changes very precisely, it achieves a five to ten-fold betterment in performance across all the metrics. Table 2 illustrates empirical results on images shown in Fig. 5. Reinforcing the results shown in Table 1 and visual results in Fig. 5, our method gives far better numerical results than Canny. Similarly, Table 3 illustrates the empirical results of our method on 27 testing patches of Sentinel - 1 SAR imagery. Here, results from the Canny edge detector have been omitted due to sub-optimal results. Hence, we only show the results of the proposed method. Our method performs equally well across all metrics without requiring preprocessing techniques like speckle reduction. Table 4 indicates the results for images shown in Fig. 6. All these results demonstrate the ability of the proposed model to learn features necessary for predicting lead boundaries in different modalities.

7   Conclusion

This work proposes an automatic system to detect sea ice leads from World-View and Sentinel SAR imagery. Since leads contain open water, they are dark and visually distinct from the neighboring sea ice. Hence taking advantage of this visual difference, we formulate identifying leads as an edge detection task. We detect the edges of these leads using the U-Net deep learning network. Furthermore, we use an edge detection specific loss function for better prediction. Finally, we show that our method works on multiple modalities and provides a pipeline for future research in detecting sea ice leads from visual data.

Acknowledgement. This work was supported by the Office of Naval Research, Arctic and Global Prediction Program as part of the Sea Ice Dynamics Experiment (SIDEx) under award number N00014-19-1-2606. The authors would like to thank Dr. Jennifer Hutchings, Dr. Chris Polashenski, Dr. Andy Mahoney, and other members of the SIDEx team for their contributions to this work in the form of data collection and invaluable input and feedback.

References

1. National snow and ice data center. https://nsidc.org/data/polar-stereo/ps_grids. html (2020), Accessed 05 Oct 2022
2. https://earth.esa.int/eogateway/missions/worldview (2022)
3. Sentinel online. https://sentinel.esa.int/web/sentinel/home (2022), Accessed 13 May 2022
4. Canny, J.: A computational approach to edge detection. IEEE Trans. Pattern Anal. Mach. Intell. **PAMI-8**(6), 679–698 (1986). https://doi.org/10.1109/TPAMI.1986. 4767851
5. Deng, R., Shen, C., Liu, S., Wang, H., Liu, X.: Learning to predict crisp boundaries. In: Proceedings of the European Conference on Computer Vision (ECCV), pp. 562–578 (2018)
6. He, J., Zhang, S., Yang, M., Shan, Y., Huang, T.: Bi-directional cascade network for perceptual edge detection. In: Proceedings of the IEEE/CVF Conference on Computer Vision and Pattern Recognition, pp. 3828–3837 (2019)
7. He, K., Zhang, X., Ren, S., Sun, J.: Deep residual learning for image recognition. In: Proceedings of the IEEE Conference on Computer Vision and Pattern Recognition, pp. 770–778 (2016)
8. Hoffman, J.P., Ackerman, S.A., Liu, Y., Key, J.R.: The detection and characterization of arctic sea ice leads with satellite imagers. Remote Sens. **11**(5), 521 (2019)
9. Ioffe, S., Szegedy, C.: Batch normalization: accelerating deep network training by reducing internal covariate shift. In: International Conference on Machine Learning, pp. 448–456. PMLR (2015)
10. Lee, S., et al.: Arctic sea ice thickness estimation from cryosat-2 satellite data using machine learning-based lead detection. Remote Sens. **8**(9) (2016). https://doi.org/ 10.3390/rs8090698, https://www.mdpi.com/2072-4292/8/9/698
11. Liang, Z., Ji, Q., Pang, X., Zhao, X., Li, G., Chen, Y.: An entropy-weighted network for polar sea ice open lead detection from sentinel-1 SAR images. IEEE Trans. Geosci. Remote Sens. 1 (2022). https://doi.org/10.1109/TGRS.2022.3169892
12. McIntire, T., Simpson, J.: Arctic sea ice, cloud, water, and lead classification using neural networks and 1.6-/spl mu/m data. IEEE Trans. Geosci. Remote Sens. **40**(9), 1956–1972 (2002). https://doi.org/10.1109/TGRS.2002.803728
13. Nair, V., Hinton, G.E.: Rectified linear units improve restricted boltzmann machines. In: International Conference on Machine Learning (2010)
14. Onana, V.D.P., Kurtz, N.T., Farrell, S.L., Koenig, L.S., Studinger, M., Harbeck, J.P.: A sea-ice lead detection algorithm for use with high-resolution airborne visible imagery. IEEE Trans. Geosci. Remote Sens. **51**(1), 38–56 (2013). https://doi.org/ 10.1109/TGRS.2012.2202666
15. Reiser, F., Willmes, S., Heinemann, G.: A new algorithm for daily sea ice lead identification in the arctic and antarctic winter from thermal-infrared satellite imagery. Remote Sens **12**(12), 1957 (2020)
16. Röhrs, J., Kaleschke, L.: An algorithm to detect sea ice leads by using AMSR-e passive microwave imagery. Cryosphere **6**(2), 343–352 (2012)
17. Ronneberger, O., Fischer, P., Brox, T.: U-net: convolutional networks for biomedical image segmentation. In: Navab, N., Hornegger, J., Wells, W.M., Frangi, A.F. (eds.) MICCAI 2015. LNCS, vol. 9351, pp. 234–241. Springer, Cham (2015). https://doi.org/10.1007/978-3-319-24574-4_28
18. Schnell, R., et al.: Lidar detection of leads in arctic sea ice. Nature **339**(6225), 530–532 (1989)

19. Simonyan, K., Zisserman, A.: Very deep convolutional networks for large-scale image recognition. arXiv preprint arXiv:1409.1556 (2014)
20. Zakharova, E.A., et al.: Sea ice leads detection using saral/altika altimeter. Mar. Geodesy **38**(sup1), 522–533 (2015)

Uncertainty Analysis of Sea Ice and Open Water Classification on SAR Imagery Using a Bayesian CNN

Xinwei Chen$^{(\boxtimes)}$, K. Andrea Scott , and David A. Clausi

University of Waterloo, Waterloo, ON N2L 3G1, Canada
{xinwei.chen,ka3scott,dclausi}@uwaterloo.ca

Abstract. Algorithms designed for ice-water classification of synthetic aperture radar (SAR) sea ice imagery produce only binary (ice and water) output typically using manually labelled samples for assessment. This is limiting because only a small subset of samples are used which, given the non-stationary nature of the ice and water classes, will likely not reflect the full scene. To address this, we implement a binary ice-water classification in a more informative manner taking into account the uncertainty associated with each pixel in the scene. To accomplish this, we have implemented a Bayesian convolutional neural network (CNN) with variational inference to produce both aleatoric (data-based) and epistemic (model-based) uncertainty. This valuable information provides feedback as to regions that have pixels more likely to be misclassified and provides improved scene interpretation. Testing was performed on a set of 21 RADARSAT-2 dual-polarization SAR scenes covering a region in the Beaufort Sea captured regularly from April to December. The model is validated by demonstrating; (i) a positive correlation between misclassification rate and model uncertainty and (ii) a higher uncertainty during the melt and freeze-up transition periods, which are more challenging to classify. Integration of the Iterative Region Growing with Semantics (IRGS) unsupervised segmentation algorithm with the Bayesian CNN outputs generates improved classification results, with notable improved results via visual inspection even when sample-based classification rates are similar.

Keywords: SAR imagery · ice-water mapping · uncertainty

1 Introduction

The monitoring of Arctic sea ice plays a crucial role in ship navigation, the safety of transportation in northern communities, and in understanding climate change. Over the past few decades, different types of remote sensing data have been employed for sea ice monitoring. Among these, the spaceborne synthetic aperture radar (SAR) is advantageous due to its high spatial resolution, polarimetric capability, and flexible imaging modes [1]. Since the microwave energy radiated

© Springer Nature Switzerland AG 2023
J.-J. Rousseau and B. Kapralos (Eds.): ICPR 2022 Workshops, LNCS 13645, pp. 343–356, 2023.
https://doi.org/10.1007/978-3-031-37731-0_26

and received by SAR is able to pass through clouds, the measurements are highly independent of atmospheric influences. In addition, as the imaging mechanism is triggered by surface roughness and subsurface physical properties, different ice types can be distinguished. Starting from 1978, more than a dozen satellite-based SAR observing systems have been developed by different countries that are useful for sea ice monitoring.

Among different sea ice monitoring tasks, the discrimination of open water from sea ice provides key information to both marine forecasting on synoptic scales and longer climate-scale simulations [3]. In the past two decades, multiple machine learning (ML)-based methods, which can map high dimensional data to an array of outputs, have been proposed for automated ice-water classification using dual-polarized SAR imagery. Methods include neural networks (NNs) [4], Markov random fields (MRFs) [5], support vector machines (SVMs) [6,7], random forest [8], conditional random fields (CRFs) [9], and convolutional neural networks (CNNs) with different structures [10–13]. Although relatively high classification accuracies have been reported in these studies, the predictions are not always trustworthy, especially during the melting season where ice and water are difficult to distinguish based on visual interpretation. In fact, only two of the studies mentioned above [6,9] have considered data obtained during the melt season. In addition, the performance evaluation of the model on the whole scene is normally limited to visual inspection and comparison with the sea ice chart. Therefore, to obtain more reliable and in-depth interpretation of classification results, it is necessary to investigate the uncertainty in the model prediction.

In Bayesian modeling, predictive uncertainty can be decomposed into two different sources, i.e., aleatoric and epistemic uncertainties. Aleatoric uncertainty (also known as data uncertainty) arises from the inherent variability of the data distribution, which is irreducible [15]. In contrast, epistemic uncertainty (also known as model uncertainty) refers to uncertainty caused by the model, which can in principle be reduced on the basis of additional information [16]. In general, the uncertainty decomposition and quantification help us locate errors inherent in the observations and evaluate the confidence of the model when making predictions for different scenarios. For operational sea ice mapping, the uncertainties may be useful to flag regions in the predictions that should be checked manually by an analyst [17].

In this paper, a model based on a Bayesian CNN is proposed to classify sea ice and water in dual-polarized SAR imagery while providing uncertainty maps along with predictions. The rest of the paper is organized as follows. The SAR imagery dataset used in this work is introduced in Sect. 2. Section 3 illustrates the Bayesian CNN model for predictions and uncertainty quantification, together with the iterative region growing using semantics (IRGS) algorithm for image segmentation. Experimental results with analysis are presented in Sect. 4. Finally, conclusion and future work of this research are given in Sect. 5.

2   Data Overview

The dataset used in this study for model training and testing is provided by Mac-Donald, Dettwiler and Associates (MDA) Ltd. It consists of 21 scenes obtained from the C-band SAR satellite RADARSAT-2 in the Beaufort Sea, north of Alaska, as shown in Fig. 1. They were all captured in the ScanSAR wide mode with HH and HV-polarizations being provided and an incidence angle ranging from 20° to 49°. Since the images were collected from April to December in the year 2010, the model and results can be evaluated under a variety of conditions (e.g., different seasons, ice concentrations). The pixel spacing is 50 m and the size of each image is around 10000 × 10000 pixels. To improve computational efficiency, the original images are downsampled using 4 × 4 block averaging. The image analysis charts that cover the locations of SAR imagery provided by a Canada Ice Service (CIS)-trained analyst are used to obtain reference for the labeling of training samples. For each scene, a land mask is provided to exclude pixels of the land from the study. More information about the dataset can be found in several previous works concerning sea ice classification and concentration estimation [18,19].

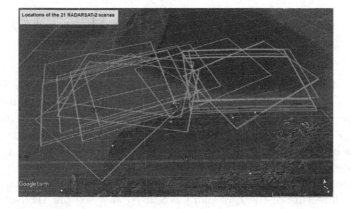

Fig. 1. Locations of the 21 RADARSAT-2 scenes used in this study.

3   Ice-Water Classification with Uncertainty

3.1   Bayesian CNN with Variational Inference

Previous studies have shown that given a neural network, model uncertainty can be obtained by representing the network weights probabilistically. These models are called Bayesian neural networks (BNNs). To make these models operationally practical, several techniques have been incorporated into the training of a BNN, such as variational inference (VI) [20], local reparameterization trick (LRT) [21], and Monte Carlo (MC) estimates. Based on these techniques, the Bayesian CNN was first developed by Gal and Ghahramani [22], which models a distribution over each kernel. The LRT was then introduced to Bayesian CNN by Shridhar et al. [23] to make it more computable. Here the main techniques and workflow of our classification model based on the Bayesian CNN will be described.

Suppose the weights in our Bayesian CNN model are denoted as $\mathbf{w}$, where w_j represents each individual weight in $\mathbf{w}$. The modeling of distributions over $\mathbf{w}$ refers to the learning of the posterior probability distribution $p(\mathbf{w}|\mathcal{D})$, where $\mathcal{D}$ represents a set of training examples with image patches and their corresponding labels. However, due to the large number of weights, $p(\mathbf{w}|\mathcal{D})$ is intractable. Therefore, the VI technique is applied, which uses an approximate distribution $q_\theta(\mathbf{w}|\mathcal{D})$ to be as similar as possible to $p(\mathbf{w}|\mathcal{D})$ by minimizing their Kullback-Leibler (KL) divergence. In our Bayesian CNN model, the distributions of $\mathbf{w}$ are assumed to conform to Gaussian distributions, which means $q_\theta(\mathbf{w}|\mathcal{D}) = \prod_j \mathcal{N}(w_j|\mu, \sigma^2)$. Finding the optimized parameters θ_{opt} (i.e., consisting of μ_{opt} and σ^2_{opt}) can be approximated by minimizing the following tractable cost function [24]

$$
\begin{aligned}
\mathcal{F}(\mathcal{D}, \theta) &\approx \sum_{i=1}^{n} \log q_\theta(\mathbf{w}^{(i)}|\mathcal{D}) - \log p(\mathbf{w}^{(i)}) - \log p(\mathcal{D}|\mathbf{w}^{(i)}) \\
&\approx \sum_{i=1}^{n} \log \prod_j \mathcal{N}(w_j^{(i)}|\mu, \sigma^2) + \log \prod_j \mathcal{N}(w_j^{(i)}|0, \sigma_p^2) \\
&\quad - \log p(\mathcal{D}|\mathbf{w}^{(i)}),
\end{aligned}
\tag{1}
$$

where $\mathbf{w}^{(i)}$ denotes the ith MC sample of weights drawn from the variational posterior $q_\theta(\mathbf{w}|\mathcal{D})$ and n is the number of draws. $p(\mathbf{w}^{(i)})$ is a Gaussian prior and the distribution of each weight can be expressed as $p(w_j^{(i)}) \sim \mathcal{N}(0, \sigma_p^2)$. The final term is the likelihood term. Following Equation (4) in [25], to calculate the activations of each layer in the Bayesian CNN, the LRT proposed by Kingma and Welling [26] is implemented to sample layer activations directly, which is more computationally efficient than sampling on the weights. In this work, the network architecture of the Bayesian CNN used is based on AlexNet proposed by Krizhevsky et al. [27] as it is able to produce accurate classification results (as shown in Table 1) with relatively simple architecture.

3.2   Uncertainty Estimation

Since the output from the Bayesian CNN after the fully connected layer is probabilistic, the ice-water classification output is therefore a predictive distribution. Given a certain sample $\mathbf{w}^{(i)}$, the corresponding predictive distribution can be expressed as $p_{\mathbf{w}^{(i)}}(y^*|x^*)$, where x^* is a new image patch data and y^* is its predicted class. In classification tasks, the overall predictive uncertainty can be obtained from predictive variance $\mathrm{Var}_q(p(y^*|x^*))$. To decompose the overall predictive uncertainty into aleatoric and epistemic uncertainty, the method proposed by Kwon *et al.* [28] is used due to its direct computation from predictive probabilities and direct interpretation of the predictive variance. The decomposition of predictive variance [28] can be expressed as

$$\mathrm{Var}_q(p(y^*|x^*)) = \mathbb{E}_q[y^* y^{*T}] - \mathbb{E}_q[y^*]\mathbb{E}_q[y^*]^T$$

$$= \underbrace{\frac{1}{T} \sum_{t=1}^{T} \mathrm{diag}(\hat{p}_t) - \hat{p}_t \hat{p}_t^T}_{\text{aleatoric}} \tag{2}$$

$$+ \underbrace{\frac{1}{T} \sum_{t=1}^{T} (\hat{p}_t - \bar{p})(\hat{p}_t - \bar{p})^T}_{\text{epistemic}},$$

where $\hat{p}_t = \mathrm{Softmax}(f_{\mathbf{w}^{(t)}}(x^*))$ ($f_{\mathbf{w}^{(t)}}(x^*)$ is the output before the softmax layer) and $\bar{p} = \frac{1}{T} \sum_{t=1}^{T} \hat{p}_t$, T is the pre-defined number of samples. Detailed derivation of the decomposition can be found in the Appendix of Kwon *et al.* [28]. It can be observed from (2) that each uncertainty can be interpreted meaningfully. For example, in our binary ice-water classification task, if the output probability of being classified as ice and the probability of being classified as water are close to each other, that means the uncertainty mainly comes from the data itself and will result in relatively large values in the aleatoric part of (2). In contrast, if the model is uncertain about the classification result, its predictive probabilities in each sampling may have a relatively large variance, which leads to relatively large element values in the epistemic part of (2). In addition, to generate uncertainty quantification result for each pixel, the diagonal elements in each part are summed together (non-diagonal terms are either close to zero or negative), which results in one value for aleatoric uncertainty and a separate value for epistemic uncertainty.

3.3 Combination with IRGS Algorithm

Although the pixel-based classification results can be obtained directly from the Bayesian CNN, they are susceptible to local noise and do not preserve the ice-water boundary information well. Hence, similar to the previous implementation [6,29], the unsupervised IRGS segmentation algorithm proposed by Yu and Clausi [30] is performed to identify homogeneous regions using an unsupervised hierarchical approach, which will be illustrated below. Then, each region is labeled as either ice or water class by taking a majority voting scheme on the Bayesian CNN classification results of all pixels within that region. The flowchart of the algorithm combining IRGS is shown in Fig. 2. First, the watershed segmentation proposed by Vincent and Soille [31] is applied to the HH channel, which

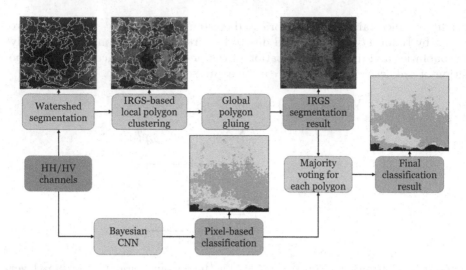

Fig. 2. Combination with IRGS algorithm to generate final classification result

segments the image into a number of autopolygons. For each autopolygon, the IRGS algorithm is then performed on a local scale and clusters the region into 6 artbitrary classes. As illustrated in [30], IRGS is an extension of the traditional MRF contextual model in which the objective functions are formulated by gradually increased edge penalty (GIEP) functions. Those objective functions can be optimized by a novel region growing (merging) scheme. Finally, the region merging scheme is conducted on a global scale to the whole scene, which first converts autopolygon boundaries into region boundaries and then merges regions in different autopolygons into 12 arbitrary classes. The implementation of IRGS on both local and global scales can be regarded as a "glocal" classification scheme. Nevertheless, since whether each class belongs to either ice or water is still unknown, the Bayesian CNN pixel-based ice-water classification results of the whole scene are introduced to label each glocal autopolygon based on a majority voting scheme, which produces the final classification results. In this study, the IRGS algorithm is implemented on the MAp-Guided Ice Classification (MAGIC) system developed by Clausi et al. [32].

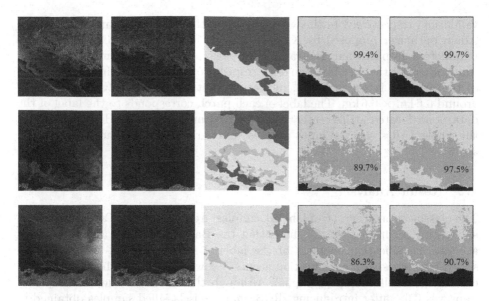

Fig. 3. First and second columns: examples of SAR scenes (scene dates from top to bottom: 20101027, 20100730, and 20100816) in HH and HV channels, respectively. Third column: the image analysis charts for each scene. Different colors represent different sea ice concentration levels. For example, the light blue and red represent open water and 90%+ sea ice concentration, respectively. Fourth column: classification results of the scenes on the same rows using Bayesian CNNs, with ice and water indicated by yellow and blue, respectively. Fifth column: classification results after combining IRGS algorithm. The classification accuracy of the labeled samples is listed on each scene. (Color figure online)

4   Experimental Results

4.1   CNN Model Training

Based on sea ice charts and visual observation, we label certain numbers of data points in each scene manually for training and validating the Bayesian CNN model. Specifically, instead of simply labeling on certain regions, scribble-based annotations are drawn in both ice and water regions. Each of the 10th point in every 10 data points is included into the training set, which prevents the labeled samples from being highly correlated with each other. The number of labeled points for each scene is given in the second and third columns in Table 1. Similar to Leigh et al. [6], the leave-one-out training scheme is adopted for model training. Specifically, to test the performance of the model on the labeled samples in a certain scene, all samples in the other 20 scenes are used for model training, with a percentage of 80% and 20% samples for training and validation, respectively. In this way, a total of 21 CNN models are trained. The Adam optimizer proposed by Kingma and Ba [33] is used to optimize all the parameters. In particular, the variational parameters θ are optimized by taking the gradient of the cost function with respect to μ and σ. The input patch size of the network is set to be 33, indicating that each patch covers an area of around 6.6 km × 6.6 km. The label of each patch corresponds to the label of the data point located at its center. Therefore, to make pixel-based predictions on the whole SAR scene, the input patches are overlapping with each other with a stride of 1.

4.2 Result Analysis

The classification accuracy of labeled samples are presented in Table 1. An average testing accuracy of 97.2% shows that the Bayesian CNN is able to perform accurate classification on most of the labeled samples (noted that there are still three scenes with classification accuracy lower than 90% which will be discussed in the following paragraphs). Although the overall testing accuracy only improves 0.6% after introducing IRGS, many misclassified samples obtained in the melting seasons have been corrected, especially in scene 20100730, where the classification accuracy is improved by 7.8%. While a testing accuracy of 97.8% is only around 1.4% higher than that obtained by Leigh *et al.* [6] using the same dataset, one scene (scene date 20100816) was removed from study in this previous work due to the challenges associated with classifying this scene. In this work, this scene is still retained since it was obtained in the melting season with complex ice-water boundaries and would be important for the study concerning uncertainty.

Nevertheless, since the labeled data points only consist of a small portion of all the pixels in the scenes, it is necessary to further evaluate the performance of the model by visually inspecting the classification results of the whole scene. A few examples of scene classification results consisting of both ice and water samples are shown in Fig. 3. It can be observed that the classification results produced by the Bayesian CNN do not delineate the complex ice-water boundaries and surrounding details (e.g., small floes and wispy looking ice) very well. In contrast, after introducing IRGS segmentation results (as shown in fifth column of Fig. 3), the detailed ice-water boundaries with wispy ice and small floes surrounded are well preserved. Besides, most of the noise-like misclassifications have been eliminated. Therefore, it can be concluded that a combination of Bayesian CNN and IRGS algorithm further improves the classification results.

Table 1. Numbers of labeled samples and the classification accuracy of labeled samples for each scene

Scene date	# of ice	# of water	Testing (%) (Bayesian CNN only)	Testing (%) (with IRGS)
20100418	0	191617	99.9	100
20100426	0	247420	99.9	100
20100510	15357	274494	99.9	100
20100524	46537	253900	99.0	99.6
20100605	6941	262942	97.5	97.5
20100623	107845	211812	99.9	99.9
20100629	32819	130951	99.7	99.6
20100712	25360	123510	98.1	99.1
20100721	50010	63192	100	99.9
20100730	49596	42753	89.7	97.5
20100807	45462	13400	96.9	100
20100816	64329	53444	86.3	90.7
20100907	121003	0	99.9	100
20100909	115469	7990	99.9	99.9
20101003	93027	42070	99.5	100
20101021	125690	42770	77.8	75.7
20101027	66151	71672	99.4	99.7
20101114	41096	67983	99.6	96.0
20101120	0	239720	99.5	100
20101206	0	239252	99.4	99.5
20101214	0	203292	99.5	100
Sum/Average	1006692	2784184	97.2	97.8

However, limitations still exist. For misclassified pixels within large homogeneous regions, which can be observed in the scenes in the last row of Fig. 3, introducing IRGS cannot correct all misclassifications effectively. That is probably caused by the blurry ice-water boundaries. In contrast, the open water region of the scene date 20101021 (which is not presented here due to page limit) consists of rough textures caused by high wind speeds, which looks totally different from the relatively smooth water surface in the other scenes and eventually leads to lower classification accuracy among the whole dataset.

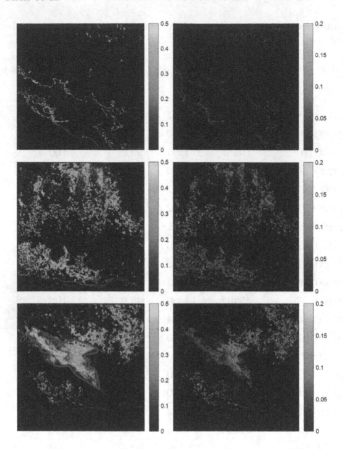

Fig. 4. Aleatoric (left column) and epistemic (right column) uncertainty maps of the scenes presented in Fig. 3 calculated from Bayesian CNN predictions. First to the third rows: uncertainty maps of scene dates 20101027, 20100730, and 20100816. An example of an open water region that is misclassified is outlined in red. (Color figure online)

4.3   Uncertainty Analysis

Uncertainty maps of the three scenes in Fig. 3 calculated from the Bayesian CNN outputs are presented in Fig. 4 for analysis. The sampling number T in (2) is set to be 5. Although a larger T can be more accurate in approximating the real predictive variance, it will be very time-consuming in computation. We also find that by choosing a larger T, the uncertainty values stay basically the same. It looks apparent that those misclassified pixels/regions (e.g., regions outlined in red in Fig. 4) tend to have high uncertainty values in both aleatoric and epistemic maps. To further analyze this, Fig. 5 is presented to show the relationship between aleatoric/epistemic uncertainty and misclassification rate calculated from labeled data points. For aleatoric uncertainty, the misclassification rate increases linearly with uncertainty. In contrast, there is a significant increase in misclassification rate when epistemic uncertainty exceeds 0.001, fol-

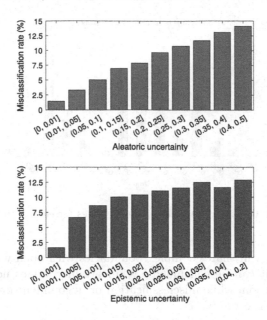

Fig. 5. The relationship between aleatoric/epistemic uncertainty and misclassification rate calculated from the labeled data points.

lowed by a linear increase, gradually flattening out with after around 0.03. High uncertainty can also be observed in regions with intermediate sea ice concentrations where it is difficult to determine the exact class label. Besides, most of the ice-water boundaries can be well delineated in uncertainty maps as pixels on and beside the boundaries tend to have brighter intensities. Even in the scene with large areas of misclassifications (e.g., scene date 20100816), a strong contrast of uncertainty values on the two sides of the "true" ice-water boundaries helps users know where the model makes either confident or probably erroneous predictions.

An overview of uncertainty values for all scenes is shown in Fig. 6. The main source of uncertainty comes from the aleatoric part as the values of aleatoric uncertainty are nearly 10 times larger than the values of epistemic uncertainty, which is consistent with other studies concerning uncertainty quantification in computer vision tasks [28,34]. This can also be accounted for by the complex backscattering mechanisms on different surface conditions across different incidence angles. By comparing uncertainty values obtained different seasons, it is obvious that the average uncertainty values in the melting season are much higher compared to other times of the year, especially for scene dates 20100712, 20100730, 20100807 and 20100816. The low uncertainty values for the scene obtained on scene 20100907 are due to the fact that only pure water is present in that scene. As ice began to freeze up again in fall, the uncertainty values decrease gradually (except for the scene obtained on scene 20101021 which has been explained in Subsection B), which is plausible as the ice is forming and

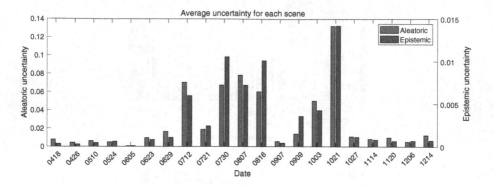

Fig. 6. The average uncertainty values for each scene.

no longer wet yet still shares complex boundaries with open water. By looking back to Table 1, it can be concluded low uncertainty values normally indicate accurate classification, while misclassification or unconfident predictions can be inferred by high uncertainty.

5   Conclusion

By assuming each weight in a CNN follows a certain Gaussian distribution, a Bayesian CNN is built to conduct pixel-wise classification between sea ice and open water in SAR imagery with both epistemic and aleatoric uncertainty. The IRGS algorithm is introduced into the workflow to segment each SAR scene into homogeneous polygons, which are then used to further improve the Bayesian CNN classification result by preserving detailed ice-water boundaries and eliminating noise-like misclassifications.

Results generated from multiple dual-polarized SAR scenes collected from RADARSAT-2 in the Beaufort Sea show that while relatively high classification accuracy on labeled samples can be achieved, factors such as rough water surface under high wind speeds and the blurry ice-water boundaries during the melting season degrade the accuracy and confidence of our model predictions significantly. Therefore, apparently it is not sufficient to evaluate the reliability of model predictions only by looking into the classification accuracy of labeled samples and visual inspection. Since it has been demonstrated that the misclassification rate increases as the increase of uncertainty, the uncertainty maps calculated from the Bayesian CNN outputs provide extra information that facilitates us to locate the correct ice-water boundaries and pixels that might be misclassified. Scenes that are obtained during the melting season generally have the highest mean uncertainty values, followed by scenes obtained during freeze-up.

The proposed method is able to conduct accurate classification on more than 97% of the labeled pixels and highlight regions with high uncertainty that should be inspected manually by an expert. Nevertheless, more SAR imagery data should be included to train a model that performs better under certain scenarios (e.g., high wind speeds, melting season). Besides, since in recent years many advanced CNNs have been proposed for more complex classification tasks, it is worthwhile to convert them into Bayesian CNNs as well and see if the classification performance can be further improved. In addition, it is also necessary to introduce the uncertainty analysis to sea ice typing, which is a more challenging classification task in SAR-based sea ice monitoring.

References

1. Li, X.-M., Sun, Y., Zhang, Q.: Extraction of sea ice cover by Sentinel-1 SAR based on support vector machine with unsupervised generation of training data. IEEE Trans. Geosci. Remote Sens. **59**(4), 3040–3053 (2021)
2. Lyu, H., Huang, W., Mahdianpari, M.: A meta-analysis of sea ice monitoring using spaceborne polarimetric SAR: advances in the last decade. IEEE J. Sel. Top. Appl. Earth Obs. Remote Sens. **15**, 6158–6179 (2022)
3. Xie, T., Perrie, W., Wei, C., Zhao, L.: Discrimination of open water from sea ice in the Labrador sea using quad-polarized synthetic aperture radar. Remote Sens. Environ. **247**, 111948 (2020)
4. Karvonen, J.A.: Baltic sea ice SAR segmentation and classification using modified pulse-coupled neural networks. IEEE Trans. Geosci. Remote Sens. **42**(7), 1566–1574 (2004)
5. Ochilov, S., Clausi, D.A.: Operational SAR sea-ice image classification. IEEE Trans. Geosci. Remote Sens. **50**(11), 4397–4408 (2012)
6. Leigh, S., Wang, Z., Clausi, D.A.: Automated ice-water classification using dual polarization SAR satellite imagery. IEEE Trans. Geosci. Remote Sens. **52**(9), 5529–5539 (2013)
7. Zakhvatkina, N., Korosov, A., Muckenhuber, S., Sandven, S., Babiker, M.: Operational algorithm for ice-water classification on dual-polarized RADARSAT-2 images. Cryosphere **11**(1), 33–46 (2017)
8. Tan, W., Li, J., Xu, L., Chapman, M.A.: Semiautomated segmentation of Sentinel-1 SAR imagery for mapping sea ice in Labrador coast. IEEE J. Sel. Top. Appl. Earth Obs. Remote Sens. **11**(5), 1419–1432 (2018)
9. Zhang, Y., et al.: Sea ice and water classification on dual-polarized sentinel-1 imagery during melting season. Cryosphere Discuss. 1–26 (2021)
10. Boulze, H., Korosov, A., Brajard, J.: Classification of sea ice types in Sentinel-1 SAR data using convolutional neural networks. Remote Sens. **12**(13), 2165 (2020)
11. Ren, Y., Li, X., Yang, X., Xu, H.: Development of a dual-attention U-Net model for sea ice and open water classification on SAR images. IEEE Geosci. Remote Sens. Lett. **19**, 1–5 (2021)
12. Wang, Y.-R., Li, X.-M.: Arctic sea ice cover data from spaceborne synthetic aperture radar by deep learning. Earth Syst. Sci. Data **13**(6), 2723–2742 (2021)
13. Lyu, H., Huang, W., Mahdianpari, M.: Eastern arctic sea ice sensing: first results from the RADARSAT constellation mission data. Remote Sens. **14**(5), 1165 (2022)
14. Jiang, M., Xu, L., Clausi, D.A.: Sea ice-water classification of RADARSAT-2 imagery based on residual neural networks (ResNet) with regional pooling. Remote Sens. **14**(13), 3025 (2022)
15. Abdar, M., et al.: A review of uncertainty quantification in deep learning: techniques, applications and challenges. Inf. Fusion **76**, 243–297 (2021)

16. Hüllermeier, E., Waegeman, W.: Aleatoric and epistemic uncertainty in machine learning: An introduction to concepts and methods. Mach. Learn. **110**(3), 457–506 (2021)

17. Asadi, N., Scott, K.A., Komarov, A.S., Buehner, M., Clausi, D.A.: Evaluation of a neural network with uncertainty for detection of ice and water in SAR imagery. IEEE Trans. Geosci. Remote Sens. **59**(1), 247–259 (2020)

18. Li, F., Clausi, D.A., Wang, L., Xu, L.: A semi-supervised approach for ice-water classification using dual-polarization SAR satellite imagery. In: Proceedings of the IEEE Conference on Computer Vision and Pattern Recognition Workshops, pp. 28–35 (2015)

19. Wang, L., Scott, K.A., Xu, L., Clausi, D.A.: Sea ice concentration estimation during melt from dual-pol SAR scenes using deep convolutional neural networks: a case study. IEEE Trans. Geosci. Remote Sens. **54**(8), 4524–4533 (2016)

20. Graves, A.: Practical variational inference for neural networks. Adv. Neural Inf. Process. Syst. **24** (2011)

21. Kingma, D.P., Salimans, T., Welling, M.: Variational dropout and the local reparameterization trick. Adv. Neural Inf. Process. Syst. **28** (2015)

22. Gal, Y., Ghahramani, Z.: Bayesian convolutional neural networks with bernoulli approximate variational inference, arXiv preprint arXiv:1506.02158 (2016)

23. Shridhar, K., Laumann, F., Liwicki, M.: A comprehensive guide to bayesian convolutional neural network with variational inference, arXiv preprint arXiv:1901.02731 (2019)

24. Blundell, C., Cornebise, J., Kavukcuoglu, K., Wierstra, D.: Weight uncertainty in neural network. In: Proceedings of Machine Learning Research, PMLR, pp. 1613–1622 (2015)

25. Shridhar, K., Laumann, F., Liwicki, M.: Uncertainty estimations by softplus normalization in bayesian convolutional neural networks with variational inference, arXiv preprint arXiv:1806.05978 (2018)

26. Kingma, D.P., Welling, M.: Auto-encoding variational bayes, arXiv preprint arXiv:1312.6114 (2014)

27. Krizhevsky, A., Sutskever, I., Hinton, G.E.: Imagenet classification with deep convolutional neural networks. Adv. Neural Inf. Process. Syst. **25** (2012)

28. Kwon, Y., Won, J.-H., Kim, B.J., Paik, M.C.: Uncertainty quantification using bayesian neural networks in classification: application to biomedical image segmentation. Comput. Stat. Data Anal. **142**, 106816 (2020)

29. Ghanbari, M., Clausi, D.A., Xu, L., Jiang, M.: Contextual classification of sea-ice types using compact polarimetric SAR data. IEEE Trans. Geosci. Remote Sens. **57**(10), 7476–7491 (2019)

30. Yu, Q., Clausi, D.A.: IRGS: image segmentation using edge penalties and region growing. IEEE Trans. Pattern Anal. Mach. Intell. **30**(12), 2126–2139 (2008)

31. Vincent, L., Soille, P.: Watersheds in digital spaces: an efficient algorithm based on immersion simulations. IEEE Trans. Pattern Anal. Mach. Intell. **13**(06), 583–598 (1991)

32. Clausi, D., Qin, A., Chowdhury, M., Yu, P., Maillard, P.: Magic: map-guided ice classification system. Can. J. Remote Sens. **36**(sup1), S13–S25 (2010)

33. Kingma, D.P., Ba, J.: Adam: a method for stochastic optimization, arXiv preprint arXiv:1412.6980 (2014)

34. Kendall, A., Gal, Y.: What uncertainties do we need in bayesian deep learning for computer vision? Adv. Neural Inf. Process. Syst. **30** (2017)

A Two-Stage Road Segmentation Approach for Remote Sensing Images

Tianyu Li[1]([✉]) [iD], Mary Comer[1] [iD], and Josiane Zerubia[2,3] [iD]

[1] Purdue University, West Lafayette, IN, USA
li2516@purdue.edu
[2] Inria, Sophia Antipolis, Valbonne, France
[3] Université Côte d'Azur, Nice, France

Abstract. Many road segmentation methods based on CNNs have been proposed for remote sensing images in recent years. Although these techniques show great performance in various applications, there are still problems in road segmentation, due to the existence of complex backgrounds, illumination changes, and occlusions due to trees and cars. In this paper, we propose a two-stage strategy for road segmentation. A probability map is generated in the first stage by a selected network (ResUnet is used as a case study in this paper), then we attach the probability map image to the original RGB images and feed the resulting four images to a U-Net-like network in the second stage to get a refined result. Our experiments on the Massachusetts road dataset show the average IoU can increase up to 3% from stage one to stage two, which achieves state-of-the-art results on this dataset. Moreover, from the qualitative results, obvious improvements from stage one to stage two can be seen: fewer false positives and better connection of road lines.

Keywords: Remote sensing · Road segmentation · Convolutional neural network (CNN) · Two stage learning

1 Introduction

With the development of new technology in satellites, cameras and communications, massive amounts of high-resolution remotely-sensed images of geographical surfaces have become accessible to researchers. To help analyze these massive image datasets, automatic road segmentation has become more and more important. The road segmentation result can be used in urban planning [28], updating geographic information system (GIS) databases [1] and road routing [8].

Traditionally, researchers designed road segmentation algorithms based on some hand-crafted features [12,14,16], such as the contrast between a road and its background, the shape and color of road, the edges and so on. The segmentation results are highly dependent on the quality of these features. Compared to manually selected features, the rise of convolutional neural networks (CNN) [10,21] provides a better solution to road segmentation, with features generated by learning from labelled training data. Many CNN-based methods have

© Springer Nature Switzerland AG 2023
J.-J. Rousseau and B. Kapralos (Eds.): ICPR 2022 Workshops, LNCS 13645, pp. 357–370, 2023.
https://doi.org/10.1007/978-3-031-37731-0_27

been proposed for road segmentation. For instance, in [22], Ronneberger et al. proposed the U-Net convolutional network for biomedical image segmentation, which has been shown to work well for road segmentation also. Zhang et al. [25], built a deep residual U-Net by combining residual unit [11] with U-Net. Zhou et al. [27] proposed D-LinkNet, consisting of ResNet-34 pre-trained on ImageNet, and a decoder. Feng et al. [9] proposed an attention mechanism-based convolution neural network to enhance feature extraction capability. A Richer U-Net was proposed to learn more details of roads in [24]. Yang et al. [23] proposed a SDUNet which aggregates both the multi-level features and global prior information of road networks by densely connected blocks. Although the performance of these networks has been successfully validated on many public datasets, the segmentation results are far from perfect due to several factors, such as the complexity of the background, occlusions by cars and trees, changes of illumination and the quality of training datasets.

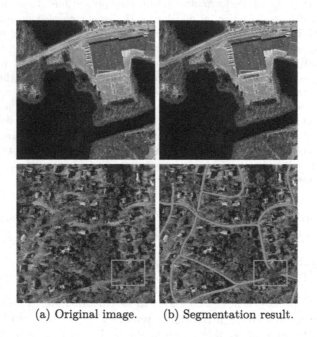

(a) Original image.   (b) Segmentation result.

Fig. 1. Illustration of false positives and broken roads (Images taken from Massachusetts dataset [20]). In (b), green represents true positive (TP), red represents false positive (FP), blue represents false negative (FN).

For example, two of the most common problems in road segmentation are: false positives, such as the red pixels in the orange box of the first row of Fig. 1(b), and road connection problems, such as the broken road in the orange box of the second row of Fig. 1(b). To solve the two problems listed above, a post-processing algorithm is usually applied to the segmented binary images. In [9],

Feng et al. used a heuristic method based on connected-domain analysis to reconstruct the broken roads. Inpainting [4,6] is also a popular way to connect broken roads. Since these methods only consider the output from a previous network, they lack information from the original images. Specifically, false connection is unavoidable. In, Fig. 2, the roads in the two red boxes are disconnected. However, they would likely be falsely connected by a post-processing [17] method without checking the original image.

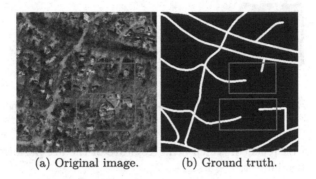

(a) Original image.   (b) Ground truth.

Fig. 2. An example of potential false connections.

In [5], Cheng et al. proposed a cascaded convolutional neural network (CasNet) which consists of two end-to-end networks, one aimed at road segmentation and the other one at centerline extraction. Zhou et al. [26], proposed a universal iteration reinforcement (IterR) model for post-processing which considers both the previous segmentation results and the original images. The IterR model improves the IoU score of segmentation results over 1% in their application. Inspired by these approaches, a two-stage road segmentation method aiming to improve the accuracy and connectivity of roads is proposed in this paper. The first stage is a preliminary segmentation of roads with a selected network (in our case study, ResUnet is used). Then a UNet-like network is applied to enhance the segmentation results by learning from the segmentation behavior of the network in stage one along with the original image.

The main contributions of this research are as follows:

1. A two-stage road segmentation training strategy: the network trained in stage one is used to generate the training samples for stage two. To be specific, when an RGB training sample is fed to the trained network in stage one, a probability map and a weight map are generated. The probability map is attached to the RGB training sample as a 4 dimension input to the network in stage two. The weight map is used for calculating the loss function in stage two.

2. Comprehensive experiments on the Massachusetts dataset [20] to show the proposed method can improve the segmentation results from the first stage to the second stage up to 3% in IoU score. A final IoU of 0.653 and F1-score

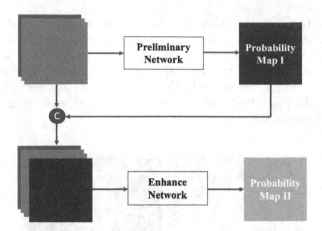

Fig. 3. The diagram of the two-stage segmentation approach.

of 0.788 can be reached, which achieves state-of-the-art performance on the Massachusetts dataset.

2   Methodology

The diagram of the two-stage segmentation approach is given in Fig. 3. A probability map is generated by the preliminary network (ResUnet in our case study) in stage one. Then it is attached to the original RGB image before being fed into the enhance network in stage two. Finally we use a threshold (0.5 in our case) to binarize the probability map II as the refined segmentation result.

2.1   Training Sample Generation

The road segmentation task is taken as a supervised learning problem in most deep learning based methods. Usually, the training samples are randomly cropped from high resolution training images (size 1500×1500 in the Massachusetts dataset) and followed by augmentation, such as rotation, flipping and so on. The number of original training images is limited in most applications due to the high cost of manual labeling. However, there are two neural networks in our two-stage segmentation approach, thus it is essential to generate the training samples for each stage properly. Instead of splitting the original training images into two parts, we use the whole training set to generate the training samples (eg. 512×512) for the network in stage one after random cropping and augmentation. After getting the trained network in stage one, another group of training samples are randomly generated in the same way from the same original training images as stage one.

From our experiments, the performance of the ResUnet (or other networks) for stage one is reasonable with the metric IoU of no less than 0.25. Based on this observation, we filter the second group of training samples by removing bad samples for which the trained network in stage one produced an IoU below a threshold T ($T = 0.25$ in our experiments). After the filtering process, we have a probability map for each of the new training samples. By attaching the probability map to each filtered training sample, four-dimensional training samples are generated for stage two. Figure 4 shows an example of training samples for stage two. The four-dimensional sample is constructed by the RGB channels Fig. 4(a) and the probability map Fig. 4(b).

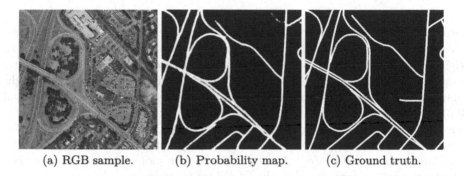

(a) RGB sample.   (b) Probability map.   (c) Ground truth.

Fig. 4. An example of training sample for stage two.

2.2 CUnet for Stage Two

The main task of the network in stage two is to remove false positives and connect the broken roads in the preliminary segmentation results. A UNet-like network (CUnet) is applied in stage two. It is just the vanilla UNet with a small change: a skip connection from the fourth dimension (the probability map) to the output is added for learning the residual between ground truth and probability map. The structure of a five layer CUnet is given in Fig. 5, where d_f is the expanded dimension in the first layer. The CUnet tested in our experiments has seven layers with $d_f = 32$.

2.3 Loss Function for CUnet

The binary cross-entropy (BCE) loss function is widely applied in deep learning segmentation [15] tasks. For road segmentation in remote sensing images, considering the imbalance between positive and negative pixels, Feng et al. [9] introduced a categorical balance factor into the BCE, which gives higher weight to negative pixels. In [24], an edge-focused loss function is introduced to guide the network to pay more attention to the road edge areas by giving the pixels

362   T. Li et al.

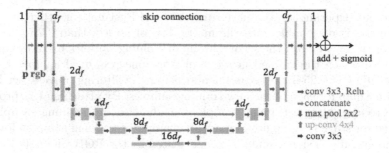

Fig. 5. A five layer CUnet.

close to edges a higher weight. Inspired by these weighted BCE loss functions, we formulate a weighted BCE loss function by strengthening the attention to the pixels (key pixels) with value larger than a threshold δ in the probability map (the 4th dimension of the input to CUnet). Figure 6(c - f) shows the weight map generated from the probability map in Fig. 6(b) with $\delta = 0.5, 0.1, 0.05$ and 0.01, respectively. When δ is large (eg. Fig. 6(c)), the disconnection part of a road may not be taken as key pixels. When δ is small (eg. Fig. 6(f)), many false alarms are included as the key pixels. In our experiment, we select $\delta = 0.05$ by trial and error (eg. Fig. 6(e)). As we expect to give more attention to these key pixels, a weight is introduced to the BCE loss function as:

$$L_{wbce} = -\frac{1}{MN} \sum_{i=1}^{MN} d_i[y_i log p_i + (1 - y_i)log(1 - p_i)] \tag{1}$$

where y_i is the true value of pixel i's category, $p_i \in (0,1)$ is the prediction value for pixel i; M is the number of pixels in one training sample; N is the batch size; d_i is the weight for pixel i:

$$d_i = \begin{cases} 1 & \text{if pixel i is not a key pixel} \\ w & \text{if pixel i is a key pixel} \end{cases} \tag{2}$$

$w > 1$ is the weight for the key pixels.

From [27], a joint loss function, which combines BCE loss and the Dice coefficient in Eq. (3), has achieved good performance in road segmentation in many datasets.

$$L_{dice} = 1 - \frac{2TP}{2TP + FP + FN} \tag{3}$$

where TP, FP, FN are the number of true positives, false positives and false negatives based on the prediction and ground truth in one batch of samples.

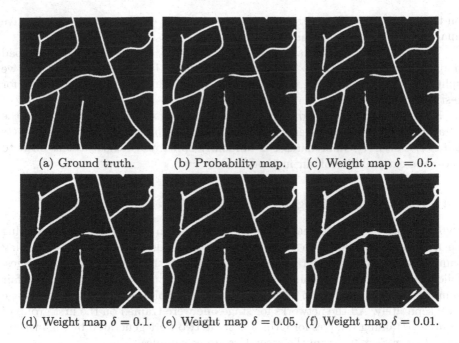

(a) Ground truth.   (b) Probability map.   (c) Weight map $\delta = 0.5$.

(d) Weight map $\delta = 0.1$. (e) Weight map $\delta = 0.05$. (f) Weight map $\delta = 0.01$.

Fig. 6. An example of key pixels in weight map with different threshold δ.

Consequently, we combine the weighted BCE loss and the Dice coefficient as:

$$L = L_{wbce} + L_{dice} \qquad (4)$$

3   Experiments

To verify the effectiveness of our method, comprehensive experiments were conducted on the Massachusetts dataset [20]. A case study based on ResUnet for stage one is performed to select the weight parameter w in Eq. (2). Then several popular networks for segmentation such as UNet [22], SegNet [2], ResUnet [25] and D-LinkNet [27], are used for the preliminary segmentation in stage one. We will show the improvements from the CUnet in stage two for each case by quantitative and qualitative analysis. In the end, we also test our method on DeepGlobe dataset [7] to verify the extensiblity of our method.

3.1   Datasets

The Massachusetts dataset [20] is a public dataset created by Mihn and Hinton. The dataset includes 1171 images, each with size 1500 × 1500 and resolution of 1 m. The 1171 images were split into training set (1108), validation set (14) and test set (49) by the creators. All the networks in our experiments were trained on the training set. Quantitative evaluation is made on the test set. Qualitative analysis is made on both validation set and test set.

The DeepGlobe road dataset [7] contains 6226 images with labelled road maps, each with size 1024×1024 and resolution of 0.5 m. Following [3,19], we split the annotated images into 4696 images for training and 1530 images for testing.

Since the training set and test set in the Massachusetts dataset are split by the creators, our main experiments in Sect. 3.3, 3.4 are based on the Massachusetts dataset. The DeepGlobe dataset is randomly split by us, thus we test on it to show the extensibility of our method.

3.2   Experiment Settings

Pytorch was used to implement all the networks in our experiments, running on a workstation with two 24Gb Titan RTX GPUs. The 512×512 training samples were generated by randomly cropping from the original training images, followed by flipping, randomly rotating and changing the brightness. For fair comparison, we created two groups of training samples, for stage one and stage two, separately. All the networks for stage one were trained on the first group of samples. Training samples for CUnet in stage two were generated by the method described in Sect. 2.1 from the second group of samples.

We set the threshold $\delta = 0.05$ for generating the probability map I in Fig. 3 to include more potential road pixels. The selection of parameter w is discussed in Sect. 3.3.

For the training process, the learning rate is set to 0.0001, batch size is 8. To prevent the networks from overfitting, the training samples were divided into training subset and validation subset with ratio 0.95 and 0.05, respectively. Early stopping was applied once the validation loss stopped decreasing for 10 epochs continuously. The training process was the same for all the networks trained in our experiments.

Evaluation metrics include precision, recall, F1-score, and IoU, which are defined as follows:

$$Precision = \frac{TP}{TP + FP} \tag{5}$$

$$Recall = \frac{TP}{TP + FN} \tag{6}$$

$$F1 = \frac{2 \times precision \times recall}{precision + recall} \tag{7}$$

$$IoU = \frac{TP}{TP + FP + FN} \tag{8}$$

where TP represents true positive, FP represents false positive, FN represents false negative.

3.3 Selection of Parameter w

In the joint loss function (Eq. (4)), which combines the weighted BCE loss and the Dice coefficient, w controls the degree of attention we put on the key pixels. Intuitively, if we put too much attention on the key pixels, this may result in false classification for other pixels. Thus we made a sensitivity test for w. In this test, ResUnet is taken as the network for stage one, we set $w = 1, 1.03, 1.05, 1.11$, respectively for training the CUnet in stage two. When $w = 1.0$, every pixel in the training sample gets the same weight, Eq. (4) returns to the Dice + BCE loss rather than Dice + weighted BCE. The ResUnet in stage one is trained with the Dice + BCE loss. Table 1 presents the evaluation results on the 49 test images. As we can see, the results from all four CUnets in stage two are much better than the result from the ResUnet in stage one. The best IoU and F1-score are reached when $w = 1.03$. Thus we set $w = 1.03$ for the experiments in the following sections.

Table 1. Test results for different w: S1 means stage one (ResUnet), S2 means stage two (CUnet).

Stage	w	IoU	F1	Prec	Recall
S1	1.0	0.6328	0.7723	0.7783	0.7708
S2	1.0	0.6455	0.7820	**0.7973**	0.7715
	1.03	**0.6530**	**0.7877**	0.7927	**0.7864**
	1.05	0.6529	0.7857	0.7941	0.7847
	1.11	0.6486	0.7834	0.7946	0.7779

Table 2. Comparison experiments on the Massachusetts dataset.

Stage-Network	IoU	F1	Prec	Recall
S1 UNet8	0.6120	0.7565	0.7344	0.7837
S2 CUnet	0.6433	0.7804	0.7913	0.7729
S1 UNet32	0.6407	0.7781	0.7922	0.7686
S2 CUnet	0.6474	0.7832	0.7999	0.7716
S1 SegNet	0.6377	0.7758	0.7834	0.7728
S2 CUnet	0.6476	0.7832	**0.8031**	0.7685
S1 ResUnet	0.6328	0.7723	0.7783	0.7708
S2 CUnet	0.6530	0.7877	0.7927	0.7864
S1 D-LinkNet	0.6263	0.7677	0.7761	0.7621
S2 CUnet	**0.6534**	**0.7880**	0.7901	**0.7885**

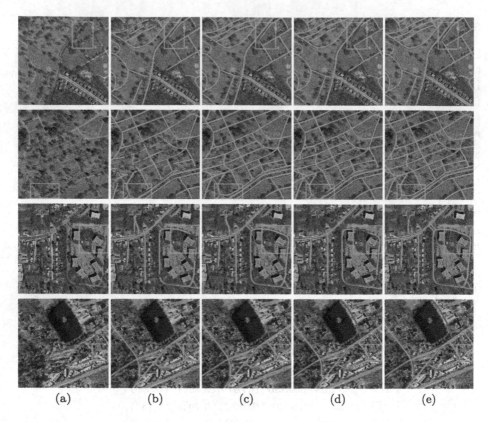

(a)   (b)   (c)   (d)   (e)

Fig. 7. Segmentation results from the Massachusetts dataset: green represents true positive (TP), red represents false positive (FP), blue represents false negative (FN). (a): Original image; (b): ResUnet; (c): ResUnet+CUnet; (d) D-LinkNet; (e) D-LinkNet+CUnet. (Color figure online)

3.4   Test on the Massachusetts Dataset

To further validate the two-stage segmentation method, we used five networks for the preliminary segmentation in stage one, UNet8 (a 7-layer UNet with $d_f = 8$), UNet32, SegNet, ResUnet and D-LinkNet, all trained with Dice + BCE loss. For each case, a CUnet was trained for stage two with $w = 1.03$ in Dice + weighted BCE loss. Table 2 presents the quantitative comparison of the results from stage one and stage two for each case. As shown in Table 2, the IoU and F1-score improved a lot from stage one to stage two for all cases. The highest IoU 0.6534 and F1-score 0.7880 are reached in the case based on D-LinkNet. Compared with the D-LinkNet case, ResUnet case achieved very close IoU 0.6530 and F1-score 0.7877, but lower recall and higher precision.

Since the two-stage approach obtained the highest IoUs in Table 2 with ResUnet and D-LinkNet as the stage-one network, we only compare with their qualitative results in this section. Figure 7 gives four examples to show the performance of our method on the broken roads from preliminary segmentations. In the segmentation results, green represents true positive (TP), red represents false positive (FP), blue represents false negative (FN). In the orange box of the first row and the second row of Fig. 7, there is a small lane which is close to the wider avenue and partially occluded by trees. ResUnet and D-LinkNet failed to fully connect the road in the segmentation results in stage one. These broken roads were successfully reconnected in stage two by CUnet. In the third row of Fig. 7, the road is adjacent to a parking lot which has the same color as the road. The performance of ResUnet and D-LinkNet are not satisfactory for this case. Again, the CUnet improved the results a lot for both ResUnet and D-LinkNet. In the last row of Fig. 7, CUnet extracted the whole road in the orange box for the ResUnet case. However, it failed to extract the complete road for the D-LinkNet case. For the ResUnet case, the task is to connect broken lines, but for the D-LinkNet case, the CUnet needs to rediscover the missing road. This demonstrates that the performance of CUnet in stage two is dependent on the output from stage one.

In conclusion, for both ResUnet and D-LinkNet cases, the CUnet can help to enhance the road connections significantly.

3.5 Test on the DeepGlobe Dataset

To verify the extensibility of our method, we test ResUnet + CUnet and D-LinkNet + CUnet methods on the DeepGlobe dataset [7]. Table 3 shows the comparison results between ResUnet + CUnet and D-LinkNet + CUnet. The IoU increases from 0.6364 to 0.6514 for the D-LinkNet + CUnet case. For the case of ResUnet, the IoU is relatively low in stage one, however, the IoU reaches 0.6456 in stage two, which can be attributed to the re-discoverability of the CUnet. Figure 8 shows four examples from the DeepGlobe dataset. Although the image resolution and road type in the DeepGlobe dataset are different from the Massachusetts dataset, our method shows similar improvement from stage one to stage two.

Table 3. Quantitative results on the DeepGlobe dataset.

Stage-Network	IoU	F1	Prec	Recall
S1 ResUnet	0.5693	0.7117	0.7343	0.7233
S2 CUnet	0.6456	0.7733	0.7635	**0.8085**
S1 D-LinkNet	0.6364	0.7670	0.7644	0.7941
S2 CUnet	**0.6514**	**0.7780**	**0.7758**	0.8040

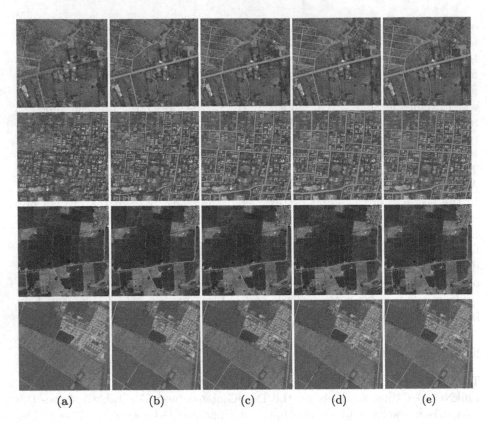

(a)   (b)   (c)   (d)   (e)

Fig. 8. Segmentation results from the DeepGlobe dataset: green represents true positive (TP), red represents false positive (FP), blue represents false negative (FN). (a): Original image; (b): ResUnet; (c): ResUnet+CUnet; (d) D-LinkNet; (e) D-LinkNet+CUnet. (Color figure online)

4   Conclusions and Perspectives

In this paper, a two-stage segmentation strategy is proposed for road segmentation in remote sensing images. The network in stage one gives preliminary segmentation results. In stage two, a proposed CUnet is applied to enhance the result from stage one. The experimental results on the Massachusetts dataset show that this strategy works for many different CNNs selected in stage one, with the enhanced segmentation results being better than the preliminary results not only in precision, but also in recall. Moreover, the qualitative results show that this strategy can alleviate the broken road problem to some extent. In future work, we plan to apply this two-stage segmentation strategy to other segmentation applications, such as roof segmentation in remote sensing images and blood vessel segmentation [13,18] in retina fundus images.

Acknowledgements. Josiane Zerubia thanks the IEEE SPS Distinguished Lecturer program which enabled her to give several talks in the USA in 2016-2017 and to start this collaboration with Prof. Comer and her PhD student (Tianyu Li) in Purdue.

References

1. Bachagha, N., Wang, X., Luo, L., Li, L., Khatteli, H., Lasaponara, R.: Remote sensing and GIS techniques for reconstructing the military fort system on the Roman boundary (Tunisian section) and identifying archaeological sites. Remote Sens. Environ. **236**, 111418 (2020)
2. Badrinarayanan, V., Kendall, A., Cipolla, R.: SegNet: a deep convolutional encoder-decoder architecture for image segmentation. IEEE Trans. Pattern Anal. Mach. Intell. **39**(12), 2481–2495 (2017)
3. Batra, A., Singh, S., Pang, G., Basu, S., Jawahar, C.V., Paluri, M.: Improved road connectivity by joint learning of orientation and segmentation. In: IEEE/CVF Conference on Computer Vision and Pattern Recognition (CVPR), pp. 10377–10385 (2019)
4. Bertalmio, M., Sapiro, G., Caselles, V., Ballester, C.: Image inpainting. In: Proceedings of the 27th Annual Conference on Computer Graphics and Interactive Techniques, SIGGRAPH 2000, pp. 417–424. ACM Press/Addison-Wesley Publishing Co., USA (2000)
5. Cheng, G., Wang, Y., Xu, S., Wang, H., Xiang, S., Pan, C.: Automatic road detection and centerline extraction via cascaded end-to-end convolutional neural network. IEEE Trans. Geosci. Remote Sens. **55**(6), 3322–3337 (2017)
6. Cira, C., Kada, M., Manso-Callejo, M., Alcarria, R., Sanchez, B.B.: Improving road surface area extraction via semantic segmentation with conditional generative learning for deep inpainting operations. ISPRS Int. J. Geo-Inf. **11**(1) (2022)
7. Demir, I., et al.: Deepglobe 2018: A challenge to parse the earth through satellite images. In: IEEE/CVF Conference on Computer Vision and Pattern Recognition Workshops (CVPRW) (2018)
8. Etten, A.V.: City-scale road extraction from satellite imagery v2: road speeds and travel times. In: Proceedings of the IEEE/CVF Winter Conference on Applications of Computer Vision (WACV), March 2020
9. Feng, D., Shen, X., Xie, Y., Hu, J., Liu, Y.: Efficient occluded road extraction from high-resolution remote sensing imagery. Remote Sens. **13**, 4974 (2021)
10. Gu, J., et al.: Recent advances in convolutional neural networks. Pattern Recogn. **77**, 354–377 (2018)
11. He, K., Zhang, X., Ren, S., Sun, J.: Deep residual learning for image recognition. In: IEEE Conference on Computer Vision and Pattern Recognition (CVPR), pp. 770–778 (2016)
12. Hinz, S., Baumgartner, A.: Automatic extraction of urban road networks from multi-view aerial imagery. ISPRS J. Photogramm. Remote. Sens. **58**(1–2), 83–98 (2003)
13. Hoover, A.D., Kouznetsova, V., Goldbaum, M.: Locating blood vessels in retinal images by piecewise threshold probing of a matched filter response. IEEE Trans. Med. Imaging **19**(3), 203–210 (2000)
14. Hu, J., Razdan, A., Femiani, J., Cui, M., Wonka, P.: Road network extraction and intersection detection from aerial images by tracking road footprints. IEEE Trans. Geosci. Remote Sens. **45**(12), 4144–4157 (2007)

15. Jadon, S.: A survey of loss functions for semantic segmentation. In: IEEE Conference on Computational Intelligence in Bioinformatics and Computational Biology (CIBCB), pp. 1–7 (2020)
16. Li, T., Comer, M., Zerubia, J.: A connected-tube MPP model for object detection with application to materials and remotely-sensed images. In: IEEE International Conference on Image Processing (ICIP), pp. 1323–1327 (2018)
17. Li, T., Comer, M., Zerubia, J.: Feature extraction and tracking of CNN segmentations for improved road detection from satellite imagery. In: 2019 IEEE International Conference on Image Processing (ICIP), pp. 2641–2645 (2019)
18. Li, T., Comer, M., Zerubia, J.: An unsupervised retinal vessel extraction and segmentation method based on a tube marked point process model. In: IEEE International Conference on Acoustics, Speech and Signal Processing (ICASSP), pp. 1394–1398 (2020)
19. Lu, X., et al.: Cascaded multi-task road extraction network for road surface, centerline, and edge extraction. IEEE Trans. Geosci. Remote Sens. **60**, 1–14 (2022)
20. Mnih, V.: Machine Learning for Aerial Image Labeling. Ph.D. thesis, University of Toronto (2013)
21. Mnih, V., Hinton, G.E.: Learning to detect roads in high-resolution aerial images. In: Daniilidis, K., Maragos, P., Paragios, N. (eds.) ECCV 2010. LNCS, vol. 6316, pp. 210–223. Springer, Heidelberg (2010). https://doi.org/10.1007/978-3-642-15567-3_16
22. Ronneberger, O., Fischer, P., Brox, T.: U-Net: convolutional networks for biomedical image segmentation. In: Navab, N., Hornegger, J., Wells, W.M., Frangi, A.F. (eds.) MICCAI 2015. LNCS, vol. 9351, pp. 234–241. Springer, Cham (2015). https://doi.org/10.1007/978-3-319-24574-4_28
23. Yang, M., Yuan, Y., Liu, G.: SDUNet: road extraction via spatial enhanced and densely connected UNet. Pattern Recogn. **126**, 108549 (2022)
24. Zao, Y., Shi, Z.: Richer U-Net: learning more details for road detection in remote sensing images. IEEE Geosci. Remote Sens. Lett. **19**, 1–5 (2022)
25. Zhang, Z., Liu, Q., Wang, Y.: Road extraction by deep residual U-Net. IEEE Geosci. Remote Sens. Lett. **15**(5), 749–753 (2018)
26. Zhou, K., Xie, Y., Gao, Z., Miao, F., Zhang, L.: FuNet: a novel road extraction network with fusion of location data and remote sensing imagery. ISPRS Int. J. Geo-Inf. **10**(1) (2021)
27. Zhou, L., Zhang, C., Wu, M.: D-LinkNet: LinkNet with pretrained encoder and dilated convolution for high resolution satellite imagery road extraction. In: IEEE/CVF Conference on Computer Vision and Pattern Recognition Workshops (CVPRW), pp. 192–1924 (2018)
28. Zhou, M., Sui, H., Chen, S., J. Wang, X.C.: BT-RoadNet: a boundary and topologically-aware neural network for road extraction from high-resolution remote sensing imagery. ISPRS J. Photogramm. Remote Sens. **168**, 288–306 (2020)

YUTO Tree5000: A Large-Scale Airborne LiDAR Dataset for Single Tree Detection

Connie Ko, Yeonjeong Jeong, Hyungju Lee, and Gunho Sohn[✉]

Department of Earth and Space Science and Engineering, Lassonde School of Engineering,
York University Toronto, Toronto, ON M2M 2P5, Canada
{cko,yjjeong,hyungju,gsohn}@yorku.ca

Abstract. Despite the computer vision community showing great interest in deep learning-based object detection, the adaptation to tree detection has been rare. There is a notable absence of proper datasets for automatic tree detection with deep convolutional neural networks to create and update tree inventories using LiDAR information. There are some publicly accessible benchmark datasets, but the domains are mostly forest. This paper introduces YUTO (York University Teledyne Optech) Tree5000, a novel LiDAR benchmark dataset for nearly 5000 individual trees in an urban context. It represents 142 species at York University in Toronto, Ontario, Canada. Semi-automatic techniques were applied to construct 3D bounding boxes for each tree using publicly available data such as Google Earth (GE) images and Google Street View (GSV), field-collected data, and airborne LiDAR. This dataset includes (1) a manually verified LiDAR dataset with four segmentation classes, (2) field-collected tree inventory data with specifications covering nearly 4.3 km^2, (3) manually adjusted GPS treetop locations, (4) semi-automatically generated 2D tree boundary information, and (5) 3D tree bounding boxes information. Unlike other research that utilized 2D images of their dataset to evaluate with a 2D detection algorithm, we use 3D LiDAR point cloud to detect trees. We evaluated the performance of the following eight algorithms on the benchmark dataset and analyzed the results: second, PointPillars, PointRCNN, VoxelRCNN, PVRCNN, PartA2, PyramidRCNN, and PVRCNN++. Mainly, we discuss the utilization of airborne LiDAR and existing 3D detection networks when developing new algorithms.

Keywords: Tree detection · object detection · deep learning · LiDAR

1 Introduction

With the advent of high-resolution remote sensing sensors and more sophisticated image analysis technologies such as deep convolutional neural network (DCNN), delineating individual tree crowns (ITCs) would be more achievable and useful for forest inventory management. Instead of delineating forest stands, the outcome of the ITCs allows foresters to assess their contents at a single tree level, as well as at a larger object scale by regrouping them into forest stands. Over the last decade, airborne lidar sensor (ALS) has become a primary data source for generating the single tree inventory. This popularity

© Springer Nature Switzerland AG 2023
J.-J. Rousseau and B. Kapralos (Eds.): ICPR 2022 Workshops, LNCS 13645, pp. 371–385, 2023.
https://doi.org/10.1007/978-3-031-37731-0_28

is primarily due to foliage penetration with high point density and three-dimensional positioning accuracy provided by the ALS. However, post-data acquisition processing for accomplishing ITCs using ALS is a tedious and costly task. Thus, there is an urgent demand to improve the accuracy and efficiency of driving individual tree information using ALS.

Recently, we have been observing the huge success of DCNN, especially in visual data analytics, which largely outperforms shallow or non-learnable vision methods. The power of the DCNNs comes from the computation of probabilities by combining features estimated through deeply stacked convolutional layers. This handcrafted feature-free architecture makes the problem of learning representation easier and more robust. However, DCNNs require a much larger scale of data to learn a few million parameters for generating accurate probabilities. In this context, many researchers have made large efforts to provide various datasets obtained with LiDAR sensors supporting the advancement of DCNN research. These benchmarks include: KITTI [1], H3D [2], Waymo Open [3], and nuScenes [4] for the 3D object detection task and Oakland [5], ISPRS [6], Semantic3D [7], Paris-Lille-3D [8], SemanticKITTI [9], and Toronto3D [10]. For the 3D segmentation task. Mostly, existing benchmarks have been acquired by mobile LiDAR sensors (MLS) for 3D object detection, segmentation, depth estimation and simultaneous localization and mapping (SLAM) purposes. The MLS benchmarks provide a wide horizontal and vertical field of view suitable for autonomous driving applications. For environmental applications such as forest inventory management, ALS is preferred due to greater coverage areas with a birds-eye-view (BEV). Compared to MLS, finding a publicly available ALS benchmark or existing tree benchmark built based on ALS that focuses on forest trees is not easy. There is a lack of ALS-based tree benchmarks in an urban setting. Forest trees develop differently than urban trees. Numerous urban trees are usually planted and situated as part of urban planning concepts, whereas forest trees grow naturally. Thus, there is a demand for accessing an urban tree benchmark processed by ALS.

To bridge the gap between the need for and availability of ALS-based tree benchmarks, we created a large-scale tree benchmark dataset for the community to advance DCNNs for detecting single trees. Our dataset has been compiled in an urban environment. It includes both planted trees (which often have little or no overlap) and naturally grown trees (typically have a significant degree of overlap) in woodlots. This study details how we constructed our dataset using ALS obtained in the leaf-on season, fieldwork, and publicly available imagery such as Google Street View (GSV) and Google Earth (GE) as supplementary information for annotation. Our new dataset includes the following: 1) segmented ALS dataset with four classes validated manually (Fig. 1a); 2) field-collected tree data including specific information about each tree; 3) manually adjusted GPS treetop locations (Fig. 1b); 4) semi-automatically generated boundaries of individual tree crowns (Fig. 1c); 5) generated 3D bounding boxes representing individual trees (4) (Fig. 1d). The main contributions of this work are:

(1) Generate a new urban tree benchmark for 3D single tree detection using ALS;
(2) Develop a unique workflow of the semi-automatic fusing tree inventory database with ALS data; and

(3) Conduct a comparative analysis of the SOTA DCNNs for 3D object detections using our new tree benchmark.

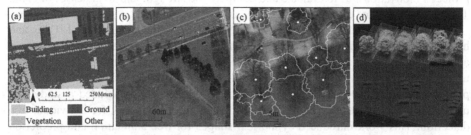

Fig. 1. YUTO Tree5000 Benchmark (a) An example of the classified (segmented) point cloud after human inspection, (b) white dots are the examples of tree location (c) white lines are the examples of derived tree boundaries, (d) examples of the 3D tree bounding box.

2 Related Work

2.1 LiDAR Benchmark Datasets for Trees

We discuss a few publications relating to benchmarking projects, focusing on the usage of LiDAR datasets in the forestry area. The first project in this area was "Tree Extraction" (2005–2008) [11, 12], which was sponsored by the European Spatial Data Research Organization (EuroSDR) and the International Society for Photogrammetry and Remote Sensing (ISPRS) Commission II. Twelve individuals participated in the United States of America, Canada, Norway, Sweden, Finland, Germany, Austria, Switzerland, Italy, Poland, and Taiwan. The purpose of this project was to assess the quality, accuracy, and feasibility of employing ALS to extract the following information about individual trees: tree position (x and y coordinates of the trunk), tree crown delineation, tree height, and crown base height (or volume of the tree crown). The same dataset is also used for another publication in 2016 [16]. Motivated by developing sustainable and adaptive management of mountain forest resources, the research project NEWFOR (New Technologies for a better mountain FORest timber mobilization) benchmarked eight ALS-based single tree detection algorithms between 2011 to 2014 [13]. Eight areas were studied for this project. Acquisition dates for the ALS data range from the year 2005 to the year 2013, with point densities ranging from 5 to 121 points (pts) / m^2. This project included four sensors (Riegl LMS-Q560, Riegl LMS-Q680i, Optech ALTM 3100, and Leica ALS 70), with study areas ranging from 0.3 ha to 1.2 ha. The study established a correlation between autonomous tree spotting techniques and forest inventory data. [14] conducted a benchmarking study for comparing the performances of tree detection algorithms. Between 2006 and 2008, five ALS datasets were acquired with the point densities ranging from 1.5 to 30 pts / m^2. The sizes of the study sites ranged from 0.05 to 0.64 ha. The ALS scanners used for this study were the Optech ALTM 3100, TopoSys Harrier 56, Toposys Falcon II and TopEye MKII. Six tree detection algorithms were tested. The project concluded that the algorithms' performance was affected by the forest structures, tree density and clustering. In 2014, the EuroSDR and Finnish Geospatial Research Institute launched the international TLS (Terrestrial Laser Scanning) benchmarking project. The project's motivation was to evaluate and compare the strength and weaknesses of using TLS for tree attribute extraction [15]. 18 algorithms were tested with 24 sample plots.

In 2020, [17] released a benchmark dataset for trees, including RGB, LiDAR and hyperspectral data, to detect trees in 2D BEV. The point density of the LiDAR dataset was approximately 5 pts / m^2. Bounding boxes were annotated in 2D, and RGB images were used for training the network. Benchmark evaluation was performed with the DeepForest python package developed by the authors [17]. Recently, [18] included a study that used 10,864 hand-label ground truth trees for testing one network for individual tree detection. This work introduced cylindrical shapes for tree annotation and prediction and reported that the circular (2D) mAP was 0.5–1 percentage point higher. The point density was reported as 16.6 pts / m^2 for the first return. The authors also decided to remove the height and z coordinate from their loss functions, as a result, the core of the prediction and evaluation were performed in 2D. Also, the fusion of segmentation and detection results was performed outside of the DCNN by complex postprocessing. Thus, if the dataset was to be released to the community, training and testing of the dataset would not be performed in an end-to-end manner. Unfortunately, the authors did not mention whether they would publicize this dataset. Their conclusion said that "the DCNNs trained on this ground truth would not necessarily learn to correctly find individual trees or tree points, but rather to emulate the training data". In contrast, our benchmark dataset provides learning and detection of individual trees. We summarized the related benchmark datasets described in Table 1..

As discussed, large-scale LiDAR benchmark datasets do not have tree-related data, whereas existing tree benchmark datasets are primarily conducted in forest environments. Also, many of these datasets are not publicly available. Amongst these studies, point density varies from 2 to 28 pts / m^2. Unlike [17], our bounding boxes are 3D instead of 2D, allowing 3D detectors to be seamlessly applied. Finally, unlike [18], we tested our benchmark dataset with eight SOTA 3D object detectors without postprocessing, based on only (x, y, z) as input and releasing our dataset to the public, benefiting the community. Our dataset addresses tree detection in an urban context by recognizing the distinction between urban and forest trees. Also, our point density is superior to that of other publicly accessible benchmark datasets. This benchmark dataset addresses the bottleneck of data availability for trees.

2.2 Tree Detection Studies

The requirements for the urban tree inventory are different from the forest inventory. Often, urban tree inventory is at the individual level [19], whereas forest inventory is an area based [20]. Along with tree presence, data such as species, dbh (diameter at breast height), and tree height are recorded [19]. Compared to forest inventory, the precise location of a tree is critical for urban tree inventory. Thus, the location error must be less than the distance between tree locations and the tree crown diameter to avoid confusion regarding individual tree locations. However, due to the lack of availability of ALS benchmarks for individual trees, current studies are biased towards implementing image

Table 1. Summary of the existing tree benchmark studies

Citation	Point density [pts/m^2]	Availability	Environment	Platform	Evaluation
[11, 12, 16]	2	no	forest	ALS	Non-DL
[13]	28	yes	forest	ALS	Non-DL
[14]	12	no	forest	ALS	Non-DL
[15]	n/a	no	forest	TLS	Non-DL
[17]	5	yes	forest	ALS	DL
[18]	17	no	urban	ALS	DL
Ours, 2022	**119; (104 first return)**	**yes**	**urban**	**ALS**	**DL**

data such as street-view images. The most significant shortcoming of such an approach is that the tree's location is derived from multi-view triangulation. Since many cities in Canada, including the City of Toronto [19], City of Guelph [21], City of Mississauga [22], and City of Markham [23], have conducted historical urban tree inventory based on field inspection. It would be logical to update such inventory by matching the newly updated physical locations of the individual tree to their existing database. Unfortunately, the field-collected data does not contain the precise tree location information to enable accurate matching. For example, it is recorded in [19] that *"The positioning shown is not accurate as the tree data has been geographically coded to the parcel address, and this will incorrectly indicate the tree location within the private parcel"*. To address this problem, it is imperative that cities update their inventory database with novel tree detection methods that can be linked to the existing tree inventory.

We identified the following studies for tree detection in urban environments. [24] and [25] used panoramic and overhead images of an area of interest. [26] used a marker-controlled watershed algorithm on the airborne LiDAR data for tree detection. [27] used street images and Part Attention Network for Tree Detection (PANTD). Their work addresses the important problem of occlusion, which is one of the biggest challenges in tree detection and is inspired by the occlusion-aware R-CNN proposed by [28]. [29] uses street-level imagery and Mask R-CNN for tree detection, and tree location was estimated from depth. These related works are based on 2D object detection. In contrast, our work is focused on using ALS and 3D object detection to understand the objects' real-world sizes and positions.

3   Benchmark Dataset

This benchmark dataset has been derived from two primary sources: ALS data and field-collected data.

3.1 LiDAR Data Acquisition

The airborne LiDAR acquisition took place on 23 September 2018 with ALS sensors Galaxy-PRIME, owned by Teledyne Optech, in Toronto, Ontario. The average flying height for the mission was 1829m above ground level. York University Keele campus area (same extent as field data) covers approximately 4.3 km^2 spanning 1.8 km in the north-south direction and 2.4 km in the east-west direction. The average point density was calculated by dividing the total number of points recorded by the area of flight coverages. Due to overlap in some areas, the overall average point density is approximately 119 pts / m^2.

3.2 Field Collected Data

The field data was collected in 2014, 2016 and 2017. Unfortunately, we could not utilize the database owned by the City of Toronto because of its incompleteness. Thus, we conducted our fieldwork to generate a new single tree inventory for this study. In the field, the location of the tree trunk was recorded with a handheld GPS. Items recorded include: 1) Common name; 2) Dbh [cm]; 3) Tree height to base of crown [m]; 4) Total height [m]; 5) Location description; 6) Latitude, longitude; 7) Status and status date; 8) Tree crown width; 9) Ownership; 10) Tree conflicts with objects such as sidewalk, signs, trees, wires, other structures; and 11) Tree health such as broken branch, dead branches, a cavity in trunk or branches, and weak yellow foliage observed. 5717 trees with 142 species were recorded in total. Figure 2 shows the frequency distribution of the top 15 tree species. A summary of the statistics of the recorded trees is provided in Table 2..

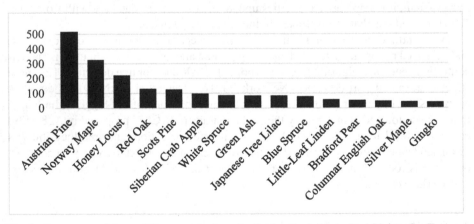

Fig. 2. Frequency of the top 15 tree species from the field-collected data, York University, Toronto.

4 Data Processing

The workflow was designed to combine the tree inventory database with ALS tree data semi-automatically (Fig. 3). We automated most of the process but retained human inspection at several locations to rectify any errors caused by the automation. After

Table 2. Summary of the statistics of field-collected trees.

	Maximum	Minimum	Mean	Standard deviation
DBH [cm]	88.50	0.50	23.37	13.48
Tree Height [m]	27.97	0.07	10.35	4.30
Crown Width [m]	21.50	0.20	6.17	3.13

automatic point cloud classification, we carefully fixed misclassified points by a human vision in the first inspection step. The second inspection step corrected location errors of the trees caused by GPS in the field. GSV images and GE images were utilized in this process. We also identified trees in the tree inventory that no longer exist in the field, which was finally removed from the dataset. The third inspection step was to ensure that tree boundaries were being drawn on the tree crowns with no field data and to ensure that the bounding box height was reasonable. A final inspection was performed to review the generated 3D bounding boxes.

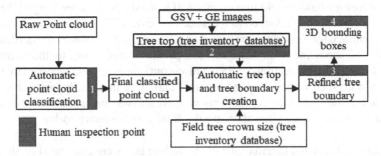

Fig. 3. Workflow for semi-automatic tree benchmark creation

4.1 Point Cloud Classification

ALS point cloud classification (segmentation) was performed with two sets of software, LAStools [38] and TerraScan [39]. After the automatic classification, we manually validated the classification results with TerraScan to correct all the misclassified points. An example of the classified point cloud can be found in Fig. 1(a). The output of this process yields a four-classes dataset (ground, vegetation, building and other).

4.2 Tree Annotation with 3D Bounding Boxes

The generation of tree annotations was semi-automatic and used the (1) ALS data, (2) GPS locations and (3) tree crown widths obtained from the fieldwork.

The recorded field data was not accurate enough to provide automatic tree annotation. The two most significant errors arose from GPS and field tree crown measurement. To correct the errors from GPS, we manually inspected the individual trees and corrected the (x, y) of the GPS location to the observed treetop using GSV and GE. Of 5717 field-collected trees, we removed 633 trees because they could not be identified in the ALS dataset during the second inspection point (Fig. 3). These could be trees that existed during field visits but were removed in 2018 when ALS data was collected. We retained 5084 2D bounding boxes in the data. We applied the marker-controlled watershed segmentation method [40] to our ALS dataset to refine and obtain a more accurate tree crown size. The algorithm first calculated CHM (Canopy Height Model) from classified ALS data. The next step is to apply a smoothing operator, in this case, a Gaussian smoothing, before detecting the local maximums as treetops and delineating the tree crowns referred to as watersheds. Despite its efficiency and effectiveness, this method relies on the magnitude of smoothing. If smoothing is too small, this method will result in many false positives (FP), and if smoothing is too large, this method will result in a large number of false negatives (FN).

To address the ambiguity of smoothing, we significantly increased the sensitivity of local maximum detections. Thus, many FP for treetops would be generated, and a single tree crown would be split into many small watersheds. We then merged the small, detected watersheds that belonged to the same tree crown. This way, a small watershed could be identified for more than one tree, thus allowing for tree crown overlap detection. The watershed candidates were selected for a particular tree crown by the overlapping circle generated from the recorded GPS location containing the field recorded tree crown width. If a watershed was overlapped by more than 30% in area, the watershed would be assigned to the same tree crown. This method allowed one small watershed to be identified by two or more trees allowing the final tree boundary to have overlapping areas.

Finally, the width and length of the 3D bounding box were calculated by the differences between maximum x and y coordinate and the minimum x and y coordinate of the finally derived tree boundary, respectively. For height, the maximum and minimum according to the z-axis of the 3D bounding box were calculated using the ten largest z values of points in the 16% center and minimum z value of points in total over the 2D BEV bounding box. Figure 1(d) illustrates an example of the visualization of the tree bounding box. In this final inspection stage (inspection point 4, Fig. 3), we retained all bounding boxes with lower than 97% overlap with another box in BEV. We kept these highly overlapped bounding boxes because of the understory and trees growing too close, and only one tree crown was visible from the ALS data. We separated 4496 from 5084 trees for this version of benchmark data: 59% of the bounding boxes had less than 40% overlap; 30% of the bounding boxes had 40–80% overlap; 11% of the bounding boxes had more than 80% overlap. The amount of overlap was interpreted as the percentage of trees occluded by another tree. The wide variety of overlapping bounding boxes marks one of the uniqueness of our dataset and will be discussed further in the discussion section.

5   Experiments

5.1   Baseline Models

For evaluation of our benchmark dataset, we selected eight SOTA networks from the OpenPCDet toolbox [41]. We acknowledge the vast literature related to object detection, but a complete survey of the topic is beyond the scope of this paper. Table 3. summarizes the networks we use for validation.

Table 3. List of networks we use for benchmark

Network	Citation	Stage	Point or Voxel Based	Anchor
SECOND	[30]	1-Stage	Voxel	Anchor
PointPillars	[31]	1-Stage	Voxel	Anchor
PointRCNN	[32]	2-Stage	Point	Anchor Free
Part-A2	[33]	2-Stage	Both	Both
PV-RCNN	[34]	2-Stage	Both	Anchor
PyramidRCNN	[35]	2-Stage	Both	Anchor
VoxelRCNN	[36]	2-Stage	Voxel	Anchor
PVRCNN++	[37]	2-Stage	Both	Both

5.2   Dataset Setting

First, the data from multiple flight paths were merged, then split into 60m x 60m data tiles. Second, truncated trees at the edge of the tiles were included in the datasets to allow the detection of partial trees. We also removed any bounding boxes that were less than $1m^2$ in BEV generated during the tiling process. In the end, we generated 5577 3D bounding boxes, including the partial trees. Third, vegetation points classified but not included in the bounding box in section IV-A were removed. This was because there were missed trees during the field survey, and we must have removed those trees. It was necessary not to include these not labelled trees in the dataset because it may confuse the networks. Forth, we normalized the height of the data with [38] to fulfil the assumption that the base bounding box height is equal to 0 for the networks. Finally, we split our data tiles randomly into training (80%), validation (10%), and test (10%) datasets.

5.3   Experimental Setting

All experiments were conducted on the OpenPCDet. Unless specified, we used the default hyperparameters applied for the KITTI dataset using the OpenPCDet toolbox [41].

Maximum Number of Voxels. Most baseline models assume that point cloud data is sparse because it would be acquired from a mobile platform, e.g., KITTI dataset. Hence, many detection networks seek effective sampling methods for boosting performance. Conversely, our tree data, acquired through an airborne platform, is much denser. To illustrate the differences, Fig. 4 (a) shows an example of KITTI data in BEV and (b) shows an example of our data in BEV. In this example, 5.3% and 96.6% of the pixels contain ALS points in (a) and (b). Due to this difference, the more voxels we use for the voxel-based networks, the better results we should get. Table 4. illustrates the differences between the default and the maximum number of voxels resulting in different IoU.

Table 4. Validation Results from default ratio and 100%.

Maximum number of voxels		AP	AP
Train	Test	(IoU = 0.3)	(IoU = 0.5)
4300 (7.5%)	10700 (18.7%)	0.695	0.532
57600 (100%)	**57600 (100%)**	**0.756**	**0.594**

Our experiments used the maximum number of voxels that GPU memory allows, 57600 for PointPillars and 150000 for others.

Number of Proposals. Most 2-stage methods use the top-100 of the RPN results when inferencing. However, when we used this default value, the 2-stage networks performed worse than the 1-stage networks and were not what we expected. Furthermore, we observed that all 2-stage networks had very high precision and low recall at the default values. Therefore, we hypothesized that more RPN proposal was required. As a result, we changed top-100 to top-500 to match the training phase. As a result, we achieved higher AP for voxel-based 2-stage networks compared to 1-stage networks. Table 5. shows the test results of voxel-based 2-stage methods improved dramatically.

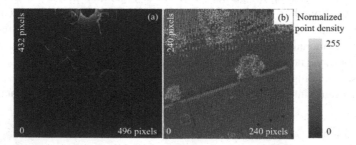

Fig. 4. (a) an example of BEV of KITTI dataset (b) an example of our dataset

Table 5. AP, precision and recall for IoU = 0.3.

Network	AP	Precision/Recall	AP	Precision/Recall
Part-A2	0.53	0.88/0.55	0.71	0.65/0.77
PV-RCNN	0.56	0.90/0.57	0.73	0.70/0.77
PyramidRCNN	0.57	0.870.58	0.79	0.77/0.83
VoxelRCNN	0.60	0.86/0.61	0.75	0.64/0.80
PV-RCNN++	0.55	0.89/0/57	0.72	0.62/0.78

Anchors. The tree in our dataset varies in size. This size variation directly affected determining the number of anchors and their sizes. We tested 1 to 5 anchors for the dataset where anchor sizes are derived from K means++. Our test shows that two anchor sizes [5.1, 4.8, 6.6] and [9.7, 9.3, 12.0] should be used. We then applied these values to all anchor-based networks.

Optimization. We used Adam optimizer with an initial learning rate 0.0003, and weight decay 0.0001. According to the baseline model's learning speed, the training was stopped learning up to 100 or 200 epochs.

Postprocessing. Since many overlapped trees were gathered as a cluster, the default NMS threshold was too low for trees. Tree clusters were detected as 1 TP at default NMS, resulting in many FNs. Hence, we increased the NMS to 0.4 to retain some of these overlapping trees.

5.4 Experimental Results

Figure 5 shows the BEV and 3D average precision (AP) at different IoU thresholds for all networks tested.

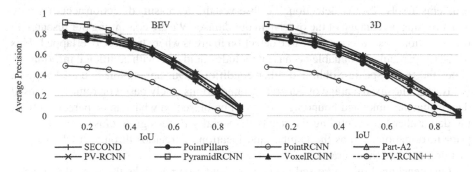

Fig. 5. AP at different IoU threshold for 8 networks at (a) BEV and (b) 3D

From Fig. 5, it was observed that the difference between BEV AP and 3D AP was small, indicating it was easier to predict values according to the z-axis and, therefore, more essential to find the methods to predict accurate BEV bounding box.

The only point-based network, PointRCNN, performed the worst for tree detection for both BEV AP and 3D AP. This was because PointRCNN draws sample points randomly, making the input data structure very sparse. Unlike instances such as cars and bicycles in the dataset created for autonomous driving, trees often overlap. To compare the prediction performance concerning overlap (occlusion), Fig. 6 shows that the higher the overlap ratio, the FN is being predicted, that is, a drop in recall.

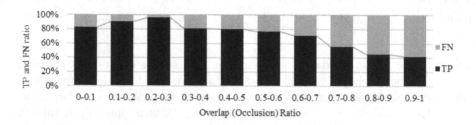

Fig. 6. True positive (TP), false negative (FN) distribution with different tree overlap (occlusion) ratio at IoU > 0.3.

6 Discussion

Our dataset is unique that it includes annotations for trees with varying degrees of occlusion. It ranges from trees that have no intersections with other trees or other things to trees with a high degree of occlusion with other objects and intersect with other trees. Although including highly overlapped trees (up to 97% overlapped in BEV) inevitably degraded our detection performance, it is essential to include these problematic cases because they are prevalent in urban green spaces such as parks and woodlots. Similar to pedestrian detection in crowded scenes, occlusion is one of the most complicated problems to solve for tree detection. We observed the decreasing detection accuracy with an increasing percentage of the overlap in our dataset. We are continuing our research in this direction to address accurate tree detection in areas where trees are overlapped. This dataset is particularly valuable because it includes field data with additional information about the trees' species, dbh, and other conditions. Our annotation is built based on fieldwork. The disadvantage of generating annotations solely based on remotely sensed data is that the annotated bounding boxes will be biased on what can be perceived from the data rather than capturing the reality. Especially if trees grow close to each other, prior information such as the number and location of treetops through fieldwork will increase annotation accuracy.

Our benchmark was assessed using eight detection networks that are all available. Our workflow applies to larger-scale annotation projects, and future studies will include the enlargement of the YUTO 5000 Tree. Our current experiments identified two best performing networks, PyarmidRCNN and VoxelRCNN, under different IoU thresholds. Second, we expected the anchor-free networks would perform better than the anchor-based network; however, this is not the case. We think this is probably due to the difficulty of predicting the size of the bounding boxes without prior knowledge of the object width-length-height ratio. Third, 2-stage detectors perform better than 1-stage due to the refinement of the second stage. However, to achieve this, we had to adjust the NMS settings at the test stage, allowing more proposal boxes to be proposed for the second refining stage. We concluded that a new network or additional network modules must be designed to improve tree detection further. We also want to emphasize that the SOTA network experiments give us insight into tree datasets rather than suggesting the best network for tree detection.

7 Conclusion

This paper presents a workflow for creating a single-tree benchmark dataset for tree detection and evaluating it using eight networks. Existing benchmark datasets for urban object detection do not include tree detection, and existing forest benchmark datasets do not have publicly accessible 3D bounding box annotations. The development and availability of our benchmark dataset will establish a critical common ground for training networks suited for updating urban tree inventories in the community. We tested eight SOTA 3D detectors to understand the applicability of existing networks designed for MLS applied to ALS. With preliminary success, we consider a new design is required to address the complexity of tree data. In addition, we recently obtained ALS data for the same area in both leaf-on and leaf-off seasons and spectral data in the acquisition. All are being processed now and will be included in future benchmark releases.

Acknowledgement. This research project has been supported by the Natural Sciences and Engineering Research Council of Canada (NSERC) 's Collaborative Research and Development Grant (CRD) – 3D Mobility Mapping Artificial Intelligence (3DMMAI) and Teledyne Geospatial Inc. We'd like to thank Andrew Sit (Product Manager), Burns Forster (Innovation Manager) and Chris Verheggen (SVP R&D) for supporting ALS data acquisition and postprocessing.

References

1. Geiger, A., Lenz, P., Urtasun, R.: Are we ready for autonomous driving? In: The KITTI vision benchmark suite. 2012 IEEE CVPR, pp. 3354–3361 (2012)
2. Patil, A., Malla, S., Gang, H., Chen, Y.-T.: The H3D dataset for full-surround 3D multi-object detection and tracking in crowded urban scenes. arXiv:1903.01568. [Cs] (2019)
3. Sun, P., et al.: Scalability in perception for autonomous driving: Waymo open dataset. In: 2020 IEEE/CVF Conference on Computer Vision and Pattern Recognition (CVPR), pp. 2443–2451 (2020)
4. Caesar, H., et al.: nuScenes: a multimodal dataset for autonomous driving. arXiv:1903.11027. [Cs, Stat] (2020)
5. Munoz, D., Bagnell, J.A., Vandapel, N., Hebert, M.: Contextual classification with functional max-margin Markov networks. In: 2009 IEEE Conference on Computer Vision and Pattern Recognition, pp. 975–982 (2009)
6. Rottensteiner, F., et al.: The ISPRS benchmark on urban object classification and 3D building reconstruction. ISPRS Ann. Photogramm., Remote Sens. Spat. Inf. Sci. **I–3**, 293–298 (2012)

7. Hackel, T., Savinov, N., Ladicky, L., Wegner, J.D., Schindler, K., Pollefeys, M.: Semantic3D.Net: a new large-scale point cloud classification benchmark. arXiv:1704.03847. [Cs] (2017)
8. Roynard, X., Deschaud, J.-E., Goulette, F.: Paris-Lille-3D: a large and high-quality ground-truth urban point cloud dataset for automatic segmentation and classification. Int. J. Robot. Res. **37**(6), 545–557 (2018)
9. Behley, J., et al.: SemanticKITTI: a dataset for semantic scene understanding of LiDAR sequences. In: 2019 IEEE/CVF International Conference on Computer Vision (ICCV), pp. 9296–9306 (2019)
10. Tan, W., et al.: Toronto-3D: a large-scale mobile LiDAR dataset for semantic segmentation of urban roadways. In: 2020 IEEE/CVF Conference on Computer Vision and Pattern Recognition Workshops (CVPRW), pp. 797–806 (2020)
11. Kaartinen, H., et al.: An international comparison of individual tree detection and extraction using airborne laser scanning. Remote Sens. **4**(4), 950–974 (2012)
12. Kaartinen, H., Hyyppä, J.: european spatial data research tree extraction official publication, no. 53 (2008). http://www.eurosdr.net/sites/default/files/uploaded_files/eurosdr_publication_ndeg_53.pdf
13. Eysn, L., et al.: A benchmark of Lidar-based single tree detection methods using heterogeneous forest data from the alpine space. Forests **6**(5), 1721–1747 (2015)
14. Vauhkonen, J., et al.: Comparative testing of single-tree detection algorithms under different types of forest. Forestry **85**(1), 27–40 (2011)
15. Liang, X., et al.: International benchmarking of terrestrial laser scanning approaches for forest inventories. ISPRS J. Photogramm. Remote. Sens. **144**, 137–179 (2018)
16. Wang, Y., et al.: International benchmarking of the individual tree detection methods for modeling 3-D canopy structure for Silviculture and forest ecology using airborne laser scanning. IEEE Trans. Geosci. Remote Sens. **54**(9), 5011–5027 (2016)
17. Weinstein, B.G., Marconi, S., Aubry-Kientz, M., Vincent, G., Senyondo, H., White, E.P.: DeepForest: a Python package for RGB deep learning tree crown delineation. Methods Ecol. Evol. **11**(12), 1743–1751 (2020)
18. Schmohl, S., Narváez Vallejo, A., Soergel, U.: Individual tree detection in Urban ALS point clouds with 3D convolutional networks. Remote Sens. **14**(6), 1317 (2022). https://doi.org/10.3390/rs14061317
19. Open Data Dataset. Open.toronto.ca. https://open.toronto.ca/dataset/street-tree-data/. Accessed11 Mar 2022
20. Forest Resources Inventory. ontario.ca. https://www.ontario.ca/page/forest-resources-inventory. Accessed11 Mar 2022
21. Street trees in Guelph. City of Guelph. https://guelph.ca/living/environment/trees/street-tree-ownership. Accessed11 Mar 2022
22. City-owned Tree Inventory. Data.mississauga.ca. https://data.mississauga.ca/datasets/city-owned-tree-inventory/explore?location=43.609902%2C-79.674385%2C11.90. Accessed11 Mar 2022
23. Street Trees. Data-markham.opendata.arcgis.com. https://data-mark-ham.opendata.arcgis.com/datasets/293d80c24bf54a4f8ab66bddaeaab184_0/about. Accessed11 Mar 2022
24. Wegner, J.D., Branson, S., Hall, D., Schindler, K., Perona, P.: Cataloging public objects using aerial and street-level images—Urban trees. In: 2016 IEEE Conference on Computer Vision and Pattern Recognition (CVPR), pp. 6014–6023 (2016)
25. Branson, S., Wegner, J.D., Hall, D., Lang, N., Schindler, K., Perona, P.: From google maps to a fine-grained catalog of street trees. ISPRS J. Photogramm. Remote. Sens. **135**, 13–30 (2018)

26. Matasci, G., Coops, N.C., Williams, D.A.R., Page, N.: Mapping tree canopies in urban environments using airborne laser scanning (ALS): a vancouver case study. Forest Ecosyst. **5**(1), 31 (2018)
27. Xie, Q., Li, D., Yu, Z., Zhou, J., Wang, J.: Detecting trees in street images via deep learning with attention module. IEEE Trans. Instrum. Meas. **69**(8), 5395–5406 (2020)
28. Zhang, S., Wen, L., Bian, X., Lei, Z., Li, S.Z.: Occlusion-aware R-CNN: detecting pedestrians in a crowd. arXiv:1807.08407. [Cs] (2018)
29. Lumnitz, S., Devisscher, T., Mayaud, J.R., Radic, V., Coops, N.C., Griess, V.C.: Mapping trees along urban street networks with deep learning and street-level imagery. ISPRS J. Photogramm. Remote. Sens. **175**, 144–157 (2021)
30. Yan, Y., Mao, Y., Li, B.: SECOND: sparsely embedded convolutional detection. Sensors **18**(10), 3337 (2018)
31. Lang, A.H., Vora, S., Caesar, H., Zhou, L., Yang, J., Beijbom, O.: PointPillars: fast encoders for object detection from point clouds. arXiv:1812.05784. [Cs, Stat] (2019)
32. Shi, S., Wang, X., Li, H.: PointRCNN: 3D object proposal generation and detection from point cloud. arXiv:1812.04244. [Cs] (2019)
33. Shi, S., Wang, Z., Shi, J., Wang, X., Li, H.: From points to parts: 3D object detection from point cloud with part-aware and part-aggregation network. arXiv:1907.03670. [Cs] (2020)
34. Shi, S., et al.: PV-RCNN: point-voxel feature set abstraction for 3D object detection. In: 2020 IEEE/CVF Conference on Computer Vision and Pattern Recognition (CVPR), pp. 10526–10535 (2020)
35. Mao, J., Niu, M., Bai, H., Liang, X., Xu, H., Xu, C.: Pyramid R-CNN: towards better performance and adaptability for 3D object detection. arXiv:2109.02499. [Cs] (2021)
36. Deng, J., Shi, S., Li, P., Zhou, W., Zhang, Y., Li, H.: Voxel R-CNN: towards high performance voxel-based 3D object detection. arXiv:2012.15712. [Cs] (2021)
37. Shi, S., et al.: PV-RCNN++: point-voxel feature set abstraction with local vector representation for 3D object detection. arXiv:2102.00463. [Cs] (2022)
38. LAStools. rapidlasso GmbH. https://rapidlasso.com/LAStools/. Accessed11 Mar 2022
39. TerraScan - Terrasolid. https://terrasolid.com/products/terrascan/. Accessed11 Mar 2022
40. DFT - Tutorial 2. Mparkan.github.io. https://mparkan.github.io/Digital-Forestry-Toolbox/tutorial-2.html. Accessed11 Mar 2022
41. GitHub - open-mmlab/OpenPCDet: OpenPCDet Toolbox for LiDAR-based 3D Object Detection. (2022). https://github.com/open-mmlab/OpenPCDet. Accessed11 Mar 2022

Spatial Layout Consistency for 3D Semantic Segmentation

Maryam Jameela and Gunho Sohn[✉]

Department of Earth and Space Science and Engineering Lassonde School of Engineering, York University, Toronto, ON M3J 1P3, Canada
{maryumja,gsohn}@yorku.ca

Abstract. Due to the aged nature of much of the utility network infrastructure, developing a robust and trustworthy computer vision system capable of inspecting it with minimal human intervention has attracted considerable research attention. The airborne laser terrain mapping (ALTM) system quickly becomes the central data collection system among the numerous available sensors. Its ability to penetrate foliage with high-powered energy provides wide coverage and achieves survey-grade ranging accuracy. However, the post-data acquisition process for classifying the ALTM's dense and irregular point clouds is a critical bottleneck that must be addressed to improve efficiency and accuracy. We introduce a novel deep convolutional neural network (DCNN) technique for achieving voxel-based semantic segmentation of the ALTM's point clouds. The suggested deep learning method, Semantic Utility Network (SUNet) is a multi-dimensional and multi-resolution network. SUNet combines two networks: one classifies point clouds at multi-resolution with object categories in three dimensions and another predicts two-dimensional regional labels distinguishing corridor regions from non-corridors. A significant innovation of the SUNet is that it imposes spatial layout consistency on the outcomes of voxel-based and regional segmentation results. The proposed multi-dimensional DCNN combines hierarchical context for spatial layout embedding with a coarse-to-fine strategy. We conducted a comprehensive ablation study to test SUNet's performance using 67 km x 67 km of utility corridor data at a density of $5pp/m^2$. Our experiments demonstrated that SUNet's spatial layout consistency and a multi-resolution feature aggregation could significantly improve performance, outperforming the SOTA baseline network and achieving a good F1 score for pylon (89%), ground (99%), vegetation (99%) and powerline (98%) classes.

Keywords: Semantic Segmentation · Airborne LiDAR · Utility Network · Spatial Layout · Coarse-to-Fine

1 Introduction

Conducting a safe, efficient, and accurate inspection for utility network management is vital to grid stability and resilience for protecting our economy.

J.-J. Rousseau and B. Kapralos (Eds.): ICPR 2022 Workshops, LNCS 13645, pp. 386–400, 2023.
https://doi.org/10.1007/978-3-031-37731-0_29

Traditionally, the utility network inspection is performed by a ground crew to manage vegetation encroachment or monitor the physical condition of the utility infrastructure [13]. Recently, operating an unmanned aerial vehicle (UAV) for utility inspection is gaining popularity to reduce the cost of data collection [31] [22]. However, it is still an open challenge to operate UAVs for completing data collection covering entire utility corridors due to strict flying regulations, short operation time, and limited spatial coverage. Thus, ALTM has become a central data acquisition platform for many utility network inspection projects. ALTM acquires dense point clouds to represent the utility infrastructure and its surrounding environment with survey-grade ranging accuracy [15]. A high-powered laser beam can penetrate foliage, enabling three-dimensional (3D) vegetation encroachment analysis at a single tree level [12] [28]. However, performing visual perception tasks such as labeling point clouds with semantic attributes from ALTM point clouds is still costly and conducted by laborious and error-prone manual work. Thus, there is an urgent demand to automate the post-data acquisition process to minimize human intervention. Recently, DCNN has out-performed previous state-of-the-art (SOTA) machine learning techniques with large margins in computer vision [27]. DCNN's most significant advantage is learning high-level features from data in an incremental manner. This deep feature representation generally generalizes DCNN's performance easier than other machine learning techniques. Recently several research groups have proposed the successful design of deep neural networks for achieving semantic segmentation using point clouds [23,24,27]. Though, neither have utilized the spatial layout found through the infrastructures, especially for utility corridors nor embedded the spatial layout for global context. This limitation inspired us to propose a network that deals with hierarchical spatial consistency that can later be generalized for any standard layout segmentation problem.

This research thoroughly investigates the utility corridor dataset. Firstly, the study unraveled spatial layout consistency. It identifies the hierarchy between regions (corridor and non-corridor) and object classes such as ground, towers, powerlines, and vegetation as shown in Fig. 1. Secondly, it utilizes the hierarchical spatial layout consistency by combining multi-dimensional input. Finally, it explores the science of human vision and information extraction for decision-making as a hierarchy. We proposed SUNet which combines two networks: one classifies point clouds at multi-resolution with object categories in three dimensions and another predicts two-dimensional regional labels distinguishing corridor regions from non-corridors. A significant innovation of the SUNet is that it imposes spatial layout consistency on the outcomes of voxel-based and regional segmentation results. SUNet also has a multi-resolution feature aggregation module in a three-dimensional network for enhancing the receptive field for minority class prediction. The following sections will discuss related work, proposed methodology, experiments, and results.

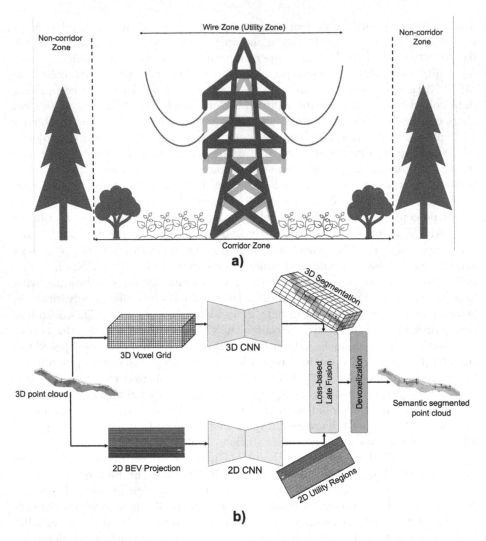

Fig. 1. SUNet is a multi-dimensional and multi-resolution network which imposes the spatial layout consistency (1a) through 2D bird's-eye view (BEV) of utility regions on the outcomes of 3D segmentation network via loss-based late fusion (1b).

2   Literature Review

We will discuss various groups of semantic segmentation methods for 3D point clouds and the importance of spatial layout in this section.

2.1   Semantic Segmentation

Semantic segmentation for 3D point cloud has improved significantly in the last decade, especially after the mainstream use of deep learning for computer vision.

Most of the research focused on utilizing intrinsic, extrinsic, and deep features for semantically labeling each point with an enclosing object or region [7]. One of the major limitations observed is the lack of focus on imposing spatial layout consistency from the real world for segmentation and global context embedding. Existing methods can be divided into three sections, i) statistical segmentation, ii) machine learning-based classification networks and iii) deep learning-based segmentation networks.

Geometrical Segmentation. Multiple existing methods treat utility corridor segmentation as a geometrical problem. These methods extract lines, cluster point clouds, and classify them using neighborhood votes, density, and height-based features [16]. These methods have shown tremendous improvement over time. The major limitations of these techniques are preprocessing, feature crafting, and the requirement of extensive domain knowledge. Most of these methods require multiple steps of filtering to segment the regions [10]. These techniques are not robust for raw large-scale dense 3D point clouds [12].

Machine Learning Based Utility Classification. Previous literature dealing with utility object classification, powerline reconstruction, and extraction has shown exemplary performance [11]. These methods employ support vector machines [28], random forest [13,15], decision trees, and balanced/unbalanced learning. These systems use either 3D voxels or 2D grid projections and handcraft features from eigenvalues to facilitate decision-making by providing distinguishing information [22]. Most of these techniques have shown limitations on 3D large-scale datasets. Deep learning and computer vision provided the ability to encode features that helps in decoding information for almost every computer vision task, including segmentation and classification. It liberated researchers from possessing extensive domain knowledge required for crafting features. It also generalizes the solutions across datasets and sensors.

Deep Learning-Based Segmentation Networks. Deep learning research has provided academic and commercial communities with a strong foundation for integrating artificial intelligence in post-processing, analysis, and predictive models. Semantic segmentation of point cloud has shown high performance using 3D voxels and 2D bird-eye view. These representations inherently come with the limitation of quantization errors despite providing an efficient boost to performance. The new batch of methods pioneered by PointNet [23] began to use raw point cloud directly as input to deep learning network which was extended by PointNet++ [24], KPConv introduced continuous kernels [27] and RandLA is state of the art network [7]. These networks have shown impressive and comparable performance on most segmentation benchmarks; such as Semantic3D [4], SensatUrban [6], or DublinCity [32]. Though, neither have utilized the spatial regularity found through the infrastructures, especially for utility corridors nor embedded the spatial layout for global context. This limitation inspired us to propose a SUNet.

2.2 Spatial Layout

Several studies in cognitive science, architectural design, and civil engineering utilize the spatial layout and relationships of objects with respect to each other [1]. This relationship helps our brains to understand the context of the scene and interpret it for decision-making. Convolution neural networks were designed to extract this spatial relationship but for learning global context spatial regularities needed to be embedded in the network such as railway lane extractions, road lane detection [9] and 3D model of the building [5]. Various other studies have been able to demonstrate how small objects such as cars on the side of a road will be easily detected based on the spatial relationship which might otherwise be ignored [26]. Our study is inspired by this research to use the spatial relationship between corridor non-corridor regions and objects present in these regions to demonstrate the importance of spatial layout embedding.

3 Methodology

SUNet is a multi-dimensional and multi-resolution network. We propose to decode the spatial consistency between layout and objects of interest. It consists of two networks; two-dimensional regional prediction network [25], which constrains the predictions of another three-dimensional network through loss-based late fusion.

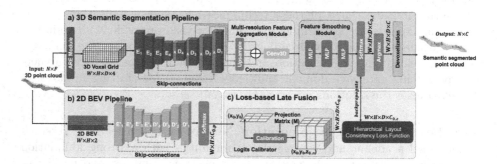

Fig. 2. The overall architecture of SUNet: Point cloud is preprocessed into voxel grid and BEV. These are separately processed by a multi-resolution 3D semantic segmentation pipeline and 2D BEV pipeline for regional prediction to impose the spatial layout consistency on 3D objects through loss-based late fusion.

3.1 3D Semantic Segmentation Pipeline

Overall network architecture is illustrated in Fig. 2. 3D segmentation network is a U-shaped multiresolution encoder-decoder [2,8]. It extracts features from a three-dimensional voxel grid to predict semantic labels for object classes [19]. In particular, this network extracts four feature maps E_1, E_2, E_3, and E_4. As shown in Fig. 2 E_n constructs output feature map D_n with series of operations including additive attention applied on D_{n-1} and E_n, two 3×3x3 convolution operations followed by batch normalization and relu activation. It results in four output feature maps { D_1, D_2, D_3,D_4 } with dimensions $\frac{H}{2l} \times \frac{W}{2l} \times \frac{D}{2l} \times 32l$ for output D at level l. These feature maps represent the deep multi-resolution output which in terms of semantic segmentation provides a multi-receptive field for segmenting objects and areas of different sizes. These feature maps are then passed through a multi-resolution feature aggregation module to incorporate knowledge and context from all levels. The final part of the pipeline is the feature smoothing module which eliminates noisy and cluttered predictions and delivers the confidence score against each class. This is passed by a loss-based late fusion module to refine and constrain using spatial layout consistency and back-propagate the loss to better learning deep features.

Additive Attention Module. In multi-resolution encoder-decoder architecture, downsampling can result in an overpopulation of false positives for small objects with significant shape variance. An additive attention gate can fix those localization problems and reduce misclassification [19]. This module learns multiple attention co-efficient for each class and produces the activated feature maps pruned to suppress the irrelevant information. These attention gates take input from previous layer of decoder D_1 for D_2 and encoder feature map of same level E_2 and generate attention co-efficient α to take element-wise summation with feature map E_2.

Multi-resolution Feature Aggregation Module. Our proposed module aggregates the feature maps from { D_1, D_2, D_3,D_4 } by upsampling and concatenating. Aggregated feature map then passes through 1×1x1 convolution. It helps in generating a feature map that eliminated the error introduced by upsampling of the decoder for minority class prediction.

Feature Smoothing Module. It is an optional module that has three multilayer perceptron (MLP) operations to smooth the feature maps. It evenly distributes the feature mean and variances. We plugged this module to remove the misclassification by a minimum margin.

3.2 2D BEV Pipeline

The biggest challenge for semantic segmentation is to integrate a larger receptive field and global context into the network for spatially informed prediction. Humans' judgment of scene semantics largely relied on their ability to grasp the global context. Our three-dimensional segmentation network is limited to local context and lacks coarser details of the scene for encoding spatial layout and global correlation of the objects. Our 2D BEV pipeline fuse this information through loss based late fusion module. Two-dimensional network is a multi-resolution encoder-decoder shown in Fig. 2 as a regional semantics block [25]. It consists of the four feature maps $\{E'_1, E'_2, E'_3, E'_4\}$ which constructs four output maps $\{D'_1, D'_2, D'_3, D'_4\}$. This network takes BEV of a complete 3D point cloud scene and predicts regional classes probability tensor of shape $W \times H \times C_p$.

3.3   Loss Based Late Fusion

This is a key module that is further divided into two sub-modules. The following sections will discuss this in detail.

Logits Calibrator. This module is straightforward calibration that takes the projection matrix between 3D voxels and 2D BEV and converts the 2D logits for regional classes of shape $W \times H \times C_p$ to 3D representation $W \times H \times D \times C_p$ by exploring the one-to-many relationship.

Hierarchical Layout Consistency (HLC) Loss Function. The proposed loss function takes advantage of hierarchy by penalizing the misclassification of object classes in the incorrect regions (corridor and non-corridor). Our loss function is a key element of late fusion module for fusing the context from a local and global scale. It takes 3D predictions from 3D pipeline and refines them through a global spatial layout extracted from 2D pipeline to bridge the gap of the larger receptive field. It evaluates the target class correlation $y_m^{P_c}$ to penalize the prediction of x_m weighted by w_p, w_c to reduce loss for better prediction as shown in Eq. 1. These co-occurrence weights for our experiments was 10.0 and 8.0 respectively and could be tuned. P is total number of parent classes which is two and C is total number of child classes.

$$L = \frac{1}{M} \sum_{p=1}^{P} \sum_{c=1}^{C} \sum_{m=1}^{M} (w_p w_c) \times (y_m^{P_c} \times (log(h_\Theta(x_m, c, p)))) \tag{1}$$

3.4   Voxelization and BEV Projection

Input representation of the 3D point cloud for our segmentation network is a voxel grid. We preprocess the raw point cloud onto the voxel grid and calculate a mean representing all the points residing in the 3D voxel. The network maintains a projection matrix from the voxel grid to the raw point cloud for easy label projection. This voxel grid provides a trade-off between efficiency and effectiveness based on the selection of voxel size.

BEV is a 2D view of a 3D point cloud. Our 2D BEV pipeline takes XY projection of a 3D scene where each pixel represents the residing points.

XY-projection gave the most optimal BEV for extracting global context for regional and object prediction. Our projection matrix M between BEV and 3D voxel grid provides projection compatibility between feature spaces to fuse 2D and 3D predictions for better utilization of spatial layout consistency.

3.5 Absolute and Relative Elevation Module

The data analysis showed non-homogeneous areas where points belonging to the same classes could be on different elevations. Hence, we incorporate local pillar-based normalization from Eq. 3 which uses the min elevation of each column and the maximum elevation of the scene for normalization and calculates over the whole point cloud $\{i \ni N, N = total\,points\}$.

Global Normalization:

$$Absolute\,Elevation_i = 1 + \frac{z_i}{z_{max\_global}} \tag{2}$$

Local Normalization:

$$Relative\,Elevation_i = \frac{(z_i - z_{min\_local})}{(z_{max\_scene} - z_{min\_local})} \tag{3}$$

Table 1. Ablation Study on importance of feature engineering over F1-Score; Occ: No. of Occupancy Points, AE: Absolute Elevation, RE: Relative Elevation and NR: Number of Returns

Methods	Features	Pylon (%)	Ground (%)	Veg (%)	Powerline (%)
Baseline	Occ + AE + NR	77.0	93.0	97.0	91.0
SUNet (ours)	Occ + AE + NR +RE	84.0	99.0	99.0	98.0

4   Experiments and Results

We conducted ablation studies based on feature engineering, loss and proposed modules. Experiments assess test set on the ground, pylon, powerline, and vegetation classes. These four classes are important for the utility industry for predictive maintenance (Fig. 3).

4.1   Dataset

Data is collected using a Riegl Q560 laser scanner over $67km^2$ in Steamboat Springs, Colorado, USA. Data is later divided into train and test sets for experiments. The first $8km^2$ of the dataset is used for testing and the remaining data is used for training the network. There is a total of 67 non-overlapping scenes each containing more than two million points with an average density

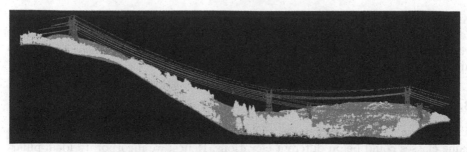

Groundtruth

SUNet+ ARE Module

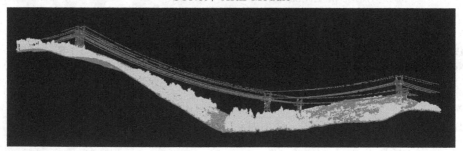

SUNet + ARE Module + MFA

Fig. 3. Visualization of results; Groundtruth, SUNet+ ARE (ours) and SUNet + ARE + Multiresolution feature aggregation module (ours). Blue: pylon, red: powerline, green: high vegetation and dark-green: ground (Color figure online)

Table 2. Comparison of baseline 3D Attention UNet (3D AUNet) to proposed SUNet and ablation study of modules multiresolution feature aggregation (MFA), and feature smoothing (FS) on recall (R), precision (P) and F1 score (F1).

Methods	Pylon (%)			Ground (%)			Veg (%)			Powerline (%)		
	R	P	F1	R	P	F1	R	P	F1	R	P	F1
3D AUNet (baseline)	72.0	84.0	77.0	93.0	94.0	93.0	97.0	97.0	97.0	84.0	98.0	91.0
SUNet+MFA+FS (ours)	78.0	97.0	87.0	**100**	99.0	**100**	99.0	99.0	99.0	**99.0**	97.0	98.0
SUNet+MFA (ours)	**82.0**	**96.0**	**89.0**	99.0	**99.0**	99.0	**99.0**	**99.0**	**99.0**	98.0	**99.0**	**99.0**

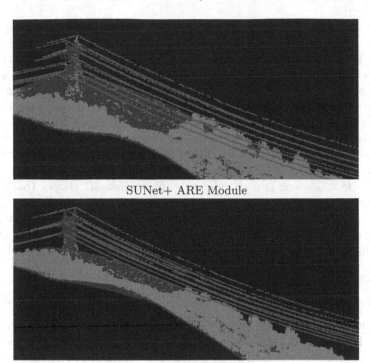

SUNet+ ARE Module

SUNet + ARE Module + MFA

Fig. 4. Visualization of Errors; SUNet+ ARE (ours) and SUNet + ARE + Multiresolution feature aggregation module (ours). Blue: pylon, red: powerline, green: high vegetation and dark-green: ground (Color figure online)

of $5pp/m^2$. We manually labeled our ground truth using Terrasolid point cloud processing software. Labels were generated through extensive domain knowledge and technical expertise. Our training dataset had five classes powerline, pylon, low vegetation, ground, and medium-high vegetation. We merged low vegetation into ground class as the most ground is covered by low vegetation. We also labeled our regional classes based on utility community literature. Powerlines and pylons are in the corridor region and (3–10) m away from the pylon is a non-corridor region.

4.2 Experimental Configuration

We took half of the scenes to pretrain our 2D regional prediction network for global regional prediction of spatial layout. Each scene is divided into four subscenes by GPS time of flight line. These subscenes are then projected on a 640×640 2D BEV grid of each pixel size= $1m^2$. Each grid has two feature channels, mean elevation, and the number of occupancy points per pixel. The input size of the 2D network is $640 \times 640 \times 2$ and the output is $640 \times 640 \times 3$ which is the regional classes' confidence score. We pretrained the network with

$batchsize = 1$ and total epochs of 100 with K-cross validation to avoid overfitting. We augmented our dataset using horizontal flip, vertical flip and random rotation. The network is trained on two GPU RTX 6000; training time is between 4–5 hours, and inference takes about 30 s. Our voxel grid is generated over each subscene and the size is $640 \times 640 \times 448$ with a voxel size of $1m^3$. Each batch consists of maximum elevation of the whole scene to provide network the complete view to better deal with vertical context. Feature channels consist of absolute and relative elevation as discussed in methodology, number of occupancy points, and a number of returns. We have conducted a feature engineering study to select these features which will be discussed in the following section. SUNet outputs $32 \times 32 \times 448 \times 5$ which is a confidence score against 3D classes (background, pylon, powerline, vegetation, and ground). Later, the final prediction assigns a true label based on the highest confidence score and project voxels labels on points using the project matrix. SUNet is trained on two GPU RTX 6000 for 100 epochs; training time is between 48–60 hours, and inference takes about 2–3 mins.

4.3 Evaluation Metrics

We selected precision, recall, and F1 score for evaluating the performance of our network. The precision determines the total number of predicted samples out of the total instances of the class. Recall measures correctly predicted samples out of the total predicted sample of the class. F1 score shows the balance between precision and recall.

4.4 Feature Engineering

We progressively developed a feature engineering study and used a number of occupancy points and absolute elevation and number of returns as input. Our feature engineering study was also inspired by [15] to develop absolute and relative elevation modules to deal with non-homogeneous surfaces. SUNet with ARE module shows a drastic improvement in the powerline, pylon, and ground classes as shown in Table 1.

Table 3. Ablation Study on importance of loss function over F1-Score; WCE: Weighted Cross Entropy and HLC: Hierarchical Layout Consistency Loss

Methods	Loss Function	Pylon	Ground	Veg	Powerline
Baseline	WCE	82.0	94.0	97.0	91.0
SUNet (ours)	HLC	**84.0**	**99.0**	**99.0**	**98.0**

4.5 Loss Functions

We proposed HLC loss function to impose the spatial layout consistency over the 3D object segmentation. As shown in Table 3 the remarkable increase in the performance of all classes especially pylon and ground classes.

4.6   Module Based Ablation Study

Later, we had dived into a module-based ablation study. We decided on four features and plugged different combinations of modules to observe the performance. SUNet used attention UNet [19] as the backbone showing improvement in all classes, especially the pylon and powerline classes. This validates the significance of global context from the 2D network to refine predictions based on regional spatial layout embedding. We then introduced multi-resolution feature aggregation and feature smoothing modules. We aggregated features from all scales of the backbone network and that improved the precision of the pylon to 97%. It shows that the pylon which is the smaller object and minority class is ignored by the downsampling. Though feature smoothing didn't show any large impact on recall for pylon class. All other classes are already reaching (98–99)%. We removed the feature smoothing module and recall for pylon class 82% improved which showed that feature smoothing was causing an error due to the structural similarity of tree and pylon.

4.7   Error Analysis

The 2D regional prediction network has room for improvement. It is the reason that the pylon class is still below 90% in the recall. Feature smoothing improved the precision of the pylon class as shown in Table 2. Though, Lower parts of pylons are misclassified as trees and isolated points labeled as powerlines. These errors are due to structural similarity of tree and pylon in terms of point density and data distribution as shown in Fig. 4.

5   Conclusion

In this work, we demonstrated that proposed SUNet with loss based late fusion contributes to embedding spatial layout. It also proved multi-resolution feature aggregation module incorporate the broader context for decision making. These experiments have verified conceptual inspiration and hypothesis i.e.; hierarchical layout spatial consistency combined with coarse-to-fine strategy can facilitate a development of deep semantic segmentation model for predictive analysis. Our future work will focus on improving the performance of regional predictions and generalization of the proposed network on various sensors.

Acknowledgment. This research project has been supported by the Natural Sciences and Engineering Research Council of Canada (NSERC)'s Collaborative Research and Development Grant (CRD) - 3D Mobility Mapping Artificial Intelligence (3DMMAI) and Teledyne Geospatial Inc. We'd like to thank Leihan Chen (Research Scientist), Andrew Sit (Product Manager), Burns Forster (Innovation Manager) and Chris Verheggen (SVP R& D).

References

1. Brosamle, M., Holscher, C.: Architects seeing through the eyes of building users, a qualitative analysis of design cases. In: 2007, International Conference on Spatial Information Theory (COSIT2007), pp. 8–13, 01 2007
2. Çiçek, Ö., Abdulkadir, A., Lienkamp, S.S., Brox, T., Ronneberger, O.: 3D U-Net: learning dense volumetric segmentation from sparse annotation. In: Ourselin, S., Joskowicz, L., Sabuncu, M.R., Unal, G., Wells, W. (eds.) MICCAI 2016. LNCS, vol. 9901, pp. 424–432. Springer, Cham (2016). https://doi.org/10.1007/978-3-319-46723-8_49
3. Guan, H., Yu, Y., Li, J., Ji, Z., Zhang, Q.: Extraction of power-transmission lines from vehicle-borne lidar data. Int. J. Remote Sens. **37**(1), 229–247 (2016). https://doi.org/10.1080/01431161.2015.1125549
4. Hackel, T., Savinov, N., Ladicky, L., Wegner, J.D., Schindler, K., Pollefeys, M.: Semantic3D.Net: a new large-scale point cloud classification benchmark. CoRR abs/1704.03847 (2017). https://arxiv.org/abs/1704.03847
5. Haldekar, M., Ganesan, A., Oates, T.: Identifying spatial relations in images using convolutional neural networks. In: 2017 International Joint Conference on Neural Networks (IJCNN), pp. 3593–3600 (2017). https://doi.org/10.1109/IJCNN.2017.7966308
6. Hu, Q., Yang, B., Khalid, S., Xiao, W., Trigoni, N., Markham, A.: Towards semantic segmentation of urban-scale 3D point clouds: a dataset, benchmarks and challenges. CoRR abs/2009.03137 (2020). https://arxiv.org/abs/2009.03137
7. Hu, Q., et al.: RandLA-Net: efficient semantic segmentation of large-scale point clouds. CoRR abs/1911.11236 (2019). https://arxiv.org/abs/1911.11236
8. Isensee, F., Kickingereder, P., Wick, W., Bendszus, M., Maier-Hein, K.H.: Brain tumor segmentation and radiomics survival prediction: contribution to the BRATS 2017 challenge. CoRR abs/1802.10508 (2018). https://arxiv.org/abs/1802.10508
9. Jeon, W.G., Kim, E.M.: Automated reconstruction of railroad rail using helicopter-borne light detection and ranging in a train station. Sens. Mater. **31**, 3289 (2019). https://doi.org/10.18494/SAM.2019.2433
10. Jung, J., Che, E., Olsen, M.J., Shafer, K.C.: Automated and efficient powerline extraction from laser scanning data using a voxel-based subsampling with hierarchical approach. ISPRS J. Photogramm. Remote. Sens. **163**, 343–361 (2020). https://doi.org/10.1016/j.isprsjprs.2020.03.018
11. Jwa, Y., Sohn, G.: A multi-level span analysis for improving 3d power-line reconstruction performance using airborne laser scanning data. ISPRS - Int. Arch. Photogramm., Remote Sens. Spat. Inf. Sci. **38**, 97–102 (2010)
12. Jwa, Y., Sohn, G., Kim, H.: Automatic 3D powerline reconstruction using airborne lidar data. IAPRS **38**, 105–110 (2009)
13. Kim, H., Sohn, G.: 3D classification of powerline scene from airborne laser scanning data using random forests. IAPRS **38**, 126–132 (2010). https://doi.org/10.13140/2.1.1757.4409
14. Kim, H., Sohn, G.: Random forests based multiple classifier system for powerline scene classification, vol. XXXVIII-5/W12, 08 2011. https://doi.org/10.5194/isprsarchives-XXXVIII-5-W12-253-2011
15. Kim, H., Sohn, G.: Point-based classification of power line corridor scene using random forests. Photogramm. Eng. Remote Sens. **79**, 821–833 (2013). https://doi.org/10.14358/PERS.79.9.821

16. Liu, Y., Li, Z., Hayward, R., Walker, R., Jin, H.: Classification of airborne lidar intensity data using statistical analysis and hough transform with application to power line corridors. In: 2009 Digital Image Computing: Techniques and Applications, pp. 462–467 (2009). https://doi.org/10.1109/DICTA.2009.83

17. Mottaghi, R., et al.: The role of context for object detection and semantic segmentation in the wild. In: Proceedings of the IEEE Computer Society Conference on Computer Vision and Pattern Recognition. pp. 891–898. IEEE Computer Society, September 2014. https://doi.org/10.1109/CVPR.2014.119. publisher Copyright: 2014 IEEE.; 27th IEEE Conference on Computer Vision and Pattern Recognition, CVPR 2014; Conference date: 23-06-2014 Through 28-06-2014

18. Nan, Z., et al.: A joint object detection and semantic segmentation model with cross-attention and inner-attention mechanisms. Neurocomputing **463**, 212–225 (2021). https://doi.org/10.1016/j.neucom.2021.08.031, https://www.sciencedirect.com/science/article/pii/S0925231221012157

19. Oktay, O., et al.: Attention U-Net: learning where to look for the pancreas. CoRR abs/1804.03999 (2018). https://arxiv.org/abs/1804.03999

20. Peng, J., Nan, Z., Xu, L., Xin, J., Zheng, N.: A deep model for joint object detection and semantic segmentation in traffic scenes. In: 2020 International Joint Conference on Neural Networks (IJCNN), pp. 1–8 (2020). https://doi.org/10.1109/IJCNN48605.2020.9206883

21. Petras, K., ten Oever, S., Jacobs, C., Goffaux, V.: Coarse-to-fine information integration in human vision. Neuroimage **186**, 103–112 (2019). https://doi.org/10.1016/j.neuroimage.2018.10.086

22. Pu, S., et al.: Real-time powerline corridor inspection by edge computing of UAV Lidar data. ISPRS - Int. Arch. Photogramm., Remote Sens. Spat. Inf. Sci. XLII-2/W13, 547–551 (2019). https://doi.org/10.5194/isprs-archives-XLII-2-W13-547-2019

23. Qi, C.R., Su, H., Mo, K., Guibas, L.J.: PointNet: deep learning on point sets for 3D classification and segmentation. CoRR abs/1612.00593 (2016). https://arxiv.org/abs/1612.00593

24. Qi, C.R., Yi, L., Su, H., Guibas, L.J.: PointNet++: deep hierarchical feature learning on point sets in a metric space. CoRR abs/1706.02413 (2017). https://arxiv.org/abs/1706.02413

25. Ronneberger, O., Fischer, P., Brox, T.: U-Net: convolutional networks for biomedical image segmentation. CoRR abs/1505.04597 (2015). https://arxiv.org/abs/1505.04597

26. Rosman, B., Ramamoorthy, S.: Learning spatial relationships between objects. Int. J. Robot. Res. **30**, 1328–1342 (2011). https://doi.org/10.1177/0278364911408155

27. Thomas, H., Qi, C.R., Deschaud, J., Marcotegui, B., Goulette, F., Guibas, L.J.: KPConv: flexible and deformable convolution for point clouds. CoRR abs/1904.08889 (2019). https://arxiv.org/abs/1904.08889

28. Wang, Y., Chen, Q., Liu, L., Zheng, D., Li, C., Li, K.: Supervised classification of power lines from airborne lidar data in urban areas. Remote Sens. **9**(8) (2017). https://doi.org/10.3390/rs9080771https://www.mdpi.com/2072-4292/9/8/771

29. Yang, J., Huang, Z., Huang, M., Zeng, X., Li, D., Zhang, Y.: Power line corridor LiDAR point cloud segmentation using convolutional neural network. In: Lin, Z., et al. (eds.) PRCV 2019. LNCS, vol. 11857, pp. 160–171. Springer, Cham (2019). https://doi.org/10.1007/978-3-030-31654-9_14

30. Zhao, J., et al.: The fusion strategy of 2D and 3D information based on deep learning: a review. Remote Sens. **13**(20) (2021). https://doi.org/10.3390/rs13204029, https://www.mdpi.com/2072-4292/13/20/4029

31. Zhou, M., et al.: Automatic extraction of power lines from UAV lidar point clouds using a novel spatial feature. ISPRS Ann. Photogramm., Remote Sens. Spat. Inf. Sci. IV-2/W7, 227–234 (2019). https://doi.org/10.5194/isprs-annals-IV-2-W7-227-2019, https://www.isprs-ann-photogramm-remote-sens-spatial-inf-sci.net/IV-2-W7/227/2019/
32. Zolanvari, S.M.I., et al.: Dublincity: Annotated lidar point cloud and its applications. CoRR abs/1909.03613 (2019). https://arxiv.org/abs/1909.03613

Computer Vision for Analysis
of Underwater Imagery (CVAUI)

Preface

It is our great pleasure to present you the workshop proceedings of the ICPR. This is a dummy text, to be replaced by the introduction of the workshop and challenge chairs.

We received 44 workshop proposals on a broad set of topics related to computer vision. The high quality of the proposals made the selection process rather difficult. Owing to space limitation, 27 proposals were accepted, among which two proposals were merged to form a single workshop due to overlapping themes.

The final 26 workshops complemented the main conference program well. The workshop topics present a good orchestration of new trends and traditional issues, as well as fundamental technologies and novel applications. We would like to thank all the workshop organizers for their unreserved efforts to make the workshop sessions a great success.

August 2022

Xiang Bai
Giovanni Farinella
Laurence Likforman
Jonathan Wu
Marco Bertini
Dimosthenis Karatzas

From TrashCan to UNO: Deriving an Underwater Image Dataset to Get a More Consistent and Balanced Version

Cyril Barrelet[1](✉) , Marc Chaumont[1,3] , Gérard Subsol[1] ,
Vincent Creuze[1] , and Marc Gouttefarde[2]

[1] Research-team ICAR, LIRMM, Univ Montpellier, CNRS, Montpellier, France
`cyril.barrelet@lirmm.fr`
[2] Research-team DEXTER, LIRMM, Univ Montpellier, CNRS, Montpellier, France
[3] Univ Nîmes, Nîmes, France

Abstract. The multiplication of publicly available datasets makes it possible to develop Deep Learning models for many real-world applications. However, some domains are still poorly explored, and their related datasets are often small or inconsistent. In addition, some biases linked to the dataset construction or labeling may give the impression that a model is particularly efficient. Therefore, evaluating a model requires a clear understanding of the database. Moreover, a model often reflects a given dataset's performance and may deteriorate if a shift exists between the training dataset and real-world data.

In this paper, we derive a more consistent and balanced version of the TrashCan [6] image dataset, called UNO, to evaluate models for detecting non-natural objects in the underwater environment. We propose a method to balance the number of annotations and images for cross-evaluation. We then compare the performance of a SOTA object detection model when using TrashCAN and UNO datasets. Additionally, we assess covariate shift by testing the model on an image dataset for real-world application. Experimental results show significantly better and more consistent performance using the UNO dataset.

The UNO database and the code are publicly available at:
https://www.lirmm.fr/uno and
https://github.com/CBarrelet/balanced_kfold.

Keywords: underwater imagery · underwater trash · inbalanced dataset · Deep Learning

1 Introduction

Recently, interest in cleaning up the seabed has increased, motivated by the growth of underwater macro-litter pollution [2]. Monitoring the presence of macro-litter on the seabed, in particular by optical acquisition, has become a very active research topic [10]. Deep Learning (DL) approaches are then adapted to

© Springer Nature Switzerland AG 2023
J.-J. Rousseau and B. Kapralos (Eds.): ICPR 2022 Workshops, LNCS 13645, pp. 403–414, 2023.
https://doi.org/10.1007/978-3-031-37731-0_30

detect, localize, and identify macro-litter in the underwater environment, which is very variable. Moreover, these approaches should run fast, which is crucial if we want to guide Remotely Operated underwater Vehicles (ROV) to pick macro-litter.

The availability of video datasets as DeepSeaWaste [5][1] or TrashCan [7][2] allowed researchers to design DL networks to classify [13,16] and localize [9,11] macro-litter within underwater images. Figure 1 shows some images from these two datasets.

Fig. 1. Images from the DeepSeaWaste (left) and TrashCan (right) datasets.

The DeepSeaWaste dataset [5] is composed of 544 underwater macro-litter images taken by the Japan Agency of Marine-Earth Science and Technology (JAMSTEC) [1]. The 76 classes are descriptive, such as *ashtray*, *bottle*, or *rope*, but they are entirely unbalanced, considering that the number of examples ranges from 1 to 12. In fact, 43 classes have only two examples at most. Moreover, some images have multiple labels. The limited number of images for some classes makes the training or evaluation of classification tasks difficult.

The TrashCan dataset [7] is a semantically-segmented database composed of 7,212 images that were primarily extracted consecutively from 312 different video sequences taken by JAMSTEC, since 1982, in the Sea of Japan. It is an improved version of the Trash-ICRA19 dataset [4]. 16 to 22 classes are represented depending on the version, such as *ROV* (which includes any part of the ROV carrying the camera), animals (which are defined by specific classes such as *animal_crab*, *animal_eel*, *animal_fish*), plant, and trash which is also divided into specific subclasses such as *trash_metal* or *trash_fishing_gear*. However, the classes are poorly balanced, particularly the *ROV* category, which represents up to 33% of all annotations. We also visually assessed that many annotations are incorrect, poorly localized, or missing. Notice that some metadata, such as the depth, date, or time, are directly overlayed on the images, which could introduce some artifacts in the learning process.

---

[1] https://www.kaggle.com/henryhaefliger/deepseawaste.
[2] https://conservancy.umn.edu/handle/11299/214865.

Another problem occurs in the evaluation. When we use the standard k-fold cross-validation method, we split the dataset into k sub-datasets, and, for each fold, we keep k-1 sub-datasets for constituting the training dataset, and the last one becomes a test dataset. Thus, we get k detection/localization accuracies that we average to estimate an overall accuracy. In the TrashCan dataset, the 7,212 images were extracted consecutively from videos sequences, so 2 images might be very similar if they belong to the same sequence, especially if the ROV is moving very slowly or is stable. Consequently, if in the k-fold evaluation process, we randomly distribute the images over the k sub-datasets, we will have images of a given sequence both in the training and the test datasets. As these images may be very close, they may artificially boost the overall performance.

In conclusion, there are very few available underwater macro-litter datasets, and they suffer from a strong imbalance between classes, many annotation errors, and temporal consistency, which make many images of the dataset very close. In this work, we propose to take the TrashCan dataset, which is the most complete and relevant one for macro-litter detection and localization in the underwater environment, and derive a new version that will be more consistent and balanced. In the following, we describe our method. Notice that even if the methodology is focused on a specific dataset, it could be used to derive other image datasets presenting the same limitations.

The rest of the paper is organized as follows. Section 2 describes the deriving process itself (frame selection, class fusion, text suppression, and re-labeling) in order to obtain a new dataset called UNO (for Underwater Non-natural Object), which is publicly available. Section 3 describes, in particular, a methodology (available on the GitHub[3]) to get k-folds, ensuring that images of the same video are only in one training or evaluation dataset, thereby resulting in a good balance of frames and bounding boxes. In Sect. 4, the state-of-the-art YOLOv5 [9] detector is used to compare performances using TrashCan and its derived version UNO as training or evaluation datasets. We also evaluate the effect of using TrashCan or UNO as the training dataset on the generalization ability by evaluating performances on images of the AQUALOC dataset [3], which presents a significant covariate shift.

2   UNO Dataset Construction

2.1   Label Redefinition

Our objective in using the TrashCan dataset is to develop methods to detect or localize macro-litter, but the dataset also includes non-litter classes such as *animal*, *plant*, or *ROV*. The trash class itself is decomposed into 8 distinct classes with 142 to 2,040 examples per class. In order to mitigate class imbalance and the ambiguity of trash definition, we decided to consider a more general problem

---

[3] https://github.com/CBarrelet/balanced_kfold

of object localization by fusing all the trash classes as the *ROV* one into a unique class that we call *Non-natural Object*. This postpones the classification step to future work.

2.2   Text Removal

As we can see in Figs. 1 and 2, some metadata are directly overlayed as text in the images. Therefore, we must remove it as it may disturb the detection process in the learning or test phase if the text is considered as an object.

More precisely, the text is always on the top and bottom parts of the image. We thus decided to suppress the top and the bottom of the frame leading to cropped images with smaller heights. To this end, we set up an automatic processing consisting in first, detecting the text, secondly estimating the average ordinate (y-axis) for the top and the bottom text line, and third cropping the middle region of the image (see Fig. 2, column 2). More practically, we train a YOLOv5 extra-large model for text detection on the COCO-Text dataset [15] with the recommended hyperparameters from [9] and a batch size of 28, achieving a precision (P) of 0.71, a recall (R) of 0.56, and a mAP@.5 of 0.621. Since the precision remains relatively low, we keep only the detected text which y coordinate is within the mean ± std of all y coordinates of the detected texts. In fact, the detected text laying outside this interval is considered as false positive and then removed.

2.3   Relocalization

TrashCan has a non-negligible part of the labels that either are incorrect, missing, or which corresponding bounding boxes (BB) are imprecisely located. We relocated every BB w.r.t. the following rules. First, we modify the border delimitation between objects and bounding boxes, assuring a perfect pixel tightness. We removed all misplaced BB and tried to avoid overlapping BB that might cause a performance drop. Secondly, we annotated missing objects from frame to frame. Furthermore, we chose to add some complex examples. Indeed, objects are barely recognizable from a human perspective because of depth, luminosity, and turbidity, in the underwater environment. So for a labeled object in a given frame, we checked for the same object in the previous frames even if its appearance is unclear and added the frame to the dataset.

2.4   Discussion on the Derived UNO Dataset

In Fig. 2, we can see in the TrashCan images that the ROV (up), which partly appears on the bottom and the upper right of the image is delineated by two different BB which are much larger than the ROV parts and (bottom) that the plastic bottle is not labeled. The UNO images are cropped parts of the TrashCan images in order to delete non-significant content as the text and the BBs were resized in order to better fit the non-natural objects.

Original: *TrashCan*   Derived: *UNO*

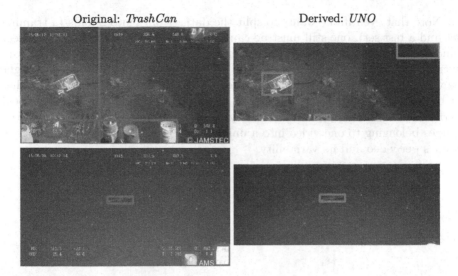

Fig. 2. Images and annotations from TrashCan (left) and UNO (right) datasets. We can see how the UNO images were cropped in order to delete artefactual content (in particular the text) and how some BB were resized or added to fit better the non-natural objects.

After the process, the UNO dataset consists of 279 video sequences with 5,902 frames and 10,773 bounding boxes labeled with the unique Non-natural object class.

We pointed out some limitations directly linked to the localization and the shape of the objects. We included some overlapping BBs while minimizing their number to limit confusion at evaluation time. Moreover, thin diagonally shaped objects, such as ropes, could confuse the model at the training stage. Indeed, a thin diagonally shaped object covers just a small portion of its BB, while the background covers the rest. We could have used polygonal BB and pixel-wise labels to improve diagonally-shaped object detection. Nevertheless, we labeled them with classic rectangle BB because of their rare occurrence.

3 A Methodology for a Well-Balanced K-Fold

When a dataset contains a small number of images, the best way to properly evaluate the accuracy of a DL network is to split the dataset in k-folds and circularly use $(k-1)$ folds as the learning dataset and the last fold for the test dataset. This results in a total of k learning phases, each evaluated on a different fold. Finally, one can average all the results in an overall performance indicator (i.e., accuracy) and compute the standard deviation. This last value can be considered as an indicator of generalizability and can be used in a Student's t-test on the performance indicator to decide if a network is better than another.

Note that even if one wants to split the dataset only into 2 folds (a training set and a test set), one still must be cautious. In the case of TrashCan, a direct random split introduces a bias. As mentioned, the frames of the dataset are extracted consecutively from the videos. A frame n and $n + 1$ of a video might be very similar, and they may be assigned one in the training set and the other in the test set. As they are very close, they may artificially boost the model performance. Therefore, the correct way to split the dataset is to group all the frames belonging to one video into a unique fold. Figure 3 shows the number of frames per video and its variability.

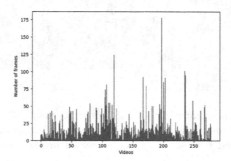

Fig. 3. Number of frames for the 279 videos.

Moreover, in order to get comparable learning phases in the cross-validation process, we must ensure that we have the same number of BB in each fold. In conclusion, we have to split the dataset into k-folds (in the following, we fixed k to 5) with both balanced frames and BB numbers, while keeping all the frames of a video in a unique fold. This problem is known as the bin packing problem [12] since we want to fill $k = 5$ folds at the best (with the video frame constraint), knowing their targeted capacity is approximately the total number of frames and BB divided by 5.

As we are looking for approximately the same number of frames and the same number of BB in each frame, we will minimize both the standard deviation σ_F of the number of frames per fold and the standard deviation σ_{BB} of the number of BB. Due to the pertinence of both the frames and the BB numbers, we choose to consider σ_F and σ_{BB} equally. Thus, the problem can then be written as the following optimization:

$$f^* = arg \min_{f \in \{1..5\}^{279}} (\sigma_F + \sigma_{BB}) \tag{1}$$

With f a 279-tuple, i.e., $f \in \{1, ..., 5\}^{279}$, corresponding to the assignment of 279 videos to 1 of the 5 folds. There are 5^{279} different 279-tuples which is very large.

An approximate but fast and easy solution to find the best assignment f is to create 100,000,000 k-folds by shuffling the videos and filling each fold to their targeted capacity. Then, we select the k-fold assignment minimizing Eq. 1.
Table 1 shows the distribution obtained in our best k-fold. The result seems reasonable since both σ_F and σ_{BB} are very low.

Table 1. Optimal 5-fold distribution with video, frame and BB numbers by fold.

Fold	Video	Frames	BBs
1	63	1180	2159
2	64	1182	2137
3	49	1185	2152
4	44	1179	2163
5	57	1176	2162
Mean	55.4	1189.2	2154.6
σ	7.81	3.00	9.60

More generally, since a different video database could lead to a scattered distribution, one may privilege a standard deviation over another in favor of a more balanced version. Hence, the problem could be rewritten as the following optimization:

$$f^* = arg \min_{f \in \{1..5\}^N} \left((1 - \alpha)\, \sigma_F + \alpha\, \sigma_{BB} \right) \tag{2}$$

With f a N-tuple, i.e., $f \in \{1, ..., 5\}^N$, corresponding to the assignment of N videos to 1 of the 5 folds, and $\alpha \in [0, ..., 1]$ a weighting parameter.

4   Experiments and Results

In this section, the UNO dataset is benchmarked with YOLOv5m [9]. As a recall, the UNO dataset contains 279 videos, 5,902 frames, and 10,773 bounding boxes. All bounding boxes contain a non-natural object; YOLOv5m is then a one-class detector.

4.1   Experiments

We chose the YOLOv5m [9] model pre-trained on ImageNet at a 640 × 640 pixels resolution. We used transfer learning from its pre-trained weights to keep the previous knowledge. We chose the SGD optimizer and the OneCycle scheduler, with initial and final learning rates of 0.0032 and 0.000384, respectively, while setting the warmup at 20% of the total epochs. In addition, we set the batch

Table 2. Results on different dataset achieved using YOLOv5m

Training set	Evaluation set	Split	P (%)	R (%)	F1 (%)	mAP@.5 (%)
TrashCan	TrashCan	Random	83.1	76.5	79.7	80.8
TrashCan	TrashCan	K-folded	57.1 ± 5.2	60.1 ± 5.5	58.4 ± 4.2	56.6 ± 6.3
TrashCan	UNO	K-folded	64.2 ± 5.0	58.2 ± 2.9	60.9 ± 2.6	60.8 ± 4.2
UNO	**UNO**	**K-folded**	**68.7 ± 4.3**	**66.2 ± 1.5**	**67.3 ± 1.5**	**68.8 ± 1.2**

Table 3. Covariate shift results using YOLOv5m

Training set	Evaluation set	Split	P (%)	R (%)	F1 (%)	mAP@.5 (%)
TrashCan	AquaLoc	K-folded	59.8 ± 6.3	52.9 ± 3.8	55.7 ± 1.6	52.5 ± 1.9
UNO	**AquaLoc**	**K-folded**	**61.2 ± 3.1**	**51.2 ± 6.2**	**55.6 ± 4.5**	**55.2 ± 4.7**

size to 28, which is the maximum according to our GPU capability (NVIDIA[4] Quadro RTX 6000 with 24Go VRAM). We set the IoU threshold to 0.2 between predictions and labels for evaluation. We also used data augmentation given in the YOLOv5 fine-tuning V5.0 version, such as color transformation, rotations, translations, scaling, shearing, flip-UP, flip-LR, mosaic, and mixup.

As mentioned, we ran five training of 300 epochs each and five tests for every experiment. Each experiment took approximately seven hours.

4.2   Results

UNO Benchmark and Improvement with Respect to TrashCan. Table 2 shows the results of various experiments with the same settings and k-fold to compare TrashCan and UNO databases.

In the first row, we evaluate the results without k-folding, using a regular random split to show the bias linked to datasets containing consecutive frames. The results are biased because both the training and validation sets contain similar frames, leading to excellent results (P = 83.1%, R = 76.5%, F1 = 79.7%, and mAP@0.5 = 80.8%) but an erroneous conclusion. Then, we use a correct distribution preventing consecutive frames to be in both training and validation sets, i.e. using our k-fold methodology. Thus, the following rows indicate the correct evaluation, where P, R, and mAP@.5 are below 70%.

In the second row, we evaluate the TrashCan model using our k-fold methodology, resulting in P = 57.1 ± 5.2%, R = 60.1 ± 5.5%, F1 = 58.4 ± 4.2%, and mAP@.5 = 56.6 ± 6.3%, whereas in the third row, we evaluate the same model but on the UNO validation split to see its performance on a cleaner version, resulting in P = 64.2 ± 5.0%, R = 58.2 ± 2.9%, F1 = 60.9 ± 2.6%, and mAP@.5 = 60.8 ± 4.2%. The latter shows an overall improvement indicating the importance of a clean evaluation set.

Finally, we give the UNO model evaluation on its validation set in the fourth row. The results increase by almost 10 points (P = 68.7 ± 4.3%, R = 66.2 ±

---

[4] https://www.nvidia.com/.

1.5%, F1 = 67.3 ± 1.5%, and mAP@.5 = 68.8 ± 1.2%). Moreover, when trained on the UNO database, YOLOv5 obtained much lower standard deviation results. UNO has thus better properties when it comes to comparing networks.   Figure 4

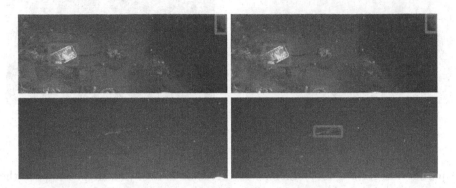

Fig. 4. Localization results on UNO images for models trained on the same subpart of TrashCan and UNO datasets, respectively.

gives a visual comparison of both the TrashCan and UNO models (the actual annotations are visible in Fig. 2). In the upper row, although the TrashCan model could localize the plastic bottle, it did not localize the bottom part of the ROV as the UNO model does. In the bottom row, we can see that the TrashCan model cannot localize the small piece of wood.

Covariate Shift Test. Given that the TrashCan dataset contains videos taken in deep water since 1982, we want to test the generalization with recent images. So we labeled 150 frames from 3 videos taken from the AquaLoc dataset [3] which were acquired in the Mediterranean sea in shallow water (see Fig. 5).

Given that the image's color, the lightness, the turbidity, the objects, and the environment differ a lot from those taken by JAMSTEC, we concluded that the distribution of both datasets is unlikely to be similar. Thus, we can test the generalization of a model by testing the covariate shift.

Table 3 shows both models' results on the covariate shift dataset. While we found no noticeable difference in the F1-score for both models, the UNO model obtains a higher mAP@.5 score than TrashCan. We assumed an actual improvement since we correlated the mAP@.5 results with a Student's t-test and failed to reject the NULL hypothesis (which means both models are equivalent), with a p-value greater than 0.05 (p-value = 0.49).

Even though a model could generalize with a relatively low amount of incorrect examples, the quality of the evaluation set determines its actual performance. Indeed, the larger the database is, the least the bad quality examples influence the overall performance. We see relatively low performances for TrashCan and UNO models regarding covariate shift testing. Indeed, JAMSTEC and

Fig. 5. Images from AquaLoc [3].

AquaLoc images are very different as the color and object shapes impact the overall distribution. Moreover, a biological phenomenon called marine biological fouling makes the detection task more difficult. Marine fouling occurs when organisms grow on underwater objects. However, because it almost does not form in deep water due to the lack of light, JAMSTEC images do not cover that variability. In order to keep the gain having a pre-trained network on the UNO database but targeting use on images having a domain shift, one can envisage performing domain adaptation [14], or generative methods [6]. This is postponed to future works.

5   Conclusion

In this paper, we first selected images from TrashCan containing at least one object, set their label as a unique class, and removed the text from the images by cropping them using YOLOv5 trained on COCO-Text as a text detector. Then, we relocated every bounding box following determined rules (pixel-perfect tightness, overlapping limitation) to obtain UNO, a new dataset of underwater non-natural objects.

Secondly, we proposed a methodology (script given online) to compare networks using a well-balanced k-fold and concluded from network comparisons that UNO exhibits better properties than TrashCan.

Thirdly, we evaluated both TrashCan and UNO using YOLOv5m with the same k-fold and hyperparameters for a fair comparison.

Finally, we evaluated the learning efficiency in deploying conditions with a covariate shift test, using underwater images taken from AQUALOC for Trash-Can and UNO models, and provided these images on UNO website.

As mentioned, UNO contains only one class because of the class imbalance of TrashCan. However, one could overlay this issue by creating a well-balanced underwater litter database or using few-shot classification methods [8,17]. Moreover, the covariate shift test indicates poor detection performances for TrashCan and UNO. Because JAMSTEC images do not cover the variability of AQUALOC (shallow water, fouling, object shapes, turbidity, and luminosity), one could envision performing domain adaptation [14] or generative methods [6] to keep the gain of having a pre-trained network on the UNO database.

Acknowledgements. This research has received funding from the European Union's Horizon 2020 research and innovation program under grant agreement No 101000832 (Maelstrom project).

References

1. JAMSTEC: Japan Agency for Marine Earth Science and Technology. https://www.jamstec.go.jp/e/
2. Canals, M., et al.: The quest for seafloor Macrolitter: a critical review of background knowledge, current methods and future prospects. Environ. Res. Lett., November 2020. https://doi.org/10.1088/1748-9326/abc6d4. publisher: IOP Publishing
3. Ferrera, M., Creuze, V., Moras, J., Trouvé-Peloux, P.: AQUALOC: an underwater dataset for visual-inertial-pressure localization. Int. J. Rob. Res. **38**(14), 1549–1559 (2019). https://doi.org/10.1177/0278364919883346
4. Fulton, M., Hong, J., Islam, M.J., Sattar, J.: Robotic detection of marine litter using deep visual detection models. In: 2019 International Conference on Robotics and Automation (ICRA) (2019). https://doi.org/10.1109/ICRA.2019.8793975
5. Haefliger, H.: Deepseawaste (2019). https://www.kaggle.com/henryhaefliger/deepseawaste
6. Hong, J., Fulton, M., Sattar, J.: A generative approach towards improved robotic detection of marine litter. In: 2020 IEEE International Conference on Robotics and Automation (ICRA) (2020)
7. Hong, J., Michael, F., Sattar, J.: TrashCan: a semantically-segmented dataset towards visual detection of marine debris. arXiv (2020). https://conservancy.umn.edu/handle/11299/214865
8. Hu, Y., Pateux, S., Gripon, V.: Squeezing backbone feature distributions to the max for efficient few-shot learning. Algorithms (2022). https://doi.org/10.3390/a15050147, https://hal.archives-ouvertes.fr/hal-03675145
9. Jocher, G., et al.: ultralytics/yolov5: v6.0 - yolov5 (2021). https://doi.org/10.5281/zenodo.5563715
10. Madricardo, F., et al.: How to deal with seafloor marine litter: an overview of the state-of-the-art and future perspectives. Front. Mar. Sci. (2020). https://doi.org/10.3389/fmars.2020.505134, https://www.frontiersin.org/article/10.3389/fmars.2020.505134
11. Ren, S., He, K., Girshick, R., Sun, J.: Faster R-CNN: towards real-time object detection with region proposal networks. IEEE Trans. Pattern Anal. Mach. Intell. (2015). https://doi.org/10.1109/TPAMI.2016.2577031
12. Schwerin, P., Wäscher, G.: The bin-packing problem: A problem generator and some numerical experiments with FFD packing and MTP. Int. Trans. Oper. Res. (2006). https://doi.org/10.1111/j.1475-3995.1997.tb00093.x
13. Tan, M., Le, Q.: EfficientNet: Rethinking model scaling for convolutional neural networks. In: Chaudhuri, K., Salakhutdinov, R. (eds.) Proceedings of the 36th International Conference on Machine Learning. Proceedings of Machine Learning Research, vol. 97. PMLR (2019). https://proceedings.mlr.press/v97/tan19a.html

14. Tzeng, E., Hoffman, J., Saenko, K., Darrell, T.: Adversarial discriminative domain adaptation. In: 2017 IEEE Conference on Computer Vision and Pattern Recognition (CVPR). IEEE Computer Society, Los Alamitos, CA, USA (2017). https://doi.org/10.1109/CVPR.2017.316, https://doi.ieeecomputersociety.org/10.1109/CVPR.2017.316
15. Veit, A., Matera, T., Neumann, L., Matas, J., Belongie, S.: Coco-text: dataset and benchmark for text detection and recognition in natural images (2016), https://arxiv.org/abs/1601.07140
16. Wu, H., Xin, M., Fang, W., Hu, H.M., Hu, Z.: Multi-level feature network with multi-loss for person re-identification. IEEE Access (2019). https://doi.org/10.1109/ACCESS.2019.2927052
17. Zhang, H., Cao, Z., Yan, Z., Zhang, C.: Sill-net: feature augmentation with separated illumination representation (2021)

Towards Depth Fusion into Object Detectors for Improved Benthic Species Classification

Matthew Dawkins[1]([✉]), Jon Crall[1], Matt Leotta[1], Tasha O'Hara[2], and Liese Siemann[2]

[1] Kitware Inc., 1712 Route 9. Suite 300, Clifton Park, NY 12065, USA
matt.dawkins@kitware.com
[2] Coonamessett Farm Foundation, 277 Hatchville Rd, E Falmouth, MA 02536, USA

Abstract. Coonamessett Farm Foundation (CFF) conducts one of the optical surveys of the sea scallop resource using a HabCam towed vehicle. The CFF HabCam v3 collects 5+ images per second, providing a continuous track of imagery as it is towed over scallop grounds. Annotations from HabCam images are translated into biomass estimates through a multi-step process that relies on adequate image subsampling and accurate scallop counts and measurements. Annotating images is the most time-consuming part of generating these reliable scallop biomass estimates. Reliably automating this process has the potential to increase annotation rates and improve biomass estimation, addressing questions about scallop patchiness and distribution over small-to-large scales on scallop grounds. Furthermore, optical survey images provide a wealth of raw data that is not consistently utilized. An additional high priority goal is to provide data for improving flounder stock assessments because the incidental bycatch of non-target species could have negative impacts on the long-term sustainability of the fishery. Kitware, Inc developed the Video and Image Analytics for Marine Environments (VIAME) system for analysis of underwater imagery with support from the NOAA Automated Image Analysis Strategic Initiative. CFF collaborated with Kitware to develop improved automated detectors for scallop classes (live scallops, swimming scallops, and clappers) and flounder by incorporating depth disparity information obtained from stereo image pairs collected during surveys. The accuracy and precision of these new detectors, with depth information incorporated, was contrasted against that of single-image detectors when utilized upgraded deep learning networks. A few methods were investigated, including early and late fusion of the depth information.

Keywords: Deep Learning · Depth Maps · Scallops · Computer Vision

1 Introduction

The Atlantic sea scallop (*Placopecten magellanicus*) is the focus of one of the most valuable fisheries on the east coast of the United States (NMFS 2020). The continued profitability of the fishery has depended on reliable surveys of the scallop stock. Biomass estimates are currently generated yearly using the results of federal and industry-funded surveys of the resource, with three out of four industry surveys conducted using optical

© Springer Nature Switzerland AG 2023
J.-J. Rousseau and B. Kapralos (Eds.): ICPR 2022 Workshops, LNCS 13645, pp. 415–429, 2023.
https://doi.org/10.1007/978-3-031-37731-0_31

survey equipment in recent years (NEFMC 2019, 2020). NEFSC conducts a combined optical/dredge survey. Three of the optical surveys use HabCam towed vehicles to collect imagery, with the vehicles operated by CFF (Fig. 1A), WHOI, and NEFSC. These systems collect 5+ images per second, providing a continuous track of imagery (Fig. 1B) as they are towed along predetermined tracks across important scallop grounds (Fig. 1C).

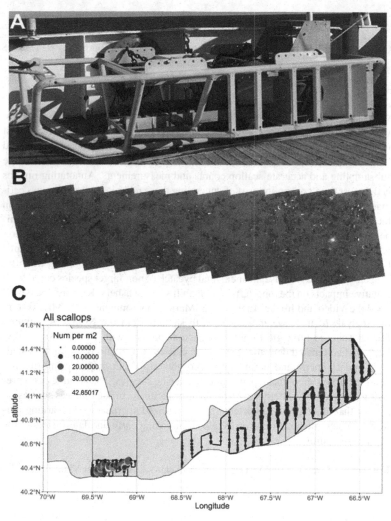

Fig. 1. (A) HabCam V3, operated by Coonamessett Farm Foundation. (B) Mosaic of images from the 2017 HabCam V3 survey. (C) Track and distribution of scallops from the 2020 industry HabCam survey on Georges Bank

1.1 Scallop Stock Assessment

Annotations from HabCam images are translated into biomass estimates through a multi-step process that relies on adequate image subsampling (i.e., annotation rate) and accurate scallop counts and measurements. Based on information collected during HabCam camera calibration, scallop lengths in pixels are converted in shell heights in millimeters. The field of view (FOV) of each image is also calculated to estimate optical survey coverage. Each shell height (SH) measured from the HabCam images is converted to a meat weight (MW) in grams using published location-specific SHMW equations that include depth as a covariate (e.g., Hennen & Hart 2012). Biomass per meter^2 is calculated by summing all MWs in an image and dividing by the FOV of that image. Biomass in a defined stock area is estimated using a combination of a hurdle generalized additive model (GAM) and ordinary kriging (OK) (Chang et al. 2017). The hurdle GAM (quasi-binomial distribution for the presence/absence model and quasi-Poisson distribution for the positive model) is used to estimate the large-scale trends in biomass with respect to latitude, longitude, and depth. Kriging on the model residuals improves estimates over smaller scales.

Annotating images is the most time-consuming part of generating reliable scallop biomass estimates. NEFSC currently annotates 1:50 images collected during their surveys, while CFF annotates 1:200 to 1:400 images. During recent HabCam v3 surveys by CFF, 25–30% of annotated images included live sea scallops. The NEFSC scallop group examined scallop abundance along a HabCam track line and estimated that a minimum of 50 images needed to be sampled over every 1000 m to generate stable abundance estimates from the models used to generate biomass estimates in their surveys (presented at the March 2015 Peer Review Meeting of Sea Scallop Survey Methodologies summarized in Maguire 2015). The closer track lines in the more intensive industry surveys (Fig. 1C) relax these annotation rate requirements, although improved annotation rates would ultimately lead to more confidence in the model inputs. The very short timeline between survey cruises and deadlines for submitting biomass estimates makes higher annotation rates difficult to achieve, but increasing image annotation rate continues to be a goal for CFF and other optical survey groups. Reliably automating scallop image annotations could increase annotation rates for all of the optical surveys, improving estimates of biomass and addressing questions about scallop patchiness and distribution over small-to-large scales on scallop grounds.

Annotation of scallops in HabCam images is complicated by the need to distinguish between live and dead scallops to generate accurate counts for biomass estimates. Human annotators differentiate between live and dead scallops based on a suite of characteristics (Fig. 2), with trained annotators confident in their decisions ~88% of the time (Maguire 2015). Gaping - one characteristic of dead scallops - as well as the presence of depressions created by live scallops (Shumway & Parsons 2016), could be more easily detected using stereo images.

Distinguishing between scallops resting on the sea floor and those swimming in the water column is important for accurate sizing of scallops in survey images. Scallop lengths are overestimated when measured in two versus three dimensions, with errors increasing as scallops swim off the sea floor (Fig. 3). Because the scallop weights used

Characteristics of live scallops

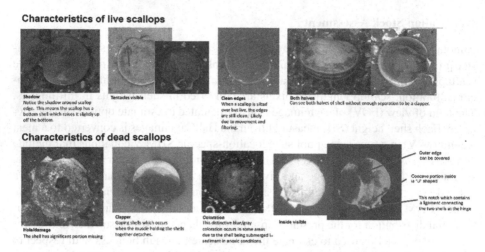

Fig. 2. Characteristics of live and dead scallops, adapted from Maguire (2015).

in stock biomass estimations are derived from shell height/meat weight equations, over-estimation of scallop lengths translates directly into overestimations of scallop biomass. Consequently, increasing the use of stereo images for scallop length estimations would have a direct impact on stock assessments.

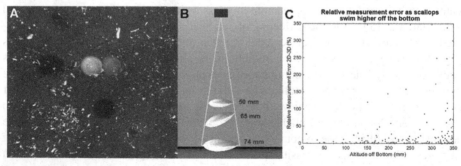

Fig. 3. Impact of swimming scallops locations in the water column on the estimation of scallop lengths. (A) Stereo image of swimming scallops, colored for 3D viewing, showing the characteristic shadows used for identification. (B) Schematic highlighting changes in real (shown) vs. estimated size as scallops move off the bottom or change their angle relative to horizontal. All three scallops in the example would have estimated 74-mm shell heights based on pixel coverage and camera altitude using a single 2D image. (C) Plot showing increasing measurement error as scallops move higher off the bottom (adapted from in Maguire 2015).

1.2 Use of HabCam Images for Flounder Stock Estimations

Optical survey images provide a wealth of raw data that is not consistently used at this time. One high priority goal for these images is to build capacity to provide data for improving flounder stock assessments because the incidental bycatch of non-target species could have negative impacts on the long-term sustainability of the scallop fishery. Bycatch of yellowtail flounder (*Limanda ferruginea*) and windowpane flounder (*Scopthalmus aquosus*) continues to impact catch levels and quota, thereby putting the continued sustainability of the scallop fishery at risk (O'Keefe & DeCelles 2013). Flounders are relatively rare in scallop optical survey images, with fewer than 1% of annotated images from recent HabCam v3 surveys including any flounder species. Moreover, identifying flounder in survey images can be difficult. Flounder can change their body patterns to camouflage on different substrates (Fig. 4), and they often bury themselves in finer substrates like sand. Consequently, there is a need for increasing image annotation rates with a focus on flounder and a more reliable method for detecting flounder in survey images. Stereo disparities have been used to improve flounder detection algorithms, taking advantage of changes in bottom topography caused by flounder presence (Fig. 5).

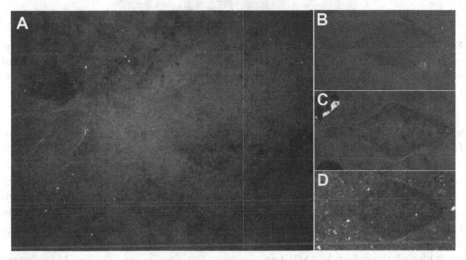

Fig. 4. Images of yellowtail flounder taken during the 2015 HabCam v3 survey. (A) A single image with at least five yellowtail flounder. Flounders with (B) uniform, (C) light mottle, and (D) dark mottle body patterns

1.3 VIAME (Video and Image Analytics for Marine Environments)

VIAME is an open-source system for analysis of underwater imagery developed by Kitware (Clifton Park, NY) with support from the NOAA Automated Image Analysis Strategic Initiative. It was originally designed as an integration platform for several different video and image processing algorithms (Dawkins et al. 2017), but has since evolved into an end-to-end toolkit for producing analytics on an archive of imagery and/or video. At the core of VIAME is an image processing system which can link C/C++, Python, and MATLAB processing nodes together into a graph-like pipeline architecture. This can be used to easily build sequences of image processing algorithms without recompiling any

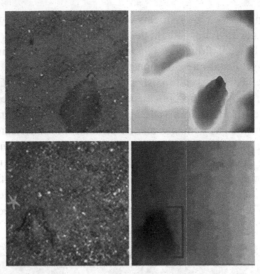

Fig. 5. Image segmentation of flounder using stereo disparities. (Top pair) Flounder resting on the surface is highlighted in red (red = close to blue = far). Adapted from presentations summarized in Maguire (2015). (Bottom pair) Flounder in a depression is highlighted in black (white = close to black = far) using the depth approach described further in Sect. 2.2. (Color figure online)

source code or writing software, enabling rapid experimentation and re-use of different functional modules. For example, a common HabCam processing sequence consists of an image color correction module followed by a scallop detector. Using VIAME, different color correction modules can be tested with the same scallop detector simply by changing the pipeline configuration. Alongside the pipelined image processing system are a number of standalone utilities for object detector model training, output detection visualization, groundtruth annotation, detector evaluation (a.k.a. scoring), and image archive search.

Although the default VIAME detection and classification models provide a substantial amount of functionality, there are many marine science image and video annotation problems that they do not address. Consequently, VIAME includes the capability for end-users to apply VIAME algorithms to new datasets and problems without any programming or knowledge of machine learning. Leveraging annotation user interfaces (web or desktop), there are two deep-learning capabilities in VIAME that enable users to create object detectors, classifiers and other analytics. Through image search and interactive query refinement, users can quickly build a complete detection and classification capability for a novel problem, then run it on imagery or video. For more challenging analytical problems, users can manually annotate images, then train a deep-learning based detection and classification capability specific to their problem.

However, the model generation methods in VIAME did not make use of stereo imagery prior to this effort, a limitation that this project was designed to address so that any user with stereo data would be able to create a detector which exploits depth information. Stereo data collection is very common across the NOAA FSCs and the marine science community in general, as stereo enables 3D measurements of scallops, fish, flora and even habitat. Stereo also significantly improves automated detection and classification under difficult conditions as indicated above for HabCam data, and also for many other underwater video collections such as small fish against cluttered backgrounds. Adding a complete stereo capability to VIAME will have broad impact across a wide spectrum of marine scientists using VIAME now and in the future.

2 Project Objectives and Methods

This ongoing effort aims to improve the accuracy of automated detectors for scallop categories (e.g., swimming scallops, live vs. dead scallops), expanding the useful data generated from optical surveys with the goal of generating more accurate and precise biomass estimates. It also aims to improve the detection of and annotation rates for key bycatch species, specifically flounder. To accomplish this, we have been investigating and measuring the performance of algorithms which fuse depth information in order to: (1) improve detection of scallops and differentiate between live, dead, and swimming scallops and (2) detect and count flounder, fish that are difficult to reliably distinguish due to their camouflage abilities, changing body patterns, and tendency to bury themselves in sandy substrates.

2.1 Image Set Acquisition and Consolidation

Stereo image pairs from the 2017 to 2019 HabCam v3 surveys were utilized for the initial experiments described in this paper. Because swimming scallops and flounder are rare and dead scallops (other than clappers) are not normally annotated for the traditional scallop assessment surveys, we examined over 260,000 images from the 2019 survey for the presence of swimming or dead scallops and flounder. Images with these organisms were aggregated and annotated. In total 8,048 jpgs and 8,048 paired stereo tifs with over 400,000 annotations were generated by domain experts at CFF, which are available for download on viame.kitware.com alongside the depth maps used in experiments.

2.2 Improved Camera Calibration and Stereo Image-Pair Alignment

Using checkerboard images collected during underwater calibration sessions for the HabCam v3 system, the raw intensity stereo pairs were first used to develop camera calibration matrices. For both calibration and depth map formulation, scripts were developed on top of the OpenCV toolkit (Bradski et al. 2008). The calibrations were used to generate both 3D sea floor models and 2D stereo depth disparity maps. Optimizations for the camera calibration process include an improved procedure that estimates camera intrinsic parameters independently of extrinsics, and also does not perform model selection to avoid overfitting with too many distortion parameters (which earlier versions of the software and the raw OpenCV functions lacked). Following calibration and rectification, 2D disparity maps were generated using the approach described in Hirschmuller et al. (2007).

2.3 Development of Improved RGB and Stereo Auto-detection Algorithms

We tested a range of object detectors for scallops and flounder using both three-channel Red Green Blue (RGB) image inputs as a baseline, alongside images with depth information incorporated (RGBD images) through use of depth disparities derived from the stereo pairs. Depth disparity information was fused early or late within the detection networks to determine which option resulted in better detections of scallop classes and flounder (Fig. 6). To accomplish this, we created a custom train and test harness, Netharn (https://gitlab.kitware.com/computer-vision/netharn), with additional utility scripts contained in https://github.com/viame/bioharn, built around the PyTorch (Paszke et al. 2019) and MMDetection (Chen et al. 2019) open-source python packages. This framework supports inputting arbitrary secondary or even tertiary channels for use with model trainings, so they are applicable not just to depth fusion but also other auxiliary data such as motion, infrared, or hyperspectral channels alongside RGB. Results from detectors developed using stereo information were compared to an alternative method using secondary chip classifiers (Fig. 7). In each case, pre-trained weights (trained on COCO) were used to initialize the network, and in the case of late fusion, both forks of the network. The methods used included the following:

- Cascade Region-Convolutional Neural Networks (Cai et al. 2018) with and without *early depth fusion*, with RGBD images treated as 4-channel inputs,
- Mask RCNN (He et al. 2017) with and without *late depth fusion*, with RGB images and depth in separate streams that produced feature maps that were summed into a single scoring map, and
- Reclassification based on *secondary chips* created from regions that were detected using Cascade R-CNN, using a separate (and independent) secondary classification network (ResNext101, Xie et al. 2017) on top of the entire Cascade RCNN network.

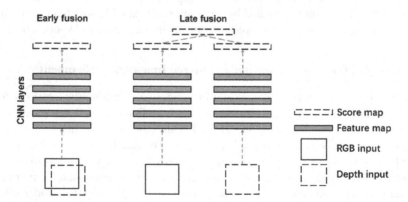

Fig. 6. Early vs. late fusion of stereo depth information. For early fusion, RGB images were joined with depth maps at the start to create a 4-channel input. For late fusion, RGB images and depth maps were processed in separate streams, and the resulting feature maps were summed to create final scoring maps. Figure modified from Li et al. 2017.

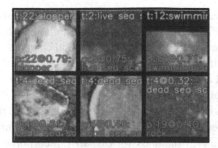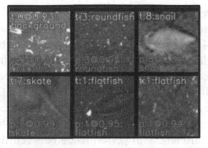

Fig. 7. Examples of secondary chips used for object classification as an independent secondary optimization (green, truth, blue, predicted). (Color figure online)

2.4 3D Model Generation

Recalibration with the calibration optimizations described in Sect. 2.2 provided the data needed to generate 3D sea floor models that could be viewed in MeshLab, open-source software for processing, editing, and viewing 3D triangular meshes (http://www.mes hlab.net/). The 3D models provided striking visual representations of the seafloor and the locations of scallops and flounder in the water column (Fig. 8). While we have yet to utilize these 3D meshes within the fused detectors, in favor of the simpler-to-integrate 2D disparity maps, we are currently investigating methods to accomplish this.

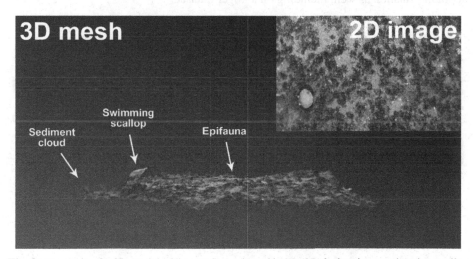

Fig. 8. Example of a 3D model of the sea floor viewed in MeshLab showing a swimming scallop and the sediment cloud it generated when jetting off the sea floor.

2.5 Preliminary Scallop Detector Comparisons

The inclusion of depth information via early fusion improved the mean average precision (mAP) of swimming scallop detection by 0.02 (Table 1 and Fig. 9A). No improvements were seen for other scallop classes using early fusion, with average precision values decreasing slightly for live scallops by −0.004 and more significantly for clappers by −0.04 (Table 1 and Fig. 9A). Discrimination between swimming scallops and clappers was slightly improved with the addition of depth information through early fusion (Fig. 10A). Late fusion of depth information improved detection average precision for swimming scallops by 0.05 and live scallops by 0.04 (Table 1 and Fig. 9B), with improvements to all categories when considering depth information. Note: while comparing consistent networks for early and late fusion may have been more beneficial to consistently contrast the differences in performance between the two methods for disparity incorporation, training resources were limited during the course of our initial effort and we simultaneously wanted to compare Mask and Cascade-RNN. Simultaneously one possible reason for reduced contribution of early fusion could have been the use of seed weights for the RGB feature but random weight initialization for the depth channel, possibly reducing its contribution. Both of these are issues we want to further investigate in the near future.

While the mAP improvements from object detectors with secondary chip auxiliary classifiers were higher than those incorporating depth information for the auxiliary scallop categories (swimmers, clappers), with the average precision values increasing for swimming scallops by 0.10 and clappers by 0.20 (Table 1), live scallop mAP decreased which indicates a higher false alarm rate when considering the large annotation class imbalance between the three categories. Due to these results, however, an additional future experiment we aim to run in are secondary chip classifiers with the addition of depth information as well, including on a larger dataset.

Table 1. Shifts in Mean Average Precision (mAP) values from best model runs.

Name/type	Live scallops	Swimming scallops	Clappers	Flounder
Cascade Faster-RCNN + Depth (Early Fusion)	−0.004	0.02	−0.02	−0.03
Mask RCNN + Depth (Late Fusion)	0.04	0.05	NA	0.03
Cascade Faster-RCNN + Secondary classifier	−0.05	0.10	0.20	0.04

2.6 Preliminary Flounder Detector Results

The inclusion of depth information via early fusion did not improve detection of flounder in the above experiment, with average precision decreasing by 0.04 (Table 1 and Fig. 9A). The opposite trend was seen when using secondary chip classifiers, with average precision increasing by 0.04. It should be noted, however, that in the above experiment models were trained jointly across all scallop categories and flounder categories together, which are vastly biased towards scallops due to large class imbalances in the training sets (with orders of magnitudes of more scallop's present). When models are fine-tuned only for flounders (i.e., only training the detectors over a single flounder category) results

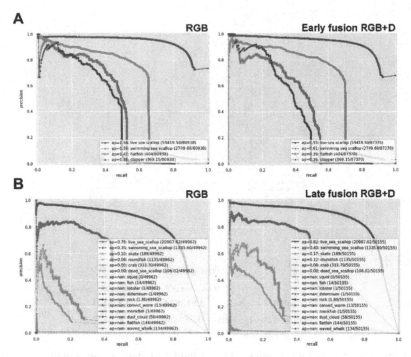

Fig. 9. Precision-Recall curves for detectors using only RGB images as inputs vs. (A) RGB images with a depth layer added as a fourth channel using early fusion and (B) RGB images and depth maps with the two joined using late fusion.

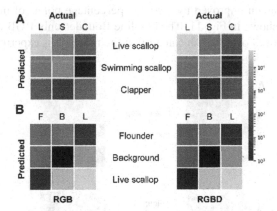

Fig. 10. Confusion matrices showing the performance of the RGB vs. RGBD early fusion detectors for classifying (A) live scallops, swimming scallops, and clappers and (B) flounder, background regions, and live scallops.

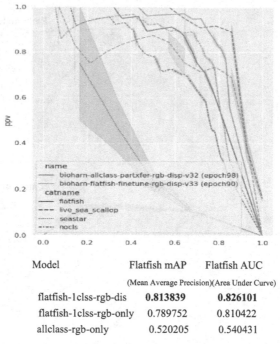

Model	Flatfish mAP	Flatfish AUC
	(Mean Average Precision)	(Area Under Curve)
flatfish-1clss-rgb-dis	**0.813839**	**0.826101**
flatfish-1clss-rgb-only	0.789752	0.810422
allclass-rgb-only	0.520205	0.540431

Fig. 11. Results when fine-tuning models just for flatfish (1 class) as opposed to training across multiple classes (allclass). In this case the all-class model was trained on not just on scallops and flatfish, as in Fig. 9, but also 10 other species (sea stars, roundfish, etc....).

with depth information improved by a couple percentage points of mean average precision (mAP), as shown in Fig. 11. The baseline flounder-only RGB detector was also significantly improved over flatfish category in the multi-class experiments (Fig. 12).

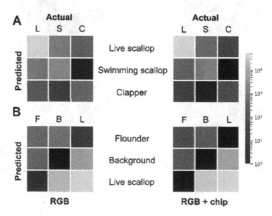

Fig. 12. Confusion matrices showing the performance of the RGB vs. RGB + chip detectors for classifying (A) live scallops, swimming scallops, and clappers and (B) flounder, background regions, and live scallops

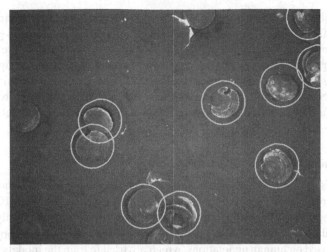

Fig. 13. Examples of the variability in the appearance of clappers (yellow circles). (Color figure online)

3 Evaluation and Conclusions

3.1 Improve Scallop Subcategory Discrimination

The addition of depth information from stereo image pairs through early and late fusion improved classification of swimming scallops but not clappers significantly. Classification of live scallops was improved with late fusion but not early fusion. These results were unexpected. We hypothesized that stereo information would improve discrimination between live scallops, swimming scallops, and clappers based on characteristics like distance off bottom for live vs. swimming scallops and gape distance for live scallops vs. clappers. While stereo information improved discrimination of swimming scallops slightly, it was less than expected. In hindsight, this result may not be surprising because human annotators do not have trouble discriminating swimming scallops in RGB images when shadows are present (Fig. 3), and the object detector models could use the same visual cue. The lack of model improvement for detecting clappers could be due to variability in the orientation and therefore appearance of clappers (Fig. 13). This variability also makes it difficult for human annotators to distinguish between live scallops, dead scallops, and clappers.

3.2 Detect and Count Flounder

The addition of depth information from stereo image pairs did not improve detection of flounder as much as expected, although there was an improvement with late fusion of depth information by a few percentage points. Training of flounder detectors using RGB and RGBD imagery was complicated because flounders are sparse targets in the HabCam image archive. Even with all the HabCam survey images provided by CFF and NEFSC data from 2015 (~10,000 images for training and ~10,000 images for testing), there are only ~2100 annotations of flounder. While this number of annotations is good enough for training initial models, deep learning is traditionally performed on more annotations. Model average precision may have decreased with the use of RGBD images and early fusion because the depth map characteristics for a flounder can differ significantly, with some flounder being closer to the camera lens than the sediment when resting on the surface but further from the camera lens when they have buried themselves or dug a hollow in the sediment (Fig. 5).

3.3 Discussion and Future Research

Live scallops are still occasionally scored as background regions and vice versa using RGB images with and without secondary chip classification and RGBD images (Figs. 10B and 11B). This may occur because human annotators mistakenly label rocks or other bivalves that are not annotated as scallops (Fig. 14). Because object detector models are based on human annotations, which are used to train the models and quantify their skill, inaccurate human annotations would have impacts at all stages.

CFF, in collaboration with Kitware, has recently received a new grant from the Scallop RSA program to develop new algorithms to improve automated classification of benthic habitats in HabCam imagery and incorporate automated measurement of target organisms, including scallop shell height measurements, into the VIAME system. Because this effort will expand automated detection beyond organism detection to habitat classification, it could reduce the number of mistaken classifications of background regions as target organisms and lead to better use of image databases for delving into questions about ecology and habitat changes. As part of the newly funded project, CFF plans to investigate habitat preferences of pre-recruit scallops using HabCam imagery collected over multiple years in Closed Area II and the southern flank of Georges Bank and in the Elephant Trunk and Hudson Canyon access areas in the Mid-Atlantic.

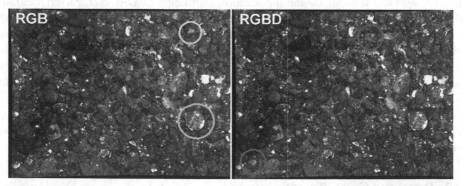

Fig. 14. Annotation and object detection model issues. The annotated RGB image included an incorrectly labeled live scallop that was actually a rock (yellow circle). The model trained on RGB images did not detect the rock and label it as a scallop, but it did miss a correctly labeled scallop (blue circle). The model trained on RGBD images did detect this scallop, but it also incorrectly labeled two rocks as scallops (red circles). (Color figure online)

References

Bradski, G., Kaehler, A.: Learning OpenCV: Computer vision with the OpenCV library. O'Reilly Media, Inc. (2008)

Cai, Z., Vasconcelos, N.: Cascade r-cnn: delving into high quality object detection. In: Proceedings of the IEEE Conference on Computer Vision and Pattern Recognition, pp. 6154–6162 (2018)

Chang, J.H., Shank, B.V., Hart, D.R.: A comparison of methods to estimate abundance and biomass from belt transect surveys. Limnol. Oceanogr. Methods **15**, 480–494 (2017)

Chen, K., et al.: MMDetection: Open mmlab detection toolbox and benchmark. arXiv preprint arXiv:1906.07155 (2019)

Dawkins, M., et al.: An open-source platform for underwater image and video analytics. IEEE Winter Conf. Appl. Comput. Vis. **2017**, 898–906 (2017)

He, K., Gkioxari, G., Dollár, P., Girshick, R.: Mask r-cnn. In: Proceedings of the IEEE International Conference on Computer Vision, pp. 2961–2969 (2017)

Hennen, D.R., Hart, D.R.: Shell height-to-weight relationships for Atlantic sea scallops (*Placopecten magellanicus*) in offshore US waters. J. Shellfish Res. **31**, 1133–1144 (2012)

Hirschmuller, H.: Stereo processing by semiglobal matching and mutual information. IEEE Trans. Pattern Anal. Mach. Intell. **30**(2), 328–341 (2007)

Li, Y., Zhang, J., Cheng, Y., Huang, K., Tan, T.: Semantics-guided multi-level RGB-D feature fusion for indoor semantic segmentation. IEEE Int. Conf. Image Process. **2017**, 1262–1266 (2017)

Maguire, J.J.: Summary Report of the Review of Sea Scallop Survey Methodologies and Their Integration for Stock Assessment and Fishery Management (2015). https://www.nefsc.noaa.gov/saw/scallop-2015/pdfs/scallop-surveys-review-summary-report-april-9.pdf

National Marine Fisheries Service (NMFS). Fisheries of the United States 2018. Current Fishery Statistics No. 2018. 167 p. (2020)

New England Fishery Management Council (NEFMC). Atlantic Sea Scallop Fishery Management Plan Framework Adjustment 30 (2019). https://s3.amazonaws.com/nefmc.org/190307-FW30-Final-Submission.pdf

NEFMC. Scallop Fishery Management Plan Framework Adjustment 32 (2020). https://s3.amazonaws.com/nefmc.org/Framework-32-Final-Submission_signed-FONSI.pdf

O'Keefe, C., DeCelles, G.: Forming a partnership to avoid bycatch. Fisheries **38**, 434–444 (2013)

Paszke, A., et al.: Pytorch: an imperative style, high-performance deep learning library. Adv. Neural Inf. Process. Syst. **32** (2019)

Shumway, S.E., Parsons, G.J. (eds.): Scallops: Biology, Ecology, Aquaculture, and Fisheries, p. 1196. Elsevier Publishing, Amsterdam Netherlands (2016)

Xie, S., Girshick, R., Dollár, P., Tu, Z., He, K.: Aggregated residual transformations for deep neural networks. In: Proceedings of the IEEE Conference on Computer Vision and Pattern Recognition, pp. 1492–1500 (2017)

Automatic Evaluation of Herding Behavior in Towed Fishing Gear Using End-to-End Training of CNN and Attention-Based Networks

Orri Steinn Guðfinnsson[(✉)], Týr Vilhjálmsson, Martin Eineborg,
and Torfi Thorhallsson

Department of Engineering, Reykjavik University, Reykjavík, Iceland
{orri17,tyr17,martine,torfith}@ru.is

Abstract. This paper considers the automatic classification of herding behavior in the cluttered low-visibility environment that typically surrounds towed fishing gear. The paper compares three convolutional and attention-based deep action recognition network architectures trained end-to-end on a small set of video sequences captured by a remotely controlled camera and classified by an expert in fishing technology. The sequences depict a scene in front of a fishing trawl where the conventional herding mechanism has been replaced by directed laser light. The goal is to detect the presence of a fish in the sequence and classify whether or not the fish reacts to the lasers. A two-stream CNN model, a CNN-transformer hybrid, and a pure transformer model were trained end-to-end to achieve 63%, 54%, and 60% 10-fold classification accuracy on the three-class task when compared to the human expert. Inspection of the activation maps learned by the three networks raises questions about the attributes of the sequences the models may be learning, specifically whether changes in viewpoint introduced by human camera operators that affect the position of laser lines in the video frames may interfere with the classification. This underlines the importance of careful experimental design when capturing scientific data for automatic end-to-end evaluation and the usefulness of inspecting the trained models.

Keywords: Fish behavior classification · Deep action recognition networks · End-to-end training · Attention maps

1 Introduction

Deep networks have been successfully employed to detect human actions in short video sequences without explicit representation of the actors or objects [1]. The models are trained end-to-end by providing only a single action label for each sequence. No explicit representations, such as objects, locations, or tracks, are extracted or provided. Instead, the model learns an implicit representation from the data and the associated action labels during training. This promises certain

© Springer Nature Switzerland AG 2023
J.-J. Rousseau and B. Kapralos (Eds.): ICPR 2022 Workshops, LNCS 13645, pp. 430–444, 2023.
https://doi.org/10.1007/978-3-031-37731-0_32

optimality of the representation concerning the imagery and the action classes, side-steps failure modes of intermediate object detection or tracking algorithms, and eliminating the manual labor of annotating every frame in a sequence. On the downside, the resulting model is essentially a black box and raises the question of what information in the images the model uses as a base for its predictions.

Results reported in the literature are typically obtained by training on a large set of video sequences sourced from the internet (e.g., UCF-101 [2] consisting of 13 320 video clips and 101 action classes). Although varied, the sequences generally depict reasonably framed, well-lit scenes with the quality expected from modern color video cameras.

In contrast, underwater imagery used in fisheries research is often captured in low-visibility environments using monochrome cameras and may be further restricted by using ambient illumination for unobtrusive observation.

The number of available samples can also be limited. However, in many deep learning applications, good results have been reported on small datasets using transfer learning, i.e., by fine-tuning a model pre-trained on a large dataset.

This paper investigates how state-of-the-art deep action recognition networks perform when trained end-to-end on a relatively small set of underwater video sequences. The dataset consists of underwater videos of fish obtained in experimental fishing trials, along with action labels encoding a behavior observed by an expert in fishing technology.

The fact that the models do not explicitly predict the location of the fish in each frame means that the reasoning behind the predicted class is not readily verified. In an attempt to elucidate the reasoning, the activation maps [3] learned by these networks are inspected for evidence that the model is attentive to the area where the fish is observed.

After introducing the dataset and the action recognition algorithms, the performance of the trained models is presented. This is followed by an inspection of the trained models using activation maps. Finally, the difference between observed and expected activation sources is discussed and further explored to identify possible sources of bias in the dataset that could adversely affect the accuracy of the model predictions.

2   Background

2.1   Related Work

Although there exists substantial literature proposing novel deep learning methods for tasks using underwater imagery (e.g., [4–6]), there is not much that offers insight into the difficulties associated with working with data of this kind. Most underwater imagery used in deep learning features scenes of shallow water ecosystems or footage captured close to the ocean surface. As such, these scenes do not suffer from problems accompanied by bad lighting conditions or noisy backgrounds. While reading through the available literature, we could not find any works using video data captured using a moving camera featuring deep seabed scenes similar to ours. [6] uses a dual-stream network for action classification and deals with high clutter video data. However, the videos are captured in an aquaculture environment, with the fish behaving more predictably, lacking distinct poses, as the fish mostly swim in a circle and only pass the camera moving from right to left. In [7] the authors use a novel action descriptor and fish action data to classify fish movement. They also compare their results to state-of-the-art methods. Their dataset is comparable in size to ours with 95 videos but only contains shallow water scenes.

2.2   Annotated Video of Fish Behaviour

The dataset used in this paper consists of underwater videos [8] recorded from a camera mounted on an experimental trawl, viewing the area immediately in front of the trawl. The trawl is unique in that a virtual structure projected by lasers has replaced the forward section of the trawl, as can be seen in Fig. 1. The recordings were made to evaluate the effectiveness of herding fish using directed light. The work reported here examines if the evaluation can be automated, allowing an evaluation to run continuously over extended trials without human effort.

The fishing trials [8] were conducted in April 2018 off the Snæfellsnes peninsula, W-Iceland, at a water depth between 80 and 120 m, where daylight is strongly attenuated. The observations span two hauls conducted on separate days totaling two hours. An enhanced CCD low-light monochrome camera (Kongsberg oe15-100c) was mounted on the trawl via a remotely controllable pan-tilt head to allow fishing gear specialists to observe the fish behavior in real-time. No additional camera lighting was used in order not to affect the behavior.

The analog video stream was digitized to 8-bit depth and stored frame-by-frame in JPEG-compressed image format at a high-quality setting. Post-operation, the videos were played back at half speed by an expert who registered the behavior of each observed fish as showing either no response, weak response, or strong response together with a time-stamp.

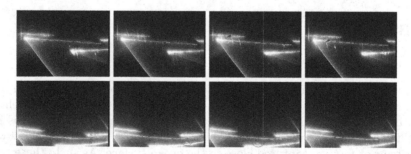

Fig. 1. Example frames from the underwater videos. The top row shows an example from the No Reaction (NR) class, while the bottom row shows an example from the Reaction (R) class. A red circle marks the location of the fish. (Color figure online)

2.3   Two-Stream Convolutional Networks

The Two-stream Convolutional Network [1] is a neural network architecture proposed for action recognition in videos. The network is composed of two parallel Convolutional Neural Networks (CNNs): a spatial stream and a temporal stream that each produces as output a prediction of the action class. The input to the spatial stream is a single video frame, while the input to the temporal stream is a stack of adjacent optical flow images. The output of the two streams is then fused by adding the softmaxed class score. Note that the two streams are trained separately; thus, the output of one stream does not affect the other.

2.4   Transformers

Transformer networks [9] were originally proposed as an alternative to recurrent neural networks used in natural language processing (NLP). Transformers learn to attend to prior words in a sequence, providing a significant improvement on NLP problems while drastically reducing training time. More recently, transformers have been adapted to various computer vision tasks [10,11]. In the Vision Transformer [12] a pure transformer is used for image classification by dividing each image down into a sequence of patches and using attention mechanisms to capture relationships between different areas of an image. Transformer architectures can be divided into two categories: hybrid transformers, where the transformer architecture is accompanied by a recurrent or a convolutional network, and a pure transformer, where the architecture is based only on attention mechanisms. Transformers have been similarly adapted to video classification tasks by applying the attention mechanism to sequences of frames. Two recent examples are the "TimeSformer" [10] and "ViViT" [11], that both have demonstrated competitive results on multiple video classification benchmarks.

2.5   Visualizing Activation Maps

Gradient-weighted Class Activation Mapping or Grad-CAM [3] is a method that uses the gradients of a target class to produce a map that indicates the regions of an input image that are most important for predicting the target class. These activation maps can be used to explain failure modes (causes of apparently unreasonable predictions), identify dataset biases, and provide an intuitive approach for tuning a model.

3   Methods

3.1   Dataset

Scene Complexity. Before training the models on the dataset, we observed some aspects of the dataset that might introduce difficulties for the models. We list a few of them below.

- The videos have a moving background that often contains objects that are easily mistaken for fish.
- The scene is dark, and the fish have natural camouflage that matches the seabed.
- The videos contain lasers which complicate the background further.
- The videos contain a time-stamp.
- Interpreting and classifying fish actions for data labeling is not straightforward, which results in samples of various lengths. (Every fish response is different.)
- The fishes are most often small compared to the scene.

Given the facts mentioned above and the fact that deep learning architectures have a tendency to use flaws found in a dataset to their advantage when trying to find features that separate samples of different classes, it is essential to understand how a model interprets the data it is being fed so as to avoid misinterpreting the results. Good performance is meaningless if the correct conclusion is derived from flawed arguments.

Dataset Generation. For the work presented here, short video clips of around 1-second duration (approx. 30 frames) were extracted from the video recordings (Sect. 2.2) around each registered observation and sorted by the time of capture.

For experimentation, the weak reaction samples were omitted from the dataset, and samples were added where no fish was visible. Each video clip in the resulting dataset was thus labeled as belonging to one of three classes: Reaction (R), No Reaction (NR), and No Fish (NF). Example frames from two classes can be seen in Fig. 1. The distribution of the sequence length (Fig. 2) is similar across the three classes.

The dataset was split into training, validation, and testing sets for training and validation. For a more accurate statistical evaluation, a total of 10 random splits were generated. The number of clips of each class in each set can be seen in Table 1.

As the viewing direction of the camera can be controlled by a human operator, the camera field of view is not identical in every sample in the dataset but has some variation, as can be seen in Fig. 1.

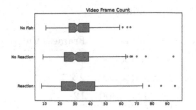

Fig. 2. The frame count distribution is shown as a box-plot for each of the three classes in the dataset.

Table 1. The class distributions for the data splits. All ten splits contained the same number of samples from each class, i.e., all ten training sets contained 144 "No fish" samples, all validation sets contained 39 "No Reaction" samples, and so on.

Class	Training	Validation	Testing	Total
NF	144	36	20	200
NR	154	39	21	214
R	151	38	21	210
Total	449	113	62	624

3.2 Data Pre-processing

Before training, the input images were cropped to exclude a time-stamp imprinted in the top left corner of each frame.

The optical flow images used as an input to the temporal stream in the two-stream network were created using the Farnebäck method [13]. The method's input parameters were adjusted slightly by experimentation to obtain a more accurate motion estimate from the videos.

3.3 Model Architectures

The two-stream network used here differs from the original [1] in that, we sample eight uniformly distributed frames from a video, send them individually into the spatial stream, and average the classification output for each frame. For the input to the temporal stream, instead of stacking the x- and y-components of the optical flow (as discussed in [1]), we compute the total optical flow and stack that with the original frames in the video. The architecture used for both streams in the two-stream network is a resnet18 CNN [14]. The hybrid model was built using a resnet18 as a feature extractor, a VisionTransformer encoder with five layers and five heads, and a classifier consisting of an AdaptiveMaxPool1d layer, a dropout layer, and finally, a fully connected layer. The timeSformer model used the base configuration of visionTransformer with divided space-time attention. The patch size used for timeSformer was 16×16.

3.4 Training Procedure

The hyperparameters used when training the models are shown in Table 2. Hyperparameter optimization was conducted using grid search. A range of values were tested for each hyperparameter.

Using more frames per video and a larger image size has been shown to improve performance for video classification tasks [12]. However, due to the large number of parameters these models have and the resulting memory consumption, we choose our parameters by balancing performance and training time.

Table 2. Hyperparameters in training

Model	Learning rate	Epochs	Batch size	Image size	Frames/Video
Spatial CNN	$1e-4$	200	4	300×300	8
Temporal CNN	$1e-4$	200	4	300×300	2×7
Hybrid	$1e-6$	100	4	300×300	12
TimeSformer	$1e-6$	100	3	224×224	8

Transformer architectures have also been shown to benefit significantly from pretraining due to the same reasons [10]. Both the two-stream and hybrid models used a resnet18 pre-trained on ImageNet [15]. The hybrid encoder was trained from scratch as pretrained weights were not readily available. The timeSformer used a VisionTransformer, pretrained on ImageNet. The final model for each split was chosen using early stopping, based on cross-entropy loss values computed on the corresponding validation set during training.

The spatial CNN and the TimeSformer network used a random horizontal flip for data augmentation. No data augmentation was used for the temporal CNN and the hybrid transformer model. Note that for the spatial and temporal CNNs, a learning rate scheduler was used where the learning rate decreases by a factor of 10 if the model does not improve for ten epochs.

4   Experiments

Three network models were trained to predict fish behavior using the training dataset. Section 4.1 presents a statistical evaluation of the performance of the trained models using common performance measures. Sections 4.2 and 4.3 provide observations on the image attributes used by the models based on the Grad-CAM activation maps together with the predicted probability (PP) of individual classes. The PP is computed by applying the softmax function to the model output, which puts the output values for all the classes on the interval (0,1) and the sum of the values equal to 1. Then the values can be interpreted as probabilities. The general softmax function is given by the formula

$$\sigma(x_i) = \frac{e^{x_i}}{\sum_0^{N_c-1} e^{x_i}} \tag{1}$$

where x_i is the model output for class, i, and N_c is the number of classes.

4.1   Comparing Model Performance

All three models were tuned on a single split, split 0, before being trained on splits 1 through 10 and evaluated on the test sets. Two metrics were used to evaluate the performance of each model, the overall accuracy and the F1 score for the NF class. The F1 score, given by Eq. 2, is used to quantify each model's ability to recognize the difference between a video containing a fish and a video that does not.

$$F_1 = 2 \times \frac{precision \times recall}{precision + recall} = 2 \times \frac{tp}{tp + \frac{1}{2}(fp + fn)} \tag{2}$$

Table 3. Comparison of the accuracy achieved by each model on splits 1–10. The mean accuracy for each model across all splits is highlighted in the last column, along with the respective standard deviation.

Data split	1	2	3	4	5	6	7	8	9	10	
Two-Stream	67.74	64.52	61.29	59.68	59.68	62.90	70.97	66.13	54.84	66.13	**63.39 ± 4.45**
Spatial	56.45	66.13	58.06	58.06	58.06	67.74	58.06	67.74	56.45	54.84	**60.16 ± 4.73**
Temporal	67.74	62.90	56.45	56.45	54.84	59.68	69.35	69.35	53.23	64.52	**61.45 ± 5.83**
Hybrid	56.45	45.16	59.68	53.23	48.39	56.45	56.45	50.00	48.39	61.29	**53.55 ± 5.09**
TimeSformer	64.52	62.90	62.90	58.06	54.84	61.29	59.68	54.84	62.90	61.29	**60.32 ± 2.77**

Table 3 shows the 10-fold accuracy achieved by each model. As shown in the table, the two-stream network achieves the highest accuracy. Of the transformer models, the pure transformer model outperforms the hybrid model. Interestingly, the best performing splits for the hybrid model seem to be the worst for the timeSformer. This trend is much less apparent in the F1 scores, as seen in Table 4, mainly because the performance gap is significantly increased.

Table 4. Comparison of the F1 score achieved by each model on splits 1–10 for the NF class. The mean F1 score for each model across all splits is highlighted in the last column, along with the respective standard deviation.

Data split	1	2	3	4	5	6	7	8	9	10	
Two-Stream	78.26	78.26	70.59	70.83	73.08	71.43	80.85	71.70	68.00	73.17	**73.62 ± 3.91**
Spatial	72.22	68.57	82.93	70.83	68.00	82.05	70.27	71.43	63.16	63.64	**71.31 ± 6.29**
Temporal	78.26	73.91	64.15	66.67	69.23	69.77	76.00	76.00	67.92	76.19	**71.81 ± 4.60**
Hybrid	70.59	46.15	66.67	61.54	54.55	53.33	63.16	54.90	54.55	64.00	**58.94 ± 7.03**
TimeSformer	78.26	73.68	69.57	68.18	66.67	66.67	68.18	75.00	74.42	75.00	**71.56 ± 3.71**

4.2   Class Activation Maps

For both the two-stream network and the hybrid network, the class activation maps targeted the final convolutional block in the resnet18. For the timeSformer model, we used the norm1 layer in the last encoder block.

Laser Line Positions Affected by the Camera View. We looked at the Grad-CAMs from every model for all the test splits, and they all showed a similar trend. Consistently, the most activity was on the lasers and the neighboring pixels, as clearly shown in Figs. 3 and 4. There are some exceptions to this, but generally, this was the case.

Figure 3 shows a Grad-CAM example from test set 2. In this case, the TimeSformer correctly predicted the video as belonging to class R with a relatively high confidence of 75.15%. The fish is clearly seen in the frame, yet according to the Grad-CAM, the model does not deem it an important factor in determining the class of the video. This is not a unique example; in fact, most if not all of the Grad-CAMs observed showed this pattern in some capacity. There are cases, such as the one shown in Fig. 4, where the model also considers the fish, but we assume that the reason for that is that the fish is apparent in common laser area.

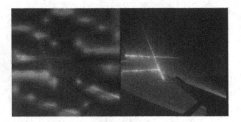 

Fig. 3. The Grad-CAM (left) shows activation mostly occurs around the laser, with no activation around the fish, even though the fish is clearly visible in the original frame (right) as it covers a portion of the laser, close to the center of the image. The model still classifies the video correctly and with high confidence.

Fig. 4. The Grad-CAM (left) shows activation around the lasers and the fish. The red color around the fish indicates high activation. However, the activation is likely due to fish covering an area where the model expects the laser to shine brightly. (Color figure online)

Inclusion of a Time-Stamp in the Frame. The original video frames include a time-stamp in the top left corner that was cropped away in pre-processing. The activation maps of models trained on the uncropped image data (Fig. 5) show strong activation around the time-stamp. However, on close inspection, the activation appears to be most strongly focused on the day and the minute within the hour.

This indicates that the model may be basing its prediction on the time of day observed in the training samples.

Max Sequence Length - Padding Frames. As previously mentioned, increasing the length of a video sequence has been shown to increase the accuracy of video classification models. The same is valid for increasing the number of data samples for training. The consequence of attempting to achieve both is

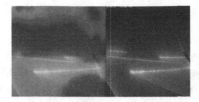

Fig. 5. An example of the model's activation around the time-stamp in the top-left corner of the video frame.

that the samples can be of different lengths. Coupled with the fact that different actions take different amounts of time to complete, it is very probable that some samples will be longer than others. Since deep learning models cannot take input of variable size, this becomes a problem. The simplest solution for this problem is to limit all video sequences to the length of the shortest video in the dataset. Nevertheless, this can have severe adverse effects if the difference between the longest and shortest video is significant. Another method for combating this problem is to pad shorter videos with zeros up to a certain length, which can also have adverse effects. Figure 6 shows an example of a padding frame used in an experiment with a sequence length of 40, along with the corresponding Grad-CAM. In this experiment, several different sequence lengths were tested to see if performance could be enhanced using data only from class R and NR. Although the performance seemed to improve with a larger sequence length, the observed improvement was due to the model using the number of padding frames to classify class R videos. Generally, when using padding frames, the model should regard the empty frames as irrelevant information and, in turn, ignore them. However, as Fig. 6 indicates, the model is extracting features from the empty frames. The PP for class R videos containing padding frames was also found to be 100% in all cases. Furthermore, the PP for all videos containing padding frames was also found to be 100% for class R, i.e., the model always classified videos containing padding frames as class R, with 100% certainty.

As detailed in Fig. 2, the dataset contains videos as short as eight frames and videos that are over 75 frames long. A closer examination of the average video length for each class shows that the R class contains shorter videos on average compared to the NR class. This is the most likely explanation for the increase in reaction class accuracy as the sequence length increases.

Fig. 6. Class activation of a padding frame. In the ideal situation, the Grad-CAM (left) and the original frame (right) would be the same as the Grad-CAM would not show any activation. However, as seen in the Grad-CAM, the padding frame has very high activation, meaning the model deems the empty frame critical to the classification.

4.3   Potential Classification Bias

Figure 7 shows the average PP per video across all 10 splits on the validation dataset. The order of the videos in the validation dataset corresponds to the order in which the video clips were created from the raw video footage. The average PP curves from each model follow a similar trend, indicating an underlying bias in the dataset.

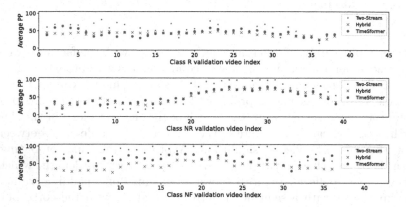

Fig. 7. The average predicted probability (PP) for every video in the validation sets based on its class.

As mentioned in Sect. 2.2, the camera's viewing direction could be remotely controlled by the camera operator. It is indeed observed that the viewing direction is not the same across all samples, causing the position of the lasers to differ between samples, which could be a source of bias. To further examine the possibility of a human-introduced bias, the videos in the dataset were manually grouped into 16 camera views according to viewing direction (Fig. 8).

Using the results from the best performing network (two-stream), a separate confusion matrix was created for the samples within each camera view. The confusion matrices (Fig. 10) contain the combined predictions across all ten validation sets. The figure also gives the prevalence of classes in each camera view in the form of a bar plot, from which it is apparent that the dataset is far from being balanced within each view. The bar plots accompanying each confusion matrix contain the class distribution for each camera view over the whole dataset. Figure 9 shows the combined confusion matrix across all ten validation sets, along with the class distribution in the dataset. In contrast to Fig. 10, Fig. 9 shows that there is little imbalance in the classes in the dataset, when camera views are not taken into account.

As Fig. 10 shows, the two-stream network often predicts the most frequently occurring class in each camera view, which could explain its relatively high accuracy on the dataset, despite the Grad-CAMs indicating that the models rarely recognize the fish. Note that the confusion matrices shown in Figs. 9 and 10 only show results from the two-stream network. However, the confusion matrices for the transformer networks were highly similar to the ones shown in the figures.

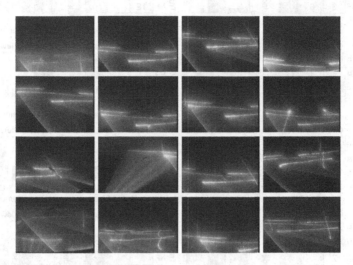

Fig. 8. Example frames from the 16 different camera views show how the position of the lasers differs between the views. Within each view, the position of the prominent laser lines is subtly modulated by the terrain and the motion of the trawl.

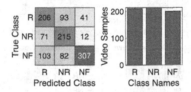

Fig. 9. The combined confusion matrix from all validation splits, along with the class distribution in the dataset.

The models would consistently predict the most prevailing class for most camera views shown in Fig. 10. However, there are cases where the confusion matrices do not follow the class distribution, e.g., camera views 4, 7, 11, and 16, which might indicate subtle differences in the scenes contained within the camera view that is only recognized by the model. Additionally, there are cases (e.g., views 1, 3, and 6) where the model accurately predicts the actual class of the video despite the actual class not being the prevailing class in the distribution. This could also indicate that the model partly learns to look at the fish in the scene.

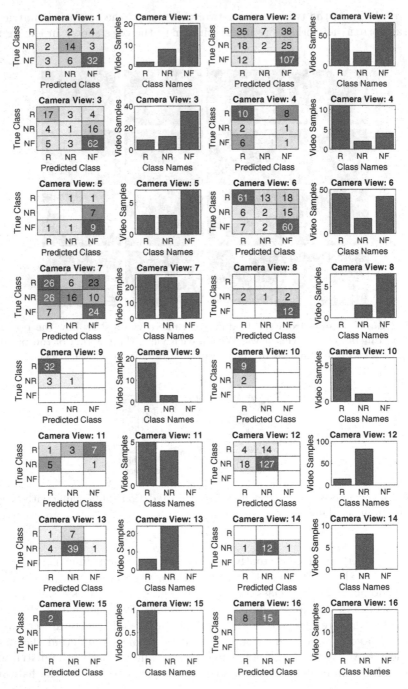

Fig. 10. Confusion matrices for each of the 16 views and the distribution of samples in each view. With few exceptions, the samples are far from being balanced across the three classes.

5 Conclusions

The paper compares the performance of three action recognition network architectures on a relatively small dataset. The dataset consists of short underwater video sequences of fish behavior in front of an unconventional trawl. The dataset is challenging due to the videos having a moving background, the fish blending in with the cluttered environment, the lasers apparent in the scene may confuse the networks, and the fish is most often small compared to the scene. Each model was evaluated on ten random splits, and performance metrics such as the F1 score for the NF class and the total accuracy were recorded. The two-stream network achieved 63.39% 10-fold accuracy and 73.62% F1 score, the highest of the tested models.

Grad-CAMs indicate that the models are predominantly attentive to the location of the laser lines in the image. Only rarely a fish also appears in the region of activation, as shown in Fig. 4. This mainly occurs when the fish is in the vicinity of the lasers. Given that the models consistently achieve an accuracy above guess rate, this observation points to an underlying bias between the location of the lasers in the frame and the presence and reaction of the fish. Therefore the classification of adjacent videos was examined since adjacent videos are more likely to have the same camera view. Figure 7 clearly shows a trend that the models classify adjacent videos the same. By observing the NR subplot, on average, the first half of the NR videos are incorrectly classified by the models, whereas the second half is correctly classified. Similar trends can be found in the other classes, but the trend is most apparent in the NR class.

To further examine if there is an underlying bias in the dataset, the videos in the dataset were grouped into 16 different camera views, as shown in Fig. 8. The confusion matrices for each camera view (Fig. 10) showed that the algorithms mostly predicted the most frequent class for the corresponding camera view. This might explain the relatively high accuracy of the algorithms on the dataset even though the Grad-CAM indicated that the models showed little to no attention to the fish in the frames.

When training end-to-end networks, care must be taken not to introduce a bias into the data being processed. As seen in this work, the models learned the dataset to some extent but not as intended due to bias introduced by human tampering.

Acknowledgements. This work is partly supported by the Rannís Technology Development Fund under grant number 2010831-0612.

References

1. Simonyan, K., Zisserman, A.: Two-stream convolutional networks for action recognition in videos. In: Advances in Neural Information Processing Systems, vol. 27 (2014)
2. Soomro, K., Zamir, A.R., Shah, M.: Ucf101: a dataset of 101 human actions classes from videos in the wild. arXiv preprint arXiv:1212.0402 (2012)

3. Selvaraju, R.R., Cogswell, M., Das, A., Vedantam, R., Parikh, D., Batra, D.: Grad-CAM: visual explanations from deep networks via gradient-based localization. Int. J. Comput. Vis. **128**(2), 336–359 (2019)

4. Jalal, A., Salman, A., Mian, A., Shortis, M., Shafait, F.: Fish detection and species classification in underwater environments using deep learning with temporal information. Ecol. Informat. **57**, 101088 (2020)

5. Siddiqui, S., et al.: Automatic fish species classification in underwater videos: exploiting pretrained deep neural network models to compensate for limited labelled data. ICES J. Marine Sci. **75**, 05 (2017)

6. Måløy, H., Aamodt, A., Misimi, E.: A spatio-temporal recurrent network for salmon feeding action recognition from underwater videos in aquaculture. Comput. Electron. Agricult. **167**, 105087 (2019)

7. Rahman, S.A., Song, I., Leung, M., Lee, I., Lee, K.: Fast action recognition using negative space features. Exp. Syst. Appl. **41**(2), 574–587 (2014)

8. Thorhallsson, T., et al.: Trawling with light, RANNIS Technology Development Fund, Project 153487–0613, Technical Final Report, [In Icelandic] (2018)

9. Vaswani, A., et al.: Attention is all you need. Adv. Neural Inf. Process. Syst. **30** (2017)

10. Bertasius, G., Wang, H., Torresani, L.: Is space-time attention all you need for video understanding? In: Meila, M., Zhang, T. (eds.) Proceedings of the 38th International Conference on Machine Learning, ser. Proceedings of Machine Learning Research (PMLR), 18–24 Jul 2021, vol. 139, pp. 813–824 (2021)

11. Arnab, A., Dehghani, M., Heigold, G., Sun, C., Lučić, M., Schmid, C.: Vivit: a video vision transformer. In: Proceedings of the IEEE/CVF International Conference on Computer Vision (ICCV), October 2021, pp. 6836–6846 (2021)

12. Dosovitskiy, A., et al.: An image is worth 16x16 words: Transformers for image recognition at scale. In: International Conference on Learning Representations (2021)

13. Farnebäck, G.: Two-frame motion estimation based on polynomial expansion. In: Bigun, J., Gustavsson, T. (eds.) Image Analysis, pp. 363–370. Springer, Heidelberg (2003)

14. He, K., Zhang, X., Ren, S., Sun, J.: Deep residual learning for image recognition. In: IEEE Conference on Computer Vision and Pattern Recognition (CVPR), vol. 2016, pp. 770–778 (2016)

15. Deng, J., Dong, W., Socher, R., Li, L.-J., Li, K., Fei-Fei, L.: Imagenet: a large-scale hierarchical image database. In: IEEE Conference on Computer Vision and Pattern Recognition, vol. 2009, pp. 248–255 (2009)

Separating Particles from Plankton Images

Nina S. T. Hirata ⬚, Alexandre Morimitsu⬚, and Antonio Goulart⬚

Institute of Mathematics and Statistics, University of São Paulo, São Paulo, Brazil
nina@ime.usp.br

Abstract. Plankton studies using imaging technologies require processing tools to help taxonomic identification of the objects captured in the
images. A great deal of the captured object images correspond to different type of particles (such as detritus). Not being able to filter out
these images means higher costs associated with transmission, storage
and further processing. In this work we investigate how well deep neural
networks are able to separate particles from plankton and what are the
main causes of classification error. We find out that most classification
errors are related to ambiguity and thus further studies and tools to deal
with ambiguities are needed.

Keywords: Plankton image · detritus · class ambiguity · deep learning

1   Introduction

In plankton ecosystem studies, there is great interest in quantifying abundance,
taxonomic diversity and distribution of the organisms in different parts of the
ocean [5]. For these type of investigations, sensors based on imaging technology
are being constantly improved and used for *in situ* collection of data [5].

Organism images are usually cropped from a larger image corresponding
to the field of view of the camera. To detect regions of interest containing
objects in these large images, a combination of image processing techniques
such as background subtraction, binarization and connected component detection is employed. The problem of identifying the taxonomic class of a plankton
can be modelled as an image classification problem. To build datasets for supervised training algorithms, usually individual object images are manually labeled.
Nowadays, deep learning based methods are being widely employed for classification [6,7,10].

When using *in situ* imaging devices, the need for high magnification to capture detailed information limits the depth of view, resulting in many out-of-
focus objects. In general, the distribution of the original collection from which
a dataset of images is built is not clear. Based on our own experience, it seems
reasonable to assume that many of the object samples captured in the images
are not plankton or are of too poor quality and thus they are discarded. Even

© Springer Nature Switzerland AG 2023
J.-J. Rousseau and B. Kapralos (Eds.): ICPR 2022 Workshops, LNCS 13645, pp. 445–459, 2023.
https://doi.org/10.1007/978-3-031-37731-0_33

after discarding the poor quality ones, training datasets usually contain not only plankton images but also images of other particles and objects such as detritus, bubble, or artifacts of the imaging process. We use the term particle to refer to any objects that are regarded as non-plankton. In fact, when we analyze some of the commonly used plankton image datasets for training and evaluating recognition algorithms, we find out that a considerable percentage of the instances correspond to particles (see details in Sect. 3.1).

Unless one is interested in studying particles, there is no need to keep and process this large percentage of particle images. The ability to effectively filter out particles, perhaps right at the beginning of the processing pipeline, would mean less data to be stored and processed. For instance, suppose we are interested in monitoring certain species at some fixed location. A device equipped with a camera and limited processing capabilities could be used to capture images from time to time, crop objects of interest from the images, and send only the set of objects of interest to a server for further analysis. The ability to separate objects of interest from the rest is crucial to reduce transmission cost. Even in situations where transmission is not an issue, the ability to better filter out particles could facilitate building customized image datasets, or reduce storage requirements and subsequent processing costs in general.

Motivated by the above issues, in this work we are interested in evaluating deep neural network models for the task of separating particles from plankton images. We would like to understand how challenging this task is and if there are common misclassification patterns. We report an initial study using three datasets and two convolutional neural network architectures. Some background is provided in Sect. 2, and details of the datasets, network architectures and training procedures are presented in Sect. 3. In Sect. 4, we report and discuss the results. In particular, for a qualitative analysis we use t-SNE projection maps; a detailed examination of specific regions in the map reveals potential ambiguous or wrong labels as the main causes of prediction errors. Conclusions and ideas for future work are presented in Sect. 5.

2   Background

Traditional approaches for plankton image classification are based on image processing pipelines that involve segmentation and feature extraction steps. Segmentation consists in determining the precise contours of the object of interest in the image and feature extraction consists in finding a discriminative representation of these objects. Frequently used features include metrics related to the shape, topology and texture of the objects. A challenge in this process is to design algorithms for segmentation and feature extraction that are robust to image content variations. In contrast, deep neural networks process the input images directly. It is generally accepted that their multiple layers play the role of finding rich representations that lead to good classification results [1]. A side effect of this flexibility is the requirement of a larger amount of training data.

Transfer learning methods have been demonstrated to be effective in reducing the requirement of large labeled datasets for training deep neural networks.

Typically, weights of a network, pre-trained on data of another domain, are used as the starting point. Then the network is further trained with data of the target domain. For plankton images, there is a number of studies reporting deep learning based classification methods where training was performed using transfer learning [6,9,11].

In general, particle detection in imaging based plankton observation projects seems to be based on some pre-processing steps aiming to simply discard poor quality object images. This results in a large number of objects that are particles, representing noise added to the subsequent processing tasks such as image labeling, dataset building or classifier training. This is particularly critical as it will slow down expert-dependent tasks such as labeling and label verification. Most existing training datasets include a few classes of particles and when training plankton classifiers, they are treated just as additional classes. An effective particle filtering could also benefit plankton recognition algorithms.

3 Methods

3.1 Datasets

We use three distinct datasets. The first two are in-house datasets containing *in situ* collected images, while the third one is a public dataset containing scanned images of net collected organisms. For each dataset, we regroup the original classes into two classes: *plankton* (blue) and *particle* (red), as illustrated in the histograms of Fig. 1. Notice that a large fraction of the images correspond to *particle*. Details of each dataset are presented next.

D1: It contains samples collected at a southeast coastal area of Brazil. It is an unbalanced dataset originally comprised of 56,725 images divided into 75 classes. We rename three classes (*bubbles*, *detritus* and *shadow*) as *particle*, and the remaining 72 classes as *plankton*. This results in 31,519 (55.56%) images in the *plankton* class and 25,206 (44.44%) images in the *particle* class. Practically all instances in the *particle* class are from the original classes *detritus* and *shadow*.

D2: It contains samples collected at a northeast coastal area of Brazil. It is an unbalanced dataset originally comprised of 703,388 images divided into 57 classes. We rename seven original classes (*detritus*, *shadow*, *det_dot*, *bolha*, *borda*, *det_agg* and *shadow_dots*) as *particle* and the remaining 50 classes as *plankton*. This results in a dataset where 415,267 (59.04%) images are in the *plankton* class and 288,121 (40.96%) images are in the *particle* class (practically the totality of the samples in this class are from the original *detritus*, *shadow*, and *det_dot* classes).

ZooScan [2]: A description of the dataset can be found in the cited reference. It is reported that samples were collected with various nets and individual object images were generated following [3]. It contains, 1,433,278 images sorted into 93 classes. We rename seven classes (*artefact*, *badfocus_artefact*, *bubbles*, *detritus*, *fiber_detritus*, *scale* and *seaweed*) as *particle* (48.78%) and the remaining ones (51.22%) as *plankton*.

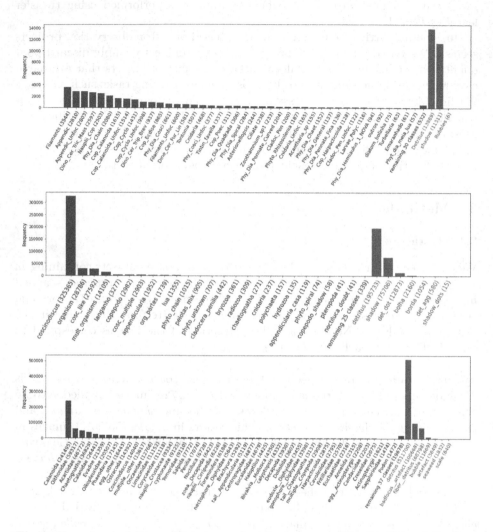

Fig. 1. From top to bottom: Histogram of original classes of the D1, D2 and ZooScan datasets, where classes in blue are regarded as *plankton* and those in red are regarded as *particle*. The number after the name of each class indicates its frequency. Classes with few samples were grouped together for better legibility. (Color figure online)

3.2   Convolutional Neural Network Architectures

We use two convolutional neural network (CNN) architectures, namely MobileNetV2 [4] and InceptionResNetV2 [12]. MobileNetV2 is a lightweight architecture (2,259,265 parameters) while InceptionResNetV2 is a larger one

(54,338,273 parameters). In both cases, we add a fully-connected one node layer at the end, after the flattened global pooling layer, to perform binary classification.

3.3 Training and Evaluation

For each dataset, a training/test split (stratified according to the original classes) following the proportions 85%/15% is built. *Particle* is regarded as the positive class (label 1) and *plankton* as the negative class (label 0). Networks are trained and validated using the full or part of the training set while evaluation and analysis are done on the test set.

For each training, about 17.65% of instances are used for validation while the rest is used for weight adjustment. The training/validation partition is stratified with respect to the binary classes (but not the original classes), and is automatically generated by TensorFlow (the deep learning framework used in this work). We use the binary cross-entropy loss function and Adam optimizer, and apply rotation and horizontal flips to augment the data. The initial weights are transferred from the network trained on ImageNet and the fully connected layer is trained for 10 epochs with learning rate 10^{-4}, and then fine-tuning is applied afterwards to the last 40% of the layers of the network with learning rate 10^{-5}, to adapt the weights of these layers to our problem. Early stopping with patience 10 (that is, if no reduction is detected in the validation loss of the last 10 training epochs) is used to reduce overfitting, and if early stopping happens, weights from 10 epochs prior are recovered and used as the final model.

For the evaluation of a trained network, we generate its prediction for the test set and compute the confusion matrix. We also use t-SNE algorithm [8] to project the features computed by the network. In general terms, features extracted from the images can be seen as points in a high-dimensional space, and t-SNE computes a similarity measure based on the distance between each pair of points. Then, it maps each point into a low-dimensional space (2-d in our case) by solving an optimization problem, trying to obtain an arrangement of the points in such a way that their distances in the 2-d space reflect their dissimilarities in the high-dimensional space. Therefore, assuming that similar images have similar features, we expect t-SNE to preserve closeness in the projected scatterplot. In Fig. 2, we show the projection of features, extracted using InceptionResNetV2, of 2000 random images from the D1 dataset. Each point in the projection is replaced with a miniaturized version of the corresponding image. We see that similar images are grouped together.

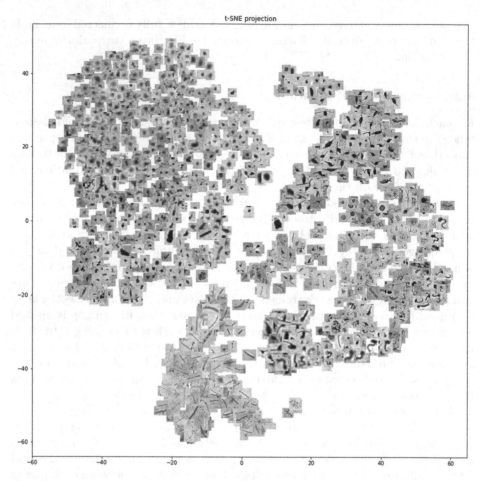

Fig. 2. The t-SNE projection of a sample of 2000 random images from the D1 dataset, with features extracted using the InceptionResNetV2.

4   Results and Discussion

4.1   Comparing the Two CNN Models

We first evaluate the two CNN architectures on the D1 and D2 datasets. Figure 3 shows the learning curves for the D1 dataset. For both architectures we see an initial steady convergence. For InceptionResNetV2, oscillations are observed later on; however as we use early stopping, we decided to use the model corresponding to weights where the curve is stable and leave further investigation of the oscillations as future work. For the D2 dataset, similar behavior was observed (not shown).

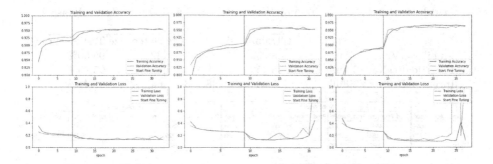

Fig. 3. From left to right: training curves for the D1 dataset using the MobileNetV2, InceptionResNetV2 (mini-batch size 32) and InceptionResNetV2 (mini-batch size 64).

Some details of the training and classification accuracy are shown in Table 1. The top block tables refer to the D1 dataset and the bottom block to the D2 dataset. For the D1 dataset, we used the full training set. Both networks achieve similar accuracy, varying from 95.36% to 95.50%. Confusion matrix shows that InceptionResNetV2 (batch size 64) presents higher accuracy with respect to *plankton* and lower accuracy with respect to *particle* when compared to MobileNetV2.

For the D2 dataset, some variations of training set size have been tested. We note that InceptionResNetV2, using only 10% of the training data, achieves similar performance of MobileNetV2 using 100% of training data. We also note that when the number of instances in each original class was limited to a maximum of 10K, accuracy dropped to 89.37%. This might be due to smaller accuracies on more frequent classes. We also did not train InceptionResNetV2 on the full training set, as 10% was already yielding good results and training on the full dataset would take a long time. We leave further investigation of these aspects for future work. Confusion matrix shows that InceptionResNetV2 (batch size 64) presents a slightly better performance than MobileNetV2. From here on, regarding InceptionResNetV2, we consider the one trained with batch size 64.

In terms of classification accuracy, both architectures perform similarly well on both sets. Thus, we use the t-SNE algorithm to project features from the last layer, right before the classification node of the network, to verify if there are other differences between them. Figure 4 shows the projection maps for the D1 test images. For each architecture, the projection is shown twice; the graphs on the left are colored according to the ground-truth labels, while the graphs on the right are colored according to the predictions of the networks. Red indicates *particle* and blue indicates *plankton*. The map of features extracted using MobileNetV2 are on the top part and those using InceptionResNetV2 are on the bottom part of the figure. Similar plots for the D2 dataset are shown in Fig. 5.

Table 1. Results of the training for the D1 (top) and D2 (bottom) datasets

Network	Training set	Training size	Test size	Batch size	Test Accuracy
MobileNetV2	Full	48,252	8,473	32	95.50%
InceptionResNetV2	Full	48,252	8,473	32	95.36%
InceptionResNetV2	Full	48,252	8,473	64	95.47%

		MobileNetV2				InceptionResNetV2			
Correct label	Total	Pred. Plankton	Pred. Particle	Pred. Plankton (%)	Pred. Particle (%)	Pred. Plankton	Pred. Particle	Pred. Plankton (%)	Pred. Particle (%)
Plankton	4694	4499	195	95.846	4.154	4572	122	97.401	2.599
Particle	3779	184	3595	4.869	95.131	229	3550	6.060	93.940
Total	8473	4683	3790			4801	3672		

Network	Training set	Training size	Test size	Batch size	Test Accuracy
MobileNetV2	Full	597,908	105,480	32	95.04%
InceptionResNetV2	10,000 cap	89,766	105,480	32	89.37%
InceptionResNetV2	10%	59,819	105,480	32	95.22%
InceptionResNetV2	10%	59,819	105,480	64	95.93%

		MobileNetV2				InceptionResNetV2			
Correct label	Total	Pred. Plankton	Pred. Particle	Pred. Plankton (%)	Pred. Particle (%)	Pred. Plankton	Pred. Particle	Pred. Plankton (%)	Pred. Particle (%)
Plankton	62265	59006	3259	94.766	5.234	59834	2431	96.096	3.904
Particle	43215	1877	41338	4.343	95.657	1790	41425	4.142	95.858
Total	105480	60883	44597			61624	43856		

As shown in the projections, overall we note that *particle* class instances are grouped on one side and *plankton* class instances on the other side of the maps. However, the projection maps generated using InceptionResNetV2 show two clearly separated clusters of points, while the ones generated with MobileNetV2 do not have the same characteristic. Based on this, we assume that although both models are achieving similar accuracy, InceptionResNetV2 is being able to perform a better separation of the two classes. Thus, from here on, we will restrict discussion to InceptionResNetV2 only. We note, however, that MobileNetV2 is much faster regarding prediction time, being able to process about 2150 images per second, while InceptionResNetV2 process about 150 images per second. These results were obtained on a RTX3070 Mobile with 8GB of VRAM, using batches of 32 images for each forward pass of the network.

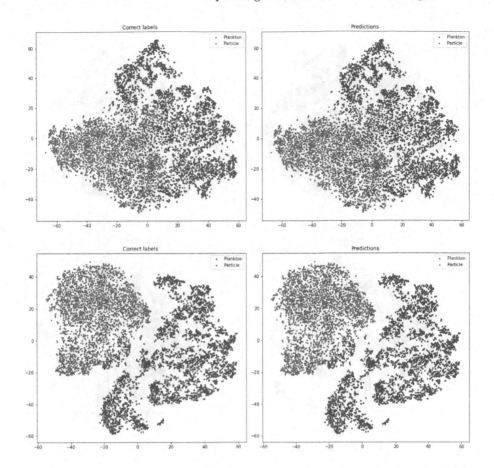

Fig. 4. t-SNE projection of D1 test images using MobileNetV2 (top) and InceptionRes-NetV2 (bottom). In the graphs on the left, points are colored according to the ground truth and, on the right, according to the predictions of each network.

4.2   Error Analysis

The t-SNE plots of Fig. 4 and 5 call attention to the fact that ground-truth labels and network predictions present distinct color patterns in the projection. Since two images with similar features are likely to be classified as being of the same class, it is expected that network prediction generates homogeneous colored regions. This is consistent with what is seen in the t-SNE plots. On the other hand, considering coloring according to the ground-truth label, it is not clear why there are *plankton* instances mixed in regions that are predominantly occupied by *particle* instances and vice-versa.

In order to understand the disagreement between ground-truth labels and network predictions, we examine in detail three regions of the plot from the D2 dataset. The regions are highlighted in Fig. 5, using boxes of three colors:

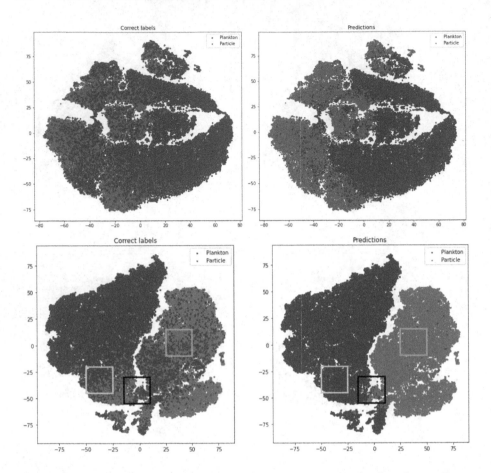

Fig. 5. t-SNE projection of D2 test images using MobileNetV2 (top) and using Inception ResNetV2 (bottom). Ground-truth labels (left) and predictions (right). Boxes highlight regions for further analysis (see text).

– **Black**: frontier between the two classes
– **Cyan**: a region where the network classifies every point as plankton despite ground-truth label indicating there are *particles*
– **Magenta**: a region where the network classifies most points as particles but fails to recognize some plankton.

In Fig. 6 we show, for each region, 24 images. The left side shows 12 *plankton* and the right side shows 12 *particle* images (according to ground-truth label) randomly selected from each region. The text above each individual image shows the network output, where scores lower than 0.5 are considered as *plankton* and those higher than 0.5 are considered as *particle*. As expected, in the region at the frontier of the two classes we see scores around 0.5, indicating that those instances are in the classification frontier. In the cyan and magenta regions,

Correct class: Plankton ┊ Correct class: particle

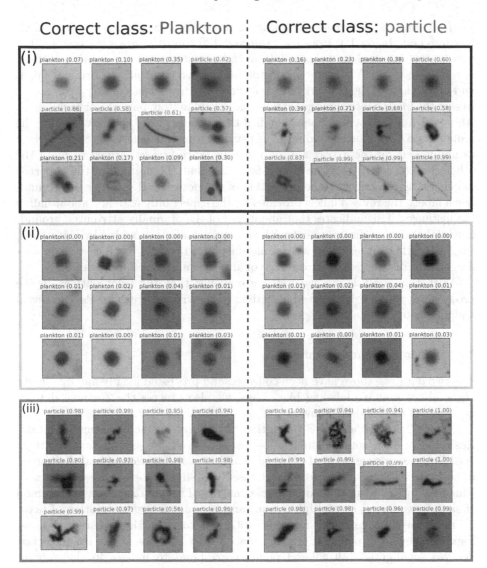

Fig. 6. Sample images from the black, cyan and magenta rectangles highlighted in the bottom plot in the left panel of Fig. 5. For each region, 12 images are from the *plankton* class (left column) and 12 images from the *particle* class (right column). The text above each image indicates the predictions by the InceptionResNetV2.

scores are closer to 0 (*plankton*) and 1 (*particle*), respectively. Although according to the ground-truth label half of the images shown for each region correspond to network classification error, we could say that the group of 12 images on the left side is visually not much different from the group of 12 images on the right side.

To further analyze these results, we selected 240 images for revision of labels by an expert, being 120 from the cyan and 120 from the magenta regions. For each region, we randomly chose 60 from the *plankton* class and another 60 from the *particle* class. When presenting the images for revision, the original labels and predictions of the network were removed to reduce bias. We asked the expert to sort the images into three general categories: plankton, particle, or ambiguous. About 92% of the revised labels matched the outputs of the network. Among the remaining 8%, all corresponding to network error cases, most were categorized as ambiguous by the expert and only one instance was confirmed to be of the other class (true error). Note that this means that the opinion of the expert is in general agreement with the prediction of the network. Regarding the ground-truth labels, the revised labels provided by the expert only matched about half of the instances. This indicates that about half of the originally attributed ground-truth labels are in disagreement with the revised labels provided by the expert, suggesting that either there were some mislabeled images or that some images are hard to distinguish, due to image quality or ambiguous appearance.

With this analysis, we have strong evidence that the color outliers in the projections, where color is given according to the ground-truth labels, can reveal ambiguous or mislabeled images.

4.3   A More General Dataset

The two datasets above have been collected and processed locally and one might argue about possible labeling bias. Thus, we also process the ZooScan dataset in a similar way as done above.

Figure 7 shows the t-SNE projection of features extracted using Inception-ResNetV2 and the confusion matrix on test set. As can be seen, the same pattern of differences between ground-truth label and network prediction is also observed in this case. The accuracy for this dataset was slightly below the other cases. This may just confirm the more complex nature of this dataset as it is the union of samples collected by multiple groups and contains a larger variation of taxa.

Here we show an error analysis restricted to a particular original class. Figure 8 shows the t-SNE projection map of test samples of the original class *detritus* highlighted (all colored points correspond to images in the *detritus* class). In fact, most *detritus* instances are colored red, indicating that the network predicted them correctly as *particle*. However, there is a number of them colored blue, meaning the network predicted them wrongly as *plankton*. The 10 images shown by the side of the projection map is a random selection of instances with classifications scores ranging from values close to 0 to values close to 1. According to the network prediction, considering 0.5 as the threshold to separate the two classes, the first 5 images on the top row are *plankton* while the 5 in the bottom row are *particle*. In fact, the first image shown is clearly a *plankton*, revealing a wrong label in the original dataset.

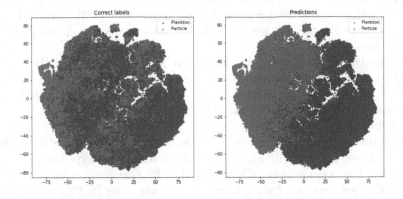

Correct label	Total	Pred. Plankton	Pred. Particle	Pred. Plankton (%)	Pred. Particle (%)
Plankton	110078	103752	6326	94.253	5.747
Particle	104871	9163	95708	8.737	91.263
Total	214949	112915	102034		

Fig. 7. ZooScan: t-SNE projections of the correct classes (left) and of the labels predicted by InceptionResNetV2 (right). At the bottom, the confusion matrix.

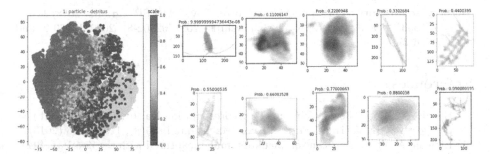

Fig. 8. ZooScan: Instances of the *detritus* class. Prediction score varies from 0 (blue, meaning plankton) to 1 (red, meaning *particle*). See details in text. (Color figure online)

5 Conclusion

In this initial study, the experiments show that deep neural networks, using transfer learning, are able to separate *particle* from *plankton* with good accuracy. We tested two networks, MobileNetV2 and InceptionResNetV2. The first is a lightweight model and trains faster than the second and, under standard training setting, both achieve similar accuracy. By inspecting the t-SNE projections of features extracted with these networks, we judged that InceptionResNetV2 is performing a better separation. By visually inspecting some specific regions with misclassifications we note that many of the misclassified instances are, actually, visually similar objects that represent ambiguous cases (with a second opinion that disagrees with the first one). We also find out that some errors are actually wrongly labeled cases.

To improve understanding and results, it seems natural that the next step should focus on quantifying and better characterizing the causes of error. By doing so, we could obtain more accurate *particle* detectors. We point out the usefulness of visualization tools, such as t-SNE plots, as they are able to capture some global patterns of the entire dataset. Then, studying specific regions of the plot may reveal details such as common misclassification causes as shown in this study. It should be noted that the task of separating some types of objects from others could be analogously tailored for specific taxonomic classes of interest against the rest, and analysis similar to the ones done in this work could be applied. It might even be possible to quantify ambiguity or uncertainty associated to individual taxonomic classes, an information that could help when taking practical decision based on plankton indicators. From a strictly computational point of view, future work includes optimizing network training setup for the task, investigating effects of highly unbalanced class distributions for this particular task, possibly considering a multi-label classification formulation of the problem, and evaluating practical impacts of an improved *particle* filtering in the processing pipeline.

Acknowledgements. This work is supported by FAPESP (grants 2018/24167-5, 2017/25835-9 and 2015/22308-2; fellowships 2021/02902-8, 2020/15170-2 and 2022/09376-2).

References

1. Bengio, Y., Courville, A., Vincent, P.: Representation learning: a review and new perspectives. IEEE Trans. Pattern Anal. Mach. Intell. **35**(8), 1798–1828 (2013)
2. Elineau, A., et al.: ZooScanNet: plankton images captured with the ZooScan. SEANOE (2018). https://doi.org/10.17882/55741
3. Gorsky, G., et al.: Digital zooplankton image analysis using the ZooScan integrated system. J. Plankton Res. **32**(3), 285–303 (2010)
4. Howard, A.G., et al.: MobileNets: Efficient Convolutional Neural Networks for Mobile Vision Applications. arXiv abs/1704.04861 (2017)
5. Lombard, F., et al.: Globally consistent quantitative observations of planktonic ecosystems. Front. Mar. Sci. **6**, 196 (2019)
6. Lumini, A., Nanni, L.: Deep learning and transfer learning features for plankton classification. Eco. Inform. **51**, 33–43 (2019)
7. Luo, J.Y., et al.: Automated plankton image analysis using convolutional neural networks. Limnol. Oceanogr. Methods **16**(12), 814–827 (2018)
8. van der Maaten, L., Hinton, G.: Visualizing data using t-SNE. J. Mach. Learn. Res. **9**(86), 2579–2605 (2008)
9. Orenstein, E.C., Beijbom, O.: Transfer learning and deep feature extraction for planktonic image data sets. In: 2017 IEEE Winter Conference on Applications of Computer Vision (WACV), pp. 1082–1088 (2017)

10. Pastore, V.P., Zimmerman, T.G., Biswas, S.K., Bianco, S.: Annotation-free learning of plankton for classification and anomaly detection. Sci. Rep. **10**, 12142 (2020)
11. Rodrigues, F.C.M., Hirata, N.S.T., Abello, A.A., Cruz, L.T.D.L., Lopes, R.M., Hirata Jr., R.: Evaluation of transfer learning scenarios in plankton image classification. In: Proceedings of the 13th International Joint Conference on Computer Vision, Imaging and Computer Graphics Theory and Applications (VISAPP), vol. 5, pp. 359–366. INSTICC, SciTePress (2018)
12. Szegedy, C., Ioffe, S., Vanhoucke, V., Alemi, A.: Inception-v4, Inception-ResNet and the Impact of Residual Connections on Learning, arXiv: abs/1602.07261 (2016)

Automated Blue Whale Photo-Identification Using Local Feature Matching

Marc Lalonde[1]([⊠]) [ID], David Landry[1], and Richard Sears[2]

[1] Computer Vision Team, Computer Research Institute of Montreal,
Montreal, QC, Canada
{marc.lalonde,david.landry}@crim.ca
[2] Mingan Island Cetacean Study, 285 rue Green, St. Lambert, QC, Canada
rsblues@polysoft.com

Abstract. Automated photo-identification of blue whale individuals has received little attention over the years compared to humpback and right whales, most likely because of the difficulty of the task: blue whales are identified using the low-contrast pigmentation of their skin (light and dark shades of grey displayed in patches of varying sizes). This paper explores the use of three local feature matching techniques (SIFT, L2-Net and LoFTR) for blue whale photo-identification and compares their performance to that of a baseline method (Pose Invariant Embeddings, or PIE) which has been used for humpback whale identification. We conduct experiments using a rich dataset made of 3129 images of 807 unique individuals acquired over a 40-year period. Results show a large difference in performance between all methods, with LoFTR outperforming the other three by a large margin. Measured top-1 and top-10 accuracies (76.7% and 80.3% respectively) suggest that LoFTR is suitable for the robust matching of images of blue whales.

Keywords: Image matching · deep learning · blue whale photo-identification

1 Introduction

Photo-identification has proven to be an essential non-intrusive tool for long-term studies of several marine mammal species since the 1970s, and is particularly useful for wide-ranging species, whether in inshore waters or over whole oceanic basins. Maintaining photographic catalogs of known individuals has become essential to gathering a large variety of long-term natural history data, such as dispersal, distribution, migratory patterns, as well as critical habitat use in feeding and reproduction. Long-term photo-identification based data are essential to life history studies, in order to determine age at sexual maturity, mortality rates, life span, etc. Mark-recapture population studies, where pigmentation patterns unique to individuals recognizable over time with equal probability of being

© Springer Nature Switzerland AG 2023
J.-J. Rousseau and B. Kapralos (Eds.): ICPR 2022 Workshops, LNCS 13645, pp. 460–473, 2023.
https://doi.org/10.1007/978-3-031-37731-0_34

Fig. 1. Random samples showing image diversity in pose/viewpoint, color, year of acquisition (1997/2008/2014)

sighted and re-sighted have been widely used to estimate population size. In addition to the collection of photo-identification data, it is vital to maintain and preserve photographic catalogues with accompanying sighting data of individuals of each species studied. Each catalogue should be reviewed and updated with better quality images and new individuals added each year to improve accuracy of data, which enables better research analysis and results.

The first marine mammal studies to use photo-identification made use of variances in dorsal fin shape and saddle pigmentation patches on the backs of killer whales (Orcinus orca). This was followed by photo-identification studies of right whale (Eubalaena glacialis and australis) using images of the varying callosity patterns found on their heads. By the mid 70s photo-identification of baleen whales such as the humpback (Megaptera novaeangliae) based on photographs of the ventral fluke pattern were well underway, which was followed in quick order by photo-identification studies of fin (Balaenoptera physalus), sperm (Physeter marcrocephalus), and minke Balaenopteera acutorostrata) whales. And in 1979 began the first such study of blue whale (Balaenoptera musculus) using photographs of their characteristic mottled pigmentation pattern.

Clear, well-exposed and contrasted photographs of well-marked animals are more easily recognized over time. Matching of individuals in ever-larger catalogues is time consuming, generally poorly funded yet vital to long-term studies. Computerized matching systems are expected to reduce the time involved in matching, the number of false matches, accelerate analysis, and allow researchers to more effectively update catalogues. The purpose of this paper is to evaluate algorithms that might be at the core of such a matching system, with specific emphasis on the identification of blue whale individuals. The main contributions are:

– Blue whale photo-identification based on local features. Three methods are explored: SIFT, L2-Net and LoFTR. To the best of our knowledge, this paper is the first addressing automated photo-identification for this species of whale.
– Performance comparison with an embeddings-based method that serves as a baseline.

The remainder of the paper is organized as follows. Section 2 lists previous works regarding whale photo-identification using automatic and semi-automatic methods, while Sect. 3 describes some candidate methods based on local feature matching as well as a baseline method applied successfully to the identification of humpback whales. Section 4 reports some photo-identification results over a challenging dataset, followed by a discussion and perspective of future work in Sect. 5.

2   Previous Work

Animal re-identification is an important tool used by ecologists to estimate populations as well as their dynamics [16]. Re-identification based on visual cues (photos, videos) is particularly appealing due to its non-intrusive character and lower cost compared to other means, and naturally, computer vision techniques play an increasingly useful role in standardizing the re-identification process. Schneider et al. [14] report that a large set of computer vision techniques have been employed to re-identify elephants, tigers, sharks, chimpanzees, lemurs, etc. In particular, photo-identification of whale individuals by means of automatic image comparisons has evolved since the early work of [10]. A short literature review highlights the fact that some specific whale species have attracted a lot of attention, most notably humpback [13] and right whales [2]. Humpback whale individuals can be distinguished due to the high-contrast color patterns on their fluke, while right whales bear callosities on their head that form a unique pattern, much like a human fingerprint. With the increasing popularity of deep learning methods, efficient solutions have been proposed in the recent years, with [11] reporting a top-10 accuracy rate of 93% for humpback whales and [2] a top-5 accuracy of 94.9% for right whales. As for blue whales, they are identified based primarily on their skin pigmentation patterns (even though they can be affected by desquamation [12]) but also on the shape of the dorsal fin and presence of scars on their flanks. The only work dedicated to blue whale photo-identification is a series of contributions by Gendron et al. [3,4,12] based on the semi-automatic analysis of the visual appearance of the dorsal fin. After manual selection of a region of interest centered on the fin, its shape is extracted, a SIFT-like signature is computed and classification is performed in order to assign the shape to one of six possible classes ("Left/Right Falcate", "Left/Right Hooked", "Left/right Triangular"). The classification is then used by an expert to complete the photo-identification process.

This work focuses on automated photo-identification of blue whales, a species that has received much less attention. Two approaches are considered:

- Local feature (i.e. keypoint) matching, which is heavily used for robust image matching [7], is a generic approach capable of finding correspondences between pairs of images. In this work, some state-of-the-art matching methods are tested to evaluate their ability to find matches between images of the same blue whale individual.
- The PIE algorithm [11], which is based on the computation and classification of an embedding that characterizes the appearance of an individual, is designed to be generic and not species specific, so it appears to be a good baseline candidate for blue whale photo-identification.

3 Methodology

This section describes the approach of using local feature matching techniques to perform photo-identification of blue whales. The hypothesis is that these methods will exploit the unique properties of an individual's skin pigmentation pattern to find dense, pixel-wise correspondences between pairs of images from the same individual, despite challenging image acquisition conditions (low contrast, waves, variations in lighting and pose/viewpoint, skin flaking, etc.). Three methods are considered in this paper: SIFT (handcrafted point extractor and descriptor), L2-Net (handcrafted point extractor, learned descriptor) and LoFTR (machine learning-based point extractor and descriptor). And as mentioned earlier a baseline method (PIE) is also described.

3.1 SIFT

SIFT [9] is an emblematic algorithm in computer vision, being used in a large variety of situations. It consists of a multi-scale keypoint extractor that also computes for each keypoint a distinctive descriptor designed to be invariant to changes in illumination, image scale/rotation, minor viewpoint changes, and image noise. These properties are crucial for robust object recognition as object appearance in real-world images may vary significantly. In this work, the Root-SIFT [1] extension is used.

3.2 L2-Net

L2-Net is a neural network architecture that can be trained to transform a local image patch into a 128-dimensional descriptor with invariance properties similar to SIFT: image patches whose descriptors are very close in Euclidean space should be similar in appearance, i.e. they should come from different images of the same object. The fully convolutional network architecture being rather simple, the quality of the descriptor arises from careful design of the loss function as well as the sampling strategy behind the selection of negative patches during training. In this work, patch extraction is performed using scripts provided by the Image Matching Benchmark [6] (based on the SIFT keypoint extractor).

3.3 LoFTR

LoFTR [15] is a state-of-the-art method for local image feature matching between images that favors pixel-wise dense matches. LoFTR distinguishes itself from SIFT as the local features are learned rather than hand-crafted; it also differs from more recent methods by the use of the Transformer architecture in order to 1) increase the receptive field of the local feature extractor (compared to CNNs) and 2) take advantage of positional encoding to increase its ability to find correspondences in 'indistinctive' regions. This latter feature might be crucial given the low contrast that characterizes the pigmentation patterns of blue whales. Finally, the authors report good results even in the presence of motion blur, yet this type of image noise is expected to be common in a whale photo-identification context as some of the dataset images are captured from a moving boat. This work uses the authors' implementation on GitHub [17] with the 'outdoor' pre-trained model.

3.4 Baseline Method: PIE

The PIE (Pose Invariant Embeddings) method [11] uses an InceptionV3 model to produce embeddings which can then serve as prototypes for a kNN classifier, where the number of classes corresponds to the number of individuals to identify. The InceptionV3 model (pretrained on ImageNet) is trained with the triplet loss function, which optimizes the model's representation so that embeddings of the same individual are close in embedding space but far from those of other individuals. An analysis of the learned representation with the t-SNE algorithm shows good invariance properties in terms of pose, viewpoint and small occlusions. The selection of the kNN classifier as a decision tool yields the interesting property that new individuals can be easily added to the proposed system without need for network retraining (their embeddings are simply added to the pool of prototypes). In their main application context (Manta ray re-identification), the authors ensure proper computation of the embeddings by manually cropping the images around the individual's natural markings.

3.5 Dataset

The dataset used for the experiments comes from a collection of images and metadata amassed over the last 40 years in the Gulf of St. Lawrence (Canada). It consists of a set of 3129 images of the right-side dorsal of 807 blue whale individuals. The dataset is quite imbalanced as most (388) of the individuals are associated with two images only (two sightings), while 47 individuals have at least 10 images associated to them. Image quality, which is qualitatively evaluated by an expert cetologist, varies from average (grade C) to very good (grade A) and horizontal resolution can be as low as 250 pixels. These variations can be explained by the time span of the (continuous) data acquisition campaign: for example, 10% of the dataset images have been captured before 1995. Some image samples are shown in Fig. 1. An additional category termed the catalog (CAT), similar to the image gallery used by face recognition algorithms, allows researchers to optimize their search efforts.

It is interesting to note that the size of this dataset is considerably larger in terms of image quantity and number of individuals than those surveyed by [14]; in addition, the long image acquisition time span makes the dataset even more challenging to use.

3.6 Matching Strategy - Local Features

In the proposed application context, a query image containing an unidentified blue whale and the set of M reference images (each of which being associated to an individual) are resized to standard dimensions, i.e. 720×192 pixels. A fine-tuned Mask R-CNN [5] object detector localizes the blue whale in each image and generates a mask that allows the removal of surrounding background (water, waves, sky, etc.). This mask is eroded in order to prevent matches that might appear along the edge of the whale's body: those are likely spurious matches caused by e.g. the presence of 'wave foam' produced by the moving whale. Finally, all three keypoint matching methods return a list of correspondences between the query image and each of the reference images. In addition, LoFTR also determines a confidence value for each correspondence (between 0 and 1). Some keypoint matching examples computed by LoFTR are shown in Fig. 2: good matches are found between the query and the reference images despite their low, non-uniform contrast, and despite mask errors that may prevent matches on a sizeable portion of the body. The query image is paired with every reference image in the database. For each pair, a simple matching score is computed which is equal to the number of matches between the two images. The most likely candidates for the unknown blue whale are those for which the matching score is the highest. Another strategy can take advantage of LoFTR's capability to attach a confidence value to a correspondence: the matching score S may then be defined as

$$S = \sum_{i=N-n}^{N} C_i$$

where n represents the number of top confidence values to sum up during the computation of the matching score, N is the number of correspondences found for a given pair and C is the sorted set of confidence values. Algorithm 1 describes the processing steps.

Algorithm 1. Compute matching score S using LoFTR confidence values. Keypoints kp_q and kp_r are extracted from query and reference images respectively; c is a keypoint matching confidence value.

Require: query_image, ref_image {input RGB images mutiplied by their RCNN masks}
Ensure: $n > 0$
    $q \leftarrow$ resize(query_image)
    $r \leftarrow$ resize(ref_image)
    $q \leftarrow$ erode(q)
    $r \leftarrow$ erode(r)
    $matches =$ match(q, r) {list of (kp_q, kp_r, c)}
    $C \leftarrow []$
    for all (kp_q, kp_r, c) in $matches$ **do**
        C.add(c)
    end for
    $RC \leftarrow$ reverse_sort(C)
    $S \leftarrow$ sum$(RC[0 : n])$

3.7   Matching Strategy - PIE

The initial dataset is reduced to the set of individuals having at least three images associated to them. The resulting subset (419 individuals, 2353 images) is then partitioned into training, validation and test sets (60/20/20) which are used to fine-tune a pretrained InceptionV3 network with a triplet loss and a semi-hard triplet mining strategy. The use of a triplet loss during the training phase constrains the batch preparation process since it must ensure that the same individual is not represented in both training and test sets. The last layer of the pretrained model is resized to match the selected dimension for the embedding space (1024, although other dimensions such as 512, 2048 and 4096 have also been tested). The network is trained using the Adam optimizer (learning rate $= 10^{-5}$), with the first five layers frozen. As mentioned earlier, an object detector is used to localize and crop the blue whale, then the cropped regions are simply resized to 224×224 pixels. Empirical hyperparameter exploration has guided the choice of the following parameters: batch size $= 32$, triplet loss margin $= 7$, number of kNN neighbors $= 25$. These cropped regions may also be preprocessed using the mask produced by the object detector, in order to mask out the background surrounding the whale (water, sky).

4   Results

The local feature matching methods have been tested on the complete dataset described in Sect. 3.5 according to the following protocol: 1) for each individual w among the 807 individuals of the dataset, an image $Image_w^{(i)}$ is picked randomly among the list of images $Image_w$ associated to this individual and it is compared to the rest of the dataset images. 2) For each comparison, a matching score is

Table 1. Matching results for the tested methods

Method	Top-1	Top-10
SIFT	25%	31%
L2-Net	37%	44%
LoFTR	75.2%	79.4%
LoFTR with confidence	76.7%	80.3%
PIE (baseline) without mask	18.0%	51.9%
PIE (baseline) with mask	13.7%	43.8%

computed, either equal to the number of correspondences found or the sum of the confidences of the best correspondences (Algorithm 1). 3) The rank of the best matching image $Image_k^{(j)}$ (where $j \neq i$ when $k == w$) is saved. 4) Top-1 and top-10 accuracies are then computed.

Results are given in Table 1. The performance spread between the various methods is likely due to the challenging diversity of the dataset. LoFTR outperforms the other methods by a large margin.

The PIE method has been tested using the protocol described in Sect. 3.7, and the results are reported in the bottom rows of Table 1. Two observations are drawn from these results. First, the accuracy numbers are fairly low, which can be an indication that the problem to solve is difficult. Second, results without background are counter-intuitively worse: this might be due to 1) errors in the masks provided by the Mask R-CNN, 2) overestimated classification performance as the background erroneously influences the decision, or 3) training skews induced by the background removal process [8].

4.1 Additional Results with LoFTR

The results obtained with LoFTR prompted additional analyses in order to better characterize its performance. Unsurprisingly, image quality does affect performance: tests limited to images of best quality yield a top-1 accuracy of 86.8%. Inspection of cases of matching failures points out image resolution as the main cause: mean resolution for quality 'A' images is 1400×700 but it drops to 860×256 for quality 'Catalog' images. Figure 3 and Fig. 4 illustrate the impact of image quality/resolution and year of acquisition on identification accuracy (see Fig. 5 for some visual examples). In some cases, non-matches between good-quality images of the same individual may happen, likely because of bad pose/viewpoint (Fig. 6 and Table 2).

As far as parameter n of the matching algorithm (Algorithm 1) is concerned, its effect on overall performance quickly plateaus, as seen in Fig. 7. Its value was set experimentally to 25 based on visual inspection.

The impact of the mask has also been quantified. Recall that the keypoint correspondences that participate in the image matching process are those belonging to the foreground (whale) while the background regions are simply ignored.

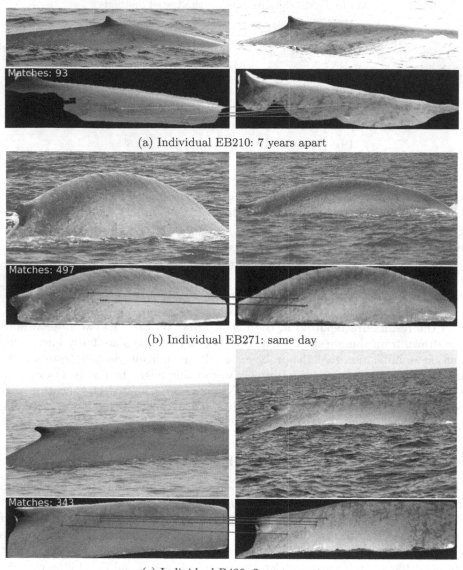

(a) Individual EB210: 7 years apart

(b) Individual EB271: same day

(c) Individual B430: 3 years apart

Fig. 2. Examples of good matches on pairs from three individuals. For each sub-figure, the original pair is shown (top row), with the masked version highlighting the top 5 keypoint matches (bottom row). The degree of redness of the lines connecting matching keypoints is proportional to the matching confidence.

Table 2. Matching results for the LoFTR-based method over different subsets (n = 25)

Dataset subset	Description	Top-1	Top-10
Entire dataset	807 individuals 3129 images	76.7%	80.3%
Quality A	299 individuals 503 images	86.8%	88.6%
Quality AB	603 individuals 1632 images	80.9%	83.6%
Quality Catalog	467 individuals 694 images	66.0%	71.4%

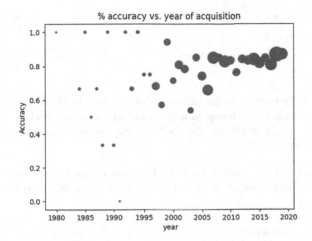

Fig. 3. (LoFTR) Impact on accuracy of year of acquisition of the query image. Bubble size represents the number of samples for the corresponding year.

Overall matching performance drops when masking is removed, likely because of spurious correspondences in non-whale areas of the images; interestingly, the decision rule that takes into account the keypoint correspondence confidence helps reduce the drop, as seen in Table 3.

5 Discussion

The large difference in performance between the methods that are studied in this paper is likely explained by the unique properties of the LoFTR method: ability to find correspondences in low-contrast areas (typical of the skin pigmentation of blue whales), robustness to viewpoint variations, robustness to motion blur, etc. Moreover, dense extraction of local features not only circumvents issues caused by imperfect background masks but also shows some tolerance to changes in visual appearance of the blue whale's skin (induced by changing physiological/environmental conditions [12]). Besides, the testing protocol has been made

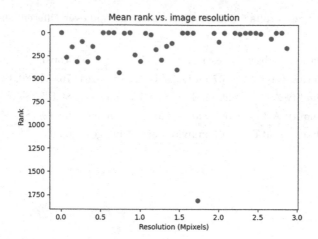

Fig. 4. (LoFTR) Impact of image resolution on ranking of the best same-class candidate: a low-resolution query image of a given individual is less likely to match another image of the same individual (ideally, the best same-class candidate should be ranked first, i.e. rank = 0)

Table 3. Classification accuracy for LoFTR. 'Sum of confidence values' is described in Algorithm 1. 'Match count' is the number of correspondences between query and reference images.

Experiment		Accuracy	
Matching score	Mask	Top-1	Top-10
Sum of confidence values	With mask	76.7%	80.3%
	Without mask	59.4%	68.2%
Match count	With mask	75.2%	79.4%
	Without mask	50.8%	60.5%

particularly challenging since the query images were chosen at random from a pool of images with varying degrees of quality: one expected use-case will involve freshly captured high-quality images to be matched against the current dataset, thus favoring higher recall performance. Also, note that good matching performance in general militates against optimization of the size of the image catalog (e.g. by keeping the 'best' images of each individual only), since the algorithm is perfectly capable of sifting through a large image collection in order to find the best match.

Fig. 5. Examples of challenging query images that fail to give a good match.

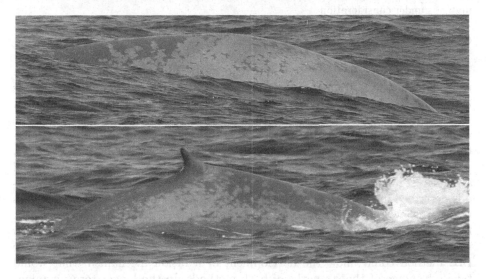

Fig. 6. Failed match between images from the same individual: relative pose is too different, i.e. there is no overlap between the two non-submerged body areas.

As far as PIE is concerned, its under-performance for blue whale classification can be explained by several factors. Firstly, PIE originally featured a manual ROI selection step. It may be affected negatively by the proposed automated ROI selection process (object detector). Tuning the detector to target the flank area, or the area under the dorsal fin, might help in alleviating this. Secondly, the identifying features of blue whales exhibit a lot less contrast than those of humpback whales, which could make the recognition more difficult.

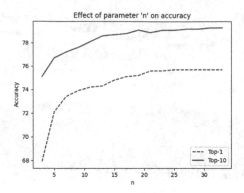

Fig. 7. (LoFTR) Impact of parameter n on accuracy: n is the number of best candidate matches under consideration.

6 Conclusion

This paper addresses the automated blue whale photo-identification problem using four methods from the literature: three local feature matching methods (SIFT, L2-Net and LoFTR) and a baseline method called PIE (Pose Invariant Embeddings). The reported results indicate that LoFTR is more suited to blue whale photo-identification because of its better capacity to capture low resolution, low contrast features.

As near-term future work, better mask creation via a properly fine-tuned semantic segmentation model is under way and this should benefit all methods described in this paper. Moreover, inspection of the image matching results tends to show that LoFTR either performs very well or breaks down rapidly. Fine-tuning LoFTR with whale images might help but a more fruitful approach would consider a complementary strategy: For instance, improvements to the PIE method could allow the development of a fusion mechanism that would take advantage of the strengths of both methods. In the longer term, it might be interesting to complement them with an edge-based technique that would focus on the shape of the dorsal fin rather than the skin pigmentation. Therefore, allowing an alternate technique to populate the top-10 list to be submitted to the whale specialist might contribute to improve the recall rate by catching individuals with a distinctive dorsal fin.

Acknowledgment. The authors would like to thank Ministry of Economy and Innovation (MEI) of the Government of Quebec for the continued support. The authors would also like to thank Julien Métais for implementing, tuning and testing the PIE algorithm during his internship at CRIM.

References

1. Arandjelović, R., Zisserman, A.: Three things everyone should know to improve object retrieval. In: IEEE Conference on Computer Vision and Pattern Recognition (2012)

2. Bogucki, R., Cygan, M., Khan, C.B., Klimek, M., Milczek, J.K., Mucha, M.: Applying deep learning to right whale photo identification. Conserv. Biol. **33**(3), 676–684 (2019). https://doi.org/10.1111/cobi.13226. https://conbio.onlinelibrary.wiley.com/doi/abs/10.1111/cobi.13226

3. Carvajal-Gámez, B.E., Trejo-Salazar, D.B., Gendron, D., Gallegos-Funes, F.J.: Photo-id of blue whale by means of the dorsal fin using clustering algorithms and color local complexity estimation for mobile devices. EURASIP J. Image Video Process. **2017**(1), 1–13 (2017). https://doi.org/10.1186/s13640-016-0153-2

4. Gendron, D., De, A., Cruz, L.: A new classification method to simplify blue whale photo-identification technique. J. Cetacean Res. Manag. **12**, 79–84 (2012)

5. He, K., Gkioxari, G., Dollár, P., Girshick, R.B.: Mask R-CNN. CoRR abs/1703.06870 (2017). https://arxiv.org/abs/1703.06870

6. Jin, Y., et al.: Image matching across wide baselines: from paper to practice. Int. J. Comput. Vision **129**(2), 517–547 (2020)

7. Karami, E., Prasad, S., Shehata, M.S.: Image matching using sift, surf, brief and orb: performance comparison for distorted images. arXiv abs/1710.02726 (2017)

8. Khani, F., Liang, P.: Removing spurious features can hurt accuracy and affect groups disproportionately. In: Proceedings of the 2021 ACM Conference on Fairness, Accountability, and Transparency, FAccT 2021, pp. 196–205. Association for Computing Machinery, New York (2021). https://doi.org/10.1145/3442188.3445883

9. Lowe, D.G.: Distinctive image features from scale-invariant keypoints. Int. J. Comput. Vis. **60**(2), 91–110 (2004). https://doi.org/10.1023/B:VISI.0000029664.99615.94

10. Mizroch, S., Beard, J., Lynde, M.: Computer assisted photo-identification of humpback whales. In: Report of the International Whaling Commission, pp. 63–70 (1990)

11. Moskvyak, O., Maire, F., Armstrong, A.O., Dayoub, F., Baktash, M.: Robust re-identification of manta rays from natural markings by learning pose invariant embeddings. arXiv abs/1902.10847 (2019)

12. Ramos-Arredondo, R.I., Carvajal-Gámez, B.E., Gendron, D., Gallegos-Funes, F.J., Mújica-Vargas, D., Rosas-Fernández, J.B.: Photoid-whale: blue whale dorsal fin classification for mobile devices. PLoS ONE **15**(10), 1–19 (2020). https://doi.org/10.1371/journal.pone.0237570

13. Ranguelova, E., Huiskes, M., Pauwels, E.: Towards computer-assisted photo-identification of humpback whales, vol. 3, pp. 1727–1730 (2004). https://doi.org/10.1109/ICIP.2004.1421406

14. Schneider, S., Taylor, G., Linquist, S., Kremer, S.: Past, present, and future approaches using computer vision for animal re-identification from camera trap data. Methods Ecol. Evol. **10**(4), 461–470 (2018). https://doi.org/10.1111/2041-210X.13133

15. Sun, J., Shen, Z., Wang, Y., Bao, H., Zhou, X.: LoFTR: detector-free local feature matching with transformers. In: IEEE Conference on Computer Vision and Pattern Recognition (2021)

16. Vidal, M., Wolf, N., Rosenberg, B., Harris, B.P., Mathis, A.: Perspectives on individual animal identification from biology and computer vision. Integr. Comp. Biol. **61**, 900–916 (2021)

17. ZJU3DV: LoFTR: Detector-free local feature matching with transformers (2021). https://github.com/zju3dv/LoFTR

Toward Data-Driven Glare Classification and Prediction for Marine Megafauna Survey

Joshua Power[1]([✉])(iD), Derek Jacoby[2](iD), Marc-Antoine Drouin[3](iD),
Guillaume Durand[3], Yvonne Coady[2], and Julian Meng[1]

[1] University of New Brunswick, Fredericton, NB E3B 5A3, Canada
{josh.jgp,jmeng}@unb.ca
[2] University of Victoria, Victoria, BC V8P 5C2, Canada
{derekja,ycoady}@uvic.ca
[3] National Research Council Canada, Ottawa, ON K1A 0R6, Canada
{Marc-Antoine.Drouin,Guillaume.Durand}@nrc-cnrc.gc.ca

Abstract. Critically endangered species in Canadian North Atlantic waters are systematically surveyed to estimate species populations which influence governing policies. Due to its impact on policy, population accuracy is important. This paper lays the foundation towards a data-driven glare modelling system, which will allow surveyors to preemptively minimize glare. Surveyors use a detection function to estimate megafauna populations which are not explicitly seen. A goal of the research is to maximize useful imagery collected, to that end we will use our glare model to predict glare and optimize for glare-free data collection. To build this model, we leverage a small labelled dataset to perform semi-supervised learning. The large dataset is labelled with a Cascading Random Forest Model using a naïve pseudo-labelling approach. A reflectance model is used, which pinpoints features of interest, to populate our datasets which allows for context-aware machine learning models. The pseudo-labelled dataset is used on two models: a Multilayer Perceptron and a Recurrent Neural Network. With this paper, we lay the foundation for data-driven mission planning; a glare modelling system which allows surveyors to preemptively minimize glare and reduces survey reliance on the detection function as an estimator of whale populations during periods of poor subsurface visibility.

Keywords: aerial survey · image quality metric · glare · neural networks · marine megafauna · machine learning · data-driven mission planning

1 Introduction

The efficacy of protecting critically endangered North Atlantic Right Whales and other megafauna is in part governed by the ability to provide accurate

Supported by National Research Council Canada.

J.-J. Rousseau and B. Kapralos (Eds.): ICPR 2022 Workshops, LNCS 13645, pp. 474–488, 2023.
https://doi.org/10.1007/978-3-031-37731-0_35

population estimates to decision-making entities. Population surveys through Atlantic Canadian waters are evaluated through systematic aerial surveys coordinated by the Department of Fisheries and Oceans Canada (DFO). While on assignment, Marine Mammal Observers (MMOs) collect sighting data and note weather conditions. Images collected from survey missions are used during post-processing to assess weather conditions that impede surface and subsurface visibility i.e., glare and sea state.

This information is in turn used to inform the formulation of parameters that make up the detection function. The detection function is used to fill in gaps where megafauna are not explicitly seen and are defined in [15] by [6,7,17,18], where glare is identified as a dominant feature. To tune these parameters images are classified into four categories based on the confidence with which MMOs can detect individuals: *None* - very low chance of missing, *Light* - greater chance of detecting than missing, *Moderate* - greater chance of missing than detecting, and *Severe* - certain to miss some. Examples of these glare intensities are shown in Fig. 1. Manually labelling these images is labour-intensive and subjective. This leads to a misrepresentation of survey visibility, which consequently leads to a misrepresentation of detection function parameters, and an inaccurate population estimation.

This project aims to provide a better estimation of megafauna populations by automating post-processing tasks to remove inter-viewer subjectivity. Additionally, this research aims to develop data-driven mission planning capabilities to aid in glare mitigation by providing pilots with pre-flight and real-time flight paths that minimize glare while on effort. To accomplish this we propose machine learning models trained with context-aware data informed by our reflectance model (Image formation model, Sect. 3).

2   Literature Review

Before this project, a glare classification method using a cascaded Random Forest (RF) architecture was developed and presented in [23]. Contributions to the design of this classifier come from three glare-related fields: architectural applications in glare prediction, specularity detection and removal (also referred to as glare detection and removal), and the ocean remote sensing community. The most notable contribution from the architectural applications field found that tree-based ensemble techniques perform particularly well on noisy subjective data [32] and paved the way for the selection of the CRFM used in the preliminary classifier.

Glare (also referred to as specularity or highlight) detection and removal commonly rely on specularity maps to produce specular free images [4,13]. Specular maps are capable of extracting glare intensity quality metrics but are too computationally expensive to support the needs of this research. The dichromatic reflection model and corresponding dielectric plane are found to be important when identifying specularity [1,14,25,26,30]. Other methods use a subset of the HIS colour space [34,36], which are similar to ours. A Convolutional Neural

Network (CNN) approach was used in [35] to remove glare on a car's license plate. Note, all methods reviewed in this section do not identify the severity of specularity, which, as it pertains to this research relies on subjective human input.

The ocean remote sensing community addressed glare modelling based on the view angle of the observer, the sun orientation, and by assuming ocean waves are capillary waves [20,21] which are dependent on wind speed [8,19]. While the findings of the remote sensing community are not leveraged in the model shown in [24] they are leveraged in the current iteration of the model and justify the implementation of data-driven mission planning, meaning, glare prediction as opposed to classification. The variable of interest, glare, is heavily correlated with the orientation of the sun as it is the dominant light source illuminating the scene under study [16]. The sun's orientation at any given point at or near the earth's surface is predictable and cyclical [29]. Intuition leads us to believe that coupling the sun's predictable position with the orientation of the aircraft should explain most instances of glare.

Given the scenes' reliance on the sun, a related and extensively researched field to glare prediction is photovoltaic (PV) power forecasting. [2] investigated using time series neural networks (NN) to predict solar irradiance. In the study, three separate experiments are explored using different parameters as NN inputs. The study finds the most influential inputs to be the hour of the day, the azimuth and zenith angle of the sun, wind speed, and wind direction. These findings line up nicely with the ocean sensing communities' glare modelling findings. Short-term solar forecasting with Gated Recurrent Units (GRUs) and Long Short-Term Memory (LSTM) were evaluated in [33] the study found that the addition of cloud cover and multivariate deep learning methods significantly improved performance.

3   Image Formation Model

The image formation model introduced in [23] is illustrated in Fig. 1, this model is used to inform decisions relating to the design of our existing machine learning models. The aircraft tasked with conducting aerial surveys to monitor megafauna is a custom-modified de Havilland Twin Otter 300 equipped with two Nikon D800 cameras interfaced with an onboard GPS receiver to monitor the position and altitude of the aircraft which is coupled to a given image in the form of metadata. The bearing of the aircraft is inferred from the coordinates associated with successive images. For either camera, the incident angle of pixel (x, y) at timestamp t with respect to the ground is $\overrightarrow{O_t}(x, y)$. To compute the sun's relative azimuth and elevation with respect to the aircraft, astronomical data and the timestamp t is used, and is referred to as $\overrightarrow{S_t}$.

The Bidirectional Reflectance Distribution Function (BRDF) of ocean water is denoted Q, three vectors are used to define this property, observer viewing angle, light incidence angle, and surface normal. The three vector representation we use is equivalent to the two-vector representation usually used [9,22] because all vectors are defined with respect to a local coordinate system aligned with gravity. The intensity of the image I_t taken at time t is defined as

$$I_t(x,y) = R\left(\int_{2\pi} Q(\overrightarrow{O_t}(x,y), \overrightarrow{\Omega}, \overrightarrow{N}_t(x,y)) L(\overrightarrow{\Omega}, \overrightarrow{S_t}, \overrightarrow{N}_t(x,y)) \, d\overrightarrow{\Omega}\right) \quad (1)$$

where R is the response function of the aquisition device (camera), $\overrightarrow{N}_t(x,y)$ is the normal of the micro-facet of the wave on the ocean surface viewed by pixel (x,y) at time t, $\overrightarrow{S_t}$ is the sun's radiance and cloud coverage [9], and $L(\overrightarrow{\Omega}, \overrightarrow{S_t}, \overrightarrow{N}_t(x,y))$ represents the scenes radiance from the sky, i.e. a measure of the scatter or reflected light from particles in the atmosphere from direction $\overrightarrow{\Omega}$. It is expected that L will vary significantly when $\overrightarrow{S_t}$ changes. Additionally, [20,21] find that $\overrightarrow{N}_t(x,y)$ can be modelled as a random variable that depends on the wind speed $\overrightarrow{V}$. The severity of the glare at time t is denoted g_{tc} for classification (4 classes) and g_{tp} for prediction (3 classes)

$$g_{tc} \in \{None, Light, Moderate, Severe\}.$$

$$g_{tp} \in \{None, Intermediate, Severe\}.$$

Moreover, g_{tc} depends on R, Q, $\overrightarrow{O_t}$ (for all pixels) , $\overrightarrow{S_t}$ and $\overrightarrow{V}$. Explicitly,

$$g_{tc} = G(I_t, R, \overrightarrow{O_t}, Q, \overrightarrow{S_t}, \overrightarrow{V}). \quad (2)$$

Using the image formation model of Eq. 1, the known quantities in Eq. 2, the function Q [22], and using numerical models to infer meteorological conditions affecting the scene, a model can be designed to suit the needs of this research. The problems we aim to address are: with classification, given $\overrightarrow{O_t}$, $\overrightarrow{S_t}$, $\overrightarrow{V}$, and the image I_t, how can we predict the value of g_{tc}. Likewise with the prediction of g_{tp} how do we the same without the image, I_t.

4   Methodology and Experimental Results

4.1   Datasets

A workflow diagram is provided in Fig. 2 which illustrates the generation and use of all datasets and models. Reference this diagram as required to gain further insight in the proceeding sections.

The Department of Fisheries and Oceans Canada (DFO) kindly provided two datasets containing imagery and associated metadata. One is much smaller (2.7 GB) and is nicknamed FIT and the other is much larger (2.42 TB), nicknamed CAM3.

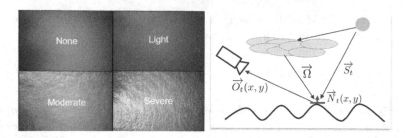

Fig. 1. Left: Glare intensity classes analyzed by MMOs, courtesy of [23]. Top left: *None* glare class. Top right: *Light* glare class. Bottom left: *Moderate* glare class. Bottom right: *Severe* glare class. **Right:** The image formation model, which attempts to encompass the constraints of our real-world system.

The FIT dataset has been applied to the preliminary cascaded Random Forest Model (CRFM) classifier which was introduced in [23]. The difference between the CAM3 dataset and the FIT dataset is substantial. The FIT dataset has data from 15 different flights and does not have sufficient temporal resolution to extract key information such as plane orientation. The CAM3 dataset has data from 33 different flights spanning an average of 5 h with pictures taken at scattered intervals ranging between 1 and 30 s. The geographic bounding box that defines the CAM3 study area is found within latitudes 41° and 49° and longitudes of −55° and −68°. Flights occur between the months of August and November between 10:00 and 22:00 (UTC). Note the FIT dataset's primary use in this manuscript is to train a model to generate pseudo-labels of the CAM3 dataset.

Since the CAM3 dataset is unlabelled it was processed prior to its use in this research. The process of labelling these data uses existing classifiers to label instances, rejecting classifications below a given confidence threshold to limit labelling error (see Sect. 4.3). Moreover, classifications from the CRFM were limited to three classes where the *None* and *Severe* classes remain, and *Light* and *Moderate* classes are combined into a new class named *Intermediate*. Limiting labelling to three classes in this fashion is justified to support data-driven mission planning but falls short for detection function parameters, as the detection function requires all four classes as input.

4.2   Feature Selection and Extraction

Because the FIT dataset is small and incompatible with deep learning methods such as CNN, we use a small set of features $\mathcal{F}$ extracted from the histogram of the I channel of the HSI colour space of the image I_t. The feature set $\mathcal{F}$ comprises of all imagery-specific features as described in [23]: Saturation, Max Index, Max, Skew, and Width. Width has not been previously defined, it uses the same bin counting procedure as Skew but adds the resulting continuous bin values as opposed to subtracting them. The feature set $\mathcal{F}$ is also extracted from the CAM3 dataset to remain consistent with the FIT dataset.

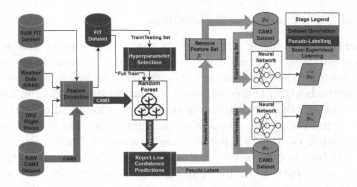

Fig. 2. The workflow diagram above illustrates the interactions between all datasets and models in this manuscript. The **dataset generation stage** illustrates how datasets are combined to create the resulting features used in the Random Forest and Neural Network architectures employed in this paper. The **pseudo-labelling stage** depicts how datasets are used to implement the naïve pseudo-labelling approach utilized in this research. The **Semi-Supervised Learning Stage** exhibits how the pseudo-labelled CAM3 dataset is used for glare classification, g_{tc}, and glare prediction, g_{tp}.

The remaining features are all extracted from metadata, i.e. timestamp, latitude, longitude, and altitude. From this, the position of the sun with respect to the aircraft, $\vec{S_t}$, is determined. Additionally, as mentioned in Sect. 3, the bearing of the aircraft is inferred from the coordinates associated with successive images. The bearing is then normalized with the positions of the mounted cameras to determine the feature $\vec{O_t}$. It is worth noting some imagery from the CAM3 dataset was missing associated metadata (GPS information). To combat missing geotags GPS tracks were procured from DFO which were used to infer missing GPS information. In the event that the nearest GPS track value is greater than 2 min away from the point of interest, the image is deemed unrecoverable.

The feature set $\vec{M}$ represents all meteorological features which pertain to wind ($\vec{V}$), cloud cover, and sea state (which is an approximation of $\vec{N_t}$). Meteorological information was downloaded from the Copernicus Climate Data Store [11], which uses ERA 5 (the 5th generation European Centre for Medium-Range Weather Forecasts) to reanalyze meteorological forecasts. $\vec{M}$ is made up of the following data variables: Maximum individual wave height, Mean direction of total swell, Mean direction of wind waves, Mean period of total swell, Mean period of wind waves, Mean wave direction, Mean wave period, Significant height of combined wind waves and swell, Significant height of wind waves, High cloud cover, Low cloud cover, Medium cloud cover, Total cloud cover, Cloud above aircraft. All data variables can be found from Copernicus with the exception of Cloud above aircraft which is a binary feature indicating whether or not there is a cloud formation above the coordinate of interest.

4.3   Semi-supervised, Pseudo-labelling

Semi-supervised learning is often used to effectively train models with many instances of unlabelled data and few instances of labelled data. Many approaches exist for semi-supervised learning, however, two dominating methods are pseudo-labelling methods [3,28] and consistency regularization [5,31]. The method utilized in this paper is a naïve implementation of pseudo-labelling methods. First, in order to generate pseudo-labels, a model had to be selected. An analysis of model confidence on the FIT dataset was investigated using four and three-class CRFMs based on the same architecture as our previous work [23]. Hyper-parameters, tree depth and number of estimators (trees), for both RF models present in the CRFM were selected using the same elbow method described in our previous work [23]. 500 iterations of 5-fold-cross validation are then executed on the untrained models with specified hyper-parameters. The extra 499 iterations of cross-validation is carried out with the intent of accounting for unseen samples during the RF bootstrap aggregation process, this results in a total of 2500 validation results (500 iterations times 5-folds of validation results). Three-class and four-class CRFM results are shown in Table 1 where a contrast between four-class and three-class performance is observed. The three-class model observed better performance; this model was selected to limit pseudo-labelling error. The new iteration of the CRFM differs from the previous classifier in two capacities, one being an output stage limited to three classes and the other being new features that incorporate meteorological conditions affecting the scene under study, $\vec{M}$. While executing five-fold-cross validation on the three-class CRFM with the FIT dataset, the probability and success of each resulting classification was recorded. This process was used to determine an appropriate probability threshold when classifying the CAM3 dataset. The probability threshold is used to limit pseudo-labelling error within an appropriate confidence interval. The resulting probability distribution generated from the FIT dataset is observed in the top of Fig. 3. From this distribution, assuming that the FIT dataset is ergodic, one

Table 1. CRFM performance. The number of trees and tree depth are denoted by the symbol T and M respectively.

Four-Class CRFM (T = 17, M = 13)				
(n = 279)	Precision	Recall	F-Score	Accuracy
None	89.84	89.04	89.33	75.78
Light	62.19	59.09	59.56	
Moderate	59.54	58.50	58.47	
Severe	81.50	82.84	81.92	
Three-Class CRFM (T = 11, M = 15)				
None	93.31	88.12	90.53	83.57
Intermediate	77.51	82.08	79.55	
Severe	83.01	80.59	81.53	

can approximate appropriate probability thresholds. The probability selection process is illustrated in the bottom left of Fig. 3. Here the probability threshold is chosen when the predicted labelling error is less than or equal to 0.1, resulting in 90% confidence tolerance in unsupervised labels generated from the CRFM. The bottom right of Fig. 3 is a predictive measure of how much data might be rejected during classification which can, in turn, be used as a measure of FIT dataset ergodicity when compared to CAM3 rejections as well as CRFM model generalizability.

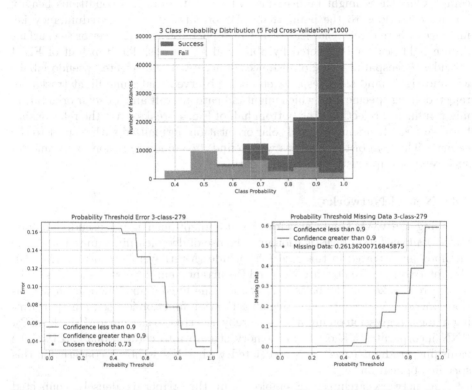

Fig. 3. Semi-supervised labelling procedure. **Top:** Model probability distributions. **Bottom left:** Probability threshold selection. **Bottom right:** Probability threshold missing data prediction.

To take full advantage of the FIT dataset prior to labelling, model hyperparameters were tuned as previously specified until they achieved an accuracy of plus or minus 1 % of the expected accuracy from cross-validation. Once, hyperparameters were tuned and appropriate model accuracy was achieved, the entire FIT dataset was used to train the CRFM used to label CAM3 data. This process resulted in 100 931 labelled images, 15.833% of the CAM3 dataset was rejected during classification. From the accepted labels, 200 were randomly selected to be manually checked against their pseudo-labels. This subset achieved an accuracy of 91% which is within the confidence bounds anticipated. It was also observed that many of the miss-classified images had either large rocks or land impacting the scene. To mitigate this as best as possible a high-resolution sea-land mask was procured to filter out any samples taken overland. This process results in a loss of 2818 images, and a sea-only CAM3 dataset with 98 113 images, of which, 56% are from the *None* glare class, 33% from *Intermediate*, and 11% are from *Severe*.

It is expected that rejected pseudo-labels consist of more complex instances of glare which could not be captured due to limitations of the FIT dataset. These complex instances might be occasions where meteorological conditions heavily impact conditions to the point that solar orientation reaches redundancy i.e. instances where direct solar iridescence is impacted by cloud cover or sea surface diffuse light scatter is affected by abnormal sea states. The top half of Fig. 4 provides a geospatial visual of instances of accepted and rejected pseudo-labels, left and right-hand sides respectively. It is observed that some flight tracks are rejected along specific lines which might indicate aircraft and/or solar orientation might influence rejection. The bottom half of Fig. 4 breaks down the relationship between aircraft orientation and solar orientation normalized with respect to the camera. The goal of this analysis was to find a common rejection quadrant. No such relationship exists with current data.

4.4   Neural Networks

Labelling the CAM3 dataset with the aforementioned naïve pseudo-labelling method allows for an investigation into the use of deep-learning approaches. The methods investigated in this research includes Multilayer Perceptrons (MLPs), also referred to as feedforward NNs and Recurrent Neural Networks (RNNs). The perceptron makes up the basis of NNs and usually contains a non-linear activation function. A perceptron missing an activation function is essentially performing a linear regression on input data, hereby, referred to as Linear MLP (LMLP). RNN incorporates a short-term memory stream into conventional MLPs. The vanishing gradient caveat [27] associated with RNN is not a concern for this specific application.

The network architecture employed in this paper is densely connected between all layers, with 27 nodes ($\mathbb{R}^{27}$) in the input layer, 256 ($\mathbb{R}^{256}$) in both hidden layers, and 3 nodes ($\mathbb{R}^{3}$) in the output layer. The CAM3 dataset was split into a training portion (80%) and a testing portion (20%), testing and training sets contained similar class proportions. A cross-entropy loss function is used to adjust model weights. Additionally, to combat dataset class imbalance class weights in the loss function are adjusted to be inversely proportional to class frequency in the training set as shown in Eq. 3. The training and testing sets are normalized separately on a feature by feature basis using Eq. 4. Hyperparameter selection for each NN model undergoes the same Edisonian process but is guided by monitoring training and testing loss and accuracy functions and tweaking parameters that generate more interpretable results. Learning rates were adjusted between 1e-7 and 0.1 during the tuning process. Hidden layer depths of 1 and 2 were investigated. The number of nodes within said layers

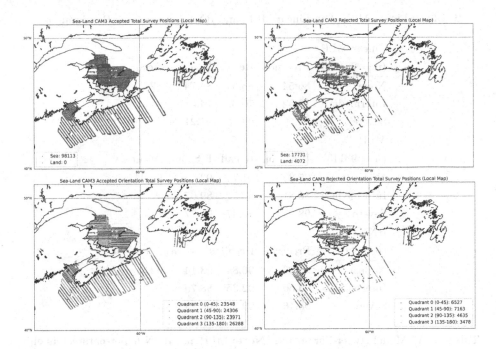

Fig. 4. Rejection analysis as it pertains to orientation. **Top left:** Accepted pseudo-label survey positions. **Top right:** Rejected pseudo-label survey positions. **Bottom left:** Accepted pseudo-label survey positions broken down by normalized orientation. **Bottom right:** Rejected pseudo-label survey positions broken down by normalized orientation. Created using Basemap and extension of Matplotlib [12]. Flight tracks provided by DFO [10].

ranged between 8 and 256. The number of epochs investigated ranged from 40 to 300 and was guided by monitoring the loss function. Both the Adam and LBFGS optimizers were investigated. Linear and non-linear MLP, as well as RNN performance is observed in Table 2. Hyper-parameters used to tune these models are delineated in Table 3.

$$W_i = \frac{\#samples}{\#classes\,\#instances} \tag{3}$$

$$\overrightarrow{F_{norm}} = \frac{\overrightarrow{F_{col}} - min(\overrightarrow{F_{col}})}{max(\overrightarrow{F_{col}}) - min(\overrightarrow{F_{col}}) + 1e^{-6}} \tag{4}$$

To investigate glare prediction, g_{tp}, we remove the feature set $\mathcal{F}$ from the dataset, this removes all imagery components. What remains is what was extracted from image metadata. Without the feature set $\mathcal{F}$, 22 features remain, changing the input layer to 22 nodes ($\mathbb{R}^{22}$). Using metadata only on MLP and RNN results in what is shown in Table 4 using the same hyper-parameters shown in Table 3.

Table 2. Linear MLP, Non-Linear MLP, and RNN Performance Predicting g_{tc}

Linear MLP				
(n = 98113)	Precision	Recall	F-Score	Accuracy
None	86.54	83.02	84.74	82.76
Intermediate	72.52	76.62	74.51	
Severe	95.50	98.98	97.21	

MLP				
(n = 98113)	Precision	Recall	F-Score	Accuracy
None	95.82	91.72	93.73	92.94
Intermediate	86.81	92.72	89.67	
Severe	98.07	99.47	98.77	

RNN				
(n = 98113)	Precision	Recall	F-Score	Accuracy
None	95.56	90.84	93.14	92.31
Intermediate	85.50	92.35	88.79	
Severe	98.16	99.33	98.74	

Table 3. All Model Hyper-Parameters. **Note:** MLP and RNN hyper-parameters only defer in Epoch, additionally, LMLP is an abbreviation for Linear MLP in this table

RNN Hyper-Parameters			
Learning Rate	0.01	Hidden Layer Activation	None (LMLP), ReLU (Others)
Hidden Layers	[256, 256]	Batch Size	[8192, 8192]
Epochs	80 (RNN), 50 (MLP)	Norm. Data	Yes
Optimizer	Adam		

Table 4. MLP, and RNN Performance Predicting g_{tp}

Metadata Only MLP				
(n = 98113)	Precision	Recall	F-Score	Accuracy
None	94.89	88.75	91.72	89.22
Intermediate	82.82	88.59	85.61	
Severe	83.61	93.29	88.18	

Metadata Only RNN				
(n = 98113)	Precision	Recall	F-Score	Accuracy
None	94.43	88.13	91.18	88.71
Intermediate	82.08	88.12	85.00	
Severe	83.59	93.21	88.14	

5   Conclusion and Future Works

The generation of a large-scale dataset from sequential streams of imagery is necessary to advance the capabilities of this research. To suit this requirement a new dataset was generated using existing classifiers on newly acquired data, the CAM3 dataset. To label the CAM3 dataset an investigation into confidence tolerances and their effect on missing data was pursued. Note that this methodology assumes the FIT dataset is ergodic and places importance on limiting model labelling error based on the confidence tolerance, it makes decisions independent of missing error metrics. Choosing probability thresholds in this manner results in the labelling of 100 931 images from the CAM3 dataset. 15.83% of the CAM3 dataset was rejected by the RF classifier. This is close to the predicted 26.13% which might indicate two things: one, the CRFM classifier generalizes well to new data; two, the FIT dataset is ergodic. The 200 pseudo-labelled images randomly selected for manual evaluation yielded a 91% accuracy which is within the 90% confidence tolerance. Since land-based obstructions obscured many of the images analyzed during manual evaluation a high-resolution land-sea mask was employed to remove tainted imagery as best as possible.

15.833% of the original CAM3 dataset is made up of rejected pseudo-labels. It is expected that these rejected labels are partly made up of instances where certain glare conditions are present regardless of solar orientation. These aberrant conditions are of particular interest to our research goals, as they constitute a means of predicting and mitigating glare irrespective of solar orientation. Hence, they constitute a flight plan unencumbered by certain time of day constraints.

A preliminary investigation into features that may impact pseudo-label rejection was performed, observing solar orientation normalized with respect to the camera. This small investigation yielded insufficient explanations, contrary to visual intuition. One reason for this might relate to the way the FIT dataset extracts aircraft bearing. To draw more concrete conclusions, we propose the following future work for pseudo-labelling. The FIT dataset's aircraft bearing feature will be re-analyzed using GPS tracks as opposed to the nearest available image which constitutes sparse instances of consecutive samples. This will be done to determine aircraft orientation more reliably. The re-analyzed FIT dataset will then be used once again in the same fashion presented in this manuscript. In order to gain a better understanding of pseudo-labelling bias, an investigation into the impact of all features on rejection will also be investigated.

The image formation model and the relationship between influencing features in glare forecasting and solar forecasting remain at the forefront of this research's guiding principles. Access to the pseudo-labelled CAM3 dataset allowed for an investigation into deep learning models such as MLP and RNN. They were investigated as a means of developing glare classification and prediction systems using features relating directly to imagery (used in classification only), solar orientation, and meteorological factors such as wind conditions, sea surface state, and cloud cover.

Glare classification was first probed from a linear regressor constructed from a MLP without an activation function, trained and tested on the CAM3 dataset, to assess the complexity of the application. The result of this process yields an 82.76% accuracy, which is similar to the accuracy of our three-class CRFM, 83.57% trained and tested on the FIT dataset. Modest performance from linear regression might indicate that much of the CAM3 dataset is easily explainable. Adding a non-linear ReLU activation functions to MLP results in a significant boost to performance, 92.94% accuracy. RNN sees slightly lower performance with an accuracy of 92.32%. Glare prediction which does not use imagery to predict glare severity is examined and achieves promising results. Metadata only MLP and RNN attain accuracies of 89.22% and 88.71% respectively. It is observed that across all non-linear model results *None* class precision remains high between 94.43% and 95.82%. This is likely due to pseudo-labelling bias from CRFM which is designed to perform best on *None* class precision as it was identified that miss classifying a *None* glare image would have the highest consequence on the detection function.

Thoroughly understanding the factors influencing glare severity and how those factors impact the ability to spot megafauna is a central element to our ability to successfully estimate species populations and contribute to the longevity and conservation of critically endangered species. Predictive path planning based on an accurate glare model presents a reliable means of maximizing surface and subsurface visibility and increasing population estimation accuracy.

Acknowledgements. The authors would like to thank Mylene Dufour, Marie-France Robichaud, and Maddison Proudfoot for their dedicated work in labelling and preparing the FIT dataset used in our experiments. Stephanie Ratelle provided us with valuable insight on the challenges associated with megafauna surveys. The authors would also like to thank both Stephanie and Elizabeth Thompson for their crucial role in promptly granting us access to the CAM3 dataset and its associated flight tracks. Their experience in conducting systematic aerial surveys throughout eastern Canadian waters was essential to our work.

References

1. Akashi, Y., Okatani, T.: Separation of reflection components by sparse non-negative matrix factorization. Comput. Vis. Image Underst. **146** (2015). https://doi.org/10.1016/j.cviu.2015.09.001
2. Alzahrani, A., Kimball, J.W., Dagli, C.: Predicting solar irradiance using time series neural networks. Procedia Comput. Sci. **36**, 623–628 (2014). https://doi.org/10.1016/j.procs.2014.09.065
3. Arazo, E., Ortego, D., Albert, P., O'Connor, N.E., McGuinness, K.: Pseudo-labeling and confirmation bias in deep semi-supervised learning. In: 2020 International Joint Conference on Neural Networks (IJCNN), pp. 1–8. IEEE (2020)
4. Artusi, A., Banterle, F., Chetverikov, D.: A survey of specularity removal methods. Comput. Graph. Forum **30**(8), 2208–2230 (2011). https://doi.org/10.1111/j.1467-8659.2011.01971.x
5. Berthelot, D., Carlini, N., Goodfellow, I., Papernot, N., Oliver, A., Raffel, C.A.: MixMatch: a holistic approach to semi-supervised learning. In: Advances in Neural Information Processing Systems, vol. 32. Curran Associates, Inc. (2019)

6. Buckland, S.T., Anderson, D.R., Burnham, K.P., Laake, J.L., Borchers, D.L., Thomas, L.: Introduction to distance sampling: estimating abundance of biological populations. Technical report, Oxford (United Kingdom) Oxford University Press (2001)
7. Buckland, S.T., Anderson, D.R., Burnham, K.P., Laake, J.L., Borchers, D.L., Thomas, L.: Advanced Distance Sampling: Estimating Abundance of Biological Populations. OUP, Oxford (2004)
8. Cox, C., Munk, W.: Measurement of the roughness of the sea surface from photographs of the sun's glitter. J. Opt. Soc. Am. 44(11), 838–850 (1954). https://doi.org/10.1364/JOSA.44.000838
9. Foley, J.D., van Dam, A., Feiner, S.K., Hughes, J.F.: Computer Graphics: Principles and Practice, 2nd edn. Addison-Wesley Longman Publishing Co., Inc., Boston (1990)
10. Gosselin, J.F., Lawson, J., Ratelle, S.: DFO Science Twin Otter Marine Mammal Surveys: Unprocessed aircraft imagery and aerial tracks (2018)
11. Hersbach, H., et al.: ERA5 hourly data on single levels from 1979 to present. Copernicus Climate Change Service (C3S) Climate Data Store (CDS) (2018). https://doi.org/10.24381/cds.adbb2d47
12. Hunter, J.D.: Matplotlib: a 2D graphics environment. Comput. Sci. Eng. 9(3), 90–95 (2007). https://doi.org/10.1109/MCSE.2007.55
13. Khan, H.A., Thomas, J.-B., Hardeberg, J.Y.: Analytical survey of highlight detection in color and spectral images. In: Bianco, S., Schettini, R., Trémeau, A., Tominaga, S. (eds.) CCIW 2017. LNCS, vol. 10213, pp. 197–208. Springer, Cham (2017). https://doi.org/10.1007/978-3-319-56010-6_17
14. Klinker, G., Shafer, S., Kanade, T.: The measurement of highlights in color images. Int. J. Comput. Vision 1(1), 7–32 (1988)
15. Lawson, J.W., Gosselin, J.F.: Distribution and Preliminary Abundance Estimates for Cetaceans Seen during Canada's Marine Megafauna Survey-a Component of the 2007 TNASS. Fisheries and Oceans Canada, Science (2009)
16. Mardaljevic, J., Andersen, M., Roy, N., Christoffersen, J.: Daylighting metrics: is there a relation between useful daylight illuminance and daylight glare probabilty? In: Proceedings of the Building Simulation and Optimization Conference BSO12. No. CONF (2012)
17. Marques, F.F., Buckland, S.T.: Incorporating covariates into standard line transect analyses. Biometrics 59(4), 924–935 (2003)
18. Marques, T.A., Thomas, L., Fancy, S.G., Buckland, S.T.: Improving estimates of bird density using multiple-covariate distance sampling. Auk 124(4), 1229–1243 (2007)
19. Mobley, B.: Light and Water: Radiative Transfer in Natural Waters. Academic Press, San Diego (1994)
20. Mobley, C.D.: The Optical Properties of Water In Handbook of Optics, 2nd edn. McGraw-Hill, New York (1995)
21. Mobley, C.D.: Estimation of the remote-sensing reflectance from above-surface measurements. Appl. Opt. 38(36), 7442–7455 (1999)
22. Morel, A., Voss, K.J., Gentili, B.: Bidirectional reflectance of oceanic waters: a comparison of modeled and measured upward radiance fields. J. Geophys. Res. Oceans 100(C7), 13143–13150 (1995). https://doi.org/10.1029/95JC00531. https://agupubs.onlinelibrary.wiley.com/doi/abs/10.1029/95JC00531

23. Power, J., Drouin, M.A., Durand, G., Thompson, E., Ratelle, S.: Classifying glare intensity in airborne imagery acquired during marine megafauna survey. In: OCEANS 2021: San Diego – Porto, pp. 1–7 (2021). https://doi.org/10.23919/OCEANS44145.2021.9705752

24. Power, J., et al.: Real-time mission planning simulations from geospatial data. In: 2021 IEEE/ACM 25th International Symposium on Distributed Simulation and Real Time Applications (DS-RT), pp. 1–2 (2021). https://doi.org/10.1109/DS-RT52167.2021.9576133

25. Shafer, S.: Using color to separate reflection components. Color. Res. Appl. **10**(4), 210–218 (1985)

26. Shen, H.L., Zhang, H.G., Shao, S.J., Xin, J.: Chromaticity separation of reflection component in single images. Pattern Recogn. **41**, 2461–2469 (2008). https://doi.org/10.1016/j.patcog.2008.01.026

27. Sherstinsky, A.: Fundamentals of recurrent neural network (RNN) and long short-term memory (LSTM) network. Physica D **404**, 132306 (2020). https://doi.org/10.1016/j.physd.2019.132306

28. Shi, W., Gong, Y., Ding, C., Tao, Z.M., Zheng, N.: Transductive semi-supervised deep learning using min-max features. In: Proceedings of the European Conference on Computer Vision (ECCV), pp. 299–315 (2018)

29. Soulayman, S.: Comments on solar azimuth angle. Renew. Energy **123**, 294–300 (2018)

30. Suo, J., An, D., Ji, X., Wang, H., Dai, Q.: Fast and high quality highlight removal from a single image. IEEE Trans. Image Process. **25**(11), 5441–5454 (2016). https://doi.org/10.1109/TIP.2016.2605002

31. Tarvainen, A., Valpola, H.: Mean teachers are better role models: weight-averaged consistency targets improve semi-supervised deep learning results. In: Advances in Neural Information Processing Systems, vol. 30 (2017)

32. Wagdy, A., Garcia-Hansen, V., Isoardi, G., Allan, A.: Multi-region contrast method -a new framework for post-processing HDRI luminance information for visual discomfort analysis. In: Proceedings of the Passive and Low Energy Architecture Conference 2017: Design to Thrive – Foundations for a Better Future (2017)

33. Wojtkiewicz, J., Hosseini, M., Gottumukkala, R., Chambers, T.L.: Hour-ahead solar irradiance forecasting using multivariate gated recurrent units. Energies **12**(21), 4055 (2019). https://doi.org/10.3390/en12214055

34. Yang, J., Liu, L., Li, S.Z.: Separating specular and diffuse reflection components in the HSI color space. In: 2013 IEEE International Conference on Computer Vision Workshops, pp. 891–898 (2013). https://doi.org/10.1109/ICCVW.2013.122

35. Ye, S., Yin, J.L., Chen, B.H., Chen, D., Wu, Y.: Single image glare removal using deep convolutional networks. In: 2020 IEEE International Conference on Image Processing (ICIP), pp. 201–205 (2020). https://doi.org/10.1109/ICIP40778.2020.9190712

36. Zimmerman-Moreno, G., Greenspan, H.: Automatic detection of specular reflections in uterine cervix images. In: Reinhardt, J.M., Pluim, J.P.W. (eds.) Medical Imaging 2006: Image Processing, vol. 6144, pp. 2037–2045. SPIE (2006). https://doi.org/10.1117/12.653089

Repeatability Evaluation of Keypoint Detection Techniques in Tracking Underwater Video Frames

Ghulam Sakhi Shokouh$^{(\boxtimes)}$ [ID], Baptiste Magnier [ID], Binbin Xu [ID],
and Philippe Montesinos [ID]

EuroMov Digital Health in Motion, Univ Montpellier, IMT Mines Ales, Ales, France
{ghulam-sakhi.shokouh,baptiste.magnier,binbin.xu,
philippe.montesinos}@mines-ales.fr

Abstract. Keypoint(s) or corners, as a stable feature possessing the
defined characteristics of a robust point of interest remain an active
research field for machine vision researchers due to its applications in
motion capture, image matching, tracking, image registration, 3D reconstruction, and object recognition. There exist different techniques for
keypoint detection; this paper focuses on direct computation on the
gray-level analysis of interest point detection because of its straightforward implementation. In this contribution, an objective comparison of
12 state-of-the-art keypoint detection techniques; an application to feature matching have been executed in the context of underwater video
sequences. These videos contain noise and all geometric and/or photometric transformations. Experiments are led on 5 videos containing in
total 10 000 frames, evaluating the repeatability of the keypoints detectors. These detectors are evaluated on these complex videos by computing statistics-based repeatability, but also as a function of the Zero-Mean
Normalized Cross-Correlation (ZNCC) scores.

Keywords: Corner detection · filtering · repeatability · underwater
imagery · keypoint detection · AQUALOQ dataset · ZNCC

1 Introduction and Motivation

The importance and interest in keypoint detection (i.e., corner or junction as a
stable interest point) in a digital image lies notably in its application in image
matching, tracking, motion estimation, panoramic stitching, object recognition,
and 3D reconstruction. Image matching through feature tracking is extensively
used in many real-time applications including autonomous driving, security
surveillance, and manufacturing automation [18]. Corner detection techniques
can be effectively applied in these applications depending on their repeatability
ratio. The reason for the corner detection's wide range of applications is that
the corner is easier to localize than other low-level features such as edges or
lines, particularly taking into consideration the correspondence problems (e.g.,

© Springer Nature Switzerland AG 2023
J.-J. Rousseau and B. Kapralos (Eds.): ICPR 2022 Workshops, LNCS 13645, pp. 489–503, 2023.
https://doi.org/10.1007/978-3-031-37731-0_36

aperture problem in matching). Hence, an objective evaluation of the frequently applied corner detection techniques by direct computation on the gray-level analysis relating to their real-time application is primarily invaluable, an example is available in [7].

The image matching and feature tracking in complex real-time scenes such as underwater videos are extremely challenging [5]. In this type of image sequence, concerning all types of image transformation (rotation, scale, affine transformations, translation, etc.), photometric transformation (illumination, occlusion, clutter, etc.), and various types of noises plus moving particles in different directions, the robustness of interest point, can be truly evaluated both objectively and visually. Repeatability is the main evaluation metric widely used for interest point matching, where the obtained points must be independent of varying image conditions [12,14,15,18]. In this work, the repeatability rate of the 12 commonly applied corner detection operators are objectively evaluated on the challenging underwater video dataset [5].

In the literature, several approaches for detecting corners and junctions in digital images have been developed: (i) involving contour chains [2], (ii) using templates [17,23] or, (iii) by image filtering techniques. Mainly, the corner detection operators via the direct computation on the gray-level analysis corresponding to the label (iii) can be categorized in three general approaches: Hessian based [3], curvature analysis [1,4,10,22,24,26], and structure tensor based [6,8,9,13,16,19]. These methods are easily developed by image filtering because they involve only image convolutions horizontally and vertically. Therefore, they can be implemented with less computational time on different devices, see details in [7]. This paper is devoted to an extensive evaluation of filtering-based corner detection methods via repeatability performance measurement in video sequences consisting of frames with different types of transformations. It is to mention that the terms corner, junction, salient point, keypoint, and interest point are used synonymously in this work.

2 Studied Keypoint Detectors by Gray-level Direct Computation

In this section, a set of corner detection techniques including the general scheme and the related parameters have been investigated. There are different approaches to determining the cornerness measure by direct computation using filtering techniques. Generally, in image filtering, the first or second derivatives may be utilized to determine corners in an image. Considering a gray-level image I, its partial derivatives are:

- $I_x = \frac{\partial I}{\partial x}$, the 1st image derivative along the x axis,
- $I_y = \frac{\partial I}{\partial y}$, the 1st image derivative along the y axis,
- $I_{xx} = \frac{\partial^2 I}{\partial x^2}$, the 2nd image derivative along the x axis,
- $I_{yy} = \frac{\partial^2 I}{\partial y^2}$, the 2nd image derivative along the y axis,
- $I_{xy} = \frac{\partial^2 I}{\partial x \partial y}$, the crossing derivative of I.

These image derivatives can be calculated by convolving the image with the [1 0 −1] or the [1 0 −2 0 1] masks in the x and/or y directions for the first and second derivatives, respectively [20]. The first derivatives are useful for the detection of step and ramp edges, whereas the second derivatives are convenient for the contour extraction of types: line, roof edges as ridge/valley features. Regarding the image surface, corners are defined as the curvature extremum along the edge line [16]. Usually, approaches to detect directly corners on the gray scale level use filtering techniques by combining image derivatives of the 1st and 2nd order, then by computing the Hessian matrix, the curvature or the structure tensor. All the necessary technical details of the studied corner detection methods including mainly the formula, denomination, parameter(s), and name of the authors are listed by year of publication in Table 1.

2.1 Determinant of the Hessian Matrix

Mathematically, the Hessian matrix $(\mathcal{H})$ indicates significant values near edges, through which corners can be estimated by the large variations of intensity values in both x and y directions. Indeed, $\mathcal{H}$ represents a square matrix of 2nd order partial derivative of image intensity; it is often computed and is useful in feature detection and characterization:

$$\mathcal{H} = \begin{pmatrix} I_{xx} & I_{xy} \\ I_{xy} & I_{yy} \end{pmatrix}. \tag{1}$$

In that respect, Beaudet [3] uses the image 2nd derivative for calculating the determinant of $\mathcal{H}$, which is related to Gaussian curvature of the image surface [11]. The computation is straightforward because it combines only three 2nd image derivatives. Even though this technique is rotation invariant, it is sensitive to noise and unstable against scale changes.

2.2 Curvature Analysis

Technically, these techniques are based on the change of gradient direction along an edge contour and/or image surface curvature. They can be easily computed by the combination of the image derivatives of 1st and 2nd order. The pioneer work in this category was originally led by Kitchen and Rosenfeld (KR) who defined the cornerness measure for each pixel intensity based on the change of 2nd order gradient direction along the edge weighted by the local gradient magnitude [10]. Theoretically, the gradient feature vector ∇I is normal to the edge and hence projecting the change of gradient direction along the edge and multiplying the result by the local gradient magnitude $|\nabla I|$ results the final cornerness measure. Inspired by this initial contribution of Kitchen and Rosenfeld [10], other related techniques were developed by Zuniga and Haralick [26], Blom et al. [4], Wand and Brady [22]. Zheng et al. [24] and Achard et al. [1] uses a smoothed image with a Gaussian of parameter ρ and then the combination of its derivatives with the derivatives of the non-smoothed image. The cornerness measure for each technique is listed in the Table 1.

Table 1. Cornerness measure formulas computed from image derivatives. Here, $\overline{I_x}$, $\overline{I_y}$, $\overline{I_{xx}}$, $\overline{I_{yy}}$ and $\overline{I_{xy}}$ denote the convolutions with a Gaussian with a standard deviation $\sigma > 0$ of images derivatives I_x, I_y, I_{xx}, I_{yy} and I_{xy} respectively. As a reminder, (λ_1, λ_2) represents the eigenvalues of the structure tensor $\mathcal{M}$.

Name	Cornerness Measure/Formula	Parameter(s)	Reference(s)	Year
DET	$DET(\mathcal{H}) = I_{xx}I_{yy} - I_{xy}^2$	–	[3]	1978
KR	$\dfrac{I_x^2 I_{yy} - 2 \cdot I_x I_y I_{xy} + I_y^2 I_{xx}}{I_x^2 + I_y^2}$	–	[10]	1982
ZH	$\dfrac{KR(I)}{|\nabla I|} = \dfrac{I_x^2 I_{yy} - 2 \cdot I_x I_y I_{xy} + I_y^2 I_{xx}}{\left(I_x^2 + I_y^2\right)^{3/2}}$	–	[26]	1983
F	$\dfrac{Det(\mathcal{M})}{Trace(\mathcal{M})} = \dfrac{\lambda_1 \lambda_2}{\lambda_1 + \lambda_2} = \dfrac{\lambda_1 \lambda_2}{|\nabla \overline{I}|^2} = \dfrac{\overline{I_x}^2\,\overline{I_y}^2 - \overline{I_{xy}}^2}{\overline{I_x}^2 + \overline{I_y}^2}$	ρ	[6,13]	1987
HS	$Det(\mathcal{M}) - k \cdot (Trace(\mathcal{M}))^2 = \overline{I_x}^2\,\overline{I_y}^2 - \overline{I_{xy}}^2 - k \cdot \left(\overline{I_x}^2 + \overline{I_y}^2\right)^2$	$\rho,\ k$	[8]	1987
BB	$|\nabla I| \cdot KR(I) = I_x^2 I_{yy} - 2 \cdot I_x I_y I_{xy} + I_y^2 I_{xx}$	–	[4]	1992
Ro	$Det(\mathcal{M}) = \lambda_1 \lambda_2 = \overline{I_x}^2\,\overline{I_y}^2 - \overline{I_{xy}}^2$	ρ	[16]	1994
KLT	$Min(\lambda_1, \lambda_2)$	ρ	[19]	1994
RTC	$\dfrac{(1 + I_x^2)I_{yy} - 2 \cdot I_x I_y I_{xy} + (1 + I_y^2)I_{xx}}{\left(1 + I_x^2 + I_y^2\right)^{3/2}}$	–	[22]	1995
GD	$I_x^2 I_{yy}^2 + I_y^2 I_{xx}^2 - \dfrac{\overline{I_x}^2\,\overline{I_{yy}}^2 + \overline{I_y}^2\,\overline{I_{xx}}^2}{\left(\overline{I_x}^2 + \overline{I_y}^2\right)^2} \cdot \left(I_x{}^2 + I_y{}^2\right)^2$	ρ	[24]	1999
ABD	$\dfrac{I_x^2 \overline{I_y}^2 + I_y^2 \overline{I_x}^2 - 2 \cdot I_x I_y \overline{I_x I_y}}{\overline{I_x}^2 + \overline{I_y}^2}$	ρ	[1]	2000
KZ	$\dfrac{1}{\left(\lambda_1^{-p} + \lambda_2^{-p}\right)^{1/p}}$	$\rho,\ p > 0$	[9]	2005

2.3   Structure Tensor

The third group uses the symmetric structure tensor $\mathcal{M}$:

$$\mathcal{M} = \begin{pmatrix} \overline{I_x^2} & \overline{I_x I_y} \\ \overline{I_x I_y} & \overline{I_y^2} \end{pmatrix}, \tag{2}$$

where $\overline{\bullet}$ indicates convolution with a low-pass filter; here a Gaussian filter of standard deviation ρ is considered (see Eq. (3) with a parameter ρ instead of σ).

The structure tensor is derived from the gradient structure tensor, which is achieved through, computing the Cartesian product of the gradient vector with itself at each point of the image. Spatial averaging of this tensor, usually with a Gaussian filter, leads to the structure tensor. As to note that averaging is needed as the plain gradient tensor has only one non-zero eigenvalue and therefore represents only innately edge features. Spatial averaging, here tied to ρ parameter, distributes this information over a neighborhood, and points that receive contributions/input from edges with different orientations will have two positive eigenvalues, which allows them to be recognized as intrinsically 2D. Eigenvectors of the gradient structure tensor indicate local orientation, whereas eigenvalues λ_1 and λ_2 give the strength or magnitude as a measure of eigenvalues in flat regions are very small (negligible), in the edges λ_1 or λ_2 is small depending on the horizontal or vertical edge, and noticeably both values λ_1 and λ_2 are large in corner points.

Based on this assumption, various corner measurement formulations have been proposed; they are listed and denominated in the Table 1 and summarized here:

- Fostner [6] and Noble [13] use an auto-correlation matrix $\mathcal{M}$ with the function F to identify salient points, which converges toward the point closest to all the tangent lines of the corner in a neighborhood and is a least-square solution. The function combines the eigenvalues, aiming to classify the keypoints from other types of local features.
- Harris and Stephens [8] also named as Plessey operator is based on principal curvature of local auto-correlation using first order derivative. This operator's response is theoretically isotropic, but often computed in anisotropic way. This cornerness measure HS yields two positive values at corners and two negative values in the case of straight edges. HS and F methods differ only in their criterion determination because the Fostner algorithm disregards the parameter k ($k > 0$) introduced in Harris and Stephens by computing a fraction.
- Rohr used a parametric model fitting as a point of maximal curvature in the direction of the steepest slope [16]. He convolved an analytical corner model with a Gaussian and adjusted the parameter of the model by a minimization technique to have the model near the observed signal. It is remarkable that this algorithm corresponds to HS technique for a value $k = 0$.
- Shi and Tomasi estimated that the corners are primitives which remain more stable for tracking, contrary to other features [19]. Consequently, the minimum eigenvalue between λ_1 and λ_2 of matrix $\mathcal{M}$ is conserved for a salient point along a video; then this detector led to the well-known KLT (Kanade-Lucas-Tomasi) feature tracker.
- Kenney et al. [9] combines λ_1 and λ_2 with a cornerness measure which is constrained by the numbers of required axioms to satisfy. The axioms mainly formulate the isotropy condition (rotation invariant corner), orthonormality of the matrix M, constant eigenvalues relating to the norm, and finally definition of the maximum value of the isotropic point over the set of constant eigenvalues. As detailed in [9], KZ detector technique is equivalent modulo for the choice of a suitable matrix norm and a normalization constant to:
  - ☐ F when $p = 1$,
  - ☐ KLT when $p \to +\infty$,
  - ☐ $\sqrt[p]{2}$R for $p \to 0$.

  In our experiments, p is fixed to 2.

These six corner detection techniques have in common the tensor $\mathcal{M}$, which is tied to the same low-pass filter parameter, here denoted ρ: the standard deviation of the Gaussian. This ρ value is identical for each compared technique in the experiment presented in the next section.

2.4   Detection of a Corner: Final Step

For corner extraction, the final step concerns the binarization of the detected salient points or corners. The obtained features from the techniques presented in Subsects. 2.1–2.3 and listed in the Table 1 compute cornerness measure by applying non-maximum suppression where the local maxima are tied to the corner positions (here a window of size 15×15 is chosen to avoid too close keypoints). Eventually, corner points are highlighted by thresholding the extracted points or by setting the number of corner points to be detected objectively (this last solution was adopted in our experiments).

3   Keypoint Repeatability Assessments

Repeatability measure is the defacto standard and is commonly applied for the performance characterization of salient point detectors [15, 21]. The repeatability rate measures the detector's robustness in being able to detect the same features in the condition of image perturbations (e.g., a corner detector that is robust in the condition of image perturbation is rated as a highly repeatable detector). To pursue a vigorous evaluation of techniques detailed and nominated in Table 1, our experiments are carried out on a specific database containing strong perturbations, as reported in Table 2 and detailed in the next subsection.

Table 2. Experimental protocols of selected videos in the AQUALOC dataset.

Sequence №	№ of Frames	Description of image transformation
Video sequence 1	1000	rotation, affine, illumination, scale
Video sequence 2	2000	rotation, affine, illumination, perspective
Video sequence 3	2000	rotation, illumination, homogeneous, scale
Video sequence 4	2000	rotation, illumination, occlusion, translation
Video sequence 5	3000	rotation, illumination, affine, scale, clutter

3.1   Experimental Protocol

In this assessment, the repeatability rate is considered as the percentage of the total number of points that are repeated between two subsequent video frames in the AQUALOQ dataset[1]. This dataset is an underwater video sequence dedicated to the localization of underwater vehicles navigating close to the seabed. These videos have been recorded from remotely operated vehicles equipped with a monocular monochromatic camera. The image data is complex in consisting of all types of geometric and photometric transformation plus different types of

---

[1] The AQUALOC Dataset [5] is available at: https://www.lirmm.fr/aqualoc/.

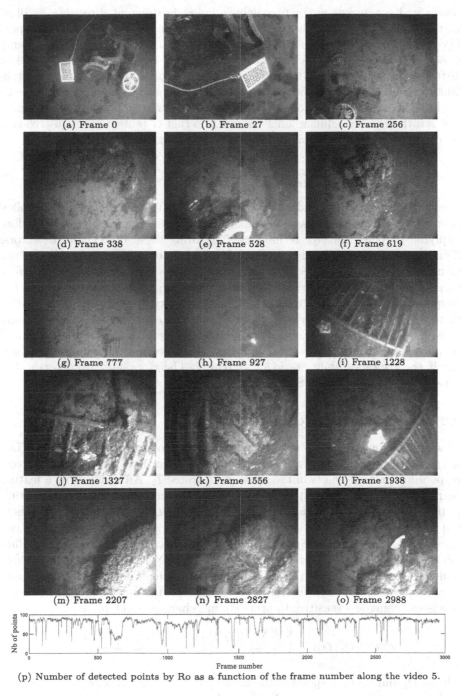

(a) Frame 0   (b) Frame 27   (c) Frame 256

(d) Frame 338   (e) Frame 528   (f) Frame 619

(g) Frame 777   (h) Frame 927   (i) Frame 1228

(j) Frame 1327   (k) Frame 1556   (l) Frame 1938

(m) Frame 2207   (n) Frame 2827   (o) Frame 2988

(p) Number of detected points by Ro as a function of the frame number along the video 5.

Fig. 1. Selected images of video 5 of AQUALOC dataset [5] for visual explanation of all types of transformation and noises, images of size 512×640.

noises and concurrent moving particles moving in different directions as illustrated in the Fig. 1. Nevertheless, the frame movements are very smooth, denoting a small inter-frame distance. For our statistical experiments, we randomly selected 5 videos with different numbers of frame sequences. With a total of 10 000 frames, video 1 includes 1000 frames, videos 2, 3 and video 4 contain 2000 frames, finally, video 5: 3000 frames, as listed and detailed in the Table 2.

In order to remove the noise in the image and obtain more relevant keypoints, the zeroth order two-dimensional Gaussian kernel G is used for regularization by convolution with the image [25]. Its equation is given by:

$$G(\sigma, x, y) = \frac{1}{2\pi\sigma^2} \cdot e^{-\frac{x^2+y^2}{2\sigma^2}} \text{ with } \sigma \in \mathbb{R}_+^*, \ (x, y) \in \mathbb{R}^2, \tag{3}$$

where σ represents the standard deviation of the Gaussian G and (x, y) the pixel coordinates. Hence, the images are smoothed with G of parameter $\sigma = 1$ before applying keypoint detector techniques. Regarding these 12 keypoint detectors, detailed in Sect. 2 and listed in Table 1, all of them detect the 100 best points per frame. The choice of ρ parameter value for the detectors consisting of ρ parameter, is usually made empirically because a too large value can delocalizes the keypoint position and will "disrupt" the repeatability. Indeed, when the ρ value increases from certain threshold, the keypoints can get misplaced increasingly (see example in [15]) and some of them could be merged. Meanwhile, too small ρ value is a restricting threshold, limiting the detection of structure and will result the low repeatability ratio for matching. Therefore, for each detector, the ρ value is estimated in the Sect. 3.2.

3.2   Evaluation via ZNCC Process

Tracking by matching the features is defined as obtaining the features (i.e., keypoints) in the first frame I_1 of the video sequence and then finding the corresponding pairs of points in the subsequent frame I_2. After detecting a feature point in I_1, a feature point in I_2 is generally estimated and located by computing the intensity variation between a patch in I_1 and patches in I_2. There are several straightforward metrics to estimate the similarity between the two intensity patches, such as Sum of Squared Differences (SSD), Sum of Absolute Difference (SAD), Normalized Cross-Correlation (NCC), and Zero-Mean Normalized Cross-Correlation (ZNCC). For our assessments, the ZNCC is chosen as the optimal evaluation metric in matching and tracking, because it is more precise as being less sensitive to proportional changes of intensity:

$$\text{ZNCC}(\Omega_1, \Omega_2) = \frac{\sum_i^N \sum_j^N [(\Omega(i,j) - \mu_1).(\Omega_2(i,j) - \mu_2)]}{N^2 \cdot \sigma_1 \cdot \sigma_2}, \tag{4}$$

where, Ω_1 and Ω_2 correspond to the frame patches of size $N \times N$ pixels, (μ_1, σ_1) and (μ_2, σ_2) are the mean and standard deviations of the intensities of the patches Ω_1 and Ω_2 respectively. In case where a keypoint is calculated in a homogeneous region: $\sigma_1 = 0$ or $\sigma_2 = 0$, consequently Eq. (4) does not compute a value in the desired range, so $\text{ZNCC}(\Omega_1, \Omega_2) = 1 - |\mu_1 - \mu_2|$. The ZNCC computes the similarity measures between the two equally sized image patches (I_1, I_2), and gives a scalar in the range $[-1; 1]$. The value/score between $[0; 1]$ indicates the ratio of positive correlativity of the features. The closer to 1 the score is, the similarity between the patches is. As there are small displacements between each frame in the studied dataset, consequently, the ZNCC descriptor is applicable for matching because patches spatially close to another patch in the subsequent frame will obtain a positive ZNCC score.

In the evaluation process, for scoring the repeatability ratio of each studied feature detector, three statistical metrics are first computed, namely: (i) mean of matched points (percentage of matched points exactly), (ii) Standard deviation (Std) of matched points and (iii) ZNCC mean for each frame. Thereafter, in order to obtain an evaluation as objective as possible, the feature point detectors having a ρ parameter are compared by varying this parameter. Indeed, ρ is increasing from 0.5 to 4.5 by a step of 0.5 and the repeatability ratio is estimated for each scale, see Sect. 3.2. Consequently, the Table 3 reports the mean and Std of matched points as a function of the video number for each detector (and best ρ). To complete the evaluation, a final score is computed in Eq. (5) to estimate the reliability of the detectors as a function of 3 entities:

- $\mathcal{M}_{Matched}$: the usual mean of matched points among 100 detected points along the 5 videos.
- $Std_{Matched}$: the usual standard deviation of matched points along the 5 videos.
- $\mathcal{M}_{ZNCC}$: the mean of ZNCC scores for all the matched points along the 5 videos.

These 3 values are displayed in Fig. 2(a)–(d) as a function of the ρ values regarding the 7 feature detectors: F, H, R, KLT, GD, A and K. Usually, it is worth noting that the $Std_{Matched}$ and $\mathcal{M}_{ZNCC}$ score can be inversely proportional to the number of detected points; an example, a detector can match few number of points by having a low $Std_{Matched}$ value, as ZH in Table 3. Furthermore, $\mathcal{M}_{Matched}$, $Std_{Matched}$ and $\mathcal{M}_{ZNCC}$ are normalized and the final score is computed by:

$$\mathcal{T}_S = \frac{a \cdot \mathcal{N}(\mathcal{M}_{Matched}) + b \cdot \mathcal{N}(Std_{Matched}) + c \cdot \mathcal{N}(\mathcal{M}_{ZNCC})}{a + b + c}, \tag{5}$$

where $\mathcal{N}$ represents the normalization function, and (a, b, c): 3 positive coefficients such that $(a + b + c) = 1$. In our experiments, $a = 0.4$, $b = 0.3$ and $c = 0.3$ to correspond to weights such that the mean of detected points remains the main entity. The Fig. 2(d) reports different scores as a function of the ρ variation. This total score is also computed for the detector without ρ parameters, namely: DET, KR, ZH, BB and RTC. Finally, all the statistics are reported in the Table 4. The more the $\mathcal{T}_S$ score is close to 1, the more the feature detector is qualified as suitable for repeatability. On the contrary, a score close to 0 indicates a low reliability of a detector.

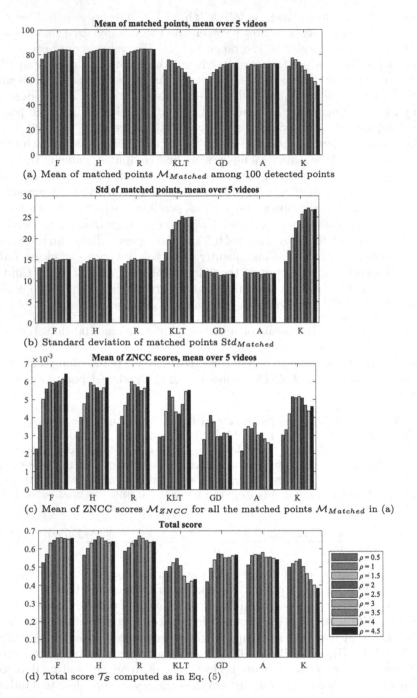

(a) Mean of matched points $\mathcal{M}_{Matched}$ among 100 detected points

(b) Standard deviation of matched points $Std_{Matched}$

(c) Mean of ZNCC scores $\mathcal{M}_{ZNCC}$ for all the matched points $\mathcal{M}_{Matched}$ in (a)

(d) Total score $\mathcal{T}_{S}$ computed as in Eq. (5)

Fig. 2. Matched and repeatability statistics as function of ρ values for 7 filtering techniques averaged on 5 videos: ρ values in the range of 0 to 4.5

Table 3. Percentage and Std of detected points per video

Detector	Video 1		Video 2		Video 3		Video 4		Video 5	
	Mean	Std	Mean	Std	Mean	Std	Mean	Std	Mean	Std
DET	81.9	7.6	76.4	14.6	80.1	13.1	68.7	15.7	77.9	11.9
KR	76.9	7.1	70.6	13.9	74.6	12.0	64.6	14.4	71.5	11.0
ZH	8.3	5.1	10.3	9.0	11.7	6.8	10.1	8.5	12.2	9.1
F	**90.2**	8.7	81.8	17.0	77.0	17.9	**88.8**	11.6	**84.5**	15.4
HS	90.1	8.6	**82.0**	17.0	**77.2**	17.7	88.5	12.4	82.9	16.5
BB	84.6	7.9	77.9	15.3	81.5	13.5	10.1	8.6	79.3	12.7
Ro	90.1	8.6	**82.0**	17.0	**77.2**	17.7	88.5	12.4	82.9	16.5
KLT	81.0	9.5	70.1	23.1	57.3	29.1	86.5	12.0	71.6	27.5
RTC	82.2	7.7	76.6	14.8	80.6	13.2	71.3	16.2	78.2	12.0
GD	64.4	11.8	68.8	12.9	64.6	13.2	71.2	9.2	69.6	12.0
A	78.1	7.0	71.1	13.4	67.1	13.8	73.8	10.0	72.0	12.5
KZ	86.3	9.9	71.7	23.7	57.8	29.6	87.4	12.1	72.2	27.8

Scale ρ Parameter Fitting. Depending on the ρ parameter, the detectors F, H, and R shows the highest stability for different scale ratio as presented in the Fig. 2(d) total score $\mathcal{T}_S$. Here, the detectors, KLT and K total score decreases for ρ values greater than 2.5, whereas the detectors GD and A produce average total score values. Correspondingly, the statistics tied to the best scores regarding ρ parameter of these detectors are reported in the Table 4, as for statistics in the Table 3. It is important to note that values are rounded in Table 3; whereas original/exact values serve for Table 4.

Usual Statistical Evaluation. The mean ZNCC values for each operator demonstrate the cumulative average similarity or correlation of only the corresponding patches in the given image sequences; they are also reported in the Table 4. The obtained values are all positive values, implying certain similarities and measures of repeatability of the corresponding matched points. Nevertheless, the mean ZNCC values are a function of matched points per detected points. As an example, the mean ZNCC values for the two detectors Ro and ZH (best versus worse detectors) correspond to the number of matched points per total number of detected points. It is to note that, a solid interpretation of the obtained values is complicated as each different operator's performances with different types of image transformation, occlusion and noises vary widely, as illustrated in Fig. 1. To be recalled again, for this experiment the displacement of frames are smooth and small, so keypoints in consecutive frames should not be too far spatially from the successive frames in the experimental videos. As an example, the detector DET shows a high percentage of matched corner points in the first video sequences; however, in the video 4, drastic changes in scores appear relating to the different transformations (81.9 against 68.7 in Table 3).

Table 4. Main repeatability statistical scores of matched points, mean ZNCC (rounded here) and final conclusive scores $\mathcal{T}_S$ in Eq. (5).

Detector	DET	KR	ZH	F	HS	BB	Ro	KLT	RTC	GD	A	KZ
ρ parameter	–	–	-	3	2.5	–	2.5	2	–	2	2.5	2
$\mathcal{M}_{Matched}$	76.62	71.11	10.92	83.90	83.41	66.15	83.40	72.79	77.36	67.83	72.01	73.66
$Std_{Matched}$	13.01	12.04	8.09	14.76	15.22	12.06	15.21	22.03	13.19	11.85	11.89	22.39
$\mathcal{M}_{ZNCC}$	0.008	0.007	0.15	0.006	0.006	0.010	0.006	0.005	0.008	0.004	0.003	0.005
$\mathcal{T}_S$, see Eq. (5)	0.34	0.32	0.07	0.66	0.66	0.30	0.67	0.55	0.35	0.57	0.58	0.54

Hence, the repeatability ratio is always dependent on the type of image transformation. Another example concerns a group of structure tensor based techniques having ρ scale parameter. Even though the detector Ro, HS, and F obtained the optimal matching score, signifying higher stability of repeatability in keypoint detection, HS (well-known Harris) as often called the benchmarking corner detector has not obtained the highest matching score among all, concerning the effects of image transformation detailed in Table 2. Furthermore, the detectors A, GD, KLT, and KZ have shown significant repeatability scores in the descending order. Besides the detectors, RTC, DET, KR and BB have shown low final scores $\mathcal{T}_S$ which their Std of matched points is also low. This objective repeatability assessment enables a valuable choice of the ρ scale parameter. Indeed, a bad ρ value regarding F, HS or Ro detectors ($\rho = 0.5$ or 1, see Fig. 2) produces poor statistics than BB detector which is one of the least reliable detector (see Table 4). To conclude this part, since the movement of the camera is smooth, a score correlated to ZNCC constitutes a technique to assess the keypoint detectors –enabling to estimate the optimum ρ parameter–. Finally, the detector ZH repeatability score is the lowest, conveying that in the condition of numerous image transformations and noises (such as underwater videos), this detector is unreliable to use; and this drawback is mainly due to sensitivity of this detector to strong illumination changes.

To conclude this part, since the movement of the camera is smooth, a score correlated to ZNCC constitutes a technique to assess the repeatability of the keypoint detectors and enabling to estimate the optimum ρ parameter for several keypoint detectors.

Visual Results. In Fig. 3(a), 50 random frame sequences have been chosen to illustrate the curves of the percentage of matched points. The 100 detected points along the sequence are displayed in blue in the first frame, while the linked points by the ZNCC are plotted in green in the Fig. 3(b)–(m). Visually the Ro, HS, and F are the best keypoint detection methods with smooth lines whereas the ZH, GD, KR and A detectors seem not stable because the displayed lines are sharped (zig-zag), illustrating the misplacement in the images of the Figs. 3 (c)-(d)-(k)-(l), reflecting the weak reliability of these techniques.

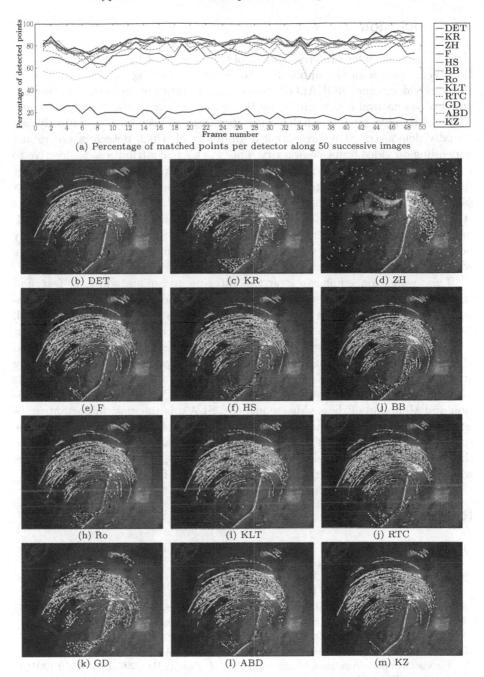

(a) Percentage of matched points per detector along 50 successive images

(b) DET   (c) KR   (d) ZH

(e) F   (f) HS   (j) BB

(h) Ro   (i) KLT   (j) RTC

(k) GD   (l) ABD   (m) KZ

Fig. 3. 100 matched keypoints on a sequence of 50 images. In (b)–(m), detected points appear in blue along the sequence, while links are in green. (Color figure online)

4   Conclusion

In this paper, an extensive investigation of the 12 state-of-the-art keypoint detection techniques with the application to feature matching in the context of a complex video scene (AQUALOQ: containing all types of image transformation and various natural noises caused by the water and sand) has been conducted. The repeatability rate of each detection operator has been both statistically and visually demonstrated in presenting a guideline of which detectors are robust depending on video frame complexity. This work can contribute as a directive to the practitioners of this domain for choosing the appropriate keypoint detectors relating to the specific application (i.e., Ro, HS, and F exemplify the robust salient point detectors with the highest stability). The scale parameter ρ of the studied keypoint detectors have been studied for an objective and complete evaluation. The results show that KLT and Harris-Stephens (HS), two particularly popular detectors, perform well but not the best among the 12 tested, especially when the ρ parameter is not well selected.

This evaluation emphasizes on the filtering technique which is fast and straightforward than other approaches along with the keypoint matching methods (ZNCC) which is few time-consuming and can be easily implemented. Accordingly, the filtering techniques are useful for certain cases of image processing and optimization which are either used independently or can be used alongside with deep learning models either in pre-processing or post-processing stages.

In closing, this study could be performed on SLAM (Simultaneous Localization and Mapping) of these video sequences. SLAM is the most important problems in the pursuit of building truly autonomous mobile robots. With SLAM the spatial map of environment while simultaneously localizing the robot relative to this model can be acquired. The SLAM of this keypoint detection techniques will realize many new general purpose applications of mobile robotics.

References

1. Achard, C., Bigorgne, E., Devars, J.: A sub-pixel and multispectral corner detector. In: ICPR, pp. 959–962 (2000)
2. Awrangjeb, M., Guojun, L., Clive, F.: Performance comparisons of contour-based corner detectors. IEEE TIP **21**(9), 4167–4179 (2012)
3. Beaudet, P.R.: Rotationally invariant image operators. In: ICPR 1987, pp. 579–583
4. Blom, J., Haar Romeny, B.M., Koenderink, J.J.: Affine invariant corner detection. Doctoral Dissertation (1992)
5. Ferrera, M., Creuze, V., Moras, J., Trouv, P.P.: AQUALOC: an underwater dataset for visual-inertial-pressure localization. Int. J. Robot. Res. **38**, 1549–1559 (2019)
6. Forstner, W., Gulch, E.: A fast operator for detection and precise location of distinct points, corners and circular features. In: Fast Processing of Photogrammetric Data 1987, pp. 281–305
7. Haggui, O., Tadonki, C., Lacassagne, L., Sayadi, F., Bouraoui, O.: Harris corner detection on a NUMA manycore. Future Gener. Comput. Syst. **88**, 442–452 (2018)

8. Harris, C.G., Stephens, M.J.: A combined corner and edge detector. In: Alvey Vision Conference, pp. 147–151 (1988)
9. Kenney, C.S., Zuliani, M., Manjunath, B.S.: An axiomatic approach to corner detection. In: CVPR, vol. 1, pp. 191–197 (2005)
10. Kitchen, L.J., Rosenfeld, A.: Gray-level corner detection. Pattern Recogn. Lett. **1**, 95–102 (1982)
11. Lipschutz, M.-M.: Differential Geometry. McGfaw-Hill, New York (1969)
12. Mokhtarian, F., Mohanna, F.: Performance evaluation of corner detectors using consistency and accuracy measures **102**(1), 81–94 (2006)
13. Noble, J.A.: Finding corners. Image Vis. Comput. **6**(2), 121–128 (1988)
14. Rey-Otero, I., Delbracio, M., Morel, J.M.: Comparing feature detectors: a bias in the repeatability criteria. In: ICIP, pp. 3024–3028 (2015)
15. Rodehorst, V., Koschan, A.: Comparison and evaluation of feature point detectors. In: International Symposium Turkish-German Joint Geodetic Days (2006)
16. Rohr, K.: Localization properties of direct corner detectors. Math. Imag. Vis. **4**, 139–150 (1994)
17. Rosten, E., Porter, R., Drummond, T.: Faster and better: a machine learning approach to corner detection. TPAMI **32**(1), 105–119 (2008)
18. Schmid, C., Mohr, R., Bauckhange, C.: Evaluation of interest point detectors. IJCV **37**, 151–172 (2010)
19. Shi, J., Tomasi, C.: Good features to track. In: CVPR, pp. 593–600 (1994)
20. Shokouh, G.-S., Magnier, B., Xu, B., Montesinos, P.: Ridge detection by image filtering techniques: a review and an objective analysis. PRIA **31**(2), 551–570 (2021)
21. Tuytelaars, T., Mikolajczyk, K.: Local invariant feature detectors: a survey. Now Found. Trends **3**, 177–280 (2008)
22. Wang, H., Brady, M.: Real-time corner detection algorithm for motion estimation. IVC **13**(6), 695–703 (1995)
23. Xia, G., Delon, J., Gousseau, Y.: Accurate junction detection and characterization in natural images. IJCV **106**(1), 31–56 (2014)
24. Zheng, Z., Wang, H., Teoh, E.-K.: Analysis of gray level corner detection. Pattern Recognit. Letters **20**(2), 149–162 (1999)
25. Canny, J.: A computational approach to edge detection. IEEE Trans. Pattern Anal. Mach. Intell. 6PAMI-8, 679–698 (1986)
26. Zuniga, O.-A., Haralick, R.-M.: Corner detection using the facet model. Pattern Recognit. Image Process., 30–37 (1983)

Underwater Fish Tracking-by-Detection: An Adaptive Tracking Approach

Divya Velayudhan$^{(\boxtimes)}$, Adarsh Ghimire , Jorge Dias , Naoufel Werghi , and Sajid Javed

Khalifa University of Science and Technology, Abu Dhabi, UAE
{100058254,100058927,naoufel.werghi,sajid.javed}@ku.ac.ae

Abstract. High distortion and complex marine environment pose severe challenges to underwater tracking. In this paper, we propose a simple, template-free Adaptive Euclidean Tracking (AET) approach for underwater fish tracking by regarding tracking as a specific case of instance detection. The proposed method exploits the advanced detection framework to track the fish in underwater imagery without any image enhancement techniques. The proposed method achieves comparable performance on the DeepFish dataset, with 22% and 14% improvement in precision and success over state-of-art trackers.

Keywords: Underwater Tracking · Object Detection · Adaptive search

1 Introduction

Underwater tracking plays a critical role in preserving aquatic ecosystems by monitoring marine life and their behavioral responses to distinct environmental conditions [32,34]. Fish are sensitive to environmental variations and toxicants, and their responses are often closely monitored to assess water quality [8,20]. Moreover, underwater fish tracking has gained traction due to the increasing interest in aquaculture. Integrating fish farms with advanced computer vision techniques to overcome the errors in human inference for identifying different fish species, estimating the population, and studying their behavior, will play an essential role in transforming the aquaculture industry [18].

However, underwater imagery poses several challenges to tracking, including variations in illumination, poor resolution, complex marine environment, scale variations, occlusion, weather conditions, and murky waters [14]. The intrinsic characteristics of marine life further complicate underwater tracking, such as fewer inter-class differences (where distinct categories of fish look similar) and camouflage (ability to blend into the environment). Figure 1 shows sample images from the DeepFish dataset [25], where it is quite difficult to identify the fishes.

Several recent studies have attempted to address the issues in underwater imagery using deep learning-based approaches. Few works [3,7,9] have employed

---

D. Velayudhan and A. Ghimire—Authors make equal contributions to this work.

© Springer Nature Switzerland AG 2023
J.-J. Rousseau and B. Kapralos (Eds.): ICPR 2022 Workshops, LNCS 13645, pp. 504–515, 2023.
https://doi.org/10.1007/978-3-031-37731-0_37

Fig. 1. Sample images from DeepFish dataset, which are too hazy to recognize the fishes, spotted here with the red bounding boxes. (Color figure online)

image pre-processing techniques for visual enhancement prior to underwater detection and tracking [22]. Some research works used Gaussian Mixture Model (GMM) [23] in detecting fish with Kalman filter [30] for tracking [10,16,26,27]. One of the early works in tracking fish employed covariance modeling to match the candidate objects [28]. Chuang *et al.* [4] studied multi-object fish tracking with underwater mobile cameras using deformable multiple kernels by leveraging histogram features. In [13], CNN features were incorporated in a two-phase graph-based method. Huang *et al.* [12] studied underwater multi-target fish tracking and used Gaussian mixture model [23] to extract region proposals from the foreground, followed by template matching using SURF [1] and CNN features. Recently, a deep hungarian network [33] was employed to track fish by leveraging spatial and appearance cues to estimate the similarity between the predictions [19]. Nevertheless, these studies are either based on hand-crafted features, require rigorous parameter tuning, or employ template matching approach, which fails under drastic appearance changes.

Recently few works [11,29] have attempted to exploit the advanced frameworks in object detection to develop efficient trackers, as tracking can be regarded as a particular case of detection tailored to a specific instance. In effect, many popular tracking algorithms are motivated by research in the object detection community, including bounding box regression (in MDNet [15]), region proposal networks (in SiamRPN [17]), and precise localization of bounding boxes (applied in ATOM [5]). Huang *et al.* [11] utilized a target guidance block fused into the detector, and a meta-learning classifier to differentiate between different instances. Meanwhile, Wang *et al.* [29] employed meta-learning to convert an object detector into a tracker through domain adaptation. Their approach involves offline training on large sequences and then online fine-tuning.

Following a similar line of investigation, this paper proposes a simplified approach to underwater fish tracking by regarding tracking as a specific case of instance detection. We propose transforming an object detector into an efficient tracker while preserving the overall architecture of the base detector without the addition of any new components. An adaptive euclidean tracking (AET) algorithm is developed to distinguish between the different instances and track the fish through the sequence. We employed Faster R-CNN [24] as the base detector in this work, but the proposed AET approach can be plugged into any detector. The proposed AET approach was evaluated on the DeepFish dataset [25] without using images from that dataset while training the detector. The Deep-Fish dataset is meant originally for classification, segmentation, and localization tasks. We divided the dataset into twenty sequences and manually annotated it for single object tracking. For a comprehensive evaluation, we considered trackers from each prominent tracking family based on Deep Correlation Filters (DCF) [5], Siamese network-based [17], and transformer-driven trackers [35]. The proposed AET algorithm outperforms the baseline trackers on the DeepFish dataset. The main contributions are summarized as follows:

- Simple and efficient algorithm for tracking fish underwater without any pre-processing techniques for image enhancement, that can be fused with any state-of-the-art detectors.
- AET method performs competitively without using any DeepFish training images.
- Better performance on tracking underwater fish when compared with baseline trackers.
- Manual annotation of DeepFish dataset for single object tracking.

The rest of this paper is structured as follows. Section 2 provides a detailed explanation of the proposed method. The experimental setup and dataset description is included in Sect. 3, while Sect. 4 discusses the results and finally conclusions are presented in Sect. 5.

2   Proposed Method

This work focuses on transforming a generic object detection model into an underwater tracker without additional architectural remodeling or online training, using a simple Adaptive Euclidean tracking algorithm. As illustrated in Fig. 2, the proposed framework has two major components: the Detection pipeline and the proposed Adaptive Euclidean Tracker (AET). The Detection pipeline is composed of two sub-modules: an object detector and a proposal filter. We employed Faster R-CNN as the object detector in the proposed system. An in-depth description of the Faster R-CNN and its training is detailed in Subsect. 2.1. The candidate object proposals generated by the detector are filtered before being passed to the proposed tracker. The AET algorithm helps in distinguishing between the different fish instances and tracking the target through the sequence, as described comprehensively in the Subsect. 2.2. The detection pipeline and the adaptive euclidean tracker are detailed in the following subsections.

2.1   Detection Pipeline

The detection pipeline is a major component of the proposed framework, consisting of two sub-modules: the Object Detector and the Proposal Filtering Module.

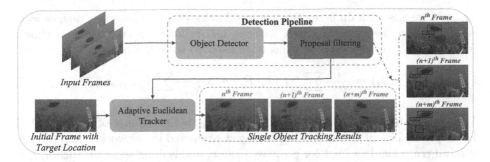

Fig. 2. Schematic diagram of the proposed framework. The input frames are fed into the detection pipeline. The proposal filter returns a collection of high confidence candidate objects/fishes (represented by the black bounding boxes), which are passed to the Adaptive Euclidean Tracker. The AET uses the target location in the initial frame to generate results (represented by blue bounding boxes). (Color figure online)

Any state-of-the-art object detector can be used within the Detection pipeline. However, we employed Faster R-CNN, a deep convolutional neural network-based object detector. The candidate proposals generated by the detector are screened by the Proposal filter to limit unnecessary computation inside AET.

Object Detector: Faster R-CNN [24] integrates the Region Proposal Network (RPN), unlike its predecessors to generate proposals. In short, the RPN predicts the probability of an anchor containing objects, which are then examined by the classification and regression branches. To facilitate the detection of fishes in underwater imagery, we have trained the generic object detector on a limited public dataset. The training routine is detailed below:

Detector Training Routine: Unlike contemporary trackers [2,5], which use several huge (often four) datasets for offline training, we used a minimalized approach by training the Faster R-CNN on a small public dataset [6] using the standard alternate training scheme.

The alternate training approach is highly suitable for training big networks on limited datasets. The strategy trains distinct parts of the network by freezing the other parts allowing the network to be more generalized. In our training strategy, we employed the following steps with weights from imagenet-pretrained model:

1. Freeze the backbone and train the Region Proposal Network (RPN) and detection network
2. Freeze the RPN and detection network, and unfreeze the backbone and train it
3. Freeze backbone again, and train the RPN and detection network simultaneously.

The dataset contains underwater footage of only two species of fish (luderick and Australian bream) from seagrass habitats in Australia. It is a small collection of 4,281 images with different lighting and backgrounds. These raw images were used to train the Faster R-CNN without using image enhancement methods. The loss function as shown in 1 has been used to train the network.

$$L(P_i, t_i) = \frac{1}{N_{cls}} \sum_i L_{cls}(P_i, P_i^*) + \lambda \frac{1}{N_{reg}} \sum_i P_i^* L_{reg}(t_i, t_i^*) \tag{1}$$

Where, i is an anchor index in a mini-batch, N_{cls} is the number of classes and P_i is the probability of anchor i being an object predicted by network. The P_i^* is the ground truth label and is 1 for positive anchor, and is 0 for negative anchor. t_i is a vector representing the 4 bounding box coordinates predicted by the network, and t_i^* is the ground truth bounding box of positive anchor. The L_{cls} is log loss over two classes (object vs. not object) and L_{reg} is the smooth $L1$ loss.

Proposal Filtering Module: The major task of this module is to filter out the low probability candidates predicted by the detector as fish to avoid unnecessary computations during tracking. Since the detector outputs several objects that may look like fish with lower confidence, it is necessary to avoid unnecessary computations and make the tracking system computationally efficient. In fact, the thresholding technique has been used to remove those candidates, since the detector also outputs the probability of candidate being a fish. We have set the threshold to 0.5 throughout the experimentation, meaning, the candidates with probability less than 50% are rejected by this module. However the impact of different thresholds can be explored as well.

2.2   Adaptive Euclidean Tracking Algorithm

The proposed AET algorithm helps differentiate between the detected candidates in a frame and guides the underwater tracking of the target fish. AET employs a simple approach and takes only the target location in the initial frame as input. The algorithm then tracks the detected instance in the subsequent frames within an adaptive search region whose bounding box center coordinates have the least L2-norm. The search region(r) plays a critical role in overcoming distractions, especially when the target fish is occluded. When the target is not detected due to occlusion or image blur the detector is prevented from detecting fish outside the search region. However, it is essential to modify the search area adaptively to account for the erratic movements of the aquatic life. Hence the variation in the center coordinates between adjacent frames is used to analyze the movement trend and adapt the search area accordingly as shown in Eq. 2 and 4. If the target moves slowly, then the search region is limited. In contrast, the search region is increased for fast-moving targets. Furthermore, tracking using the center coordinates as opposed to the bounding box coordinates also helps in better performance, making it less dependent on higher precise detection results. The pseudo-code of the proposed AET approach is presented in Algorithm 1.

Algorithm 1: Proposed Adaptive Euclidean Tracking Algorithm

---

1 **Input:** Frame sequence $\{F_i\}_{i=1}^{N}$ where N is the total number of frames, initial bounding box B_1, detector model $h\,(x:\theta)$, search radius r.

2 **Output:** Tracking Results $\{B_i\}_{i=1}^{N}$

3 Compute centre c of bounding box B_1 as (c^x, c^y)

4 $\hat{r} \leftarrow r$

5 **for** $i \leftarrow 2, ..., N$ **do**

6 $\quad$ Detect all fish within the search region of centre c and radius $\hat{r}$

7 $\quad$ Get bounding boxes and scores as $\{B_{det}^{j}, s_j\}_{j=1}^{M}$, where M is the number of detections.

8 $\quad$ **if** all $s_j \leq 0.5$ **then**

9 $\quad\quad\mid$ $B_i \leftarrow B_{i-1}$

10 $\quad\quad\mid$ **continue**

11 $\quad$ **end**

12 $\quad$ Compute $\{c_{det}^{j}\}_{j=1}^{M}$.

13 $\quad$ Update c with the centre value $\{c_{det}^{j}\}_{j=1}^{M}$ having the least L2 norm.

14 $\quad$ Update B_i with the corresponding bounding box values.

15 $\quad$ Compute $d_i \leftarrow max\,(c_i^x - c_{i-1}^x, c_i^y - c_{i-1}^y)$;

16 $\quad$ **if** $i \geq 3$ **then**

17 $\quad\quad\mid$ Compute movement trend $t_i \leftarrow \frac{d_i + d_{i-1}}{2}$

18 $\quad\quad\mid$ Update search radius, $\hat{r} \leftarrow r + \frac{t_i}{2}$

19 $\quad$ **end**

20 **end**

$$T_i = \frac{d_i + d_{i-1}}{2} \tag{2}$$

Where, T_i is the movement trend. d_i and d_{i-1} are the ith and $i-1^{th}$ frame target bounding boxes centers respectively. It is computed using Eq. 3.

$$d_i = max\left(c_i^x - c_{i-1}^x, c_i^y - c_{i-1}^y\right) \tag{3}$$

Where, c_i^x and c_i^y are the center of target along x and y axis in i^{th} frame. Similarly, c_{i-1}^x and c_{i-1}^y are the center of target along x and y axis in $i - 1^{th}$ frame.

$$\hat{r} = r + \frac{t_i}{2} \tag{4}$$

Where, $\hat{r}$ is the update rule for search radius which updates with respect to initial radius and trend line, so that it does not explode. The search radius r is set to be greater than the size of the bounding box in the initial frame.

3   Experimental Setup

This section explores the dataset description, and experimental protocols used to assess the performance of the proposed AET algorithm for tracking fish underwater.

3.1   Dataset

DeepFish is a public benchmark comprised of over forty thousand images with high resolution (1,920 × 1,080) collected from twenty distinct marine ecosystems in Australia [25]. The dataset contains three subsets (FishClf, FishLoc and FishSeg), each intended for classification, localization, and segmentation tasks. Thus, it includes label-level, point-level and mask-level annotations. In order to utilize the dataset for single object tracking, we divided it into twenty sequences and manually annotated it, and used all the sequences for the evaluation.

3.2   Experimental Protocols

Training and Implementation
Faster R-CNN was trained on a limited dataset using a single NVIDIA GTX 1660Ti on Intel(R) Core(TM) i7-10750H CPU@2.60 GHz processor with 24 GB RAM. The detector was trained for 15 epochs on each alternating training scheme with a batch size of 12, using SGD optimizer with an initial learning rate of 0.01, momentum of 0.9, and weight decay of 0.0005. The framework was then evaluated on DeepFish dataset.

Evaluation Protocols and Tracker Selection
We have used the One Pass Evaluation (OPE) protocol [31] to study the performance of the proposed tracking algorithm and compared it with other trackers in terms of precision, normalized precision, and success. While precision measures the distance in pixels between the tracking output and the ground truth, success computes the intersection over union (IoU) between the two. Since precision is sensitive to target size and resolution, we have used normalized precision [21]. We have chosen trackers from each of the most prominent families: ATOM [5] from DCF family, SiamRPN [17] from Siamese family, and TrTr [35] from Transformer family.

4   Results

This section discusses the evaluation results of the proposed AET on DeepFish dataset. The overall performance of the trackers is shown in Fig. 3. From the result, we can see that our proposed AET tracker achieves the best performance in the dataset in both precision and success with scores of 0.677 and 0.796 respectively. The transformer tracker, TrT, has the second-best precision of 0.452 while the ATOM has the second-best success of 0.656. In fact, our AET

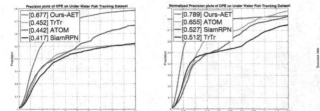
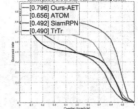

Fig. 3. Precision, Normalized Precision, and Success plots on DeepFish dataset. Our approach outperforms all other methods by a large margin in AUC, reported in the legend.

Fig. 4. Proposed framework exploits the detector to track the fish in blurry (Fig. (A) and (C)) and the camouflaged (Fig. (B) images, without any pre-processing. The red and green bounding boxes show the groundtruth and predictions respectively. (Color figure online)

tracker achieves 22% and 14% improvement in precision and success respectively, compared with the other SOTA trackers, proving its superiority.

The possible reason for the lower performance of the state-of-the-art trackers is the highly distorted underwater imagery (Fig. 1), which limits the extraction of relevant and distinguishable features, resulting in poor performance. On the other hand, the proposed framework takes advantage of the advanced detection framework to identify the fishes, despite the haziness, camouflage, and sudden appearance variation. Figure 4 illustrates samples images from different sequences, where the proposed framework was successful in identifying the fish, while SOTA trackers failed. However, it is to be noted that the proposed framework was never trained on the DeepFish dataset. It was subjected to only minimal training (with just two types of fish), and yet the proposed network is capable of identifying the fish.

The proposed AET algorithm uses L2-norm to track the fish within an adaptive search region. Hence it is essential to visualize the results when other fishes cross the target. Figure 5 illustrate two such scenarios. The proposed framework performs well because of its ability to analyze the target movement and modify the search area adaptively. The search region increases if the target moves faster and shrinks if it slows down.

Fig. 5. Qualitative results of the proposed AET method. Top and bottom rows show tracking results on two different sequences when the other fishes cross the target. The red and green bounding boxes show the groundtruth and predictions respectively. Please zoom in for visualization. (Color figure online)

Fig. 6. Visualization results where the detector fails due to camouflage and haziness in the images.

Furthermore, a few failure scenarios are shown in Fig. 6 and Fig. 7. The detector fails to identify the fish in Fig. 6 due to the haziness. This can be overcome by extended training of the Faster R-CNN on a larger dataset. The detector makes a false prediction in the sequence (in third image) in Fig. 7, causing a large variation in the centre coordinates. This increases the search region in the subsequent frames, ultimately tracking the wrong candidate. From these results we can infer that proper training of the detector can improve the performance even further. The tracker is purposefully designed to be simple by just utilizing the euclidean distance, however the performance of the framework can be further enhanced by incorporating additional visual features.

Fig. 7. Visualization of a failure case. The detector makes false prediction on the third image in the sequence, causing the tracker to lose its target.

5   Conclusion

In this work, we proposed a simple, template-free Adaptive Euclidean Tracking (AET) approach for underwater fish tracking by regarding tracking as a specific case of instance detection. The proposed method exploits the advanced state-of-art detection framework to achieve comparable performance on Deep-Fish dataset, with 22% and 14% improvement in precision and success over state-of-art trackers. For future work, we plan to fuse a light-weight module for encoding the target features to provide additional supervision for the AET algorithm.

Acknowledgments. This publication acknowledges the support provided by the Khalifa University of Science and Technology under Faculty Start Up grants FSU-2022-003 Award No. 84740 0 0401.

References

1. Bay, H., Ess, A., Tuytelaars, T., Van Gool, L.: Speeded-up robust features (SURF). Comput. Vis. Image Underst. **110**(3), 346–359 (2008)
2. Bhat, G., Danelljan, M., Gool, L.V., Timofte, R.: Learning discriminative model prediction for tracking. In: Proceedings of the IEEE/Cvf International Conference on Computer Vision, pp. 6182–6191 (2019)
3. Boudiaf, A., et al.: Underwater image enhancement using pre-trained transformer. In: Sclaroff, S., Distante, C., Leo, M., Farinella, G.M., Tombari, F. (eds.) ICIAP 2022. LNCS, vol. 13233. pp. 480–488. Springer, Cham (2022). https://doi.org/10.1007/978-3-031-06433-3_41
4. Chuang, M.C., Hwang, J.N., Ye, J.H., Huang, S.C., Williams, K.: Underwater fish tracking for moving cameras based on deformable multiple kernels. IEEE Trans. Syst. Man Cybern. Syst. **47**(9), 2467–2477 (2016)
5. Danelljan, M., Bhat, G., Khan, F.S., Felsberg, M.: Atom: accurate tracking by overlap maximization. In: Proceedings of the IEEE/CVF Conference on Computer Vision and Pattern Recognition, pp. 4660–4669 (2019)
6. Ditria, E.M., Connolly, R.M., Jinks, E.L., Lopez-Marcano, S.: Annotated video footage for automated identification and counting of fish in unconstrained seagrass habitats. Front. Mar. Sci. **8**, 160 (2021)
7. Fabbri, C., Islam, M.J., Sattar, J.: Enhancing underwater imagery using generative adversarial networks. In: 2018 IEEE International Conference on Robotics and Automation (ICRA), pp. 7159–7165. IEEE (2018)
8. Gerlai, R., Lee, V., Blaser, R.: Effects of acute and chronic ethanol exposure on the behavior of adult zebrafish (Danio Rerio). Pharmacol. Biochem. Behav. **85**(4), 752–761 (2006)
9. Guo, Y., Li, H., Zhuang, P.: Underwater image enhancement using a multiscale dense generative adversarial network. IEEE J. Oceanic Eng. **45**(3), 862–870 (2019)
10. Hossain, E., Alam, S.S., Ali, A.A., Amin, M.A.: Fish activity tracking and species identification in underwater video. In: 2016 5th International Conference on Informatics, Electronics and Vision (ICIEV), pp. 62–66. IEEE (2016)
11. Huang, L., Zhao, X., Huang, K.: Bridging the gap between detection and tracking: a unified approach. In: Proceedings of the IEEE/CVF International Conference on Computer Vision, pp. 3999–4009 (2019)

12. Huang, R.J., Lai, Y.C., Tsao, C.Y., Kuo, Y.P., Wang, J.H., Chang, C.C.: Applying convolutional networks to underwater tracking without training. In: 2018 IEEE International Conference on Applied System Invention (ICASI), pp. 342–345. IEEE (2018)

13. Jäger, J., Wolff, V., Fricke-Neuderth, K., Mothes, O., Denzler, J.: Visual fish tracking: combining a two-stage graph approach with CNN-features. In: OCEANS 2017-Aberdeen, pp. 1–6. IEEE (2017)

14. Jesus, A., Zito, C., Tortorici, C., Roura, E., De Masi, G.: Underwater object classification and detection: first results and open challenges. arXiv preprint arXiv:2201.00977 (2022)

15. Jung, I., Son, J., Baek, M., Han, B.: Real-Time MDNet. In: Ferrari, V., Hebert, M., Sminchisescu, C., Weiss, Y. (eds.) ECCV 2018. LNCS, vol. 11208, pp. 89–104. Springer, Cham (2018). https://doi.org/10.1007/978-3-030-01225-0_6

16. Lantsova, E., Voitiuk, T., Zudilova, T., Kaarna, A.: Using low-quality video sequences for fish detection and tracking. In: 2016 SAI Computing Conference (SAI), pp. 426–433. IEEE (2016)

17. Li, B., Yan, J., Wu, W., Zhu, Z., Hu, X.: High performance visual tracking with siamese region proposal network. In: Proceedings of the IEEE Conference on Computer Vision and Pattern Recognition, pp. 8971–8980 (2018)

18. Li, D., Du, L.: Recent advances of deep learning algorithms for aquacultural machine vision systems with emphasis on fish. Artif. Intell. Rev. **55**, 1–40 (2021)

19. Martija, M.A.M., Naval, P.C.: SynDHN: multi-object fish tracker trained on synthetic underwater videos. In: 2020 25th International Conference on Pattern Recognition (ICPR), pp. 8841–8848. IEEE (2021)

20. Masud, S., Singh, I., Ram, R.: Behavioural and hematological responses of cyprinus carpio exposed to mercurial chloride. J. Environ. Biol. **26**(2 Suppl), 393–397 (2005)

21. Müller, M., Bibi, A., Giancola, S., Alsubaihi, S., Ghanem, B.: TrackingNet: a large-scale dataset and benchmark for object tracking in the wild. In: Ferrari, V., Hebert, M., Sminchisescu, C., Weiss, Y. (eds.) ECCV 2018. LNCS, vol. 11205, pp. 310–327. Springer, Cham (2018). https://doi.org/10.1007/978-3-030-01246-5_19

22. Panetta, K., Kezebou, L., Oludare, V., Agaian, S.: Comprehensive underwater object tracking benchmark dataset and underwater image enhancement with GAN. IEEE J. Oceanic Eng. **47**, 59–75 (2021)

23. Rasmussen, C.: The infinite gaussian mixture model. In: Advances in Neural Information Processing Systems 12 (1999)

24. Ren, S., He, K., Girshick, R., Sun, J.: Faster R-CNN: towards real-time object detection with region proposal networks. In: Advances in Neural Information Processing Systems 28 (2015)

25. Saleh, A., Laradji, I.H., Konovalov, D.A., Bradley, M., Vazquez, D., Sheaves, M.: A realistic fish-habitat dataset to evaluate algorithms for underwater visual analysis. Sci. Rep. **10**(1), 1–10 (2020)

26. Sharif, M.H., Galip, F., Guler, A., Uyaver, S.: A simple approach to count and track underwater fishes from videos. In: 2015 18th International Conference on Computer and Information Technology (ICCIT), pp. 347–352. IEEE (2015)

27. Shiau, Y.H., Chen, C.C., Lin, S.I.: Using bounding-surrounding boxes method for fish tracking in real world underwater observation. Int. J. Adv. Rob. Syst. **10**(7), 298 (2013)

28. Spampinato, C., Palazzo, S., Giordano, D., Kavasidis, I., Lin, F.P., Lin, Y.T.: Covariance based fish tracking in real-life underwater environment. In: VISAPP (2), pp. 409–414 (2012)

29. Wang, G., Luo, C., Sun, X., Xiong, Z., Zeng, W.: Tracking by instance detection: a meta-learning approach. In: Proceedings of the IEEE/CVF Conference on Computer Vision and Pattern Recognition, pp. 6288–6297 (2020)

30. Welch, G., Bishop, G., et al.: An Introduction to the Kalman Filter. University of North Carolina at Chapel Hill, Chapel Hill (1995)

31. Wu, Y., Lim, J., Yang, M.H.: Object tracking benchmark. IEEE Trans. Pattern Anal. Mach. Intell. **37**(9), 1834–1848 (2015). https://doi.org/10.1109/tpami.2014.2388226

32. Xia, C., Fu, L., Liu, Z., Liu, H., Chen, L., Liu, Y.: Aquatic toxic analysis by monitoring fish behavior using computer vision: a recent progress. J. Toxicol. **2018** (2018)

33. Xu, Y., Osep, A., Ban, Y., Horaud, R., Leal-Taixé, L., Alameda-Pineda, X.: How to train your deep multi-object tracker. In: Proceedings of the IEEE/CVF Conference on Computer Vision and Pattern Recognition, pp. 6787–6796 (2020)

34. Yang, L., et al.: Computer vision models in intelligent aquaculture with emphasis on fish detection and behavior analysis: a review. Arch. Comput. Meth. Eng. **28**(4), 2785–2816 (2021)

35. Zhao, M., Okada, K., Inaba, M.: TRTR: Visual tracking with transformer. arXiv preprint arXiv:2105.03817 (2021)

Understanding and Mitigating Demographic Bias in Biometric Systems (UMDBB)

Preface

With recent advances in deep learning obtaining hallmark accuracy rates for various computer vision applications, biometrics is a widely adopted technology for recognizing identities, surveillance, border control, and mobile user authentication. However, over the last few years, the fairness of this automated biometric-based recognition and attribute classification methods have been questioned across demographic variations by media articles in the well-known press, academic, and industry research. Specifically, facial analysis technology is reported to be biased against darker-skinned people like African Americans, and women. This has led to the ban of facial recognition technology for government use. Apart from facial analysis, bias is also reported for other biometric modalities such as ocular and fingerprint and other AI systems based on biometric images such as face morphing attack detection algorithms. Despite existing work in this field, the state-of-the-art is still in its initial stages. There is a pressing need to examine the bias of existing biometric modalities and the development of advanced methods for bias mitigation in existing biometric-based systems.

The first edition of the International Workshop on Understanding and Mitigating Demographic Bias in Biometric Systems (UMDBB) was held in conjunction with the 26th edition of the International Conference on Pattern Recognition (ICPR) at Montréal, Canada in 2022. This workshop provided the forum for addressing the recent advancement and challenges in the field of fairness of AI in the context of biometrics. *The workshop aimed to increase awareness of demographic effects, and recent advances and provide a common ground of discussion for academicians, industry, and government.* The format of the workshop included two invited talks and seven oral paper presentations. The workshop was a full-day event. After a thorough and accurate peer review process, these 7 papers were accepted for presentation and publication in the proceedings as full-length papers. The review process focused on the quality of the papers and their scientific merit. In compliance with the main conference protocol, we adopted a single-blind review policy, and each paper was reviewed by a minimum of two independent, expert reviewers. After collecting the reviews, final decisions were made based on the reviews received and discussions by the organizers. The accepted papers covered a range of topics including the impact of GAN-induced attribute manipulation on face recognition, use of PGAN-based synthetic face images for bias mitigation of facial recognition, deep generative views for bias mitigation of gender classifier, age and gender classification applied to finger vein images, a demographic balanced database of finger hypercubes, brief audit of post-pandemic biometrics, and statistical methods for assessing differences in false non-match rates across demographic groups. The two invited talks were given by Prof. Karl Ricanek from the University of North Carolina, Wilmington, and Dr. Nisha Srinivas from Trueface.

This workshop provided an international forum where researchers from the United States, Europe, Canada, and Asia had the opportunity to share a common vision of the recent advances and the path forward in the field of Fairness in AI.

September 2022   Ajita Rattani
                                                                 Michael King

Workshop Organization

Organizers

Ajita Rattani   Wichita State University, USA
Michael King   Florida Institute of Technology, USA

Technical Program Committee

Ajita Rattani   Wichita State University, USA
Michael King   Florida Institute of Technology, USA
Kevin Bowyer   University of Notre Dame, USA
Arun Ross   Michigan State University, USA
Karl Ricanek   University of North Carolina Wilmington, USA
John Howard   MdTF.org, USA
Emanuela Marasco   George Mason University, USA
Krishnapriya Kottakkal Sugathan   Valdosta State University, USA
Mark Burge   Federal Bureau of Investigation, USA
Nisha Srinivas   Trueface, USA
Yevgeniy Sirotin   SAIC, USA

Can GAN-Induced Attribute Manipulations Impact Face Recognition?

Sudipta Banerjee[1]([✉])[ID], Aditi Aggarwal[1], and Arun Ross[2][ID]

[1] International Institute of Information Technology, Hyderabad, India
sudipta.b@iiit.ac.in, aditi.aggarwal@students.iiit.ac.in
[2] Michigan State University, East Lansing, USA
rossarun@cse.msu.edu

Abstract. Impact due to demographic factors such as age, sex, race, etc., has been studied extensively in automated face recognition systems. However, the impact of *digitally modified* demographic and facial attributes on face recognition is relatively under-explored. In this work, we study the effect of attribute manipulations induced via generative adversarial networks (GANs) on face recognition performance. We conduct experiments on the CelebA dataset by intentionally modifying thirteen attributes using AttGAN and STGAN and evaluating their impact on two deep learning-based face verification methods, ArcFace and VGGFace. Our findings indicate that some attribute manipulations involving eyeglasses and digital alteration of sex cues can significantly impair face recognition by up to 73% and need further analysis.

Keywords: Face recognition · Generative adversarial network (GAN) · Attribute manipulation

1 Introduction

Demographic attributes (race, age and sex) [9,14], face and hair accessories or attributes (glasses, makeup, hairstyle, beard and hair color) [28], and data acquisition factors (environment and sensors) [22,24] play an important role in the performance of automated face recognition systems. Demographic factors can potentially introduce biases in face recognition systems and are well studied in the literature [1,15,21]. Work to mitigate biases due to demographic factors are currently being investigated [8,20]. Typically, some of these attributes can be modified *physically*, *e.g.*, by applying hair dye or undergoing surgery. But what if these attributes are *digitally* modified? Individuals can alter their facial features in photos using image editors for cheekbone highlighting, forehead reduction, etc. The modified images, with revised features, may be posted in social media websites. But do such manipulations affect the biometric utility of these images? Assessing the impact of digital retouching on biometric identification accuracy was done in [4]. With the arrival of generative adversarial networks (GANs), the possibilities of automated attribute editing have exploded [11,16–18]. GANs

© Springer Nature Switzerland AG 2023
J.-J. Rousseau and B. Kapralos (Eds.): ICPR 2022 Workshops, LNCS 13645, pp. 521–535, 2023.
https://doi.org/10.1007/978-3-031-37731-0_38

can be used to change the direction of hair bangs, remove facial hair, change the intensity of tinted eyeglasses and even add facial expressions to face images. With GANs for facial age progression [29], a person's appearance can seamlessly transit from looking decades younger to appearing as an elderly individual. Note that the user does not have to be a deep learning expert to edit attributes in face images. Several smartphone-based applications have such attribute modifications in the form of filters, *e.g.*, FaceApp [7]. Open-source applications make it easy to modify an image by uploading the image, selecting the attribute to be edited, using a slider to regulate the magnitude of the change, and downloading the edited photo. The entire process can be easily accomplished in under five minutes [5]. Recently, mask-aware face editing methods have emerged [26].

Motivation: Although the intent of using image editing routines stems from personal preferences, they can be misused for obscuring an identity or impersonating another identity. The style transfer networks are typically evaluated from the perspective of visual realism, *i.e.*, how realistic do the generated images look? However, we rarely investigate the impact of such digital manipulations on biometric face recognition. Work has been done to localize the manipulations [13], estimate the generative model responsible for producing the effects [30], and gauge the robustness of face recognition networks with respect to pose and expression [10]. But we need to investigate GAN-based attribute manipulations from the perspective of biometric recognition. Studying the influence of digital manipulations of both demographic and facial attributes on face images is pivotal because an individual can use the edited images in identification documents. Therefore, it is imperative to assess the impact of GAN-based attribute manipulations on biometric recognition to evaluate the robustness of existing open-source deep learning-based face recognition systems [23]. **Our objective is to conduct an investigative study that examines the impact of attribute editing (thirteen attributes) of face images by AttGAN [11] and STGAN [17] on two popular open-source face matchers, namely, ArcFace [6] and VGGFace [27].**

The remainder of the paper is organized as follows. Section 2 describes image attribute editing GANs and open-source face recognition networks analyzed in the work. Section 3 describes the experimental protocols followed in this work. Section 4 reports and analyzes the findings. Section 5 concludes the paper.

2   Proposed Study

In this work, we investigate how GAN-induced attribute manipulations affect face recognition. In the process, we will review the following research questions through our study.

1. Does GAN-based attribute editing only produce perceptual changes in face images?
2. Are there certain attribute manipulations that are more detrimental than others on face verification performance?

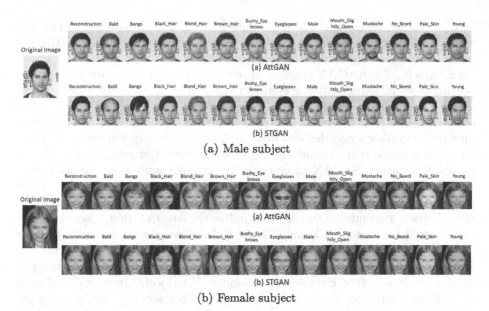

Fig. 1. Examples of attribute-manipulated images using AttGAN and STGAN for a (a) male subject and a (b) female subject. To demonstrate the ability of the GAN as a faithful autoencoder, 'Reconstruction' images are also displayed.

3. Is the impact of GAN-based manipulations consistent across different face recognition networks?

To answer the above questions, we used two GAN-based image editing deep networks, *viz.*, AttGAN and STGAN to modify thirteen attributes on a set of face images from the CelebA dataset. The edited images are then compared with the original face images in terms of biometric utility using two deep learning-based face recognition networks, namely, ArcFace and VGGFace. We hypothesize that digital manipulations induced using GANs can alter the visual perceptibility of the images, but more importantly, affect the biometric utility of the images. Note that these attributes are not originally present in the images: they are artificially induced. Although such manipulations may seem innocuous, they can produce unexpected changes in the face recognition performance and should be handled cautiously. We now discuss the GANs used for attribute manipulation and the deep face networks considered in this work.

AttGAN [11]: It can perform binary facial attribute manipulation by modeling the relationship between the attributes and the latent representation of the face. It consists of an encoder, a decoder, an attribute classification network and a discriminator. The attribute classifier imposes an attribute classification constraint to ensure that the generated image possesses the desired attribute. Reconstruction learning is introduced such that the generated image mimics the original image, *i.e.*, only the desired attribute should change without compromising the integrity of the remaining details in the image. Finally, adversarial learning maintains the overall visual realism of the generated images. The network allows high quality facial attribute editing with control over the attribute intensity and accommodates changes in the attribute style.

STGAN [17]: AttGAN employs an encoder-decoder structure with spatial pooling or downsampling that results in reduction in the resolution and irrecoverable loss of fine details. Therefore, the generated images are susceptible to loss of features and look blurred. Skip connections are introduced in AttGAN that directly concatenate encoder and decoder features and can improve the reconstruction image quality but at the expense of reduced attribute manipulation ability. In contrast, STGAN adopts selective transfer units that can adaptively transform the encoder features supervised by the attributes to be edited. STGAN accepts the difference between the target and source attribute vector, known as the difference attribute vector, as input unlike the AttGAN that takes the entire target attribute vector as input. Taking the difference vector results in more controlled manipulation of the attribute and simplifies the training process.

VGGFace [27]: "Very deep" convolutional neural networks are bootstrapped to learn a N-way face classifier to recognize N subjects. It is designed such that the network associates each training image to a score vector by using the final fully connected layer that comprises N linear predictors. Each image is mapped to one of the N identities present during training. The score vector needs fine-tuning to perform verification by comparing face descriptors learned in the Euclidean space. To that end, triplet-loss is employed during training to learn a compact face representation (projection) that is well separated across disjoint identities.

ArcFace [6]: Existing face recognition methods attempt to directly learn the face embedding using a softmax loss function or a triplet loss function. However, each of these embedding approaches suffer from drawbacks. Although softmax loss is effective on closed-set face recognition, the face representations are not discriminative enough for open-set face recognition. Triplet loss can cause a huge number of face triplets for large datasets, and semi-hard triplet mining is challenging for effective training. In contrast, additive angular margin loss (ArcFace) optimises the geodesic distance margin by establishing correspondence between the angle and arc in normalized hypersphere. Due to its concise geometric interpretation, ArcFace can provide highly discriminative features for face recognition, and has become one of the most widely-used open-source deep face recognition networks.

3   Experiments

We used 2,641 images belonging to 853 unique individuals with an average of ~3 images per subject from the CelebA [19] dataset for conducting the investigative study in this work. Next, we edited each of these images to alter 13 attributes, one at a time, using AttGAN and STGAN to generate $2{,}641 \times 13 \times 2 = 68{,}666$ manipulated images. We used the codes and pre-trained models provided by the original authors of AttGAN [3] and STGAN [25] in our work. The

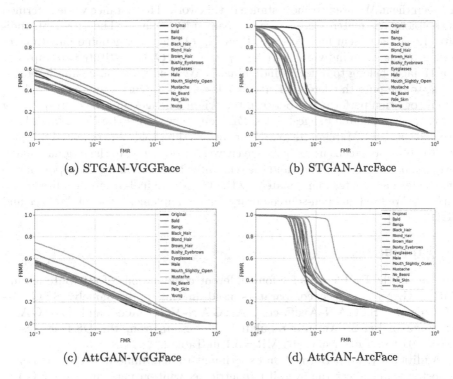

(a) STGAN-VGGFace

(b) STGAN-ArcFace

(c) AttGAN-VGGFace

(d) AttGAN-ArcFace

Fig. 2. DET curves obtained for all pairs of GANs (for attribute editing) and deep face recognition networks (for biometric matching). (a) STGAN-VGGFace, (b) STGAN-ArcFace, (c) AttGAN-VGGFace and (d) AttGAN-ArcFace.

list of attributes edited are as follows: *Bald, Bangs, Black_ Hair, Blond_ Hair, Brown_ Hair, Bushy_ Eyebrows, Eyeglasses, Male, Mouth_ Slightly_ Open, Mustache, No_ Beard, Pale_ Skin,* and *Young.* We selected these thirteen attributes as they were modified using the original AttGAN and STGAN models. Examples of GAN edited images are presented in Figs. 1(a) and 1(b). Note that the attributes are applied in a toggle fashion. For example, the *Male* attribute changes the face image of the male individual by inducing makeup to impart a feminine appearance (see Fig. 1(a) ninth image from the left), while the same attribute induces facial hair in the face image of the female subject to impart a masculine appearance (see Fig. 1(b) ninth image from the left). We can also observe that the manipulations are not identical across the two GANs and can manifest differently across different sexes. For example, attribute *Bald* is more effectively induced by STGAN compared to AttGAN and has a more pronounced effect on male images than female images (see Figs. 1(a) and (b) second image from the left). To perform quantitative evaluation, we compared an original image (I_i) with its respective attribute manipulated image (O_j) using a biometric comparator, $\mathcal{B}(I_i, O_j)$, where $\mathcal{B}(\cdot, \cdot)$ extracts face representations from each image and computes the vector distance between them. We used cosine distance in this work. The distance value is termed as the biometric match score between a pair of face images. The subscripts indicate the subject identifier. If $i = j$, then (I_i, O_j) forms a genuine pair (images belong to the same individual). If $i \neq j$, then (I_i, O_j) constitutes an impostor pair (images belong to different individuals). We used the genuine and impostor scores to compute the detection error trade-off (DET) curve, and compared the face recognition performance between the original images and the corresponding attribute manipulated images. In the DET curve, we plot False Non-Match Rate (FNMR) vs. False Match Rate (FMR) at various thresholds. We repeated this process to obtain fourteen curves, viz., one curve corresponding to the original images (original-original comparison) and the remaining thirteen curves corresponding to the thirteen attributes manipulated by the GAN (original-attribute edited comparison). We used an open-source library for the implementation of ArcFace and VGGFace [2].

4   Findings

We present the DET curves for four different combinations of attribute manipulating GANs and face comparators used in this work, namely, **STGAN-VGGFace**, **STGAN-ArcFace**, **AttGAN-VGGFace** and **AttGAN-ArcFace** in Fig. 2. We also tabulated the results from the DET curves at FMR = 0.01 in Table 1 and at FMR = 0.1 in Table 2.

Additionally, we performed an experiment to determine how the number of impostor scores affect the overall biometric recognition performance for GAN-edited images. The number of scores corresponding to genuine pairs was $\sim$10K, and the number of scores corresponding to impostor pairs was $\sim$7M. Due to memory constraints, we selected a subset of impostor scores for plotting the DET curves. We randomly selected impostor scores, without replacement, in factors of 5X, 10X, 50X and 100X of the total number of genuine scores (10K). This resulted in 50K, 100K, 500K and 1M impostor scores, respectively. We observed that the DET curves obtained by varying the number of impostor scores from the AttGAN-ArcFace combination are almost identical. See Fig. 3. Therefore, for the remaining three combinations, we used the entire set of genuine scores but restricted to utilizing one million impostor scores.

Analysis: In Table 1, we reported the results @FMR = 0.01. We observed that the attribute 'Eyeglasses', a *facial* attribute produced the **highest** degradation in the biometric recognition performance (see the red colored cells). AttGAN-ArcFace achieved FNMR = 0.98 compared to the original performance of FNMR = 0.25 @FMR = 0.01 (reduction in performance by 73%). Note that we reported the reduction as the difference between the FNMR obtained for modified images and the original images. The DET curve indicated as *Original* in Fig. 2 denotes the face recognition performance computed using only the unmodified images. AttGAN-VGGFace achieved FNMR = 0.52 compared to the original performance of FNMR = 0.32 @FMR = 0.01 (reduction in performance by 20%). STGAN-ArcFace achieved FNMR = 0.31 compared to the original performance of FNMR = 0.25 @FMR = 0.01 (reduction in performance by

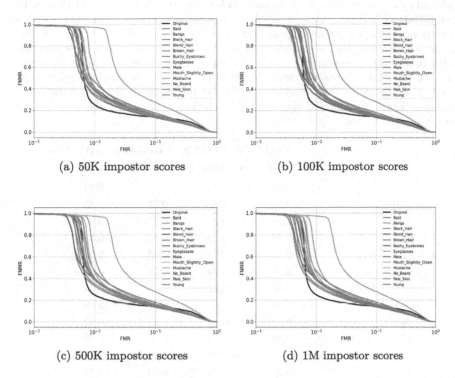

(a) 50K impostor scores

(b) 100K impostor scores

(c) 500K impostor scores

(d) 1M impostor scores

Fig. 3. DET curves of AttGAN-ArcFace obtained after varying the number of impostor scores (a) 50K, (b) 100K, (c) 500K and (d) 1M. We varied the number of impostor scores with respect to the number of genuine scores (∼10K) in factors of 5X, 10X, 50X and 100X, respectively. Note the DET curves show minimal variations.

6%). STGAN-VGGFace achieved FNMR = 0.39 compared to the original performance of FNMR = 0.32 @FMR = 0.01 (reduction in performance by 7%). The **second highest** degradation was caused due to the change in 'Male', a *demographic* attribute. AttGAN-ArcFace achieved FNMR = 0.47 compared to the original performance of FNMR = 0.25 @FMR = 0.01 (reduction in performance by 22%). AttGAN-VGGFace achieved FNMR = 0.43 compared to the original performance of FNMR = 0.32 @FMR = 0.01 (reduction in performance by 11%). STGAN-ArcFace achieved FNMR = 0.30 compared to the original performance of FNMR = 0.25 @FMR = 0.01 (reduction in performance by 5%). STGAN-VGGFace achieved FNMR = 0.42 compared to the original performance of FNMR = 0.32 @FMR = 0.01 (reduction in performance by 10%). STGAN-ArcFace achieved FNMR = 0.18 compared to the original performance of FNMR = 0.25 @FMR = 0.01 (improvement in performance by 7%) for the attribute 'Pale_Skin'. In Table 2, we reported the results @FMR = 0.1. We observed that the attributes seem to improve the recognition performance by up to 4% in FNMR for STGAN-ArcFace. On the contrary, for the remaining

Table 1. Face recognition performance: False Non-Match Rate (FNMR) at a False Match Rate **(FMR) = 0.01** for attribute manipulated images. The red colored cells correspond to the maximum degradation (if any) in the biometric recognition performance compared to the original in each column. The green colored cells correspond to the maximum improvement (if any) in the biometric recognition performance compared to the original in each column. Identical performance results in multiple colored cells within a column. Note majority of the attributes resulted in degradation. The attribute 'Eyeglasses' caused the worst degradation in biometric recognition performance followed by the 'Male' attribute.

	STGAN-VGGFace	STGAN-ArcFace	AttGAN-VGGFace	AttGAN-ArcFace
Original	0.32	0.25	0.32	0.25
Bald	0.34	0.22	0.35	0.40
Bangs	0.28	0.23	0.35	0.57
Black_Hair	0.29	0.20	0.33	0.35
Blond_Hair	0.30	0.21	0.33	0.39
Brown_hair	0.26	0.19	0.31	0.34
Bushy_Eyebrows	0.30	0.22	0.35	0.40
Eyeglasses	0.39	0.31	0.52	0.98
Male	0.42	0.30	0.43	0.47
Mouth_Slightly_Open	0.26	0.21	0.32	0.38
Mustache	0.28	0.20	0.34	0.45
No_Beard	0.28	0.20	0.33	0.41
Pale_Skin	0.27	0.18	0.34	0.40
Young	0.31	0.22	0.37	0.40

three sets, *viz.*, STGAN-VGGFace, AttGAN-ArcFace and AttGAN-VGGFace, we continued to observe a drop in recognition performance with 'Eyeglasses' resulting in the worst drop in performance by 14%, followed by 'Male' resulting in the second highest drop in performance by 7%. Now, let us review the questions posited at the beginning of the paper.

Question #1: Does GAN-based attribute editing only produce perceptual changes in face images?

Observation: **No.** GAN-based attribute editing not only alters the perceptual quality of the images but also significantly impacts the biometric recognition performance. See Tables 1 and 2, where a majority of the attributes strongly degraded the face recognition performance.

Table 2. Face recognition performance: False Non-Match Rate (FNMR) at a False Match Rate **(FMR)** = **0.1** for attribute manipulated images. The red colored cells correspond to the maximum degradation (if any) in the biometric recognition performance compared to the original in each column. The green colored cells correspond to the maximum improvement (if any) in the biometric recognition performance compared to the original in each column. Identical performance results in multiple colored cells within a column. Note @FMR = 0.1, STGAN-ArcFace (attribute editing using STGAN and face matching using ArcFace) caused the least degradation in face recognition.

	STGAN-VGGFace	STGAN-ArcFace	AttGAN-VGGFace	AttGAN-ArcFace
Original	0.10	0.14	0.10	0.14
Bald	0.12	0.12	0.11	0.16
Bangs	0.09	0.11	0.11	0.17
Black_Hair	0.09	0.10	0.11	0.14
Blond_Hair	0.10	0.11	0.10	0.15
Brown_hair	0.08	0.10	0.10	0.14
Bushy_Eyebrows	0.09	0.11	0.11	0.16
Eyeglasses	0.13	0.13	0.19	0.28
Male	0.17	0.14	0.16	0.18
Mouth_Slightly_Open	0.08	0.10	0.10	0.15
Mustache	0.09	0.10	0.10	0.16
No_Beard	0.08	0.10	0.10	0.16
Pale_Skin	0.08	0.10	0.10	0.16
Young	0.10	0.11	0.13	0.16

Question #2: Are there certain attribute manipulations that are more detrimental than others on face verification performance?

Observation: **Yes.** Editing of 'Eyeglasses' attribute caused a significant degradation in FNMR by up to 73% @FMR = 0.01 for AttGAN-ArcFace. It was followed by the 'Male' attribute that caused the second highest degradation in FNMR by up to 22% @FMR = 0.01 for AttGAN-ArcFace. Surprisingly, a facial attribute, 'Eyeglasses' and a demographic attribute, 'Male', when edited separately, were responsible for significant degradation in the biometric recognition performance in a majority of the scenarios.

Question #3: Is the impact of GAN-based manipulations consistent across different face recognition networks?

Observation: **No.** The impact of GAN-based attribute manipulations on face recognition depends on two factors, firstly, which GAN was used to perform the attribute editing operation, and secondly, which face recognition network was used to measure the biometric recognition performance. For example, the 'Bald' attribute caused degradation in the performance for AttGAN, *irrespective* of which face matcher was used. However, the same attribute caused improvement in the face recognition accuracy for STGAN when ArcFace was used as the face matcher, but caused reduction in the recognition performance when VGGFace was used as the face comparator. Similar findings were observed for the 'Bangs' attribute.

Fig. 4. Examples depicting 'Male' attribute edited using STGAN and AttGAN, respectively, in male (top row) and female (bottom row) individuals. AttGAN output images appear to contain more visual artifacts compared to STGAN outputs.

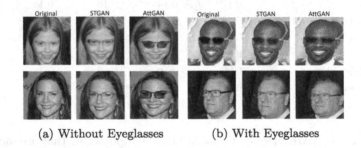

(a) Without Eyeglasses   (b) With Eyeglasses

Fig. 5. Examples depicting 'Eyeglasses' attribute edited using STGAN and AttGAN, respectively, in original images (a) Without Eyeglasses and (b) With Eyeglasses. Note in images containing eyeglasses, the GANs fail to remove the glasses completely, instead they lighten the shades of the eyeglasses or the glass rims. STGAN outputs appear better for images with and without eyeglasses.

To investigate the possibility of **dataset-specific bias**, we selected 495 images from the Labeled Faces in-the-Wild (LFW) dataset [12] belonging to 100 individuals, and applied attribute editing using AttGAN. AttGAN resulted in the worst drop in performance on the CelebA dataset, so we employed it for this experiment. This is done to examine whether the impact of attribute editing on face recognition performance manifests across datasets. Next, we computed the face recognition performance between the original and the attribute-edited images using ArcFace and VGGFace comparators and observed the following results. 'Eyeglasses' attribute editing resulted in the worst degradation in the performance by 83% while using ArcFace and by 37% while using VGGFace in terms of FNMR at FMR $= 0.01$. It was followed by 'Bangs' attribute resulting in

Table 3. Face recognition performance: False Non-Match Rate (FNMR) at a False Match Rate **(FMR)** = **0.01/0.1** for attribute manipulated images on the **LFW dataset**. The red colored cells correspond to the maximum degradation (if any) in the biometric recognition performance compared to the original in each column. Note *all* of the attributes resulted in degradation. 'Eyeglasses' caused the worst degradation in biometric recognition performance.

	AttGAN-ArcFace	AttGAN-VGGFace
Original	0.17/0.11	0.39/0.17
Bald	0.39/0.16	0.57/0.27
Bangs	0.86/0.26	0.71/0.39
Black_Hair	0.33/0.14	0.56/0.27
Blond_Hair	0.36/0.14	0.59/0.27
Brown_hair	0.33/0.14	0.59/0.31
Bushy_Eyebrows	0.50/0.20	0.68/0.35
Eyeglasses	0.99/0.43	0.77/0.49
Male	0.26/0.11	0.47/0.23
Mouth_Slightly_Open	0.30/0.12	0.51/0.23
Mustache	0.36/0.16	0.56/0.28
No_Beard	0.33/0.14	0.55/0.26
Pale_Skin	0.33/0.14	0.56/0.26
Young	0.32/0.13	0.55/0.26

second-highest degradation in the performance by 69% while using ArcFace and by 32% while using VGGFace in terms of FNMR at FMR = 0.01. See Table 3.

To investigate the possibility of **GAN-specific artifacts**, we compared the 'Reconstructed' images with the attribute edited images, specifically, the 'Eyeglasses' and 'Male' attribute edited images, to evaluate the face recognition performance. This is done to assess whether face recognition performance is affected solely by attribute editing or influenced by GAN-specific artifacts. Note that 'Reconstructed' images are faithful reconstruction of 'Original' images that demonstrate the fidelity of the GAN as an effective autoencoder. See Table 4 for FNMR at FMR = 0.01 and 0.1 for Reconstructed-Reconstructed, Reconstructed-Eyeglasses and Reconstructed-Male comparisons. We observed similar degradation in performance when comparing attribute edited images with GAN-reconstructed images by up to 47% for 'Eyeglasses' attribute and by up to 12% for 'Male' attribute in terms of FNMR at FMR = 0.01. The results indicate that AttGAN has an overall weaker reconstruction and attribute editing capability than STGAN.

The implications of our findings are as follows. Bias due to naturally prevalent demographic factors in automated face recognition systems can be further aggravated when attributes are digitally modified. Digitally altering the sex

Table 4. Face recognition performance: False Non-Match Rate (FNMR) at a False Match Rate **(FMR) = 0.01/0.1** for attribute manipulated images. We report the face recognition performance by comparing 'Reconstructed' images with 'Eyeglasses' attribute and 'Male' attribute edited images.

	STGAN-VGGFace	STGAN-ArcFace	AttGAN-VGGFace	AttGAN-ArcFace
Reconstructed	0.30/0.08	0.21/0.10	0.42/0.12	0.49/0.20
Eyeglasses	0.38/0.12	0.27/0.11	0.50/0.19	0.96/0.29
Male	0.42/0.16	0.28/0.12	0.47/0.20	0.46/0.19

cues (denoted by 'Male' attribute) can be considered as manipulating a demographic attribute. It involves adding facial hair to images of female individuals and adding makeup to impart feminine appearance to images of male individuals. See Fig. 4. These artificial manipulations affect face recognition performance. Surprisingly, altering a facial attribute like 'Eyeglasses' caused an excessive degradation in face recognition performance. Modifying the 'Eyeglasses' attribute involves adding glasses to individual face images where no eyeglasses are present and removing eyeglasses in the images where the individual is wearing one. See Fig. 5. AttGAN struggles with addition as well as removal of eyeglasses from the images, and, instead, produces visually apparent artifacts that might be responsible for significant degradation in the biometric recognition performance. Removal of glasses is particularly hard: the GANs are only able to lighten the lens shades or the color of the eyeglass frames, but not completely remove the glasses. To check for any statistical variation between the results produced by AttGAN for the 'Eyeglasses' attribute, we repeated the experiment with the original images five times. Each time, we followed the same procedure and executed basic attribute editing and not attribute sliding (sliding regulates the intensity of attribute modification). We obtained exactly identical results for each of the five runs, *i.e.,* a decrease by 73% in FNMR @FMR = 0.01. On the LFW dataset, 'Eyeglasses' attribute resulted in a decrease by up to 83% in FNMR @FMR = 0.01, while 'Bangs', also a type of facial attribute, reduced the biometric recognition performance by up to 69%. Therefore, we observed that 'Eyeglasses' attribute editing reduced the biometric recognition performance considerably on both CelebA and LFW datasets. Although the exact reason responsible for significant degradation in face recognition performance caused by 'Eyeglasses' attribute editing is unknown, we speculate that the attribute manipulations may produce severe changes in texture around the facial landmarks resulting in the drop in face recognition performance.

Therefore, our findings indicate that digitally modified attributes, both demographic and facial, can have a major impact on automated face recognition systems and can potentially introduce new biases that require further examination.

5 Conclusion

In this paper, we examined the impact of GAN-based attribute editing on face images in terms of face recognition performance. GAN-generated images are typically evaluated with respect to visual realism but their influence on biometric recognition is rarely analyzed. Therefore, we studied face recognition performance obtained using ArcFace and VGGFace after modifying thirteen attributes via AttGAN and STGAN on a total of ~68,000 images belonging to 853 individuals from the CelebA dataset. Our findings indicated some interesting aspects: (i) Insertion or deletion of eyeglasses from a face image can significantly impair biometric recognition performance by up to 73%. Digitally modifying the sex cues caused the second highest degradation in the performance by up to 22%. (ii) There can be an artificial boost in the recognition accuracy by up to 7% depending on the GAN used to modify the attributes and the deep learning-based face recognition network used to evaluate the biometric performance. Similar observations were reported when tested on a different dataset. Our findings indicate that attribute manipulations accomplished via GANs can significantly affect automated face recognition performance and need extensive analysis. Future work will focus on examining the effect of editing multiple attributes simultaneously, in a single face image, on face recognition.

References

1. Albiero, V., Zhang, K., King, M.C., Bowyer, K.W.: Gendered differences in face recognition accuracy explained by hairstyles, makeup, and facial morphology. IEEE Trans. Inf. Forensics Secur. **17**, 127–137 (2022)
2. ArcFace and VGGFace implementation. https://pypi.org/project/deepface/. Accessed 18 May 2022
3. AttGAN implementation. https://github.com/LynnHo/AttGAN-Tensorflow. Accessed 18 May 2022
4. Bharati, A., Singh, R., Vatsa, M., Bowyer, K.W.: Detecting facial retouching using supervised deep learning. IEEE Trans. Inf. Forensics Secur. **11**(9), 1903–1913 (2016)
5. Chen, H.J., Hui, K.M., Wang, S.Y., Tsao, L.W., Shuai, H.H., Cheng, W.H.: Beauty-Glow: on-demand makeup transfer framework with reversible generative network. In: IEEE/CVF Conference on Computer Vision and Pattern Recognition (CVPR), pp. 10034–10042 (2019)
6. Deng, J., Guo, J., Xue, N., Zafeiriou, S.: ArcFace: additive angular margin loss for deep face recognition. In: IEEE/CVF Conference on Computer Vision and Pattern Recognition (CVPR), pp. 4685–4694 (2019)
7. FaceApp. https://www.faceapp.com/. Accessed 17 May 2022
8. Gong, S., Liu, X., Jain, A.K.: Jointly de-biasing face recognition and demographic attribute estimation. In: Vedaldi, A., Bischof, H., Brox, T., Frahm, J.-M. (eds.) ECCV 2020. LNCS, vol. 12374, pp. 330–347. Springer, Cham (2020). https://doi.org/10.1007/978-3-030-58526-6_20
9. Grother, P., Ngan, M., Hanaoka, K.: Face Recognition Vendor Test (FRVT) Part 3: Demographic Effects. NIST IR 8280 (2019). https://nvlpubs.nist.gov/nistpubs/ir/2019/NIST.IR.8280.pdf

10. Gutierrez, N.R., Theobald, B., Ranjan, A., Abdelaziz, A.H., Apostoloff, N.: MorphGAN: controllable one-shot face synthesis. In: British Machine Vision Conference (BMVC) (2021)

11. He, Z., Zuo, W., Kan, M., Shan, S., Chen, X.: AttGAN: facial attribute editing by only changing what you want. IEEE Trans. Image Process. **28**(11), 5464–5478 (2019)

12. Huang, G.B., Ramesh, M., Berg, T., Learned-Miller, E.: Labeled faces in the wild: a database for studying face recognition in unconstrained environments. Technical report 07–49, University of Massachusetts, Amherst, October 2007

13. Huang, Y., et al.: FakeLocator: robust localization of GAN-based face manipulations via semantic segmentation networks with bells and whistles. ArXiv (2022)

14. Klare, B.F., Burge, M.J., Klontz, J.C., Vorder Bruegge, R.W., Jain, A.K.: Face recognition performance: role of demographic information. IEEE Trans. Inf. Forensics Secur. **7**(6), 1789–1801 (2012)

15. Krishnan, A., Almadan, A., Rattani, A.: Understanding fairness of gender classification algorithms across gender-race groups. In: 19th IEEE International Conference on Machine Learning and Applications (ICMLA), pp. 1028–1035 (2020)

16. Kwak, J., Han, D.K., Ko, H.: CAFE-GAN: arbitrary face attribute editing with complementary attention feature. In: Vedaldi, A., Bischof, H., Brox, T., Frahm, J.-M. (eds.) ECCV 2020. LNCS, vol. 12359, pp. 524–540. Springer, Cham (2020). https://doi.org/10.1007/978-3-030-58568-6_31

17. Liu, M., et al.: STGAN: a unified selective transfer network for arbitrary image attribute editing. In: IEEE/CVF Conference on Computer Vision and Pattern Recognition (CVPR), pp. 3668–3677 (2019)

18. Liu, S., Li, D., Cao, T., Sun, Y., Hu, Y., Ji, J.: GAN-based face attribute editing. IEEE Access **8**, 34854–34867 (2020)

19. Liu, Z., Luo, P., Wang, X., Tang, X.: Deep learning face attributes in the wild. In: Proceedings of International Conference on Computer Vision, December 2015

20. Mirjalili, V., Raschka, S., Ross, A.: PrivacyNet: semi-adversarial networks for multi-attribute face privacy. IEEE Trans. Image Process. **29**, 9400–9412 (2020)

21. NIST Study Evaluates Effects of Race, Age, Sex on Face Recognition Software. https://www.nist.gov/news-events/news/2019/12/nist-study-evaluates-effects-race-age-sex-face-recognition-software. Accessed 4 May 2022

22. Phillips, P.J., Flynn, P.J., Bowyer, K.W.: Lessons from collecting a million biometric samples. Image Vis. Comput. **58**, 96–107 (2017)

23. Ross, A., et al.: Some research problems in biometrics: the future beckons. In: International Conference on Biometrics (ICB), pp. 1–8 (2019)

24. Sgroi, A., Garvey, H., Bowyer, K., Flynn, P.: Location matters: a study of the effects of environment on facial recognition for biometric security. In: 11th IEEE International Conference and Workshops on Automatic Face and Gesture Recognition, vol. 02, pp. 1–7 (2015)

25. STGAN implementation. https://github.com/csmliu/STGAN. Accessed 18 May 2022

26. Sun, R., Huang, C., Zhu, H., Ma, L.: Mask-aware photorealistic facial attribute manipulation. In: Computational Visual Media, vol. 7, pp. 363–374 (2021)

27. Taigman, Y., Yang, M., Ranzato, M., Wolf, L.: DeepFace: closing the gap to human-level performance in face verification. In: IEEE Conference on Computer Vision and Pattern Recognition, pp. 1701–1708 (2014)

28. Terhörst, P., et al.: A comprehensive study on face recognition biases beyond demographics. IEEE Trans. Technol. Soc. **3**(1), 16–30 (2022)

29. Yang, H., Huang, D., Wang, Y., Jain, A.K.: Learning face age progression: a pyramid architecture of GANs. In: IEEE/CVF Conference on Computer Vision and Pattern Recognition, pp. 31–39 (2018)
30. Yu, N., Davis, L., Fritz, M.: Attributing fake images to GANs: learning and analyzing GAN fingerprints. In: IEEE/CVF International Conference on Computer Vision, pp. 7555–7565 (2019)

Using PGAN to Create Synthetic Face Images to Reduce Bias in Biometric Systems

Andrea Bozzitelli, Pia Cavasinni di Benedetto, and Maria De Marsico$^{(\boxtimes)}$ (iD)

Department of Computer Science, Sapienza University of Rome, Rome, Italy
{bozzitelli.1647510,cavasinnidibenedetto.1665706}@studenti.uniroma1.it,
demarsico@di.uniroma1.it

Abstract. This work does not aim to advance the state of the art for face demographic classification systems, but rather to show how synthetic images can help tackle demographic unbalance in training them. The problem of demographic bias in both face recognition and face analysis has often been underlined in recent literature, with controversial experimental results. The outcomes presented here both confirm the advantage of using synthetic face images to add samples to under-represented classes and suggest that the achieved performance increase is proportional to the starting unbalance.

Keywords: Face Demographic Classification · Demographic Bias · Training data re-balancing · Synthetic Images

1 Introduction

The analysis reported in this paper quantitatively assesses how solving the possible unbalance in age, gender, and ethnicity of training face sets can positively affect the performance of demographic classification systems [7]. Above all, it determines that the improvement is directly proportional to the initial unbalance: the greater the unbalance, the greater the advantage of re-balancing the training dataset. It is worth underlining that face demographic classification can be both useful in itself, and also provide soft biometric information to be used in a complementary way with the face trait. In a more complex architecture, that information can be used as a preliminary filter for recognition [4,14]. The classification of the demographic attributes of a face can be used in a cascade to trigger a specific recognizer trained on faces with the same characteristics. Strategies aiming at a preliminary correct demographic classification may alleviate the often discussed problem of demographic bias in face recognition. However, also such correct classification calls for well-balanced training datasets. This work proposes an approach to balancing.

Ethical Guidelines for Trustworthy AI [2] contain 4 principles of reliability that aim at a compromise between technological progress and respect for human

© Springer Nature Switzerland AG 2023
J.-J. Rousseau and B. Kapralos (Eds.): ICPR 2022 Workshops, LNCS 13645, pp. 536–550, 2023.
https://doi.org/10.1007/978-3-031-37731-0_39

rights. They are (1) Respect for human autonomy; (2) Prevention of harm; (3) Fairness; (4) Explicability. UTKface [27] is the popular starting dataset used for the experiments. It is quite unbalanced with respect to age, gender, and ethnicity. This can cause biased training on the underrepresented classes, which is a critical ethical issue, especially with social or cultural minorities. This clashes with the third principle and could lead to the violation of other principles as well if a system based on machine learning or deep learning biased algorithms does not give equal opportunities or causes unjustified prejudice to people of a certain age, gender, or ethnicity. It is possible to improve the fairness of the demographic classification by re-balancing the existing training data. From a different point of view, in the case of biometrics, and especially face, personal data need to be treated in a more careful way because there is a greater possibility of colliding with human rights. Their collection, processing, use, and especially their disclosure raises delicate issues. Joining these considerations, it is interesting to asses whether the collection of additional data can be substituted by the creation of synthetic images. Two issues have encouraged the deepening of this theme:

i) checking the feasibility of using synthetic images for system training, given the increasingly restrictive data privacy protection rules (i.e., art. 13 of GDPR UE/2016/679[1]);

ii) assessing a quantitative relationship between balancing the training classes by adding synthetic images and the possible accuracy improvement of the demographic classification.

These goals were tackled by using a deep learning GAN-based algorithm to create synthetic images of people's faces with specific attributes of age, gender, and ethnicity. The model underlying the image synthesis is A2F_P (Attributes to Faces - Progressive), inspired by the Att2MFace network [5]. The obtained images were added to UTKface to improve the performance of a demographic classification system. The analysis of the re-balancing effect entails comparing the performance of two models relying on a CNN (Convolutional Neural Network) architecture for the classification of age, gender, and ethnicity. The training phases of the two models, called Model_Unbal and Model_Bal, respectively use the unbalanced training set and the re-balanced one after the addition of synthetic images for the underrepresented classes.

2 Related Work

The possible demographic bias in face recognition algorithms has long been a controversial topic in the biometric community. One of the first experimental works to analyze a possible other-race effect in face recognition [21] compares the results of a so-called Western algorithm, the fusion of eight algorithms from Western countries, and a so-called East Asian algorithm, from five algorithms from East Asia. They were tested on all the available East Asian and Caucasian

---

[1] https://gdpr-info.eu/.

face pairs from the FRVT 2006 database [22]. At low false acceptance rates, the Western algorithm recognized Caucasian faces more accurately than East Asian ones and the contrary happened for the East Asian algorithm. The more systematic 2012 study in [14] relies on a large-scale analysis of face recognition performance on race/ethnicity, gender, and age. The analysis considers six face recognition algorithms, three commercial off-the-shelf (COTS) systems, two face recognition algorithms that do not use training data (Uniform Local Binary Patterns (LBP) [19] and Gabor Features [23]), and a trainable face recognition algorithm, the Spectrally Sampled Structural Subspace Features algorithm [14]. The conclusions seem to be confirmed by more recent works with different approaches: the female, Black, and younger groups are generally more difficult to recognize for all matchers. Training on datasets well distributed across all demographics is critical to reduce face matcher vulnerabilities on specific demographic cohorts. At the same time, recognition performance generally improves on any cohort when submitting its probes to systems trained exclusively on that same race/ethnicity/age. Therefore the authors of [14] suggest a human-in-the-loop approach, where an operator can choose among a suite of multiple face recognition systems, trained on different demographic cohorts, based on the human evaluation of the demographic information of a given probe. Since this is not always possible, e.g., in unattended conditions, [4] suggests a similar multi-expert strategy with a final automatic selection of the most reliable response. As an alternative, a robust preliminary demographic classification can channel the input towards the specialized recognizer. A recent study [6] draws similar conclusions: demographic factors can have a large influence on various currently biased biometric algorithms. Biometric performance is lower for females and youngest subjects, and the classification of demographics from facial images is lower for dark-skinned females. Deep learning has not solved the problem completely. Several works have focused on gender bias. Using a quite small dataset, [11] reports higher false match rates for under-40 African-American and Caucasian females. African-American females achieve a higher false match rate also when over 40. The study in [3] reports the results of using the same COTS matcher on images from eleven different automated kiosks, while the experiments in [16] use deep CNN matchers and datasets from the IARPA Janus program to assess the effect of various covariates. Both studies report a lower accuracy for females. Training data appears of paramount importance to produce a fair matching.

Collecting huge collections of personal images is a hard and time-consuming task, also subject to privacy-preserving regulations. Adding synthetic data seems to be a viable strategy that deserves exploration. Effective strategies should allow the creation of synthetic images possibly tuning different combinations of demographic characteristics. Three recent examples are especially interesting, all relying on Generative Adversarial Networks (GANs) [8]. The approach in [1] provides a tool for measuring demographic bias on recognition. It exploits a GAN (Generator) to synthesize "transects". These are grids of images, obtained by traversing the generator's latent space in selected attribute-specific directions to modify synthetic faces accordingly. The directions are learned using randomly sampled faces and human annotators. A different approach to image synthesis maps visual attributes onto new images, as in [26]. A vector of visual attributes is extracted from a natural language description; afterward, this vector is combined with learned latent factors to generate image samples. Along a similar line, [25] proposes a synthesis approach based on attribute-labels and starts by learning text feature representations capturing important visual details. A Deep Conditional Convolutional Generative Adversarial Network (DCGAN) [20] is used to edit/modify images based on attributes to implement an image-to-image translation. It is possible to create images with associated class labels also with AC-GAN [18], that exploits auxiliary classifiers. During the training phase, the generator receives input data related to the class of the image to be generated, while the discriminator has the task of providing both a probability distribution related to the sources and a probability distribution on the class labels. The excellent results in the use of AC-GAN in [5] led to taking inspiration from the proposed Att2MFace network to create synthetic images to use in the present study to balance age, gender, and ethnicity attributes. The mentioned work also relies on PGANs (Progressive Generative Adversarial Network) [13] to create high-resolution synthetic images. This network inspired the architecture used in this work: a more detailed presentation is included in Sect. 3.

3   Materials and Methods

3.1   UTKface Dataset

The dataset for this study is UTKface[2]. It contains over 20,000 face images annotated with age, gender, and ethnicity, with significant variation in, e.g., pose, expression, illumination, occlusion, and resolution. Age is 0–116, gender is either 0 (male) or 1 (female), and race is an integer from 0 to 4 (White, Black, Asian, Indian, and Others including Hispanic, Latino, Middle Eastern).

Some preliminary cleaning operations slightly reduced the number of images. The first skimming entailed the supervised removal of about 30 either damaged or occluded images. At the end of this process, the dataset contained 23,672 elements. A further removal involved images with some missing data (3 images). It was immediately evident that the *Others* ethnicity class is too generic and with too many disparate ethnicities included. This could cause confusion in the somatic features used by the networks and the production of synthetic images with mixed and far-fetched somatic traits. While the former can be realistic in the real world, the latter could have created a bias. After some preliminary tests, the adopted strategy was to drop this class and then delete included samples.

As far as age is concerned, a different redefinition strategy was adopted based on macro-classes: 1) 'children', denoting people under 15 years old; 2) 'young', denoting people between 15 and 24 years old; 3) 'adult', denoting people between 25 and 64 years old; 4) 'senior', denoting people between 65 and 84 years old; 5) 'old', denoting people over 85 years old. The resulting total number of images was 21,981. As a result of these changes, the resulting dataset classes present

---

[2] https://susanqq.github.io/UTKFace/.

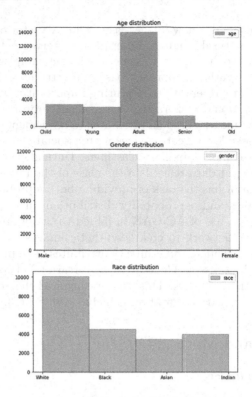

Fig. 1. Demographic distribution in the reorganized UTKFace dataset.

the distributions in Fig. 1. The "Adult" samples are the majority compared to all the other samples, while "Old" are poorly represented, "Males" are more than "Females", and regarding Ethnicity, the predominant value is "White", while "Asian" is a minority. Table 1 further summarizes the number of samples for every combination of attributes with the respective percentage of images in the dataset. The unbalance for some combinations is dramatic, for example there are only 6 samples for Old Indian Males. Given the small number of deleted images, except for the "Others" groups that were inhomogeneous, the re-organization is not responsible for the unbalance. The last label re-organization step was the mapping of categorical to binary data encoding by One-Hot, a binary-matrices representation of data better suited for learning algorithms. Every possible feature becomes a column of the matrix. These columns are populated with the value 1.0 if the sample has the corresponding characteristic, and 0.0 otherwise.

3.2   Att2MFace Network

The network Att2MFace proposed in [5] is designed to generate synthetic images of faces from precise visual attributes and for different modalities. The goal is achieved by combining the concept of PGAN and AC-GAN, with the addition

Table 1. Number of images and percentages of combinations of demographic attributes.

Gender	Ethnicity	Age	# Samples	Percentage
Male	White	Child	710	3.23 %
		Young	486	2.21 %
		Adult	3606	16.41 %
		Senior	576	2.62 %
		Old	85	0.39 %
	Black	Child	86	0.39 %
		Young	245	1.11 %
		Adult	1823	8.29 %
		Senior	139	0.63 %
		Old	19	0.09 %
	Asian	Child	509	2.32 %
		Young	137	0.62 %
		Adult	780	3.55 %
		Senior	118	0.54 %
		Old	28	0.13 %
	Indian	Child	246	1.12 %
		Young	175	0.80 %
		Adult	1750	7.96 %
		Senior	83	0.38 %
		Old	6	0.03 %
Female	White	Child	780	3.55 %
		Young	666	3.03 %
		Adult	2453	11.16 %
		Senior	485	2.21 %
		Old	212	0.96 %
	Black	Child	109	0.50 %
		Young	346	1.57 %
		Adult	1675	7.62 %
		Senior	54	0.25 %
		Old	22	0.10 %
	Asian	Child	461	2.10 %
		Young	414	1.88 %
		Adult	911	4.14 %
		Senior	28	0.13 %
		Old	44	0.20 %
	Indian	Child	297	1.35 %
		Young	383	1.74 %
		Adult	992	4.51 %
		Senior	26	0.12 %
		Old	16	0.07 %

of modules called multimodal stretch-in (in the discriminator) and multimodal stretch-out (in the generator) to manage multimodality. These modules guarantee effective training with the features of the same subject on each modality. The multimodal stretch-in modules perform embeddings to simultaneously synthesize all the multimodal faces, while the multimodal stretch-out modules are introduced in order to discriminate the different modalities. These two kinds of modules allow the network to provide multiple output representing the face image in different modalities. Att2MFaces is a GAN with a generator G that takes in input two elements, a noise vector that represents a starting noise image in the form of an array of random values, and an attribute vector in the form of an array whose values are 1 when the attribute is true, or 0 otherwise. The attributes taken into account are related to the characteristics of the face, such as open mouth, beard, mustache, male, young, etc. Gender is present, ethnicities are not explored, while for age there is only the young attribute. The focus of the authors is on multimodality. In fact, they manage three different datasets with visible, thermal, polar, sketch, and infrared modalities, namely ARL Multi-modal Face Dataset [12], CelebA-HQ dataset [13], and CASIA NIR-VIS 2.0 Face Database [15]. The discriminator D reads both generated images by G and real images from the dataset and gives feedback either real or fake to the generator, inducing a cascade update of the weights of the entire GAN. To summarize, the output of the model is a set of images depicting the same face but in different modalities (thanks to stretch-in and stretch-out modules), which respect the input attributes (thanks to AC-GAN) and with high resolution (thanks to PGAN). The underlying idea of PGAN is to grow both the generator G and the discriminator D in a progressive way, starting from a low-resolution image and adding layers to the two networks during training, increasing the resolution step by step. The output of Att2MFace network is a set of synthetic images representing the same face but in different modalities, including visible light, near-infrared, and a sketch. See [5] for further details on AttMFace architecture.

3.3   Face Image Synthesis by A2F_P - Attributes to Faces - Progressive

A2F_P uses the strategies of the Att2MFaces, i.e. a PGAN to process high-resolution images while maintaining stability, and enjoining the characteristics of AC-GAN to produce images with specific attributes. Multimodality is not taken into account, since the focus is on age, gender and ethnicity attributes that are the core of this study. As a consequence, in A2F_P it is not necessary to use the multimodal stretch-in and multimodal stretch-out modules since we are only interested in demographic attributes in a single modality. It is worth underlining that the aim of this work is not to propose a new architecture but to remodel a successful existing one to use it for the work purposes. The input of the entire network in the training phase is composed of real images and labels. The dataset also changes since for A2F_P the starting dataset is the re-organized version of the UTKface dataset, i.e., visible face images with relative labels for the attributes to be studied. Space constraints only allow presenting some basic detail of the A2F_P Generator and Discriminator.

Generator. The generator has as its objective the creation of synthetic images starting from a few elements (an initial random image and the attributes of the face) and gradually growing thanks to the feedback given by the discriminator. Given a binary visual attribute vector v_a and a noise vector z (random noise starting image as in [5]), the generator G aims to generate an image compliant with the attribute vector:

$$G(v_a, z) = x_a \qquad (1)$$

Figure 2 shows a basic representation of a generator. Its input is a binary visual attribute vector v_a to synthesize an image with specific characteristics. In the example, the input to the generator G is the vector relative to an adult

Caucasian man, and any noise vector z. The result is an image that agrees with the attributes specified in the input. The generator G network consists of:

1. Normalization Layers, based on pixel-wise equalization that prevents the escalation of the magnitude of the signal.
2. Equalized Linear12 Layers apply a linear transformation to the data as a linear function.
3. Equalized Conv2D13 Layers apply a 2D Convolution to the data: it maps a 2D array of features into another two-dimensional array of different sizes by applying a function based on the weighted average.
4. LeakyReLU activation function, defined as follows:

$$LeakyReLU = \begin{cases} x, & \text{if } x > 0 \\ negative\_slope \times x, & \text{otherwise} \end{cases} \quad (2)$$

With $negative\_slope$ (leakiness) that controls the angle of the negative slope. It is by default $1e - 2$.

As a result of the progressive training, the generator network will contain fewer layers at the beginning and more layers at the end. At each training phase, the size of the image to be generated is increased, starting from 4×4 up to 256×256. The first block of the complete network can be defined as an MLP that has the potential to map attribute vector and noise vector onto a latent space. This block is composed of a Normalization Layer, an Equalized Linear Layer and the LeakyReLU activation function. The input shape of the Normalization Layer is 532, where this value is given by the following formula:

$$input\_shape = dim(z) + dim(v_a) \quad (3)$$

Where $dim(z)$ is the dimensionality of the noise vector $z \in R^{512}$, and $dim(v_a)$ is the dimensionality of the attribute vector $v_a \in R^{d_a}$, with d_a the possible values of the attributes. After the initial block, there are n blocks that map the features from one resolution to another, for each scale of the image. A block of this kind contains two Conv2Ds with 3×3 kernel and padding 1, each followed by the LeakyReLU activation function and the Normalization Layer.

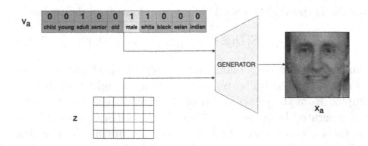

Fig. 2. Face generation from age, gender, and ethnicity attributes.

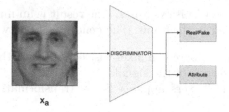

Fig. 3. Discriminator D.

Discriminator. The discriminator has to understand if the image passed by the generator is real or fake and to identify the output attributes of the image (Fig. 3). During training, it receives both images generated by the network and real images from the dataset. The better the discriminator performs in its tasks, the more the generator will produce meticulous images. Given an image, the discriminator D aims to output real/fake feedback and an attribute vector:

$$D(x_a) = d_f, d_a \tag{4}$$

The discriminator consists of the same layers of the generator but, while the generator upscales for each transition block, the discriminator downscales. The input shape starts from $16 \times 256 \times 256$ and ends with $256 \times 4 \times 4$ due to all Conv2D with LeakyReLU activation function and pixel-wise normalization. At the end of feature reduction, two different Equalized Linear levels allow returning d_f and d_a outputs (Fig. 3).

Progressive Training. GAN progressive training starts from a very small resolution of images, up to a larger resolution, e.g., 1024×1024. A2F_P maximum resolution is 256×256. Whenever the resolution grows, a transition block, consisting of several layers as described, is added both to the generator G and to the discriminator D. In A2F_P, the model is composed of exactly 7 progressive training steps with resolutions 4×4, 8×8, 16×16, 32×32, 64×64, 128×128, and 256×256 (Fig. 4). To balance the effects of the step-by-step addition of layers and to allow their correct interpolation, there is an auxiliary trainable α weight, initialized to 0.

As in [5], the Adam optimizer was chosen to update the weights of the network based on training data; WGAN-GP loss was adopted [9] defined as:

$$\mathcal{L} = \mathbb{E}[D(x)] - \mathbb{E}[D(x')] + \lambda_{gp}\mathbb{E}[\|(\nabla_{x^*} - D(x^*)\|_2 - 1)^2] \tag{5}$$

where x and x' are the real image and the synthesized image, x^* is implicitly defined as an element sampled uniformly along straight lines between pairs of points sampled from the distribution of the real images and the distribution of the images generated by generator [9]; D is the output probability score, while $\mathbb{E}[D(x)]$ is the expected value to have a certain output by the discriminator. $\mathbb{E}[D(x)] - \mathbb{E}[D(x')]$ is the original critic loss and $\lambda_{gp}\mathbb{E}[\|(\nabla_{x^*} - D(x^*)\|_2 - 1)^2]$ is the gradient penalty. The generator tries to minimize this loss, while discriminator

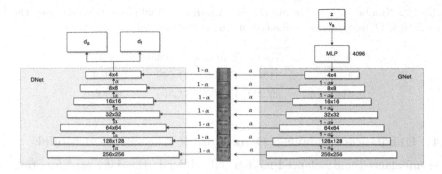

Fig. 4. Progressive training.

Fig. 5. Progressively generated images.

tries to maximize it. Figure 5 shows the generation of some images. Filling the dataset with too many synthetic images could be detrimental. A t threshold was established to balance the sample number for each attribute. All the groups that exceeded the t threshold were down-sampled, while all those with a number of samples less than the threshold t underwent an up-sampling with synthetic images. The value of t was set to 500, which gave the best results in the testing and performance evaluation phases and maintained the image number in line with the real dataset. After this, each of the 5 Age classes, 2 Gender classes, and 4 Ethnicity classes contained about 4,000, about 10,000, and about 5,000 images, respectively.

Table 2. Number of images for the two models. Unbalanced training uses the re-organized UTKface dataset, balanced one used the derived balanced dataset

Training	Total	Training	Validation	Test
Unbalanced	21,981	15,386	1,649	4,946
Balanced	20,000	14,000	1,500	4,500

3.4 Unbalanced/Balanced Demographic Classification Models

The unbalanced and balanced models only differ in the data used for training, either the re-organized UTKface dataset or its balanced version, with 70% images for training and 30% for testing, with the validation set being 25% of the test set. The CNN used for age, gender, and ethnicity classification is inspired by Network A in [24], with independent networks that are trained separately to predict the age, gender, and ethnicity of an input face image x. Changes were made to make the network adequate both to the size of the images in the dataset, and to have three distinct outputs, one for each attribute treated.

$$CNN(x) = (a, g, e) \tag{6}$$

The structure of the convolutional network is defined as:

1. Input Block: images of size $200 \times 200 \times 3$ are loaded as Tensor; a spatial convolution is applied, with 3×3 kernel and ReLU activation function; the output is $200 \times 200 \times 32$.
2. Conv Block: it maps features as the size of the input image is reduced; it contains a Convolution, a Normalization, and a Max Pooling layer; the Conv Block is repeated five times.
3. Embedding: this is a level of convergence; the Global Max Pooling encapsulates all features in a shape 192 layer.
4. Output Blocks: they represent the three final outputs related to the characteristics of a subject in an image; they are two Dense Layers for each detection to be carried out: the first of 128 units with ReLU activation function, and the second with the number of units related to the considered attributes of each class with Softmax activation function.

The loss chosen for every output layer is the categorical cross-entropy with Softmax activation function. The study used the RMSprop optimizer [10]. It performed better than Adam in training, by reducing the loss/accuracy variations between epochs. The best resulting training configuration had batches of 64 elements, for 10 epochs of 240 steps. Table 2 shows the number of images used with the two models. Although fewer than the original set, the images are better category-balanced. Synthetic ones were only used for training.

4 Experimental Results and Discussion

The PGAN was run on a Nvidia GeForce GTX 1070 video card. This GPU device exploits the CUDA. The results show better demographic classification when

Table 3. Results training with the unbalanced vs. balanced dataset

MODEL_UNBAL

Class	Accuracy	AVG Pecision	AVG Recall	AVG F1-Score
Age	0.76	0.68	0.56	0.58
Gender	0.88	0.87	0.88	0.87
Ethnicity	0.79	0.76	0.78	0.78

MODEL_BAL

Class	Accuracy	AVG Pecision	AVG Recall	AVG F1-Score
Age	0.91 (+20%)	0.91 (+34%)	0.91 (+62%)	0.91 (+57%)
Gender	0.92 (+4%)	0.92 (+5%)	0.93 (+6%)	0.92 (+6%)
Ethnicity	0.90 (+14%)	0.90 (+18%)	0.90 (+15%)	0.90 (+15%)

training with a balanced set of data. Table 3 reports the results in terms of Accuracy, Average Precision (over the attribute values), Average Recall, and Average F1-Score for both unbalanced and balanced training. The performance metrics generally improve, as expected, but most of all the improvement is directly proportional to the initial unbalance for the specific demographic trait. Reminding Fig. 1, the highest difference in attribute value frequencies was related to Age, followed by Ethnicity, while a much better balance was already found for Gender. Table 3 clearly shows a dramatic improvement for Age, with Accuracy increasing by 20% and AVG F1-score by even 57%. The improvement for Ethnicity is definitely lower, and the improvement for Age is an order of magnitude lower on all metrics. Even deeper insight can be gained by looking at the chart bars in Fig. 6 for every attribute/value. Precision for Child and Recall for Adult can be affected by the age intervals, and actually, F1-score slightly decreases only for Adult value. This may suggest adopting different age intervals. Finally, it is interesting to compare the achieved results with NIST FRVT 2015 on gender classification [17]. This large-scale evaluation of facial gender classification baselined accuracy against a large dataset of visa and mugshot images collected under well-controlled pose, illumination, and facial expression. The results are generally better than those achieved in the present work, even after the balanced training. However, the latter refer to a dataset of face images in the wild. Although the purpose of this work is not to challenge the state of the art, this consideration adds interest to the proposal.

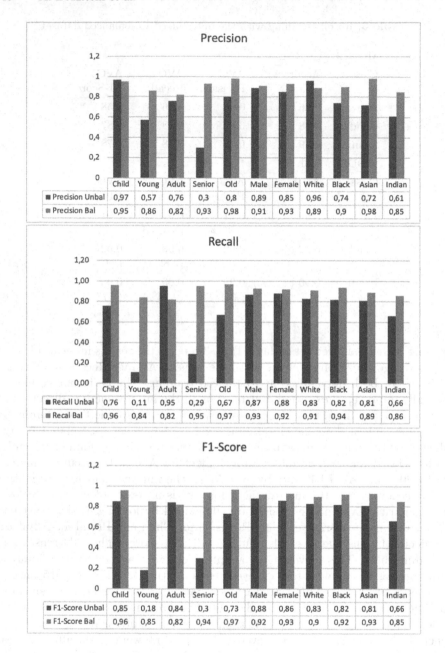

Fig. 6. Precision, Recall, and F1-score for the single values of each attribute.

5   Conclusion

This work confirms that the re-balancing of face image training datasets improves the general accuracy of demographic classification. Re-balancing was achieved here using PGAN-created synthetic images, an interesting alternative to the collecting of new real personal images. The results further clearly show a per-class improvement that is directly proportional to the initial class unbalance. In the future, to compare with A2F_P, other networks, e.g., DC-GAN, StyleGAN, or StyleGANv2 could be used for synthesis, or training images could be synthesized from one dataset to test over another one. A different demographic classification could be compared with Model_Bal. Finally, it would be interesting to augment training data directly for face recognition, to evaluate the effect on performance, in particular for the originally underrepresented demographic groups.

References

1. Balakrishnan, G., Xiong, Y., Xia, W., Perona, P.: Towards causal benchmarking of biasin face analysis algorithms. In: Ratha, N.K., Patel, V.M., Chellappa, R. (eds.) Deep Learning-Based Face Analytics. ACVPR, pp. 327–359. Springer, Cham (2021). https://doi.org/10.1007/978-3-030-74697-1_15
2. European Commission: High-Level Expert Group on AI. Ethics guidelines for trustworthy AI (2019). https://digital-strategy.ec.europa.eu/en/library/ethics-guidelines-trustworthy-ai. Accessed 20 July 2023
3. Cook, C.M., Howard, J.J., Sirotin, Y.B., Tipton, J.L.: Fixed and varying effects of demographic factors on the performance of eleven commercial facial recognition systems. IEEE Trans. Biom. Behav. Identity Sci. 40(1), 2 (2019)
4. De Marsico, M., Nappi, M., Riccio, D., Wechsler, H.: Leveraging implicit demographic information for face recognition using a multi-expert system. Multimedia Tools Appl. 76(22), 23383–23411 (2017)
5. Di, X., Patel, V.M.: Multimodal face synthesis from visual attributes. IEEE Trans. Biom. Behav. Identity Sci. 3(3), 427–439 (2021)
6. Drozdowski, P., Rathgeb, C., Dantcheva, A., Damer, N., Busch, C.: Demographic bias in biometrics: a survey on an emerging challenge. IEEE Trans. Technol. Soc. 1(2), 89–103 (2020)
7. Garcia, R.V., Wandzik, L., Grabner, L., Krueger, J.: The harms of demographic bias in deep face recognition research. In: 2019 International Conference on Biometrics (ICB), pp. 1–6. IEEE (2019)
8. Goodfellow, I., et al.: Generative adversarial nets. In: Ghahramani, Z., Welling, M., Cortes, C., Lawrence, N., Weinberger, K. (eds.) Advances in Neural Information Processing Systems, vol. 27. Curran Associates, Inc. (2014). https://proceedings.neurips.cc/paper/2014/file/5ca3e9b122f61f8f06494c97b1afccf3-Paper.pdf
9. Gulrajani, I., Ahmed, F., Arjovsky, M., Dumoulin, V., Courville, A.C.: Improved training of Wasserstein GANs. In: Advances in Neural Information Processing Systems 30 (2017)
10. Hinton, G., Srivastava, N., Swersky, K.: Neural Networks for Machine Learning - Lecture 6e - rmsprop: Divide the gradient by a running average of its recent magnitude. https://www.cs.toronto.edu/~tijmen/csc321/slides/lecture_slides_lec6.pdf. Accessed 05 June 2022
11. Howard, J.J., Blanchard, A.J., Sirotin, Y.B., Hasselgren, J.A., Vemury, A.R.: An investigation of high-throughput biometric systems: results of the 2018 department of homeland security biometric technology rally. In: 2018 IEEE 9th International Conference on Biometrics Theory, Applications and Systems (BTAS), pp. 1–7. IEEE (2018)

12. Hu, S., et al.: A polarimetric thermal database for face recognition research. In: Proceedings of the IEEE Conference on Computer Vision and Pattern Recognition Workshops, pp. 119–126 (2016)

13. Karras, T., Aila, T., Laine, S., Lehtinen, J.: Progressive growing of GANs for improved quality, stability, and variation. In: International Conference on Learning Representations (2018)

14. Klare, B.F., Burge, M.J., Klontz, J.C., Bruegge, R.W.V., Jain, A.K.: Face recognition performance: role of demographic information. IEEE Trans. Inf. Forensics Secur. **7**(6), 1789–1801 (2012)

15. Li, S., Yi, D., Lei, Z., Liao, S.: The CASIA NIR-VIS 2.0 face database. In: Proceedings of the IEEE Conference on Computer Vision and Pattern Recognition Workshops, pp. 348–353 (2013)

16. Lu, B., Chen, J.C., Castillo, C.D., Chellappa, R.: An experimental evaluation of covariates effects on unconstrained face verification. IEEE Trans. Biom. Behav. Identity Sci. **1**(1), 42–55 (2019)

17. Ngan, M., Grother, P.J., Ngan, M.: Face recognition vendor test (FRVT) performance of automated gender classification algorithms. US Department of Commerce, National Institute of Standards and Technology (2015)

18. Odena, A., Olah, C., Shlens, J.: Conditional image synthesis with auxiliary classifier GANs. In: International Conference on Machine Learning, pp. 2642–2651. PMLR (2017)

19. Ojala, T., Pietikainen, M., Maenpaa, T.: Multiresolution gray-scale and rotation invariant texture classification with local binary patterns. IEEE Trans. Pattern Anal. Mach. Intell. **24**(7), 971–987 (2002)

20. Perarnau, G., Van De Weijer, J., Raducanu, B., Álvarez, J.M.: Invertible conditional GANs for image editing. arXiv preprint arXiv:1611.06355 (2016)

21. Phillips, P.J., Jiang, F., Narvekar, A., Ayyad, J., O'Toole, A.J.: An other-race effect for face recognition algorithms. ACM Trans. Appl. Percept. (TAP) **8**(2), 1–11 (2011)

22. Phillips, P.J., et al.: FRVT 2006 and ICE 2006 large-scale experimental results. IEEE Trans. Pattern Anal. Mach. Intell. **32**(5), 831–846 (2010). https://doi.org/10.1109/TPAMI.2009.59

23. Shen, L., Bai, L.: A review on gabor wavelets for face recognition. Pattern Anal. Appl. **9**(2), 273–292 (2006)

24. Srinivas, N., Atwal, H., Rose, D.C., Mahalingam, G., Ricanek, K., Bolme, D.S.: Age, gender, and fine-grained ethnicity prediction using convolutional neural networks for the East Asian face dataset. In: 2017 12th IEEE International Conference on Automatic Face & Gesture Recognition (FG 2017), pp. 953–960. IEEE (2017)

25. Wang, Y., Dantcheva, A., Bremond, F.: From attributes to faces: a conditional generative network for face generation. In: 2018 International Conference of the Biometrics Special Interest Group (BIOSIG), pp. 1–5. IEEE (2018)

26. Yan, X., Yang, J., Sohn, K., Lee, H.: Attribute2Image: conditional image generation from visual attributes. In: Leibe, B., Matas, J., Sebe, N., Welling, M. (eds.) ECCV 2016. LNCS, vol. 9908, pp. 776–791. Springer, Cham (2016). https://doi.org/10.1007/978-3-319-46493-0_47

27. Zhang, Z., Song, Y., Qi, H.: Age progression/regression by conditional adversarial autoencoder. In: Proceedings of the IEEE Conference on Computer Vision and Pattern Recognition, pp. 5810–5818 (2017)

Deep Generative Views to Mitigate Gender Classification Bias Across Gender-Race Groups

Sreeraj Ramachandran and Ajita Rattani[(✉)]

School of Computing, Wichita State University, Wichita, USA
sxramachandran2@shockers.wichita.edu, ajita.rattani@wichita.edu

Abstract. Published studies have suggested the bias of automated face-based gender classification algorithms across gender-race groups. Specifically, unequal accuracy rates were obtained for women and dark-skinned people. To mitigate the bias of gender classifiers, the vision community has developed several strategies. However, the efficacy of these mitigation strategies is demonstrated for a limited number of races mostly, Caucasian and African-American. Further, these strategies often offer a trade-off between bias and classification accuracy. To further advance the state-of-the-art, we leverage the power of generative views, structured learning, and evidential learning towards mitigating gender classification bias. We demonstrate the superiority of our bias mitigation strategy in improving classification accuracy and reducing bias across gender-racial groups through extensive experimental validation, resulting in state-of-the-art performance in intra- and cross dataset evaluations.

Keywords: Fairness and Bias in AI · Deep Generative Views · Generative Adversarial Networks

1 Introduction

Gender is one of the important demographic attributes. Automated gender classification[1] refers to automatically assigning gender labels to biometric samples. It has drawn significant interest in numerous applications such as demographic research, surveillance, human-computer interaction, anonymous customized advertisement system, and image retrieval system [19,26,41,66].

---

[1] Studies in [25,49] have shown the inherent problems with gender and race classification. While the datasets used in this study use an almost balanced dataset for the training, it still lacks representation of entire large demographic groups, effectively erasing such categories. We compare the gender and racial categories specified in these datasets to past studies, not to reaffirm or encourage the usage of such reductive classifications.

Supported by National Science Foundation (NSF).

© Springer Nature Switzerland AG 2023
J.-J. Rousseau and B. Kapralos (Eds.): ICPR 2022 Workshops, LNCS 13645, pp. 551–569, 2023.
https://doi.org/10.1007/978-3-031-37731-0_40

Companies such as Amazon, Microsoft [5], and many others have released commercial software containing an automated gender classification system from biometric facial images.

Over the last few years, published research has questioned the fairness of these face-based automated gender classification systems across gender and race [5, 28, 38, 47]. A classifier is said to satisfy group fairness if subjects in both the protected and unprotected groups have an equal chance of being assigned to the positively predicted class [62]. Existing gender classification systems produce unequal rates for women and people with dark skin, such as African-Americans. Studies in [39, 56] have also evaluated the gender bias of facial analysis based deepfake detection and BMI prediction models. Further, studies in [29, 30] have evaluated the bias of ocular-based attribute analysis models across gender and age-groups.

To mitigate the bias of the gender classification system, several solutions have been developed by the vision community. These solutions are based on regularization strategies [43], attention mechanism [35] and adversarial debiasing [2, 65], data augmentation techniques [7], subgroup-specific classifiers [10], and oversampling the minority classes using Generative Adversarial Networks(GANs) [48].

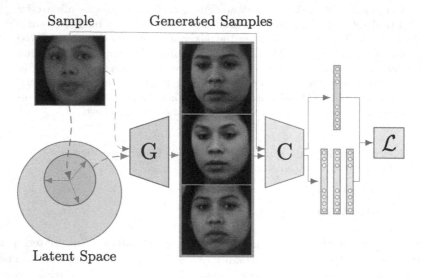

Fig. 1. Input samples are projected into a latent space and augmentations are generated. The loss function minimizes the distance between the embedding along with the classification loss.

Often the aforementioned mitigation strategies offer a trade-off [2, 65] between the fairness and classification task. Further, the efficacy of these strategies are demonstrated on limited number of races; mostly African-American and Caucasian [5, 38]. A bias mitigation strategy that offer fairness across several inter-sectional subgroups without compromising the gender classification accuracy is still an **open challenge** [57].

To further advance the state-of-the-art, this paper proposes a solution that combines the power of structured learning, deep generative views, and evidential learning theory for classifier's uncertainty quantification, for bias mitigation of the gender classification algorithms. We observe that the locally smooth property of the latent space of a Generative Adversarial Network (GAN) model facilitates the generation of the perceptually similar samples. The augmentation strategies that exploit the local geometry of the data-manifold are more powerful in general when used in a consistency regularization style setting. We chose the latent space of the GAN model to be a surrogate space for the data-manifold and therefore sampled augmentations from the latent space called deep generative views.

Specifically, the facial images of the training set are inverted to the GAN latent space to generate a latent code by training an encoder of the trained StyleGAN. The generated latent code is perturbed to produce variations called *neighboring views* (deep generative views) of the training images. The original training samples along with the neighboring views are used for the gender classifier's training. The regularization term is added to the loss function that enforces the model to learn similar embedding between the original images and the neighboring views. Lastly, a reject option based on uncertainty quantification using evidential deep learning is introduced. The reject option is used to discard samples during the test time based on the quantification of the uncertainty of the classifier's prediction. Figure 1 shows the schema of the proposed approach based on obtaining generative views by projecting the original samples into the latent space.

The proposed bias mitigation strategy has the **dual advantage** of enhancing the classifier's representational ability as well as the fairness, as demonstrated through extensive experimental evaluations. Also, its generality allows it to be applied to any classification problem, not just face-based gender classification.

In summary, the main **contributions** of this paper are as follows:

- A bias mitigation strategy for deep learning-based gender classifiers that leverages and combines the power of GAN to produce deep generative views, structured learning, and evidential learning theory for uncertainty quantification.
- We demonstrate the merit of our proposed bias mitigation strategy through experimental analysis on state-of-the-art facial attribute datasets, namely, FairFace [31], UTKFace [71], DiveFace [37] and Morph [50], and ocular datasets namely, VISOB [42] and UFPR [69].
- Extensive experiments demonstrate the dual advantage of our approach in improving the representational capability as well as the fairness of the gender classification task, thus obtaining state-of-the-art performance over existing baselines most of the time.

2   Related Work

Fairness in Gender Classification: In [5], authors evaluated the fairness using commercial SDKs and observed least accuracy rates for dark-skinned females.

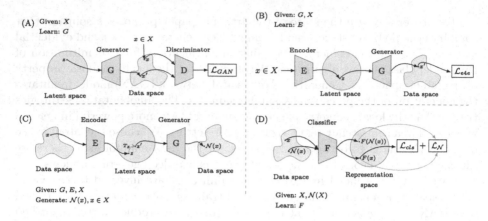

Fig. 2. Overview of the proposed method. (A) Training a GAN to learn the input image data distribution, X. (B) Training an Encoder model, E to learn to project input image, x to the latent space. (C) Generating Neighbour Views by first projecting input image into latent space using E, applying perturbation in latent space, then using G to generate. (D) Training the Classifier, F using both the input image and its neighbors.

Studies in [52,58] proposed data augmentation and two-fold transfer learning for measuring and mitigation bias in deep representation. Attribute aware filter drop was proposed in [40] and regularization strategy in [59] are used to unlearn the dependency of the model on sensitive attributes. In [10], a multi-task Convolution Neural Network (MTCNN) is proposed, that use a joint dynamic loss to jointly classify race, gender and age to minimize bias. A data augmentation strategy called fair mixup is proposed in [7], that regularize the model on interpolated distributions between different sub-groups of a demographic group. An auto-encoder that disentangle data representation into latent sub-spaces is proposed by [43]. Using GANs to generate balanced training set images w.r.t protected attributes was proposed in [48]. Recently OpenAI released its large scale language-image pretraining model called CLIP [45] which was trained contrastively on 400M image-text pairs and demonstrated its exceptional performance as well as bias on both zero-shot and fine-tuning setting on gender classification tasks.

GANs for Real Image Editing: Advancements in GANs [3,14,21–24,46] enable us to produce increasingly realistic images that can replicate variations in training data. Specifically, the learnt intermediate latent space of the Style-GAN [22–24] represents the distribution of the training data more efficiently than the traditional Gaussian latent space. By leveraging the disentangling properties of the latent space as shown in [8,17,51,54,61,68], extensive image manipulations could be performed. Once we invert the input image into the learned latent space, we can modify real images in a similar way. High-quality inversion methods (i) can properly reconstruct the given image, and (ii) produce realistic and semantically meaningful edits. Optimization methods [1,9,33] optimize the latent code by minimizing error for an individual image, whereas faster encoder-based methods [16,44,61] train an encoder to map images to the latent space.

Once inverted, manipulations can be done on the given image by finding "walking" directions that control the attribute of interest. Studies in [11,12,54] use supervised techniques to find these latent directions specific to attributes. Whereas studies in [17,63,64] find directions in an unsupervised manner, requiring manual identification of the determined directions later and [55] using a closed-form factorization algorithm for identifying top semantic latent directions by directly decomposing the pre-trained weights.

Structured Learning, Ensembling of Deep Generative Views: Studies in [4,15,27,36] have shown that combining feature inputs with a structured signal improves the overall performance of a model in various scenarios such as Graph Learning and Adversarial learning. These structured signals either implicit (adversarial) or explicit (graph) are used to regularize the training while the model learns to accurately predict (by minimizing supervised loss) [60] by maintaining the input structural similarity through minimizing a neighbor loss. Recently [6] proposed a test-time ensembling with GAN-based augmentations to improve classification results.

3   Proposed Approach

Figure 2 illustrates the overview of the proposed approach. The process involves training a generative model to produce different views of a given input image. The training images are projected to the latent space of the generator. The variations to the input images are produced using augmentation in the latent space. These generative views act as a structured signal and are used along with the original images to train the downstream gender classifier. Therefore, by injecting prior knowledge into the learning process through the learned latent space and by enforcing local invariance properties of the manifold when used as a consistency regularizer, the classifier's performance is significantly improved. This helps propagate the information contained in the labeled samples to the unlabeled neighboring samples. The proposed strategy of leveraging neighbor views is used during classifier's training, the test images are used as it is during the test-time.

3.1   GAN Preliminaries

A GAN [14] consists of a generator network (G) and a discriminator network (D) involved in a min-max game, where G tries to fool D by producing realistic images from a latent vector z and D gets better at distinguishing between real and generated data. We employ the StyleGAN2 [24] generator in this study. Previous works have shown that the intermediate W space, designed to control the "style" of the image is better able to represent images than the original latent code z with fine-grained control and better disentanglement. In a StyleGAN2 generator, a mapping network M maps z to $w \in W$ and G generates the image x, given w. i.e. $x = G(M(z))$.

3.2   Projecting Images into GAN Latent Space

To alter an image x with the generator, we must first determine the appropriate latent code that generates x. GAN inversion refers to the process of generating the latent code for a given image x. For GAN inversion, there are optimization-based methods as well as encoder-based methods that offer various trade-offs between edit-ability, reconstruction distortion, and speed. We specifically use the *encoder4editing* method (e4e) [61]. e4e use adversarial training to map a given real image to a style code composed of a series of low variance style vectors, each close to the distribution of W. We can generate the reconstruction, x', which is closer to the original x using the given style vectors and the generator, G.

3.3   Generating Views Using Pretrained GAN

For generating views, we use existing latent editing methods. We specifically employ SeFA [55], a closed-form factorization technique for latent semantic discovery that decomposes the pre-trained weights directly. Unsupervised, SeFa determines the top k semantic latent directions. To produce alternate views, we randomly select an arbitrary set of semantic latent directions and sample distances from a Gaussian distribution for latent space traversal for each image x. The generator then uses these updated style vectors to generate the views. In the case of latent vectors occurring in poorly defined i.e., warped region of latent space which may produce non-face images, a simple MTCNN-based [70] face detector is utilized to screen out the non-faces.

3.4   Structured Learning on Deep Generative Views

Let $x_i \in X$ be the input sample. We obtain its corresponding latent style vector w_i using e4e. We may apply SeFA on w_i to obtain $N(w_i) = \{w_i^1, \ldots, w_i^m\}$, where m is a hyperparameter representing the number of neighbours, the neighbouring latent vectors. Using the pretrained StyleGAN generator we may produce the neighbouring views $N(x_i) = G(N(w_i))$.

During training each batch will contain samples with pairs of original sample x_i and the generated neighbours $N(x_i)$. Both x_i and $N(x_i)$ are used in the forward pass but only x_i is backpropagated and used for calculating batch statistics in the normalization layers. This is because of the distributional difference between the real and generated images. The total loss, $\mathcal{L}_{total}$ is given by

$$\mathcal{L}_{total} = \mathcal{L}_{cls}(y_i, y_i') + \alpha \sum_{x_j \in \mathcal{N}(x_i)} \mathcal{L}_{\mathcal{N}}(h_\theta(x_i), h_\theta(x_j)) \tag{1}$$

where $\mathcal{L}_{cls}(y_i, y_i')$ is the classification loss, α is a hyperparameter, $\mathcal{L}_{\mathcal{N}}$ is any distance function that can be used to calculate the distance between the sample embedding and the neighbour embedding and $h_\theta(x)$ is the sample embedding from the neural network. For our experiments, we use Jensen-Shannon Divergence [67] to calculate the distance between the sample embedding and the neighbour embedding.

3.5 Evidential Deep Learning for Quantifying Uncertainty

In standard classifier training where prediction loss is minimized, the resultant model is ignorant of the confidence of its prediction. A study in [53] proposed explicit modeling of uncertainty using subjective logic theory by applying a Dirichlet distribution to class probabilities. Thus, treating model predictions as subjective opinions, and learning the function that collects the evidence leading to these opinions from data using a deterministic neural net. The resulting predictor for a multi-class classification problem is another Dirichlet distribution, the parameters of which are determined by a neural net's continuous output.

Let us assume that $\alpha_i = \alpha_{i1}, \dots, \alpha_{ik}$ is the parameters of a Dirichlet distribution for the classification of a sample i, then $(\alpha_{ij} - 1)$ is the total evidence, e_j estimated by the network for the assignment of the sample i to the jth class. The epistemic uncertainty can be calculated from the evidences e_i using

$$u = \frac{K}{S_i} \tag{2}$$

where K is the number of classes and $S_i = \sum_{j=1}^{K}(e_j + 1)$ [53] proposes the following loss function in this scenario:

$$\mathcal{L}_i = \sum_{j=1}^{K}(y_{ij} - \hat{p}_{ij})^2 + \frac{\hat{p}_{ij}(1 - \hat{p}_{ij})}{S_i + 1} \tag{3}$$

$$\mathcal{L}_{edl} = \sum_{i=1}^{N} \mathcal{L}_i + \lambda_t \sum_{i=1}^{N} KL[D(\boldsymbol{p}_i | \tilde{\boldsymbol{\alpha}}_i) || D(\boldsymbol{p}_i | \langle 1, \dots, 1 \rangle)] \tag{4}$$

where $\boldsymbol{y}_i$ is the one-hot vector encoding of ground-truth and $\boldsymbol{p}_i$ is the class-assignment probabilities given by $\hat{p}_k = \alpha_k / S$.

We use the estimated uncertainty as the basis for rejection, similar to reject-option-based classification [20], where a test sample in low confidence region is rejected based on the model's confidence values. The provided model of uncertainty is more detailed than the point estimate of the standard softmax-output networks and can handle out-of-distribution queries, adversarial samples as well as samples belonging to the critical region. Therefore a high uncertainty value of a test sample suggests the model's under-confidence. And we use this uncertainty estimate as the basis for rejecting samples during test time rather than using the softmax probabilities.

4   Experiments and Results

4.1   Datasets Used

For all our experiments we used the FairFace [31] as our training dataset. Testing was done on the test set of the FairFace as well as DiveFace [37], UTKFace [71] and Morph [50] datasets.

Table 1 shows the characteristics of these datasets used in our study.

Table 1. Datasets

Dataset	Images	Races
FairFace	$100k$	White, Black, Indian, East Asian, Southeast Asian, Middle Eastern, Latino Hispanic
DiveFace	$150k$	East Asian, Sub-Saharan, South Indian, Caucasian
UTKFace	$20k$	White, Black, Indian, Asian
Morph	$55k$	White, Black

4.2   Gender Classification

For our experiments on gender classification, we used FairFace as our training dataset. The FairFace dataset was also used for training the StyleGAN2 generator as well as the e4e encoder that was subsequently used to generate the neighbouring views.

Generating Neighbouring Views: For pretrained StyleGAN2, we use the official StyleGAN2-ADA implementation pretrained on high quality FFHQ-256 face dataset [23] and used transfer learning on the FairFace training set with images resized to 256×256. We obtained a Fréchet inception distance (FID) [18] of 4.29, similar perceptual quality as of FFHQ on StyleGAN [23]. The uncurated images generated by the trained generator are shown in Fig. 3.

For pretraining e4e, we use the official e4e implementation with the pretrained StyleGAN2 generator from above and the FairFace training set. Figure 3 shows uncurated reconstructions by the encoder. Finally, for generating the views, the training set images are first inverted using e4e and then we use SeFA to choose the top k semantic latent directions. We pick distances in both positive and negative directions randomly. For our experiments we initially generate 56 neighbors

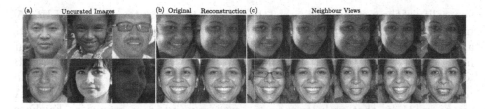

Fig. 3. (a) Uncurated images generated by StyleGAN2 trained on FairFace. (b) Images reconstructed using the trained e4e encoder and pretrained StyleGAN2 generator. (c) Generative views created by selecting top semantic latent directions with SeFA and randomly sampling along those directions.

per image, to have a wide variation of views. We then use a pretrained MTCNN face detector to detect faces on the generated images and remove non-faces to ensure a clean dataset sampled from the well-defined region of latent space. Figure 3 shows examples of generated variations.

Training the Classifier: For our experiments, we use a baseline *EfficientNetV2-L* pretrained on ImageNet as a gender classification model. Our proposed method based on deep generative views and structured learning, denoted by *Neighbour Learning (NL)*, is applied to this model. We also compare our results with a sensitive-attribute aware multi-task classifier (MT) [10], with race as the secondary attribute.

Further, we combine both NL and MT and evaluate their performance (third configuration). And finally, our last configuration which also has the ability to predict uncertainty, combines NL, and MT and replaces the final classification head of the gender classifier with an evidential layer (EDL) and replaced cross-entropy loss with an evidential loss.

For all our experiments, we use an RMSProp optimizer with a cosine annealing schedule with an initial learning rate of 4×10^{-4} and weight decay of 1×10^{-5}. We use a batch size of 128 across 2 RTX8000 GPUs, with label smoothing of 0.1, and *autoaugment* policy for data augmentation. For NL, α is set to 2, and the number of neighbors, m to 7 for the final configuration. We also apply *lazy regularization* to speed up the training, inspired by StyleGAN, where we apply the costly NL regularization every n batch. For our final model, we set this hyperparameter value to 2. For evaluation, we used the *Degree of Bias (DoB)* [13], the standard deviation of classification accuracy across different subgroups, as well as *Selection Rate (SeR)* [32], the ratio of worst to best accuracy rate, as a metric for evaluation of the fairness.

Table 2 show the results on the FairFace validation set. The empirical results suggest that the proposed method NL improves the fairness of the model as well as the overall accuracy, outperforming both baseline and multi-task aware setup (MT). Combining NL with MT and evidential deep learning (EDL) further improves the performance by reducing the DoB to 1.62 and with an accuracy of 94.70%. To compare with the state of the art as well as to evaluate the generality of the method, we applied the same to the vision tower of the CLIP [45] model. We used the ViT-L/14 version of the model with pretrained weights and added a final linear classification head for the configuration. Applying our method to the CLIP model [45], an already SOTA method, improved the DoB while maintaining the accuracy. As most studies constraint the bias evaluation to a simple white vs non-white subjects, we restrict our comparisons to SOTA methods [34,45] that evaluate fairness across multiple-race groups on FairFace and observed our method either outperformed or enhanced the models that were pretrained on huge datasets such as WebImageText($400M$) [45] and Instagram ($3.5B$) [34].

Table 2. Gender classification results of the proposed method across gender-race groups when trained and tested on FairFace.

Configuration	Gender	Black	East Asian	Indian	Latino Hispanic	Middle Eastern	Southeast Asian	White	Average ↑	DoB ↓	SeR ↑
A Baseline	Male	91.24	94.08	95.88	93.06	97.54	92.93	94.30	94.27	2.01	91.96
	Female	89.70	94.95	94.50	96.02	95.96	96.18	94.18			
B + NL (LR = 2)	Male	91.24	95.24	96.15	94.83	97.79	94.01	95.63	94.67	1.67	**93.78**
	Female	91.81	94.70	94.89	95.18	96.21	95.29	93.04			
C + NL (No LR)	Male	91.74	95.62	96.41	95.08	97.91	94.29	95.45	**95.06**	1.67	93.68
	Female	91.68	95.08	95.94	96.63	95.96	95.59	93.87			
D + MT	Male	91.61	94.85	94.82	94.45	97.91	94.56	95.99	94.58	1.73	92.83
	Female	90.89	94.05	95.28	95.90	96.21	93.82	93.77			
E + MT + NL	Male	91.86	94.98	96.81	93.69	97.79	93.20	94.92	94.59	1.66	93.48
	Female	91.41	94.95	95.41	95.66	95.45	94.12	94.08			
F + MT + NL + EDL	Male	91.86	94.85	95.35	94.58	97.79	92.65	94.83	94.70	**1.62**	93.62
	Female	91.55	95.73	95.41	96.02	95.71	94.41	95.02			
G CLIP + Linear	Male	94.99	96.78	97.21	96.72	98.77	96.05	97.78	**96.76**	1.10	95.36
	Female	94.19	96.63	97.25	97.83	96.71	96.62	96.47			
H + NL	Male	95.12	96.78	97.21	96.72	98.52	95.92	97.15	96.70	**0.99**	**95.87**
	Female	94.45	96.90	96.59	97.71	97.22	96.18	96.99			
I + MT + NL + EDL	Male	95.37	96.78	97.08	97.10	98.89	95.92	97.15	96.70	1.00	95.38
	Female	94.32	96.63	96.46	97.11	97.22	96.75	96.78			
Instagram + Linear [34]	Male	92.50	93.40	96.20	93.10	96.00	92.70	94.80	93.77	1.73	93.66
	Female	90.10	94.30	95.00	94.80	95.00	94.10	91.40			

Cross Dataset. Evaluations were done on UTKFace, DiveFace, and Morph Datasets. Table 3 shows cross-dataset results. In the calculation of DoB for datasets where the test set is not balanced across demographic groups, a weighted standard deviation was used instead of a standard deviation. For DiveFace and Morph, various configurations improved the overall fairness over the baseline whereas it was not the case for UTKFace. It must also be noted that across all datasets the proposed method improved the overall classification accuracy regardless.

Rejecting Samples Based on Uncertainty as Threshold. For evidential learning, we replace the classification head such that, it outputs parameters of a

Table 3. Cross-dataset evaluation of the proposed model.

	UTKFace			DiveFace			Morph		
	DoB ↓	Avg. Acc ↑	SeR ↑	DoB ↓	Avg. Acc ↑	SeR ↑	DoB ↓	Avg. Acc ↑	SeR ↑
Baseline	**1.96**	94.67	**92.60**	0.74	98.45	97.71	7.67	96.26	74.89
MT	3.01	94.25	88.89	0.78	98.34	97.67	10.01	95.02	69.97
NL (LR = 2)	2.55	94.54	90.11	**0.49**	98.49	**98.48**	8.99	95.95	70.68
NL (No LR)	2.26	**94.76**	91.55	0.51	**98.60**	98.39	7.72	**96.41**	74.84
MT + NL	2.31	94.47	90.91	0.77	98.40	97.52	6.69	96.21	78.06
MT + NL + EDL	2.27	94.50	91.53	0.83	98.37	97.43	**6.26**	96.32	**78.98**
CLIP + LP	1.86	**96.58**	92.91	0.68	**99.08**	97.90	**0.89**	**99.46**	**97.04**
CLIP + NL	**1.60**	96.47	**94.59**	0.62	99.02	**98.09**	1.39	99.19	95.43
CLIP + MT + NL + EDL	2.04	96.52	92.85	0.69	99.04	97.81	1.10	99.26	96.33

Dirichlet Distribution. We also replace the classification loss $\mathcal{L}_{cls}$ with the evidential loss term defined by Eq. 4. For our experiments, removing the annealing coefficient λ_t worked better. We may calculate the uncertainty of the prediction using Eq. 2. This uncertainty is used as a threshold to reject/accept the prediction of the model.

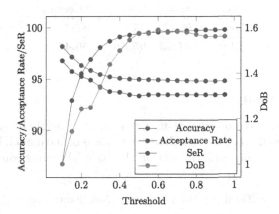

Fig. 4. Model behaviour at various uncertainty thresholds

Figure 4 shows the behavior of the model at different uncertainty thresholds. The choice of uncertainty threshold is application dependent. Although it is to be noted, at a threshold of 0.2 the model rejects only 4% of all images and at the same time improving the overall accuracy +2% and reducing the DoB to 1.25 from 1.62.

Effectiveness on Other Biometric Modalities. In order to analyze the generalizability of our method across different biometric modalities, we also conducted similar experiments on an ocular and a periocular dataset. For ocular analysis across gender, we used the VISOB [42] dataset. Table 4 shows the condensed results on VISOB dataset. The proposed method improved the accuracy as well as the DoB. For periocular analysis, we used the UFPR Periocular [69] dataset. For this dataset, since race annotations are not available, we present the results across gender only. Table 5 shows the results on UFPR dataset. As can be seen, the proposed method improved accuracy across gender even for ocular and periocular biometrics.

Table 4. Gender classification results of the proposed method across gender when trained and tested on VISOB dataset.

Config	Avg. Acc ↑	DoB ↓	SeR ↑
Baseline	87.95	15.27	48.37
NL	**89.17**	**14.18**	**52.51**

Table 5. Gender classification results of the proposed method across gender when trained and tested on UFPR dataset.

Config	Male ↑	Female ↑	Overall ↑
Baseline	96.13	95.13	95.60
NL	**97.13**	**95.88**	**96.47**

4.3   Ablation Study

Neighbour Size. We observe that increasing the neighbor size of a sample improves the overall accuracy as well as the fairness of the model. For the ablation study, we conducted our experiments on the base NL configuration (Table 6).

Table 6. Ablation Study: Neighbour Size

Neighbour Size	Avg. Acc ↑	DoB ↓	SeR ↑
1	94.35	1.95	92.20
3	94.58	1.69	92.69
5	94.50	1.73	93.39
7	**94.67**	**1.67**	**93.78**

Lazy Regularization. The lazy regularization value is chosen as a trade-off between training speed and the overall performance. The model works best when n is 1, i.e. no lazy regularization. Although this particular configuration is the best of all, we decided to stick with the $n = 2$ configuration considering the speed trade-off (Table 7).

Table 7. Ablation Study : Lazy Regularization

n	Avg. Acc ↑	DoB ↓	SeR ↑
1	**95.06**	**1.67**	93.68
2	94.67	**1.67**	**93.78**
4	94.94	1.79	93.21
8	94.92	1.72	92.96

Distance Metrics. The distance function $\mathcal{L}_{\mathcal{N}}$ for neighbor regularization can be any function that can compute the distances between embedding. We evaluated L2 and Jensen-Shannon (JS) Divergence. Though cosine similarity and KL divergence are also possibilities. Experiments proved JS Divergence to be a better distance function for the model (Table 8).

Table 8. Ablation Study : Distance Metrics

Distance Metric	Avg. Acc ↑	DoB ↓	SeR ↑
L2	**94.76**	1.71	92.91
JS Div	94.67	**1.67**	**93.78**

Effect of Generated Views on Backpropagation. The generated views are solely used for calculating the regularization term from the embeddings in the proposed approach, not for backpropagation or batch statistics calculation. We test this by using backpropagation to train a model using generated views, and we discover that the bias is substantially higher when generated views dominate the data distribution, despite the total accuracy improving marginally (Table 9).

Table 9. Ablation Study : With BackProp vs Without BackProp

Config	Avg. Acc ↑	DoB ↓	SeR ↑
With BackProp	**94.79**	2.11	91.14
Without BackProp	94.67	**1.67**	**93.78**

5 Conclusion and Future Work

Several studies have demonstrated that deep learning models can discriminate based on demographic attributes for biometric modalities such as face and ocular. Existing bias mitigation strategies often offer the trade-off between accuracy and fairness. In this study, we proposed a bias mitigation strategy that leverages the power of generative views and structured learning to learn invariant features that can improve the fairness and classification accuracy of a model simultaneously. We also propose a rejection mechanism based on uncertainty quantification that efficiently rejects uncertain samples at test time. Extensive evaluation across datasets and two biometric modalities demonstrate the generalizability of our proposed bias mitigation strategy to any biometric modality and classification task. While the training process we currently uses pregenerated neighbour samples, future research would explore ways to generate neighbor samples during the training phase to take into account the needs of the task at hand. Further, we will evaluate the efficacy of our proposed approach in mitigating bias for other computer vision tasks such as deepfake and biometric spoof attack detection.

Acknowledgement. This work is supported from National Science Foundation (NSF) award no. 2129173. The research infrastructure used in this study is supported in part from a grant no. 13106715 from the Defense University Research Instrumentation Program (DURIP) from Air Force Office of Scientific Research.

References

1. Abdal, R., Qin, Y., Wonka, P.: Image2StyleGAN: how to embed images into the StyleGAN latent space? In: 2019 IEEE/CVF International Conference on Computer Vision, ICCV 2019, Seoul, South Korea, 27 October–2 November 2019, pp. 4431–4440. IEEE (2019). https://doi.org/10.1109/ICCV.2019.00453
2. Adeli-Mosabbeb, E., et al.: Representation learning with statistical independence to mitigate bias. In: IEEE Winter Conference on Applications of Computer Vision, WACV 2021, Waikoloa, HI, USA, 3–8 January 2021, pp. 2512–2522. IEEE (2021). https://doi.org/10.1109/WACV48630.2021.00256
3. Brock, A., Donahue, J., Simonyan, K.: Large scale GAN training for high fidelity natural image synthesis. In: 7th International Conference on Learning Representations, ICLR 2019, New Orleans, LA, USA, 6–9 May 2019. OpenReview.net (2019). https://openreview.net/forum?id=B1xsqj09Fm
4. Bui, T.D., Ravi, S., Ramavajjala, V.: Neural graph learning: training neural networks using graphs. In: Proceedings of the 11th ACM International Conference on Web Search and Data Mining, WSDM 2018, pp. 64–71. Association for Computing Machinery, New York (2018). https://doi.org/10.1145/3159652.3159731
5. Buolamwini, J., Gebru, T.: Gender shades: intersectional accuracy disparities in commercial gender classification. In: Friedler, S.A., Wilson, C. (eds.) Conference on Fairness, Accountability and Transparency, FAT 2018. Proceedings of Machine Learning Research, New York, NY, USA, 23–24 February 2018, vol. 81, pp. 77–91. PMLR (2018). http://proceedings.mlr.press/v81/buolamwini18a.html
6. Chai, L., Zhu, J., Shechtman, E., Isola, P., Zhang, R.: Ensembling with deep generative views. In: IEEE Conference on Computer Vision and Pattern Recognition, CVPR 2021, virtual, 19–25 June 2021, pp. 14997–15007. Computer Vision Foundation/IEEE (2021). https://openaccess.thecvf.com/content/CVPR2021/html/Chai_Ensembling_With_Deep_Generative_Views_CVPR_2021_paper.html
7. Chuang, C., Mroueh, Y.: Fair mixup: fairness via interpolation. In: 9th International Conference on Learning Representations, ICLR 2021, Virtual Event, Austria, 3–7 May 2021. OpenReview.net (2021). https://openreview.net/forum?id=DNl5s5BXeBn

8. Collins, E., Bala, R., Price, B., Süsstrunk, S.: Editing in style: uncovering the local semantics of GANs. In: 2020 IEEE/CVF Conference on Computer Vision and Pattern Recognition, CVPR 2020, Seattle, WA, USA, 13–19 June 2020, pp. 5770–5779. Computer Vision Foundation/IEEE (2020). https://doi.org/10.1109/CVPR42600.2020.00581

9. Creswell, A., Bharath, A.A.: Inverting the generator of a generative adversarial network. IEEE Trans. Neural Netw. Learn. Syst. **30**(7), 1967–1974 (2019). https://doi.org/10.1109/TNNLS.2018.2875194

10. Das, A., Dantcheva, A., Bremond, F.: Mitigating bias in gender, age and ethnicity classification: a multi-task convolution neural network approach. In: Leal-Taixé, L., Roth, S. (eds.) ECCV 2018. LNCS, vol. 11129, pp. 573–585. Springer, Cham (2019). https://doi.org/10.1007/978-3-030-11009-3_35

11. Denton, E., Hutchinson, B., Mitchell, M., Gebru, T.: Detecting bias with generative counterfactual face attribute augmentation. CoRR abs/1906.06439 (2019). http://arxiv.org/abs/1906.06439

12. Goetschalckx, L., Andonian, A., Oliva, A., Isola, P.: GANalyze: toward visual definitions of cognitive image properties. In: 2019 IEEE/CVF International Conference on Computer Vision, ICCV 2019, Seoul, South Korea, 27 October–2 November 2019, pp. 5743–5752. IEEE (2019). https://doi.org/10.1109/ICCV.2019.00584

13. Gong, S., Liu, X., Jain, A.K.: DebFace: de-biasing face recognition. CoRR abs/1911.08080 (2019). http://arxiv.org/abs/1911.08080

14. Goodfellow, I., et al.: Generative adversarial nets. In: Ghahramani, Z., Welling, M., Cortes, C., Lawrence, N., Weinberger, K.Q. (eds.) Advances in Neural Information Processing Systems, vol. 27. Curran Associates, Inc. (2014). https://proceedings.neurips.cc/paper/2014/file/5ca3e9b122f61f8f06494c97b1afccf3-Paper.pdf

15. Goodfellow, I.J., Shlens, J., Szegedy, C.: Explaining and harnessing adversarial examples. In: Bengio, Y., LeCun, Y. (eds.) 3rd International Conference on Learning Representations, ICLR 2015, Conference Track Proceedings, San Diego, CA, USA, 7–9 May 2015 (2015). http://arxiv.org/abs/1412.6572

16. Guan, S., Tai, Y., Ni, B., Zhu, F., Huang, F., Yang, X.: Collaborative learning for faster StyleGAN embedding. CoRR abs/2007.01758 (2020). https://arxiv.org/abs/2007.01758

17. Härkönen, E., Hertzmann, A., Lehtinen, J., Paris, S.: GANSpace: discovering interpretable GAN controls. In: Larochelle, H., Ranzato, M., Hadsell, R., Balcan, M., Lin, H. (eds.) Advances in Neural Information Processing Systems 33: Annual Conference on Neural Information Processing Systems 2020, NeurIPS, Virtual, December 2020, pp. 6–12 (2020). https://proceedings.neurips.cc/paper/2020/hash/6fe43269967adbb64ec6149852b5cc3e-Abstract.html

18. Heusel, M., Ramsauer, H., Unterthiner, T., Nessler, B., Hochreiter, S.: GANs trained by a two time-scale update rule converge to a local Nash equilibrium. In: Guyon, I., et al. (eds.) Advances in Neural Information Processing Systems, vol. 30. Curran Associates, Inc. (2017). https://proceedings.neurips.cc/paper/2017/file/8a1d694707eb0fefe65871369074926d-Paper.pdf

19. Jain, A., Huang, J.: Integrating independent components and linear discriminant analysis for gender classification. In: 6th IEEE International Conference on Automatic Face and Gesture Recognition, FGR 2004, 17–19 May 2004, Seoul, Korea, pp. 159–163. IEEE Computer Society (2004). https://doi.org/10.1109/AFGR.2004.1301524

20. Kamiran, F., Karim, A., Zhang, X.: Decision theory for discrimination-aware classification. In: 2012 IEEE 12th International Conference on Data Mining, pp. 924–929 (2012). https://doi.org/10.1109/ICDM.2012.45

21. Karras, T., Aila, T., Laine, S., Lehtinen, J.: Progressive growing of GANs for improved quality, stability, and variation. In: 6th International Conference on Learning Representations, ICLR 2018, Conference Track Proceedings, Vancouver, BC, Canada, 30 April–3 May 2018. OpenReview.net (2018). https://openreview.net/forum?id=Hk99zCeAb

22. Karras, T., Aittala, M., Hellsten, J., Laine, S., Lehtinen, J., Aila, T.: Training generative adversarial networks with limited data. In: Larochelle, H., Ranzato, M., Hadsell, R., Balcan, M., Lin, H. (eds.) Advances in Neural Information Processing Systems 33: Annual Conference on Neural Information Processing Systems 2020, NeurIPS 2020, Virtual, December 2020, pp. 6–12 (2020). https://proceedings.neurips.cc/paper/2020/hash/8d30aa96e72440759f74bd2306c1fa3d-Abstract.html

23. Karras, T., Laine, S., Aila, T.: A style-based generator architecture for generative adversarial networks. In: IEEE Conference on Computer Vision and Pattern Recognition, CVPR 2019, Long Beach, CA, USA, 16–20 June 2019, pp. 4401–4410. Computer Vision Foundation/IEEE (2019). https://doi.org/10.1109/CVPR.2019.00453

24. Karras, T., Laine, S., Aittala, M., Hellsten, J., Lehtinen, J., Aila, T.: Analyzing and improving the image quality of StyleGAN. In: 2020 IEEE/CVF Conference on Computer Vision and Pattern Recognition, CVPR 2020, Seattle, WA, USA, 13–19 June 2020, pp. 8107–8116. Computer Vision Foundation/IEEE (2020). https://doi.org/10.1109/CVPR42600.2020.00813

25. Keyes, O.: The misgendering machines: Trans/HCI implications of automatic gender recognition. Proc. ACM Hum. Comput. Interact. 2(CSCW), 88:1–88:22 (2018). https://doi.org/10.1145/3274357

26. Khan, S., Ahmad, M., Nazir, M., Riaz, N.: A comparative analysis of gender classification techniques. Middle-East J. Sci. Res. 20, 1–13 (2014). https://doi.org/10.5829/idosi.mejsr.2014.20.01.11434

27. Kipf, T.N., Welling, M.: Semi-supervised classification with graph convolutional networks. In: 5th International Conference on Learning Representations, ICLR 2017, Conference Track Proceedings, Toulon, France, 24–26 April 2017. OpenReview.net (2017). https://openreview.net/forum?id=SJU4ayYgl

28. Krishnan, A., Almadan, A., Rattani, A.: Understanding fairness of gender classification algorithms across gender-race groups. In: Wani, M.A., Luo, F., Li, X.A., Dou, D., Bonchi, F. (eds.) 19th IEEE International Conference on Machine Learning and Applications, ICMLA 2020, Miami, FL, USA, 14–17 December 2020, pp. 1028–1035. IEEE (2020). https://doi.org/10.1109/ICMLA51294.2020.00167

29. Krishnan, A., Almadan, A., Rattani, A.: Investigating fairness of ocular biometrics among young, middle-aged, and older adults. In: 2021 International Carnahan Conference on Security Technology (ICCST), pp. 1–7 (2021). https://doi.org/10.1109/ICCST49569.2021.9717383

30. Krishnan, A., Almadan, A., Rattani, A.: Probing fairness of mobile ocular biometrics methods across gender on VISOB 2.0 dataset. In: Del Bimbo, A., et al. (eds.) ICPR 2021. LNCS, vol. 12668, pp. 229–243. Springer, Cham (2021). https://doi.org/10.1007/978-3-030-68793-9_16

31. Kärkkäinen, K., Joo, J.: FairFace: face attribute dataset for balanced race, gender, and age (2019)

32. Lin, F., Wu, Y., Zhuang, Y., Long, X., Xu, W.: Human gender classification: a review. Int. J. Biom. 8(3/4), 275–300 (2016). https://doi.org/10.1504/IJBM.2016.10003589

33. Lipton, Z.C., Tripathi, S.: Precise recovery of latent vectors from generative adversarial networks. In: 5th International Conference on Learning Representations, ICLR 2017, Workshop Track Proceedings, Toulon, France, 24–26 April 2017. OpenReview.net (2017). https://openreview.net/forum?id=HJC88BzFl

34. Mahajan, D., et al.: Exploring the limits of weakly supervised pretraining. In: Ferrari, V., Hebert, M., Sminchisescu, C., Weiss, Y. (eds.) ECCV 2018. LNCS, vol. 11206, pp. 185–201. Springer, Cham (2018). https://doi.org/10.1007/978-3-030-01216-8_12

35. Majumdar, P., Singh, R., Vatsa, M.: Attention aware debiasing for unbiased model prediction. In: IEEE/CVF International Conference on Computer Vision Workshops, ICCVW 2021, Montreal, BC, Canada, 11–17 October 2021, pp. 4116–4124. IEEE (2021). https://doi.org/10.1109/ICCVW54120.2021.00459

36. Miyato, T., Maeda, S., Koyama, M., Ishii, S.: Virtual adversarial training: a regularization method for supervised and semi-supervised learning. IEEE Trans. Pattern Anal. Mach. Intell. (2017). https://doi.org/10.1109/TPAMI.2018.2858821

37. Morales, A., Fiérrez, J., Vera-Rodríguez, R., Tolosana, R.: SensitiveNets: learning agnostic representations with application to face images. IEEE Trans. Pattern Anal. Mach. Intell. 43(6), 2158–2164 (2021). https://doi.org/10.1109/TPAMI.2020.3015420, https://doi.org/10.1109/TPAMI.2020.3015420

38. Muthukumar, V.: Color-theoretic experiments to understand unequal gender classification accuracy from face images. In: IEEE Conference on Computer Vision and Pattern Recognition Workshops, CVPR Workshops 2019, Long Beach, CA, USA, 16–20 June 2019, pp. 2286–2295. Computer Vision Foundation/IEEE (2019). https://doi.org/10.1109/CVPRW.2019.00282

39. Nadimpalli, A.V., Rattani, A.: GBDF: gender balanced DeepFake dataset towards fair DeepFake detection (2022). https://doi.org/10.48550/ARXIV.2207.10246. https://arxiv.org/abs/2207.10246

40. Nagpal, S., Singh, M., Singh, R., Vatsa, M.: Attribute aware filter-drop for bias-invariant classification. In: 2020 IEEE/CVF Conference on Computer Vision and Pattern Recognition Workshops (CVPRW), pp. 147–153 (2020). https://doi.org/10.1109/CVPRW50498.2020.00024

41. Ngan, M., Grother, P.: Face recognition vendor test (FRVT) - performance of automated gender classification algorithms (2015). https://doi.org/10.6028/NIST.IR.8052

42. Nguyen, H.M., Reddy, N., Rattani, A., Derakhshani, R.: VISOB 2.0 - the second international competition on mobile ocular biometric recognition. In: Del Bimbo, A., et al. (eds.) ICPR 2021. LNCS, vol. 12668, pp. 200–208. Springer, Cham (2021). https://doi.org/10.1007/978-3-030-68793-9_14

43. Park, S., Kim, D., Hwang, S., Byun, H.: README: representation learning by fairness-aware disentangling method. CoRR abs/2007.03775 (2020). https://arxiv.org/abs/2007.03775

44. Perarnau, G., van de Weijer, J., Raducanu, B.C., Álvarez, J.M.: Invertible conditional GANs for image editing. CoRR abs/1611.06355 (2016). http://arxiv.org/abs/1611.06355

45. Radford, A., et al.: Learning transferable visual models from natural language supervision. CoRR abs/2103.00020 (2021). https://arxiv.org/abs/2103.00020

46. Radford, A., Metz, L., Chintala, S.: Unsupervised representation learning with deep convolutional generative adversarial networks. In: Bengio, Y., LeCun, Y. (eds.) 4th International Conference on Learning Representations, ICLR 2016, Conference Track Proceedings, San Juan, Puerto Rico, 2–4 May 2016 (2016). http://arxiv.org/abs/1511.06434

47. Raji, I.D., Buolamwini, J.: Actionable auditing: investigating the impact of publicly naming biased performance results of commercial AI products. In: Conitzer, V., Hadfield, G.K., Vallor, S. (eds.) Proceedings of the 2019 AAAI/ACM Conference on AI, Ethics, and Society, AIES 2019, Honolulu, HI, USA, 27–28 January 2019, pp. 429–435. ACM (2019). https://doi.org/10.1145/3306618.3314244

48. Ramaswamy, V.V., Kim, S.S.Y., Russakovsky, O.: Fair attribute classification through latent space de-biasing. In: IEEE Conference on Computer Vision and Pattern Recognition, CVPR 2021, Virtual, 19–25 June 2021, pp. 9301–9310. Computer Vision Foundation/IEEE (2021). https://openaccess.thecvf.com/content/CVPR2021/html/Ramaswamy_Fair_Attribute_Classification_Through_Latent_Space_De-Biasing_CVPR_2021_paper.html

49. Randall, D.W.: Geoffrey Bowker and Susan Leigh Star, sorting things out: classification and its consequences - review. Comput. Support. Coop. Work. **10**(1), 147–153 (2001). https://doi.org/10.1023/A:1011229919958

50. Ricanek, K., Tesafaye, T.: MORPH: a longitudinal image database of normal adult age-progression. In: 7th International Conference on Automatic Face and Gesture Recognition (FGR06), pp. 341–345 (2006). https://doi.org/10.1109/FGR.2006.78

51. Richardson, E., et al.: Encoding in style: a StyleGAN encoder for image-to-image translation. In: IEEE Conference on Computer Vision and Pattern Recognition, CVPR 2021, Virtual, 19–25 June 2021, pp. 2287–2296. Computer Vision Foundation/IEEE (2021). https://openaccess.thecvf.com/content/CVPR2021/html/Richardson_Encoding_in_Style_A_StyleGAN_Encoder_for_Image-to-Image_Translation_CVPR_2021_paper.html

52. Ryu, H.J., Adam, H., Mitchell, M.: InclusiveFaceNet: improving face attribute detection with race and gender diversity. In: Workshop on Fairness, Accountability, and Transparency in Machine Learning, pp. 1–6, March 2018

53. Sensoy, M., Kaplan, L.M., Kandemir, M.: Evidential deep learning to quantify classification uncertainty. In: Bengio, S., Wallach, H.M., Larochelle, H., Grauman, K., Cesa-Bianchi, N., Garnett, R. (eds.) Advances in Neural Information Processing Systems 31: Annual Conference on Neural Information Processing Systems 2018, NeurIPS 2018, Montréal, Canada, December 2018, pp. 3–8 (2018). https://proceedings.neurips.cc/paper/2018/hash/a981f2b708044d6fb4a71a1463242520-Abstract.html

54. Shen, Y., Gu, J., Tang, X., Zhou, B.: Interpreting the latent space of GANs for semantic face editing. In: 2020 IEEE/CVF Conference on Computer Vision and Pattern Recognition, CVPR 2020, Seattle, WA, USA, 13–19 June 2020, pp. 9240–9249. Computer Vision Foundation/IEEE (2020). https://doi.org/10.1109/CVPR42600.2020.00926

55. Shen, Y., Zhou, B.: Closed-form factorization of latent semantics in GANs. In: IEEE Conference on Computer Vision and Pattern Recognition, CVPR 2021, Virtual, 19–25 June 2021, pp. 1532–1540. Computer Vision Foundation/IEEE (2021). https://openaccess.thecvf.com/content/CVPR2021/html/Shen_Closed-Form_Factorization_of_Latent_Semantics_in_GANs_CVPR_2021_paper.html

56. Siddiqui, H., Rattani, A., Ricanek, K., Hill, T.: An examination of bias of facial analysis based BMI prediction models. In: Proceedings of the IEEE/CVF Conference on Computer Vision and Pattern Recognition (CVPR) Workshops, pp. 2926–2935, June 2022

57. Singh, R., Majumdar, P., Mittal, S., Vatsa, M.: Anatomizing bias in facial analysis. CoRR abs/2112.06522 (2021). https://arxiv.org/abs/2112.06522

58. Smith, P., Chen, C.: Transfer learning with deep CNNs for gender recognition and age estimation (2018)

59. Tartaglione, E., Barbano, C.A., Grangetto, M.: EnD: entangling and disentangling deep representations for bias correction. In: IEEE Conference on Computer Vision and Pattern Recognition, CVPR 2021, virtual, 19–25 June 2021, pp. 13508–13517. Computer Vision Foundation/IEEE (2021)

60. TensorFlow: the neural structured learning framework. https://www.tensorflow.org/neural_structured_learning/framework

61. Tov, O., Alaluf, Y., Nitzan, Y., Patashnik, O., Cohen-Or, D.: Designing an encoder for StyleGAN image manipulation. ACM Trans. Graph. **40**(4), 133:1–133:14 (2021). https://doi.org/10.1145/3450626.3459838

62. Verma, S., Rubin, J.: Fairness definitions explained. In: Proceedings of the International Workshop on Software Fairness, FairWare 2018, pp. 1–7. Association for Computing Machinery, New York (2018). https://doi.org/10.1145/3194770.3194776

63. Voynov, A., Babenko, A.: Unsupervised discovery of interpretable directions in the GAN latent space. In: Proceedings of the 37th International Conference on Machine Learning, ICML 2020, 13–18 July 2020, Virtual Event. Proceedings of Machine Learning Research, vol. 119, pp. 9786–9796. PMLR (2020). http://proceedings.mlr.press/v119/voynov20a.html

64. Wang, B., Ponce, C.R.: A geometric analysis of deep generative image models and its applications. In: 9th International Conference on Learning Representations, ICLR 2021, Virtual Event, Austria, 3–7 May 2021. OpenReview.net (2021). https://openreview.net/forum?id=GH7QRzUDdXG

65. Wang, T., Zhao, J., Yatskar, M., Chang, K., Ordonez, V.: Balanced datasets are not enough: estimating and mitigating gender bias in deep image representations. In: 2019 IEEE/CVF International Conference on Computer Vision, ICCV 2019, Seoul, South Korea, 27 October–2 November 2019, pp. 5309–5318. IEEE (2019). https://doi.org/10.1109/ICCV.2019.00541

66. Wayman, J.: Large-scale civilian biometric systems-issues and feasibility. In: Proceedings of Card Tech/Secur Tech ID, vol. 732 (1997)

67. Wikipedia: Jensen-Shannon divergence, May 2022. https://en.wikipedia.org/wiki/Jensen-Shannon_divergence

68. Wu, Z., Lischinski, D., Shechtman, E.: StyleSpace analysis: disentangled controls for StyleGAN image generation. In: IEEE Conference on Computer Vision and Pattern Recognition, CVPR 2021, Virtual, 19–25 June 2021, pp. 12863–12872. Computer Vision Foundation/IEEE (2021)

69. Zanlorensi, L.A., Laroca, R., Lucio, D.R., Santos, L.R., Britto, A.S., Menotti, D.: UFPR-periocular: a periocular dataset collected by mobile devices in unconstrained scenarios (2020). https://doi.org/10.48550/ARXIV.2011.12427. https://arxiv.org/abs/2011.12427

70. Zhang, K., Zhang, Z., Li, Z., Qiao, Y.: Joint face detection and alignment using multi-task cascaded convolutional networks. CoRR abs/1604.02878 (2016). http://arxiv.org/abs/1604.02878

71. Zhang, Z., Song, Y., Qi, H.: Age progression/regression by conditional adversarial autoencoder. In: IEEE Conference on Computer Vision and Pattern Recognition (CVPR). IEEE (2017)

Statistical Methods for Assessing Differences in False Non-match Rates Across Demographic Groups

Michael Schuckers[1](✉), Sandip Purnapatra[2], Kaniz Fatima[2], Daqing Hou[2], and Stephanie Schuckers[2]

[1] Mathematics, Computer Science and Statistics, St. Lawrence University, Canton, NY, USA
schuckers@stlawu.edu
[2] Computer and Electrical Engineering, Clarkson University, Potsdam, NY, USA
{purnaps,fatimak,dhou,sschucke}@clarkson.edu

Abstract. Biometric recognition is used across a variety of applications from cyber security to border security. Recent research has focused on ensuring biometric performance (false negatives and false positives) is fair across demographic groups. While there has been significant progress on the development of metrics, the evaluation of the performance across groups, and the mitigation of any problems, there has been little work incorporating statistical variation. This is important because differences among groups can be found by chance when no difference is present. In statistics this is called a Type I error. Differences among groups may be due to sampling variation or they may be due to actual difference in system performance. Discriminating between these two sources of error is essential for good decision making about fairness and equity. This paper presents two novel statistical approaches for assessing fairness across demographic groups. The first methodology is a bootstrapped-based hypothesis test, while the second is simpler test methodology focused upon non-statistical audience. For the latter we present the results of a simulation study about the relationship between the margin of error and factors such as number of subjects, number of attempts, correlation between attempts, underlying false non-match rates(FNMR's), and number of groups.

1 Introduction

Biometric recognition is a technology that has broad application for border security, e-commerce, financial transactions, health care, and benefit distribution. With its explosion in use, there are concerns about the fairness of solutions across the broad spectrum of individuals, based on factors such as age, race, ethnicity, gender, education, socioeconomic status, etc. In particular, since biometric recognition has a possibility of error, both false negatives (false rejection) and false positives (false acceptance), the expectation is that solutions have performance which are "fair" across demographic groups. Buolamwini, et. al. found that gender classification based on a single face image had a higher error rate for darker-skinned females with a high 34.7% error rate, compared to other groups (intersections of skin types and genders) [1,2]. While focused on gender

© Springer Nature Switzerland AG 2023
J.-J. Rousseau and B. Kapralos (Eds.): ICPR 2022 Workshops, LNCS 13645, pp. 570–581, 2023.
https://doi.org/10.1007/978-3-031-37731-0_41

classification rather then face recognition, these papers brought considerable attention to this issue. Others found demographic differences in face recognition for some algorithms and systems [3,4].

To quantify the equitability of the various face recognition algorithms, multiple metrics have been proposed to evaluate fairness. ProposedFairness Discrepancy Rate (FDR) weights the two types of errors seen in biometric recognition (false accept and false reject rates), either equally or otherwise, and balances FDR across groups [5]. The U.S. National Institute of Standards and Technology (NIST) introduced the Inequity Rate (IR) metrics for face recognition algorithm performance testing and [6] proposed two interpretibility criterion for biometric systems, i.e. Functional Fairness Measure Criteria (FFMC) and Gini Aggregation Rate for Biometric Equitability (GARBE). In other artificial intelligence (AI) research, evaluation metrics include demographic parity, equalized odds, and equal opportunity [7–10].

However, with all of these active research and analyses, there has been limited contribution towards recommending appropriate statistical methods for determining when two or more groups are "equal" or not. This is essential, as any metric when measured in a sample, will have uncertainty which is a function of variability, correlation, number of groups, and other factors. This uncertainty can be measured through statistical methods, e.g. confidence intervals, to determine the likelihood that differences are found by chance or are a true difference. Given that exact "equality" is unlikely, if not impossible, for a set of groups, these methods allow for appropriate conclusions to be drawn from results.

This paper focuses on statistical methods for fairness solely for false negatives. Biometric solutions used widely by the public are typically based on "verification" or one-to-one matching. A false negative error is when the correct individual is falsely rejected, e.g., does not match their enrollment on a mobile device, passport, bank, or government benefits provider. This "error" may block an individual from accessing benefits which they are entitled to. The goal of this paper is to consider the statistical methods to address differences in false non-match rates based on number of subjects, number of attempts, correlation in attempts, and number of possible demographic groups in the test. The number of subjects and number of attempts can decrease the variability as the number of subjects and attempts increase; whereas, incorporating the correlation between number of attempts may increase sample variability. Most importantly, the number of demographic groups being compared impacts the variation as an increased number of groups increases the chances that a difference between groups may be found "by chance", and thus adjustments need to be made in the test due to this effect, often called multiplicity [11].

This paper develops two approaches to detecting differences in FNMR's between demographic groups. Additionally, we explore the trade-off among variation parameters based on simulations of a hypothetical equity study. In addition to giving guidance on expected outcomes of such a study, this paper will provide suggestions for "practical" thresholds that could be used for when to say that a group is different that would minimize the possibility that difference was based upon chance alone. In the next section we discuss related statistical work that has been done to assess differences in FNMR's between groups. Section 3 introduces the basic statistical structures needed to estimate variation in FNMR estimation. A bootstrap hypothesis test for the equality of FNMR across G groups is presented in Sect. 4, as well as a simplified alternative that yields a margin of error for detecting differences among groups. That section also includes results of a simulation study. We summarize and discuss this work and possible alternatives in Sect. 5.

2 Related Work

In this section, we discuss other work on statistical methods for comparison of bioauthentication across demographic groups. The NIST Information Technology Laboratory (ITL) quantifies the accuracy of face recognition algorithms for the demographic groups of sex, age, and race [3]. A component of the evaluation focuses on FNMR for one-to-one verification algorithms on four large datasets of photographs collected in U.S. governmental applications (domestic mugshots, immigration application photos, border crossing, and visa applications). For high-quality photos, FNMR was found to be low and it is fairly difficult to measure false negative differentials across demographics. Compared to high-quality application photos, the FNMR is higher for lower-quality border crossing images. Similar observations regarding image quality have been made by others, e.g. [4]. A measure of uncertainty is calculated for each demographic group based on a bootstrapping approach. In bootstrapping, the genuine scores are sampled 2000 times and the 95% interval is plotted providing bounds for each group. No method was presented to suggest when an algorithm might be "fair" under uncertainty. A notional approach might be to declare an algorithm fair if the intervals plotted overlap across all combinations of groups. This, however, does not fully address the possibility of Type I errors.

Cook et al. [4] examined the effect of demographic factors on the performance of the eleven commercial face biometric systems tested as part of the 2018 United States Department of Homeland Security, Science and Technology Directorate (DHS S&T) Biometric Technology Rally. Each participating system was tasked with acquiring face images from a diverse population of 363 subjects in a controlled environment. Biometric performance was assessed by measuring both efficiency (transaction times) and accuracy (mated similarity scores using a leading commercial algorithm). The authors quantified the effect of relative facial skin reflectance and other demographic covariates on performance using linear modeling. Both the efficiency and accuracy of the tested acquisition systems were significantly affected by multiple demographic covariates including skin reflectance, gender, age, eyewear, and height, with skin reflectance having the strongest net linear effect on performance. Linear modeling showed that lower (darker) skin reflectance was associated with lower efficiency (higher transaction times) and accuracy (lower mated similarity scores) [4]. While statistical significance of demographic factors was considered based on a linear model of match scores, this approach may not be applicable for assessing commercial systems which operate at a fixed threshold.

de Freitas Pereira and Marcel [5] introduce the Fairness Discrepancy Rate (FDR) which is a summary of system performance accounting for both FNMR and FMR. Their approach uses a "relaxation constant" rather than trying to assess the sampling variation or statistical variation between FNMR's from different demographic groups. Howard et al. [6] present an evaluation of FDR noting its scaling problem. To address this scaling problem, the authors propose a new fairness measure called Gini Aggregation Rate for Biometric Equitability (GARBE).

Other research has also performed extensive evaluations of face recognition across demographic groups, e.g. [12], but have not presented statistical methods as part of their work.

3   Variance and Correlation Structure of FNMR

Statistical methods for estimation of FNMR's are dependent upon the variance and correlation of matching decisions. In this section, we present the basic statistical structures for a single FNMR following [13]. This structure forms the basis for the statistical methods that we present in the next sections. Let D_{iij} represent the decision for the jth pair of captures or signals collected on the ith individual, where n is the number of individuals, $i = 1, \ldots, n$ and $j = 1, \ldots, m_i$. Thus, the number of sample pairs that are compared for the ith individual is m_i, and n is the number of different individuals being compared. The use of m_i implies that we are allowing the number of comparisons made per individual to vary across individuals. We then define

$$D_{iij} = \begin{cases} 1 \text{ if } j^{th} \text{ pair of signals from individual } i \\ \quad \text{ is declared a non-match,} \\ 0 \text{ otherwise.} \end{cases} \tag{1}$$

We assume for the D_{iij}'s that $E[D_{iij}] = \pi$ and $V[D_{iij}] = \pi(1 - \pi)$ represent the mean and variance, respectively. Thus, π represents the FNMR. We assume that we have a stationary matching process within each demographic group and implicit in this assumption is that we have a fixed threshold within each group. Our estimate of π, the process FNMR, will be the total number of errors divided by the total number of decisions:

$$\hat{\pi} = [\sum_{i=1}^{n} \sum_{j=1}^{m_i} D_{iij}]/[\sum_{i=1}^{n} m_i]. \tag{2}$$

Following Schuckers [14, 15], we have the following correlation structure for the D'_{iij}s:

$$Corr(D_{iij}, D_{i'i'j'}) = \begin{cases} 1 \text{ if } i = i', j = j' \\ \rho \text{ if } i = i', j \neq j' \\ 0 \quad otherwise. \end{cases} \tag{3}$$

This correlation structure for the FNMR is based upon the idea that the there will only be correlations between decisions made on signals from the same individual but not between decisions made on signals from different individuals. Thus, conditional upon the error rate, there is no correlation between decisions on the ith individual and decisions on the i'^{th} individual, when $i \neq i'$. The degree of correlation is summarized by ρ. Then we can write the variance of $\hat{\pi}$, the estimated FNMR, as

$$V[\hat{\pi}] = N_{\pi}^{-2} \pi(1 - \pi)[N_{\pi} + \rho \sum_{i=1}^{n} m_i(m_i - 1)] \tag{4}$$

where $N_\pi = \sum_{i=1}^{n} m_i$. An estimator for ρ is given by:

$$\hat{\rho} = \frac{\sum_{i=1}^{n} \sum_{j=1}^{m_i} \sum_{\substack{j'=1 \\ j' \neq j}}^{m_i} (D_{iij} - \hat{\pi})(D_{iij'} - \hat{\pi})}{\hat{\pi}(1 - \hat{\pi}) \sum_{i=1}^{n} m_i(m_i - 1)}. \tag{5}$$

Models like that found in (3) are known as intra-individual or intra-class models and have been studied extensively in the statistics literature, e.g. Fleiss et al. [16], Williams [17] or Ridout et al. [18]. The parameter ρ in the models above represents the intra-class correlation. This measures the degree of similarity between the decisions made on each individual. If the decisions on each individual are varying in a way that suggests that the decisions are not dependent upon the individual then ρ is zero, meaning that the observations are uncorrelated. Negative values of ρ are possible but such values suggest that decisions on signals from the same individual are less similar to each other than they are to all of the other decisions. This seems unlikely to be the case in the context of biometric authentication. Several authors, including Fleiss et al. [16], have suggested using the following alternative way of writing (4)

$$V[\hat{\pi}] = N_\pi^{-1} \pi(1 - \pi)(1 + (m_0 - 1)\rho) \tag{6}$$

where $m_0 = \frac{\sum_{i=1}^{n} m_i^2}{N_\pi}$. If $m_i = m$ for all i, then $N_\pi = nm$ and the variance of $\hat{\pi}$ from (6) becomes $V[\hat{\pi}] = (nm)^{-1} \pi(1 - \pi)(1 + (m - 1)\rho)$.

The intra-class correlation has a direct relationship with the variance of $\hat{\pi}$. As ρ increases, the variance in both cases increases. This is a consequence of the lack of independent information from each individual. If ρ is large, then each additional decision on a previously observed individual is providing little new information.

4   Statistical Methods for Multiple FNMR's

To evaluate and assess if different FNMR's are *detectably* different[1], we need to understand the variation due to sampling. In equity studies across different demographic groups, we need to account for the sampling variation from each of the G groups. For what follows we will assume that there are G demographic groups across multiple dimensions. For example, if a study wants to compare four ethnic groups, five education levels, three genders and five age groups, then $G = 4 + 5 + 3 + 5 = 17$. Methods for comparisons of different demographic groups on their FNMR's generally involve comparing FNMR's across three or more categories. These methods are more advanced and more sophisticated than those for comparing two groups or for comparing a single group to a specific value. See [13] for methods involving one or two FNMR's. Below we present and discuss statistical methods for determining if there are detectable differences between FNMR's among G independent groups. This single methodology is preferable to testing multiple times which yields potentially higher rates of Type I errors. Below we begin with a bootstrap hypothesis test and that is followed by a simplified version that may be more easily understood by a broad audience.

---

[1] We are using detectably different here in place of significantly different. See [19].

4.1 Bootstrap Hypothesis Test

Since the individuals and decisions are independent between groups, we bootstrap each group separately to mirror the variability in the sampling process. As with an analysis of variance (ANOVA), we use a test statistic similar to the usual F-statistic and then we compare the observed value to a reference distribution composed of bootstrapped values. Formally, our hypotheses are: $H_0 : \pi_1 = \pi_2 = \pi_3 = \ldots = \pi_G$, vs H_1 : at least one π_g is different .

1) Calculate

$$F = \frac{\left[\sum_{g=1}^{G} N_{\pi}^{(g)} (\hat{\pi}_g - \hat{\pi})^2 \right] / (G-1)}{\left[\sum_{g=1}^{G} N_{\pi}^{(g)} \hat{\pi}_g (1 - \hat{\pi}_g)(1 + (m_0^{(g)} - 1)\hat{\rho}_g) \right] / (N-G)} \tag{7}$$

for the observed data where

$$\hat{\pi} = \frac{\sum_{g=1}^{G} N_{\pi}^{(g)} \hat{\pi}_g}{\sum_{g=1}^{G} N_{\pi}^{(g)}}, \; \hat{\pi}_g = \frac{\sum_{i=1}^{n_g} \sum_{j=1}^{m_i^{(g)}} D_{iij}^{(g)}}{\sum_{i=1}^{n_g} m_i^{(g)}} \tag{8}$$

and $N = \sum_{g=1}^{G} N_{\pi}^{(g)}$. Here $\hat{\pi}$ is the (weighted) average of the FNMR's across the G groups.

2) For each group g, sample n_g individuals with replacement from the n_g individuals in the gth group. Denote these selected individuals by $b_1^{(g)}, b_2^{(g)}, \ldots, b_{n_g}^{(g)}$. For each selected individual, $b_i^{(g)}$, in the gth group take all the $m_{b_i^{(g)}}$ non-match decisions for that individual. Call these selected decisions $D_{b_i^{(g)} b_i^{(g)} j}^{(g)}$'s with $j = 1, \ldots, m_{b_i^{(g)}}$ and calculate

$$\hat{\pi}_g^b = \frac{\sum_{i=1}^{n_g} \sum_{j=1}^{m_{b_i^{(g)}}} D_{b_i^{(g)} b_i^{(g)} j}^{(g)}}{\sum_{i=1}^{n_g} m_{b_i^{(g)}}} - \hat{\pi}_g + \hat{\pi}. \tag{9}$$

3) Repeat the previous two steps some large number of times, K, each time calculating and storing

$$F_{\pi} = \frac{\left[\sum_{g=1}^{G} N_{\pi}^{(g)} (\hat{\pi}_g^b - \bar{\pi}^b)^2 \right] / (G-1)}{\left[\sum_{g=1}^{G} N_{\pi}^{(g)} \hat{\pi}_g^b (1 - \hat{\pi}_g^b)(1 + (m_0^{(g)b} - 1)\hat{\rho}_g^b) \right] / (N-G)}. \tag{10}$$

Here $\bar{\pi}^b$ represents the calculations given above applied to the bootstrapped matching decisions,

$$\bar{\pi}^b = \frac{\sum_{g=1}^{G} N_{\pi}^{(g)b} \hat{\pi}_g^b}{\sum_{g=1}^{G} N_{\pi}^{(g)b}}, \tag{11}$$

where $N_{\pi}^{(g)b} = \sum_{i=1}^{n_g} m_{b_i^{(g)}}$. The values for $\hat{\rho}_g^b$ and $m_0^{(g)b}$ are found by using the usual estimates for those quantities applied to the bootstrapped decisions from the gth group.

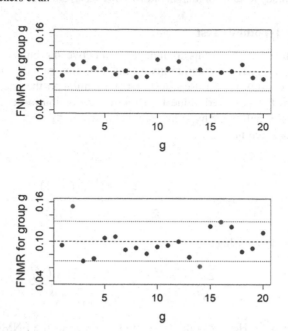

Fig. 1. The top subfigure has all $G = 20$ group FNMR's fall between the bounds (dotted lines) generated by adding and subtracting a margin of error, M, from the overall FNMR (dashed lines), while the bottom subfigure has three subgroups (in red) that fall outside of these bounds. (Color figure online)

4) Then the *p-value* for this test is $p = \frac{1 + \sum_{\varsigma=1}^{K} I_{\{F_{\pi} \geq F\}}}{K + 1}$.
5) We will conclude that at least one of the FNMR's is different from the rest if the *p-value* is small. When a significance level is designated, then we will reject the null hypothesis, H_0, if $p < \alpha$.

We adjust our bootstrapped sample statistic, here $\hat{\pi}^b$, to center their distributions of the FNMR's in each group in accordance with the null hypothesis of equality between the G FNMR's. In this case we center with respect to our estimate of the FNMR, $\hat{\pi}$, assuming all of the FNMR's are identical.

4.2 Simplified Alternative Methodology for Broad Audience Reporting

The methods of the previous subsection may be difficult to explain to a broad, non-technical audience. Consequently, in this section, we propose a methodology for simplifying the testing of multiple FNMR's across demographic groups. That is, we will conclude that a particular subgroup g has a different FNMR if its observed FNMR is outside of the interval created by taking the average FNMR, $\hat{\pi}$, and adding and subtracting a margin of error, M. This methodology is more straightforward for explaining to decision makers and to wide audiences and takes advantage of the common usage of the margin of error.

In order to generate a single margin of error for all G groups, we bootstrap the differences of each FNMR from the overall FNMR, then use the distribution of the maximal absolute differences to obtain M. This approach is the following:

1) Calculate the estimated overall FNMR, $\hat{\pi}$ and the estimated FNMR for each group, $\hat{\pi}_g$, for $g = 1,\ldots,G$.
2) Sample with replacement the individuals in each group following Step 2) of the bootstrap approach above and calculate $\hat{\pi}_g^b$, the scaled bootstrapped estimated FNMM for group g.
3) Calculate and store $\phi = \max_g |\hat{\pi}_g^b - \hat{\pi}|$ using the notation from Eq. 9 of the bootstrap approach.
4) Repeat the previous two steps K times where K is large, say more than 500.
5) Determine M by finding the $1 - \alpha/2^{th}$ percentile from the distribution of ϕ.

The maximal differences, the ϕ's, are calculated from each group FNMR which are scaled to (subtracted from) the overall mean, so the distribution for ϕ that assumes variation if all of the FNMR's are equal. From this approach a range, $(\hat{\pi} - M, \hat{\pi} + M)$,

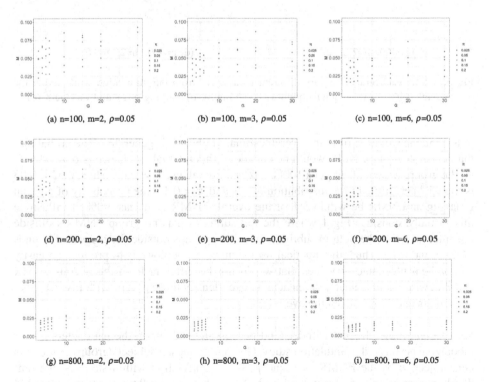

(a) n=100, m=2, ρ=0.05   (b) n=100, m=3, ρ=0.05   (c) n=100, m=6, ρ=0.05

(d) n=200, m=2, ρ=0.05   (e) n=200, m=3, ρ=0.05   (f) n=200, m=6, ρ=0.05

(g) n=800, m=2, ρ=0.05   (h) n=800, m=3, ρ=0.05   (i) n=800, m=6, ρ=0.05

Fig. 2. Results of simulation study for margin of error (M) as a function of number of individuals (n), number of attempts (m), correlation between attempts (ρ), and FNMR (π). Subfigures are organized by columns where m increases from left to right and by rows where n increases from top to bottom. Each figure plots M versus G for fixed $\rho = 0.05$ and with different values for π denoted by color.

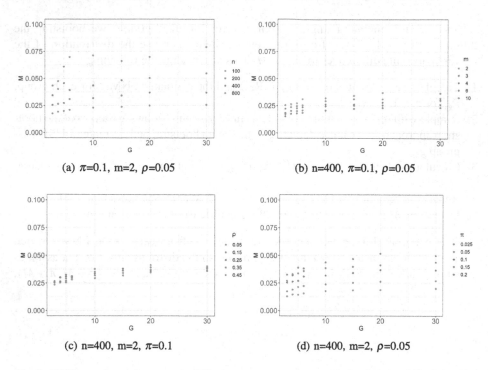

(a) π=0.1, m=2, ρ=0.05

(b) n=400, π=0.1, ρ=0.05

(c) n=400, m=2, π=0.1

(d) n=400, m=2, ρ=0.05

Fig. 3. Within each graph we vary different parameters from our simulation while fixing the others: each color is a varying n (subfigure a); varying m (b); varying ρ (c); and varying π (d)

of acceptable variation from the overall estimated FNMR, is generated. The probability that a sample group FNMR would be outside of this interval by chance is $\alpha \times 100\%$ if all the groups are equal. To get a $100(1-\alpha)\%$ interval, use $\alpha = 0.05$. Thus, if $M = 0.03$ is the 95th percentile of the distribution of ϕ's and $\hat{\pi} = 0.10$, the probability of a group g having an FNMR be within 3% of the overall FNMR is at least 90%. To illustrate this visually, consider Fig. 1 where the top subfigure has no group FNMR's outside our interval while the bottom subfigure has three groups outside the generated bounds of 0.07 and 0.13. Thus, the practical use of this methodology is to produce an easily comprehensible range of values that would not be different from the overall FNMR and, likewise, yield a clearly delineated way to identify those groups with FNMR's that are statistical different from the overall mean.

Simulation Study. To better understand how M depends upon the parameters of our model, we performed a simulation study. Given G groups, n subjects/group, m attempts per subject, π as the FNMR rate, and ρ as the correlation within subjects, we randomly generated false non match rates, $\hat{\pi}_g$, for each group 1000 times and calculated M as above. We ran all combinations of the following values for each parameter: $\pi = 0.025, 0.05, 0.10, 0.15, 0.20$, $\rho = 0.05, 0.15, 0.25, 0.35, 0.45$, $n = 100, 200, 400, 800$, $m = 2, 3, 4, 6, 10$ and $G = 3, 4, 5, 6, 10, 15, 20, 30$. Our values for ρ were selected to cover the values for estimated intra-individual correlations found in [13]. We fixed α at 0.05

for these simulations. Figures 2 and 3 show summaries of the results of these simulations with M rounded to three decimal places with $\alpha = 0.05$ in all cases. Figure 2 shows simulation results for various values of n, the subfigure rows, m, the subfigure columns and π, colors within each subfigure while the intra-individual correlation ρ was fixed at 0.05 for these graphics. Within each subfigure, we have plotted M versus G and denoted different values of π by different colors. From each subfigure, we can see that M grows as G increases though the amount of increase in M slows as G gets larger than 10. Moving down subfigure rows, ie. as n increases we see that M decreases. Similarly, going from left to right across subfigure columns, i.e. as m increases we see decreases in M. Within each subfigure we can see that M becomes smaller as π decreases. In Fig. 3, we have plotted M versus G and varied a single parameter (denoted by different colors) in each subfigure at the values given above while fixing the other parameters at $n = 400$, $\pi = 0.10$, $\rho = 0.05$ and $m = 2$. From these values, we can see the impact of n, the number of individuals per group has the largest impact on M, followed by π, the overall FNMR, then m, the number of attempts per individual, and ρ the intra-individual decision correlation. Only ρ is negatively associated with the size of M. The impacts of m and ρ are tied together because of the nature of FNMR data. While not shown in either of these figures, our simulations show that there is a positive, though not linear, relationship between ρ and M.

5 Discussion

Equity and fairness in biometrics are important issues. The declaration of differences between demographic groups is a consequential one. Such conclusions about differences between groups need to be statistically sound and empirically based. In this paper, we have proposed two approaches for testing for statistically detectable differences in FNMR's across G groups. Our first approach uses the F-statistic as a metric and builds a reference distribution for that statistic via bootstrapping. As mentioned above, this methodology, while valid and appropriate, is not easy to explain. Our second approach attempts to remedy this drawback. The second approach is to bootstrap maximal differences among the FNMR's in the G groups assuming a known equal FNMR across all groups, then generates a margin of error, M, to be added and subtracted to the overall FNMR for delineating which groups or subgroups are statistically different from the overall mean. The latter approach has an advantage of being simpler and similar to other colloquial margins of error. From our simulation study of this simpler approach, we have confirmed that the number of groups, G, and the number of individuals tested, N, substantially impact the margin of error. Likewise though to a lesser extent the intra-individual correlation, ρ, and the number of attempts per individual, m, impact the size of M. Our simplified approach uses the maximal absolute difference from the overall FNMR across the G groups. Using this distribution we generate an interval that is the overall FNMR plus and minus a margin of error M where M is based upon the distribution of the maximal absolute difference. Both of these methods, because they rely solely on thresholded decision data are applicable for testing commercial systems.

Both of our approaches in this paper have considered differences from the overall FNMR. But reasonable alternatives such as $\max_g \left(\frac{\hat{\pi}_g}{\hat{\pi}}, \frac{\hat{\pi}}{\hat{\pi}_g} \right)$ might be of interest. The importance of being able to generate a reference distribution to allow for an appropriate comparison to the observed statistics is critical to any statistical evaluation regardless of the functional form of the variation.

This paper has looked at false non-match rate but similar methods and approaches exist for other common measures of bioauthentication performance including failure to enrol rates, failure to acquire rates and false match rates. See [13] for approaches for testing and comparing differences among multiple groups for these metrics.

Acknowledgment. This work was supported by grants from the US National Science Foundation CNS-1650503 and CNS-1919554, and the Center for Identification Technology Research (CITeR).

References

1. Buolamwini, J., Gebru, T.: Gender shades: intersectional accuracy disparities in commercial gender classification. In: Proceedings of Machine Learning Research, Conference on Fairness, Accountability, and Transparency, pp. 1–15 (2018)
2. Buolamwini, J.A.: Gender shades: intersectional phenotypic and demographic evaluation of face datasets and gender classifiers, M.Sc. Thesis (2017). http://hdl.handle.net/1721.1/114068. Accessed 10 Jul 2022
3. Grother, P., Ngan, M., Hanaoka, K.: Face recognition vendor test (FRVT) part 3: demographic effects. United States National Institute of Standards and Technology, Technical report, NIST.IR 8280 (2019). https://doi.org/10.6028/NIST.IR.8280
4. Cook, C.M., Howard, J.J., Sirotin, Y.B., Tipton, J.L., Vemury, A.R.: Demographic effects in facial recognition and their dependence on image acquisition: an evaluation of eleven commercial systems. IEEE Trans. Biometrics Behav. Identity Sci. 1(1), 32–41 (2019)
5. de Freitas Pereira, T., Marcel, S.: Fairness in biometrics: a figure of merit to assess biometric verification systems. IEEE Trans. Biometrics Behav. Identity Sci. 4(1), 19–29 (2022)
6. Howard, J.J., Laird, E.J., Sirotin, Y.B., Rubin, R.E., Tipton, J.L., Vemury, A.R.: Evaluating proposed fairness models for face recognition algorithms. arXiv preprint arXiv:2203.05051 (2022)
7. Hardt, M., Price, E., Srebro, N.: Equality of opportunity in supervised learning, Technical report (2016). https://doi.org/10.48550/arXiv.1610.02413
8. Bellamy, R.K.E., et al.: AI Fairness 360: an extensible toolkit for detecting and mitigating algorithmic bias. IBM J. Res. Develop. 63(4/5), 4:1–4:15 (2019)
9. IBM: AI Fairness 360. IBM toolkit. https://aif360.mybluemix.net/. Accessed 11 Jul 2022
10. Osoba, O.A., Boudreaux, B., Saunders, J., Irwin, J.L., Mueller, P.A., Cherney, S.: Algorithmic equity: a framework for social applications. RAND Corporation, Technical report (2019)
11. Hsu, J.: Multiple Comparisons: Theory and Methods. Chapman & Hall/CRC (1996)
12. Krishnapriya, K.S., Albiero, V., Vangara, K., King, M.C., Bowyer, K.W.: Issues related to face recognition accuracy varying based on race and skin tone. IEEE Trans. Technol. Soc. 1(1), 8–20 (2020)
13. Schuckers, M.E.: Computational Methods in Biometric Authentication. Springer, London (2010). https://doi.org/10.1007/978-1-84996-202-5
14. Schuckers, M.E.: Theoretical statistical correlation for biometric identification performance. In: Proceedings of the International Conference on Acoustics, Speech, and Signal Processing (ICASSP) (2008)

15. Schuckers, M.E.: A parametric correlation framework for the statistical evaluation and estimation of biometric-based classification performance in a single environment. IEEE Trans. Inf. Forensics Secur. **4**, 231–241 (2009)
16. Fleiss, J.L., Levin, B., Paik, M.C.: Statistical Methods for Rates and Proportions. Wiley (2003)
17. Williams, D.A.: The analysis of binary responses from toxicological experiments involving reproduction and teratogenicity. Biometrics **31**, 949–952 (1975)
18. Ridout, M.S., DemÉtrio, C.G.B., Firth, D.: Estimating intraclass correlation for binary data. Biometrics **55**, 137–148 (1999)
19. Wasserstein, R.L., Lazar, N.A.: The ASA statement on p-values: context, process, and purpose. Am. Stat. **70**(2), 129–133 (2016). https://doi.org/10.1080/00031305.2016.1154108

Deep Learning Based Age and Gender Recognition Applied to Finger Vein Images

Georg Wimmer[✉][iD], Bernhard Prommegger[iD], and Andreas Uhl[iD]

Department of Artificial Intelligence and Human Interfaces, University of Salzburg,
Jakob-Haringer-Strasse 2, 5020 Salzburg, Austria
{gwimmer,bprommeg,uhl}@cs.sbg.ac.at

Abstract. Finger vein recognition deals with the identification of subjects based on their venous pattern within the fingers. It was shown in previous work that biometric data can include more than only identity related information like e.g. age, gender and ethnicity. In this work, deep learning based methods are employed to find out if finger vein image data includes information on the age and gender of the subjects. In our experiments we use different CNNs and different loss functions (triplet loss, SoftMax loss and Mean Squared Error loss) to predict gender and age based on finger vein image data. Using three publicly available finger vein image datasets, we show that it is feasible to predict the gender (accuracies of up to 93.1%). By analyzing finger vein data from different genders we found out that the finger thickness and especially the total length over all finger veins are important features to differentiate between images from male and female subjects. On the other hand, estimating the age of the subjects hardly worked at all in our experiments.

Keywords: finger vein recognition · age · gender

1 Introduction

Biometric systems extract identity related information to use it for person recognition or identification. However, biometric data can include more than only identity related information. For example, humans can deduce a lot of information from images of the face of a person like age, gender and ethnicity.

Previous works predicted both the age and gender of subjects based on face images [18,29], voice recordings [15], gait [21], ear [28] and also using less intuitive biometric traits for age and gender prediction like finger prints [6] and EEG recordings [13]. Furthermore, iris (ocular) images have been used to predict age [19] and gender [1,23]. Reviews about the demographic bias in biometrics are presented in [5,22].

This project was partly funded from the FFG KIRAS project AUTFingerATM under grant No. 864785 and the FWF project "Advanced Methods and Applications for Fingervein Recognition" under grant No. P 32201-NBL.

J.-J. Rousseau and B. Kapralos (Eds.): ICPR 2022 Workshops, LNCS 13645, pp. 582–596, 2023.
https://doi.org/10.1007/978-3-031-37731-0_42

In this work we analyze the demographic bias in biometric finger vein image data with respect to the age and gender of the subjects. Research on soft-biometrics showed that privacy-sensitive information can be deduced from bio-metric templates of an individual. Since these templates are expected to be used for recognition purposes only, this raises major privacy issues. We aim to find out if these privacy issues also apply for finger vein data with regard to age and gender information.

Two medical studies [7,14], showed that there is no noticeable influence of age on the size of the veins but the size of the veins is in general bigger for men as for woman.

In [4], the authors claim that common finger vein recognition systems are not able to recognize age and gender from finger vein images. However, the considered finger vein recognition systems were purely trained for subject recognition and not to recognize the age or gender of the subjects. There are also previous publications that developed methods specifically for age and gender recognition based on vein images. However, these publications either use a heavily biased experimental setup and/or show serious errors in the experimental setup by speaking of age and gender recognition while actually doing subject recognition:

- [2,3]: In these two papers from the same authors Local Binary Pattern (LBP) operators are employed together with a nearest neighbor classifier to estimate the age and gender based on finger vein [2] and palm vein [3] images. What the authors actually did is to assign an image the age/gender of its nearest neighbor. The systematical error in the experimental setup is that they did not exclude comparisons between images from the same finger and subject. As the nearest neighbor of nearly each image is an image from the same finger, these two papers do misrepresent a subject recognition as an age/gender recognition.
- [25]: In this publication a 2-layer network combined with a linear SVM classifier is applied for gender recognition of hand dorsal vein images. In the publication there is no splitting in training and evaluation data (same data is used for training and evaluation), which heavily biases the experiments and makes the results unusable.

So this is the first paper for age and gender recognition based on finger vein images with methods specifically trained to predict the age and gender of the subjects without a heavily biased or incorrect experimental setup. In the experiments we employ CNN-based methods for gender and age recognition on three publicly available finger vein image datasets. The CNNs are trained using various loss functions that are suited for age respectively gender recognition. Furthermore, this is the first paper that analyses what features are really different between male and female finger vein images.

2   Databases

In the experiments, three publicly available finger vein datasets are employed. All of them provide - next to the vein images - also information on age and gender

Table 1. The number of subjects, instances and samples of each of the three employed finger vein image datasets.

Database	Subjects	Instances	Samples
PLUS-FV3	76	456	2268
UTFVP	60	360	1440
MMCBNU	100	600	6000

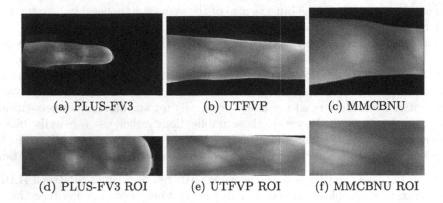

(a) PLUS-FV3   (b) UTFVP   (c) MMCBNU

(d) PLUS-FV3 ROI   (e) UTFVP ROI   (f) MMCBNU ROI

Fig. 1. Exemplar finger vein images of the three datasets. In the top row we show the original finger vein image and in the bottom row the ROI extracted versions of the images above.

of the acquired subjects. The first dataset is a combination of the PLUSVein-FV3 [12] and the PROTECT Multimodal DB [8] further donated as PLUS-FV3. Due to missing age and gender information, two out of the 78 subjects have been omitted. The other datasets are the UTFVP [24] and the MMCBNU [16]. The number of subjects, instances and image samples are listed in Table 1. The experiments are applied to the original finger vein images as well as to images that are reduced to the region of interest (ROI) using a ROI extraction technique based on [17]. In Fig. 1, example images (original ones as well as ROI extracted version of the images) are presented for each dataset.

3   Methods

Since age and gender recognition are quite different tasks to handle we employ different CNN-based approaches with different loss functions for the two tasks which also results in different performance measures for different approaches. Since the datasets are mostly quite inbalanced with respect to the number of images per gender (see Table 2) and the age distribution among the subjects (see Fig. 2, black bars), the CNN training is applied using balanced batch sampling (each batch contains the same number of images per class) to mitigate the bias in the data. For all experiments, the CNNs are trained using 2-fold cross validation.

The CNNs are trained on one fold and evaluation is applied on the other one and then vice versa. The images of half of the subjects are in one fold and the images of the remaining subjects are in the other fold. All CNNs are trained for 400 epochs using nets that were pretrained on the ImageNet database. Data augmentation is applied by first resizing the input images to a size of 229×229 and then extracting a patch of size 224×224 at a random position of the resized image (± 5 pixels in each direction). As performance measures we report the mean accuracy over the two folds and partly also the mean Equal Error Rate (EER) over the two folds.

3.1 Methods for Gender Recognition

To train a CNN to recognize the gender based on finger vein images, each image of the training fold is assigned to the class (male or female) of the respective subject. In that way the CNN can learn similarities between images of the same class (gender) and differences between images of different classes. For more meaningful results and to see if different methods produce different results, two quite different CNN approaches are applied with very different loss functions for CNN training and also different CNN architectures:

1. Triplet loss: Same as in a previous publication on finger vein recognition [26], we employ the triplet loss function for CNN training. Per training step, the triplet loss requires three input images at once (a so called triplet), where two images belong to the same class (the anchor image and a sample from the same class, further denoted as positive) and the third belongs to a different class (further denoted as negative). The triplet loss learns the network to minimize the distance between the anchor and the positive and maximize the distance between the anchor and the negative. The triplet loss using the squared Euclidean distance is defined as follows:

$$L(A, P, N) = \max(\|f(A) - f(P)\|^2 - \|f(A) - f(N)\|^2 + \alpha, 0), \qquad (1)$$

where A is the anchor, P the positive and N the negative. α is a margin that is enforced between positive and negative pairs and is set to $\alpha = 1$. $f(x)$ is an embedding (the CNN output of an input image x). So the CNN is trained so that the squared distances between all embeddings of finger vein images from the same class (gender) is small, whereas the squared distance between embeddings of any pairs of finger vein images from different classes is large. As CNN architecture we employ the SqueezeNet [10], a neural networks with low memory requirements. The size of the last layers convolutional filter is adapted so that a 256-dimensional output (embedding) is produced. As first performance measure we compute the EER, where the similarity score between two finger vein images is defined as the inversed euclidean distances between the CNN outputs of two images. As second performance measure we compute the (Rank-1) accuracy. Since CNNs that were trained with the triplet loss produce an feature vector (embedding) for each input image instead of a class prediction (like CNNs trained with the SoftMax loss), a classifier is required to obtain gender predictions. Ftor this we employ a linear SVM to predict the gender based on the CNN outputs. Same as the CNNs, the SVM is trained on the training fold while evaluation is applied on the images of the evaluation fold.

2. SoftMax loss: Another obvious choice for this 2-class gender classification problem is to employ the widely known SoftMax loss function to train a CNN. As net architecture we employ the DenseNet-161 [9]. Since the CNN predicts gender directly without generating any feature vector output per image, we only report the accuracy and not the EER, for which distances between images would be required.

As can be observed in Table 2, only the PLUS-FV3 dataset is somehow balanced with respect to the gender distribution of the subjects. The other two datasets consist of distinctly more male subjects than female ones. So for a better overview on the CNN classification outcomes, we not only report the accuracy over the whole dataset but also the percentage of images from female subjects that were correctly classified as female (ACC women) and the percentage of images from male subjects that were correctly classified as male (ACC men).

The gender recognition experiments are applied to the original images as well as to the ROI extracted images. The original images have the advantage that the images contain information on the length and thickness of the fingers, while the ROI extracted images have the advantage of a higher image resolution since the images need to be resized to the required CNN input size (224×224) and by downsizing only the part of the image containing the finger the resolution is higher than by downsizing the whole image.

3.2 Methods for Age Recognition

For all age recognition experiments, we only employ the ROI extracted images. This is done because the length and thickness of the fingers does not matter for age recognition. Age recognition will probably be a more difficult task than gender recognition, since there are no known differences in the vein structure depending on the age of the subjects (see [14]). Because of that, we do not directly start with a direct estimation of the age but firstly conduct an experiment to find out if CNNs are at least able to discriminate between finger vein images of young and old subjects. For this, we divide the datasets in two classes, with one class consisting of all images of subjects under 25 years and the other class of all images of subjects over 45 years. The images of all subjects with an age between 25 and 45 years are removed for this experiment. If the CNNs are not even capable to differentiate between these two age groups, then all further experiments to estimate the age of subjects based on finger vein images would probably be futile. For this experiments we employ the same methods (SqueezeNet trained with triplet loss and DenseNet trained with SoftMax loss) as in the gender recognition experiment. Similar to the gender recognition experiment, the datasets are quite unbalanced with respect to the number of images per class and hence we once again not only report the overall accuracy but also the percentage of correctly classified images of the class containing all subjects under 25 years age and of the class containing all subjects above 45 years age.

In a second and more difficult experiment, we aim to directly estimate the age of the subjects using a CNN trained with the mean squared error (MSE) loss function. For this experiment we use all images of the datasets contrary to the previous one. As net architecture we employ ResNeXt101 [27]. For training, each finger vein image of the training fold is assigned to the age of the according subject so that the CNN can learn to estimate the age based on finger vein images. For the images of the evaluation fold, an age estimation is made using the trained CNN. Then the folds for training and validation are exchanged. In this experiments we do not classify images like in the previous experiments but directly estimate the age of the subjects from the images. Thus, we need to apply different performance measures in this experiment and report the mean absolute error (MAE) over all images:

$$MAE = \frac{1}{N} \sum_{i=1}^{N} |y_i - \hat{y}_i|, \tag{2}$$

where N is the number of images of the dataset, $\hat{y}_i$ the CNN's age prediction of image i and y_i the actual age of the image's subject. Furthermore, we divide the images into several age groups with an age group having a range of 10 years. Then we compare the actual number of images per age group with the number of images that are correctly and incorrectly predicted to the considered age group. Additionally, we present the mean over the CNN age predictions over all images per age group.

4   Results

4.1   Gender Recognition

In Table 2, we present the gender recognition results using the SoftMax loss trained CNN (along with the number of images per gender) and in Table 3 the results using the triplet loss trained CNN. For the triplet loss trained net we report the EER additional to the accuracy. We can observe that on all three datasets accuracies between about 79 and 93% are achieved for both kinds of CNNs. In general, the accuracies for the two kinds of CNNs are similar. For the PLUS-FV3 and UTFVP dataset, the classification rates are between about 76% and 87% for images from female subjects and between 84% and 97% for images from male subjects. In case of the MMCBNU dataset, the inbalance between the number of male and female subjects is huge (nearly 5 times as much men as women) which probably leads to the fact that most images are predicted to be male by the CNNs, even the images from women. For the ROI images of the MMCBNU dataset, about 50% of the images from female subjects are classified correctly but for the original images only 10–15% of the images from female subjects are classified correctly. In the discussion we will analyze if the inbalance between the number of images from male and female subjects is actually the reason that most of the images of the MMCBNU dataset are predicted to be male.

Table 2. Gender classification results (accuracy (ACC) in %) using SoftMax loss trained CNNs

Databases	Images per gender		ACC		
	women	men	overall	women	men
PLUS-FV3 (ROI)	951	1317	81.7	76.4	86.0
MMCBNU (ROI)	1020	4980	87.5	49.3	93.4
UTFVP (ROI)	384	1056	90.5	78.8	96.3
PLUS-FV3 (Orig.)	951	1317	86.1	84.0	88.2
MMCBNU (Orig.)	1020	4980	79.3	10.1	93.5
UTFVP (Orig.)	384	1056	92.2	82.1	97.1

Table 3. Gender recognition (EER in %) and classification results (ACC in %) using triplet loss trained CNNs

Databases	EER	ACC		
		all	women	men
PLUS-FV3 (ROI)	34.2	80.3	73.3	84.0
MMCBNU (ROI)	27.1	88.6	51.4	96.1
UTFVP (ROI)	18.3	92.1	83.6	96.4
PLUS-FV3 (Original)	29.4	84.4	78.3	89.5
MMCBNU (Original)	46.9	80.3	14.6	93.9
UTFVP (Original)	13.8	93.1	86.5	96.7

In general, it does not matter whether we use the original finger vein images or the ROI extracted images with respect to the results, except for the MMCBNU dataset.

4.2 Age Recognition

2-Class Age Recognition Experiment: In Table 4 we present the results for the 2-class age recognition experiment, where all images of subjects under 25 years of age are assigned to one class and all images of subjects over 45 years are assigned to the other one. On all three datasets, the images from the class with fewer images are misclassified clearly more often than the images from the class with more images. The differences in the results of the two classes are even more pronounced than in the gender recognition experiments. For the MMCBNU dataset, nearly all images are predicted to belong to the class with distinctly more samples (<25). We can observe that at least for the PLUS-FV3 and the UTFVP dataset, the prediction of the age class is clearly better than random assignment with classification rates of up to nearly 90% for the UTFVP dataset and up to 76% for the PLUS-FV3 dataset.

Age Estimation Experiment: In Fig. 2 we present the number of images per age group for all three datasets as well as outcomes of the age recognition

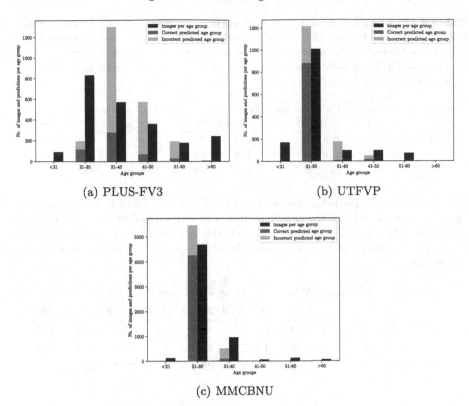

(a) PLUS-FV3   (b) UTFVP

(c) MMCBNU

Fig. 2. Actual number of images per age group (black bars) compared to the number of CNN age predictions that are correctly (green bar) and incorrectly (orange bar) assigned to an age group (Color figure online)

experiment for images at different age groups. The age of the subjects is estimated using the CNN trained with the MSE loss. Each age group except the first (till 20) and last one (over 60) has a range of 10 years. The black bar shows the number of images per age group, the green bar the number of images that are correctly predicted to the considered age group and the orange bar the number of images that are incorrectly predicted to the considered age group. So if we add up the numbers of the orange and green bar for an age group, then we get the number of images whose CNN age estimate is within the range of the age group under consideration. In Fig. 2 we can observe that only the PLUS-FV3 dataset has a at least somehow balanced distribution of subjects across the different age groups. The other two datasets mainly consist of subjects at an age between 21 and 30. We can observe that most of the images on all datasets are predicted to the age group that contains the mean age over a dataset. In case of the two datasets UTFVP and MMCBNU, this is also the age group that contains the majority of image samples. In case of the PLUS-FV3 dataset, where the images are distributed over several different age groups, most images are predicted to the wrong age group (31–40 years).

Table 4. CNN results for grouping the images in two classes, where one class comprises all images below an age of 25 years and the other one all images above 45 years. For the triplet loss trained CNNs we present the accuracy and the EER in %, for the SoftMax loss trained CNNs we only present the accuracy. Furthermore, we present the number of images per class.

Database	Nr. of images		CNN results with Triplet loss				CNN results with SoftMax		
	<25	>45	EER	ACC overall	ACC<25	ACC>45	ACC overall	ACC<25	ACC>45
PLUS-FV3	297	657	40.3	76.0	63.3	83.9	74.0	58.9	85.1
MMCBNU	1440	240	51.0	83.6	97.2	6.7	85.1	99.4	0.0
UTFVP	672	167	26.4	89.7	99.4	59.7	87.4	98.8	50.7

Table 5. CNN age prediction results using the MSE-loss. The left column shows the mean age per dataset and the middle columns the Mean Absolute Error (MAE) of the CNN and of the method that simply predicts the mean age for all samples (MP). The right side columns present the mean over the CNN age predictions over all images per age group

Databases	Mean age	MAE		Mean CNN prediction per age group					
		CNN	MP	0–20	21–30	31–40	41–50	51–60	>60
PLUS-FV3	38.5	11.4	11.5	33.4	36.2	38.8	37.2	41.6	44.7
MMCBNU	27.7	4.5	4.5	24.9	27.0	26.8	28.8	25.9	26.6
UTFVP	28.4	5.9	6.2	25.1	26.4	25.9	32.1	31.9	-

In Table 5, we present the CNN results on all three datasets using the Mean Absolute Error (MAE) in years as performance measure. To get an understanding if the MAE results of the proposed CNN age prediction method are good or rather not, we compare the MAE of the CNN with the MAE of a method denoted as 'mean prediction' (MP). This method simply assigns the mean age (average age over the ages of all subjects from a dataset) to each image of the dataset. In addition, we present the mean over the CNN age estimates separately for the images of each age group. For example, if we consider the age group '0–20', it means that we present the average over all CNN age estimates from images of subjects between the ages of 0 and 20 years. We can observe in Table 5 that the MAE of the CNN is only slightly better or equal as the MAE for predicting the mean age for each image of the dataset (MP). So the age estimation using our CNN does not work well.

When we observe the mean CNN predictions per age group on the PLUS-FV3 dataset (the two other datasets mainly consist of images from subject with an age between 21 and 30, which limits the information we can extract from the results of these two datasets), then we can see that the CNN age predictions on finger vein images from subjects of higher age are indeed higher as the age predictions on images of subjects from lower age. However, the CNN predictions are clearly too close to the mean age over the dataset (38.5) and hence too high for images of younger subjects and too low for images of older subjects.

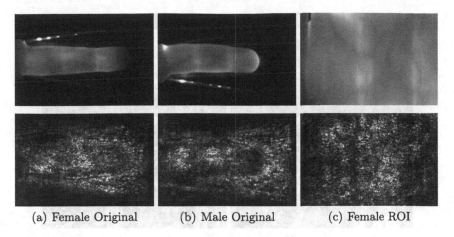

(a) Female Original   (b) Male Original   (c) Female ROI

Fig. 3. CNN visualizations using Vanilla backpropagation of male and female finger vein images using original as well as ROI images. Top row: original image, bottom row: saliency map

5 Discussion

In this section we aim to find out which features enable the CNNs to discriminate between genders using a gradient based CNN visualization technique. Furthermore, we want to find which differences actually do exist between male and female finger vein images by analyzing segmentation masks of the fingers and manual extracted segmentations of the finger vein structure. In addition, we want to find the cause for the poor gender recognition result on the MMCBNU dataset. Age recognition clearly did not work and hence there is no need to discuss the results any further.

The idea behind gradient based CNN visualization techniques is to compute the gradient of the network's prediction with respect to the input, holding the weights fixed. This determines which pixels of an input image need to be changed the least to affect the prediction the most. In this work we employ gradient visualization using Vanilla Backpropagation [20] to get the saliency maps of images. With these saliency maps we can measure the relative importance of each pixel to the ultimate prediction by the model. In Fig. 3 we present the saliency maps of three different finger vein images from the PLUS-FV3 dataset (two original images and one ROI image) using a CNN that was trained to predict the gender with the SoftMax loss function. From the saliency maps of the two original images (one of a man's finger and one of a woman's finger) we can observe that image regions from the background that are surrounding the finger have an impact on the CNN predictions as high as image regions within the finger. This indicates that the finger thickness and length are features used by the CNN to determine the gender. By segmenting the fingers on the UTFVP dataset (using the segmentation method for the ROI extraction) and computing the finger thickness, we found that the fingers of male subjects are in average

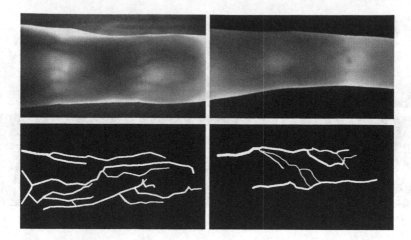

Fig. 4. Two example images of the UTFVP dataset (top row) and their manually extracted segmentation masks (bottom row) from the $UTFVP_{seg}$ dataset.

15% thicker than those of female subjects. For the ROI image, the saliency map is fairly uniform across the regions of the finger without any clear visible correspondence to the vein pattern, so no conclusion can be drawn about what features are important for the CNN to predict the gender.

As already mentioned in the introduction, it was shown in a medical study that the cross section area of veins is in general bigger for men as for women. We now aim to verify if that is also the case for the finger veins using a dataset containing manually segmented veins from finger vein images. This dataset [11], further denotes as UTFVP$_{seg}$, contains 388 segmentation masks from images of the UTFVP dataset. 292 segmentation masks are from male subjects and 92 from female subjects. UTFVP$_{seg}$ includes at least one segmentation mask per finger of the UTFVP dataset, for some fingers it includes two. In Fig. 4 we show two finger vein images of the UTFVP dataset and their segmentation masks from the UTFVP$_{seg}$ dataset. We can observe that the segmentation masks only cover the clearly visible finger veins but not the very fine ones that are hardly visible. In addition, the segmentation masks do not perfectly match the finger vein thickness, but the masks are still much better than for finger vein pattern extraction techniques like Maximum Curvature (MC) and Principle Curvature (PC), which do absolutely not reflect the actual vein thickness.

By analyzing the average vein thickness using the segmentation masks, we can find out if there are differences in the vein thickness depending on the gender of the subjects. This is done by first computing the size of the area of the finger vein structure by counting the number of pixels in the segmentation masks that are indicating a vein. Secondly, we compute the summed up length over all finger veins by applying skeletonization to the segmentation mask and summing up the number of pixels of the skeletonized finger vein segmentation mask. By dividing the area of the finger vein structure by its lengths we get the average finger

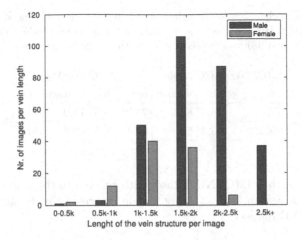

Fig. 5. Bar plot showing the distribution of the summed up length of the finger vein structure on the images of the UTFVP$_{seg}$ database for the two genders

vein thickness/diameter of a finger vein image. Now by averaging the average finger vein thickness over all images per gender we can find out if there are truly differences between men and women with respect to the finger vein thickness. It turned out that the mean vein diameter for finger vein images of men is 8.6 pixels whereas the mean vein diameter for finger vein images of women is 8.5 pixels. So there is hardly any difference between the genders.

However, we found out that the summed up length over all finger veins of an image is for male subjects about 1.4 times higher in average than for female subjects. That means that there are clearly more well visible finger veins for men as for women. Figure 5 presents the distribution of the vein length on the UTFVP$_{seg}$ database of male and female subjects, where the length of the vein structure is defined as the sum of the pixels of the skeletonized segmentation mask. The higher length of the vein structure in finger vein images of male subjects could be one of the reasons that the CNNs were able to determine the gender based on finger vein images.

Finally, we want to find out if the inbalance of the MMCBNU dataset data with respect to the gender distribution (only 17% of the images are from female subjects) is the reason that so much images of female subjects were predicted as male. For this we apply a gender recognition experiment to a subset of the MMCBNU dataset consisting of all 17 female subjects but only 17 of the 83 male subjects (we simply chose the first 17 male subjects of the dataset). So, in total the sub dataset consists of 1020 images of female subjects and 1020 images from male subjects. The gender recognition experiments are employed exactly the same as for the original dataset, except using the smaller but balanced subset of the MMCBNU dataset. In Table 6 we present the results of this experiment.

As we can observe in Table 6, female images are predicted with about the same accuracy as male images on the balanced MMCBNU sub dataset. So the

Table 6. Gender classification results (ACC in %) on a balanced subset of the MMCBNU dataset (ROI as well as original images) using CNNs trained with the triplet loss (SVM results) and CNNs trained with the SoftMax loss

MMCBNU	ACC triplet			ACC SoftMax		
	all	women	men	all	women	men
ROI	78.5	82.0	74.2	75.6	75.9	74.2
Original	53.4	50.4	57.1	51.5	49.8	54.3

huge inbalance of the MMCBNU dataset with respect to the gender distribution was actually the reason that so many female images were classified incorrectly on the MMCBNU dataset.

6   Conclusion

In our experiments on three public finger vein image datasets we showed that it is indeed feasible to predict the gender based on finger vein images. For the UTFVP dataset we achieved accuracies of up to 93.1%, for the PLUS dataset accuracies of up to 86.1% and for the MMCBNU dataset accuracies of up to 88.6%. However, it should be noted that the data sets used are rather small and unbalanced in terms of the number of images from male and female subjects and therefore predictions are more accurate for the larger group (male). In general, it did not matter which CNN architecture or loss function was used. As the results for original and ROI images (which contains no shape or background information) are similar, one can conclude that the finger region itself contains enough information to predict gender. However, we showed that the thickness and length of the fingers are important features for the CNNs to discriminate between the genders. Furthermore, there is a big difference between the genders with respect to the length of the finger vein structure. In average, the summed up length of the finger vein structure for male subjects is about 1.4 times higher than for female subjects.

The experiments to estimate the age based on finger vein images did not perform well. For two of the three datasets, it did work at least to some extent to differentiate between young (>25) and old subjects (>45), but on the MMCBNU dataset nearly all images were predicted as male. The direct estimation of the age using a MSE loss trained CNN did not work at all and only performed slightly better than simply predicting the mean age over all subjects for all images.

References

1. Bobeldyk, D., Ross, A.: Analyzing covariate influence on gender and race prediction from near-infrared ocular images. IEEE Access **7**, 7905–7919 (2019). https://doi. org/10.1109/ACCESS.2018.2886275

2. Damak, W., Boukhris Trabelsi, R., Damak Masmoudi, A., Sellami, D., Nait-Ali, A.: Age and gender classification from finger vein patterns. In: Madureira, A.M., Abraham, A., Gamboa, D., Novais, P. (eds.) ISDA 2016. AISC, vol. 557, pp. 811–820. Springer, Cham (2017). https://doi.org/10.1007/978-3-319-53480-0_80

3. Damak, W., Trabelsi, R.B., Masmoudi, A.D., Sellami, D.: Palm vein age and gender estimation using center symmetric-local binary pattern. In: Martínez Álvarez, F., Troncoso Lora, A., Sáez Muñoz, J.A., Quintián, H., Corchado, E. (eds.) CISIS/ICEUTE -2019. AISC, vol. 951, pp. 114–123. Springer, Cham (2020). https://doi.org/10.1007/978-3-030-20005-3_12

4. Drozdowski, P., et al.: Demographic bias: a challenge for fingervein recognition systems? In: 2020 28th European Signal Processing Conference (EUSIPCO), pp. 825–829 (2021). https://doi.org/10.23919/Eusipco47968.2020.9287722

5. Drozdowski, P., Rathgeb, C., Dantcheva, A., Damer, N., Busch, C.: Demographic bias in biometrics: a survey on an emerging challenge. CoRR abs/2003.02488 (2020). https://arxiv.org/abs/2003.02488

6. Falohun, A., Deborah, F., Ajala, F.: A fingerprint-based age and gender detector system using fingerprint pattern analysis. Int. J. Comput. Appl. 136, 975–8887 (2016). https://doi.org/10.5120/ijca2016908474

7. Gagne, P., Sharma, K.: Relationship of common vascular anatomy to cannulated catheters. Int. J. Vasc. Med. 2017 (2017)

8. Galdi, C., et al.: Protect: pervasive and user focused biometrics border project - a case study. IET Biometrics 9(6), 297–308 (2020). https://doi.org/10.1049/iet-bmt.2020.0033

9. Gao, H., Liu, Z., Weinberger, K.Q.: Densely connected convolutional networks. CoRR abs/1608.06993 (2016). http://arxiv.org/abs/1608.06993

10. Iandola, F.N., Moskewicz, M.W., Ashraf, K., Han, S., Dally, W.J., Keutzer, K.: Squeezenet: alexnet-level accuracy with 50x fewer parameters and <1mb model size. CoRR abs/1602.07360 (2016). http://arxiv.org/abs/1602.07360

11. Jalilian, E., Uhl, A.: Enhanced segmentation-CNN based finger-vein recognition by joint training with automatically generated and manual labels. In: Proceedings of the IEEE 5th International Conference on Identity, Security and Behavior Analysis (ISBA 2019), pp. 1–8. IDRBT (2019)

12. Kauba, C., Prommegger, B., Uhl, A.: Focussing the beam - a new laser illumination based data set providing insights to finger-vein recognition. In: Proceedings of the IEEE 9th International Conference on Biometrics: Theory, Applications, and Systems (BTAS 2018), Los Angeles, California, USA, pp. 1–9 (2018, accepted)

13. Kaushik, P., Gupta, A., Roy, P.P., Dogra, D.P.: EEG-based age and gender prediction using deep BLSTM-LSTM network model. IEEE Sens. J. 19(7), 2634–2641 (2019). https://doi.org/10.1109/JSEN.2018.2885582

14. Kröger, K., Ose, C., Rudofsky, G., Roesener, J., Weiland, D., Hirche, H.: Peripheral veins: influence of gender, body mass index, age and varicose veins on cross-sectional area. Vasc. Med. 8(4), 249–255 (2003). https://doi.org/10.1191/1358863x03vm508oa

15. Kwasny, D., Hemmerling, D.: Gender and age estimation methods based on speech using deep neural networks. Sensors 21(14), 4785 (2021). https://doi.org/10.3390/s21144785. https://www.mdpi.com/1424-8220/21/14/4785

16. Lu, Y., Xie, S.J., Yoon, S., Wang, Z., Park, D.S.: An available database for the research of finger vein recognition. In: 2013 6th International Congress on Image and Signal Processing (CISP), vol. 1, pp. 410–415 (2013). https://doi.org/10.1109/CISP.2013.6744030

17. Lu, Y., Xie, S.J., Yoon, S., Yang, J., Park, D.S.: Robust finger vein ROI localization based on flexible segmentation. Sensors **13**(11), 14339–14366 (2013)
18. Rwigema, J., Mfitumukiza, J., Tae-Yong, K.: A hybrid approach of neural networks for age and gender classification through decision fusion. Biomed. Signal Process. Control **66**, 102459 (2021). https://doi.org/10.1016/j.bspc.2021.102459. https://www.sciencedirect.com/science/article/pii/S1746809421000562
19. Sgroi, A., Bowyer, K.W., Flynn, P.J.: The prediction of old and young subjects from iris texture. In: 2013 International Conference on Biometrics (ICB), pp. 1–5 (2013). https://doi.org/10.1109/ICB.2013.6613010
20. Simonyan, K., Vedaldi, A., Zisserman, A.: Deep inside convolutional networks: visualising image classification models and saliency maps. In: Workshop at International Conference on Learning Representations (2014)
21. Sun, Y., Lo, F.P.W., Lo, B.: A deep learning approach on gender and age recognition using a single inertial sensor. In: 2019 IEEE 16th International Conference on Wearable and Implantable Body Sensor Networks (BSN), pp. 1–4 (2019). https://doi.org/10.1109/BSN.2019.8771075
22. Sun, Y., Zhang, M., Sun, Z., Tan, T.: Demographic analysis from biometric data: achievements, challenges, and new frontiers. IEEE Trans. Pattern Anal. Mach. Intell. **40**(2), 332–351 (2018). https://doi.org/10.1109/TPAMI.2017.2669035
23. Tapia, J.E., Perez, C.A., Bowyer, K.W.: Gender classification from the same iris code used for recognition. IEEE Trans. Inf. Forensics Secur. **11**(8), 1760–1770 (2016). https://doi.org/10.1109/TIFS.2016.2550418
24. Ton, B.T., Veldhuis, R.N.J.: A high quality finger vascular pattern dataset collected using a custom designed capturing device. In: 2013 International Conference on Biometrics (ICB), pp. 1–5 (2013). https://doi.org/10.1109/ICB.2013.6612966
25. Wang, J., Wang, G., Pan, Z.: Gender attribute mining with hand-dorsa vein image based on unsupervised sparse feature learning. IEICE Trans. Inf. Syst. **E101.D**(1), 257–260 (2018). https://doi.org/10.1587/transinf.2017EDL8098
26. Wimmer, G., Prommegger, B., Uhl, A.: Finger vein recognition and intra-subject similarity evaluation of finger veins using the CNN triplet loss. In: Proceedings of the 25th International Conference on Pattern Recognition (ICPR), pp. 400–406 (2020)
27. Xie, S., Girshick, R., Dollár, P., Tu, Z., He, K.: Aggregated residual transformations for deep neural networks. In: 2017 IEEE Conference on Computer Vision and Pattern Recognition (CVPR), pp. 5987–5995 (2017). https://doi.org/10.1109/CVPR.2017.634
28. Yaman, D., Irem Eyiokur, F., Kemal Ekenel, H.: Multimodal age and gender classification using ear and profile face images. In: Proceedings of the IEEE/CVF Conference on Computer Vision and Pattern Recognition Workshops (2019)
29. Zhang, K., et al.: Age group and gender estimation in the wild with deep ROR architecture. IEEE Access **5**, 22492–22503 (2017). https://doi.org/10.1109/ACCESS.2017.2761849

A Novel Time-Series Database of Finger Hypercubes Before and After Hand Sanitization with Demographics

Sriram Sai Sumanth$^{(\boxtimes)}$ and Emanuela Marasco

Center for Secure Information Systems, George Mason University,
Fairfax, VA 22030, USA
{ssriram2,emarasco}@gmu.edu

Abstract. During the past decade, hyperspectral imaging (HSI) has been an area of broad, innovative work in a variety of applications such as health, defense, and remote sensing. Hyperspectral images can be collected using a compact HSI imager and are referred to also as hypercubes. Currently, there are no biometric hyperspectral databases available to the community. In this paper, we create the Finger Hypercubes Sanitization with Demographics Database (FHSD) (https://github.com/cysber-CSIS/GMU-CSIS—Finger-Hypercubes-Sanitization-with-Demographics-FHSD-2022) consisting of hyperspectral images of human fingers along with their demographics (*i.e.*, age, gender, and ethnicity) captured before and after hand sanitization. This gender-balanced database consists of images pertaining to 100 subjects collected in an indoor environment with a white background under proper lighting conditions using the Resonon bench-top Pika-L hyperspectral imaging system (400–1000 nm). For each subject, multiple left and right index samples were acquired before and after sanitization. In addition to spatial information, HSI data provides 281 channels decoding a spectral component able to describe skin reflectance. Thus, this data holds great potential for enabling a more in-depth analysis of demographic differentials in fingerprints compared to conventional sensing technologies.

Keywords: Hyperspectral Imaging · Hypercubes

1 Introduction

Despite several benefits, the use of algorithmic decision systems is also associated with different risks for individuals, such as discrimination and unfair practices. In particular, biometric systems (*e.g.*, face and fingerprint recognition) have exhibited undesirable demographic differentials by yielding lower genuine scores for ethnic minorities and women. While numerous studies evaluate the fairness of various face recognition systems, these studies are limited for fingerprint recognition [15]. Over the past decade, researchers have demonstrated the possibility of predicting gender from fingerprint images. The majority of current methods for predicting gender rely on techniques based on textural properties such as ridge density [2, 15].

© Springer Nature Switzerland AG 2023
J.-J. Rousseau and B. Kapralos (Eds.): ICPR 2022 Workshops, LNCS 13645, pp. 597–609, 2023.
https://doi.org/10.1007/978-3-031-37731-0_43

Over the past ten years, sensor-based fingerprint recognition systems have been under careful examination to see if they exert racial and gender bias. It has been found that the use of Binarized Statistical Image Features (BSIF), Local Binary Patterns (LBP), and Local Phase Quantization (LPQ) were able to identify features to discriminate males from females fingerprint images with an accuracy of 88.7% using K-Nearest Neighbor. To further explore gender classification with respect to capture bias, cross-sensor evaluation was performed using local textural descriptors (LBP, and BSIF) achie-ved an accuracy of 80% [2, 15].

Recent studies found that demographic covariates may exhibit bias in fingerprint match scores obtained using automatic matchers. ROC regression techniques have been used to evaluate the impact of demographics such as age, gender, and ethnicity on the performance of the latent fingerprint automatic matchers. These techniques show that the models perform significantly better on male subjects with an AUC of 71% and 76% for the right index and thumb instances respectively. They perform even better when latent image quality has been used as an auxiliary covariate along with the demographics [4, 18, 19]. Statistical testing frameworks have also been used to evaluate biases in a commercial-off-the-shelf fingerprint matcher (VeriFinger 12.3 SDK) and a neural fingerprint matcher (DeepPrint). The highest True Match Rate (TMR) was observed in females with a TMR of 99.58% and 93.3% for Verfinger 12.3 and DeepPrint, respectively. The analysis of biases in fingerprints may be limited by existing sensing technologies; therefore, we propose to investigate the problem from a richer perspective, i.e., in the hyperspectral domain [1, 3, 5].

Over the past few years, Hyperspectral imaging (HSI) has been used across various fields such as forensic science, seed viability, environmental monitoring, and food quality checks [12]. Recently, HSI has also gained a lot of interest in biometrics and is used to analyze a person's physical and biological characteristics to authenticate and verify their identity [7–11]. These imagers collect both spectral and spatial information from the subjects and hence are more widely adopted by many security services to expand their capabilities for different biometric purposes. HSI can measure continuous spectral bands to analyze a wide spectrum of light instead of assigning primary colors (red, green, and blue) to each pixel. While a standard RGB camera acquires data across 3 channels, the hyperspectral imager collects data from 281 channels and offers a much wider spectrum. It uses fine wavelength resolution to measure the continuous spectrum of light for each pixel of the scene, not only in the visible but also in the near-infrared region [14]. Using deep learning technology in HSI analysis has advanced quickly in recent years and attracted a lot of attention. Researches have been conducted to develop deep learning models for hyperspectral image classification specifically to deal with a few labeled samples by proposing techniques to achieve good performance in such a critical scenario including autoencoders, few-shot learning, transfer learning, activate learning, and data augmentation [37].

In this paper, we create the Finger Hypercubes Sanitization with Demographics (FHSD) database which is the first one providing containing finger hypercubes from 100 subjects with demographics. The images are captured in various temporal sessions, *i.e.*, before and after applying hand sanitizer, enabling the analysis of the impact of this product on the spectral signature of finger data. The collection is multi-instance (*i.e.*, left and right index) and multi-sample (*i.e.*, three per subject).

The rest of the paper is structured as follows: Sect. 2 describes recent applications of hyperspectral technology. Section 3 presents technical details about HSI scanning methods and acquisition modes. Section 4 discusses the data collection protocol, the tools used, and the challenges faced, and Sect. 5 draws our conclusion.

2 Literature Review

Lately, subject identification and authentication using hyperspectral and multispectral imaging have gained a lot of interest due to their ability to collect spectral information from the subjects besides spatial information by acquiring their data cubes from across the different bands of the electromagnetic spectrum.

In 2008, Robila proposed an approach to study and analyze the efficiency of hyperspectral face recognition and the effectiveness of human matching based on spectral characteristics by acquiring the data in indoor and outdoor environments from over 120 bands across multiple spectra in various angles. It was performed to improve the face recognition by combining images from different sources, such as the visible and the infrared spectrum. They observed that spectral angle and data together could be used to differentiate humans [9].

In 2017, L. Di Cecilia *et al.* built an optical system and developed a method to measure the spectral reflectance of the human iris. They collected data in the spectral range of 440 to 900 nm. By performing hyperspectral analysis on the iris, its pigmentation and age-related changes could be observed over time. They also found that machine learning techniques like k-means clustering can be used to improve the evaluation of iris structural features [10]. In 2017, Dabhade *et al.* conducted a laboratory experiment to perform an analysis on human authentication using a hyperspectral face database of 120 cubes collected from 70 subjects. They performed feature extraction on the UWA HSFD database developed by the university of Western Australia using principal component analysis. They found that recognition rates of hyperspectral face images vary across different spectral bands [11].

In 2018, Jenerowicz *et al.* conducted a study to analyze the possibilities of using a pushbroom hyperspectral camera to interpret the hand biometric characteristics, such as hand shape and vein pattern of the subjects, for accurate identification. They found that data collected at 900mm (near-infrared region) could be used to better identify the hand's vascular patterns, making it a viable alternative to currently available commercial biometric systems [8].

In 2022, Marasco *et al.* conducted a study to analyze the impact of hand sanitizer on the spectral signature pertain to finger hypercubes using a subset of the proposed Finger Hypercubes Sanitization with Demographics (FHSD) database. They built a framework to perform a non-parametric classifier-based two-sample test to determine whether the spectral signals collected from the finger hypercubes before hand sanitization differs from the signal collected after hand sanitization. They found that hand sanitizer does not have a significant impact on the finger hypercubes [6].

3 Fingerprints in the Hyperspectral Domain

Electromagnetic radiation (EMR) is energy in the form of electromagnetic waves that interact with substances in various ways depending on whether it strikes a solid, liquid, or gas and undergoes one or more of the processes of reflection, absorption, and transmission. Reflection occurs when the electromagnetic radiation is reflected by the target surface upon which it is incident. The absorption process, on the other hand, occurs when the target absorbs the incident radiation. Finally, transmission occurs when the radiation passes through the target unaffected [27–30]. The physical characteristics of the target and the wavelength of the incident light determine how much light is absorbed, reflected (which the camera can capture), and transmitted by the target.

Light is an EMR within a visible region that enters human biological tissue, which undergoes multiple scattering and absorption events as it travels through it. The analeptic window spanning from 600 to 1300 nm allows significant light penetration because most tissues are weak absorbers. The penetration depth of light entering the human biological tissues is determined by the tissue's ability to absorb it [32]. This light absorbed is either converted to heat or is radiated in the form of luminescence. The EMR in this visible to the near-infrared region can penetrate the skin up to 4–5 mm [33]. Over time, long exposure of the instrument to the light will lead to accumulation of electrons, leading to dark currents, *i.e.*, a flow of charges in the absence of light. This phenomenon generates noise in the hypercubes which must be eliminated by dark current correction [31,43].

HSI systems are categorized based on the acquisition mode and on how the target's spectral and spatial information is obtained [34]. There are two main types of scanning methods: spatial (point and line) and spectral (area) scanning [35], and three ways to acquire the hypercube: point, line, and area scanning [36].

As shown in Fig. 1, point scanning (also known as whisk-broom imaging) is the most time-consuming method in which the spectrum is procured at only one spatial location at a time, and then the detector or the target is moved to acquire other points. It aids in obtaining a high spectral resolution to perform a more detailed analysis of the captured pixel [38].

Pushbroom cameras (also known as Line-scan cameras) can scan 100 times faster than point-scan cameras while still achieving high spectral resolution, see Fig. 1 [39, 40]. At a given time, the imager captures one line of pixels from the target (y-axis). Moving the camera's field-of-view (FOV) in that direction generates the other spatial dimension (x-axis) [38].

Area scan (also known as staring imaging) acquires the hyperspectral image one wavelength at a time from the target using a rotating filter or a tunable filter such as LCTF or AOTF, as shown in Fig. 1. This method requires no relative movement between the target and the imager, and the imager captures a whole spatial scene (wavelength) at each spectral band in a sequence [41]. Hyperspectral images are a stack of images collected across the electromagnetic spectrum by obtaining a continuous spectrum of wavelengths for every pixel in an image. The images are collected at different spectral bands resulting in three-dimensional data structures containing two spatial dimensions (X-Y) and one spectral dimension (λ) known as a hypercube [42]. The Resonon Pika L line scan camera was used to collect the hypercubes in this study. As the object is

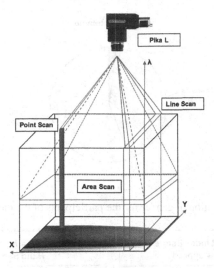

Fig. 1. Classification of different types (line, point, and area scan) of hyperspectral cameras and the amount of data each camera acquires within a single scan.

translated, it gathers data one line at a time and assembles multiple lines to complete the two-dimensional image; this line-by-line assembly of the numerous line-images results in a complete finger hypercube with spectral and spatial dimensions. The application of this system can be extended and used to distinguish demographic information such as age and gender and can also perform contactless fingerprint recognition using machine learning. As this imager collects the data across 281 spectral channels, it helps analyze the biochemical content in the finger skin for a better understanding of the effect of hand sanitizer on spectral information across the subjects over time. Therefore, our database bridges the gap between biometrics and advanced image processing, making it distinct from other databases in the biometric community.

4   The Data Collection

The hypercubes and the demographics were collected from 100 subjects. The subjects are gender-balanced, as shown in Fig. 2, and are primarily students, their families, and friends who are 18 years of age or older, free of metabolic diseases, malfunction of the genetic disorder of metabolism (e.g., diabetes), and are of normal weight. We collected data from people of various ages and backgrounds. In terms of ethnicity, 84% of the subjects are Asians/Asian Americans, 6% are Hispanic/Latino, 6% are White/Caucasians, and 4% are North African/African Americans. The subjects with known health issues and under any kind of hormone treatment are excluded from this study. Individuals with open wounds/cuts on their hands were also excluded due to the burning sensation caused by the hand sanitizer.

For each subject, six hypercubes (3 per finger) were collected from the left and right index fingers before the hand sanitizer was applied, as shown in Fig. 3. Once the hand

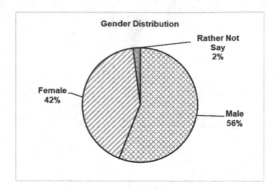

Fig. 2. Distribution of gender for the participants of the data collection.

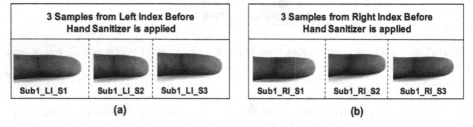

Fig. 3. Hypercube samples collected before hand sanitization: (a) Hypercubes captured from the left index before hand sanitization, and (b) hypercubes captured from the right index before hand sanitization.

sanitizer is applied, each fingerprint instance was collected three times after 1, 10, and 25 min resulting in a total of 24 hypercubes collected from each subject as shown in Fig. 4. In total this dataset comprises of 600 hypercubes collected before sanitization and 1800 hypercubes from both the fingers after hand sanitization as shown in Table 1. Therefore, it comprises a total of 2400 hypercubes collected from 100 subjects, and the total time taken for each subject during the data acquisition is 45 min. In this data collection, each finger hypercube at an instance is collected three times to better understand the spectral variations at each instance. To study demographic biases, the demographic data were also collected from the subjects via an in-person paper survey. For this collection, we used Purell hand sanitizer containing 70% ethanol, manufactured by GOJO, and subjects applied a single pump of hand sanitizer, approximately 3 ml of this product once the six hypercubes were collected before hand sanitization.

The challenges encountered during this data collection involve difficulties for some of the subjects in placing their finger directly under the camera, others faced problem to keep their finger still while the stage was moving. Some of the subjects could not look and put their finger directly under the camera due to the halogen lighting assembly being too bright. A few technical challenges faced during the initial assembly of the bench-top system are setting the stage controls and focusing the objective lens of the imager. As Pika-L is a line scan camera, the stage must move at a speed proportional to

Table 1. Details about the data collected in this study.

Sanitization	# of Subjects	Finger instance	Time (min.)	# of Samples per Subject	# of Datacubes
Before Sanitization	100	Left Index	0	3	300
		Right Index		3	300
After Sanitization		Left Index	1	3	300
			10	3	300
			25	3	300
		Right Index	1	3	300
			10	3	300
			25	3	300
				Total # of Datacubes	2400

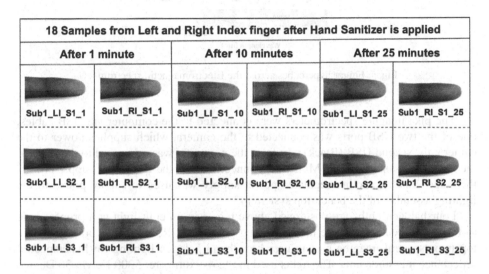

Fig. 4. The 18 hypercubes, 6 collected at each instance from the left (L) and right (R) index fingers after 1, 10 and 25 min of hand sanitization.

the imager's frame rate to acquire the target with a unit aspect ratio. The image could be elongated or shortened if the stage is too slow or too fast in comparison to the frame rate of the camera. Focusing the bench-top system's objective lens is a difficult task that is accomplished by placing a calibration sheet within the imager's field of view and rotating the lens with an allen wrench until the sheet is focused.

4.1   The Sensing Module

The data was captured by using the Resonon bench-top hyperspectral camera Pika L illustrated in Fig. 6. The resonon bench-top system comprises of a linear translation stage, mounting tower, lighting assembly, and SpectrononPro software installed on a desktop computer. The Pika L is a lightweight and compact Visible Near Infrared (VNIR) hyperspectral imager with a maximum frame rate of 165fps; it has a 23 mm lens with a spectral range of 400–1000 nm, as shown in Fig. 5, 281 spectral channels, 13.1° field of view, 2.1 nm spectral resolution, and 900 spatial pixels. The Resonon Hyperspectral cameras are line scan imagers that collect data one line at a time. The multiple line images are then pieced together line-by-line to form a final image. A linear stage assembly is used in the bench-top system, which is moved forward and backward with the help of a stage motor [43].

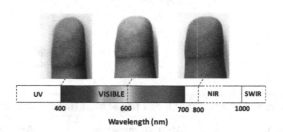

Fig. 5. Finger hypercubes across the Electromagnetic spectrum

The pika imaging spectrometers were connected to the computer via USB cables; one of the two USB ports was connected to the camera, which supplies power to the camera; the second USB (Black) port from the computer was connected to the stage of the bench-top system via the Mini USB connection, and the DC power supply powers the stage. Finally, another regulated power supply was used to supply power to the lighting assembly of the bench-top system [43].

Four halogen bulbs are positioned above the stage to emit light at a proper angle to focus the scene and create ideal scanning conditions. Resonon's laboratory bench-top hyperspectral imaging system uses broadband halogen lighting for hyperspectral reflectance measurements. The lights used in the 4-fixture are: 5300 Kelvin 36 Degree 12V 35W Halogen Flood Light Bulb. A stabilized power supply controls these lights, reducing variation caused by illumination fluctuations [43]. Since hyperspectral imaging separates light from a scene into many spectral components, the total radiation incident on a single sensor pixel is relatively small. The halogen lighting assembly provides adequate illumination at all wavelengths to acquire high-quality hyperspectral data from the bench-top system. The hyperspectral imaging system was set up with a distance of about 25 cm between the lens and the linear stage, with the lighting assembly also at the same level as the lens. Once the lighting assembly is adjusted to focus on the linear stage, the dark currents are corrected by blocking all the light entering the lens of the camera with the cap as shown in Fig. 7(a). The camera is then calibrated for response correction by placing a white tile under the lens; these corrections are performed in the same environment where the data collection was performed.

The Spectronon Pro is the software used by Resonon to control its bench-top system. It is connected to the Pika L camera via a USB cable. As shown in Fig. 6(b), this software performs all of the scans and collects hypercubes from each subject. Before performing the scans, the camera and stage parameters of the bench-top system are adjusted using the Spectronon Pro interface. It analyzes the hypercube across various wavelengths by selecting the Region of Interest (ROI) and generating the mean spectrum for each ROI in the hypercube.

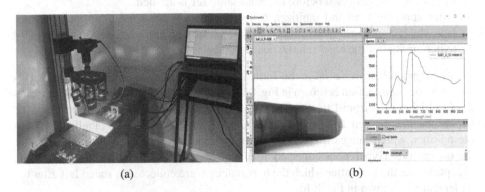

(a)   (b)

Fig. 6. The Resonon bench-top system: (a) the hyperspectral camera Pika L, and (b) the spectronon Pro interface used to collect the hypercubes from the subjects.

4.2 The Protocol

Data from each subject is collected by placing the subject's left and right index fingers under the camera. As shown in Fig. 3(a) & Fig. 3(b), each fingerprint instance is collected three times using the HSI camera before the hand sanitizer is applied. Once the hand sanitizer is applied, each fingerprint instance is collected three times after 1, 10, and 25 min as shown in Fig. 4. These images are equally distributed over both genders and are stipulated with their respective demographics. Before starting the acquisition, a white tile is placed under the camera to provide a white background while capturing the image and it is placed three holes from the right. The finger should be placed 1 cm from the border of the white surface in a way that the finger is under the camera, as shown in Fig. 7(b).

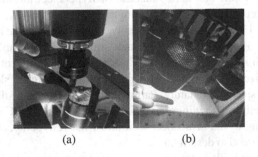

(a)   (b)

Fig. 7. (a) Dark current correction by blocking the lens (b) Placing the finger on the white surface for hypercube acquisition.

To acquire the hypercubes, subjects are asked to perform the following steps,

- The subjects are first asked to place their left index finger on the white surface under the camera without moving it, and three hypercubes are collected.
- The subjects then place their right index finger under the camera and three more hypercubes are collected before the hand sanitizer is applied.
- After applying the hand sanitizer, 6 hypercubes are collected, 3 at each instance from the left and right index fingers after 1, 10, and 25 min, resulting in a total of 18 hypercubes after the hand sanitization.

The hypercubes are saved in .bil format. The nomenclature of the hypercubes collected before sanitization is shown in Fig. 8(a). The first four digits indicate the subject's label, which ranges from 1 to 100. The two characters after the underscore denote if the hypercube is collected from the L (left) or R (right) index finger. Finally, the sample number, which ranges from S1 to S3, is indicated by the last two characters after the underscore. Hypercubes collected after sanitization are labeled similarly, with the exception that the time after which the hypercubes were collected is stated last after the underscore, as shown in Fig. 8(b).

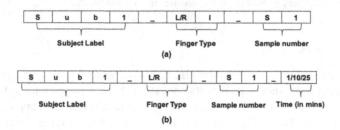

Fig. 8. (a) Nomenclature for the hypercubes collected before hand sanitization, (b) Nomenclature for the hypercubes collected after hand sanitization.

5   Conclusions

This paper presents a new biometric database of hyperspectral images of fingers pertaining to 100 subjects along with their demographics (age, gender, and ethnicity) from left and right index. Furthermore, the images were captured before and after 1, 10, and 25 min of applying a hand sanitizer. For each subject, three samples per finger were collected to study intra-class variability. The data acquisition protocol was carefully designed to minimize changes of biochemical content in finger skin reflectance and subsequently in the spectral signature. Participants with metabolic diseases and genetic disorders were not eligible to minimize variations in the spectra. Calibration and setup procedures pertaining to the instrument Resonon Pika L hyperspectral imager used in this data collection are also described.

In future work, we will: *i)* extend the experiments by considering additional commercial hand sanitizer to study how they affect the spectral and spatial features, *ii),* design algorithms for HSI gender and age estimation to understand and mitigate demographic differential in fingerprint data, and *iii)* establish a benchmark that evaluates the robustness of spectral signature with respective hand sanitization.

Acknowledgment. This work was funded by the National Science Foundation (NSF) grant #2036151.

References

1. Marasco, E.: Biases in fingerprint recognition systems: where are we at? In: 2019 IEEE 10th International Conference on Biometrics Theory, Applications and Systems (BTAS), pp. 1–5 (2019)
2. Marasco, E., Lugini, L., Cukic, B.: Exploiting quality and texture features to estimate age and gender from fingerprints. In: Biometric and Surveillance Technology for Human and Activity Identification XI, vol. 9075, pp. 112–121. SPIE (2014)
3. Jain, A.K., Deb, D., Engelsma, J.J.: Biometrics: trust, but verify. arXiv preprint arXiv:2105.06625 (2021)
4. Marasco, E., He, M., Tang, L., Tao, Y.: Demographic effects in latent fingerprint matching and their relation to image quality. In: 2022 7th International Conference on Machine Learning Technologies (ICMLT), pp. 170–179 (2022)
5. Godbole, A., Grosz, S.A., Nandakumar, K., Jain, A.K.: On demographic bias in fingerprint recognition, arXiv preprint arXiv:2205.09318 (2022)
6. Marasco, E., Tao, Y.: Mitigating the impact of hand sanitizer on the spectral signature of finger hypercubes. In: 2022 International Joint Conference on Biometrics (IJCB 2022) (2022)
7. Roui-Abidi, B., Abidi, M.: Multispectral and Hyperspectral Biometrics. In: Li, S.Z., Jain, A. (eds.) Encyclopedia of Biometrics, pp. 993–998. Springer, Boston (2009). https://doi.org/10.1007/978-0-387-73003-5_163
8. Jenerowicz, A., Walczykowski, P., Gladysz, L., Gralewicz, M.: Application of hyperspectral imaging in hand biometrics, vol. 10802, p. 108020G (2018)
9. Robila, S.A.: Toward hyperspectral face recognition. In: Image Processing: Algorithms and Systems VI, vol. 6812, pp. 296–304. SPIE (2008)
10. Di Cecilia, L., Marazzi, F., Rovati, L.: Hyperspectral imaging of the human iris, p. 104120R (2017)
11. Dabhade, S.B., Bansod, N., Rode, Y., Kazi, M., Tharewal, S., Kale, K.: Hyper spectral image analysis for human authentication, pp. 1–4 (2017)
12. GringGIS: 10 important applications of hyperspectral image (2016). https://grindgis.com/remote-sensing/10-important-applications-of-hyperspectral-image
13. Rampfesthudson: How does a hyperspectral sensor work? (2019). https://www.rampfesthudson.com/how-does-a-hyperspectral-sensor-work/
14. NIREOS: What is hyperspectral imaging? (2022). https://www.nireos.com/hyperspectral-imaging/
15. Marasco, E., Cando, S., Tang, L., Tabassi, E.: Cross-sensor evaluation of textural descriptors for gender prediction from fingerprints. In: IEEE Winter Applications of Computer Vision Workshops (WACVW), pp. 55–62. IEEE (2019)
16. Rathgeb, C., Drozdowski, P., Frings, D.C., Damer, N., Busch, C.: Demographic fairness in biometric systems: what do the experts say? arXiv preprint arXiv:2105.14844 (2021)
17. Marasco, E.: Biases in fingerprint recognition systems: where are we at? In: 2019 IEEE 10th International Conference on Biometrics Theory, Applications and Systems (BTAS), pp. 1–5. IEEE (2019)

18. Yoon, S., Jain, A.K.: Longitudinal study of fingerprint recognition. Proc. Natl. Acad. Sci. **112**(28), 8555–8560 (2015)
19. Marasco, E., He, M., Tang, L., Sriram, S.: Accounting for demographic differentials in forensic error rate assessment of latent prints via covariate-specific ROC regression. In: Singh, S.K., Roy, P., Raman, B., Nagabhushan, P. (eds.) CVIP 2020. CCIS, vol. 1376, pp. 338–350. Springer, Singapore (2021). https://doi.org/10.1007/978-981-16-1086-8_30
20. Lugini, L., Marasco, E., Cukic, B., Dawson, J.: Removing gender signature from fingerprints. In: 37th International Convention on Information and Communication Technology, Electronics and Microelectronics (MIPRO), pp. 1283–1287. IEEE (2014)
21. Marasco, E., Cukic, B., Shehab, M., Usman, R.: Attack trees for protecting biometric systems against evolving presentation attacks. In: 16th Annual IEEE International Conference on Technologies for Homeland Security (HST) (2017)
22. Marasco, E., Cukic, B.: Privacy protection schemes for fingerprint recognition systems. In: Biometric and Surveillance Technology for Human and Activity Identification XII, vol. 9457, pp. 83–96. SPIE (2015)
23. Marasco, E., Vurity, A.: Fingerphoto presentation attack detection: generalization in smartphones. In: 2021 IEEE International Conference on Big Data (Big Data), pp. 4518–4523. IEEE (2021)
24. Taherkhani, F., Dawson, J., Nasrabadi, N.M.: Deep sparse band selection for hyperspectral face recognition, arXiv preprint arXiv:1908.09630 (2019)
25. Socolinsky, D.A., Wolff, L.B., Neuheisel, J.D., Eveland, C.K.: Illumination invariant face recognition using thermal infrared imagery. In: IEEE Computer Society Conference on Computer Vision and Pattern Recognition, CVPR 2001, vol. 1, pp. I-I (2001)
26. Wikipedia: Hyperspectral imaging (2022). https://en.wikipedia.org/wiki/Hyperspectral_imaging
27. Exelis, an introduction to hyperspectral imaging (2014). https://www.ugpti.org/smartse/research/citations/downloads/Excelis-Introduction_to_HSI_Technology-2014.pdf
28. Government of canada, radiation - target interactions (2015). https://www.nrcan.gc.ca/maps-tools-publications/satellite-imagery-air-photos/remote-sensing-tutorials/introduction/radiation-target-interactions/14637
29. Howard, D.: Electromagnetic radiation absorption (2022). https://study.com/academy/lesson/electromagnetic-radiation-absorption.html
30. College of Earth and Mineral Sciences: The roads traveled most by radiation (2020). https://www.e-education.psu.edu/meteo3/l2_p4.html
31. Thorlabs, P.: Camera Noise and Temperature Tutorial (2020). https://www.thorlabs.com/newgrouppage9.cfm?objectgroup_id=10773#::text=Dark%20Shot%20Noise%20(%CF%83D,excited%20int%20the%20conduction%20band)
32. Vo-Dinh, T.: Biomedical photonics handbook, biomedical diagnostics (2014). https://books.google.com/books?hl=en&lr=&id=IY_LBQAAQBAJ&oi=fnd&pg=PP1&ots=6kuSjbZmyy&sig=zfkgBsD-F5D8Xjnv637xM1IZzlw#v=onepage&q&f=false
33. Wikipedia: Fluorescence (2022). https://en.wikipedia.org/wiki/Fluorescence
34. Kamruzzaman, M., Sun, D.-W.: Introduction to hyperspectral imaging technology. In: Computer Vision Technology for Food Quality Evaluation, pp. 111–139. Elsevier (2016)
35. Lu, G., Fei, B.: Medical hyperspectral imaging: a review. J. Biomed. Opt. **19**(1), 010901 (2014)
36. Qin, J., Chao, K., Kim, M.S., Lu, R., Burks, T.F.: Hyperspectral and multispectral imaging for evaluating food safety and quality. J. Food Eng. **118**(2), 157–171 (2013)
37. Jia, S., Jiang, S., Lin, Z., Li, N., Xu, M., Yu, S.: A survey: deep learning for hyperspectral image classification with few labeled samples. Neurocomputing **448**, 179–204 (2021)

38. Halicek, M., Fabelo, H., Ortega, S., Callico, G.M., Fei, B.: In-vivo and ex-vivo tissue analysis through hyperspectral imaging techniques: revealing the invisible features of cancer. Cancers **11**(6), 756 (2019)
39. Gowen, A.A., Feng, Y., Gaston, E., Valdramidis, V.: Recent applications of hyperspectral imaging in microbiology. Talanta **137**, 43–54 (2015)
40. Liu, Z., Yu, H., MacGregor, J.F.: Standardization of line-scan NIR imaging systems. J. Chemom. J. Chemom. Soc. **21**(3–4), 88–95 (2007)
41. Garini, Y., Young, I.T., McNamara, G.: Spectral imaging: principles and applications. Cytometry Part A J. Int. Soc. Anal. Cytol. **69**(8), 735–747 (2006)
42. Edelman, G.J., Gaston, E., Van Leeuwen, T.G., Cullen, P., Aalders, M.C.: Hyperspectral imaging for non-contact analysis of forensic traces. Forensic Sci. Int. **223**(1–3), 28–39 (2012)
43. Resonon pika l, Bozeman, MT 59715 USA (2014). https://resonon.com/Pika-L

Brief Audit of Post-pandemic Biometrics

Sudarsini Tekkam Gnanasekar, Olha Shaposhnyk, Illia Yankovyi,
and Svetlana Yanushkevich[✉]

Biometric Technologies Laboratory, Schulich School of Engineering,
University of Calgary, Alberta, Canada
syanshk@ucalgary.ca

Abstract. This paper offers a brief audit of biometric technology in the post-pandemic realm. To accomplish the audit objectives, we map a general biometric-enabled system concept onto the Emergency Management Cycle (EMC), a core doctrine to address disasters. This mapping helps identify the technology-societal gaps unveiled during the most recent pandemic. We focus on auditing the biometric-enabled watchlist for e-borders and e-health systems. In the biometric-enabled systems, fairness becomes of critical importance, while the related concept of Equity, Diversity, and Inclusion (EDI) is well suited for the generalization of fairness in biometrics. We also emphasize the need to update the biometric courses for training future technology developers.

Keywords: Biometrics · Fairness · Bias · Emergency management cycle · e-borders · e-health · Equity · Diversity · Inclusion

1 Introduction

Periodical review of biometric achievements and limitations is a common research practice, such as a summary of state-of-the-art technologies [34] as well as a review of particular areas, e.g. faces as a health status indicator [63], facial expression and emotion detection or recognition [45], age assessment from a face image [23], race identification from a face [24], and summary of expert opinions on demographic fairness in biometric systems [28,56].

A missing chain in the latest reports is a post-pandemic audit of biometric-enabled systems. In contrast to the biometric technology review, the current critical analysis of post-pandemic epidemiological countermeasures is a well-identified trend in many fields, e.g. e-health [4,52], supply-chains [33], education [61], science [60], military [41], and biometric-enabled payment systems [44]. A common research question is "Why advanced socio-technological systems were not effective or failed in a pandemic?"

Monitoring of the recent development of the biometric-enabled systems led us to the conclusion that the security that relies on the e-ID [31] has failed during the COVID pandemic. The practitioners moved, eventually, from a centralized security control to a trusted distributed platform [30]. In addition, the role of

© Springer Nature Switzerland AG 2023
J.-J. Rousseau and B. Kapralos (Eds.): ICPR 2022 Workshops, LNCS 13645, pp. 610–626, 2023.
https://doi.org/10.1007/978-3-031-37731-0_44

e-health and e-coaching systems that integrated biometrics appears to be over-valued in the pre-pandemic period. During pandemics, the simplest functions of these systems were used, such as tele-contacts with patients using smartphones [8]. These and other socio-technological failures require systematic, unbiased, and objective examination. Our study aims to contribute to the auditing of the post-pandemic biometrics. We propose:

1. A conceptual view of the biometric-enabled systems through the Emer-gency Management Cycle (EMC), – the core doctrine to solve challenges caused by disasters [20, 64]; the EMC-aware view allows to identify the socio-technological gaps of post-pandemic biometrics, and
2. A detailed audit of case examples; we chose a biometric-enabled watchlist and an e-health system where the fairness of facial recognition is one of the dominant performance factors. We also view fairness through the lenses of Equity, Diversity, and Inclusion (EDI) [5].

We argue that such an approach is rational, timely, and in demand for the following reasons. First, all computational intelligence systems are parts of EMC [4] including biometric-enabled systems. They should be designed to help prevent or minimize the likelihood of any potential pandemic (mitigation phase), to be helpful in cases of possible pandemic scenarios (preparedness phase), to be efficient against epidemiological attacks (response phase), and to be maintainable in the aftermath of the disaster (recovery phase). Intuitively, the recent pandemic disaster called for action to create the *epidemiological-conditioned* biometrics such as recognition of biometric traits in the presence of face masks and shields, sanitary gloves and other personal protective equipment [2].

Secondly, the concepts of the EDI-aware systems and fairness in biometrics are closely related. Both assess the socio-ethical categories of an object (gender, disabilities, religious affiliation, etc.) using the measures such as risk, trust, and bias [10, 71]. The users' quest for fairness of the biometric-enabled systems is expressed implicitly or explicitly through the following questions:

- Can I trust this model?
- What is the risk of my trust?
- What kind of biases can I expect?

Finally, we argue that viewing the socio-technical platform of the EMC (including the biometric-enabled sub-systems of such) through the EDI lenses is of teaching and learning value [20, 61].

After this introduction, we represent our audit strategy in Sect. 2. The general audit landscape is reported in Sect. 3. Case examples are considered in Sect. 4. Summary, conclusions and future work are provided in Sect. 6.

2   Audit Strategy

We utilize the general audit principles defined by the ISO standard [32]. This allows us to provide a systematic, unbiased, and objective examination using an application-specific auditing strategy, a critical factor of audit efficiency. In contrast, another approach, called a review, refers to an evaluation of the research field based on available information, e.g. reports and publications. An audit is the highest level of inspection with the purpose of providing critical analysis. It results in the recommendations for improvements.

Audit Material. This audit is based on the achievements of biometric technology before the COVID pandemic, during the pandemic, and during recovery. We follow the audit style of the post-pandemic criticism in the areas of healthcare [4], e-health [52], science [60], education [61], security and privacy [50], and payment systems [44]. Most of these recent works advocate for the EMC in an attempt to identify and explain socio-technological gaps. We accept the EMC-centric approach and adapt it for use in biometric-enabled systems.

2.1   4-Fold Audit Strategy

To accomplish our audit objectives, we developed a 4-fold strategy to audit post-pandemic biometric-enabled systems. The proposed strategy consists of 1) an audit content, i.e. specification of audit scope (psychological, technological, and EDI-EMC-centric), 2) the socio-technological assessments (risk, trust, and bias), and 3) an object of the audit profiling (biometric-enabled system or its components), as shown in Fig. 1). To introduce the audit strategy, we use a real-world example of the bias phenomenon.

Psychological View. An example of a bias is the so-called own-race bias, a tendency to have better recognition for faces of one's racial ingroup rather than outgroup faces [29]. The effect of social categorization on face recognition has been well established: face recognition is superior for individuals that belong to familiar social categories, such as one's age group, gender, and race. The social categorization-individuation model proposes that the ingroup biases in face recognition result from the enhanced processing of identity diagnostic features of ingroup faces and category-diagnostic features of outgroup faces. Other socio-ethical categories include impersonation and distrust (user behavioural effects in interactions with biometric devices).

Technological View. Related to example of the own-race bias, we refer to the face recognition experiments reported in [15,25,48]. As suggested in [62], the face recognition performance had 82.7% of difference in the case when gender was considered. The authors developed an unsupervised fair score normalization to combat this bias. This approach was theoretically motivated by the concept of individual fairness [17], resulting in a solution that treats similar individuals similarly and, thus, more fairly. The fairness in the face recognition algorithms can be achieved by training and testing the developed algorithms on diverse subject groups [38,48,54]. A related effect is known as the Doddington phenomenon [57,69,70]. It is described in this paper in Sect. 4.

EMC Projections. EMC is defined as a commonly accepted doctrine to manage disasters [20,64]. Accordingly to this doctrine, a society, at a certain point in time, is in one of four EMC states: mitigation, preparedness, response, and recovery. It follows from this doctrine that any socio-technological system should satisfy these states' requirements aiming to develop, improve, and apply the counter-measures.

EDI Dimensions. The EDI address emerging socio-ethical phenomena that impact various social activities [5]. Consequently, the EDI concept is also woven into various socio-technological systems [36,58]. In our work, the security checkpoint for the future e-borders is considered to be an EDI-aware system by design (see Sect. 4).

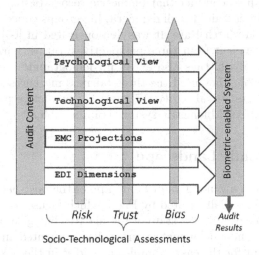

Fig. 1. The 4-fold auditing strategy for post-pandemic biometric-enabled systems which should be profiled accordingly to the specific 4-fold audit content.

For the EMC to work effectively, it is necessary to ensure the development of all four of its components and not just focus on the response phase when an emergency has already occurred. Early strategic planning makes it possible not to overload the system in times of crisis [66].

Socio-Technological Assessments. Fairness, risk, trustworthiness, biases, transparency, explainability, and interpretability become the key performance measures of biometric-enabled systems [38,54,56,62,65]. For example, following the definitions by NIST [51], risk is a "measure of the extent to which an entity is threatened by a potential circumstance or event, and typically is a function of: (i) the adverse impact, also called cost or magnitude of the harm, that would arise if the circumstance or event occurs, and (ii) the likelihood of event occurrence". Formally, risk is defined as a function F of impact (or consequences) of a circumstance or event and the probability of its occurrence.

Consider, for example, the fairness of biometric technology or an algorithm. The risk of their fairness can be assessed as follows:

$$\begin{Bmatrix} \text{Risk of} \\ \text{fairness} \end{Bmatrix} = F(\text{Impact}, \underbrace{\text{Probability}}_{\text{Fairness detection}})$$

In this model, the Impact corresponds to the actual level of system cost (e.g. traveller satisfaction from an automated border crossing in an airport), and the Probability denotes the probability of fairness measured in terms of the number of correctly classified patterns among available patterns.

In [54], the authors consider that biometric recognition systems are fair if a decision threshold τ is "fair" for all demographic groups concerning False Match Rate and False Non-Match Rate. It was demonstrated in [65] that bias in biometric systems is evident from three perspectives: ratios, fairness criteria, and intersectionality analysis. Bias also exists in demographic groups such as age, gender, and race [65]. They used the three fairness measures such as (1) equalized odds [27], (2) statistical parity [17], and (3) predictive parity [11] to show that a realistic, unbiased biometric system is impossible.

3 General Audit Landscape

This section provides a general audit landscape of the post-pandemic biometric-enabled systems. This is illustrated by Fig. 1 which focuses on the EMC projections and EDI dimensions. The state-of-the-art psychological and technological aspects of the pre-pandemic biometrics are well-documented and out of the scope of this audit, except for the case examples provided in the next section.

3.1 EMC Projections

Figure 2 represents the EMC concept [20,64] that was adapted for biometrics in this paper. Putting a biometric-enabled system into EMC resulting the following useful projections: 1) one of four emergency states/phases at a certain time, and 2) relationships between states/phases (if not specified, called "Gap"). The following tasks should be conducted through development of biometric-enabled system:

1. Discover epidemic counter-measures (Mitigation phase);
2. Prototype these counter-measures following readiness plans (Preparedness phase);
3. Operate in real-world scenarios of epidemic attack (Response phase); and
4. Switch biometric-enable system in a regular mode (Recovery phase).

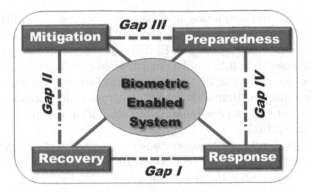

Fig. 2. Readiness of the biometric-enabled system for potential threats and its counter-measure content as specified by the EMC phases. The EMC gaps characterize by the level of the readiness.

For example, the current state of the biometric-enabled systems corresponds to the recovery phase. A reasonable explanation of the failures of some biometric-enabled systems during the recent COVID pandemic, such as the failure of security checkpoints, suggests the negligence of counter-epidemic tasks in the mitigation and preparedness EMC phases. Gaps II, III, and IV indicate the direction of these missed efforts.

3.2   EDI-Aware Biometric Systems

In the EDI-aware biometric system, diversity refers to the different users. Equity is about creating fair access to systems, opportunities, and advancement for all those different people. Inclusion is about creating an environment that cultivates a sense of belonging for all individuals to feel empowered and contribute freely.

The EDI-aware biometric system operates the common demographic and impersonation attributes, including risk, trust, and bias assessments. EDI computational aspects are audited in [1].

3.3   Pandemic-Conditioned Biometrics

The 4-fold auditing strategy (Fig. 1) provides an updated, post-pandemic sociotechnological landscape of biometric-enabled systems. The updates include:

- performance measure that account for the limitations of the usage of biometrics under the constraints posed by the personal protective equipment or gear; it includes various unwanted effects,
- computational platform that mitigates the unwanted effects by using advanced machine learning techniques,
- efficiency evaluation using various measures and the advanced machine reasoning to improve the system-level decision support, and
- privacy awareness that takes into account the exposure of health records.

In this content, impersonation and fairness effects are conditioned by epidemiological countermeasures such as personal protective equipment (e.g. face masks), and become challenging. The EMC projections add layers of complexity to the R&D of possible solutions. To illustrate this, we refer to our recent approach based on deep learning and multi-spectral face recognition [55] resulting in 99% face recognition. Remarkably, NEC[1] corporation announced the 99.9% face recognition rate for the combination of vaccination passport and periocular images of the individuals.

During the pandemic, another previously suggested technology proved itself useful, – a biometric-enabled Self-Sovereign Identity (SSI). This valuable practical outcome, SSI, satisfies the requirements of

1. a regular biometric-enabled mode, and
2. a counter-epidemic mode (IATA's current practice [30]) with future extension to epidemic-conditioned biometrics.

An arbitrary biometric-enabled system is conditioned by the diversity of the population, technology limitations and social components, including:

- disability (damage to fingers, voice, eyes);
- age (biometric traits of infants and young children, i.e. traits are acceptable only for a limited time and require updating);
- privacy (there is a risk that the biometric traits are used in an unauthorized manner by a third party);
- bias (race and gender bias, in particular);
- trust (breaking the trustworthiness between the user and the system leads to socio-technological conflict);
- forgery (biometric traits can be replaced by their synthetic copies [71]).

The EMC projections suggest updating the scope of conditions with respect to epidemiological requirements, e.g. self-sovereign identity, e-health, tracing, vaccination, and personal protective equipment. The EDI lenses suggests updating various socio-technological conditions related to risks, trust, and biases.

4   Case Examples

We introduce two case examples (watchlist and e-health) in order to assess the practical value of our audit strategy.

4.1   Biometric Enabled Watchlist for E-Borders

A biometric-enabled watchlist for e-borders is a frontier of applications of biometric technologies. In e-borders, the problem "Is this traveller on the watchlist?" is reformulated as "Assess the risk of the traveller being on the watchlist" [18].

---

[1] https://www.nippon.com/en/news/kd839443641406668800/.

In e-borders, the preferable traits include face, fingerprint and iris biometrics [22,31]. In particular, the Canada Border Services Agency has used facial matching as a way to increase the processing of arriving travellers and to offer an option for self-service [13]. Also, the biometrics used in the Primary Inspection Kiosk and the NEXUS kiosk have been transitioning from retina and fingerprint to face, specifically for facial verification. Figure 3 illustrates the procedure of a watchlist check to identify potential risks.

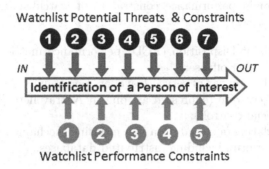

Fig. 3. Real-world watchlist check in e-borders is under set of potential threats, constraints, and performance requirements. (Color figure online)

Watchlist Tasks. Traveler risks assessment in e-borders addresses various components, including authentication and watchlist check. Watchlist is a mandatory component of e-borders. It enables the identification of individuals of interest using biometric traits and related contextual information. A biometric-enabled watchlist (or database of persons of interest) is commonly accepted by national and international security agencies, e.g. the Interpol Terrorism Watch List of fugitives and suspected terrorists, and No-Fly list of people suspected of some involvement with terrorism. In e-borders, the central problem is to improve the performance, such as throughput, and minimize the risks of border passage of an unwanted subject. Biometric-enabled watchlists for e-borders addresses many challenges such as updating or enabling infrastructure, biometric-enabled passports/IDs, the reliability of biometric traits, as well as privacy issues.

Watchlist Impact and Constraints. The identification mode of the biometric recognition system is under various potential threats and limitations on biometric modalities. (Figure 3, grey numerical arrows):

1. Fairness effects [38,54,56,62];
2. Inherent (unintentional) impersonation bias known as Doddington phenomenon [42,69], and enforced impersonation [70];
3. Social bias (e-borders is an integrated part of the country) and service bias i.e. risks of service degradation [12];
4. Leakage of information due to attack;

5. Synthetic biometric traits [71], including plastic surgery [35];
6. Vulnerabilities caused by technological factors [7];
7. Biometric traits limited to those used in e-passport [22,31].

Watchlist Performance Constraints. Performance measures of a watchlist is an integral part of a checkpoint performance, interoperability, response time, life cycle (theoretical, predicted or vendor reported, and operational or real performance), as well as the reliability and credibility of sources and information. Specifically, the main performance constraints of watchlist include (Figure 3, green numerical arrows):

1. Redress Complaint Disposition (RCD) performance metric is based on the paradigm of traveller offense;
2. Throughput (the number of served travellers per hour);
3. Operational reject rate (expressed as "one in N travellers (1:N) is wrongly directed to special control");
4. Dynamical updating of stored data via updating mechanisms, e.g. the RCD;
5. Operational platform, including distributed databases.

Formalization and Modeling of the Fairness Effects. In [68], a helpful taxonomy of assessment and prediction of fairness for algorithmic classification problems was introduced. According to this taxonomy, there are various definitions of fairness: 1) based on statistical measures, 2) based on similarity measures, and 3) based on causal reasoning. For example, work [16] is based on an understanding of the fairness of watchlist check as a statistical problem. Risks of biases using causal reasoning techniques were addressed in [40].

In [17], the fairness assessment is defined as follows. Let V be a set of individuals. Consider randomized classifiers that map individuals to distributions over outcomes $A = \{0, 1\}$. To introduce the notion of fairness, authors assume the existence of a metric on individuals $d : V \times V \to R$. Randomized mappings $M : V \to \Delta(A)$ from individuals to probability distributions over outcomes. To classify individual $x \in V$, an outcome a according to the distribution $M(x)$ must be chosen. Mapping similar people can be interpreted as the distributions assigned to those who are similar. In this formulation, fairness leads to an optimization problem. That is, fairness is achieved iff $D(M(x), M(y)) \le d(x, y)$ where D is a chosen type measurement of similarity of distributions. Various fairness measurements are compared in [68].

Formalization and Modeling of the Doddington's Effect. Doddington's phenomenon was intensively studied in the last two decades [57,69,70], and can be compared to assessing the biometric fairness. Instead of relatively stable fearless effects, Doddington's categorization of biometric traits is an unstable phenomenon; it depends on various factors such as the quality of biometric traits, algorithmic features of the processing, match score generation and the decision-making strategy at all levels of the processing hierarchy.

Doddington's likelihood was defined in [42] as a product of the probabilities of genuine subject A_G and imposter subject A_I with respect to the category D_i, where $D_1 =$ 'Sheep', $D_2 =$ 'Goat', and $D_3 =$ 'Wolf/Lamb':

$$\text{Likelihood} = P(A_G|D_i)P(A_I|D_i).$$

Similarly, Doddington's evidence was defined as the total probability [42]:

$$P(A) = \sum_{i=1}^{3} \underbrace{P(A_G|D_i)P(A_I|D_i)}_{\text{Doddington's likelihood}} P(D_i)$$

The probability $P(A)$ is called the evidence factor; it can be viewed as merely a scale factor that guarantees that the posterior probabilities sum to one, as probabilities must. The posterior probability of the Doddington's phenomenon (also a belief for evidence A) is calculated using the Bayesian profile:

$$\underbrace{P(D_i|A_G, A_I)}_{\text{Posterior}} = \underbrace{P(A_G|D_i)P(A_I|D_i)}_{\text{Doddington's likelihood}} \frac{\overbrace{P(D_i)}^{\text{Prior}}}{\underbrace{P(A)}_{\text{Evidence}}}$$

Given an unknown traveller who can be on the watchlist (A_G) or not (A_I), the Bayesian profile states that by observing the Doddington's evidence A (in the watchlist), we are able to evaluate the risks that this traveller belongs to one of the Doddington's categories, D_i. The Bayesian profile addresses updating degrees of belief upon receiving new evidence (updating the watchlist).

Watchlist for e-borders [39] is a subject of a particular interest. Papers [42,43,70] studied the watchlist performance based on the Doddington phenomenon. In the case of watchlists, gender imbalance considerably deteriorates the fairness in a biometric system, which is also referred to as the fairness effects for different demographic groups [16]. The gender and ethnicity bias, also known as a cognitive Artificial Intelligence bias, often results in an imbalanced performance for different demographics, such as failure of enrollment or failure to identify a face [25].

4.2   Fairness in Biometrics for E-Health

In e-health systems, fairness is essential in order to minimize ethical [9], social and other issues [53]. Both safety and fairness are important variables in the R&D of e-Health devices, and systems [47].

Self-monitoring using a smartphone is a part of e-health technologies and a well-established area in research and practice [21]. Monitoring of COVID-19-related stress globally in 63 countries has shown that over 70% of the respondents had greater than moderate levels of stress, with 59% meeting the criteria for clinically significant anxiety and 39% reporting moderate depressive symptoms [67].

According to [59], COVID-19 has threatened the mental health of nearly one-third of the general population: the pooled prevalence of stress, depression, and anxiety was estimated at 29.6%, 33.7%, and 31.9%, respectively. E-coaching for mental apps health is feasible across all platforms ranging from text messages to social media and for both on-demand and scheduled interactions [49]. Study [8] suggests that individualized e-technologies in community mental health settings have great potential; standardization of the intervention, development of guidelines for improving client-clinician collaboration, and conducting pilot studies are on demand.

In e-health systems, facial expressions of critical importance, e.g. features of pain (facial grimace or changes in vocal pitch or heart rate due to pain conditions), depression, and anger. Unfortunately, fairness and Doddington's phenomenon impact facial expressions too. The broader literature suggests that anger bias is racialized, with Black adults are stereotyped as angry and emotionally dysregulated [14]. These stereotypes clearly activate hostile responses in the perceiver.

Individuals are racially biased when judging the emotions of others [14]. Study [26] expand the questions of racialized emotion recognition accuracy and anger bias. Authors motivated their study that teachers may incorrectly judge children as angry for many reasons, including their own implicit and explicit racial biases. Authors concluded that racialized anger bias, while identified among prospective teachers, is likely an issue involving both individual and community-wide change. When addressing bias related to race, an essential first step is an awareness of bias, followed by the desire to reduce bias and an understanding of the contextual triggers.

Figure 4 illustrates a biometric-enabled system known as e-health concerning physiological-psychological traits: biometric, biomedical, and behaviour. Specifically, biometric traits such as 1) face-based user identification, 2) emotion detection, and 3) detection pitches of interest in voice, which are processed in conjunction with biomedical traits, 4) heart rate, 5) blood pressure, 6) other traits. Additional information is obtained from behaviour traits extracted using conversational and questionnaire techniques.

The detection and classification of the biometric traits are also the components of e-coaching for health [6,37] where the related biases are of critical importance.

5   Teaching and Learning

The teaching of biometric system design is a part of many undergraduate and graduate university programs. Systematic view on R&D of biometric-enabled systems should become a new strategy in these classes. We argue that:

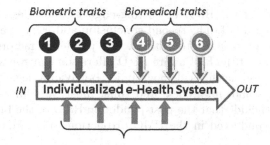

Fig. 4. A biometric system is a part of an e-health system. Decision-making in e-health is based on the fusion of biometric, biomedical, and behavior traits.

1. Including the EMC-centric design of the biometric courses advocates the forefront of biometrics and can be considered an essential part of post-pandemic R&D biometric-enabled systems. Recent publications suggest the EMC-centric view on R&D in various fields [13].
2. The EDI lenses in R&D biometric-enabled systems help correct the socio-technological vision of various effects of biometrics. For example, EDI was considered in the context of generative interactions in organizations [5].

This also concerns the training of the biometric system designers and engineers and training the users of the biometric systems.

6 Summary, Conclusion, Limitations, and Future Work

Contemporary biometric technologies are often included in the complex intelligent systems for access control, monitoring and operations of the public establishments. They are an integral part of many system architectures. Performance of biometric-enabled systems (identity recognition, certain behaviour pattern detection, accurate vitals monitoring) is evaluated in the context of the overall system. For example, in security checkpoints for e-borders, biometric-centric processes are highly parallel, often distributed, synchronized with other tasks such as object detection, and optimized in a multi-criteria space, e.g. time, risk, and user satisfaction.

As a case example, we introduced a biometric-enabled watchlist. We emphasized that the watchlist as a part of e-borders is only a partially solved biometric problem, and multiple threats and constraints to operations and performance of such systems are ever-present. Another example is e-healthcare monitoring, where an automated identification of the user's state (e.g. pain, stress, anxiety) and its fairness is affected by the accuracy of facial expression or emotion recognition.

The key motivation of this audit is the impact of the recent pandemic on the performance of biometric-enabled systems such as e-health systems and security checkpoints. Post-pandemic studies emphasize the importance of embedding the

EMC in all stages of the R&D of cutting-edge technologies. This is the first conclusion from our audit. The second conclusion addresses the need to update the concepts and technologies to mitigate the pandemic factors and unwanted effects. The concept of the EDI-aware R&D offers some answers. We argue that the biometrics factors such as demographic, behaviour, legality, and privacy, are subject to bias and unfairness and thus, must be addressed through the EDI lenses. We conclude that the post-pandemic R&D of the biometric-enabled systems shall be conducted in the EMC projections, in conjunction with EDI concepts.

There are several limitations of this audit. In particular, the post-pandemic biometric horizon should be considered in the content of the lesson learned from the 2015 European Union mass-migrant crisis [19]. The central question of the post-2015 crisis is: "Why did the advanced border policy and praxis, including biometric-enabled systems, fail [3]?" Note that the risk of globalization of migration due to the climate hazards increased. This led to an increase in the irregular migration flows, and also resulted in the reinforcement of border control, including biometric-enabled systems [46].

Acknowledgments. This project was partially supported by the Natural Sciences and Engineering Research Council of Canada through the grant "Biometric intelligent interfaces", and the Social Sciences and Humanities Research Council of Canada via NFRF project "Emergency Management Cycle-Centric R&D: From National Prototyping to Global Implementation".

References

1. Abid, N., Shmerko, V., Yanushkevich, S.: Audit of computational intelligence techniques for EDI-aware systems. In: Proceedings of IEEE International Joint Conference on Neural Networks, Padua, Italy, pp. 1–8 (2022)
2. Alonso-Fernandez, F., Raja, K.B., Raghavendra, R., Busch, C., et al.: Cross-Sensor Periocular Biometrics for Partial Face Recognition in a Global Pandemic: Comparative Benchmark and Novel Multialgorithmic Approach, arXiv arXiv:1902.08123 (2020)
3. Andersson, R.: Europe's failed 'fight' against irregular migration: ethnographic notes on a counterproductive industry. J. Ethn. Migr. Stud. **42**(7), 1055–1075 (2016)
4. Baral, P.: Health systems and services during COVID-19: lessons and evidence from previous crises: a rapid scoping review to inform the united nations research roadmap for the COVID-19 recovery. Int. J. Health Serv. **51**(4), 474–493 (2021)
5. Bernstein, R.S., Bulger, M., Salipante, P., Weisinger, J.Y.: From diversity to inclusion to equity: a theory of generative interactions. J. Bus. Ethics **167**, 395–410 (2020)
6. Beun, R.J., et al.: Improving adherence in automated e-coaching. In: Meschtscherjakov, A., De Ruyter, B., Fuchsberger, V., Murer, M., Tscheligi, M. (eds.) PERSUASIVE 2016. LNCS, vol. 9638, pp. 276–287. Springer, Cham (2016). https://doi.org/10.1007/978-3-319-31510-2_24

7. Butt, M., et al.: Towards e-passport duplicate enrollment check in the European Union. In: Proceedings of European Intelligence and Security Informatics Conference, pp. 247–251 (2013)
8. Carpenter-Song, E., et al.: Individualized intervention to support mental health recovery through implementation of digital tools into clinical care: feasibility study. Community Ment. Health J. **58**(1), 99–110 (2022)
9. Char, D.S., Shah, N.H., Magnus, D.: Implementing machine learning in health care - addressing ethical challenges. N. Engl. J. Med. **378**, 981–983 (2018)
10. Cho, J.-H., Chan, K., Adali, S.: A survey on trust modeling. ACM Comput. Surv. **48**(2), 1–40 (2015)
11. Chouldechova, A.: Fair prediction with disparate impact: a study of bias in recidivism prediction instruments. Big Data **5**(2), 153–163 (2017)
12. Clavell, G.G.: Protect rights at automated borders. Nature **543**(7643), 34–36 (2017)
13. Committee of the Whole: Binder for the Minister of Public Safety and Emergency Preparedness - July 8, 2020: Facial Recognition, Public Safety Canada (2020)
14. Correll, J., Park, B., Judd, C.M., et al.: Across the thin blue line: police officers and racial bias in the decision to shoot. J. Pers. Soc. Psychol. **92**, 1006–1023 (2007)
15. Das, A., Dantcheva, A., Bremond, F.: Mitigating bias in gender, age and ethnicity classification: a multi-task convolution neural network approach. In: European Conference on Computer Vision, pp. 1–13 (2018)
16. Drozdowski, P., Rathgeb, C., Busch, C.: Demographic Fairness in Face Identification: The Watchlist Imbalance Effect, arXiv, arXiv:2106.08049 (2021)
17. Dwork, C., Hardt, M., Pitassi, T., Reingold, O., Zemel, R.: Fairness through awareness. In: ITCS 2012: Proceedings of the 3rd Innovations in Theoretical Computer Science Conference, pp. 214–226 (2012)
18. European Union: Technical Study on Smart Borders. European Commission, Directorate General for Home Affairs and PwC (2014)
19. Estevens, J.: Migration crisis in the EU: developing a framework for analysis of national security and defence strategies. Comp. Migr. Stud. **6**, 28 (2018)
20. Fagel, M.J.: Principles of Emergency Management and Emergency Operations Centers (EOC). CRC Press, Boca Raton (2010)
21. Faurholt-Jepsen, M., et al.: The effect of smartphone-based monitoring on illness activity in bipolar disorder: the MONARCA II randomized controlled single-blinded trial. Psychol. Med. **50**, 838–848 (2020)
22. Frontex, Operational and technical security of electronic passports. Frontex Research and Development Unit, Warsaw (2011)
23. Fu, Y., Guo, G., Huang, T.S.: Age synthesis and estimation via faces: a survey. IEEE Trans. Pattern Anal. Mach. Intell. **32**(11), 1955–1976 (2010)
24. Fu, S., He, H., Hou, Z.-G.: Learning race from face: a survey. IEEE Trans. Pattern Anal. Mach. Intell. **36**(12), 2483–2509 (2014)
25. Grother, P., Ngan, M., Hanaoka, K.: Face recognition vendor test (FRVT) part 3: demographic effects. National Institute of Standards and Technology Interagency or Internal Report 8280 (2019)
26. Halberstadt, G., Cooke, A.N., Garner, P.W., et al.: Racialized emotion recognition accuracy and anger bias of children's faces. Emot. Am. Psychol. Assoc. **22**(3), 403–41 (2022)
27. Hardt, M., Price, E., Srebro, N.: Equality of opportunity in supervised learning. Adv. Neural. Inf. Process. Syst. **29**, 3315–3323 (2016)

28. Howard, J.J., Rabbitt, L.R., Sirotin, Y.B.: Human-algorithm teaming in face recognition: how algorithm outcomes cognitively bias human decision-making. PLoS ONE **15**(8), e0237855 (2020)
29. Hugenberg, K., Wilson, J.P., See, P.E., Young, S.G.: Towards a synthetic model of own group biases in face memory. Vis. Cogn. **21**(9–10), 1392–1417 (2013)
30. IATA (International Air Transport Association), Travel-Pass Initiative (2021)
31. ICAO (International Civil Aviation Organization), Machine Readable Travel Documents, Seventh Edition, Document 9303 (2015)
32. International Organization for Standardization ISO 19011:2018, Guidelines for auditing management systems (2018)
33. Ivanov, D.: Exiting the COVID-19 pandemic: after-shock risks and avoidance of disruption tails in supply chains. Ann. Oper. Res. 1–18 (2021)
34. Jain, A.K., Nandakumar, K., Ross, A.: 50 years of biometric research: accomplishments, challenges, and opportunities. Pattern Recogn. Lett. **79**, 80–105 (2016)
35. Jillela, R., Ross, A.: Mitigating effects of plastic surgery: fusing face and ocular biometrics. In: Proceedings of IEEE 5th International Conference on Biometrics: Theory, Applications and Systems, pp. 402–411 (2012)
36. Kamphorst, B.A.: Autonomy-Respectful E-Coaching Systems: Fending Off Complacency. Ph.D. thesis, Utrecht university (2020)
37. Kamphorst, B.: E-coaching systems: what they are, and what they aren't. Pers. Ubiquit. Comput. **21**(1), 625–632 (2017)
38. Krishnan, A., Almadan, A., Rattani, A.: Probing fairness of mobile ocular biometrics methods across gender on VISOB 2.0 dataset. In: Del Bimbo, A., et al. (eds.) ICPR 2021. LNCS, vol. 12668, pp. 229–243. Springer, Cham (2021). https://doi.org/10.1007/978-3-030-68793-9_16
39. Labati, R.D., Genovese, A., Muniz, E., Piuri, V., Scotti, F., Sforza, G.: Biometric recognition in automated border control: a survey. ACM Comput. Surv. **49**(2), 1–39 (2016)
40. Lai, K., Oliveira, H.C., Hou, M., Yanushkevich, S.N., Shmerko, V.: Assessing risks of biases in cognitive decision support systems. In: European Signal Processing Conference, pp. 840–844 (2021)
41. Lai, K., Yanushkevich, S.N., Shmerko, V.P.: Epidemic attack on the aircraft carrier theodore roosevelt: bridging the gaps in emergency management. J. Def. Model. Simul. (2021)
42. Lai, K., Yanushkevich, S., Shmerko, V., Eastwood, S.: Bridging the gap between forensics and biometric-enabled watchlists for e-borders. IEEE Comput. Intell. Mag. **12**(1), 17–28 (2017)
43. Lai, K., Kanich, O., Dvorak, M., Drahansky, M., et al.: Biometric-enabled watchlists technology. IET Biometrics **6**(6), 1–10 (2017)
44. Liebana-Cabanillas, F., Munoz-Leiva, F., Molinillo, S., Higueras-Castillo, E.: Do biometric payment systems work during the COVID-19 pandemic? Insights from the Spanish users' viewpoint. Financ. Innov. **8**(22), 1–25 (2022)
45. Martinez, B., Valstar, M., Jiang, B., Pantic, M.: Automatic analysis of facial actions: a survey. IEEE Trans. Affect. Comput. **10**(3), 325–347 (2019)
46. McLeman, R.: International migration and climate adaptation in an era of hardening borders. Nat. Clim. Chang. **9**, 911–918 (2019)
47. Mehrabi, N., Morstatter, F., Saxena, N., Lerman, K., Galstyan, A.: A survey on bias and fairness in machine learning. ACM Comput. Surv. **54**, 1–35 (2019)
48. Merler, M., Ratha, N., Feris, R.S., Smith, J.R.: Diversity in faces, arXiv arXiv:1901.10436 (2019)

49. Meyer, A., Wisniewski, H., Torous, J.: Coaching to support mental health apps: exploratory narrative review. JMIR Hum. Factors **9**(1), e28301 (2022)
50. Moon, H.G., Lho, H.L., Han, H.: Selfcheck-in kiosk quality and airline non-contact service maximization: how to win air traveler satisfaction and loyalty in the post-pandemic world? J. Travel Tour. Mark. **38**(4), 383–398 (2021)
51. National Institute of Standards (NIST), Security and Privacy Controls for Information Systems and Organizations. NIST Special Publication 800-53, Rev. 5 (2017)
52. Oberschmidt, K., Grünloh, C., Nijboer, F., van Velsen, L.: Best practices and lessons learned for action research in ehealth design and implementation: literature review. J. Med. Internet Res. **24**(1), 31795 (2022)
53. Osoba, O.A., Welser, W.: An Intelligence in Our Image: The Risks of Bias and Errors in Artificial Intelligence. RAND Corporation (2017)
54. Pereira, T.F., Marcel, S.: Fairness in biometrics: a figure of merit to assess biometric verification systems. IEEE Trans. Biom. Behav. Identity Sci. **4**(1), 19–29 (2022)
55. Queiroz, L., Lai, K., Yanushkevich, S., Shmerko, V.: Biometrics in the Time of Pandemic: 40% Masked Face Recognition Degradation can be Reduced to 2%, arXiv, arXiv:2201.00461 (2022)
56. Rathgeb, C., Drozdowski, P., Frings, D.C., Damer, N., Busch, C.: Demographic Fairness in Biometric Systems: What do the Experts say? arXiv, arXiv:2105.14844 (2021)
57. Ross, A., Rattani, A., Tistarelli, M.: Exploiting the Doddington zoo effect in biometric fusion. In: Proceedings of IEEE 3rd International Conference on Biometrics: Theory, Applications and Systems, pp. 1–7 (2009)
58. Sa, C., Cowley, S., Martinez, M., Kachynska, N., Sabzalieva, E.: Gender gaps in research productivity and recognition among elite scientists in the US, Canada, and South Africa. PLoS One **15**(10), 2020 (2020)
59. Salari, N., et al.: Prevalence of stress, anxiety, depression among the general population during the COVID-19 pandemic: a systematic review and meta-analysis. J. Glob. Health **16**(57) (2020)
60. Scheirer, W.: A pandemic of bad science. Bull. Atomic Sci. **76**(4), 175–184 (2020)
61. Tanase, F.-D., Demyen, S., Manciu, V.-C., Tanase, A.-C.: Online education in the COVID-19 pandemic-premise for economic competitiveness growth? Sustainability **14**(6), 3503 (2022)
62. Terhorst, P., Kolf, J.N., Damer, N., Kirchbuchner, F., Kuijper, A.: Post-comparison mitigation of demographic bias in face recognition using fair score normalization. Pattern Recogn. Lett. **140**, 332–338 (2020)
63. Thevenot, J., Lopez, M.B., Hadid, A.: A survey on computer vision for assistive medical diagnosis from faces. IEEE J. Biomed. Health Inform. **22**(5), 1497–1511 (2018)
64. US Department of Homeland Security, National Response Framework (2022). media-library/assets/documents/117791
65. Valdivia, A., Corbera-Serrajordia, J., Swianiewicz, A.: There is an elephant in the room: towards a critique on the use of fairness in biometrics, arXiv, arXiv:2112.11193 (2021)
66. VanVactor, J.D.: Strategic healthcare logistics planning in emergency management. Disaster Prev. Manag. **21**(3), 299–309 (2012)
67. Varma, P., Junge, M., Meaklim, H., Jackson, M.L.: Younger people are more vulnerable to stress, anxiety and depression during COVID-19 pandemic: a global cross-sectional survey. Prog. Neuro-Psychopharmacol. Biol. Psychiatry **109**, 110236 (2021)

68. Verma, S., Rubin, J.: Fairness definitions explained. In: IEEE/ACM International Workshop on Software Fairness, pp. 1–7 (2018)
69. Yager, N., Dunstone, T.: The biometric menagerie member. IEEE Trans. Pattern Anal. Mach. Intell. **32**(2), 220–230 (2010)
70. Yanushkevich, S.N., Eastwood, S.C., Manderson, T.L., et al.: Taxonomy and modeling of impersonation in e-border authentication. In: Sixth International Conference on Emerging Security Technologies, pp. 38–43 (2015)
71. Yanushkevich, S., Reitinger, N., Stoica, A., et al.: Inverse biometrics: privacy, risks, and trust. In: Encyclopedia of Cryptography, Security and Privacy, pp. 1–4 (2020)

Author Index

J.-J. Rousseau and B. Kapralos (Eds.): ICPR 2022 Workshops, LNCS 13645, pp. 627–629, 2023.
https://doi.org/10.1007/978-3-031-37731-0

Printed in the United States
by Baker & Taylor Publisher Services